VOICE FOR THE WORLD'S POOR

WORLD BANK MISSION STATEMENT

Our dream is a world free of poverty.

To fight poverty with passion and professionalism for lasting results.

To help people help themselves and their environment by providing resources, sharing knowledge, building capacity, and forging partnerships in the public and private sectors.

To be an excellent institution able to attract, excite, and nurture diverse and committed staff with exceptional skills who know how to listen and learn.

Our Principles

Client centered, working in partnership, accountable for quality results, dedicated to financial integrity and cost-effectiveness, inspired and innovative.

Our Values

Personal honesty, integrity, commitment; working together in teams—with openness and trust; empowering others and respecting differences; encouraging risk-taking and responsibility; enjoying our work and our families.

VOICE

SELECTED SPEECHES AND WRITINGS

FOR THE

OF WORLD BANK PRESIDENT

WORLD'S

JAMES D. WOLFENSOHN, 1995 – 2005

POOR

THE WORLD BANK
Washington, D.C.

CONTENTS

This volume of the best speeches and writings of World Bank President James D. Wolfensohn is published by the World Bank Group in recognition of Jim and Elaine Wolfensohn and their many contributions to development.

The collection was assembled by a team under the leadership of Andrew Kircher. Michael Treadway applied his superb editing skills to the manuscript. Andrea Shettle was indispensable in researching the speeches, fact-checking, and proofreading. Stephen McGroarty in the Office of the Publisher provided excellent editorial support from start to finish. Nancy Lammers and Mary Fisk managed the design and editorial production of the book. Randi Park and Monika Daniela Lynde coordinated the printing process. Simone McCourtie researched and selected the photos. The book also benefited from the advice of Gerry Rice, Rob Floyd, Candy Perque Herlihy, and Caroline Anstey. Maria Acosta supported the book team throughout the process.

In sifting through the thousands of pages of Wolfensohn's speeches and writings, the editors have tried to present some insight into the innovations, changes, and challenges of a critical and transformative decade in the World Bank's 60-year history. We hope the reader will find them illuminating, instructive, and inspiring.

AIDS	Acquired immunodeficiency syndrome
ASEAN	Association of South East Asian Nations
CDF	Comprehensive Development Framework
CGIAR	Consultative Group on International Agricultural Research
DAC	Development Assistance Committee (of the OECD)
EDI	Economic Development Institute
G-7 (-8)	Group of Seven (Eight) leading industrialized nations
GDP	Gross domestic product
GEF	Global Environment Facility
GNP	Gross national product
HIPC	Heavily indebted poor countries
HIV	Human immunodeficiency virus
IBRD	International Bank for Reconstruction and Development
ICSID	International Centre for Settlement of Investment Disputes
IDA	International Development Association
IFC	International Finance Corporation
IMF	International Monetary Fund
IMFC	International Monetary and Financial Committee
infoDev	Information for Development program
ITC	International Trade Centre
MDGs	Millennium Development Goals
MIGA	Multilateral Investment Guarantee Agency
NEPAD	New Partnership for Africa's Development
NGO	Nongovernmental organization
OAU	Organization of African Unity (now the African Union)
OECD	Organisation for Economic Co-operation and Development
PRSP	Poverty Reduction Strategy Paper
UNCTAD	United Nations Conference on Trade and Development
UNDP	United Nations Development Programme
UNESCO	United Nations Educational, Scientific, and Cultural Organization
UNICEF	United Nations Children's Fund
USAID	United States Agency for International Development
WHO	World Health Organization
WTO	World Trade Organization

On a crisp fall morning in 2004, a crowd of 2,500 gathered in Constitution Hall in Washington, D.C., and took their seats to hear the opening speeches of the Annual Meetings of the World Bank and the International Monetary Fund. A succession of speakers rose to the podium to welcome the delegations from 184 countries that together own the two institutions, which that year were marking the 60th anniversary of their founding at the Bretton Woods conference in New Hampshire in 1944.

When at last World Bank President James D. Wolfensohn stepped up to the podium to deliver his final Annual Meetings address as president, some in the audience of finance ministers and central bank governors might have expected a recitation of projects and programs planned, of trust funds replenished, of debt ratios or exchange rates. Instead they heard a stirring story about poor people.

They heard about the human drama of development, portrayed through stories of people Wolfensohn had met in the last year during his frequent visits to developing countries around the world. They heard about a farmer from the Peruvian highlands and his quest for ever more elusive water for his land and his herd. They heard about a Chinese woman in the Loess Plateau, who had improved her life thanks to a Bank project that turned arid highlands into arable cropland. And they heard about a group of young Bosnians, Croats, and Serbs, working together to put their homeland's troubles behind them and create a peaceful and more hopeful life.

As Wolfensohn spoke, a senior official of one delegation, standing in the back of the auditorium, whispered to a colleague, "Ahh, listen to that. Our guy could never get away with telling those stories. Our people wouldn't let him."

The comment was a vintage reaction to Wolfensohn, who ever since arriving at the World Bank almost 10 years before had been determined to break the mold of what a World Bank president could say and do. In his first Annual Meetings speech, he had spelled out his intention to break the "armlock" of bureaucracy on the institution. Earlier, at a press conference in Africa in his first month on the job, he had said, "I haven't come to change the face of the Bank but to express what is in the hearts of the people of the Bank."

During his 10 years and visits to more than 120 countries, Wolfensohn was prolific in speaking from the heart. This volume, *Voice for the World's Poor: Selected Speeches and Writings of World Bank President James D. Wolfensohn, 1995–2005,* captures only a small fraction of that outpouring of words—and to the extent possible some of the passion behind them.

Determined to reenergize the Bank and refocus its work on the fight against poverty, Wolfensohn used the bully pulpit of his office to urge, plead, encourage, and cajole partners, critics, and foes into uniting behind the task. In a profile of Wolfensohn's tenure in the *National Journal* in January 2005, Bruce Stokes wrote that he "gave voice to the world's poor, integrating their views into the Bank's planning."

In the process, Wolfensohn changed the face and the character of an institution that had previously been seen by many as heartless and arrogant. By describing the challenge of development in terms of people, not numbers—as he did on the stage that morning at Constitution Hall—Wolfensohn put the spotlight back on the World Bank's real purpose: fighting global poverty and helping the world's poor people forge a better life.

Anyone who has known Jim Wolfensohn or heard him speak during those 10 years can attest to the power of his improvisational style. Wolfensohn's habit of eschewing written speeches and instead "speaking from the heart" without notes is now legendary, not only to those who have worked with him but also to many in the development community who have been touched by his words.

During a press briefing with the rock star Bono in 2000 at the Bank-Fund Annual Meetings in Prague, the Irish singer praised Wolfensohn for his activism in relieving the debts of the world's poorest countries and called him the "Elvis of economics." Others have compared his speeches to jazz improvisations. In reality, and perhaps not coincidentally, Wolfensohn is a classical music enthusiast and a cellist.

If his speeches are indeed musical performances, then this collection is a sampling of his "greatest hits." But this volume offers much more than a compilation of speeches. Leafing through its pages, the reader will find a wide-ranging menu of both genres and themes: formal addresses, off-the-cuff remarks, talks at staff townhall meetings, op-eds, letters, forewords, and messages to shareholders. The editors have sifted through thousands of pages of Wolfensohn's oral and written oeuvre to find representative samples of his comments on almost all of the major development topics, from AIDS and education to infrastructure and the environment. (For the more voracious reader or the specialist interested in drilling deeper on a particular topic, the Bank's website offers a more comprehensive collection at www.worldbank.org/wolfensohn.)

The Annual Meetings speeches, all of which are included here, are especially noteworthy because they offer major insights into Wolfensohn's thinking as it evolved over the years. Each also constitutes a "State of the Bank" report to the Board of Governors. The Chairman's Messages in the Bank's Annual Reports, meanwhile, give readers a concise overview of the major

highlights of the previous year. And the selected forewords to the annual *World Development Report*—the Bank's flagship publication, which each year addresses an important dimension of current development thinking—tackle that year's theme and relate it back to the core of the Bank's mission.

This book can be approached in a variety of ways. A student of development or a researcher can jump straight to the speeches and writings that are of interest. Or a general reader can take in the volume from front to back; the pieces are arranged in chronological order, allowing a sense of the major changes and challenges that Wolfensohn and the Bank faced in the decade of his presidency.

In these pages, readers will learn about Bosnia's reconstruction in the mid-1990s, the Asian crisis of the late 1990s, the Millennium Development Goals, the trauma of the September 11 attacks, the aftermath of the Iraq war, and the outpouring of help for the victims of the tsunami of December 26, 2004. The book's geographical scope is likewise broad, with pieces on Rwanda's rebuilding, China's progress in fighting poverty, India's rise on the world scene, and Russia's development strategy. Also included are Wolfensohn's addresses at the major international summits of the decade, such as the 1995 Beijing conference on women, the 2002 Monterrey conference on financing for development, and the 2004 poverty conference in Shanghai.

The reader can also gain insight into how Wolfensohn has brought major change to the World Bank itself, whose staff of 10,000 in 109 country offices makes it the world's largest development organization. He led the modernization of the 60-year-old institution through a rapid decentralization, moving hundreds of staff overseas to the country offices and linking them all through cutting-edge technology and videoconferencing facilities. Decentralization allowed the Bank to place much more emphasis on home-grown development planning, giving borrowing countries the opportunity to put themselves in the "driver's seat" of their own development.

At the same time, readers will sense the urgency and sometimes frustration in Wolfensohn's remarks about the pace of change that he wants to bring to the institution. For example, in the early years he frequently urges the Bank's development partners to shed old stereotypes of the Bank and instead find common ground and new ways of working together.

Yet the results speak for themselves. Today, the World Bank is largely recognized by both wealthy and poorer countries as more effective than ever before in delivering results "on the ground." An independent audit of the Bank's International Development Association (IDA), which makes low-cost loans to the poorest countries, by Booz Allen Hamilton in 2004, found that IDA met and, in some areas, went beyond its performance targets.

Under Wolfensohn's leadership, the Bank's resources have been used more selectively and are increasingly focused on countries, such as Uganda and Vietnam, with strong records for good policymaking. Success rates in Bank-supported projects, as judged by its independent Operations Evaluation Department, have increased from just over 70 percent in 1995 to closer to 90 percent in recent years.

Wolfensohn broke new ground in several major policy areas, including social issues, the environment, the private sector, disabilities, culture, and interfaith dialogue. The policy changes Wolfensohn brought about can be seen in many areas of the Bank's work, but several issues stand out:

- Ten years ago, debt relief was not on the World Bank's agenda, nor was it considered a priority by the international community more widely. Today, largely thanks to Wolfensohn's drive for an initiative to help the Heavily Indebted Poor Countries, 27 impoverished countries are receiving debt relief on the order of $54 billion.
- Ten years ago, corruption was rarely mentioned in international development circles, where it was viewed as a political matter and as such beyond the Bank's purview. In 1996, at the Bank-Fund Annual Meetings, Wolfensohn gave a groundbreaking speech on the "cancer of corruption," citing it as a major burden on the poor in developing countries. Corruption is now widely recognized as a major impediment to development that must be tackled aggressively. The Bank itself is supporting some 600 anticorruption programs in nearly 100 countries and has struck more than 200 companies and individuals from its contractor list for engaging in fraud or corrupt activity.
- Ten years ago, HIV/AIDS was not always viewed as a significant issue on the development agenda. Today, the Bank is the largest provider of external resources to the developing countries for HIV/AIDS treatment and prevention initiatives.
- Ten years ago, women's issues were at best an add-on or an afterthought in development strategy. But between 1995 and 2003 the Bank committed nearly $7 billion for girls' education as well as for health, nutrition, and population projects, of which women are the major beneficiaries.
- On the environmental front, the Bank has expanded rapidly and is today the largest external provider of financing for environmental projects in the world.

The past decade has also seen the Bank refine and broaden its approach to one of its original core mandates, that of postconflict reconstruction. The Bank's efforts in Bosnia during the mid-1990s showed a new, more active approach to reconstruction that sought to provide swift assistance to survivors of the brutal conflict, while also helping cement the fragile peace accord. Since then the Bank has played a vital role in the West Bank and Gaza, Kosovo, Timor-Leste, Sierra Leone, and over 30 other countries, its expertise and finance helping to restore growth and peace.

Ten years ago, the World Bank was perceived almost solely as a lending institution. It is now equally focused on providing advice, knowledge, and global experience. The Bank also has taken advantage of the enormous potential of the Internet to help create new programs such as the African Virtual University, the Global Development Learning Network, and the Development Gateway.

Under Wolfensohn, the Bank has become more open and transparent. Wolfensohn personally encouraged efforts to reach out more to other international organizations, the private sector, and civil society. Many nongovernmental organizations (NGOs), including some that were among the Bank's most vitriolic critics, now engage in dialogue with the Bank, and many participate in the Bank's projects. It is generally more widely recognized today that, although NGO criticism will always be part of the relationship with the Bank, the critiques are seen more as constructive and worthy of review. Wolfensohn also made partnership with the private sector a central part of the Bank Group's activities.

Readers of this volume will see these changes in the World Bank and observe how Wolfensohn's thinking evolved over the 10 years of his presidency. For example, the idea that first appears in his 1996 Annual Meetings speech as the need for a "new paradigm" for development later reappears as the Comprehensive Development Framework, a holistic approach to development that links all its elements—social, structural, human, governance, environmental, economic, and financial—simultaneously. Other times it seems as if the world has evolved to catch up with his ideas. After years of Wolfensohn sounding the theme that both poor and rich countries live in "one world, not two," the September 11, 2001, attacks made it blindingly clear to everyone that "there is no wall" between developed and developing countries—that, as Wolfensohn put it in a March 2002 speech, "On September 11 the crisis of Afghanistan came to Wall Street, to the Pentagon, and to a field in Pennsylvania."

If there is one theme that shines throughout these 10 years of words, it is the focus on people, and in these pages Wolfensohn speaks frequently about the people he and his wife Elaine have met on their travels. He insists that poor people do not want charity—the issue is empowerment and how to ensure they "reach their potential." In that first Annual Meetings address in 1995, Wolfensohn speaks of the "nobility" of the people he has met in Brazil, China, Haiti, and Uganda. He goes on to say, "I have learned that the real test of development can be measured not by the bureaucratic approval process but by the smile on a child's face when a project is successful."

By telling stories of people he has met during his visits to developing countries, Wolfensohn reminds his audiences of the common humanity that unites people in wealthy countries with people in developing countries. There is the encounter in 1996 with a Muslim leader in Bosnia who has lost his wife and two daughters to a single shell, but who remains hopeful for a better future. There are the women he meets in a Rio *favela,* who proudly show him how a water project has brought them not only running water but also official recognition in society, evidenced by the printing of their names on their utility bills.

Through these stories, Wolfensohn repeatedly emphasizes that development is about more than just economics. It is about social justice and improving the daily lives of the 3 billion people who live on less than two dollars a day. This emphasis proved especially important during the aftermath of the Asian crisis, when, as markets and the press obsessed over the likely size of the next multi-billion-dollar rescue package, Wolfensohn drew attention back to the social fallout of the crisis.

"Humanizing" the World Bank was not always an easy task in an institution with more Ph.D.s than almost any other in the world. To jokingly provoke his managers and staff, Wolfensohn would occasionally speak of his pride in not being an economist, claiming that it gave him the ability to go beyond the numbers and understand the big development picture—a picture that always had human features.

If poor people and their suffering was a main theme throughout Wolfensohn's work, providing them hope for a better future was its counterpoint. From the time of his arrival at the Bank, Wolfensohn speaks about the need to provide hope to poor people. But it is in the later years of his presidency that hope emerges as a major theme. In those years, the theme is especially salient in his increasing interactions with youth groups from around the world, including at a meeting in Paris in 2003. In such meetings, Wolfensohn speaks feelingly of hope for the 1.8 billion people in the world who are under the age of 14, and the 2.8 billion who are under the age of 24—hope for jobs, opportunity, peace, and security in the post-9/11 world.

For all the focus on people, their hopes, and their dreams, however, the reader will find no cheap sentiment in these speeches and essays. The alert reader will observe Wolfensohn using his words strategically for maximum impact with the audience at hand, whether wealthy or poor, whether a group of finance ministers or a group of NGO activists, whether encouraging action on a new initiative or supporting ongoing efforts on an existing program. Wolfensohn also demonstrates an ear for the startling statistic that drives home a point. In one speech, for example, to illustrate the need for Africans to have greater confidence in their own future, Wolfensohn notes that 37 percent of African private wealth is held outside Africa, compared with only 3 percent in Asia.

Underneath the variations, however, the core of each address rests on a set of main messages delivered time and again, to ensure his points are penetrating the development debate. These core messages often start as a one-time off-hand comment, then grow to be a staple of his discourse. Often, months or years later, the same statistics and messages will show up in the speeches of others on the foreign policy and development scene, reinforcing the value of repetition to drive a point home.

Wolfensohn's constancy and determination are evident in his unrelenting support for the International Development Association, the Bank affiliate that provides concessional lending for the world's poorest countries. His advocacy helped keep IDA on the international agenda when the U.S. Congress was threatening to reduce its funding, and it played no small part in the success of the latest replenishment of the fund. In February 2005, donor countries agreed to contribute at least $34 billion during the next three years for development assistance, of which about $18 billion will come as new contributions from 40 donor countries. This represents, at a minimum, a 25 percent increase in over-all resources over the previous replenishment, the largest expansion of IDA resources in two decades.

The careful reader will also see in these speeches glimpses of Wolfensohn's past—as an investment banker, as a student at Harvard Business School, and as a child growing up in Australia. He draws on his business background, for example, to advocate for his reorganization of the Bank's bureaucracy and its decentralization to the field. He stresses the sanctity of a business deal and the importance of keeping one's word. And he speaks, often humorously, of the effect that his Australian background had on his world outlook.

As he chooses his words, Wolfensohn can often be seen seeking to strike the right balance between confident optimism and dire warnings of the dangers of inaction. On one hand, he warns of "the ticking time bomb" of the growth of youth in developing countries to underline the repercussions of ignoring young peoples' aspirations. He cautions audiences in wealthy countries against ignoring the growth of the developing world, noting that emerging markets may someday "redraw the economic map of the world." On the other hand, he inspires audiences by drawing their attention to the opportunities and possibilities of a better world if the right action is taken.

In choosing the pieces for this volume, the editors have allowed in only those words that Wolfensohn himself gave at the various venues. No "remarks as prepared for delivery" are included here—only the transcripts of what he actually said. This may sound like a small matter, but those who have worked with Wolfensohn on any of his speeches know the difference. In the end it is Wolfensohn's ability to improvise, to speak from the heart and for the moment, that sets him apart from most other speakers. So it is those words that are presented here.

Unfortunately, it was not possible to include all of Wolfensohn's remarks that have made an impression over the years, and not just because of length limitations but because some of the best addresses were not recorded. When approached about this book, one senior Bank official, present at Wolfensohn's first official trip to Africa in 1995, tells of an occasion where Wolfensohn gave off-the-cuff remarks to a state banquet. On the way to giving the speech, Wolfensohn asked only for a list of names of people to recognize, and then improvised a speech that the official described as "spellbinding" and that hit all the right "tough love messages" on poverty, government spending, and official corruption. Unfortunately, that speech was not recorded—but its impact remains with those who were there.

The speechwriters who have worked with Wolfensohn over the years describe the speechwriting process as eclectic, how he put an address together over a period of time and through a number of drafts. At less formal events, Wolfensohn would typically start with a draft and then put it aside, waiting until the event itself to gauge the atmosphere of the room before modifying the remarks so they would resonate as much as possible with the audience.

His approach on major policy addresses, such as Annual Meetings speeches, was more complex. Some on Wolfensohn's staff describe the first draft of these addresses as a rough gem such as one might find deep in a mine. Once brought to the surface, the dusky jewel is polished and smoothed through various redrafts until it is ready for display. Another compares the process to viewing a portrait that is hidden behind a curtain. With each draft that Wolfensohn revises, another piece of the curtain falls away to reveal another part of the portrait—this time the mouth, next the eyes, now the nose. Only when the speech is delivered is the portrait fully exposed for all to see in full color.

Although readers of this volume will hear much of Wolfensohn's opinions on a plethora of topics, one thing they will not hear, but that is just as important, is Wolfensohn listening. Yet one of Wolfensohn's legacies is that he did much to transform the World Bank from a top-down institution into one that listens to and learns from its critics.

What the reader also will not hear is the sound of Wolfensohn's Australian-accented voice. Although a naturalized U.S. citizen, Wolfensohn retains the accent he grew up with, which distinguishes him from previous Bank presidents who were born and raised in the United States. In a 1990 profile of Wolfensohn in his role as head of the Kennedy Center in Washington, D.C., the *Christian Science Monitor* described his voice as a "distinctive baritone, low, confiding, with an Australian angularity, an overlay of English discretion from the years he spent in London banking circles, and a bit of New York rasp."

Despite his impressive record of change at the World Bank, Wolfensohn still has his critics. Wolfensohn himself would admit to not having completed everything he had intended to achieve at the Bank. But, in the last year of his presidency, he would point to well-known development reports of previous decades, from the Pearson Commission to the Brandt Commission, to show that the links between poverty, peace, and development that he had so persistently advocated had been supported by many before him.

As the reader will find, Wolfensohn built on that foundation of ideas but also developed new ideas of his own and introduced concepts that would dramatically change the World Bank and the development landscape. By doing so, Wolfensohn has proved himself unique in the way he has brought together all the strands of development into a coherent whole, and in the passion he has brought to the bully pulpit of his position. He has energetically refocused the World Bank on poverty, and he has tirelessly drawn the attention of world leaders to the need to provide hope and a better future for the world's poor. But, above all, he has given voice to the voiceless, to those on the margins of society, to those on the outside looking in. As the reader will find in the pages of this volume, Jim Wolfensohn is truly a *Voice for the World's Poor*.

INCLUDING PEOPLE IN DEVELOPMENT

JUNE 1995 – MAY 2000

Letters to World Bank staff on first day as president

WASHINGTON, D.C. | JUNE 1, 1995

In these letters sent to all staff Bank-wide on Wolfensohn's first day on the job, he pays tribute to Lewis Preston, who preceded him as president and who died only weeks before. Wolfensohn speaks about his belief in social justice and his expectations of excellence in the institution. The letters reflect his desire for the Bank staff to work as a family, a theme to which he would often return.

Dear Colleagues:

I feel greatly privileged to join you today in your work at the World Bank Group. The achievements of the Bank, IFC and MIGA* have been considerable; you have every reason to be proud of the contribution you have made to the causes we all cherish.

The joy of my arrival is tempered by the circumstances of Lew Preston's illness and untimely death. He was a great banker and humanitarian, and I know that I can count on you to join me in seeking to complete his initiatives.

There has been much commentary in the press about my plans for the Bank Group, little or none of it originating from me. Let me then set forth as simply as I can the structure of my program.

I would like to serve four constituencies: first, our borrowers; second, those who entrust us with funds for our work; third, the important broader constituencies of support in both borrower and donor countries; and fourth, our staff and management.

To familiarize myself with the borrowers we serve, I will spend a substantial amount of time in the field during the next six months. In coordination with the Executive Directors, I will meet with government leaders, visit project sites, talk with supporters and critics alike, meet with NGOs [nongovernmental organizations] and other interest groups, within civil society—and just walk the streets. Elaine will join me on all these trips. I want to get a first-hand feel about how the Bank is doing, what is working, and what needs to be improved. I will report directly to those concerned my impressions from each trip. We can then examine issues, and where appropriate, take initiatives.

Second, I will visit our Part I shareholders.† I want to get a better sense of whether we are achieving their aims within the framework of an institution

---

* The International Finance Corporation and the Multilateral Investment Guarantee Agency, both part of the Bank Group.

† Part I shareholders are those (mostly developed) countries that contribute to the resources of the International Development Association.

which at times must balance conflicting expectations. True to the vision of our founding fathers, we need to be a proud and independent institution. We must never forget, however, that we are dependent on the support and resources of our shareholders to achieve our lofty goals. Like my predecessors, I am committed to sustaining our triple-A status as a borrower—the bedrock of our effectiveness.

Third, I will also meet with those who can assist us in our work and through whom we can better reach our goals. I will meet with the IMF [International Monetary Fund], agencies of the UN [United Nations], the regional development banks, as well as the NGO community, to further existing initiatives in a cooperative spirit. I will also meet with leaders in the private sector to further my own understanding of how we can forge this important and expanding partnership in our development work. The challenges in our world today are momentous; cooperation—not conflict—must be our goal. We must be open to outside commentary, however difficult it may be to listen. We must face issues head on and early, in order to assume business and intellectual leadership on issues affecting our activities.

Finally, let me speak to our World Bank family, without which our dreams cannot be realized. From what I can see, we are blessed with a group of dedicated and highly qualified people—diverse and caring, with a long and unique collective experience. It is much too early for me to comment on the existing climate of morale and performance in our institution. Let me communicate simply what I care about and what I expect will characterize the organization under my period as President.

First, I expect from you loyalty to the institution and to each other. By this I do not mean that there should not be dissent nor that we cannot criticize our practices or actions. But criticisms must be internal and constructive, accompanied by initiatives to solve the problems. I will regard externally voiced criticism of the Bank—of ourselves—as an indication of a desire to find alternative employment.

Second, I hope we can all recognize that the Bank Group is not some inanimate object, that it is the sum of the individuals. None of us can avoid the responsibilities for what we do. Each of our actions affects our collective image as an institution.

Third, I want us to look outwards and forward, not just to internal processes. I believe we all work here because we care about the world: we care about poverty, the environment, social justice, and many other issues which make up the dreams of the institution. These should be our guiding lights. Our organization and internal practice must serve our objectives, not dominate them.

Fourth, I expect absolute standards of excellence in our work, and in our renewal of skills.

Finally, we must have integrity in our word and in our behavior, inside and outside our institution.

I should add only that I have a very strong sense of family, not only about Elaine, Sara, Naomi and Adam, but about each one of you. You can count on me to act fairly towards you, and notwithstanding our size, I expect that each of you will care about one another.

Entering our second half century, the Bank Group is at a critical juncture in our history. The world around us has changed, and its expectations from, and demands on, our institution have become enormously complex. We should regard this as a period of opportunity.

I am truly proud to be with you at this time, looking to create an even greater institution, worthy of our dreams, and critically important to our children and those who come after them.

Sincerely yours,
James D. Wolfensohn

Dear Colleagues:

In my letter to you this morning, I set out the structure of my program for the initial few months as President.

As I mentioned, one of the constituencies I intend to serve is the staff and management of this institution—the World Bank family. I look forward to listening to and learning from all of you. To begin this dialogue, I am opening up several lines of communications.

Starting today, I plan to meet with as many of you as possible. Over the coming months, I hope to have frank conversations with you through a series of Open Houses with randomly selected groups of staff and managers, through meetings with the management teams of each Vice Presidency, and by organizing informal breakfasts and lunches with various small groups.

Innovation and creativity are important elements of the world around us. To capture your constructive suggestions I have established an All-in-One* "IDEAS-line" which I encourage you to use. Your suggestions will help me to understand the character of the institution and will play a major role in defining what needs to be done in the future. I will communicate the results of this endeavor shortly after the Annual Meetings.

Finally, let me reiterate how pleased I am to be working with you.

Sincerely yours,
James D. Wolfensohn

---

* All-in-One was the electronic mail system in use at the Bank at the time.

"WE'RE HERE FOR ONE REASON ONLY, AND THAT IS TO CHANGE THE WORLD"

Remarks at an open house for World Bank staff

WASHINGTON, D.C. | JUNE 2, 1995

In the second of many townhall meetings he would have with staff over the next 10 years, Wolfensohn shares reflections on his first day as president of the Bank. He spells out his reasons for wanting to become president, praises the quality of the staff, and appeals for teamwork across the World Bank Group.

First of all, I want to say to you, for Elaine and for myself, how delighted we are to have the chance to meet you. We don't easily have the opportunity of meeting everybody in the Bank, so what we're trying to do is the impossible, which is to have a series of functions like this, which are not so big that we don't have the opportunity to say hello individually. That will take us a little longer to get around the institution. I may have to leave it to my successor to finish. But we're going to do our best, and within the next week, I think, or the next few days that we're here, we will have another couple of receptions, and then regularly each month after that.

We hope very much that you will appreciate that what we want to do is to be close to all of you. I'm exceptionally insecure, and because of that insecurity I need to know who my friends are in the institution. And the best way to do that is to fill you up with a glass of wine, give you a piece of cheese, and hope that that will carry us forward together. And when you start getting fed up with me, I'll give you another glass of wine and another piece of cheese, and hope that that will do the trick.

On a more serious note, it's clear that we have a very big job to do together. It's a job that I described in my note to you, which I hope you will have received yesterday. And I hope you will have received a subsequent note, which says that it's my expectation and hope that you will get in touch with me on this wonderful computer line that has been set up, which I confess to you I don't know where the end of it is, and if I did, I wouldn't know how to turn on the machine. But I will very shortly. And I am extremely hopeful that we can have open access to my office, and you can be absolutely sure that I will see everything that comes in, though you may not be absolutely sure that I will respond to each one of you individually.

I think I said in my note that it's my intention to try and get a sense of what is going on and to get back to you at or about the time of the Bank-Fund meetings. There's no doubt that I will get back to some of you in the interim. But I want to assure you that I will be taking very seriously what it is you send to me, and that it is my intention to be guided very significantly by the serious observations that you make.

I'm anxious for this direct dialogue because there is a certain malaise in the institution now, which led me to put a page two on that memorandum to you. And I thought about that page two a lot, because you have to wonder why is it that you would send out a page that talks about loyalty, that talks about excellence, that talks about family, and that talks about living together and says that, if you've got problems, let's resolve them inside and not outside.

Well, the reason for that is really very simple. I've had now five weeks or so, maybe a little longer, anticipating this job, and I've been exposed to observations from the outside, many of them negative—not all of them negative, but too many of them negative. And much of that negativism has been conveyed to me by friends and associates outside the institution, who have heard these negative comments from people inside the institution. And if there are 11,000 of us, and each of us has a couple of people in our family, it means that there are 33,000 people running around Washington saying that the World Bank suffers in the following respects, or they can't stand whomever it is, and that they're waiting apprehensively for this new president who has characteristics they already dislike, and so on. In fact, the whole of the period before I got appointed was marked for me by what I read in the newspapers about what I am alleged to have said the day before, about staff cuts or about resignations of vice presidents or whatever, none of which I actually said. All of it emanated from within this institution, because apparently you've got to talk about something at the coffee meetings in the morning and in the various groupings.

I have no problem about internal criticism. I have no problem about vigorous internal criticism. But I have a big problem about destructive criticism. So if there's criticism, I welcome it, but I'd also like you to put a paragraph saying what you think should be done about it. And I would urge you not to do it with anonymous letters, too many of which I have received, telling me about individuals and telling me about systems in the Bank, and signed either J. Smith or J. Jones, or signed most recently with names of people in the Bank where there were six or seven people with the same name. Whoever is writing me those letters is pretty smart, but if I find them, they'll be out of here in 30 seconds. And if you find them, I hope you'll tell me, so that together we can throw them out in 30 seconds, because that is not the environment that we want. And as to the outside, as I said rather presumptuously in my letter, if, in a measurable time, like tomorrow, we find that people are talking down the Bank, I will accept that as a valid reason to recognize that whoever it is is not happy here and I will gently assist them to leave.

And the reason I'm saying that is not to be confrontational, and it is not for my benefit. It is that, in order to win the real battle, we have to be a team, and that's why I spoke as I did on the second page of my note to you. And if I hadn't had reason to write it, I would never have written it.

And so I ask first that, as a family, we recognize that, yes, there may be problems, but that they can be resolved, by having an open system with you and by being available. I want you to know that I am ready to tackle problems and I'm ready to tackle them head on. And I will not give you a 250-page report as my answer, giving you the alternatives from which to choose. I will consider the alternatives, and I will make a decision. And to make that decision work, I will need you to help me.

And so I hope that you share this spirit, because every one of you is here because you have a spirit and you have training and you have a competence, which is what got you into the institution. And every one of you has a dream, which is not a dream of fighting paper and internal politics. Because if it were that, why come to work? Why be here?

What is needed is a sense of mission, which I'm sure each one of you has, and a dream and a sense of something on the outside. There are those among you who live in the ecosystem of the Bank. The ecosystem of the Bank is such that you can exist in the Bank with no sense of the outside world. There are procedures, there are personnel manuals, there's health service, there's catering.

There are rumors, there's sex, there's everything you need inside the ecosystem. And the wonderful thing is that you can exist in it without ever having to think about the outside.

I don't think that's a particularly useful concept. Thank God not everyone has it, but there are too many who do. And I hope that soon no one will have that view and that whatever the current ecosystem becomes, it will be a system that serves the outside, because we're here for one reason only, and that is to change the world. It's quite a thing to change the world. The Bank has been doing it for 50 years. It's been criticized. It's made a number of notable successes and no doubt a number of notable failures. But the world is a very much better place for having had the World Bank.

And now we're coming up to the year 2000. We're in an environment where the Bank faces a lot of criticism, where there's a lot of budgetary restraint. The reason I was late today is that I was talking to certain people about IDA [the International Development Association] and the replenishments, which is an important part of our activities. There are NGOs [nongovernmental organizations] out there that love us, and too many that don't love us, and some of them that don't love us have great justification in not loving us. This is not monolithically an institution that gets everything right.

And so there are criticisms that to a degree are valid, and there are criticisms that are wholly invalid. But what we have to have is not only a dialogue inside our institution but also a dialogue outside our institution. And we need to regain something that, to an extent, I think we've lost, which is the intellectual leadership and the proactive leadership that an institution with a bunch of the brightest people in the world should assert.

And I may have a long way to go in terms of providing that intellectual leadership, but I can assure you that I'm working very hard to be an important intellectual leader in terms of development and the issues that we face. And to do that I need you, because collectively you have—and maybe individually you have—far more experience than I do and greater knowledge. But I'm a fast learner, and I can promise you I am a learner with a mission, and I am a learner who is going to work very hard to make you proud of the intellectual leadership that I hope I can give this institution.

But to give that leadership, I need your support, and I need you to be thinking in terms of proactive activity. And I need you to be thinking in terms of excellence, and I need you to be thinking in terms of training yourselves and training the people who report to you. And I need you to be thinking in terms of what the problems are and facing them squarely and early and directly, and not with 17 alternatives but with a recommendation. Because I can assure you that some elements of this Bank would be out of business if it were in the private sector, and I want to be able to say that, if this Bank were in the private sector, it would be the best private sector institution that there is in the world. And I want to be able to say to [Managing Director of the International Monetary Fund] Michel Camdessus and secretaries of the Treasury and [President of the Inter-American Development Bank] Enrique Iglesias and everybody else that I want to work with you, that *we* want to work with you, that we're not competitive in terms of turf, that we're the best partners, and the quality of what we do is the best, and the people are the best, and the sense of urgency is the greatest, and the directness is the best, and that we're not judging ourselves by theoretical models but by the effectiveness of what we do. And that is something that I hope I can bring to the organization, largely because I have made my living being effective.

And you may say that's crass and it's commercial and it's from the outside and I'm an outsider and I don't know beans about development. But actually I do know a little bit about development, and I do know a little bit about the issues. In fact, for 20 or more years, I've been interested in the issues, and I've been involved in the issues, but as an amateur. But I'm now a professional, and I gave up a lot to come here, to be the best professional heading the best professional organization there is in either the public or the private sector. And that's why I need all of you, because this is not a one-man job. This is a job for a family.

Let me just comment on that. There is something sort of interesting that an outsider observes on becoming an insider at the Bank, and that is that one keeps hearing comments about what seems to be this disembodied figure that is the Bank—that the Bank is doing this, the Bank is doing that, someone up there is doing that, the Executive Directors are doing it, the Board is doing it.

The Bank is not disembodied. The Bank is you. There is an individual responsibility on everybody. There is one on me, and there's one on every one of you in terms of what this institution is. And some people have lost that sense. They regard it as a paymaster, a provider of health services, and something to bitch about. And that's no fun.

I want everybody to come in feeling the same pride that I do. And I want a team that feels that same pride, and if you don't feel that pride, then go find pride somewhere else, because whether the team is 11,000 or 5,000 or 2,000, let's have a team that cares and that is united and that is on board.

That gets us to the issue of numbers. I haven't come in saying we will cut 30 percent or cut 10 percent or increase 20 percent. What I'm going to do in the first six months, together with Elaine, is to get out in the field and see what we think is the mission of the Bank. I am simultaneously in that first two months going to visit every sector of the Bank, and I will be dealing *en passant* with such little things as Gaza and the West Bank and Mexico's banking system and the Argentine banking system, and goodness knows what else which will come up in a random way during that period.

But my objective in that period of time is to get a sense for myself of where is our relative advantage and what is it that we're doing well, what is it that we can improve, where we should put our resources, and how we should work to that end. When I know that, I'll tell you the right size of this institution. I'm not coming in with a budgetary notion before I know what it is that we need to do. Maybe we need 22,000 people. Maybe we need 6,000 people. I don't know.

The one thing I do know is that when we know what we're doing and when we have the objectives and when we know the resources, we'll have the right number of people, and they'll be people who care and they'll be people who stand erect and who are proud to be in the institution. And it's my privilege, really, to be here at a time of change, when we're coming up to a millennium shift, at a moment when we can reexamine what's important to the Bank and what's important to the world, and where we can cast out for ourselves a program that is not just important for us but is important for our kids and for the people who come after us.

And that's why I've come here at the old age of 61 to spend my declining years in a nice comfortable job working 16 hours a day, seven days a week, for a dream. And Elaine and I came tonight and we're coming to meet all of you simply to say to you that you can count on our effort. I hope you can count on our integrity. You can count on our commitment to all of you. And you can count on our desire to be part of a family that it's fun to come to work with every day.

So thank you all for being here. Mark* will now tell me, if he's here, that I've spoken too long, but then I do, and Elaine and I will be very happy to meet any of you we haven't met, and I wish you a good weekend.

---

* Mark Malloch Brown, at that time director of external relations at the World Bank.

Address at the Fourth World Conference on Women

BEIJING | SEPTEMBER 15, 1995

This address focuses mainly on gender, with Wolfensohn pointing to education for girls as central to development, a topic not always accepted at the time by mainstream development experts. The speech is also noteworthy for the way Wolfensohn takes on criticisms of the Bank from his perspective of being president for 90 days and having visited over 20 countries.

Madame Chair, Mrs. Mongella, Mr. Kittani,* Distinguished Guests, Ladies and Gentlemen:

I arrived in Beijing last evening to find that I am sharing the platform with Prime Minister Brundtland and President Fujimori,† as well as with a representative of youth, and I must say that I am deeply honored to be in such company. I have had a morning of discussions and meetings, and I do indeed have a prepared text, which is available and which is being distributed to you. But I cannot but begin by saying that I'm very proud to be here representing the World Bank, and I am extraordinarily conscious of the important dialogue into which I am entering.

It is very difficult to ignore the importance of the arguments one hears about the World Bank: the criticisms of structural adjustment, the arguments on how unfeeling is the Bank, the notion that we apply preconceived models developed in Washington to the detriment particularly of the disadvantaged and women, and that our efforts to alleviate poverty instead increase poverty. All the things that I came to do at the World Bank appear to be perceived by many as being exactly the reverse.

I cannot but begin by saying that, in the last 90 days, I have had the opportunity to visit more than 20 countries. I've been in villages, I've been in slums, I've been in health care facilities. I've met with women's groups, I've met with NGOs [nongovernmental organizations], and, most important, I've met with my colleagues. And I want you to know that, unless I am living in a different world, the perception, at least, of the people *in* the World Bank—and my own perception—about our goals and our aspirations is that we want to work *alongside* people in poverty everywhere, to bring about sustainable development in the world, and, most particularly and most centrally, to recog-

---

* Gertrude Mongella, former minister of state for women's affairs in Tanzania, was secretary-general of the Beijing conference. Ismat Kittani was special representative of the secretary-general of the United Nations.
† Gro Harlem Brundtland, prime minister of Norway, and Alberto Fujimori, president of Peru.

nize the position of women, to recognize that much needs to be done and that we need to join with those at this conference in taking action.

I've come here today because I wanted to demonstrate personally that the World Bank is committed to the causes that you have come here for, and that my colleagues in the Bank, both in Washington and in our offices around the world, are committed to working with you. And it may well be that in the past there have been examples of things that we've done wrong. I'm sure there are many. And it may well be that in the past even our paradigms of development have not been effective. But I've learned one thing in the last 90 days, and that is that the development business is a very tough business, and that in order to make it effective, and in order to reach the sort of goals that people here are looking for, we must work together in partnership and with a sense of mutual trust and mutual commitment.

There isn't a country that I visit that I don't go through the first hour of meetings with the NGOs hearing the set pieces—about how bad the World Bank is and how unfeeling, how ignorant, how inappropriate are our policies. And after about an hour of the invective, I try and get the discussion down to at least a normal level of voice and get across the understanding that the Bank is currently the largest donor in the world to issues related to women. We are putting $5 billion annually into projects that involve quite specific issues relating to the advancement of women's rights, to human rights, and to economic opportunity.

And if we're doing it wrong, we welcome having a dialogue about it. We want to be partners with the governments that we serve, with the NGOs with whom we work, with the interest groups, and with the civil society, in order to develop in the years to come more effective mechanisms to achieve the objectives for which you're meeting here.

So, by way of introduction, I merely want to say to you that I am committed, and my colleagues are committed, and I ask you to listen to what we have to say, to advise us in whatever way you wish, but that you should regard us as a partner who is committed to the same objectives that you are.

My first trip as World Bank president was to Mali, and it was a meaningful trip. There was a young child born just as we arrived, and I've long and often thought about her since then. She has a one in four chance of going to school. She faces the prospect of stunted growth. At the age of six, she faces the prospect of brutal genital mutilation. She'll be married young. She'll have two decades of childbearing and 1 chance in 20 of dying in childbirth.

As I saw in villages throughout Africa, and in other places, the women grow most of the food. Yet they're the last to sit down at the table. They are the people who are absolutely at the center of the village life. And, if they

work hard, they'll make less than a third of a man's wage. They look for justice and opportunity. They look for financing for their ventures.

We in the World Bank are committed to working alongside these women, and I personally have been involved with them. We are, in fact, dealing with the 1.3 billion people in the world who earn less than a dollar a day, 70 percent of whom are women. But we're doing it with concessionary funds from IDA [the International Development Association], and I must say to you that the single biggest problem I'm facing now, before I can even enter into the types of projects that we'd all like to be doing, is a challenge to the very existence of IDA itself.

We are facing the possible withdrawal of some countries from the full extent of their commitments to IDA. IDA is operating on a budget of $6 billion. If that is cut, as it may well be, by a third or a half, we will have $2 billion or $3 billion less to spend worldwide on issues that directly affect the subject of this conference. So I would ask all of you to go back from this conference, to your countries, and tell people that IDA is essential to education, health, nutrition, agriculture extension, control of AIDS—all the issues that are central not only to development but particularly to the role of women. And any reduction in contributions to IDA would be a direct and immediate challenge to the activities and to the initiatives that we can take as a result of this conference.

I'd also like to say that, in terms of the activities of the Bank and the actions that we can take with regard to women, you cannot look at this in a singular, compartmentalized fashion. Development is a systemic business. One has to take an overall approach. But what I think is called for at this conference, and what is clear to us, is that women's issues *not* be just an adjunct issue, not just an add-on, but that they be central to that systemic solution. And we at the Bank are looking to increase and expand the input of those with knowledge and those with special commitment to these issues, so that, as we generate and develop our projects, we can have, right from the beginning, at the policy level and at the implementation level, a key and central role in those aspects that relate to women's rights and women's opportunities.

I might say that this move is not just a move to recognize women. It will require a change in behavior on the part of men—in the households in which we live, in the societies we build, and, may I say, in the institutions in which we work. It is crucial that this be a two-sided change, a change not only in the opportunities for women but also in the response of men who play their part.

Before this group I can say straightforwardly that, as you well know, we work with governments, and it is for you who are in government to work in partnership with us, if you so choose, in designing programs that will put the results of this conference into practice. You play the key role in removing discrimination in laws, in your institutions, and in the freedom that you allow to civil society.

But we in the development institutions can play a very important role in investing in women. We know that economic reform programs that are specifically directed to the female population pay a most effective return for the whole of society. By ensuring health care, and especially reproductive services, we give strength to the society in which you live. And, as we have shown recently in the establishment of a new microenterprise finance facility, we also recognize that, to create economic opportunity, we need to have new paradigms of development to assist women in their economic activities. This $200 million facility that we have established is just a beginning, but over 10 years it will help nearly 8 million women and their families and give 40 million family members a good start. As I said earlier, we are already expending over $5 billion in the Bank on programs specifically about women, and we are looking for ways in which we can be particularly and demonstrably effective in our efforts.

Having seen the signs outside the hall, I'm well aware that we're looking for action. And, indeed, the Bank is acting already. But nowhere is that action more important to us than in education for girls. Of the 900 million people who are illiterate in the world today, women outnumber men by two to one. And 60 percent of the 130 million children who are not attending primary school are girls. I'm well aware of the goal that was set by the 1990 World

Summit for Children,‡ of an 80 percent completion rate for primary education by 2000. We in the Bank have been exploring this area for very good and obvious reasons. I think it is well understood—and it's been repeated many times at this conference, as it's been reported to me—that the return to educating girls is not just in reading and writing, but in the development of the society. It is in health care. It is in control of population. It is in establishing a society that is just.

And so we at the Bank have been looking at yet a further goal, and we have committed our own funds to try and establish that goal, which is to increase that 80 percent goal for primary education to 100 percent by 2010. But more significant even than that, we are looking to add another goal: that 60 percent of all our children should get a secondary education, and half of them should be girls and half of them boys. We at the Bank have decided that we will increase the amount of money that we're giving to education in the primary and secondary schools from $1.1 billion a year to $1.5 billion a year, for an extra $2 billion over the next five years. And, of that $1.5 billion, we are going to set aside 60 percent for the education of girls—a total of $900 million a year for the next five years directed to the education of young girls.

This is not a trivial commitment. This is a fundamental commitment and an established policy now of the Bank. And we will be working with governments and with other institutions to try to generate an increase in giving to this particular sector. We will be increasing our own participation in it, our own personnel, and you can rely on us to be central to this activity in the years ahead.

My hope in coming to this conference is that I can establish with you that, after barely 90 days on the job as president of the World Bank, I have a deep and abiding commitment to the issues that this conference is addressing. I believe that my feelings resonate in the halls of the Bank. I am prepared to recognize that the Bank does not have all the answers, nor does anybody. I'm anxious to establish with you a partnership for the future. I'm anxious to listen. I'm anxious to be open. I'm anxious to challenge existing practices. But what I'm most anxious for is that, at the end of my time in office, I can be judged on our record of building effective programs that have at their very core the advancement of women.

Thank you so much.

---

‡ The World Summit for Children, organized by UNICEF, was held in New York in September 1990.

Address to the Board of Governors at the Annual Meetings of the World Bank and the
International Monetary Fund

WASHINGTON, D.C. | OCTOBER 10, 1995

*This first Annual Meetings speech shows clearly how Wolfensohn artfully
uses anecdotes about people he has met on his trips to the field to portray in
human terms the challenge of poverty and development. The speech is perhaps
best remembered as the one where Wolfensohn defined success as the "smile
on a child's face." But many of the themes that would guide his presidency
can also be found here: fighting poverty for a more just and peaceful world,
the debts of poor countries, ownership, knowledge, the environment, and the
internal renewal of the Bank.*

Mr. Chairman, Governors, Ladies and Gentlemen:

It gives me great pleasure to welcome you to Washington for these Annual
Meetings of the World Bank and the International Monetary Fund—my first
as president. I extend a very special welcome to the delegation from Brunei
[Darussalam], which today becomes the Bank's 179th member country.

I am greatly honored by my appointment as president of the World Bank
Group, and I wish to thank you for the confidence you have shown in elect-
ing me to this position. Elaine and I pledge to work hard and, with your help,
to make a contribution to the dream that we all share: a better world for our
children. Let me say at the outset that I feel greatly privileged to be working
with my friend [IMF Managing Director] Michel Camdessus, who is giving
me so willingly the benefit of his immense experience.

The Bank Group has a distinguished record of achievement. Since my arrival four months ago, I have visited many countries and projects and have
been gratified and encouraged by the strong partnership that exists among us,
our clients, and our member governments. I have learned that development is
a tough and complicated business. After 50 years of operation, and with new
leadership, now is a good time for the Bank Group to take stock. The world
around us has changed, and its expectations from, and demands on, our institution have become ever more complex. I regard this as a difficult period, but
one of enormous opportunity.

One thing is clear: we must continue to act, so that poverty will be alleviated,
our environment protected, social justice extended, human rights strengthened,
and women's rights advanced, all in the cause of a more just and peaceful world.
We must ensure that our organization functions at the highest level to achieve
these goals.

In embarking on this task, I am very conscious of the sadness we all feel at the tragic loss of my predecessor, Lewis T. Preston. Lew was a great banker and a humanitarian. He loved the Bank, and he and Patsy worked hard to improve its effectiveness and enhance its reputation. We are grateful for all that Lew gave to the institution, and we would like Patsy and the family to know that he will always be remembered with affection. In particular, Lew's belief that educating girls is the best investment a country can make is recognized in the Lewis T. Preston Education Program for Girls, recently established in his honor.

What are you expecting from me after my first few months with the Bank? Weighty pronouncements? Massive reorganization plans? Headline news? Instead of any of those, I am about to give a progress report, an indication of my approach to my new responsibilities, and some insight into the direction in which I would like to lead the Bank.

A Sense of Direction

To gain a sense of that direction, I have spent about a third of my time in these past four months traveling to our borrowing and lending member countries—talking and listening to government leaders, businesspeople, activists in NGOs [nongovernmental organizations], farmers, trade unionists, students, mothers and children. Elaine and I have visited dozens of the projects that the Bank is supporting, and a number of images have stayed with me:

- The woman entrepreneur I met in the small town of Katwe, Uganda, converting banana peels into charcoal briquettes and using the proceeds from her sales to improve her community. She had all the pride of the chairwoman of a multinational company as she shared with me her pencil-written records.
- Villagers in the arid province of Gansu, China, to whom a Bank-financed project delivers water through a 50-kilometer system that traverses mountains and valleys. Those villagers are using their own resources—in partnership with government experts—to invest in agriculture, roads, and education for their children.
- Slum dwellers in Port-au-Prince, Haiti, and in Salvador, Brazil, working—with our help—to install clean water and sanitation facilities and thus contribute to their own health and productivity while protecting their environment.

I saw enormous challenges: the monumental power and fragility of the Amazon and the damage done by people in need of land and in need of hope; schools in Africa, with 90 children in a class, working 10 to a book and 2 to a pencil; the appalling conditions facing the people of Gaza, where incomes have been stagnant for a decade, yet where investment and job creation must be part of any lasting peace; the islands of the South Pacific, where our environment is under attack as foreign entities seek to destroy natural forests for profit without any long-term concern for the future of the islanders.

Although my odyssey is not complete, I have learned of the tremendous diversity among the Bank's clientele: dynamic growth in East Asia and parts of Latin America, but not enough growth in much of Africa; the unique challenges of transition in Eastern Europe and the former Soviet Union; and the special needs of states that either are failing or are struggling to be born, from Burundi to Bosnia.

I have learned that the real test of development can be measured not by the bureaucratic approval process but by the smile on a child's face when a project is successful. I have learned of the power of development when people are given the chance to participate in it. Most of all, I have learned that there is nobility and capacity in the people we are trying to assist—and that there is a vital need for the World Bank Group to help with the huge, unfinished development agenda. The developing countries deserve our support for moral and social reasons. But they also need our support because they represent future growth for us all. And equitable growth means stability for our planet.

If the Bank Group is to be as effective as it can be in contributing to this goal, it must adjust to new conditions. And the key questions guiding change are these: What do you, our members, need from us today, next year, and five years and more from now? And where can we make the crucial difference? As I attempt to give a sense of my current thinking, let me organize my remarks along the following lines:

- What is the context in which the Bank operates today?
- What is the role of the Bank in development, now and in the coming years?
- What can the Bank do to achieve its objectives in an effective and accountable manner?
- What immediate and early initiatives are we taking?

The Context: A Changing World

We are, of course, operating in a context that is vastly different from that of 10 or even 5 years ago. The post–Cold War era has witnessed perhaps the most momentous changes in economic history. Country after country has moved away from command-and-control economic policies to greater reliance on markets. The rapid expansion of trade and technology has accelerated global integration, with the developing countries contributing 75 percent of the growth in world exports in recent years. There has been a transformation in private capital flows, which now total three times official development assistance. As democracy has swept the world, a host of new players have added their different strengths to the cause of development—in the private sector, among NGOs in local communities, and in civil society.

All this has raised expectations of development and made the potential for development greater than ever before. Yet the challenges, too, are growing. We have made good progress on poverty reduction in several areas, including East Asia and some parts of Latin America. But still 1.3 billion people live on a dollar a day or less. Adequate sanitation and electricity remain beyond the reach of two-fifths of the world's people. This shocking poverty is fueled by continuing rapid population growth of more than 80 million people a year worldwide, 95 percent of them in the developing countries. And it is compounded by the threat to biodiversity and the environment with continued profligate waste in the industrial world. Given current population and urban growth rates over the next generation, industrial output and energy use in the developing countries will increase fivefold, carrying a risk of irreversible environmental damage. We must heed the warnings of the [1992] Rio Earth Summit and act to protect the world for our children.

I have been encouraged by the high priority now being given to the environment by more and more developing countries and by their increasing requests for the Bank's assistance in this area. The richer nations, since they are the greatest polluters, must share this burden. Progress is being made, through collaboration on the Global Environment Facility, for instance. But much more remains to be done. Without environmental protection, development can be neither lasting nor equitable. My commitment to the task is unequivocal.

The fundamental problems of equity between rich and poor nations also exist in regions that are growing dynamically. In Latin America the poorest 20 percent of the population receive less than 4 percent of the income and have even less of the assets. In other regions, too, the gap between rich and poor is getting worse. The distribution of the benefits of growth presents one of the major challenges to stability in the world today. Social injustice can destroy economic and political advances. This is a challenge that must be addressed by the governments and leaders of the countries we work with.

We must learn more about the why and the how of income distribution. We must measure progress not only in gross domestic product per capita but also in social and environmental benefit per capita, as we are seeking to do in some of our most recent work. And we must be aware of the close relation between peace and development. We cannot ignore crises such as those in Bosnia, Gaza, and Rwanda and the challenges they present to the world development community.

The Challenge to IDA and the Need for a New Compact

It strikes me as bitterly ironic that just as we are reaching a consensus on how to address these challenges in our changing world, the threat to development assistance has never been greater. I refer here specifically to the funding crisis facing the Bank Group's concessional affiliate, the International Development Association.

As you know, IDA's basic constituency is the world's 3 billion poorest people. Ninety percent of IDA's lending goes to countries with incomes per capita below $600 a year. Using its global experience, IDA advises the poorest countries on their economic reforms. It is the largest investor in their education and environmental programs and in other vital areas, such as helping to combat AIDS.

With the help of IDA-supported projects, in the past several years alone malnutrition among infants was cut by half in 6,000 villages in India. Over

6 million textbooks were distributed to primary schools in Africa. And millions of women and children in Central America received basic nutrition.

In these ways and more, IDA is the backbone of the international effort to help the world's poorest nations help themselves. And yet, despite the record, there is a serious question about the fulfillment of some donor commitments under IDA10, the 10th replenishment of IDA's capital. Budget cutting by the U.S. Congress has led to delays and may lead to large reductions in the size of the contribution by IDA's leading donor. And for every dollar cut by the United States, IDA could lose a total of five dollars as other nations reduce their contributions proportionately.

This means that if congressional estimates of a U.S. cut of approximately 50 percent materialize, overall donor contributions to IDA in the coming 12 months could be reduced from $6 billion to under $3 billion. Achieving an adequate IDA11 for the next three years will be extraordinarily difficult if IDA10 is reduced so drastically. This is not only a threat to IDA; it is a threat to the long-term viability of multilateral financing for development.

As Michel Camdessus has pointed out, if IDA is seriously underfunded, we will be faced with a world of increasingly unstable nations. Some of the ministers here today will have to abandon plans for building human resources, expanding education for girls, increasing the supply of clean water, investing in infrastructure, or moving soldiers out of the barracks and onto small farms. There are so many urgent tasks.

The donor community needs to understand the costs of an underfunded IDA. We must explain that world citizenship has a price and that IDA is central to the whole development process. National budget-cutting exercises in the industrial countries must give due weight to international considerations. Money saved now for domestic purposes will lead to huge costs later. It is in the donors' own self-interest to maintain an adequate level of support.

Obviously, IDA and its partners in government and civil society must be accountable and must be seen to spend scarce resources wisely and well. There must be a compact: in return for the donor community's ensuring that IDA has adequate resources, recipient countries and the Bank must ensure that those resources are used even more effectively. Projects must be well managed, and corruption must be eliminated. In addition, we need to provide better information about the benefits of this important work to donor governments—and to their voters.

The Problem of Debt

In addition to resource constraints, some of the poorer countries face serious problems of overhanging debt. Yes, private capital flows have exploded, but more than 80 percent has gone to about a dozen countries. Private investment is not yet the answer for the poorer countries.

We know that there is no universal solution to the problem of overhanging debt. A case-by-case approach is necessary. With current instruments, we are already providing resources to help the majority of indebted countries meet their needs for both debt service and repayment. But, for a small number of countries, the debt overhang remains just too great. And, as it grows, new lending becomes less effective.

Roughly a quarter of the poorest countries' debt is owed to multilateral institutions such as the Bank and the Fund. We must therefore review the options for addressing the problem of the countries that cannot escape from their debt overhang. You all know that the Bank and the IMF are studying the issue. Together, we expect to make some recommendations to our boards and to bring our conclusions before the Development Committee at the Spring Meetings of our organizations. The issue is difficult and the options are many. But we believe that the problem merits serious attention and deserves a clear indication of what the Bank and the Fund can recommend.

Let me repeat: the crucial need to free up more resources—whether by reducing multilateral debt or by replenishing IDA—must be matched by the track record and by the commitment of the recipients to sound policies and effective, transparent implementation. This must be our compact.

The Role of the Bank in Development

What is the Bank's role in this compact, now and in the future? As you know, the Bank has evolved throughout its history, from an agency for postwar reconstruction 50 years ago to a global development institution today. Recently I visited Japan, where evidence of the Bank's assistance is manifest, as it is in over two dozen other countries that have "graduated" from requiring our help.

As the needs of our members have changed, the Bank has changed to meet them. The Bank Group of institutions is one result. I have already talked about the crucial importance of IDA. But there is more to the Bank Group than IDA. And there is more to the Bank Group's work than just lending.

There is the International Bank for Reconstruction and Development, whose original genius remains as valid, if not more valid, today as five decades ago: to borrow on the financial markets in order to fund long-term development through loans to governments; to use its guarantee power to mobilize additional private capital; and to transfer the lessons of development experience across countries. Like my predecessors, I am committed to sustaining the IBRD's triple-A borrowing status, because that is the bedrock of our effectiveness, allowing us to play our triple role as lender, adviser, and partner to our clients whose projects we assist.

There is the International Finance Corporation, which last year made loan and equity commitments of close to $3 billion to help develop the private sector in 67 developing countries. For every dollar the IFC invested, six additional dollars were leveraged from other sources. But this is far from being the only measure of the IFC's effectiveness. The range of its services is growing dramatically, from advice on capital market development in Vietnam to assistance with the privatization of agriculture in Russia. And it continues to push ahead on the frontier issues of private finance: support for small businesses in Africa, or establishing a biodiversity fund for Latin America. Looking to the future, I believe the IFC can extend its reach and expand its development impact.

There is also the Multilateral Investment Guarantee Agency, founded in 1988, whose goal is to stimulate private investment in developing countries by insuring against noncommercial risk. In six short years of operation, MIGA has leveraged total investment of close to $9 billion in 36 countries. The only constraint on its doing more is its very conservative capital and gearing ratio, which I would hope to take up with our shareholders at a future point.

The IBRD, IDA, the IFC, and MIGA are seeking to develop new products and instruments so that we can maximize the benefits for our clients. We have demonstrated our flexibility in a number of dramatic ways this past year, from helping to strengthen Mexico's financial sector during the peso crisis to assisting with the creation of a new microfinance program for the world's poorest. To be even more responsive to our clients' diverse needs, however, we need to strengthen our organization along "group" lines, to take advantage of our collective services and experience. And that is one of my priorities.

We have found in country after country that sound economic policies are essential for stimulating growth, creating jobs, and helping the poor. We have learned that investing in people, particularly through education programs, is the principal engine of social and economic progress. We have seen the power of the contribution of women, as the main agents for change in their families and communities. We know that infrastructure—power, transport, and telecommunications—is essential, and we will continue to support it as appropriate. At the same time, we have realized how critical it is to protect the Earth's fragile environment—our land, our forests, our water. And we recognize the great present dangers of drugs and organized crime.

For me, the big lesson from a review of our history and from my travels is that there is no single solution. I have seen how interlinked are the pieces of the development puzzle. Our programs have to be part of a comprehensive development strategy that is rooted in a country's individual needs. It is in this context that our experience can be critically important to our clients.

Let me take one example, from a village I visited in Mali. There an IDA-supported agricultural project has helped farmers increase their yields. But still they need storage capacity and transport to market. They need a marketplace that is fair and a distribution system that is not monopolistic. They need access to credit and training in how to run their own small businesses. Beyond all this, they need a legal system to protect their rights, assistance in setting up facilities for education and health, and a stable economic and political climate.

The government of Mali understands all this. But each part of the puzzle poses different problems and imposes different demands on capacities, both financial and managerial. What I have seen has brought home to me the complexity of development and the benefits that can be realized when all the pieces fall into place.

Learning from others' experience is one of the keys. The Bank Group, because it is global, is uniquely placed to assist with the networking of development experience: agricultural extension from India to Uganda, private pension funds from Chile to the Czech Republic, macroeconomic lessons from Malaysia to Ghana. The ideas are legion. The lesson is straightforward: advice is as important as money. And one of the Bank's greatest strengths is that our advice is independent. Governments trust us.

Looking to the future, I see the Bank Group's central role as helping to bring all this together in a systemic approach to development: the ideas, the financing, the people—and a knowledge of all these components and of what it takes to build a successful development program. There is an extraordinary opportunity for this institution to leverage its unique capacity to integrate development and make it truly sustainable.

Greater Effectiveness and Accountability

Although we have had notable successes in the past, the Bank's senior management and I agree that we can be even more effective in the future by sharpening our focus on the issues we are tackling and by judging our performance according to the impact in the field. Of course, orderly process in the consideration of projects is critical. But results are what matter. I believe we can strengthen the rigor of both our analysis and our implementation. We must be prepared to be held accountable—and to reward our colleagues by the tests of the marketplace.

This will help us, in turn, to be more effective in achieving our basic mission: to reduce poverty and improve the quality of people's lives. You have heard me say that we can judge development impact by the smile on a child's face. We must organize ourselves—whether it be in our private sector work, including that of the IFC and MIGA, or in our activities on environment and human development—to deliver on that smile.

We must also acknowledge that we operate in the new world I have tried to describe, with new clients and new demands. Some of our clients have access to new, alternative sources of money and advice. We think this is terrific. Our job is to make sure that we complement these alternatives and stay relevant.

To do that, we have to change the way we do business. We must focus on our clients and results and break the armlock that, I sense, bureaucracy has placed on this institution. If we do that, we will create a more profound change than any structural reorganization. I am talking here of liberating the talent and commitment of our wonderful staff and harnessing that talent and commitment directly to development. In short, I am talking about creating a "results culture."

Let me outline some of my thinking thus far on how to get there:

- Externally, we can and must build stronger partnerships.
- Internally, we can and must be a center of excellence.

The Power of Partnerships

From my experience in the private sector, I know the power of partnerships. This was reaffirmed during my recent travels.

On the Loess Plateau of China I saw peasants working with government specialists, as well as with the Bank, to protect this immense part of the global commons. I saw partnerships too, in Chiapas, Mexico, where history has cruelly denied many people the chance of an adequate life. Working with the federal and provincial authorities, the Inter-American Development Bank, the private sector, research institutes, and NGOs, we are making a new effort to alleviate poverty and relieve social tensions. In the West Bank and Gaza I saw our expanding involvement with the United Nations and the European Union in helping to build the bridge between peace and development.

I know that the Bank is already an experienced partner. But I believe we can go much further. And we can start by working more closely with our shareholders and donors. Here our executive directors play an indispensable role.

We must also deepen our collaboration, as we have begun to do, with the UN system, the IMF, and the World Trade Organization. We can expand our cooperation with the private sector, which plays an increasingly important role in development. And we can do much more to reach out to NGOs and civil society. Let me also pay tribute to the regional development banks with which we work, and to their leaders who have given me so much advice and help.

To be a good partner, we must be ready to listen to criticism and respond to constructive comment. There is no place for arrogance in the development business. I want to have a Bank that is open and ready to learn from others and that holds itself accountable. In that context, I regard our independent inspection panel as a valuable asset.

We must listen as we formulate our plans of action. Our friends are a great help. We cannot be fully effective, however, if our critics will not listen to us before they assess our positions and actions. Unconstructive and vitriolic criticism from outside does not help the people we are trying so hard to assist, and it creates a climate of resistance inside the Bank.

Everywhere I have traveled, I have met with representatives of the NGO community and civil society. We are really interdependent. But we must build mutual trust. I am committed to this endeavor.

Of all our partnerships, we must remember that the most important are those with the governments to which we lend—and the people whom they serve. It is a point worth repeating: we must get closer to our clients. This will mean continuing to strengthen our field presence while maintaining a very strong base at the center. At the same time, we must be mindful that the projects we finance are not World Bank projects—they are Chinese, Haitian, or Malawian projects. It is for the Bank to support them and advise on them. But it is for the countries to own them and be responsible for them.

Our commitment can only work with your commitment. Partnership is the key.

The Search for Excellence

Let me turn from the Bank's search for new partnerships to the search for excellence.

As I see it, there has been too much emphasis on lending volume and not enough on results on the ground; too much focus on economic reports and not enough on the effectiveness of the policy dialogue. Sometimes we have thought that solutions to our clients' problems lay in Washington rather than in the field. Making development impact the measure against which we want to be judged—and to judge ourselves—is my most important task.

As a step toward this goal, we must review our personnel and reward policies and invest more time and money in education and training for management and staff. I know we have a long history of facilitating learning for our clients. Last year alone, our Economic Development Institute reached 7,000 people from 137 countries through its seminars and programs, and a multiple of that number through its training of trainers.

But much, much more can and will be done to create an internal learning culture, through exchange of best practices and through expanded training in educational institutions and businesses throughout the world. It is also my intention to increase opportunities to enrich our culture inside the Bank through more appointments to management and staff from outside the Bank on both a permanent and a medium-term basis.

We will accept nothing less than absolute standards of excellence. We wish to be the best in our business. Continual renewal of skills and constant focus on the needs of our clients will enable us to meet those standards.

Our Immediate Initiatives

I have spoken of four main themes:

- the need for a new compact, to ensure that resources are sufficient to meet the needs of the world's poorest people, and to ensure that those resources are used with maximum efficiency
- the need to take an integrated approach to development, bringing together its different strands to ensure sustainability
- the need for the Bank Group to strengthen and expand its partnerships, both global and local
- the need for us to develop further our institutional culture—to focus on excellence and results.

If that is the general direction, here are some of my immediate priorities for the coming months:

- First, I will do everything in my power to ensure that IDA's funding is sufficient to meet the essential needs of its recipients and to prevent an irretrievable setback to the global effort to reduce poverty. I ask for your exceptional help in that effort in both IDA10 and the planning for IDA11.
- Second, we will work with the IMF and others to help resolve the issue of multilateral debt for the most heavily indebted, poorest countries.
- Third, we will accelerate and deepen the effort to work with existing and new partners, with specific measures for reaching out to the private sector, NGOs, and civil society.
- Fourth, we will launch the process of institutional change.
- Fifth, we will enhance our work with clients to attract private and public investment in high-quality projects. This will include capacity-building

initiatives for governments, the strengthening of legal and accounting systems and property rights, the marketing of opportunities, and the assurance to investors that they will have no nasty surprises in carrying out their plans.

- Sixth, and finally, we must anticipate and organize for postconflict economic development programs, when war is replaced by peace.

I see the Bank itself, fundamentally, as a partnership—because it belongs to the world, to all of us. We who work here offer you our hard work and commitment. In return, we need your support.

Once again, let me say how proud I am to head the Bank Group and how much I appreciate the opportunity to contribute to the dream that we all share—the dream of a better, more peaceful, and more just world. Together, we can make it a reality.

With Federico Mayor, James G. Speth, Carol Bellamy, and Nafis Sadik,*
published in the *International Herald Tribune*

MAY 11, 1996

*Education was a key issue in Wolfensohn's development strategy from the
beginning and throughout his tenure. This essay, co-written with the heads
of several other international institutions, reflects the partnership Wolfensohn
wanted to put in practice. Noteworthy is the contrast between high military
expenditure and inadequate education spending—a theme he would return
to frequently in later years.*

At the World Conference on Education for All, held six years ago in Thailand,
155 countries pledged to take the necessary steps to provide primary education
for all children and massively reduce adult illiteracy by the end of the decade.
We are organizing a meeting in Amman, Jordan, in June to assess what has
been done by nations and the international community to fulfill these commitments.

The balance sheet for the last six years is mixed. Much progress has been
made in terms of higher enrollments and better and more relevant education
in many countries. In particular, nine of the world's most populous nations—
Bangladesh, Brazil, China, Egypt, India, Indonesia, Mexico, Nigeria and
Pakistan—are working together. Even countries with a modest per capita GNP
such as Sri Lanka and Zimbabwe are providing primary schooling for eight or
more children out of 10.

But much more needs to be done. There are still 130 million children who
have no access to school, the majority of them girls. A large proportion, one-
third or more in many countries, do not complete primary school. Of those
who do, many do not acquire the essential skills and knowledge expected from
primary education. Far too many children will soon join the world's 885 million illiterate adults, most of whom are women. Secondary education, so vital
for development, is accessible to only 17 percent of sub-Saharan Africa's children. A much more concerted effort is needed to expand and improve educational opportunities, especially for girls and women.

It is unacceptable that a world that spends approximately $800 billion a
year on weapons cannot find the money—an estimated $6 billion per year—
to put every child in school by the year 2000. A mere one percent decrease
in military expenditures worldwide would be sufficient in financial terms. In

* Director-general of the United Nations Educational, Social, and Cultural Organization (UNESCO); administrator of the United Nations Development Programme; executive director of the United Nations Children's
Fund (UNICEF); and executive director of the United Nations Population Fund, respectively.

sub-Saharan Africa, only $2.5 billion per year would be needed to provide universal primary education. The international community and the developing world can and must invest in education, particularly in primary education, to achieve economic growth and poverty reduction.

The Amman meeting will be a milestone on the road to universal education and to its positive effects on economic development, infant survival, reproductive health, birth rates and the overall empowerment of people, especially women. Decisive and radical solutions must be found at both international and national levels to the problems that countries face in meeting the basic learning needs of their populations.

No real breakthrough will be possible unless commitment to this goal is translated into a serious rethinking of resource priorities on the part of national leaders and the international community alike.

We wish to stress our conviction that basic education for all is not only a human right, but also the cornerstone of human development. Providing access to high-quality basic education is probably the single most effective means to ensure democracy, sustainable development and peace.

Foreword to *World Development Report 1996,* published for the World Bank
by Oxford University Press

MAY 31, 1996

*This foreword is of historical interest because the 1996 report tracks the tran-
sition of countries with centrally planned economies—only a few years after
the fall of the Berlin Wall and the dissolution of the Soviet Union.*

World Development Report 1996, the 19th in this annual series, is devoted to
the transition of countries with centrally planned economies—in particular,
Central and Eastern Europe, the newly independent states of the former Soviet Union, China, and Vietnam—to a market orientation.

This transition, which affects about one-third of the world's population, has
been unavoidable. The world is changing rapidly: massive increases in global
trade and private investment in recent years have created enormous potential
for growth in jobs, incomes, and living standards through free markets. Yet
the state-dominated economic systems of these countries, weighed down by
bureaucratic control and inefficiency, largely prevented markets from functioning and were therefore incapable of sustaining improvements in human
welfare. Although these systems guaranteed employment and social services,
they did so at the cost of productivity, overall living standards, and, importantly, the environment, which has been severely damaged in some countries
by distorted prices, inefficient use of natural resources, and antiquated plant.

Necessary as the transition to the market has been, it has not been easy.
Some countries have been considerably more successful than others in implementing the key elements of change. Above all, the transition has had and will
continue to have a profound impact on people's lives. In some of the countries undergoing transition there has been a short-term drop in living standards;
in others human welfare has improved dramatically. Everywhere it has
changed the basic economic rules of the game and has irreversibly altered the
relationship between people and their political and social, not to mention economic, institutions.

This Report is devoted to exploring the experience of economies in transition, to identifying which approaches work and which do not, and to pin-
pointing the critical elements of success. It does not overgeneralize. It recognizes
that the countries it examines represent a diverse array of national histories,
cultures, and political systems; in fact, it explores the linkages between these
noneconomic factors and economic outcomes. Yet it makes a number of general points that provide valuable information to all reforming economies and
to those who care about them. It drives home the utter necessity of both lib-
eralizing economies through opening trade and market opportunities and

stabilizing them through reducing inflation and practicing fiscal discipline—and then of sticking to those policies consistently over time. It discusses the necessity of reforming enterprises and expanding the private sector, while restructuring social safety nets to deal with the social impact of the move to the market. And it makes the vital point that, in the long run, clear property rights and widespread private ownership are needed for markets to perform efficiently and equitably.

The Report also makes a major contribution in discussing the institutions that make a market-based economy work. It describes how public agencies, legal systems, financial institutions, and education and health systems can all enhance the success of market economies. These are the institutions that help set and enforce the rules that allow market transactions to proceed in a climate of confidence, that decrease the opportunities for corruption and crime, that mobilize and allocate resources, and that build human capital. And it discusses the need for transition countries to carry through with measures to integrate themselves further within the global economy. Integration into the institutions of the world trading system is an important way to help these countries nourish and sustain the reforms they have undertaken.

Beyond these essential technical and institutional elements of transition, this Report is about *people.* It is about how people can be protected from the loss of security and income that can accompany transition, how they can be helped to cope with the increased mobility and know-how required of workers in market economies, and how their children must receive the education and health care that will allow them to contribute to the prosperity to which their countries aspire. This brings us back to the very reason for transition in the first place, and the reason why this Report is needed. It is about how to unleash the enormous talents and energies of these countries' populations, and how to help them achieve their vision for a future of opportunity and well-being for all their citizens. In the end, we will gauge the success of transition not merely by statistical measures of national wealth, investment, or productivity, but also by the quality of life of the people who live in these countries.

Address to the Board of Governors at the Annual Meetings of the World Bank
and the International Monetary Fund

WASHINGTON, D.C. | OCTOBER 1, 1996

> *In this second Annual Meetings address, Wolfensohn lays out the progress
> achieved in the past year on six priorities, including IDA replenishment,
> debt relief, partnerships, the private sector, postconflict reconstruction, and
> building a results culture at the Bank itself. He foreshadows the Compre-
> hensive Development Framework by speaking of a "new paradigm" and a
> "broader, more integrated approach" to development. But this address is best
> known as his "cancer of corruption" speech, for it was here that Wolfensohn
> took on an issue that the development community had long studiously
> ignored. As this volume goes to press, the Bank has gone on to support more
> than 600 anticorruption programs and governance initiatives developed by its
> member countries.*

Mr. Chairman, Governors, Ladies and Gentlemen:

I am delighted to welcome you to these Annual Meetings. I would like to thank
the chairman for his support for our efforts, and I would like to express my deep
appreciation to [IMF Managing Director] Michel Camdessus, who has helped
me so much this year with his experience, advice, and, above all, his friendship.

Like Michel, I extend an especially warm welcome to Bosnia and Herzegovina, the World Bank's 180th member country. During my visit to Sarajevo
last April, I saw the magnitude of the challenge facing the country, and I was
profoundly moved by the courage and hope of its people. Working with them
and with all our partners, the Bank has already begun to help with the massive
task of reconstruction. Elaine and I join with everyone here in offering our
heartfelt best wishes to the citizens of Bosnia and Herzegovina for peace and
happiness in the years to come.

I have visited over 40 countries in these past 16 months. I have met with
governments and with business and nongovernmental organizations. But it is
the people, the poor and the disadvantaged, who have made the biggest impression on me. I have learned that they do not want charity; they want opportunity. They do not want to be lectured to; they want to be listened to.
They want partnership. Like all of us, they want a better life for themselves and
for their children. What I have seen in country after country is that, when they
are given a chance, the results are truly remarkable.

I have also been struck by the critical importance of history and culture.
We must build upon local tradition, not disrupt it. We must encourage the
young to respect their heritage, and we must accord dignity to the individual.

Without respect for cultural continuity and for social institutions, I believe there can be no true development.

Let me express my gratitude to the groups represented in this room, whether donor or recipient; private business, foundation, or NGO. I feel privileged to have become a member of this great community. And I believe that, by strengthening our partnership even more, we can offer the people we serve better opportunities and more hope for the future.

Working together is in everyone's interest. There are not two worlds, rich and poor; there is one world. We are linked in so many ways. Simple economics gives the industrialized countries reason enough to assist the developing countries. With their 4.5 billion people, these are the markets of tomorrow. But rich and poor countries are also linked by a host of challenges that have no respect for national borders: migration, disease, environmental degradation, famine, terrorism, and war.

More positively, we are linked by a common humanity, and we are united in a historic undertaking to improve the human condition. We must get this message across to government leaders and to voters so that we can maintain and strengthen our common effort.

The Past Year: A Progress Report

Mr. Chairman, when we met last year, I set out six immediate priorities:

- bringing IDA11, the 11th replenishment of the International Development Association, to a successful conclusion
- addressing the debt problems of the poorest countries
- building and expanding partnerships
- accelerating private sector development
- doing more to help in postconflict situations, and
- creating a "results culture" within the Bank Group.

Thanks to your support, tremendous help from our executive directors, and a great deal of effort from our management and staff, I have significant progress to report.

First, I pledged that we would do all in our power to ensure sufficient funding for IDA. The agreement reached last spring should enable IDA to lend close to $22 billion over the next three years—a remarkable achievement under the circumstances. At the same time, however, the agreement is fragile. It depends crucially on donors' understanding of each other's individual positions on the replenishment and, of course, on commitments being honored as speedily as possible. Beyond this, we must all intensify our efforts to ensure

IDA's long-term future, remembering always that it is the lifeline for 3 billion people living in the world's poorest countries.

Second, I made the commitment last year that we would work closely with our other partners to address the problem of unsustainable debt in the poorest countries. As Michel Camdessus has noted, after a year of hard work and much debate, the Bank and the IMF together have developed a proposal that is flexible, comprehensive, and responsive to debtors and creditors alike. At the Development Committee* meeting yesterday, ministers gave their strong endorsement to this proposal. Now, presuming fair burden sharing with other donors, we are ready to move ahead with debt-relief operations in selected countries. I extend my thanks to everyone who has helped in this effort, which I believe will prove a major breakthrough in the fight against poverty.

Third, I said we would build stronger partnerships. This past year I met with the leaders of the other multilateral development banks to explore better coordination of our programs. We have expanded our links with the United Nations and its agencies, with the World Trade Organization, and with the European Union. We have forged new relationships with the major foundations and with NGOs both international and local. We are building partnerships on gender issues, the environment, the social impact of economic reforms, the private sector, and other priority areas. We are also deepening partnerships with our shareholders, including efforts to benefit more from the successful development experience of our "graduates" from development lending, such as Singapore. Above all, we are strengthening partnerships with our clients, for example through the innovative program for capacity building in Africa, prepared and recommended by the African governors at these Meetings last year.

Fourth, we have stepped up our efforts to promote private sector development and to rationalize the Bank Group's activities with the private sector. The Bank is working with governments to help them improve the policies and the legal, tax, and judicial systems that are crucial for encouraging investment. We have strengthened our outreach to corporations, helping them to assess and implement projects in our client countries. We have also heard one of the messages that came through loud and clear at these Meetings last year, namely, to strengthen our guarantee program. I am pleased to report that there are 43 confirmed and probable projects in the pipeline for International Bank for Reconstruction and Development guarantees, most of them awaiting government action or investor decisions for the next step. And we are actively looking at how we can expand this program even further.

---

* The Development Committee is a grouping of finance ministers representative of the Bank's member countries that meets twice a year to discuss and advise on development issues.

The IFC [International Finance Corporation], which this year celebrates its 40th anniversary, has had a record year, leveraging more than $19 billion in support of projects worldwide. Since its founding in 1956, it has provided financing to nearly 2,000 companies in 125 countries. As you know, the IFC often works in countries where few other financial institutions are willing to go, and in the next year it will extend its reach to 16 nations where it has never worked before and where the investment climate is the toughest.

The Multilateral Investment Guarantee Agency also continues to exceed our original expectations. Its guarantees have catalyzed foreign direct investments now totaling an estimated $15 billion, and its online marketing and information service, the IPAnet, offers data and analysis on the business climate in more than 90 countries. Given the rapid growth in demand for its services, our Board will soon be discussing my recommendation for a capital increase for MIGA.

We have established a Private Sector Development Group, to pull together the catalytic strengths of our three institutions and make them more easily accessible to our private sector partners. In addition, the Bank and the IFC have initiated joint country strategies to help ensure that our activities reinforce each other and stay clearly focused on development impact.

Fifth, we have organized ourselves for postconflict work and have made great strides in improving our programs in this area. In Bosnia and Herzegovina 14 projects are being implemented, with Bank Group financing of over $325 million. In Gaza and the West Bank, our joint efforts are yielding results and have contributed to the creation of 22,000 new jobs. In Haiti we are working with a coalition of donors to help sustain peace and build economic opportunity for the poor. We are also working in Angola and Lebanon to assist with employment and reconstruction. More broadly, we will soon be presenting to our Board a policy paper aimed at strengthening our support for postconflict recovery.

Sixth, I pledged last year to build a "results culture" at the Bank, and this effort is showing tangible progress. I am extraordinarily grateful to my colleagues in the management team for their advice and support, without which none of our achievements would have been possible. We have stressed that we will not measure our performance by dollars lent or projects approved, but by our development impact—results on the ground. I cannot overstate the importance of this change. By putting quality ahead of quantity, we have fundamentally changed the incentives that guide our staff. Backed by tougher quality assurance for our work and enhanced accountability, this reorientation will result in major improvements in project design. We also have raised country portfolio issues to a higher level of attention with our clients. I myself have discussed these issues with the authorities in Russia, Brazil, and other countries. And we have launched a major review of those country portfolios with the highest concentrations of risky projects.

We are increasing our country focus through much stronger client involvement in our assistance strategies and by locating some of our country directors in our borrowing countries. We are paying greater attention to our clients' needs, with customized advisory services and important new products such as the single-currency loan, which allows our clients to borrow at an interest rate that is effectively only 50 basis points above the triple-A rate. And we are speeding up our procedures.

We are also improving our professional expertise through the creation of sectoral networks among our staff, with the first of these established in the area of human development. We are strengthening our management capacity, with a substantial executive education program as well as an exchange program with a broad range of private and public institutions. And we are investing more in our staff, including a doubling of skills training this year. In all these areas we are choosing our best women and men, who reflect our rich geographic diversity, to build a Bank staff that can work most effectively with their counterparts all over the world.

While we still have a long way to go, I believe we have made real progress toward changing the course of the institution. We now have a committed and talented team—staff and management—working to improve the Bank Group and to prepare it for the next century. There is excitement and empowerment; there is challenge and innovation. We will succeed with some initiatives, and we will fail with others. But our institution is on the move.

The Strategic Agenda

Together we have accomplished a great deal over the past 12 months. But it is just the beginning, the down payment on the bigger task that lies ahead. Together we need to look toward the challenges facing us in the new millennium.

Last year I suggested four major themes, which have evolved but which remain valid for the coming year and beyond:

- a new compact among donors, investors, and recipients, to ensure that resources are sufficient to meet the needs of the world's poorest people and that those resources are used efficiently and transparently
- a broader, more integrated approach to development, to ensure sustainability
- strengthening and expanding partnerships, both global and local, and

- continuing to pursue change in the Bank's culture to focus on excellence and results.

The New Compact

I have already mentioned IDA and the debt initiative and their critical role in catalyzing resources for development. We also need to attract more private flows to the poor countries. And then we need to work on the second part of the compact: ensuring that all resources are used efficiently.

In 1995 private flows to developing countries exceeded $170 billion, three times official flows and four times what they were just five years ago. However, 75 percent of these flows went to just 12 countries. About 50 countries, most of them very poor, received virtually no private inflows.

Our new world of open markets raises the stakes for developing countries. Investment is linked to good policies and good governance, liberal trade regimes, and high saving rates, combined with sound legal and judicial systems. Simply put, capital goes to those countries that get the fundamentals right. And we are working with our clients on those fundamentals.

Strong financial systems are key. But there are pervasive problems with prudential regulations and their enforcement. About one in five developing countries faces a banking crisis. Unproductive public expenditures and uncollected taxes are a further huge drag on these economies. That is why the Bank Group, working with the IMF, is strengthening its capacity to help our clients strengthen their financial sectors and reform their expenditure programs.

If the new compact is to succeed, we must tackle the issue of economic and financial efficiency. But we also need to address transparency, accountability, and institutional capacity. And let's not mince words: we need to deal with the cancer of corruption.

In country after country, it is the people who are demanding action on this issue. They know that corruption diverts resources from the poor to the rich, increases the cost of running businesses, distorts public expenditures, and deters foreign investors. They also know that it erodes the constituency for aid programs and humanitarian relief. And we all know that it is a major barrier to sound and equitable development.

Corruption is a problem that all countries have to confront. The solutions, however, can only be homegrown. National leaders need to take a stand. Civil society plays a key role as well. Working with our partners, the Bank Group will help any of our member countries seeking to implement national programs that discourage corrupt practices. And we will support international efforts to fight corruption and to establish voluntary standards of behavior for corporations and investors in the industrialized world.

The Bank Group cannot intervene in the political affairs of our member countries. But we can give advice, encouragement, and support to governments that wish to fight corruption, and it is these governments that will, over time, attract the larger volume of investment. Let me emphasize that the Bank Group will not tolerate corruption in the programs that we support, and we are taking steps to ensure that our own activities continue to meet the highest standards of probity.

The New Paradigm

The second element of our strategy is the need for a broader, more integrated approach to development—a new paradigm, if you will. Poverty reduction remains at the heart of everything we do. But the magnitude and complexity of the task are daunting. This fact has been brought home to me time and time again as I have met and talked with people during my travels, whether it be the coal miners of Ukraine, the Muslim women's groups of North Africa, the unemployed of Tucumán province in Argentina, or the fishermen of the Aral Sea.

Reducing poverty clearly involves the interplay of a number of issues: macroeconomic policy, private sector development, environmental sustainability, and investments in human capital—especially girls' education and early childhood development. All these elements are important. But, let's face it, at the end of the day *people* make policies and projects work. Social, cultural, and institutional factors are key to success and sustainability. In the Balochistan province of Pakistan, for example, where female enrollment rates have traditionally been among the lowest in the world, local communities and parents worked together, through a Bank-supported project, to design culturally sensitive schools and curricula. The result is that Balochistani parents are now sending their girls to school.

This is even more true at the policy level. We are all familiar with the economic record of the East Asian countries. But it was those countries' strong institutions and social cohesion that enabled them to consistently choose sound macroeconomic policies, promote rural development, and make large investments in basic education and health. And the result was rapid growth and poverty reduction.

Without the right social underpinnings, it is difficult for economic development to succeed, and virtually impossible for it to be sustained. We see this in countries that are mired in poverty—where economic growth is fragile, population is rising rapidly, children are not going to school, and, even more tragically, where they are dying from diseases we know how to prevent or cure. On a more extreme scale, we see it where the social fabric is torn and conflict has broken out. I referred earlier to the horror in Bosnia. But just last year there were some 50 major within-country conflicts worldwide. Over the past decade more than half of the world's poorest countries have experienced conflict.

The lesson is clear: economic advance requires social advance; without social development, economic development cannot take root. For the Bank this means making sure that the programs and projects we support have adequate social foundations. We can do this by designing more-participatory country strategies and programs, reflecting discussions not only with governments but also with community groups, NGOs, and private businesses; by putting more emphasis on social, cultural, and institutional issues and their interplay with economic issues in our project and analytical work; and by learning more about how the changing dynamics among public institutions, markets, and civil society affect social and economic development. I see this as a critical challenge—in fact, *the* critical challenge before us. But if we can succeed in broadening our approach in this way, I believe it will have a tremendous payoff in helping our clients achieve truly sustainable development.

The New Knowledge Partnership

The third item on the strategic agenda is partnership, and here we have made good headway over the past year. But today I want to focus on a specific form of partnership that will take on special importance as we enter the new millennium: a partnership for creating and sharing knowledge and making it a major driver of development.

Development knowledge is part of the global commons: it belongs to everyone, and everyone should benefit from it. But a global partnership is required to cultivate and disseminate it. The Bank Group's relationships with governments and institutions all over the world, together with our unique reservoir of development experience across sectors and countries, position us to play a leading role in this new global knowledge partnership.

We have been in the business of researching and disseminating the lessons of development for a long time. But the revolution in information technology increases the potential value of these efforts by vastly extending their reach. To capture this potential, we need to invest in the necessary systems, in Washington and worldwide, to enhance our ability to gather development information and experience and share it with our clients. We need to become, in effect, the Knowledge Bank.

We can do this through networking: pooling our wealth of cross-country experience, capturing the best global thinking and expertise on a given issue, and making it easily accessible to our clients and partners. We can do it by expanding the role of our Economic Development Institute, which already reaches thousands through its learning programs and is well on its way to reaching millions by harnessing teleconferencing, television, and the Internet. And we can do it by pioneering new partnerships that connect our clients with global centers of knowledge and investment. One example is our World Wide Web site, which is accessed 1.5 million times a month; another is the Information and Development Fund, through which the Bank and our partners help the poorest countries to realize the potential of information technology.

Let me stress one other point: the global knowledge partnership is not about machines. It is about people. The challenge is to harness the technology to link people together and to leverage its impact for development. That means both accumulating the right kind of knowledge and helping our clients build the capacity to use it.

The New Bank

Let me turn briefly to the fourth and final item on our strategic agenda: the Bank itself and our efforts to build a culture based on results, accountability, and excellence. To get the biggest bang from our scarce resources, we must be absolutely tough-minded. Sometimes in the past, we set overly ambitious targets and committed ourselves to objectives that were simply not realistic. That must change. We have to promise only what we can deliver and, then, deliver what we promise. This new culture of realism and results is fundamental to the changes at the Bank that I have described:

- getting closer to our clients
- developing new products, customized to our clients' needs, and
- ensuring that our products are of top quality.

To be successful, we will need new skills and new ways of working together. We need to continue the effort to invest more in our staff, to keep them at the cutting edge in their fields. And we need to become much better at working with others, tapping knowledge sources around the world to bring the very best expertise to our clients.

We have started down the road toward revitalizing our institution. It will not be done overnight, and it will require some special investment up front.

As part of the effort, we are taking a fresh look at our finances and at our fee and cost structure. We must be able to make more flexible—and better—decisions on how we use our resources.

We have before us a real opportunity to invest in the future. With your support, I am confident we can build a new Bank: a more responsive, focused institution, dedicated to learning and excellence, serving the needs of our entire membership, and reinvented to face the challenges of the 21st century.

We Have to Work Together

Mr. Chairman, I have spoken of a strategic agenda that will carry us forward to the next millennium. But we can meet it only through partnership. And that leads me back to where I began today, to my visit to Sarajevo. I met there with religious leaders: Catholic, Muslim, Orthodox, and Jewish. And I was struck by the fact that each of them spoke, not of hatred, but of the need to work together and to look to the future.

One of them, a Muslim leader, told me how he had lost his wife and two daughters to a single shell, on a single day of fighting, as they went to the market to buy some water. And yet, as I sat with him on a carpet in his mosque, he spoke of the meaning of the Koran—and of forgiveness. "We have to work together," he told me. "It's our only hope."

Working together is a challenge for us all and a responsibility for our world: for social justice, for economic opportunity, for human well-being, and for history. We are all here because we share the dream of a better world. To achieve it, we have to work together.

Thank you.

Message from the president and chairman from the 1996 World Bank *Annual Report*

OCTOBER 1996

*The Chairman's Message was an innovation Wolfensohn introduced to
the Bank's annual reports as a way of reporting personally to shareholders
on the institution's progress on a wide range of topics. Annual reports had
previously contained only an Executive Directors' report. Here Wolfensohn
touches on a number of issues from armed conflict to IDA, information
technology, and the rise of private capital flows.*

This *Annual Report,* covering July 1, 1995, to June 30, 1996, details a critical
period in the history of the World Bank Group, one of transition designed to
create an institution that is stronger, more agile, and more effective in response
to the needs of its developing-country clients.

This transition has been made necessary by the extraordinary change taking
place in the global economy, with explosive growth in worldwide trade and
private investment centering on the emerging market economies. In the 1990s,
developing countries have contributed 70 percent of the growth in global
GDP and half the growth in world trade. Private investment flows to the developing world have more than tripled, from around $44 billion in 1990 to
nearly $170 billion by the end of 1995.

Economic change is about far more than numbers. It is about change in
people's lives. For many people, this change has been for the better. Many
countries have cut their poverty rates by more than half and have expanded
access to health, education, and social services to their entire population. Far
more people now have access to economic opportunity than in the recent past.
Further, just a decade ago, only about 1 billion people lived in economies that
could be called market-oriented; today, the figure is around 5 billion people.
Meanwhile, communications technology is drawing people from around the
world closer together. Today, doctors in Africa, Latin America, or Asia can
teleconference with top medical researchers around the world; entrepreneurs
can get the latest global market information instantly; and students in the most
remote parts of the globe have the possibility of access to the world's best libraries and teaching resources. The potential of what the information revolution is unleashing is extraordinary.

But growth and prosperity cannot be taken for granted. In many of the
world's poorest countries, global change has not brought significant improvements to people's lives. We still live in a world where 1.2 billion people live
below the line of what the World Bank considers absolute poverty—$1 per
day—and in Africa, the number of poor people is expected to continue

growing into the next century. A quarter of the developing world's population lacks access to safe drinking water, and almost half of it has no electricity. One hundred thirty million children, most of them girls, are not getting the chance to go to school. In too many places the poor—and most particularly women—are shut out of the opportunities that would allow them to improve the conditions of their lives.

Despite the explosive growth in the world economy, many countries are being left behind. Seventy-five percent of private capital flows to the developing world are concentrated in just twelve countries (and East Asia receives 60 percent of the total). At the same time, official development assistance—which might have filled the gap—has fallen to its lowest point in real terms ($59 billion) in twenty-three years. And many of the world's poorest countries are so deeply in debt as to make it practically impossible for them to sustain vital economic reforms.

Armed violence continues to plague the world. Just last year, there were some fifty armed conflicts worldwide. We are all aware of the horror in Bosnia, where a quarter of a million people have been killed and unspeakable horrors committed. But Bosnia is far from the only site of such abominations. In the past decade, 70 million people have been displaced from their homes or become refugees. And the world remains under the growing threat of environmental deterioration, uncontrolled population growth, epidemic disease, and an emerging shortage of water resources.

The current change under way around the world carries great opportunities—and risks. The role of the World Bank under these conditions is to help its clients seize the opportunities, avoid the pitfalls, and—for those countries just beginning to make the transition to soundly managed market economies—build the capacity to stay on course.

This means we must stay close to our clients and develop our own ability to adapt to their changing needs. It means we must be able to respond quickly to conditions on the ground, and particularly to the challenge of postconflict situations; create innovative new mechanisms for assisting the poorest; help build sound market systems; and ensure that development is environmentally sustainable. If we are to be truly effective, we must expand and deepen our partnerships with the UN system, regional development banks, bilateral assistance agencies, nongovernmental organizations, foundations, the private sector, and others; and we must develop the professional capabilities of our own staff to the highest possible level. We must also work with the International Monetary Fund, other multilateral development banks, and the governments of creditor nations to reduce the burden of debt in the poorest reforming countries. And we must lead the way in ensuring that concessional resources—

particularly in the form of IDA [International Development Association] funds—continue to be adequate to finance our clients' development priorities.

This *Annual Report* reviews what we have already done and where we are headed in these areas, in addition to covering the Bank's ongoing development activities around the world. It provides the essential facts about Bank operations in all regions of the world and in all sectors of development.

In the end, however, the *Report* is not only about financial statistics or percentages; it is about people—the people who live in the countries we serve. It is about the immeasurable improvements that the World Bank is bringing to people's lives. In the end, this will be the gauge by which we judge our success.

THE BANKING COMMUNITY IN AN INTERDEPENDENT WORLD: OPPORTUNITIES AND CHALLENGES

Address to the Bankers' Club

LONDON | FEBRUARY 3, 1997

In this speech in the world banking and financial center that is the City of London, Wolfensohn recalls his days at the investment firm Schroders and how the World Bank has expanded his view of the world and of global issues. He urges the City and its banking community to "lift its sights" beyond profits to acknowledge its moral and social responsibility to help build a better world.

Mr. President, My Lord Mayor, Mr. Governor, My Lords Aldermen, Sheriffs, and Ladies and Gentlemen:

May I, on behalf of the guests, thank you. This is quite a night for me, Mr. President, because I have a link with the City of London from my youth. I learned about it from my father, who went to the City of London School and, by some extraordinary coincidence, became a Freeman of the City of London for organizing the Victory Parade after World War I. And one of the few things he was able to leave me that have the distinction that this does was my right by patrimony to have the Freedom of the City of London. And I recall, as an impecunious student on my way to study in the United States, dropping by this building to see if I could pick up the Freedom of the City. I was scared about one thing principally, my Lord Mayor, which was how much would it cost, given my state at that time. But I was able to get it, and I was duly handed a book titled *Rules for the Conduct of Life,* which I thought would be of enormous value to me as I progressed further.

And I learned that I had, I think, at least three privileges. One was that I could wear a drawn sword in the City. Second, that I could drive my sheep over Westminster Bridge or London Bridge, I'm not quite sure which. And, third, that I could be hanged by a silken cord, instead of something less attractive, were I to become an investment banker here.

In any event, it is, indeed, a privilege for me to be here, and one cannot but be overwhelmed by being in this glorious environment. I thank you, very much, Mr. President, for that glowing introduction. I only wish that I was still in the private sector and that I could benefit from it by gaining clients, although, with a group like this, I'm not sure there would be too much business for what I was doing.

But now I'm in a different world. Now I'm in a world of development. I'm in a world that concerns itself not with the ceremonies of tonight, and not with the wonders of the City, but with 4.7 billion people out of the 5.6 billion who live on this Earth.

I recall with enormous pleasure my time in the City. And I know very well the long and distinguished history that London and this country have had in terms of international development. I was privileged to come here to work at Schroders under the leadership of Lord Richardson, who is here tonight, and I'm thrilled that he is here to hear me speak. And I learned, as you all know, of the history of this City and the development of many of the countries around the world, of the funds you sent to the United States, to Latin America, to other parts of the world, and, of course, the assets you had sent to Australia in chains years earlier. And I know very well that you are continuing that tradition, my Lord Mayor, in inviting developing countries to share in the benefits of this City.

But the world has changed, and I've learned quite a lot since I left Schroders and since I left private practice. And what I've learned is that it's a different world. It's a world in which there are 1.2 billion people who live on less than a dollar a day, in which there are 3 billion people who live on less than two dollars a day, in which there are 1.2 billion people who don't have access to water, in which there are 120 million children who don't go to school. It's a world of many conflicts and many, many problems.

But there are also many opportunities. Because this developing world in which I'm now so heavily engaged is not another world. It's our world. We're linked with this world. We're linked with it because we share the same environment. We're linked with it because we breathe the same air. We're linked with it because our health is dependent on the health of people in those countries.

The scourge of AIDS, from which 16 million people are suffering, started in that so-called developing world. And having just returned from India, my Lord Mayor, I can tell you that, by the end of this century, which is just a short time away, if nothing is done there will be 7 million people who are HIV-positive in that country alone. We cannot ignore that.

And we're linked by crime and we're linked by migration, because migrants come from countries that do not have economic opportunity. We're linked by war. In Europe we're linked by the problems of the transition economies and what might happen should there be a nuclear mishap in those countries, which also are part of the developing world. And we're linked by food and we're linked by famine.

The developing world is not something we can opt out of. It's part of the same world we live in, and yet, from my own experience and my own time both in the City and in the United States, few of us think of it as part of us. It's only after traveling to some 40-odd countries that I have come to realize that this world is, in fact, our world.

And it's not our world just for social or moral reasons. It's our world for economic reasons. In the years since 1990, 40 percent of the growth in world GDP has come from those countries. By the turn of another 30 years, 30 percent of the world's GDP will come from those countries, as does 20 percent today.

The developing world is the source of much of our trade, so that one cannot imagine growth in the developed world without growth in the developing world. And it's quite easy to see that, in the City of London and in other international markets, we are responding to that fact. International bond issues last year for developing countries were $88 billion, a significant increase from earlier years. International banks loaned $35 billion, up from $3 billion in 1990. There is economic opportunity and we are responding.

But the problem is that, of the $230 billion in private capital that last year went to the developing world, 75 percent of it went to 12 countries only, which leaves 140 countries where there is a need for development assistance and for economic advance. And. by the way, that $230 billion in private capital compares with only $50 billion from all the official institutions. The private sector now accounts for nearly five times the amount of official assistance, up from half of official assistance seven years ago.

And you can say, "Well, what's that got to do with me? What does it have to do with us?" And I would reply that that is our future. Maybe those of us at this table can ignore it, but our children cannot, nor can our grandchildren. Because by 2025, the 5.6 billion people in this world will be 9 billion, of which 8 billion will be in the developing countries. And the major cities of this world will be in developing countries, so that we will no longer think just in terms of London, New York, and the centers of Europe. We will be thinking of Jakarta and Beijing and São Paulo, and we'll be thinking of cities in Africa, because these will be the major cities.

This is what we need to think of now, not for ourselves, but for the next generation. And it's crucial that the bankers in this City, as the home and largest center of international banking, recognize that there is something more than the profit motive behind our policies and our strategies.

We have to orient ourselves differently from the way we were trained. I'm sure that all of you, like me, were not trained to think in terms of the 4.7 billion people. It's perfectly possible to exist without knowing that they exist. But our children cannot. And we have a responsibility in the banking community to participate in bringing about a more stable world.

Development is no longer an issue of government-to-government assistance. After World War II there was practically nothing flowing to these developing countries. And there was, of course, a need to restructure Europe and other countries affected by the war. And so the international community created the Bretton Woods institutions: the World Bank and our sister institution, the International Monetary Fund. But since that time development has become much more complex. It is no longer just the two international institutions, the Bank and the Fund. At the Bank itself we've diversified, and we've founded the International Finance Corporation and MIGA [the Multilateral Investment Guarantee Agency], our insurance company, and there are now a multitude of regional development banks as well. There are also bilateral institutions. And there's the European Union.

So we have at one level the governmental contributors to development and, in addition, with the onset of freedom and with the development of markets, we have seen growth in nongovernment organizations and nonstate actors, so that there is now a partnership not just between governments but between governments and civil society. And beyond that, there is, of course, now the partnership with the private sector. And with $200 billion per year needed for infrastructure development alone in developing countries, there clearly has to be a true partnership with the private sector.

The international institutions have to change. But private institutions also have to change the way they think, not just of themselves but of how to leverage their activities and their interests to work in partnership with the governments of these countries. The governments also have to change, and they are changing.

And the opportunities are changing. We're looking at the moment at creating satellite links with 60 countries overseas. If you can imagine it, countries in Africa will be able to jump a generation in terms of research, in terms of training, and in terms of accessibility through access to the Internet and to interactive television—not only for discussions but for training sessions originating in Washington and in London and in Singapore. These aren't things of the future; they're things of today that we're acting on now.

Last week I was in Washington, and after breakfast I went next door to my conference room and I had a conversation with 12 African ministers who were sitting in Cameroon. The potential is enormous and so are the implications. Using their computers and video interchange, our children are going to be as close to Africa as they are to cities in Europe or to London.

This world is not a static world. It's a world full of expectation and hope, but it's also a world of great differences. Low-income countries today make up 56 percent of the world's population but have less than 5 percent of the world's income. Meanwhile the inequalities between rich and poor countries are growing, and within countries as well we see a great division of wealth. In Peru the difference between the top 10 percent and the bottom 10 percent is 80-fold.

Why do I raise this? Because if one group is economically disadvantaged compared with another, ultimately you will have social instability. The two things go together. They have to go together. And so we have a responsibility as bankers not just to think in terms of immediate profit, but to think also in terms of preparing a world for our children. We have the education, we have the technology, and we have the vision. And many banks in this room already have the networks. We are already out there. But we must be out there with something other than just looking for deposits and making money. We must be out there thinking in terms of contributing to a better world. If banks insist on environmental conditions in their lending, there will be environmental conditions in lending. If banks insist on labor standards, there will be labor standards. If banks join in a fight against corruption, we will at least make a hole in corruption and maybe win the battle. Corruption is not just an issue of the developing countries. There are the corruptees and there are the corruptors. And many corruptors come from developed countries, and many corruptees are clients of all of us. If we don't want the cancer of corruption to spread throughout the world, we ourselves must stand up to it.

In Washington at the moment there is a meeting of 2,000 people on microcredit. The banks can make an immense contribution to microcredit. It may not be profitable today, but one of the most effective tools in the villages and in the slums is the possibility of getting small-scale loans. I recall as vividly as if it were yesterday my trip to Uganda. I visited a slum, and I met a woman there who, together with other women, was making briquettes out of banana peel. And they would fire up the banana peel, and it would become carbon and charcoal, and they would press it together and make briquettes for heat. She had started this business with a $50 loan. And she showed me her accounts in a little exercise book with all the pride of a chairman of General Motors. And I've seen the same thing in India, where we are teaching women to run businesses—women who can't read, who use cartoonlike figures instead of words in their account books. And we're training women in basic skills.

These are things that, as chairmen, we may not need to do, but for the sake of the young people in your overseas offices you should put something into it. Give the younger people a chance to make a contribution to these societies, and to learn something themselves. I have become very humble about what there is to be learned from the cultures of developing countries. We could all learn from the culture of family in Africa.

Recently I was in Uzbekistan, at the edge of the Ural Sea, a place that is desolate because, as some of you may know, it's an environmental tragedy. This is an inland sea that is gradually shrinking and becoming salt, affecting the neighboring countries, because the water has been siphoned off for improper irrigation. And when I was there I went to a fishing village that was now 20 kilometers away from the sea. Now, having a fishing village 20 kilometers from the sea, where the people only know how to catch and dry fish, is a problem. And as a result the people there were living on $15 a month.

So we went there, to this desolate place, my wife and I, two hours in a Russian helicopter, and we met a group of scantily dressed young kids, and we talked through their teacher, who spoke some English, and we gave them some pencils and a few other things. And as we were leaving a little boy came up to me and put in my hand a five-sum note, equivalent to about 10 cents, and then scampered off. And I said to the teacher, "What is this?" And he said, "In Central Asia, when a visitor comes, we give them money for the next stage of their journey."

I can give you dozens of examples of the sort of thing one sees in the developing world. They do not want charity; they want opportunity. They have the same genomes that we have. They have the same instincts that we have. They want their kids to get an education. They want shelter, they want peace, and they want economic development.

We have a lot to learn from that world of 4.7 billion people. And it's only right that the young people within our banks should both contribute and learn, so that we can have a world in which we can profit economically, certainly, but more important, a world in which the moral and social responsibility that we owe to each other is carried forward.

I believe that the City of London and the banking community can lift its sights and, in lifting its sights, help our children and help make the world a more peaceful and stable place.

Thank you.

THE WORLD BANK AND THE EVOLVING CHALLENGES OF DEVELOPMENT

Address at a Congressional Staff Forum
sponsored by the Overseas Development Council

WASHINGTON, D.C. | MAY 16, 1997

This address was delivered at a seminar hosted by the Overseas Development Council, an independent, international policy research institution based in Washington. Wolfensohn describes the changes facing the Bank and how the Bank is reinventing itself to handle those new demands. Wolfensohn points to the challenges of living in a "singular world," speaks of the "explosion" of civil society, and describes how the Bank is decentralizing to become more effective.

In the 23 months that I have been at the World Bank, I have had the chance to travel to over 55 countries, not just to visit governments but spending 60 to 70 percent of my time in the field. My travels have allowed me to get close to the real issues facing the Bank, and what has come home to me is the remarkable quality of people in different countries, the remarkable quality of cultures, the remarkable things that we can learn from the history of others.

But the fact is that, today, 3 billion of the 4.7 billion people who live in the developing world live on less than two dollars a day, and 1.3 billion live on less than one dollar a day. A billion, three hundred million don't have clean water. One hundred and fifty million children don't go to school. Forty thousand die every day because of hunger-related diseases. Fifty million children are mentally or physically damaged because of improper or inadequate nutrition.

This world of 4.7 billion people is not a world that we can turn our backs on, either as economic creatures or as social or moral creatures. When we look at it as economic creatures, that world represents 18 percent of the world's GDP today, and in another 30 years it will represent 30 percent. It's growing at twice the rate of the OECD* countries. It represents 40 percent of the increase in trade and 50 percent of the annual increase in world product. It provides 4 million jobs for Americans. So, whether you like that world or not, it's part of our economy and it's part of our world. It's not a fringe activity or an optional extra; it's an essential element.

The developing world is also an essential element for all of us in terms of the environment. It's essential in terms of drugs and crime. It's essential in terms of migration and immigration. It's essential in terms of health and food. It's part of our world. We will not have peace and security in our world without peace and prosperity in the developing world.

---

* Organisation for Economic Co-operation and Development, whose members include most of the world's countries with high incomes per capita.

But, as we've moved into the post–Cold War era, we've begun to forget that world. Where once we worried about preventing Africa from becoming a communist staging area, or about having a communist aircraft carrier off our coast in Latin America, today we look at aid and at the multilateral institutions and ask why we need them. And the reason we need them is very simple. We need them for all the economic, social, and moral reasons I've just described. We need them because we live in a singular world. We need them because, although *we* may be able to avoid thinking about that single world for a year or two, our children surely cannot.

We also need the developing world in ways that are new and different. Why? Because the world has changed dramatically in the last 15 years. We have seen the collapse of communism and a profound movement toward market economies. Ten years ago 1 billion people lived under a market economy; today that number has increased to 5 billion. Ten years ago only 30 percent of the world's countries were democratic; today 65 percent have some form of democratic elections.

And, as the world has changed, so has the role of multilateral institutions like the Bank. Seven years ago the multilateral institutions were still working in something of a vacuum. Today, however, the Bank and its affiliate the International Development Association, which originally were almost the only entities involved in development, are joined by a host of bilateral institutions, regional development banks, the European Union, and various UN agencies, all forming part of an international group of institutions that together transfer about $45 billion a year to the developing world in official aid. But even that figure is small compared with the $244 billion that the private sector now invests each year in the developing world—five times as much as the official sector.

All that means there is a whole new dynamic in the development community. It is no longer just the U.S. Agency for International Development and the World Bank plus IDA, but a mix of multinational institutions, regional banks, and the private sector. But the private sector picture is very skewed. Last year 75 percent of private capital flows to developing countries went to only 12 countries. So the international institutions now have a whole new task before them, that of helping other developing countries create an enabling environment that will encourage private investment.

Then there is the explosion in civil society. I have just come back from Poland, where there are now 30,000 registered NGOs [nongovernmental organizations]. I traveled from there to Romania, where they are newer at it but have made considerable progress. With the Internet and with expanding interchange between peoples, the cycle time to get civil society up and running is much quicker than it ever was before.

But what is significant is not just the numbers. For us in the development business, it is crucial to be able to listen to civil society, to learn from it, and to work with it in order to make our efforts effective. There are literally hundreds of thousands, if not millions, of people in the world engaged in development on a voluntary and civic basis. This is not just a group of people who spend their time criticizing the Bank or the bilateral development agencies; these are committed individuals who are part of the development community. And although they may be part of or affiliated with international NGOs, the great majority of them are local.

So there is a whole new dimension to the Bank. It is no longer alone on Mount Olympus, as it was 50 years ago after World War II. Rather it is part of an expanding universe of bilateral, regional, and multilateral institutions. Multilateral lending is now dwarfed, in terms of available funds, by the private sector and the literally hundreds of thousands of individuals contributing from civil society.

Finally, there are the governments themselves. The key actor in terms of development in each country is, of course, the government. Our purpose is not to dole out advice or pretend that we run the country; it is to try and help ensure that governments do things that are sustainable and that they have the capacity to carry out development projects and to establish an environment in their country that will attract investment from overseas. Far more important, we are there to ensure that they can take the necessary action to give their own people the confidence to invest at home, to create savings, to establish sound financial systems, to strengthen their judicial systems, to ensure property rights—all essential conditions for development.

This is the world in which we are operating. It's a very different world from 50 years ago. And it's a world of many transcendent themes that affect development and demand our attention—the crucial importance of education, the role of women, and the environment.

What we have learned at the Bank is that development is about people. That does not mean we have to abandon infrastructure projects or basic macroeconomic planning; we know how central macroeconomic policy is to growth and to private investment. But macroeconomic policy by itself isn't enough. We must also make sure that we give adequate weight to the human dimension, that we reach down to all corners of society. If we do not do that, we fail. We simply cannot realize social peace and social justice in a country unless we do something about the human dimension of development. We cannot have sustainable economic development without social development.

What impact does all this have on the Bank? What impact does it have on the United States? One immediate, significant impact is that, to remain relevant, we at the Bank must ensure that everything we do is geared toward development effectiveness. Why? Because if we are going to convince the Congress or the legislatures of other donor countries that the Bank should stay in business, we must make absolutely sure that what we are doing is useful, sustainable, and effective. This may seem obvious, but to date most development institutions have not operated on the basis of development effectiveness.

But, to do that, we first of all have to decide how we will judge effectiveness. What is an effective education program? Suppose we can show that we are getting more girls to go to primary school for two or three years. Is that an adequate measure of our effectiveness in terms of girls' education? Clearly, it isn't. Or take rural development. You can go into rural areas and improve crop yields by planting seeds farther apart and getting corn to grow twice as high. But it's not a success if you can't store the corn, if you can't get it to market, or if you have a monopolistic system of pricing.

As we enter the 21st century, all of us—at the Bank, in the UN system, in governments, and in NGOs—have to address the issue of what effectiveness in the development business means. We all talk about poverty reduction and sustainability, but, if we are really to make a difference for those 4.7 billion people in the developing countries, we need to make sure that we can actually deliver results on the ground in a meaningful way. And that means more than raising GDP per capita. It means improving the quality of life in all its dimensions. It means bringing people into society who, for all intents and purposes, have never been allowed in before.

And so, as part of our Program of Renewal at the Bank, I have asked some of our best people to focus on this issue of effectiveness. But we also need to make sure that, as an institution, we are making the best use of our capacities. As I have said many times, if the European Bank for Reconstruction and Development or the Food and Agriculture Organization can do something better than we can, let them do it. We are not in competition with each other, and the needs are simply enormous. Poverty is not diminishing; it's increasing. The gap between the rich and the poor isn't decreasing; it's increasing. The environment is not improving; it's deteriorating. In fact, we have had a 3 percent increase in carbon emissions since Rio,[†] despite all our promises. All this has a direct impact on developed and developing countries alike.

To meet those needs, the Bank is focusing on being much more selective in its activities, in order to target those areas where it has the greatest leverage and to enter into partnerships with other players in areas where they have a comparative advantage. The Bank does not have to lead every project. We are

---

† The United Nations Conference on Environment and Development (the Rio Earth Summit) was held in Rio de Janeiro in June 1992.

now taking the view that we can lead, we can follow, or we can be in the middle. We can put our name on the project, or we can be anonymous. The most important thing is to get the job done, and that is a very significant change for our institution. And it's difficult and it takes time. But it's a change we must make.

But we realized that, if we reorganize on this basis, we cannot do everything from Washington. If you were running a bakery business covering the whole United States, you would not run it all from Washington. You would establish your bakeries around the country. If you were running an accounting or service business, you would have to be out in the field. All of the great international companies are dispersed: they have regional offices; they have local people. Why should it be different for the World Bank? Why should we fly in for three weeks, go into a village, go back to the hotel, and then fly back to Washington, and think that, if we do that four times a year, we are going to have a profound impact?

Therefore the Bank is going to disperse into the field and give authority to the people in the field. Consistent with that, we are looking at our processes and procedures with a view to getting rid of the layers of bureaucracy that have built up over the years—not only in the World Bank but in the international system in general. We are focusing on process, we are focusing on accountability, and we are focusing on dispersing authority.

We are also focusing on much greater coordination of our activities within the Bank Group. The World Bank Group is composed of the International Bank for Reconstruction and Development, which is our program that lends at market-based rates to middle-income countries; the International Finance Corporation, our institution to deal with the private sector; the Multilateral Investment Guarantee Agency, our investment insurance operation; and, of course, IDA, our concessional lending window, which is funded annually by donor countries and targeted to the poorest countries. IDA's resources, collectively, amount to a little over $6 billion a year and are replenished on a three-year cycle.

I am not here to plead for IDA. As you know, the United States is behind in its payments, but the Bank is hopeful that it will pay its arrears, and that is something to which the president and the secretaries of state and the Treasury are now committed. Let me just say that, if the United States is going to continue its leadership in the world after the East-West conflict, it would be wholly improper to drop the ball now that the ideological conflict is over. Nor would it be in America's self-interest. So whether one considers the matter on the basis of what is morally or socially right or on the basis of self-interest, there is an overwhelming case for making sure that IDA lending is maintained.

Finally, the Bank is trying to adjust to the new world of information technology. I have just come from a videoconference with 500 people in Morocco, where we are running a seminar on knowledge and information for the countries of North Africa and the Arab region. We have had some 46 different sessions there. In June we will be co-hosting a seminar in Toronto called Global Knowledge 97. Because of the excitement this initiative is generating, we expect some 2,000 people from around the world to attend.

As part of this knowledge initiative, the Bank is organizing itself as a knowledge institution, so that in two years you will be able to come into the Bank online and find out, on any development subject, what is best practice and who is dealing with projects in that particular area, complete with their telephone and facsimile numbers and Internet addresses. You will also be able to access technical literature through the Bank. The Mellon Foundation is putting 6 million pages of academic literature online, to which we will be linked. For instance, if you are interested in preschool learning, we want you to be able to see what we are doing and then link to the Department of Education in the United States, to education ministries and agencies in other countries, to UNESCO [the United Nations Educational, Scientific, and Cultural Organization], and so on. We are going to be able to weave together this fabric of knowledge, including videoconferencing facilities, across all of our offices. We have taken transponder space on the UN satellite so that every one of our offices in Africa will be linked. These new media will allow us, as an international institution, to be a fantastic agent of change and knowledge. We are positioning ourselves to be a convenor, a catalyst, and a guide in the sharing of knowledge, information, and best practice experience worldwide.

Knowledge, decentralization, private sector development, social development, aid effectiveness, selectivity, partnership, and participation. Some will say that this reorganization effort that we've begun is controversial and expensive. I believe it is just the opposite. This is leadership of a very important kind, not just because we want to make the Bank a good professional institution, but because it goes far beyond the Bank, to the issue of peace and stability in the world. The bottom line is simple and stark. If we do not create some sense of social equity and development with those 4.7 billion—soon to be 6 billion—people living in the developing world, our children will not live in peace. If we cannot create economic growth in these poorer countries, we will not have economic growth in the world. If we cannot begin to arrest environmental degradation, we will all begin to feel the effects.

This is not an issue of charity. It is not a distant concern for the United States. It is an absolutely central issue for all of us, and I hope that the World Bank Group will be a major factor in bringing about change in this area, and that we not only will achieve success but will do so with American leadership.

Published in *The Asian Wall Street Journal*

SEPTEMBER 19, 1997

Timed to appear a week before the joint Bank-Fund Annual Meetings in Hong Kong SAR, this op-ed details China's success in fighting poverty, points to its remaining challenges, and offers the Bank's continuing help in the country's development.

China and its 1.1 billion people are in the throes of two historic transitions: from command economy to market, and from a rural, agricultural society to an urban, industrial one. So far, both transitions have been spectacularly successful. China is the fastest-growing economy in the world, with per capita incomes quadrupling in the past 20 years. Between 1978 and 1995, the value of its exports and imports as a share of GDP tripled, and China was second only to the United States as a recipient of foreign direct investment.

Only two generations ago, 80% of China's population lived in absolute poverty and more than 60% of adults were illiterate; today the figures are 20% and 10% respectively. In just two generations, China has achieved income growth and improvements in living standards that took other countries two centuries to achieve—and which many countries have still not achieved.

As astonishing as all this is, it is consistent with what we at the World Bank have come to know about China. It is a country where the extraordinary is routine, and where the impossible just seems to demand a little more time and effort.

One project that we are working on with China illustrates the point. Together, we are restoring the Loess Plateau in northern China, turning it back from centuries of erosion to fertile farming land. It involves an area that is the size of France and which looks like the surface of the moon. Already farmers in the area who faced famine every few years are selling surplus food. When completed, the project will have so restored the landscape that it will actually alter the local climate.

Despite our knowledge of the country, and our close working relationship with those leading the reform process there, the Bank has still often underestimated China's potential (the country's gross domestic product today is twice what we said it would be back in 1985). The rapid growth has lifted 200 million Chinese out of absolute poverty since 1978 and has brought the country squarely on to the world stage as a strong exporter and growing consumer. In fact, so impressive is China's recent performance that it would be easy to be mesmerized by its rapid growth, to focus only on where China is headed, and lose sight of where China is.

The truth is that China is still a very poor country—people's incomes are only about half the level of those in Brazil, for example—with large, unmet needs and serious inequalities. But this confusion of performance with prosperity, or total size with individual income, is evident in the debate over whether or not China should be classified as a developing nation for the purposes of membership in the World Trade Organization. How can it be "developing," one might ask, when it is expected to be the biggest economy in the world early next century? But in reality, how can it be classified as "developed" when the average income is about $600 a year?

The World Bank is trying to help by providing both advice and finance to support many areas of China's reform program, from helping to create a real-estate market to overhauling basic employment laws. China, however, has been very much in the driver's seat.

We have lent more money to China in the 1990s than to any other country, and none has used our assistance more effectively. On the other hand, though the raw numbers look big (currently about $3 billion a year, $28.3 billion total) China receives less money per capita than any other country we lend to in East Asia.

But if development teaches anything, it is that every silver lining has a cloud. Fast growth exposes weaknesses in the economic fabric and creates new challenges which must be dealt with. The economic events unfolding elsewhere in East Asia leave no doubt on this point.

The strength of China's economy over the past two decades does not automatically guarantee that the growth will continue at the same rate in the years ahead. Indeed, for most countries, past growth is a poor indicator of future performance. Even the East Asian "tigers" see their once-booming growth figures leveling off as their economies mature. China has some real advantages, however. Its high savings rate, relative stability, large domestic market and record of economic reform bode well for future growth.

Fortunately, rapid economic growth is not the government's sole objective. Growth must be sustainable, and its benefits must reach the poor and the vulnerable—of whom there are at least 250 million in China. Critically, development needs the full and equal involvement of women in society. Growth must reduce, not worsen, inequality.

Growth must also respect and protect the environment, and that has not been the case in the past. China today is one of the most polluted countries in the world, and it faces growing demand for power generation, for urban space and resources such as water and land, and increased food production—all of which put more pressure on the environment.

Tough decisions need to be made in reshaping the role of the state. Many parts of the economy still suffer from an undesirable blurring of governmental and commercial functions, which is a holdover from the days of central planning. These poorly defined roles create conflicts of interest within government and, ultimately, could harm the economy. Greater clarity will lay the foundation for sustained rapid growth and improvement in the quality of people's lives. It is encouraging that the reports from the Chinese Communist Party Congress demonstrate a strong willingness to tackle the issue of state-owned enterprises. Both these and the financial sector require bold reform.

No country has succeeded in changing from command economy to market, and from rural to urban, at the same time. The complexity of these two transitions cannot be overstated; nor can China's resolve. Whether in the area of reforming the tax and budget system, redefining the role of the state, or providing the growing economy's massive infrastructure needs, there is a relentless quality about China's progress. It is this, as much as the significant achievements of the past 20 years, that makes us optimistic about China's future, whatever the challenges, however uncharted the waters.

Address to the Board of Governors at the Annual Meetings of the World Bank
and the International Monetary Fund

HONG KONG SAR, CHINA | SEPTEMBER 23, 1997

*The joint Bank-Fund Annual Meetings were held in Hong Kong SAR just
months after exercise of sovereignty there was returned to China. Speaking
movingly about his recent visit to a shantytown in Brazil, Wolfensohn declares
that the key development challenge of our time is inclusion, or "bringing people
into society who have never been part of it before." The issues of inclusion and
empowerment would play an important role in Wolfensohn's later speeches.
He often reminded audiences that poor people do not want charity—they want
opportunity, dignity, and a chance to provide the best for their children.*

Mr. Chairman, Governors, Ladies and Gentlemen:

I am very pleased to welcome you to these Annual Meetings of the World
Bank Group and the International Monetary Fund. I am also delighted to be
in Hong Kong. This beautiful and bustling city, which I have visited regularly
for 40 years, exemplifies the openness, dynamism, and optimism of so much
of Asia today. And so does our meeting here in this magnificent conference
center, where everything has been done impeccably. I would like to express
my thanks to our hosts, the Government of China, and the authorities here in
Hong Kong. It is impossible to imagine greater courtesy, generosity, and efficiency. We look forward to your continued progress.

China's success has been truly remarkable. Less than a generation ago, 8 in
10 Chinese eked out an existence by tilling the soil for less than a dollar a day.
One adult in three could neither read nor write. Since then, 200 million people have been lifted out of absolute poverty, and illiteracy has fallen to less than
1 in 10. China is the World Bank's largest borrower, one of our most valued
shareholders, and home to more than a quarter of our nearly 5 billion clients.
I am delighted that our partnership continues to strengthen.

This is the third time that I address you as president of the World Bank
Group, and the third time I have had the opportunity to express my deep gratitude to my friend [IMF Managing Director] Michel Camdessus, whose collaboration over the last two and a half years has been so invaluable to me. We
work ever more closely together, and I continue to benefit from his great experience and judgment.

From the beginning, one of my priorities has been to take the pulse of
development firsthand. I have now visited almost 60 countries. I have met
with governments, parliamentarians, and the private sector. I have talked with
national and international NGOs [nongovernmental organizations] on subjects

ranging from women's issues to the environment, from health to the impact of macroeconomic reform.

Wherever I go, I continue to be impressed by the people we serve—by their strength, their energy, and their enterprise, even in the most abject conditions; by the hundreds of thousands disadvantaged by war; by the millions of children without families, condemned to live on the streets; by the disabled, shut out from any kind of social support; by the plight of the poorest.

Today our clients number 4.7 billion people in over 100 countries. Three billion live on less than two dollars a day. Of those, 1.3 billion live on less than one dollar a day. One hundred million children go hungry every day; over 100 million never even get the chance to go to school.

But whether they live on the plains or in the valleys, in slums or in isolated villages, whether they speak Hindi, Swahili, or Uzbek, they have one thing in common: They do not want charity. They want a chance. They do not want solutions imposed from without. They want the opportunity to build from within. They do not want my culture or yours. They want their own. They want a future enriched by the inheritance of their past.

I have learned that people are the same wherever they are—here in this room or across the world. We all want the best for our children and our families. We all want peace and economic and physical security. We all want to live in a supportive community. We all want personal dignity.

This was vividly brought home to me six months ago when I visited a large water and sanitation project that the Bank is supporting in the *favelas* of Brazil. The project, which is now self-sustaining, brings together the local community, the private sector, and NGOs. With my host, the vice governor of the state of Rio de Janeiro, I went from one makeshift home to the next, talking with the women who live there and who used to carry water on their shoulders from the bottom of the hillside to their dwellings at the top. One after the other, they proudly showed me their running water and flushed their toilets and told me how the project had transformed their lives.

And as I walked around, more and more of the women came up to me displaying pieces of paper showing charges and receipts for a few *reais* a month. I watched and listened to this for a while until the vice governor said, "What they're showing you, Jim, is that this is the first time in their lives that their name and address have appeared on an official notice. This is the first time their existence has been officially recognized. This is the first time that they have been included in society. With that receipt they can get credit to purchase goods. With that receipt they have recognition and hope."

As I walked back down the hill, I realized that this is what the challenge of development is all about: *inclusion*. It is about bringing people into society who have never been part of it before. This is why the World Bank Group exists. This is why we are all here today: to help make it happen for people.

The State of Development in 1997

Where are we in terms of "making it happen" in 1997? In many ways this is the best of times for developing countries. Output in the developing world grew last year by 5.6 percent—the highest rate in 20 years. Foreign direct investment exceeded $100 billion—the most ever. Private capital flows totaled $245 billion—five times official development assistance. And developing countries are projected to enjoy continued strong growth over the next 10 years.

Social indicators are also improving. Life expectancy has risen more in the past 40 years than in the previous 4,000. And freedom is blossoming. Today nearly two in three developing countries use open elections to choose their national leadership, and 5 billion people live in market economies, up from 1 billion 10 years ago.

There is also much good news in each major developing region:

- Reform programs in Eastern Europe and Central Asia continue to advance, and prospects for accession to the European Union now look promising for several countries in the region.
- There is real progress in Sub-Saharan Africa, with new leadership and better economic policies. That region's gross domestic product grew 4.5 percent in 1996, up from 2 percent two years ago.
- In the Middle East and North Africa, despite political problems, efforts continue to boost regional trade and investment, improve competitiveness, and expand economic opportunity.
- In Latin America, countries have emerged from the tequila crisis with their earlier gains against hyperinflation fully intact.
- In East Asia, despite recent turbulence in financial markets, we still expect long-term growth and poverty reduction to be strong.
- In South Asia, home to 35 percent of the developing world's poor, economic growth rates over the past several years have approached 6 percent a year.

This all adds up to much to celebrate—but there is also much to lament. Yes, the glass is half full, but it is also half empty. Too many people are not enjoying the fruits of success:

- Here in East Asia, despite the economic "miracle," inequities between rural and urban areas and between the skilled and the unskilled are becoming more widespread.

- In the countries of the former Soviet Union, the old and the unemployed have become more vulnerable amid the turbulence caused by the transition from command to market economies.
- In parts of Latin America, problems of landownership, crime, drug-related violence, unequal access to education and health care, and enormous disparities in income hinder progress and threaten stability.
- In many of the world's poorest countries, population growth continues to run ahead of economic growth, eroding living standards.

The deeper tragedy is that the glass is almost totally empty for too many. Indeed, for far too many it is the worst of times, as huge disparities persist across and within countries. In too many countries, the poorest 10 percent of the population have less than 1 percent of the income, while the richest 20 percent enjoy over half. In too many countries, girls are still only half as likely as boys to go to school. In too many countries, children are impaired from birth because of malnutrition, inadequate health care, and little or no access to early childhood development programs. In too many countries, ethnic minorities face discrimination at the hands of ethnic majorities, and some even fear for their lives.

What we are seeing in the world today is the tragedy of exclusion.

The Challenge Ahead

Our goal must be to reduce these disparities across and within countries, to bring more and more people into the economic mainstream, to promote equitable access to the benefits of development regardless of nationality, race, or gender. This, *the challenge of inclusion,* is the key development challenge of our time.

You and I and all of us in this room—the privileged of the developing and the industrial world—can choose to ignore the challenge. We can choose to focus only on the successes. We can live with a little more crime, a few more wars, air that is a little bit dirtier. We can insulate ourselves from whole sections of the world for which crisis is real and daily but to the rest of us largely invisible. But we must recognize that we are living with a time bomb, and unless we take action now, it could explode in our children's faces.

If we do not act, in 30 years the inequities will be greater. With population in the developing countries growing by 80 million a year, instead of 3 billion living on less than two dollars a day, it could be as high as 5 billion. In 30 years the quality of our environment will be worse. Instead of 4 percent of tropical forests lost since the Rio Earth Summit five years ago, it could be 24 percent.

In 30 years the number of armed conflicts may be higher. Already we live in a world that last year alone saw 26 interstate wars and 23 million refugees.

One does not have to spend a long time in Bosnia or Gaza or the Great Lakes district in Africa to know that, without economic hope, we will not have peace. Without equity, we will not have global stability. Without a better sense of social justice, our cities will not be safe and our societies will not be stable. Without inclusion, too many of us will be condemned to live separate, armed, and frightened lives.

Whether you broach it from the social or the economic or the moral perspective, this is a challenge we cannot afford to ignore. There are not two worlds; there is one world. We breathe the same air. We degrade the same environment. We share the same financial system. We have the same health problems. AIDS is not a problem that stops at borders. Crime does not stop at borders. Drugs do not stop at borders. Terrorism, war, and famine do not stop at borders.

Meanwhile economic transformation is fundamentally changing the relationships between the rich and the poor nations. Over the next 25 years, growth in China, India, Indonesia, Brazil, and Russia will likely redraw the economic map of the world, as the share in global output of the developing and transition economies doubles. Today these countries represent 50 percent of the world population but only 8 percent of its GDP. Their share in world trade is a quarter that of the European Union. By 2020 their share in world trade could be 50 percent *more* than Europe's.

We share the same world, and we share the same challenge. The fight against poverty is the fight for peace, security, and growth for us all.

How, then, do we proceed? This much we know: no country has been successful in reducing poverty without sustained economic growth. Those countries that have been most successful—including, most notably, many here in East Asia—have also invested heavily in their people, have put in place the right policy fundamentals, and have not discriminated against their rural sectors. The results have been dramatic: large private capital inflows, rapid growth, and substantial poverty reduction.

The message for countries is clear: educate your people; ensure their health; give them voice and justice, financial systems that work, and sound economic policies; and they will respond, they will save, and they will attract the investment, both domestic and foreign, that is needed to raise living standards and fuel development.

But another message is also emerging. We have seen in recent months how financial markets are demanding more information disclosure, and how they are making swift judgments about the quality and sustainability of government policies based on that information. We have seen that, without sound organization and supervision, financial systems can falter, and the poor are hurt the most. We have seen how corruption flourishes in the dark, how it prevents growth and social equity, and how it creates the basis for social and political instability.

We must recognize this link between good economic performance and open governance. Irrespective of political systems, public decisions must be brought right out into the sunshine of public scrutiny—not simply to please the markets, but to build the broad social consensus without which even the best-conceived economic strategies will ultimately fail.

The Development Community as Partners

How can we in the broader development community be most effective in helping with the enormous task ahead? It is clear that the scale of the challenge is simply too great to be handled by any single one of us. Nor will we get the job done if we work at cross purposes or pursue rivalries that should have been laid to rest long ago. Name calling between civil society and multilateral development institutions must stop. We should encourage criticism, but we should also recognize that we share a common goal and that we need each other.

Partnership, I am convinced, must be a cornerstone of our efforts. And it must rest on four pillars:

First and foremost, the government and the people of developing countries must be in the driver's seat, exercising choice and setting their own objectives. Development requires much too much sustained political will to be externally imposed. It *cannot* be donor-driven. What we as a development community *can* do is help countries—by providing financing, yes, but even more important, by providing knowledge and sharing the lessons learned about the challenges and how to address them. We must learn to let go. We must accept that the projects we fund are not donor projects or World Bank projects—they are Costa Rican projects, Bangladeshi projects, Chinese projects. And development projects and programs must be fully owned by the local stakeholders if they are to succeed. We must listen to those stakeholders.

Second, our partnerships must be inclusive, involving bilateral and other multilateral institutions, the United Nations, the European Union, regional organizations, the World Trade Organization, labor organizations, NGOs, foundations, and the private sector. With each of us playing to our respective strengths, we can leverage up the entire development effort.

Third, although we should offer our assistance to all countries in need, we must be selective in how we use our resources. There is no escaping the hard fact: more people will be lifted out of poverty if we concentrate our assistance on countries with good policies than if we allocate it without regard to the policies pursued. Recent studies confirm what we already knew intuitively: that, in a good policy environment, development assistance improves growth prospects and social conditions, but in a poor policy environment, it can actually retard progress by reducing the need for change and by creating dependency.

I want to be very clear on this point: I am not espousing some Darwinian theory of development whereby we discard the unfit by the wayside. Quite the contrary, our goal is to support the fit and to help make the unfit fit. This is all about inclusion.

In Africa, for example, a new generation of leaders deserve our strongest support for the tough decisions they are making. They have vast needs and a growing capacity to use donor funds well in addressing them. We must be there for them. It is an economic and a moral imperative.

However, where aid cannot be effective because of bad policy or corruption or weak governance, we need to think of new ways of helping the *people*. The old technical assistance approaches of the past relied too heavily on foreign consultants. We can instead help countries help themselves by building their own capacity to design and implement their own development.

Finally, all of us in the development community must look at our strategies anew. We need to make that quantum leap that will allow us to make a real dent in poverty. We need to scale up, to think beyond individual donor-financed projects to larger, country-led national strategies, and beyond that to regional strategies and systemic reform. We need approaches that can be replicated and customized to local circumstances—not one agricultural project here or one group of schools there, but *country* rural and educational strategies that can help the Oaxacas and the Chiapases of this world, as well as the Mexico Citys. We need to hit hard on the key pressure points for change: adequate infrastructure in key areas, social and human development, rural and environmental development, and financial and private sector development. And we need to remember that educating girls and supporting opportunities for women—in health, education, and employment—are crucial to balanced development.

In the struggle for inclusion, all this adds up to a changed bottom line for the development community. We must think *results*—how to get the biggest development return from our scarce resources. We must think *sustainability*—how to have an enduring development impact within an environmentally sustainable framework. We must think *equity*—how to include the disadvantaged. We must focus not on the easy projects, but on the difficult—in northeast Brazil, in India's Gangetic Plain, and in the Horn of Africa. Projects there will be riskier, yes, but success will be worth all the more in terms of including more people in the benefits of development and giving more people the chance of a better life.

The World Bank Group's Response

How is the Bank Group responding to the challenge of inclusion? Last year at these meetings, I said that if the Bank Group was to be more effective, it needed to change—to get closer to our clients' real needs, to focus on quality, and to be more accountable for the results of our work. This year I want to tell you that it is happening. Not only is the Bank changing, but the need for change is now fully accepted.

I know, and you know, that the Bank has tried to change before. But there has never been this level of commitment and consensus. We are building on the mission statement articulated by my predecessor, Lewis Preston, whose untimely death prevented him from implementing his plans.

Earlier this year we launched an action program, the Strategic Compact, to renew our values and commitment to development and to improve the Bank's effectiveness. I believe the Compact is historic, not because there is agreement on every paragraph of the document, but because staff, management, and shareholders—with terrific support from our Executive Directors—are now united on the future direction of the institution. While we still have a long way to go, and while change is painful and some people are undoubtedly feeling that pain, implementation is well under way.

I really believe that this time we can succeed. And we will succeed because of our truly remarkable and dedicated staff. I do not believe a better development team exists, or one with more experience in fighting poverty.

But the Compact is not primarily about our organization and internal change; it is about our *clients* and meeting their needs more effectively. To take this beyond rhetoric, we have decentralized aggressively, moving people and resources to the field. By the end of this month, 18 of our 48 country directors with decision-making authority will be based in the countries they serve, compared with only 3 last year.

We have speeded our response time and introduced new products such as the single-currency loan and loans for innovative projects of $5 million or less that can be implemented very quickly. Working with Michel Camdessus and our colleagues in the IMF, as well as with many other partners, we have prepared debt reduction packages worth about $5 billion for six heavily indebted poor countries under the HIPC Initiative. That is not bad for an effort that did not even have a name 18 months ago. And we are moving speedily ahead to help other countries in similar distress.

The new World Bank is committed to quality. We have put in place reinvigorated country management teams, with 150 new managers selected over the last six months, and rigorous training and professional development programs have been introduced for all staff. The IFC [International Finance Corporation] has also made major changes in management and is likewise decentralizing. We have improved the quality of our portfolio, and as a result our disbursements reached a record level last year of $20 billion.

The quality of *all* our work is being enhanced by the progress we have made toward becoming a Knowledge Bank. We have created networks to share knowledge across all regions and all major sectors of development. Our Economic Development Institute is playing a leading role in this area. Last June in Toronto, working with the Canadian government and many other sponsors, the EDI brought together participants from over 100 countries for the first Global Knowledge Conference.

My goal is to make the World Bank the first port of call when people need knowledge about development. By 2000 we will have in place a global communications system, with computer links, videoconferencing, and interactive classrooms, affording our clients all around the world full access to our information bases. It will mean the end of geography as we at the Bank have known it.

We are also promoting increased accountability throughout the Bank Group. We have developed a corporate scorecard to measure our performance. We are closely monitoring compliance with our policies and continuing to work to improve the inspection process by making it more transparent and effective. And we are designing new personnel policies that explicitly link staff performance to pay and promotion.

We are also emphasizing accountability in the dialogue with our clients. Last year I highlighted the importance of tackling the cancer of corruption. Since then we have issued new guidelines to staff for dealing with corruption and for ensuring that our own processes meet the highest standards of transparency and propriety. We have also begun working with a first half-dozen of our member countries to develop anticorruption programs.

My bottom line on corruption is simple: if a government is unwilling to take action even though the country's development objectives are undermined by corruption, then the Bank Group *must* curtail its level of support to that country. Corruption, by definition, is exclusive: it promotes the interests of the few over those of the many. We must fight it wherever we find it.

But what is key to meeting the challenge of inclusion is making sure not only that we do things right, but that we do the right things. Earlier I mentioned the strategic pressure points of change. Let me say a few words about what we are doing in some of these areas.

First, in the area of *human and social development,* we are mainstreaming social issues, including support for the important role of indigenous culture, into our country assistance strategies so that we can better reach ethnic minorities, households headed by women, and other excluded groups. We are participating in programs designed by local communities to address pervasive needs, such as the EDUCO basic literacy program in El Salvador and the District Primary Education Program in India, and these programs are now being replicated by other countries. We are increasing our support for efforts at capacity building, in particular the comprehensive program initiated by the African countries last year.

Sustainable development is also critical. In the *rural sector,* which is home to more than 70 percent of the world's poor, we have completed a major rethinking of our strategy. Lending for rural projects is now up after many years of decline, supporting innovative programs such as the new, market-based approach to land reform in Brazil. On the *environmental* front, we are also supporting our clients' efforts to address the "brown" issues—clean water and adequate sanitation—that are so often neglected but are so important for the quality of the everyday lives of the poor. And, through the Global Environment Facility, the Global Carbon Initiative, and a new partnership with the World Wildlife Fund to protect the world's forests, we are continuing to advance the global environmental agenda.

With respect to the *private sector,* we are capitalizing on the synergies among the Bank, the IFC, and MIGA [the Multilateral Investment Guarantee Agency] and coordinating our activities within a single, client-focused service "window." Across the Bank Group we are ramping up our work on regulatory, legal, and judicial reform designed to help create environments that will attract foreign and domestic private capital. We are using International Bank for Reconstruction and Development guarantees to help support policy changes and mitigate risk, and we are expanding the product line of IDA [the International Development Association] to help poor countries develop their private sectors and become full participants in the global economy.

Meanwhile the IFC is working in 110 countries and in more sectors, employing a wider range of financial products than ever before. Last year saw $6.7 billion in new approvals in 276 projects. The IFC's Extending the Reach Program is targeting 33 countries and regions that have so far received very little private sector investment. Again, the goal is clear: to bring more and more marginalized economies into the global marketplace.

MIGA, too, is playing an active and enhanced role. Last year it issued a record 70 guarantee contracts for projects in 25 developing countries, including 11 where it has not worked before. I am delighted that yesterday the Development Committee* agreed to an increase in MIGA's capital that will allow it to continue to grow.

Finally, the needs of the *financial sector* have been brought sharply into focus by recent events here in East Asia. Here, too, we are scaling up our work in co-ordination with the IMF and the regional development banks, for the simple reason that, when the financial sector fails, it is the poor who suffer most. It is the poor who pay the highest price when investment and access to credit dry up, when workers are laid off, when budgets and services are cut back to cover losses. But success in the financial sector requires much more than the an-nouncement of new policies or financial packages pulled together when crisis hits. That is why we are expanding our capacity for banking and financial sys-tem restructuring—not just for the middle-income countries, but taking on the larger task of financial sector development in low-income countries. For those countries, home to the world's 3 billion poorest people, IDA remains the key instrument for addressing the challenge of inclusion. I will be coming back to you in due course to seek your support for the 12th replenishment of IDA.

The Dream of Inclusive Development

I believe we in the World Bank Group have made considerable progress in putting our own house in order in preparation for the challenges of the new millennium. Nineteen ninety-seven has been a year of significant achievement. We must push ahead with this process. We must make sure that we deliver next year's work program and that we strengthen the project pipeline and increase the resources going directly to the front line. And we must implement the find-ings of our recently completed cost-effectiveness review. But the time has also come to get back to the dream—the dream of inclusive development.

We stand at a unique moment in history, one where we have a chance to make that dream a reality. Today we have an unprecedented consensus on the policies that need to be put in place for sustainable and poverty-reducing growth. Today we have clear and unambiguous evidence of the economic and social linkages between the developing and the industrial worlds. Today we face a future where, unless we take action, our children will be condemned to live in a degraded environment and a less secure world. All we need today is the determination to focus on tomorrow and the courage to do it now.

As a development community, we face a critical choice. We can continue business as usual, focusing on a project here, a project there, all too often running

---

* The Development Committee is a grouping of finance ministers representative of the Bank's member coun-tries that meets twice a year to discuss and advise on development issues.

behind the poverty curve. We can continue making international agreements that we then ignore. We can continue engaging in turf battles, competing for the moral high ground.

Or we can decide to make a real difference. But to do that we need to raise our sights. We need to forge partnerships to maximize our leverage and our use of scarce resources. And we need to scale up our efforts and hit hard on those areas where our development impact can be greatest.

We at the Bank Group are ready to do our part, but we cannot succeed alone. Only if we all work together will we even make a dent. Only if we collectively change our attitude will we make that quantum leap. Only if, in boardrooms and ministries and city squares across the globe, we begin to recognize that, ultimately, we will not have sustainable prosperity unless we have inclusion, will we make it happen.

Let me end where I began, in that *favela* in Brazil. What I saw in the faces of the women there I have also seen in the faces of women in India showing me passbooks for their savings accounts. I have seen it in the faces of rural cave dwellers in China being offered new, productive land. I have seen it in the faces of villagers in Uganda, able for the first time to send their children to school because of the private profit they can now make through rural extension schemes.

The look in these people's eyes is not a look of hopelessness. It is a look of pride, of self-esteem, of inclusion. These are people who have a sense of themselves, a sense of tradition, a sense of family. All they need is a chance.

Each one of us in this room must take personal responsibility for making sure they get that chance. We can do it. For the sake of our children, we must do it. Working together, we will do it.

1997: THE STRATEGIC COMPACT AND A MORE EFFECTIVE FIGHT AGAINST POVERTY

Message from the president and chairman from the 1997 World Bank *Annual Report*

SEPTEMBER 1997

This message focuses on the internal reorganization of the Bank. It high-lights the Strategic Compact, a program aimed at making the institution more effective in fighting poverty.

This *Annual Report,* covering July 1, 1996, to June 30, 1997, chronicles a year of renewal at the World Bank. Strengthening partnerships and getting results in serving the poorest people in the world are two recurring themes running through these pages. Nowhere have these two objectives been better illustrated than in the strengthened working relationship that is being forged between management and staff of the World Bank and its shareholders represented by the Executive Board.

Over the last ten years the environment for the Bank's clients has changed dramatically. While official development assistance has declined, private capital flows have surged. But they have been concentrated in a comparatively small number of countries. At the same time, the role of civil society and that of the private sector have become more pronounced, governments have become more accountable for their actions, and all the players rely on the new capacity to share knowledge rapidly as a result of dramatic changes in technology.

As the Bank has recognized these developments, we have introduced new approaches to ensure that the lending and advice we provide is what our clients really need. One consequence of the reform process is of special note. Institutional change, encapsulated in the Strategic Compact, has been given momentum by a joint commitment by management and the Board to enhance the latter's role in defining policy directions.

The Executive Board's unanimous approval of the Strategic Compact last March, whereby investment in changes over the next two years will lead to a much stronger and cost-effective institution in the future, was an important step in further strengthening the relationship between the Bank and its share-holders. The Executive Board will have an integral role in monitoring the Strategic Compact and ensuring its success as management reports regularly to the Board on progress in implementing policy initiatives. We now have symmetry in the roles of management and the Board in approving projects and changes in the Bank's policies: projects are discussed as part of broader country assistance strategies, while changes in specific policies will increasingly be considered within the overall policy framework established by the Strategic Compact.

The changes the Bank is undertaking have the specific objective of making the Bank the most effective institution in the world in the fight against poverty.

We aim to reach this goal through a clearly defined business plan, which is embodied in the Strategic Compact. By fiscal year 2001, we have committed to returning our real operating costs to this year's level while providing a higher level of service and greater volume of products to our clients.

To ensure that our shareholders see a return on the investment that we are making to renew the Bank, we are building up our capacity to evaluate our institutional performance against clearly defined objectives. Fifty years after the Bank made its first loan, we are poised to enter the new millennium with fresh vigor and more attuned to our clients' needs than ever before.

Almost 5 billion people who live in our client countries deserve the benefits that an effective and competent World Bank, at the heart of a global network of development assistance, can provide.

DO WE HAVE THE COURAGE TO GRAB OUR CHANCE IN ASIA?

Published in *The Australian*

SEPTEMBER 30, 1997

These are excerpts from a speech Wolfensohn gave in Sydney on his way back to Washington from the Bank-Fund Annual Meetings in Hong Kong. It represents a direct and frank appeal to those in his home country about the importance of development, and a call for Australian leadership.

Australia has the talent to carve a wonderful future in the region—we need a leadership with the guts to take us there.

I think about Australia because I worry about the future, not because I am concerned about the life of any of you here in this room, but because I'm wondering whether Australia will in fact meet the challenge of leadership which is open to it.

I now live in the developing world. And it's a world that has 4.7 billion people and a lot of them are very poor. But they do represent 18 percent of the world's gross national product, and it's the fastest growing area of the world, and it's the most diverse area of the world and, in another 25 years, it will represent 39 percent of the world's gross national product.

And we think of it as a second world, but it isn't the second world: it's part of our world. Australia's exports to East Asia, which is part of the developing world, now amount to 60 percent of exports. To the whole of Asia, it's 75 percent of exports. We breathe the same air as this developing world. We drink the same water.

When I grew up here, we were British-oriented. I always thought of the Third World or Asia as something different. It's not.

We are not an Asian nation but we're next to Asia. I think there has been a lot of reaching out to Asia recently: the leadership on the Asia-Pacific Economic Co-operation forum, the leadership on the Association of South-East Asian Nations consultative group, work we did in Cambodia, a real sort of outreach in terms of Australian leadership.

What troubles me is whether we really believe it—whether Australia really believes that it's part of Asia, whether it really believes that our future is linked with Asia.

Why am I interfering, coming back? Why am I commenting on things that I don't know about? I'm commenting because I care and because I do have a chance to see around the world. I worry in terms of Australia's leadership, about whether we really adopt the fact that the world has changed, that Asia is the fastest growing area of the world, that we have the greatest opportunity, being on the doorstep of Asia, and that if we miss this chance, it's not you who miss the chance, it's our kids who will miss the chance. And that's where leadership comes in.

Australia is in a perfect position to take advantage of this next century. I read last night a lot of interesting phrases—we can act as a bridge to Asia, to the UK, to the sources of knowledge to the US. That's nonsense.

If you don't think the Chinese deal directly, and that the Indonesians deal directly, or the Asians deal directly, you're kidding yourselves. If you think they need Australia, they do not need Australia. And with telecommunications and communications the way they are, Australia runs the risk of being marginalised. We have 18 million people in this country. We're one-third of 1 percent of the world's population of 5.7 billion.

Ten years ago there was only one country in Asia bigger than Australia in terms of GDP and that was Japan. In five years, it will be China, Indonesia, India; these countries are growing at 9 percent a year. We may grow at 3½ percent a year.

The future of the world is dependent on the developing countries.

Australia is uniquely positioned to reach out, but we have to believe it. The remarkable thing is that, as I travel around the world, I'm received as an Australian, everywhere, and, as an Australian, people regard you as being fair, being straightforward. Not being lumbered with being American or being British, or being Dutch or being anything else, Australians have a remarkable, unique position. People like Australians. People care about Australians.

But what we have to do is to show some caring ourselves. We don't just have to receive foreign students to study here.

We should send students abroad. How wonderful it would be if we could send 5000 kids every year to Asia for two years, a sort of Australian outreach corps, to learn about Asia . . . and it would change the fabric of society.

What you cannot do is to lead without involvement. You have to get involved. And there is no chance for Australian leadership unless there's involvement, unless there's belief, unless there's a real desire to say we're going to change, we're strong enough and we're tough enough, and we're self-confident enough to be Australian and to be open to outside influences—then we can lead.

And what do we have to contribute? We have here a fantastic education system. We have a great technology. We used to be very practical. And all it requires is a bit of effort, a bit of strategy, a bit of saying: let's set the course for the next generation, let's invest now for the next generation.

What I think about Australian leadership is that it is all there, everything is there, except pushing it over the edge. We've got the people, they have the skills, the understanding, the technology, the creativity; we've got the sense of excellence and we don't have a colonial history.

And this country has absolutely everything, except the will to do it. And I beg you to have the will to do it because Australians can make a difference. And it's not for you, it's for your children.

And if you want them to grow up in a world of peace and stability, you have to act now. And that means being open in our country. It means getting rid of people in Canberra who think the other way. It means being open in your companies. It means inviting new immigrants home. It means advancing people's opportunities.

I think there is an enormous chance for Australian leadership. I think we have everything but the courage to do it. And I just hope like hell that those who are leading now will have that courage.

I look forward to sharing with you in years from now, if I am still alive, a new sense of Australia in the developing world; confident, caring, open, not hung up on race, gender or religion; and being the Australia that I remember.

Foreword to *Rural Development: From Vision to Action*, published by the World Bank

OCTOBER 1997

> *This is one of a select handful of Wolfensohn's forewords in this volume.*
> *The forewords show the specific attention Wolfensohn paid to particular*
> *themes and how he supported new research and initiatives. This piece*
> *heralds the creation of a new Bank strategy for development in rural areas.*

Reducing poverty and eliminating hunger are among the most fundamental challenges we face. Today more than 1.3 billion people are compelled to live on less than one dollar a day. More than 800 million people are going hungry, because they cannot afford to buy the food they and their families need. And the numbers of poor and hungry people will surely continue to grow unless action is taken now.

Reducing poverty and ending hunger require focused attention on the rural economy. Nearly three out of four of the world's poor and hungry people live in rural areas. Although the absolute numbers and the proportion of poor people living in cities are expected to grow rapidly, the majority of poor will continue to live in the countryside until well into the next century.

Rural people also play a critical role in protecting the environment. Agriculture is the world's biggest user of land and water resources. Agriculture both contributes to environmental degradation and suffers as a result of it.

Excess use of fertilizers and pesticides pollutes the water and destroys biodiversity, and unmanaged deforestation eliminates critical habitats and ruins watersheds. Meanwhile, water pollution and erosion reduce the productivity of farms and fisheries.

We must raise the productivity of poor people in agricultural areas and ensure that they have the capacity to market and distribute their products. These improvements not only will raise the incomes of the rural poor but also will benefit the urban poor by bringing down the price of food. We must improve the efficiency of land, water, and chemical use if we are to feed the world's population, expected to exceed eight billion by 2025, without destroying the environment.

This rural sector strategy outlines the steps the Bank and its partners must take to spur rural development. Key elements of the strategy include:

- *Taking a broad rural focus, as opposed to a narrow agricultural sector focus.* The rural sector strategy focuses on the entire rural productive system. Water resource allocation and comprehensive watershed management incorporate irrigation and drainage. The management of natural resources in sustainable production systems treats agriculture, forestry, and livestock as part of a larger

system. Human capital development, infrastructure, and social development are integrated into rural development strategies and programs.

- *Involving the entire World Bank Group in promoting rural development.* Coordination among the different actors must be greatly improved to ensure that efforts are neither duplicated nor hampered.
- *Working with partner countries and the broader international community to integrate rural development in overall country development strategies.* The rural sector strategy stresses the formulation of country assistance strategies as critical to building consensus both within the Bank Group and among stakeholders in countries.
- *Addressing long-ignored issues.* We must not be timid on issues such as land reform, and we must greatly increase our commitment to food and nutrition policy. Gender equity will be an important aspect of many of these issues.
- *Addressing old issues in new ways.* The Bank Group has acquired considerable knowledge about what works and what does not. We will implement more widely the promising new approaches. For example, we will involve stakeholders in the development and execution of projects through all stages, deliver rural financial services to the poor using new approaches, and promote sustainable resource use through community-based management.

Address to the United Nations Economic Commission for Africa

ADDIS ABABA | JANUARY 27, 1998

*In one of his most memorable speeches on Africa, Wolfensohn calls for
partnership and the end of mutual stereotyping between the multilateral
development institutions and their developing-country clients. Inspired by a
meeting in Uganda just days before with 12 leaders from eastern and southern
Africa, Wolfensohn speaks of a "new beginning" for Africa and of the
continent's chance to "move forward."*

Mr. Chairman, Dr. Salim,* Your Excellencies, and Friends:

I want to say at the outset how much I appreciate those very generous words
of introduction. They are helping me get over the nerves I feel at being in this
hall, where, 35 years ago, 31 of the historic leaders of Africa signed the charter of the Organization of African Unity: Ben Bella, Houphouët-Boigny,
Nkrumah, Nyerere, Senghor,† and all the other towering figures I see on the
beautiful mural that adorns this hall. Their images encourage and stimulate me
to try and do more for the development of this great continent.

I have much to learn. The continent of Africa is a very difficult place to describe in a few words. It is a place of enormous contrasts, a place it is very hard
to get a handle on. It is a place where any positive statement is likely to be
contradicted somewhere on the continent, a place where any negative statement is likely to be contradicted somewhere else.

Last night, as I was preparing these remarks, I started to jot down a few
thoughts about my impressions after two and a half years working as president
of the World Bank and spending time in Africa. When I speak of Africa in the
United States, I of course point out that the economic statistics have shown increases in overall GNP growth and in growth in GNP per capita, that civil society is flourishing, and that there is a new spirit of optimism, which I share.
But, even as I say that, I know that more people are dying on this continent for
reasons that could be avoided than anywhere else. I know that some parts of the
continent are wracked by chaos and conflict, and that in those parts of Africa
not only is there no growth, but in fact people are dying of malnutrition.

I know of the new leadership, those with passion, with vision, with integrity, of whom we speak with such honor and with such pride. Yet I also

---

* Salim Ahmed Salim, secretary-general of the Organization of African Unity (now the African Union).
† Ahmed Ben Bella, Kwame Nkrumah, Julius Nyerere, and Léopold Senghor were the first presidents after
independence of Algeria, Ghana, Tanzania, and Senegal, respectively; Felix Houphouët-Boigny was president
of Côte d'Ivoire from shortly after independence until 1993.

know of those of whom we do not speak with honor and pride—in fact, of whom we do not speak at all.

I know how proud we are that many African countries have reached growth rates of more than 5 percent a year. But I also know that the population is increasing at close to 3 percent a year, and that to make the sort of quantum leaps that Africa needs remains a daunting challenge and will require annual growth rates of 8 to 10 percent.

I know that we have seen improvements in education: a 78 percent primary school enrollment rate, with an increasing enrollment of girls. But I also know of the 30-odd countries that are at the same educational level as 15 years ago, where progress has stalled.

And I know of the history and culture of Africa. I have personally been enormously moved as I have traveled around the continent. In villages, slums, and middle-class areas, I have seen a reflection of its rich and diverse culture. I have seen the strength of its family values. I have seen people in absolute poverty who do not want a handout, but simply want a chance. They have dignity; they have nobility. These people are the core and the strength of Africa. And yet, in other parts of Africa, I have seen chaos and irrational killing that does no credit either to those who participate or to the continent.

Against this background of contradictions and contrasts, I am also struck by the remarkable set of crosscurrents in the ways in which people deal with each other when it comes to Africa. When people speak of the World Bank and the Bretton Woods institutions today, they automatically say, "Structural adjustment. Massive debt. Messed-up economies. Damaged lives." And even when I go to Kampala to meet with 12 African leaders, the headline in the London press tells the world—before the press conference has even been called—that the meeting is a failure, when it was, in fact, an enormous success.

There are so many images that we have of each other—set pieces, stereotypes—that box us in and keep partnership and progress out. There is the way in which some NGOs [nongovernmental organizations] speak of the World Bank, the way in which many multilateral institutions speak of governments, the way in which some speak of the private sector. Relationships have congealed in a way that affects the entire discussion on Africa.

It is time for a new beginning. It is time to stop laying the blame for past mistakes. It is time to stop claiming credit for past achievements. It is time to focus on the future, Africa's future. Last week, in this hall, the Archbishop of Canterbury talked of the "chains around Africa." We should not think of the chains of Africa; we should think of the freedom of Africa, the liberation of Africa, the chance to move forward in Africa.

From the confusing picture that I have sketched, one very important notion emerges: There is leadership in this continent. There is strength in the people of this continent. There is a humanity here that can allow Africa to break free from the stereotypes of the past and stand proudly and face the future. I see it here in Ethiopia, one of the poorest countries in Africa, a country that was wracked by chaos and conflict, a country driven to its knees. But, even in their brief six years in power, its dynamic and committed new leaders are making a difference. This remarkable group of people is facing up to a set of economic and social indicators that most people would have found extraordinarily daunting. They are doing it with courage, they are doing it with perseverance, and they are doing it with transparency. And I would just like to say to the ministers here in the audience how much I admire what you are doing and how much we at the Bank appreciate our partnership with you.

The Bank has lent over $50 billion in Africa since our first loan to Ethiopia in the 1950s. We have had a lot of experience, and we are anxious to build on the past. Have we made mistakes? Certainly. But so have we all. Development is a tough business. It is not a business for which there is a textbook where you can look up how to solve every problem. Development takes courage, it takes daring, it takes the risk of failure, and it takes partnership.

I met this week in Kampala with 12 leaders from eastern and southern Africa, including Prime Minister Meles, at a meeting convened by President Museveni.[‡] After the niceties of the introduction, we got down to the question that had brought us there. This was the first time that a group of national leaders in Africa had ever sat down with the president of the World Bank to discuss the issues facing Africa and what we could do together. It was also the first time, with or without the president of the World Bank, that the leaders themselves had sat down together for that sort of discussion in an informal setting. And what did they talk about? Let me quote from the press release:

> The leaders identified several constraints to Africa's development: inadequate levels of human development as evidenced in particular by education and health indicators, inadequate physical and social infrastructure, poor prioritization of development needs, bureaucracy and ineptitude, low value-adding capacity and unfavorable terms of trade, small and fragmented markets, an underdeveloped agricultural sector dominated by subsistence farming, limited access to Western markets, a heavy debt burden, low savings and lack of entrepreneurship, lack of research and application of technology, and lack of meaningful partner-

---

‡ Prime Minister Meles Zenawi of Ethiopia and President Yoweri Museveni of Uganda, respectively.

ship between African leaders and donors leading to identifying the wrong development priorities.

These are not my words; these are the words of the 12 presidents.

The message coming out of Kampala was a very simple one. It is a message I would like to align myself with today. That simple, positive, and powerful message said, "Let us not look back at what has happened in the past, let us look forward. Let us take a simple, business-like approach to the future. Let us stand up as equals and face the issues. Let us set an agenda for growth and development over the next 5 or 10 years." We came out of that meeting with an enormous sense of forward motion, which was shared by President [Abdou] Diouf of Senegal, with whom I will be meeting next June along with a group of other West and Central African leaders to review these results, and perhaps add to them and move further forward.

What targets did we set? It is worth outlining them because they constitute our agenda for the next few years. But before doing so, let me set one important ground rule. I said to the African leadership, "The buck stops with African leaders. The buck stops with Africa. Without strong African leadership, the World Bank, the International Monetary Fund, the multilateral institutions, the bilateral institutions, the remarkable agencies of the United Nations, the private sector, and the NGOs will all be fairly helpless to bring about meaningful and lasting changes."

I told them that I do not want to come to another meeting where we talk about World Bank projects. I reject "World Bank projects." I do not own "World Bank projects." The projects I want to see are Ivorian projects, Senegalese projects, Ethiopian projects. And unless they are owned by the African leadership and the African people, we in the Bank are not going to participate. Africa is not dependent on the World Bank—this is a continent of 48 proud countries. Recognizing that and acting on it are the basis for moving forward. African leadership was the ground rule for the targets set by the meeting in Kampala, and it must be the ground rule for all our work in Africa.

Let me now go briefly through the targets.

The first is human resource development: education for all, with no gender bias. This is a highly significant starting point for growth. I am not talking about just setting up schools, but integrated educational development. Why? Because building schools without textbooks or teachers is not education.

But education without health care is also meaningless. You cannot have 25, 30, or 40 percent of your children being damaged, nutritionally and physically, before they get to school, and expect that you are going to educate them. I have just come back from Bangladesh, where 25 percent of the children are stunted from malnutrition before they are even enrolled in school. To have a health care system that works, you need to reach out and move to the field; you need nutrition, you need family planning, and you need distributive justice.

And in Africa you need vigorously and straightforwardly to pronounce the word "AIDS" and talk about AIDS prevention. AIDS can destroy a people and a continent. It needs to be put front and center, and we need to emphasize prevention. Even though it is hard to talk about in many societies, and even though it is hard to bring out into the open, it is a fact that we must face.

We then stressed capacity building at all levels. Capacity building is crucial in the government and the public sector. But it is also crucial in the private sector, it is crucial in farmers' organizations, it is crucial in NGOs, it is crucial in the administrative and technical professions. Let me give you an example from my last 24 hours here in Ethiopia. We signed two programs, one providing $300 million for roads and one providing $200 million for electric power. Reaping the full benefits of these programs will require the sustained participation of Ethiopians from all walks of life: large and small entrepreneurs, engineers, technicians, local authorities, and village groups.

To avoid the charge that we are providing all the technical assistance from outside, which does not build capacity, we must confront the issue of how to come up with Ethiopian engineers who can build roads, when roads have not been built in this country for 50 or 60 years. Where do we get engineers who will know about prestressed concrete technology in a country where there has been none? We have to bring about technical training and capacity building at all levels.

And so I discussed with members of the cabinet this morning how to advance the country by focusing on capacity building. We talked about capacity building on a range of levels, including teaching, distance learning, using new technology, using satellite technology, setting up classrooms so that there can be an exchange of ideas over thousands of miles. But we also discussed low-tech approaches, such as wind-up radios that need no batteries, for classrooms on the air. We talked about establishing distance learning facilities here in Addis Ababa—and the Bank is prepared to finance them—with classes not only for advanced subjects but also for training at local levels, for technical skills and manual trades.

This kind of capacity building is crucial, and in Kampala the leaders strongly endorsed the African-designed initiative that was completed in 1996, called "Partnership for Capacity Building in Africa." They are now going to elevate that initiative to their level and push further forward.

We also talked about rural development and rural transformation. In a continent where 40 percent of the population live on less than one dollar a day, and where 70 percent of the poor live in rural areas, rural development is essential. But we talked not just about agricultural development, about extension services, or about increasing yields. We also talked about the fact that rural development means rural roads, it means financing, it means microcredit, it means opportunities for women, it means the opportunity to transform agricultural products, be it into clothing or into food products. We have to look at rural development systematically, so that village infrastructure, rural electrification, communications, the empowerment of farmers to make their own decisions, and administrative decentralization like that going on here in Ethiopia can all become a reality.

The leaders then spoke of private sector development. This is a requirement, and one that is not unique to Africa. The numbers are staggering. Seven years ago, net flows of private sector investment into the developing world were on the order of $30 billion a year, and official flows, from the Bank and other multilateral and bilateral institutions, were $60 billion a year. Today official development assistance has dropped from $60 billion to $45 billion, and private sector investment has gone from $30 billion to $300 billion. From being half the size of net official development assistance seven years ago, private sector external investment is now more than six times as large. And this changes the dynamics. It means the private sector has to take an ever-increasing role in development. And I do not mean just the foreign private sector; I also mean the domestic private sector.

But what do we see when we look at Africa? We see that Africa is missing out. Of $300 billion in total foreign private capital flows to the developing world, Sub-Saharan Africa received about $12 billion. And of that only $2.6 billion came in the form of direct investment—a trivial number in relation to the size and potential of this continent. But we also have to face facts. It is not just because the private sector is myopic that less than 1 percent of foreign direct investment comes to Africa. Africa needs to set itself up to *attract* private investment, and that means a clean regulatory environment; it means a judicial system that works; it means property rights, corporate law, and predictability in taxes and in relationships with governments; it means capacity building, health care, and the infrastructure necessary to go along with it. And it means corruption must be stamped out. Without these, private investors simply will not invest.

Infrastructure was the sixth item on the leaders' agenda in Kampala: rural roads to improve access to remote regions, rural water for its health benefits and the time savings for women, rural electricity, and major roads to facilitate national unity as well as international road links to speed up regional integration. These links are vital. With 48 independent states in Africa, the continent's markets are too small and fragmented. African countries need to come together to further regional development, and that, too, was one of the areas for target setting that the leaders identified as important. Progress will require reducing imbalances among countries in terms of infrastructure; harmonizing policies, especially on trade matters; and building on regional organizations such as SADC [the Southern African Development Community], COMESA [the Common Market for Eastern and Southern Africa], and the West African Economic and Monetary Union.

And then we talked about conflict prevention and resolution. What the OAU is doing in this area, under the leadership of its secretary-general, Dr. Salim, is remarkable. But you cannot have growth in Africa if people are killing one another. You cannot have growth in Africa if societies are crumbling. You cannot have growth in Africa if people are living frightened, fragile lives. What we have got to do is stop the fighting. And when the fighting stops, we must replace it with economic development, with opportunity, with hope, so that it does not start again. That is as true in Africa as it is in Bosnia, in Gaza, in Guatemala, or across the world. So what we need to do is develop that sense of justice and expectation on the part of the people of this continent.

And finally we talked about public sector reform and good governance, about training, accountability, and living wages for the people who work in government.

Two other themes cut across all our discussions: gender and the environment. For each priority set in Kampala, the specific needs and contributions of women must be identified and addressed, be it their transport needs, their access to credit, or their legal standing to own assets; be it their reproductive health and old age problems, or their education and literacy. And economic statistics need to record and to monitor the progress of both genders.

Meanwhile Africa's precious environmental resources must be nurtured. Water must be carefully managed and the soil preserved, especially in fragile ecological areas. The rich biodiversity of the continent must be preserved, by working in collaboration with the local populations who depend on their environment.

How, then, to achieve all this? This much we know. We will not succeed unless we put the congealed relationships of the past behind us and move to a new relationship. In this critical endeavor, four partners are key.

The first and most obvious set of partners is the *governments* of the countries that are developing. What can we expect of them? We can expect rigorous, predictable, and sustained good economic management; we can expect transparency, accountability, and measures to fight corruption—not just within Africa but in relationships with external partners as well. In those countries where "extraordinary expenditures"—bribes and enticements—are tax deductible, we also need to follow on the OECD convention against corruption with early action.[§]

But the issue goes beyond that. My experiences in Africa and in other places have convinced me that corruption is a tough thing to talk about. People will say, "The boss is not corrupt, but the people around him are." Or sometimes they will say, "The boss is corrupt, and the people around him wish that he was not." Sometimes they will say they are all corrupt.

We have to be able to talk about corruption. We have to be able to recognize that the biggest obstacle to social equity *is* corruption, that the biggest obstacle to including the majority of the people in the benefits of growth is corruption. Corruption, by definition, is exclusive. It promotes the interests of the few over those of the many. We have to talk about it, we have to bring it to light, and we have to fight it.

The second of the four partners is the *donor community*. Donors are important not just in terms of giving money, but because of the knowledge and expertise they can share. We all have to do a better job of working together. We cannot fight over whose flag should fly over each and every project. We cannot all send large teams to study every subject. We cannot operate in a manner that is less than cooperative and that does not add value. I am sure that, in the past, the Bank has not adhered to such rules in every case. I will just tell you now that this will not be the case in the future. We will lead when it is appropriate for us to lead, we will follow when it is appropriate for us to follow, and we will not participate at all when the job is better done by others. I give you our commitment that, from here on, this is the way we will operate.

The third partner is, of course, the *private sector*. Businesses and investors clearly need to participate fully, and we have to establish an environment that attracts private investment. But even when such an environment is in place, there is still an enormous selling job to do. Why? Because Africa's image among investors is still much worse than warranted by the risks entailed by its economic fundamentals. Let me give you a statistic that stunned me last night when I was reading. I looked at how much money Africans hold abroad, as compared with how much money Latin Americans hold abroad, or Asians hold abroad. This is a reflection of what Africans think about the investment climate on their own continent. You will be staggered to know, as I was, that 37 percent of African private wealth is held outside Africa, whereas in Asia only 3 percent is held outside, and in Latin America 17 percent. Africans have

---

§ The Convention on Combating Bribery of Foreign Public Officials in International Business Transactions was adopted by the Organisation for Economic Co-operation and Development in November 1997.

to show confidence in Africa if we are going to have foreign investment in this continent.

Finally, the fourth set of partners, and perhaps the most important, are the *NGOs and organizations of civil society*. NGOs represent an important and critical force. Not all NGOs are created equal. There are good NGOs and, I am hesitant to say it, there are bad NGOs. But where we can establish partnerships with them, the potential is enormous. Let me give you a striking example from West Africa, where we have worked with governments and NGOs in eradicating river blindness. This program is an excellent example of the type of four-way partnership I have in mind: the governments have been committed; several international institutions—WHO, UNDP, FAO,** and the World Bank—have collaborated on the basis of what each had to offer; the private sector has donated the drug; and NGOs have played an essential role in delivering it. Their involvement is helping us expand the program to the other infected parts of Africa.

Other such partnerships are under way. Last night we announced a 20-year program with SmithKline Beecham and with WHO on elephantiasis, another disease that affects the continent. And in 20 years we want to eradicate that disease, too. SmithKline is giving us a drug—you take one pill once a year, much like the drug that we are using against river blindness. Here, too, the four-way partnership will be the key to success.

That is the dream and the vision: to bring the four groups together to tackle issues in the context of long-term, nationwide programs that reach the greatest number of people we can. But to make this vision a reality, we must face other issues, none perhaps as important as debt. His Grace, the Archbishop of Canterbury, when he was here, talked about the chains of debt and colonialism. Yes, debt is a heavy burden indeed, and we should be grateful to the archbishop for his efforts. But we should deal with it not with rhetoric, but with strategy, with precision, and with practicality within the framework of the Heavily Indebted Poor Countries Initiative.

I have seen His Holiness the Pope and members of the Pontifical Council three times in the last year. In February 1998 the Bank will meet with religious leaders in London. We are talking with NGOs. We now have a chance of resolving the debt problem in Africa. The HIPC Initiative is not, perhaps, the total answer, but it is an intelligent and appropriate approach to dealing with the issue. The HIPCs' long-term debt is around $167 billion in net present value terms, with Africa accounting for about $120 billion. Of that, the share

---

** The World Health Organization, the United Nations Development Programme, and the Food and Agriculture Organization, respectively.

owed to the World Bank—that is, to IBRD [the International Bank for Reconstruction and Development] and IDA [the International Development Association]—constitutes 10 percent. So the problem is not just the Bank and IDA; the major problem lies with the creditor governments. They must be mobilized to do much more.

The Bank has $150 billion in assets: $25 billion in capital, and another $125 billion that we have borrowed. So the most that we could forgive is $25 billion, because we have to pay back the $125 billion. We could forgive $25 billion of African debt, but if we do that, there is no Bank left. We would go out of business. Clearly there is a limit to what we can do.

The same is true of IDA. We have $70 billion for IDA, and we are relying for half of IDA's replenishment on what we receive from repayments on loans already extended. If we forgive the debt owed to IDA, we do not get those repayments, and so we would have to halve the size of IDA's program. If you like that idea, we will do that, and we can close IDA. Again there is a clear, practical limit to what we can do.

The real question does not relate to the World Bank. We are intermediaries. The real question gets back to the governments that own us, the major creditors that make up the other 90 percent of what the HIPCs owe. And I think the way to gain their support is not with rhetoric, but by trying to mobilize and build momentum for the debt-relief program so that they can build on the very constructive steps already taken.

Let me also underline that the HIPC Initiative is the newest and most innovative but by no means the only instrument we have to reduce Africa's debt burden. We are using IDA reflows to cover the IBRD debt of the IDA countries—the so-called fifth dimension. Over $1 billion in relief has been provided since we started using this instrument in 1988. We have a debt facility for buying back commercial debt. We helped countries buy back $4.4 billion of their debt in the 1990s—that is equivalent to 11 percent of the combined GDPs of the countries concerned. Recently we approved a significant package that should help Côte d'Ivoire cancel about $5 billion of its commercial debt, which is equivalent to 45 percent of its GDP.

Debt is a problem. I am committed to doing something about it, and so is Michel Camdessus, [the managing director] of the International Monetary Fund. You have my promise to do everything humanly possible to solve this issue.

So my message is simple: Let us stop taking preordained positions about each other. Let us look forward. Let us analyze the problems, and let us adopt a game plan for the future. Let us set ourselves targets for how we, the four partners—governments, multilateral institutions, the private sector, and civil society—can work together. And let us judge ourselves on our results. When we get things right, let us congratulate ourselves and move forward. When we get things wrong, let us not react with recriminations and anger, but instead try and see what went wrong so we do not do it again. Unless we are united, unless we forget a lot of these preset positions, Africa will not move forward. This moment, which should be Africa's, will be lost.

Yesterday, at the museum, I saw a painting by Afework Tekele, who made the beautiful stained glass window outside Africa Hall. It was a wonderful painting. It was a painting with a perimeter about Africa, about Africa's troubles. Out there at the edge, it had a UN symbol. But in the center it had a sunrise, the sunrise of Africa—your sunrise. This is Africa's moment, a moment Africa richly deserves, a moment to seize. It is a moment to build a sunrise that will bathe us all in light.

THE WORLD NEEDS A STRONG AND INTERNATIONALLY ACTIVE JAPAN

Address at the Annual Dinner of the Japan Society

NEW YORK | JUNE 10, 1998

Here Wolfensohn appeals to a largely Japanese audience about the country's role in assisting countries coming out of the Asian crisis. Speaking of the recession in Japan, he says, "Japan has to respond, not just for Japan's sake, but because the world has come to count on Japan." Wolfensohn's familiarity with Japan, spurred by a long interest in Japanese culture, shows clearly throughout this speech.

Thank you very much, Deryck,* your excellencies, and ladies and gentlemen, and I see a number of my friends in the audience. It's not often that a public servant from Washington gets invited to such a ritzy dinner in New York. So I was delighted to have the opportunity to come up and see some old friends and to address you at this dinner. My single regret is that it wasn't two years ago. Because then I could have talked about the Asian miracle, and we would have been drinking champagne, and there would have been an atmosphere of levity and self-confidence in the room. That self-confidence I'm sure is still there, but the sense of levity is a little removed.

As you know, I have spent my time at the World Bank dealing with issues of poverty. We're an institution that is over 50 years old, and we have even more clients than Salomon Brothers, Travelers, Smith Barney, and Citibank put together. We're probably the only institution in the world that has more clients than you do, Deryck. We have 4.8 billion of them. And 3 billion of them live on less than two dollars a day, and 1.3 billion of them live on less than one dollar a day. So the function of our institution is to concern ourselves with issues of poverty, with issues of growth, with issues of the environment. And we've been doing that for some 54 years.

But we didn't start by doing that. We started as a reconstruction bank after World War II, along with our sister institution, the International Monetary Fund. And one of our client countries at that time was Japan. In fact, we made 31 loans to Japan between 1953 and 1966. If you've been on the bullet train, you should know that that had something to do with us, because we did the original financing. And if you've seen the Kurobe hydroelectric dam, that is ours, too. And I'm sure that when my predecessors acted at that time to help rebuild Japan, they never dreamed that Japan would emerge as the economic success that it is.

---

* Deryck Maughan, chairman and chief executive officer of Citigroup International and vice chairman of Citigroup, Inc.

In those days Japan was not in great shape. I can remind you that the life expectancy of Japanese women then was 54 years, and the life expectancy of men was 50 years. Today, life expectancy is 86 years for women and 77 years for men. Infant mortality in those days was 31 out of 1,000 live births; today it's 3. Only 42 percent of people of high school age went to school back then; today it is 100 percent.

But, looking beyond the statistics, Japan has developed not only in terms of its economic welfare, but also as a major contributor to the world in which we live. Of course, it has become richer by several fold; its people have grown richer at the rate of 4.5 percent a year. The United States has a gross national product of $7.5 trillion. In 1996 values, Japan's GNP was $5.2 trillion, far ahead of Germany's $2.3 trillion, France's $1.5 trillion, or the $1.1 trillion of the United Kingdom or Italy. So tonight, as we bring the United States and Japan together with $12 trillion of combined GNP, we're dealing with the principal engines of growth on our planet. And, of course, the engine of growth in Asia continues to be Japan.

And so it is that, lately, we've been looking not at assisting Japan, but at being assisted *by* Japan in resolving the issues of the Asian crisis. And I've become aware of just how involved Japan is in what is now going on in Asia. You know that nearly 20 percent of Japan's exports go to the other Asian countries of which we're speaking. And over 20 percent of those Asian countries' exports go to Japan. You also know that in the crisis, as we looked at bank exposures, we saw that Japanese banks in the five so-called crisis countries in Asia held 33 percent of all their outstanding debt. And when you look at the extended Asian experience, in China and the other countries that are not among those five, we find that Japan is lending on the order of $260 billion— more than the entire capital of the Japanese banking system.

Japan and the crisis countries of Asia are therefore considerably interdependent, both in their trade and in their broader economic activity. And Japan has a history of taking a major role in the countries in which the World Bank operates. Japan recognized very early that the developing world was the world it was going to grow in. Today those 4.7 billion people in the developing world have only 18 percent of the world's GDP, but their GDP is growing at twice the rate of that of the developed world. In another 25 years it will be 30 percent of the world's GDP. And Japan has taken a prominent and active role in that growth. Many of the companies and banks represented in this room are among those that have made the decision and got out there and helped develop the other Asian countries, as well as many others in the portfolio of the World Bank's work.

But then we hit a problem. We hit a problem that is not one of basic government mismanagement or mistakes in basic government policies. Because one has to say that what Japan and Asia did before the crisis was a recipe for considerable success. Education, communications, significant investment, high saving rates, an outward orientation—all the things that, together with fiscal balance, led us to think that these countries' growth would continue unabated. And when we started to see some signs two years ago that things might not be as good as we thought, the essential optimism that we all had for Asia stopped us, and stopped many of the countries themselves, from taking actions that they might have taken to stem the crisis. Two years ago there was a euphoria about Asia, and it was difficult to tell the Thais or the Indonesians or the Koreans that something was wrong. Maybe [Managing Director of Goldman, Sachs] Jerry Corrigan, whom I see sitting down the table here, succeeded in doing it, but we did not.

It is clear that we've hit a wall with these countries—not so much in terms of their basic fiscal policies, but because of certain activities in the private sector, and a lack of recognition on the part of the government of some of the signs that might have led them to adopt more flexible exchange rate policies, and more scrutiny of how their banks were lending. And so we ran into a problem, starting in July of last year with the recognition of Thailand's problems, and then creeping into Korea and Indonesia—the rest of the story is well known to you, and it's a story in which I'm now very much involved. I'm involved not just because this is a story that affects developing countries, but because, as with Japan, so as with the rest of the world, what happens in those countries is critically important to economic stability, and indeed peace, on our planet.

We're working to try and right some of the things that have gone wrong in these countries. We're doing many of the conventional things. We're putting together financial packages, and in that, of course, Japan has been a leader. It is one of those countries that not only has committed itself to help but has in fact paid up, with billions to Thailand, Indonesia, and Korea, and $15 billion in export credits. These are important contributions to a package that totals, for those three countries, somewhere over $100 billion, with a major amount coming from trust funds and the Asian Development Bank.

This shows that Japan is a true partner. It is trying to help with financial support. It is also trying to help us in the two things that we at the Bank have to do to try and right these countries, one at the structural level and the other at the human level. At the structural level what is imperative in these countries—and action is now being taken on this—is a sound financial structure, a sound judicial system, transparency, and openness in accounting. It had become clear that those characteristics of the management of the economy were lacking. So each of the countries has said, "We want better

bankruptcy laws. We want more effective judicial systems. We want protection of property rights. We want banking systems that work. We want supervisory mechanisms that work. We want financial control mechanisms,
both for banking and for the corporate sector. We want to encourage saving. We want to do all the things that are necessary to be part of a world
where capital flows rapidly and can move from country to country and ex-
acerbate instability."

And so these countries, which typically have not done those things, which
have been secretive, which have allowed important companies not to publish
accounts and banks not to open their books, and which have had supervisory
bodies that have not supervised, are now saying, "Let's fix these things." And
they are doing it not because that is what the Fund has prescribed, but because
they recognize that that is what they need to do to be part of the global system. And that's one of the things that we are helping with, drawing on financial help from Japan.

We're also looking at the other aspect of what is necessary in these countries. It is one that does not get headlines, but one that will determine—
manifestly so in the case of Indonesia—the region's peace and stability. And
that is the issue of people, the issue of poverty. It's the issue of employment,
which, again, doesn't make the headlines, but which has been of supreme importance in that country. We've seen the prospect of the population living on
less than one dollar a day growing by 10 percent by the end of the year, which
would put 20 million more people into poverty. Meanwhile the number of
unemployed could rise to 8 million.

And, in varying ways, so it goes with Korea and Thailand, in terms of both
their social statistics and their poverty statistics. We at the World Bank have
been looking at what happens in a system that does not have a social under-
pinning, that has been reliant on family support for people that are out of a job,
a system where for generations people earning money have sent it back to the
family in anticipation of when they might have a problem. They go back to
the womb of the family, because that *is* the social support system. In Thailand
we see workers going back to their rural villages and finding, because of the
combination of El Niño and the economic downturn, that the expected economic support is not there, and they get frustrated and they get angry. There
is an increase in crime, kids are taken out of school to protect their homes,
there's pressure on the homes, kids are put into prostitution, and there is a
general unraveling of society.

In varying degrees throughout the whole region, this pressure on society,
this issue of social support, has become a fundamental issue equivalent to the
financial issue, because whenever you make financial decisions without think-

ing of the human and social consequences, you do so at your peril. That was certainly clear in Indonesia, as it is clear in Russia, as it is clear in many parts of the world. And it is Japan that has been the leader up to now in overseas development assistance to help fund these sorts of activities—totaling over $9 billion—and focusing so much of its efforts on the social and the human. That is a great tribute to Japan.

But now Japan itself is in recession. And this recession is occurring against the background of all these interdependencies—interdependencies in terms of trade, of finance, of working on overseas assistance, in terms of being morally correct and paying its dues and helping countries that are developing. All of a sudden Japan is not growing, and the banking system is under attack. Industry has lost some of its confidence, and 4.1 percent of the labor force is unemployed. The yen is weakening, and one sees, as I have, that reduction in confidence that was so prevalent two years ago.

Japan has to respond, not just for Japan's sake, but because the world has come to count on Japan. Remember that Japan has a $5.2 trillion economy, and compare that figure with the size of the other Asian economies that have long depended on Japan. Korea's economy, which was the 11th largest in the world, is $480 billion, which is less than 10 percent the size of Japan's. Indonesia, with its 200 million people, has a $213 billion economy, less than 5 percent the size of Japan's. Thailand's economy is $177 billion, Malaysia's is $90 billion, Singapore's is $93 billion, and the Philippines' is $82 billion. Compare those numbers with Japan's $5.2 trillion, and ask yourself how important any change in Japan's economy is to those countries. We are used to thinking of such influences as coming from the United States, and too rarely do we look at the significance and importance of Japan. But here Japan is the locomotive. Japan is the country that has acted correctly, that has brought about investment, that has invested in itself, that has financed investment elsewhere, that is part of trade, that is interdependent with Asia—and now it is not doing well. Small wonder that we look to Japan with concern, not as outsiders, keen to beat up on Japanese politicians or businessmen, but because the Japanese are our partners and we're deeply concerned.

We're deeply concerned because we are aware of the steps that they've taken: 30 trillion yen last December as a financial package, with 17 trillion of it going into deposit insurance and 13 trillion to strengthen the banks, although only 2 trillion has been spent. Another package of 16 trillion yen is coming in, of which 4 trillion is in the form of tax waivers, and another 6 trillion for public works. Still, the confidence is not there, and the funds that are being released are not being spent but instead are being saved because people are worried.

As I look around the room and see the representatives of so many distinguished Japanese businesses and banks, it is clear to me that Japanese businessmen and bankers are worried. They're worried because they see the need for firm action on the part of the government and the private sector together, to make the kind of move that has characterized Japan in the past: the bold moves, the powerful moves, the strategic moves, which are necessary not just for Japan, but indeed for peace and stability in the region and for stability in the world.

Tonight's dinner is a moment to reflect on this situation. It is not a moment for enormous joy, but it is a moment to recognize that the Japanese people, and the achievements of the Japanese, are such that you must say, "Japan has everything that is needed to get it right." It has the people, it has the education, it has the resources, and all it needs to do is to act in a definitive way.

That is my hope and my expectation, because it is crucial that Japan restore the sense of confidence needed to make its economy vibrant and growing again. And I can say, in my capacity as president of the World Bank, that what Japan does will make a bigger difference than anything I can think of to the future of the 4.7 billion people for whom we work. I look with confidence toward Japan's decision-makers and hope and pray with you that, when next year's dinner comes around, what I've talked about tonight will be history.

Thank you so much.

Address to the Board of Governors at the Annual Meetings of the World Bank
and the International Monetary Fund

WASHINGTON, D.C. | OCTOBER 6, 1998

*One year after the Hong Kong SAR annual meetings, Wolfensohn
speaks about the human toll of the Asian crisis. He urges the Bank's
shareholding countries to look beyond the headlines of the financial crisis
and see the "human pain" around the world. He talks about the need
to discuss financial sector reform, but he also calls for a debate on the
foundations of development and stresses the need for a "new development
framework."*

Mr. Chairman, Governors, Ladies and Gentlemen:

This is the fourth time I stand before you as president of the World Bank Group.
At the outset I would like to express my appreciation to our chairman, Wolfgang
Ruttenstorfer,* and to my colleague and friend, Michel Camdessus,[†] for the
partnership that we have enjoyed during the past year. I would also like to pay
tribute to the work that the Fund has done in a year characterized by great turmoil, and to acknowledge the contribution that Michel and his colleagues have
made in dealing with very difficult problems at a very difficult time.

We all recognize that we meet under the shadow of a global crisis. We
come here in a united endeavor to protect the common welfare, to listen to
ideas from all quarters, and to reach out to friends and critics alike to find new
solutions. We must embrace the bold.

Mr. Chairman, I stand before you today under very different circumstances
from last year. Twelve months ago we were reporting growth in global output of 5.6 percent, the highest annual rate in 20 years. Twelve months ago
East Asia was stumbling, but no one was predicting the degree of the fall.
Twelve months ago South Asia, home to 35 percent of the world's poor, was
still nuclear test-free and seemed set to enjoy years of 6 percent growth and
perhaps more. Twelve months ago developing countries as a whole were on
a path toward strong growth over the next decade. Twelve months ago there
was optimism about Russia with its strong reformist team.

And then came a year of turmoil and travail. In East Asia estimates suggest
that more than 20 million people fell back into poverty last year, and that
growth is likely to be halting and hesitant at best for several years to come.
Russia, beset by economic and political crisis, finds itself caught between two

* Executive director from Austria at the World Bank and the IMF.
† Managing director of the IMF.

worlds and two systems, comfortable with neither. Japan, the world's second-largest economy and so crucial to East Asia's recovery, has a government committed to economic reform yet is still in recession, with a profound impact not just in Asia but around the world. It was also a year that saw nuclear tests in India and Pakistan, war threatened in Eritrea and Ethiopia, and terrorist bombs in Kenya and Tanzania.

All this was compounded by the impact of natural disaster: in Latin America, the worst El Niño in history, with its full devastating force falling most heavily on the poor; in Bangladesh, floods that kept two-thirds of the nation under water for more than two months, setting back many of the recent social and economic gains; in China, flooding of the Yangtze Basin, with an estimated 3,500 deaths, 5 million homes destroyed, and 200 million lives dislocated.

Mr. Chairman, I have spoken in the past about images of hope: of people from the slums of Brazil to the rural villages of Uganda, from the Loess Plateau in China to the hundreds of thousands of women who are finding their dignity through microcredit—people empowered to take charge of their destinies. But today I have other memories: dark, searing images of desperation, hopelessness, and decline, of people who once had hope but have it no more. I remember the mother in Mindanao, pulling her child out of school, haunted by the fear that he will never return there. I remember the family in Korea, with a mid-size scrap metal business, made destitute through lack of credit. I remember the father in Jakarta, paying a moneylender three times in interest what he himself would earn that day, falling deeper and deeper into debt, not knowing how he will ever work himself free. I remember the child in Bangkok, now condemned to work the streets, a child no longer.

Today, while we here talk of financial crisis, 17 million Indonesians have fallen back into poverty, and across the East Asian region a million children will now not return to school. Today, while we talk of financial crisis, an estimated 40 percent of the Russian population lives in poverty. Today, while we talk of financial crisis, across the world 1.3 billion people live on less than a dollar a day, 3 billion live on less than two dollars a day, 1.3 billion have no access to clean water, 3 billion have no access to sanitation, and 2 billion have no access to electric power. We talk of financial crisis while in Jakarta, in Moscow, in Sub-Saharan Africa, in the slums of India, and in the barrios of Latin America, the human pain of poverty is all around us.

The Financial Crisis

Mr. Chairman, we must address this human pain. We must go beyond financial stabilization. We must address the issues of long-term equitable growth, on which prosperity and human progress depend. We must focus on the institutional and structural changes needed for recovery and sustainable development. We must focus on the social issues. We must do all this, because if we do not have the capacity to deal with social emergencies, if we do not have longer-term plans for solid institutions, if we do not have greater equity and social justice, there will be no political stability. And without political stability, no amount of money put together in financial rescue packages will bring about financial stability.

And so, in response to the current crisis, we at the Bank have focused on putting in place the short- and the long-term measures for sustained recovery. We are working with governments on financial, judicial, and regulatory reform, on bankruptcy laws, anticorruption programs, and corporate governance—all so essential to the restoration of private sector confidence. Before the crisis hit, we had already worked on financial sector reform in 68 countries. At the request of our shareholders, we have now expanded that capacity by one-third, and we are reinforcing our leadership in corporate governance.

On the social front, we have been restructuring our existing portfolios to ensure a sharp focus on priority programs that can reach poor communities quickly. We are working to keep children in school, for example in Indonesia, where we support a program to provide scholarships for 2.5 million children. We are helping create jobs, for example in Thailand, through a new social fund. We are putting in place frameworks for social protection, for example in Korea, through a series of structural adjustment loans. Throughout the region we are trying to maintain food supplies, trying to make sure vital medicines reach the sick, trying to ensure that health and education programs continue, trying to ensure that the environment does not suffer, trying to put people first.

Mr. Chairman, we have learned that while appropriate macroeconomic plans, with effective fiscal and monetary policies, are essential in every respect, such plans alone are not sufficient. We have learned that when we ask governments to take the painful steps to put their economies in order, we can create enormous tension. It is people, not governments, that feel the pain. When we redress budget imbalances, we must recognize that programs to keep children in school may be lost, that programs to ensure health care for the poorest may be lost, that small and medium-size enterprises, which provide income to their owners and employment to many, may be starved of credit and may fail.

We have learned, Mr. Chairman, that there is a need for balance. We must consider the financial, the institutional, and the social together. We must learn to have a debate in which mathematics does not dominate humanity, where the need for often-drastic change can be balanced with protecting the interests of the poor. Only then will we arrive at solutions that are sustainable. Only then will we bring the international financial community *and* local citizens along with us.

Mr. Chairman, there has been much talk leading up to and within these Meetings of a new global financial architecture. That talk reflects a growing sentiment that something is wrong with a system in which even countries that have pursued strong economic policies over a period of years are battered by international financial markets, and where workers in those countries will be thrown out of work, their children's education interrupted, their hopes and dreams destroyed.

I believe that, in the more than half a century since the creation of the new economic architecture in the aftermath of World War II, our international economic institutions have served us well. No, they have not solved all our problems. But we are far better off with them than we would have been without them. Although poverty has not been eradicated, incomes have been raised. The Green Revolution has brought food to millions who might otherwise have starved. Some ancient scourges, such as river blindness, have been almost eradicated, and we have made progress against many others. We have gone for more than a half-century without a major global crisis. The system has withstood large shocks, such as the huge increase in oil prices of the 1970s. And in that half-century those postwar institutions have evolved with the global economy.

But we cannot pretend that all is well. We cannot close our eyes to the fact that the crisis has exposed weaknesses and vulnerabilities that we must now address. We must be bold, but we must also be realistic. We will not devise a new architecture in two days or even two weeks. But neither can we afford to lose a decade, as Latin America did in the aftermath of its crisis in the early 1980s. Too much is at stake; too many people's lives hang in the balance.

What we can do here and now is this: We can identify what needs to be done. We can recognize the problems. We can clarify our objectives. We can work to reach consensus. The problems are too big and their consequences too important to be guided by the pat answers of the past, or the fads or ideologies of the day. We must make a collective commitment to join together to build something better. Let me suggest a three-pillared approach:

- The first pillar must be *prevention*. We must understand the causes of crises and work to create economic structures that make them less frequent and less severe.
- The second pillar must be *response*. No matter how successful we are in the first task, there will be crises. We need to devise more effective ways of re-

sponding to the crises, ways that entail a better sharing of the burden, ways that do not inflict such pain on workers, small businesses, and other innocent victims.

- The third pillar must be *safety nets*. No matter how successful we are in devising fair and efficient responses—and it is clear that we have a long way to go—there will be innocent victims. Unemployment rates will rise. We must do a much better job of ensuring that these innocent victims are protected.

Mr. Chairman, at the request of finance ministers we have been working to increase collaboration between the Bank and the Fund. Ministers asked us to review our division of labor, and we have done that in a spirit of true partnership. Our roles are clearly different. The Fund's mandate covers surveillance, exchange rate matters, the balance of payments, and growth-oriented stabilization policies and their related instruments. The Bank has a mandate for the composition and appropriateness of development programs and priorities, including structural and sectoral policies, and therefore, by building a sound basis for development, a responsibility for crisis prevention.

At this moment of crisis, with private sector funds withdrawing from emerging markets, IMF resources strained, and little direct support from the more wealthy nations, we recognize the obligation to be a countercyclical lender, committed to help where help is needed, not just in the crisis countries but also for our many other clients who are excellent performers but are caught short in the current squeeze for funds in the global markets. Yes, we must help them so that *they* do not become crisis countries.

Yes, we must come in quickly in the crisis countries to make sure that social, institutional, and policy reforms can take immediate root and are integral parts of the overall program. In that way the responses to the crisis will enhance long-term recovery. Yes, we must come in quickly with emergency social assistance. But ours is a different role from that of the Fund. We can be an emergency lender, but we cannot be a liquidity lender. Given our financial structure and the need to stay within our prudent lending limits, there are trade-offs that we cannot ignore.

If we are to lend more up front, there will be less to lend for our long-term development mission: less for the International Development Association, less for the Heavily Indebted Poor Countries Initiative, and less for the poor in the crisis countries. New demands made on us will require a very careful assessment of possible needs for new resources. Today, backed by our existing capital and resources and substantial uncalled capital, we are in a very strong position, but as we move forward we must be careful not to find ourselves constrained by lack of capital.

We must also remember that we cannot be distracted from the urgent need to ensure that we have full funding for the poorest countries, through the 12th IDA replenishment and the HIPC Initiative. That must be a priority in the weeks and months ahead.

The New Approach

Mr. Chairman, when we look at the pace and the depth of global change over the last 12 months, we, like all of you in this room, ask ourselves what lessons we should learn from these experiences. We, like all of you, are asking what we can do differently in the future to try and avoid these shifts in the economic and sociopolitical landscape.

What have we observed? We see that, in today's global economy, countries can invest in education and health, can put the macroeconomic fundamentals in place, can build modern communications and infrastructure, can do all these things. But if they do not have an effective financial system, if they do not have adequate regulatory supervision or adequate bankruptcy laws, if they do not have effective competition and regulatory laws, if they do not have transparency and accounting standards, their development is endangered and will not last.

We see that countries today can move toward a market economy, can privatize, can break up state monopolies, can reduce state subsidies. But if they do not fight corruption and put in place good governance, if they do not introduce social safety nets, if they do not build the social and political consensus for reform, if they do not bring their people with them, their development is endangered and will not last.

We see that countries today can attract private capital, can build a banking and financial system, can deliver growth, can invest in people, or at least some of them. But if they marginalize the poor, if they marginalize women and indigenous minorities, if they do not have a policy of inclusion, their development is endangered and will not last.

We see, Mr. Chairman, that in a global economy it is the *totality* of change in a country that matters. Development is not just about adjustment. Development is not just about sound budgets and fiscal management. Development is not just about education and health. Development is not just about technocratic fixes. Development *is* about getting the macroeconomics right, yes, but it is also about building the roads, empowering the people, writing the laws, recognizing the women, eliminating the corruption, educating the girls, building the banking systems, protecting the environment, and inoculating the children. Development is about putting *all* the component parts in place, together and in harmony.

The need for balanced development is true for East Asia and Russia. It is true for Africa. It is true for Latin America, for the Middle East, for the transition economies of Central and Eastern Europe and Eurasia. It is true, Mr. Chairman, for us all.

The notion that development involves a totality of effort—a balanced economic and social program—is not revolutionary, but the fact remains that it is not the approach that we in the international community have been taking. Although we have had some extraordinary success over these many years with individual programs and projects, too often we have not related them to the whole. Too often we have been too narrow in our conception of the economic transformations that are required. While focusing on the macroeconomic numbers or on major reforms like privatization, we have ignored the basic institutional infrastructure, without which a market economy simply cannot function. Rather than incentives for wealth creation, there can be misplaced incentives for asset stripping.

Too often we have focused too much on the economics, without a sufficient understanding of the social, the political, the environmental, and the cultural aspects of development. We have not thought adequately about the overall structure required in a country to allow it to develop, in an integrated fashion, into the type of economy that its people and its leadership have chosen. We have not thought sufficiently about the vulnerabilities, those parts of an economy whose collapse can bring all the building blocks tumbling down; or about sustainability, what it takes to make social and economic transformation last. Unless we do, we may build a new international financial architecture. But it will be a house built on sand.

Mr. Chairman, let me suggest a concept that may help us address some of these concerns. The IMF has an overall framework within which it reviews annually with its client countries the macroeconomic performance of each country. In the wake of the current crisis, we will need a *second* framework, one that deals with the progress in the structural reforms necessary for long-term growth, that includes the human and social accounting, that deals with the environment, that deals with the status of women, rural development, indigenous peoples, progress in infrastructure, and so on.

And so in our discussions at the Bank, we have developed and are experimenting with a new approach, not one that is imposed by us on our clients, but one that they develop with our help. It is an approach that would move us "beyond projects," to think instead much more rigorously about what is required to achieve sustainable development in its broadest sense.

Mr. Chairman, we need a *new development framework.*

What might countries look for in such a framework? First, the framework would outline the essentials of good governance: transparency, voice, the free flow of information, a commitment to fight corruption, and a well-trained, properly remunerated civil service.

Second, it would specify the regulatory and institutional fundamentals essential to a workable market economy. These include a legal and tax system that guards against caprice, secures property rights, and ensures that contracts are enforced, that there is effective competition, and that there are orderly and efficient processes for resolving judicial disputes and bankruptcies. They include a financial system that is modern, transparent, and supervised adequately, free of favor, with internationally recognized accountancy and auditing standards for the private sector.

Third, our framework would call for policies that foster inclusion. That means education for all, especially women and girls; health care; social protection for the unemployed, the elderly, and people with disabilities; early childhood development; mother and child clinics that will teach health care and nurture.

Fourth, our framework would describe the public services and infrastructure necessary for communications and transport. These include not just things like rural and trunk roads, but also policies for livable cities and growing urban areas, so that problems can be addressed with urgency, not 25 years from now when they have become overwhelming. And alongside such an urban strategy, there should be a program for rural development that provides not only agricultural services but also capacity for marketing and for financing and for the transfer of knowledge and experience.

Fifth, our framework would set forth objectives to ensure the environmental and human sustainability so essential to the long-term success of development and the future of our shared planet. Water, energy, food security—these and other issues must also be dealt with at the global level. And we must ensure that the culture of each country is nurtured and enriched, so that development is firmly based and historically grounded.

Finally, all of these five components would, of course, be developed within a supportive and effective macroeconomic plan and open trade relations.

This may not be a comprehensive list, and the list will of course vary from country to country, depending on the views of government, parliamentary assemblies, and civil society. But, I would submit, it gets at the essentials.

Mr. Chairman, we must learn from the past. How a framework is developed and applied is as important as the contents of that framework. Ownership matters. Countries and their governments must be in the driver's seat, and the people must be consulted and involved. Participation matters, not only as a means of improving development effectiveness, as we know from our recent studies, but also as the key to long-term sustainability and to leverage. We must never stop reminding ourselves that it is up to each government and its people to decide what their priorities should be. We must never stop reminding ourselves that we cannot and should not impose development by fiat from above or from abroad.

Mr. Chairman, in our discussions at the Bank, we ask each other a series of simple questions. What if it were possible for governments to join together with civil society, with the private sector, to decide on long-term national priorities? What if it were possible for donors to then come in and coordinate their support, with countries in the driver's seat, with local ownership and local participation? What if it were possible for these strategies to look 5, 10, 20 years ahead, so that development could really take root and grow and could be monitored on an ongoing basis? Too ambitious, some will say, too utopian. But what if I told you it is already happening?

- In El Salvador today, a national peace commission, born of civil war, is drawing up, together with civil society, the private sector, and the government, a list of national priorities. They are doing this together so that those priorities can extend beyond the life of one government and become part of a national consensus for the future. And the same thing is happening in Guatemala and is being considered elsewhere in Latin America.
- In Accra, Ghana, last year, the government held a National Economic Forum involving policymakers, civic leaders, and large numbers of stakeholders. Out of this forum came proposals for concrete action, targets for reducing inflation, sectoral policies on agriculture and human development, and goals for macroeconomic policy.
- In India's Andhra Pradesh, a state of 70 million people, the chief minister has a program for 2020. It is a program for literacy, for improved access to health care, for livelihoods, for empowering women, for developing backward areas, for creating safety nets. It is a program with clearly monitorable targets that can be regularly checked.

El Salvador, Guatemala, Ghana, India: to these I could add others—Brazil, Mozambique—where elements of this approach have been adopted. These are not countries that have reverted to central planning. They are countries that, together with their stakeholders, are designing road maps for the future—their future—in much the same way that successful businesses do.

Mr. Chairman, hubris should not allow us to think that we at the Bank or in the donor community can be the cartographers of countries' development. But we can be important catalysts.

What I am proposing is that over the next couple of years we bring a new perspective, working with interested governments to draw up holistic frameworks that sharpen strategic vision. We would like to find two countries in each region of the developing world that we could work with to test this idea. And we will report to you all at the end of that time.

We must work with our partners in the donor community to see how, together with the participant countries, we can develop coordinated strategies, joint missions, and joint objectives, so that we can put an end to the duplication that wastes precious resources and leaves tempers and clients frayed.

Within our institution we must build on the work we have already begun, to move from a project-by-project approach to an approach that looks at the totality of effort necessary for country development, that takes the long view, that asks of every project, How does this fit into the bigger picture? How can this be scaled up to cover the whole country? How can this be rolled out over time—5, 10, 20 years—so that not only do the countries themselves fully own and participate in it, but that it becomes sustainable and part of the strategy of that society's overall development?

In some cases we will go beyond national strategies to regional strategies, to better reap the benefits of economies of scale. We must think also of global strategies to create global public goods—not only a cleaner, healthier physical environment, but also a sound international economic environment, free of the instability that is of such concern today; and the knowledge that we are increasingly recognizing as a key to successful development.

Mr. Chairman, what we are talking about is a new approach to development partnership. It is a partnership led by the governments and parliaments of the developing countries themselves, influenced by their civil society, and joined by the domestic and international private sectors and by bilateral and multilateral donors. It is a partnership that can look at measurable goals with much better marked roadmaps for achievement. Critically, it is a partnership in which we in the donor community must learn to cooperate with each other and be better team players, capable of letting go of the ball.

Let me assure you, Mr. Chairman, that we in the Bank Group are committed to such a partnership, to putting issues of turf behind us. What matters is not who leads or who follows, who has their name on a project or who remains anonymous. What matters is that we join together to get the job done.

Mr. Chairman, in normal years at this stage in my speech, I would give you a progress report on the Bank's achievements. But this is not a normal year. You will be happy to hear that I will not mention our internal renewal, nor will I tell you of our achievements or the challenges that still lie ahead. All these issues I discuss regularly with our Executive Directors, and I am extremely grateful for their advice, guidance, and hard work. I am also very encouraged by the support that I have received from ministers for our renewal program and the improvements we are making in development effectiveness, and we will of course push ahead with that program. But it seems inappropriate to talk of housekeeping when the village is burning.

Let me instead just say two things. First, I want to take this occasion to thank the World Bank Group staff for the extraordinary work that they have done this year. I am enormously proud of them. There is no better team of dedicated and motivated colleagues in the world today.

Second, I want to thank Jannik Lindbaek, executive vice president of the IFC [International Finance Corporation], and Akira Iida, executive vice president of MIGA [the Multilateral Investment Guarantee Agency], for their work over the last five years. I am delighted also to welcome Peter Woicke, who shortly takes up the leadership of the IFC, and Motomichi Ikawa, who is now leading MIGA.

The Other Crisis

Mr. Chairman, this year the headlines have been full of the financial crises. This year we are asking ourselves how we can prevent the financial crises of the future. This year we are focusing on financial architecture, corporate restructuring, and building strong safety nets, as part of both crisis prevention and crisis resolution. This year we are waking up to the fact that we do not have all the answers.

Let us not stop at financial analysis. Let us not stop at financial architecture. Let us not stop at financial sector reforms. Now is our chance to launch a global debate on the architecture, yes, but also a debate on the foundations of development. Now is our chance to show that we can take a broader and more balanced view. Now is our chance to recognize that there is a silent crisis looming on the horizon. It is a crisis of world population, which will add 3 billion more people to the planet over the next 25 years. It is a crisis of global water supply, which will see 2 billion people suffering from chronic water shortages by 2025. It is a crisis of urbanization, in which urban populations will treble over the next 30 years, and in which by 2020 two-thirds of Africa's population will live in cities—cities that today have no economic growth. Finally, it is a crisis of food security, which will require a doubling of food production over the next 30 years.

It is a human crisis, Mr. Chairman, and one from which the developed world will not be able to insulate itself. And it will not be resolved unless we address the fundamental issue of the essential interdependence of the developed and the developing worlds. It will not be met unless we begin to take a holistic approach both to development and to our own response to crisis, looking at the financial, the social, the political, the institutional, the cultural, and the environmental aspects of society all together.

The poor cannot wait on our deliberations. The poor cannot wait while we debate new architecture. The poor cannot wait until we wake up—too late—to the fact that the human crisis affects us all. The child on the streets of Bangkok needs to go back to school. The mother in the slums of Calcutta needs to survive childbirth. The father in the village in Mali needs to be able to see beyond today.

As markets tumble and the poverty numbers soar, all of us in this room have a shared responsibility and a shared interest in promoting prosperity in developing and emerging markets. As markets tumble and the poverty numbers soar, all of us in this room have a shared responsibility to put in place policies that can help these countries work their way out of crisis.

In the end, Mr. Chairman, we succeed or we suffer together. We owe it to our children to recognize now that their world is one world, linked by communications and trade, linked by markets, linked by finance, linked by environment and shared resources, linked by common aspirations. If we act now with realism and with foresight, if we show courage, if we think globally and allocate our resources accordingly, we can give our children a more peaceful and equitable world, where poverty and suffering will be reduced and where children everywhere will have a sense of hope.

This is not just a dream. This is our responsibility.

Message from the president and chairman from the 1998 World Bank *Annual Report*

OCTOBER 1998

This short message focuses on the internal changes that are improving the Bank's effectiveness.

Last year's *Annual Report* described a year of change and renewal. This year many of those changes have begun to bear fruit. Disbursements and quality are up; projects at risk are down; and our clients are reporting improvements across the institution—from more client responsiveness to more humility.

This year has seen further changes: the implementation of the Cost Effectiveness Review; further decentralization of decision-making powers to the field; a new budgeting and planning process for the first time linked to strategic objectives; and the introduction of a new human resources policy designed to end the traditional divisions between headquarters and local staff in the field, and between regular and nonregular staff. Much remains to be done. But the progress of the last twelve months provides us with a solid foundation on which to build. None of this would have been possible without the wholehearted support and guidance of our Executive Board.

For many of our clients the year has also brought profound change. We do not yet know what the long-term effects of the East Asian crisis will be, but the impact on the poor has already been savage. For all of us at the World Bank Group, the crisis has highlighted the fact that financial and social policy must go hand in hand. With the support of our shareholders we have set up the new Special Financial Operations Unit to look at financial and social issues in crisis countries on an urgent basis. We are also expanding our work on long-range financial sector reform and focusing much more attention on social assessments.

With its threat of returning millions to poverty, the crisis has also underlined the fact that, as I put it in my speech at the Annual Meetings in September 1997, the challenge of inclusion is the key development challenge of our time. Across the globe, too many people are missing out on the fruits of economic success. Our goal must be to reduce these disparities across and within countries; to bring more and more people into the economic mainstream; to promote equitable access to the benefits of development, regardless of nationality, race, or gender.

To do this we must boost our work with our partners in government and in the other donor agencies, civil society, and the private sector. We must reach out much more proactively to disadvantaged groups—especially women and indigenous peoples—and we must take a more holistic view of development itself. It is my strong belief that we will not make development meaningful, sustainable, and inclusive until we put people at the center of the development process. This means a much greater focus on country ownership and participation, a better appreciation of local conditions, and more attention to the role of culture.

You will find these themes reflected in the pages of this *Annual Report*. Taken together, they show an institution that is repositioning itself to meet the demands of a new millennium—an institution committed to results, partnerships, and inclusive development. The 4.8 billion people who are our ultimate clients deserve nothing less.

WEST BANK AND GAZA: WITHOUT ECONOMIC HOPE THERE CANNOT BE PEACE

Remarks for the Prime Minister's Jubilee Business Summit

JERUSALEM | OCTOBER 13–15, 1998

In this speech delivered by videoconference, Wolfensohn speaks on an issue that is close to his heart: Middle East peace and development. He describes the World Bank's work in the West Bank and Gaza and says that "if there is to be peace, there must be economic progress."

Mr. Chairman, Ladies and Gentlemen:

It is a very great honor for me to be able to address this meeting, and I want to thank you, my dear friend, former Israeli Prime Minister Shimon Peres, for the invitation, and also thank the prime minister [Benjamin Netanyahu] and those organizing this event for the honor that you have given the World Bank in asking us to address this session.

I very much regret that I cannot be with you in person, but, as I am sure you understand, there are a number of things going on in our world today that require me to be back in Washington. And much though I would like to be with you, I fear that I have to remain here.

The issue of economic harmony in the Middle Eastern region is something that is very dear to my heart and very dear to the heart of many of my colleagues, and in every way that we can we have tried to demonstrate our belief that, if there is to be peace, there must be economic progress. Very simply, in our work in Gaza and the West Bank, we have sought to take a lead in helping the people of that region, because we know, as I am sure all of you know, that without economic hope, there cannot be any peace.

But it is not just for defensive reasons that we are doing it. We believe very much that, in terms of opportunities for the future, regional cooperation is essential to expand markets, to build links, and to allow the people of the region to settle into a period of optimism and growth that can be supported by all areas of society.

We have taken a number of steps, as you well know, Mr. Chairman, to try and work with regional interests to bring about economic development. I recall very well last May the meeting that was held in Bethlehem with you and with [Palestinian] President [Yasser] Arafat, under the auspices of the Peres Institute and with the support of the Israeli government to establish the Peace Technology Fund, a fund of $100 million with the objective of building a base that could be used to develop both human and real potential in Gaza and the West Bank for technology enterprises. And I am very happy that, since that time, we have been successful in getting very substantial funding, and that fund is already in operation. This is a remarkable example of how, outside the peace process itself, individuals both from Israel and from Gaza and the West

Bank have come together in a common endeavor to develop economic enterprise, which itself will give hope to the people of the region.

We have also been very active and continue to be active in trying to develop other enterprises in the region. The Gaza Industrial Estates Project, which has been supported from Europe, as well as from local and international funds, is a project that quite properly is designed to expand Gaza and Israel to allow access from each side, to allow for industrial enterprises to grow and to flourish with the ability to trade on both sides of its fences.

This is a remarkable enterprise. It has not been easy. It has been fraught with issues of politics and security, but it is moving forward, and, having seen it recently, I can say that it is one of the most modern enterprises of that type that I have seen anywhere in the world, a tribute to its sponsors and to those who are supporting it.

But beyond that, we have also in our enterprise MIGA, our Multilateral Investment Guarantee Agency, a subsidiary of the World Bank, put together an insurance fund of over $20 million to try and take some of the risk of investing in Gaza and West Bank off the backs of the investors, and that remains a facilitating mechanism to allow for investment in those areas.

And, beyond that, we have established an investment fund for the communities, which allows us to get down into the villages and the towns where citizens are able to choose their projects, and where small amounts of money can be used to generate vital enterprises.

But let me stand back for a minute and make some observations about the region. We at the Bank are not politicians. We are not able to enter the peace process, and in any event it is probably beyond our competence, but what we are able to do is recognize the reality that, in the region in general, including most importantly Jordan and hopefully other countries in the region, there is the opportunity for an internal market, there is an opportunity for trade, there is an opportunity for profit, and, through that, an opportunity for employment, an opportunity for hope for the people of the region.

As a financial and development institution, it is our very strong belief that if we can together work toward a unified market, if we can together bring about the dream of the privatization of peace, we will be on the most solid ground that we can be for a better future for our children.

I assure you that we in the Bank are ready to play our full part. We look forward to learning from this conference. We look forward to meeting with you at this conference to determine ways in which we can be of assistance, and I can assure you that we will be unrelenting in our efforts to work with all of you to bring about a peaceful climate for economic development, a climate for hope for all the people of the regions.

I wish you great success in your deliberations and can assure you of our continued support.

Remarks at the World Bank–NGO Conference on Participatory Development

WASHINGTON, D.C. | NOVEMBER 19, 1998

This address is representative of the many discussions Wolfensohn had with civil society during his tenure, which marked a new, more open approach for the World Bank. His appeal for a constructive partnership comes through clearly in these brief remarks.

Thank you very much, and let me say that yesterday, when I landed on returning from a trip—literally around the world in eight days—the first thing I did was to find out what was going to happen at these meetings. I was told that I would be allowed in tomorrow afternoon, and I said, "Well, I would like to be allowed in earlier, because I feel I am part of these meetings." So I am taking the liberty of showing up early to welcome you on behalf of the Bank and to reaffirm, not only to our own NGO [nongovernmental organization] working group, but also to our co-sponsors and every one of you, just how important we think this gathering is.

In my speech at the Bank-Fund Annual Meetings last month, I laid out my vision of where I want to see the Bank going, and central to that is the need to bring all the players together if we are to achieve our objective of bringing about a better world and improving our development results. That is very clear to me, and it has been increasingly clear in the three and a half years I have been here. We want the Bank to be an institution that cherishes partnership, that believes that we are not going to get there unless we work together in a more orderly and coordinated manner, and that is prepared to listen, to learn, and to participate.

Many of you will say that those are words that do not immediately jump to mind when you think of the World Bank. Well, I guess they do not, and indeed they do not immediately jump to mind to everybody *in* the World Bank. So what we have to do as a result of these meetings is focus on the issue of participation and partnership, and confront those areas where we have made progress and those where we have not made progress. And that means looking at issues where we may be exaggerating our efforts, where we are saying things are happening and yet, when you get right down to the guts of it, they are not. It also means looking at issues we would rather not look at.

I hope that in this meeting we can start at the ground level and come to a real understanding of where we are at, so that tomorrow, when we hear the reports, you can bring up those areas where things need to be done. I hope that we can then identify those areas very clearly and unemotionally, and set some deadlines and a perspective for how we can achieve those objectives going forward.

I think that your very presence here says that the time for rhetoric about how bad we in the Bank have been, or how bad you on the other side have been, is almost over. I do not doubt that some of that will creep in, but let me say that, as far as I am concerned, I am starting from the knowledge that we have done some things right and some things wrong. And I am starting from the belief that our working together in partnership is a matter of necessity—not for ourselves, but, frankly, to achieve our objectives against poverty and the other targets that we are setting for ourselves. There is no way we can achieve those objectives acting independently, whether it be the Bank acting independently, or NGOs acting independently, or the private sector or the other multilateral institutions acting independently. We will simply not be able to help governments in developing countries, or have them lead us and help their people, unless we can do it better together.

I can give you 50 examples of where we are working at cross purposes, or where we are doing things in ways that could be done much better. That applies particularly to the Bank, because where we have not done adequate consultation and participation, it comes back and hits us later on. Just as a practical matter, we are nuts not to get the advance advice and assistance we need to try and do our job right. It is not a question of philosophy. It is a question of pragmatism. We really need to be closer together.

I can assure you that, so far as the Bank is concerned, I am determined to drive this thing forward. I think you will have seen some progress in the last couple of years, but it is nothing compared with what I hope we will be able to do in the next few years.

We have had our Operations Evaluation Department conduct an internal study of how our own staff think we are doing in our work with NGOs. They give us a few plaudits, but they also talk about how we are not effectively tapping the talents of the bilateral organizations, the foundations, and other partners, or the in-depth knowledge of NGOs. They say that we are not as flexible as we should be regarding procurement, contracting, and consulting procedures; that we overstate what we are doing with NGOs; that we do not accurately track what we are doing with NGOs; that we are doing good things on a number of projects, but that there are a lot of things we are doing badly.

So I start with this as my base. I do not think I am being deluded by our own advertising or by what I am being told by some colleagues. I am starting at a very clear-sighted level. I think that there has been a change in the institution. We now have more than 50 NGO representatives in the field. In some areas of the regions the regional consultative groups are working extremely well.

You will remember that we started with a global committee, and then, at the suggestion of the committee itself, we broke it down into regions. Some regional vice presidents are doing better than others, I think it is fair to say. So we are starting to develop some best practices, and where we are operating at best practice, it is working, I think, extremely well, and light-years from what it was.

So what I am looking for you to do during these 48 hours is essentially to review with us where we are and where we need to go. Give us your views on the level of participation. Give us your views on partnerships. And come back to us tomorrow with practical steps that you think we can take, within the framework of the limited capacity of human beings to change and of behavior patterns to change after long years behaving differently.

I have to get my colleagues in the Bank to recognize the importance of participation. We have, together, to get governments and other participants to recognize the importance of participation, because it is not always the case that we can develop best practice in one or more countries and then simply transfer it to others. This is not going to be an instant fix. This is something that we need to fix progressively, but within a tight time frame.

We are ready to do that, and I am ready to mobilize both our management and our staff to deal with it, and there will be some laggards. There will be people who will not do it. We have to find out who they are, but with the remarkable machinery of the NGO e-mail system, that is probably not going to be very difficult, given the way I myself get traced around the world. So my guess is that, if we work together, there will be plenty of ways of finding out where the success stories are, and where the success stories are not.

So I came today just to say welcome and to let you know how I very much look forward to our discussion tomorrow. I hope that it can be constructive in both directions, and that, as the Bank's behavior patterns change with respect to NGOs, maybe some NGO patterns of behavior and reactions about the Bank will also modulate a little bit, so that we can have a true and effective accomplishment together.

I wish you a very good day and a half, and I look forward to meeting you again tomorrow.

A PROPOSAL FOR A COMPREHENSIVE DEVELOPMENT FRAMEWORK

Excerpts from a memorandum to the Board of Executive Directors
and staff of the World Bank

WASHINGTON, D.C. | JANUARY 21, 1999

> *This excerpt from Wolfensohn's proposal to the Board outlines the Compre-
> hensive Development Framework (CDF) and his thinking on how it could
> move development forward on a more "comprehensive, transparent, and
> accountable" basis. The CDF is a holistic approach to development that links
> all its elements—social, structural, human, governance, environmental,
> economic, and financial—at the same time.*

To: The Board, Management, and Staff of the World Bank Group

During recent months I have been considering what I have learned in my first
three and a half years as President of the World Bank Group and am particularly grateful to all of you for the advice and guidance you have provided.
With your help, I have had a unique opportunity to visit 84 countries, Part I*
and borrowing countries alike. I have visited hundreds of projects, met with
government officials, private sector representatives, and members of civil society, from trade unions and employee organizations to religious groups, from
foundations to global and local NGOs [nongovernmental organizations] of
every type, size, and character. I have also participated in and benefited enormously from meetings with other multilateral organizations, starting with my
regular breakfast and meetings with my friend, [Managing Director of the International Monetary Fund] Michel Camdessus, and with the leaders and colleagues in the regional banks. I acknowledge my many exchanges with members
of the UN family and with bilateral agencies with whom we work extensively
throughout the year.

Obviously I believe that we and all of the above groups have contributed
significantly to the betterment of mankind and to the improvement in the lives
of many in poverty. I am convinced of the importance of consultation and
participation. But the fact remains that progress is too slow. With 3 billion
people still living under $2 a day, with growing inequity between rich and
poor, with forests being degraded at the rate of an acre a second, with 130 million children still not in school, with 1.5 billion people still not having access
to clean water, and 2 billion people not having access to sewerage, we cannot
be complacent. More than this, we must be concerned that 80 to 90 million
people are being added annually to our planet, mainly in the developing

---

* Part I countries are those (mostly developed) countries that contribute to the resources of the International
Development Association.

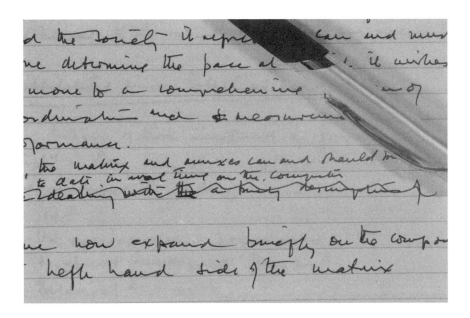

world. Two billion more souls must feed themselves by the year 2025, hampered by wars, with growing inequity, and with distortions of economies and politics as evidenced in crises from Indonesia to Russia and from Latin America to Africa. With the reduction in Overseas Development Assistance and current instability in the international financial markets, there is much to be concerned about.

Poverty Alleviation and Development Effectiveness

I have been considering the special role of our institution and its effectiveness in poverty alleviation and sustainable development. Together we have worked very hard over these last years, building on the extraordinary work done in the past, to redirect our institution to one that is results-based and not volume- or procedure-based. I am extremely grateful to all of you for the hard work that is already bearing fruit. We are fortunate because we have 54 years of experience and several institutional frameworks, including the IBRD, IDA, IFC, MIGA,[†] as well as related institutions such as the Consultative Group for International Agricultural Research—Executive Secretariat (CGIAR), the

---

† The International Bank for Reconstruction and Development, the International Development Association, the International Finance Corporation, and the Multilateral Investment Guarantee Agency, all Bank Group affiliates.

Global Environment Facility Secretariat (GEF), and the Consultative Group to Assist the Poorest (CGAP). We can be proud of our history and of the role we have played. We have extremely experienced people in most areas of development—or at least access to them. We are making use of partnerships with others who have more effective skills or broader reach of resources than we have. We are indeed learning to listen more and to be a better partner for the governments and the people we serve and for those with whom we work in the international and local communities.

In addition, I believe we have a better articulation of our role with the IMF. Broadly, our sister institution has the responsibility for macroeconomic stabilization for our client countries and for surveillance. We have the responsibility for the structural and social aspects of development. Obviously, these are not two isolated roles and we work together very closely on a day-to-day basis.

As I have said before, the two functions are like breathing in and breathing out. An appropriate macroeconomic framework is essential for our work, but the social, structural, and human agenda, which we share with the regional banks, members of the UN system, and other partners in development, is essential for the IMF, which cannot and does not prescribe in a vacuum. Together we must serve the hopes and aspirations of the people in our client countries, or our clients will not achieve their objectives in peace and stability. And together we must work with and support the work of the World Trade Organization, which is so critical to the trading arrangements and future of our client countries.

In particular areas, such as strengthening the financial systems around the world, we work together as partners with the IMF, regional banks, the BIS,[‡] and other institutions, each of us contributing according to the needs of the situation and our available human resources. Our partnerships with the international community are many and varied and serve our clients well.

Part I: A Concept—A Balance Sheet with Two Sides, a Coin with Two Sides, a Duet with Two Parts

When I think of a development framework for a country and for regions, I think of a balance sheet with two sides. On the left is the macroeconomic presentation, including the Article IV reports of the IMF, the National Income Accounts, the Balance of Payments and Trade Statistics, and all the other fi-

---

‡ The Bank for International Settlements, based in Basel, Switzerland, is an international organization that fosters cooperation among central banks and other agencies in pursuit of monetary and financial stability.

nancial and economic analyses which are at the core of our current appraisal system. All of us are used to quoting GDP statistics, interest rates, reserves statistics, percentage growth statistics, and so on as a basis for monetary and fiscal policy. Based on analysis of the information, we can decide whether a country is Part I or Part II, IDA eligible, or HIPC [Heavily Indebted Poor Countries Initiative] eligible. It is the language that Finance Ministers find comfortable, and we all use it to make decisions.

The Need for the Right-Hand Side

There is, however, a clear need for a second side which reflects more adequately an analytical framework that presents the structural, social, and human aspects. It must go beyond the familiar statistics of infant and maternal mortality, unemployment, and children in school, to address fundamental long-term issues of the structure, scope, and substance of societal development.

Let me explain this a little more, but before doing so, let me say that I am not too convinced about the imagery of a Balance Sheet. Perhaps we could speak of two sides of a coin, or two parts of a duet. What is key is that the two parts, namely, macroeconomic aspects on the one side and the social, structural and human on the other, must be considered together.

But let me return to my balance sheet example. Unlike macroeconomic analysis, which brings everything together in a familiar consolidated form, we in the development field have been less successful in giving an accountable presentation of the status of structural work and social progress. This is not surprising since multilaterals and bilaterals alike are limited by resources, experience, and reach, and none except the government of the country in question has an overall responsibility. Governments have the responsibility for putting it all together in a comprehensive review of all the elements required for growth and poverty alleviation. But we know that not all of the governments we serve have the capacity to do so, or the resources, or sometimes even the will. Nor is there an agreed framework for presentation.

We also know that we "players" in the development business are surely not accustomed to working together in harmony, neither the UN system and multilaterals with bilaterals nor NGOs with the private sector. We certainly cooperate more than we did in the past. We at the Bank are committed to strengthening such cooperation. But there is still suspicion and many historic grudges and perceptions. What is necessary is an overarching framework—an approach agreed with the government concerned—which will allow us all to work together to meet our goals for poverty alleviation and environmental sustainability. On the basis of such work, we would then be able to present a right-hand side of the Country Balance Sheet, which would allow for a more comprehensive analysis and more soundly based action.

The Comprehensive Development Framework and the International Financial Architecture

Within and without governments, in a multitude of research and private organizations, in the press and public discourse, analysis is proceeding as to how the world financial and economic system should be changed, and what role the Bretton Woods institutions [the World Bank and the IMF] are to play. I am of the personal view that with some few changes, including expanded and more transparent financial information, the basic international architecture has served us well. Of course, it can no doubt be strengthened and I am certain that many suggestions will be made. I wish to deal here with only one aspect of the debate.

The Comprehensive Development Framework I am proposing highlights a more inclusive picture of development. We cannot adopt a system in which the macroeconomic and financial are considered apart from the structural, social and human aspects, and vice versa. Integration of each of these subjects is imperative at the national level and among the global players. It is not possible to separate these subjects in Part I countries where the structure of economic and social governance exists. It is certainly not possible to separate these subjects in Part II countries where there is much less tolerance for risk due to fragile structures. A wrong step on the macroeconomic side can have dire consequences for the structural, social, and human dimensions. In addition, profligate and unbridled spending without regard to resource constraints and fiscal and monetary policy can also have dire consequences.

The Prerequisites for Sustainable Growth and Poverty Alleviation

What are the basic structural, social, and human prerequisites that should balance the macroeconomic considerations? Let me set forth my list, which we should examine and test over the next 12–18 months. But before doing so, let me make one additional important assertion. I believe that unless we think of having *all* the basic prerequisites, say over a 20-year timeframe, we will endanger and sometimes ruin the effectiveness of individual projects and programs which we undertake with our clients. Clearly not all the objectives can be approached simultaneously. The framework should not become a straitjacket. We need the flexibility to adjust to the varied conditions of each country. There will be a need for setting priorities, for phasing of action based on financial and human capacity and based on necessary sequencing to get to our objectives. But over time, all the requirements within a holistic framework must be addressed if there is to be stable, equitable, and sustainable development.

One of the reasons for developing such a comprehensive, holistic framework is to allow us to think more strategically about the sequencing of policies, programs, and projects and the pacing of reforms. While the comprehensive approach emphasizes that we must advance on all fronts, certain steps need to be taken before others.

Let me give some examples of what I mean. The fact is that the success of most projects is dependent on many assumptions extraneous to the project itself. Building new schools is of no use without roads to get the children to the schools and without trained teachers, books, and equipment. Establishing banks and financial institutions without a banking system that is supervised will lead to chaos. Initiatives to make progress creating equal opportunities for women make no sense if women have to spend many hours each day carrying clean water, or finding and gathering fuel for cooking. Seeking universal primary education without prenatal and postnatal health care means that children get to school mentally and physically damaged. Establishing a health system but doing nothing about clean water and sewerage diminishes enormously the impact of any effort. Seeking equity when government is riddled with corruption and has inefficient and untrained officials is an objective that will never be realized.

Privatization prior to establishing an effective regulatory or competition framework can be a recipe for a disaster; the benefits of lower prices for consumers may well not be achieved. We know, at least from hindsight, that part of the failures in Russia were due to paying insufficient attention to the preconditions for a market economy. Too often in the past, we have gone after the "easy" targets, saying that we would attack the more difficult (often institutional) issues later on. In doing so, we have failed to recognize the essential complementarities.

By contrast, good business strategy attempts to identify bottlenecks—the hard to solve problems that are impediments to success—and it begins by attacking these first. We must learn to apply these lessons to attack poverty and bring about development.

It is also clear to all of us that ownership is essential. Countries must be in the driver's seat and set the course. They must determine goals and the phasing, timing, and sequencing of programs. Where there is not adequate capacity in the government to do this, we must support and help them to establish, own, and implement the strategy. And we must work to achieve the strategy with our colleagues in the government, in the international development community, the civil society, and the private sector. In some countries the long and short term goals will be set by a process of public debate and consensus building led by the government with all sections of society. In other countries the establishment of goals will continue to be set more centrally.

Let me now set down a possible framework for presenting and managing a holistic approach to the structural, social, and human aspects of development:

1. Good and Clean Government
2. An Effective Legal and Justice System
3. A Well-Organized and Supervised Financial System
4. A Social Safety Net and Social Programs
5. Education and Knowledge Institutions
6. Health and Population Issues
7. Water and Sewerage
8. Power
9. Roads, Transportation, and Telecommunications
10. Sustainable Development, Environment, and Cultural Issues
11. Rural Strategy
12. Urban Strategy
13. Private Sector Strategy
14. Special National Considerations

Part II: A Proposal for a Broader Approach to Partnership and to Management of the Development Process

If we can accept for the moment that the above-mentioned listing is a plausible statement of the structural, social, and human prerequisites for sustainable development, we can now devote attention to a consideration of what is being done in these areas and by whom. It is obvious to me that there is much too little coordination of effort, much too much suspicion between participants, and in many cases a simple absence of a framework to coordinate and bring together under government guidance an agreed set of objectives and effective and accountable programs. There is too little transparency, much too little consultation, and too little accountability for performance.

We would like to test as a management tool a matrix. On the top of the chart—the horizontal axis—we list the 14 subjects referred to in Part I. On the vertical axis, we list the "players" in the development business.

The players in the development field seem to be four:

1. *Government*

At the first level, the governmental structure of a country must be in charge of the process of development strategy and implementation. Government should aspire to have programs under each of the 14 headings along the top of the matrix, and these will be entered into the grid. Obviously, the entries will have to be made in a form of shorthand and, as I just noted, annexes behind each subject heading will give fuller details. For example, an annex on Justice Systems, an annex on education, gives far more detail on each subject.

Government should include not only national programs, but provincial and state, city, and municipal to the extent that they are relevant.

2. *Multilateral and Bilateral Participants*

The listing of those involved in the programmatic thrusts is long, but let me give an incomplete but indicative listing:

- IMF [International Monetary Fund]
- UN agencies and programs
- WTO [World Trade Organization]
- European Union
- Regional development banks
- Bilateral agencies
- International organizations

All of these participants, as well as the World Bank Group, are involved in projects and programs for development. At a time of lessening resources for overseas development assistance and budgetary restraints on agencies, which reduce available human resources, each of us needs to know what the other is doing so that we can cooperate and avoid duplication of effort.

3. *Civil Society*

In all its forms, civil society is probably the largest single factor in development— if not in its monetary contribution, then certainly in its human contribution and its experience and its history.

It is by its nature somewhat disorganized, due to the diversity of groups involved, although individual projects and initiatives are often meritorious, effective, and of very long standing. There is, however, little accountability with some nongovernmental organizations. Certainly greater cooperation with governments, multilateral and bilateral agencies, and the private sector would be beneficial to all.

The list of participants in civil society is great, including, of course, elected parliamentary assemblies, which are included also in the government sector. An incomplete list is as follows:

   (i) Religions and religious organizations;
  (ii) Foundations;
 (iii) Trade unions and employee organizations;
 (iv) Employer organizations;
  (v) Nongovernmental organizations with international reach;
 (vi) Local nongovernmental organizations;
(vii) Local groups organized for consultation and for implementation of projects; and
(viii) Organizations of indigenous peoples.

Depending on local political circumstances, civil society has a greater or lesser voice, but our experience is that by engaging civil society in projects and programs, better results are achieved both with design and implementation and usually greater effectiveness, including more local ownership. I think we all recognize more and more that local ownership is the key to success and project effectiveness.

4. Private Sector

It is absolutely clear that domestic and foreign private investment is the key to economic growth and employment. It offers know-how, training, and investment, which is essential for development and for the creation of employment opportunities. Private sector involvement is essential for science and technology—a critical factor for growth in all countries. There is a responsibility on governments to provide an appropriate climate for investment, but there is also a growing understanding on the part of business leadership that it is not only morally good but good business to invest with a strong sense of social responsibility.

Conclusion

To conclude, let me say that none of this would be possible without the work being done individually by all our institutions in giving advice and support on projects and programs. Clearly this must continue with even greater efficiency and effectiveness.

What is new is an attempt to view our efforts within a long-term, holistic, and strategic approach where all the component parts are brought together. Such development should, in our judgment, be a participatory process, as transparent and as accountable as possible within the political climate prevailing in each country. This is not a return to central planning. It is a holistic and strategic approach to development based on country ownership and partnership.

What is new is the commitment to integration of effort, essential in today's global economy where overseas development is declining significantly. It is also a commitment to expanded partnerships, transparency, and accountability under the leadership of the government.

What is new is that the international financial architecture must reflect the interdependence of macroeconomic and financial with structural and social and human concerns.

I personally believe that unless we adopt this approach on a comprehensive, transparent, and accountable basis, we will fail in the global challenge of equitable sustainable development and poverty alleviation. We will fail to build a sustainable international architecture for the coming millennium.

Certainly, we should give this approach a chance, work with our chosen countries, with our partners, and measure our results in a 12 to 18 month timeframe. I am not wed to every word of this approach. I want to test it, and if it can be improved and developed so that we can all be held to higher and more accountable and comprehensive standards, then our goal of making a better and fairer world will be closer at hand.

THE RIGHT WHEEL: AN AGENDA FOR
COMPREHENSIVE DEVELOPMENT

Remarks at the International Conference on Democracy, Market Economy,
and Development

SEOUL | FEBRUARY 26, 1999

*This address came 14 months after the election of Kim Dae Jung as president
of the Republic of Korea. As Wolfensohn notes, this was the first meeting
where a World Bank president spoke under the headings of development and
democracy.*

President Kim, Distinguished Leaders, Ladies and Gentlemen:

I am absolutely delighted to have the opportunity to be with you today. I will
let you in on a little secret: this meeting is the result of some 14 months of
waiting. Just before President Kim was confirmed in office, he invited me to
his home, and as we sat down at the table, he indicated his very strong belief
in the need for reform and his commitment to a market economy and to
democracy and to changing his country.

This man certainly has convictions, and he has stuck to them. We have
seen, over the last year, the remarkable progress he has made as leader of this
great country, and how he has kept his commitment to open the debate to all
of us here: from academia, from business, from civil society, and from the
multilateral institutions. We have a chance here to talk about the fundamental issues that affect not only the future of this country but, indeed, the future
of our globe.

I should tell you a second thing: I am a little nervous. I am nervous because
I have distinguished leaders before me who can say probably better than I how
these things can be done, and because of the broad range of other distinguished
speakers who will be here in the next two days. And I am particularly nervous
because my colleague, [World Bank Chief Economist] Joe Stiglitz, has a 36-
page speech already written with some 50 footnotes. And I was told my good
friend [Nobel economics laureate] Amartya Sen has the same, except that it is
probably longer, deeper, and much more important. And I very much look
forward to hearing him also.

So I am here with you as someone who has come to the development business only in the last three years and who does not have the background of
many who are speaking. But I have had the opportunity, in these last three and
a half years, to visit 85 countries, to look at development, to look at poverty,
and to build on the experience and guidance of my 10,000 colleagues who,
collectively and with their predecessors, have established the World Bank as a
critical and important factor in the development community.

I should make one last comment in relation to my fear. I was told by my general counsel, as I was leaving, to read the regulations of the World Bank, of the Bretton Woods institutions that were formed some 50 years ago. There, in very large print, it is written that the responsibility of the Bank is to deal in economic matters. Subsequent Bank Boards have interpreted that to include social matters, but it says in Article IV that I can have no part in political matters. So it is not surprising, Mr. President, that this is the first time there has been a meeting with the World Bank that has in its heading both "development" *and* "democracy." Let me say that I will leave democracy to you, Mr. President, and to myself in my private capacity. In my public capacity what I would like to talk about is some of those aspects of development that we at the Bank find important—indeed, central—and about whose importance we have some evidence from democratic societies. And I hope we can discuss these findings with you in these two days. It is to those issues that I will be addressing my remarks.

Let me make one other preliminary comment, drawing on what the president said about the cart with two wheels. I will be dealing with the right wheel. The left wheel I interpret to be the wheel that is most often spoken of: fiscal policy, monetary policy, macroeconomics, exchange rates, interest rates, the size of rescue packages. This has been the stuff of all the headlines over the last many months in relation to the international financial crisis. And beyond that, it is the way in which we typically look at countries, that is, in the context of their GDPs. We all have the ability to examine them from economic and statistical points of view, and we have their annual accounts and their balance of payments and their budget deficits. All of that I am going to leave to the left wheel, not because it is not important, but because all too often we forget the right wheel. And that right wheel to which I am referring is the wheel that is not immediately visible when you look at your computer screen—when you look for rates, or when you look for other figures. That right wheel is the essential element of the structure of the economy and the social and the human aspects of society. As President Kim has pointed out, you cannot have one wheel without the other. Both wheels need to be there, in our consideration, simultaneously.

We at the Bank, in our approach to the structural and social, think first in terms of poverty. My colleagues at the Bank decided recently that we should have a statement of our principles. I left it to my colleagues to draw it up, and the first line of that statement is that the function of our institution is "to fight poverty with passion," because fighting poverty is at the center of our role as an institution. We are also concerned, as President Kim said, with ensuring that we do this within a global context and while preserving an environment that is sustainable and enduring. This is the vantage point from which we come to look at that right wheel.

What have we learned from looking at the issues of poverty and development in this way? A number of themes have been emerging in my thinking and in the thinking of my colleagues, which I hope very much might be discussed in the course of these two days. Let me outline some of them to you.

The first theme is *inclusion*. A couple of years ago, at my second Annual Meetings speech, I developed the proposition that there can be no real development without inclusion. We cannot leave people behind. We cannot sustain an increasing difference between rich and poor, with more and more people becoming poor and fewer and fewer seeing opportunities for wealth. We have to deal here, too, with the question of the rights of women. We have to deal with the question of those who are disabled. We have to deal with those living in poor areas within a country. We have to deal with the divisions within society. This is not just a social and moral issue—although it is that, and it is sufficiently that to merit our attention. It is also an economic issue. It is also an issue of peace and stability.

From that we move to a second theme, which is that of *corruption,* on which President Kim has already spoken eloquently. I have just come from a conference of 90 countries on that subject, in Washington just hours before I left. This is a subject, by the way, that I was not allowed to talk about when I arrived at the World Bank over three years ago. I was told there was a certain word I could not utter. It was called the C-word—C for corruption. And if you did use it, you had to use it very quietly and out of earshot.

[IMF Managing Director] Michel Camdessus and I decided that we would redefine corruption as not a political issue but an economic and social issue. And we did that at our joint Annual Meetings in 1996. Since that time we have had vigorous debate and a great focus on the topic, to the point that, at the Annual Meetings in 1997, the central item on the agenda of the Development Committee[†] was corruption.

Corruption is a cancer. Corruption is the greatest eroding factor in a society. Corruption is the largest impediment to investment. And it is not just a theoretical concept. It is a concept whose real implications become clear when children have to pay three times the price that they should for lunches. It becomes clear when people die from being given bad drugs, because the good drugs have been sold under the table. It becomes clear when farmers are robbed of their livelihood. And it becomes clear when, as I learned in a visit to Uganda recently, governments are forced to review their entire processes to uproot it. The Ugandan government had increased its investment in education

---

† The Development Committee is a grouping of finance ministers representative of the Bank's member countries that meets twice a year to discuss and advise on development issues.

and health threefold over five years, only to find that the same amount of money as in the first year was going to educational and health services, with the rest being siphoned off.

This brings me to the third *theme,* which is transparency. Transparency can be used effectively against corruption, and it is an essential factor in the smooth running of a society. And let me use that same example from Uganda to illustrate. In response to what it had found, the Ugandan government simply decided it would publish, using newspapers and radio, the amount of money it was sending to each school district and to each school. It published the names of the 10,000 teachers who were officially on the payroll. And it sent to each school an estimate of the money that it should receive. It did not send out the police force. And two years later the problem was turning around. This shows that transparency is an enormously important element in the smooth functioning of any society.

And then there is the question of *knowledge,* to which the president alluded. We are indeed in a sixth International Revolution, a revolution on which the world is building its future. I was fascinated to find that Korean industry has, with the help of advisers and with the government, produced a report titled *Knowledge for Action.* And this report, which the president recently released along with the private sector, contains 38 action items to transform this economy into a knowledge-driven economy. This represents an enormous cultural shift, one that will influence the way in which the Korean people deal with education, with culture itself, with the freedom of the individual, with the taking of risks, with the distribution of rewards. But, under President Kim's leadership, it is clear that this country is grappling with that challenge, as indeed we must hope that the whole developing world will.

Just three weeks ago I was in Côte d'Ivoire, 45 percent of whose exports are cocoa and coffee and related products. For years the farmers of that country, two and a half million of them, have received less for their output than they deserve, in fact roughly half the world price. And so we at the Bank said, "Stop the monopoly. Open it up to the market." But not much happened. The farmers still got half the world price from the traders. I went there to see what had been done. I went into the jungles, and I went to the small farms. And from there I went to a village where I was made a chief, and I was given a black hat and gold robes and looked rather wonderful. I should have worn it today.

So there I was, sitting in a hundred-year-old costume, in the middle of the village, now talking with farmers who had formed a cooperative. Then my fellow chiefs said, "Let's go to the office," and in the middle of the dirt-road village we went to the office, and there, on the left side of the room, was a computer for weighing in the coffee and the cocoa. And on the right side was another computer, this one linked to the Internet, with a young Ivorian getting quotes from the Chicago Board of Trade, from London and Paris, which he then passed along using a cellular telephone to the farmers in the region, most of them illiterate. And we came back after this, to our meeting of chiefs and farmers, and they talked to me about forward contracts, about c.i.f. and f.o.b., about prices on the Chicago Board of Trade. And I realized that a distance of a hundred years had been spanned, because of knowledge. This is not just an African experience. This is central to the role of development in the years to come.

And, as the final theme, I talk of *ownership,* which is an essential element in this development process: ownership as a result of knowledge transfer, ownership as a result of opportunity, ownership as key, because no one wants to be told what to do from the outside. It is simply not effective just to get programs nominally accepted. Those programs must be owned and developed by the people they serve. This is a form of democracy, a form of political movement in a sense. But it is also an economic issue, because with ownership you get results.

With those themes as our guide, we have approached the notion of how we in the Bank can improve what we do. With these ideas, which are not new but have been floating around, we have tried to flesh out what it is that is on that right-hand side of the cart: what it is about development that is non-financial, what it is that is truly needed to have development in a market system. These are often things that are not immediately visible, things that you can sometimes forget, Mr. President, if the balance of payments increases and if profits increase. But in the medium and the long term, these things are fundamental to development that is continuous.

Among these things I speak of good governance and of the fight against corruption. I speak of a comprehensive legal system—and not just a comprehensive system of laws that define rights—civil rights, human rights, corporate rights—but also a justice system that underpins it and that is fair, that is equitable, that is honest. I speak also of a financial system that works, that monitors and supervises banks and the private sector. Here, too, I speak of transparency: transparency in accounting, transparency in reporting clarity, in objectivity, a standard form of presentation like that now demanded of any global business. And I speak of a social system that works. It does not have to be the same social system that we have in the United States or in other Western countries. It can be based on family. It can be based on tribe. It can be based on past history. But there is a need for some social safety net, and what has been done in this country in the last 12 months is truly quite remarkable as a cultural change in that context.

Then there is the issue of education and of knowledge. There is the issue of health. There is the issue of clean water, which 1.3 billion people on our planet still do not have. There is the issue of electric power, to which 2 billion people still have no access. There is the need for roads, the need for communications, the need for a rural strategy, the need for an urban strategy, and the need for an environmental and cultural strategy. We must not forget our environment, and, in a globalized society, we must not forget our local culture.

I was fascinated that in this same report, *Knowledge for Action,* there was recognition of the fact that, if you are to have creativity, you must also have cultural creativity. You must create an environment in which people can risk, can create. The report said that Korea wants a Bill Gates and a Stephen Spielberg. If they want a Bill Gates and a Stephen Spielberg, creativity is of the essence, and that *is* culture, and it cannot and it must not be put down.

Finally, of course, we have to have a private sector environment that is conducive to investment, not just by and in large companies but in medium-size companies and in the smallest companies as well.

So there is an agenda. It is an agenda for discussion. And I would raise one last issue, the issue of how we attack this agenda. This is not an agenda that should be imposed from above. This is not government from the center. This is not central planning. What we have learned is that the decisions on priorities, the pursuit of our objectives, and the achievement of those objectives require partnership. It must be a partnership between governments; between the multilateral institutions, such as ours, and the bilateral institutions; and between the private sector and civil society in all its forms, from NGOs [nongovernmental organizations] to trade unions, from religions to foundations, from those who speak for ordinary people to the highest elites. The healthiest societies are those that allow for a free expression of views and for the shared setting of objectives.

This meeting today is an exemplification of President Kim's commitment to that objective. And for us at the Bank, it exemplifies the so-called Comprehensive Development Framework that we are now testing, where we are looking at the whole list of issues that I described, from governance to education. We are not looking at it alone, and not with any arrogant presumption that we in Washington know what should be done. Instead we are looking at it with enormous humility, because these objectives can only be achieved if we do it together, in the partnerships I have just described, with clear priorities, with transparency, and with sound judgment about what has proved effective.

We have talked today mostly about Korea, and a little about the region. But the issue that we are discussing in these two days is one that is not just about this country or this region. I cannot forget that 3 billion people in the world today live on less than two dollars a day, and that in another 25 years we will have another 2 billion people, the majority of whom will fall into that category. I cannot forget that we will need to double the production of food in the first half of the next century, on the same amount of land. I cannot forget the pressures on water. I cannot forget the growing inequities in our system. And I cannot forget these things because, as I look at the turn of the millennium, I think of the future of my children, just as you probably think of the future of yours. If we want a future of peace, if we want a future of opportunity, if we want a future for our children, we must address these issues now.

Thank you.

Remarks at the Bretton Woods Committee Annual Meeting
WASHINGTON, D.C. | JUNE 9, 1999

World Bank presidents have spoken frequently at meetings of the Bretton Woods Committee, a bipartisan, nonprofit group devoted to increasing public understanding of international financial and development issues and the role of the Bretton Woods institutions—the Bank and the International Monetary Fund—and of the regional development banks in the global economy. Wolfensohn uses the opportunity to clarify the respective roles of the Bank and IMF.

Thank you very much, Bill, Jim, and Henry.* And let me start on a personal note, which is that I am delighted that [former World Bank President] Bob McNamara is here with us today, and I heard on NPR this morning that it's his birthday. So may I wish you a happy birthday, Bob. It's great to see you in such good form.

I was given the topic today of "More Focus on the Social Sector." And I guess that this topic was suggested by my colleagues to try and give me the opportunity to differentiate somewhat the activities of the Bank from those of the Fund. You'll be hearing very shortly from Michel,[†] with whom I had breakfast today. We did not collude on what we would say, but I think he is in agreement with what I will say on that score.

Let me not touch heavily on the Fund today, other than to say that we work very closely with them, that we are respectful of and contribute to and are assisted by their efforts in surveillance, in crisis management, and in the establishment of fiscal and monetary policy. Their role in all of these matters has been so apparent in the last two years, which have been a time of extreme difficulty for [the Republic of] Korea, Thailand, Indonesia, Brazil, Russia, and all the other countries that have been affected in some way or other by the international financial crisis.

The last two years have also been very difficult for both the Fund and the Bank, and indeed for all international institutions, because the impact of this crisis has been significant worldwide. It has been significant not only for the front-line states whose names have been in the headlines, but also for the middle-level states that have been affected by the crisis through reduced access

---

* Bill Frenzel, Jim Orr, and Henry Owen, respectively, co-chairman, executive director, and founding co-chairman of the Bretton Woods Committee.
† Michel Camdessus, managing director of the International Monetary Fund.

to markets, or increases in costs, or the impact on trade. And when those impacts are added to those of the other crises we have seen—natural disasters, floods, droughts, and wars—we have had a pretty busy time. Most of the time these issues are translated in the headlines into the size of the financial package offered to the country in crisis. The financial press tends to cover them on the basis of whether it is a $17 billion package, or a $42 billion package, or a $58 billion package that has been put together. And, at that moment, confidence is thought to return.

There is an attendant argument about fiscal and monetary policy. There are the observations by the well informed on what the crisis country's exchange rate policy should be. There is a significant debate carried out in the press on the questions, always, of the economics and the numbers. And this has made us a little humble at the Bank, because when we see all this money going out and the debate focusing on that, some of us wonder what *we* do, if everything can be cured by money. And that led us to some very serious thought, not about what we have done since Bob was president of the Bank, but in terms of trying to present in a more coherent fashion something that can balance the discussion of the financial and macroeconomic considerations.

And so we started to think in terms of the focus, or, as my title says, "More Focus on the Social Sector." But it is a focus not *just* on the social sector, but more broadly on the economic and social structure with which we are charged to involve ourselves. Since the initial objectives of the Bretton Woods agreements—the reconstruction of Europe and Japan after World War II—were met, the focus of the Bank has been realigned toward, and has remained on, development, and especially the issues of poverty and sustainable development. And so the way we have tended to think about ourselves—and it is more a reordering and a shift in focus than a fundamental change—is to assert that the Bank's role, parallel to and engaged with the IMF's role, is one of addressing a number of visible and essential elements that need to be addressed for there to be growth, development, and peace in the countries we are dealing with.

We start by saying that there has to be good governance in a country. That means a decent administration, and it means confronting the issue of corruption. These are issues that, historically, we have been edging toward, but which are now front and center on the Bank's agenda. If you give a billion dollars to a country that is well run, it is no surprise that it usually does better than if you give that same billion to a country that is poorly run and subject to corruption. Governance is thus now a central, focal issue and number one on our agenda.

Number two on the agenda is the character of the legal and justice system. If a country wants to have equitable growth, if it wants to deal with the question of poverty, if it wants to deal with the differences in power between rich and poor or between people of influence and people of no influence, and if it wants to have stable development, that country must have a legal system that protects rights. It has to protect property rights. It has to protect human rights. The country must have available to it a commercial code that addresses issues of bankruptcy and sanctity of contract. That, of course, plays very much into the question of investment. But, in any event, few would deny that a coherent legal system and, may I say, an honest justice system are essential for stable growth.

Unfortunately, in many of the countries in which we operate, the legal system is not coherent, nor is the justice system very effective. Last week I was in Azerbaijan, Georgia, and Armenia, and, working with the president of Georgia, we addressed the fact that the very richest people in Georgia are the judges. And these judges were thought to be absolutely impossible to dislodge, until the president—assisted by work that we did—brought in, over furious opposition, testing of the judges. Not only were they tested, but the examinations were shown on television. And of the 200 judges who were tested, 131 were not reappointed, and meanwhile 178 new judges were appointed. This would have been unthinkable some years ago, but of course it makes an enormous difference to the potential for equitable development in Georgia.

The third thing that is needed, as is evident in Korea, Thailand, Indonesia, and many other countries, is an effective and transparent supervisory mechanism for banks, for capital markets, for corporations, and for accounts systems. In all of these areas we are working integrally with the Fund. This issue of supervision and control of financial systems also relates to poverty. The people who get hurt most in a financial crisis are rarely the rich, and not always, although sometimes, the middle class, but certainly the poor. So, for us, the very essence of development comes back again to the supervision, control, and monitoring of financial systems.

Finally, there is the social safety net. The safety net was very much put to the test in Korea, Thailand, and Indonesia, all of which suffered significant increases in poverty and unemployment during the crisis. And, in transition economies, as they have moved to privatization and market-based development, the absence of an adequate social safety net has resulted in coal miners lying on railway tracks, and in riots by teachers. There have to be support systems to replace those formerly provided by the old, inefficient state enterprises.

So the first thing I would like to say to you is that, although it does not make headlines, this work on structural reform—which is not quick work—is absolutely essential for dealing with the questions of stability and growth. And, if you think about it for a few minutes, it is obvious that that is the case. And so the focus, as my title suggests, is first and foremost on structure.

Then there are the social aspects of development that one needs to consider. These are not things that can be accomplished in one year, or three years, or in a period of one project or two projects, but only over a longer period, as part of a broader strategy for development in these countries. What are the social elements that need to be established as the focus for the Bank's work, indeed for the country's work? We have come up with our own list of priorities, which, however, are not preordained but rather suggested, because the list must be established by the countries themselves. They are not something that can or should be imposed by Washington or by any other central authority or power. It is a suggested framework for the establishment of social focus. Here we think of education and knowledge, of health care, and of water, because in another 50 years nearly half of the people on our planet will not have access to adequate water. Already 1.3 billion people do not have it. We think of sewerage, roads, rural roads, methods of communication, electric power, an environmental strategy, and a cultural strategy, because it is very important to ensure that countries keep some sense of their own cultural continuity. We think of a strategy to attract business. We think of an urban strategy, because we have more and more people moving into urbanized areas and considerable growth in the number of megacities worldwide. Within another 15 years there will be 22 megacities—cities of 10 million people or more—in developing countries. And finally, of course, we think of a rural strategy, because the great weight of poverty is still in rural areas.

These, then, become the focuses of attention, and although they are not easily encapsulated in a $17 billion figure, or a $42 billion or a $58 billion figure, without them you cannot have serious and continuing and long-term development. May I suggest also that without them you will not have peace. In the next 25 years we will add to our planet—including the existing 3 billion people who live on less than two dollars a day and the 1.4 billion who live on less than one dollar a day—another 2 billion people. These numbers are extraordinary. And yet, at the same time, overseas development assistance is diminishing, as we heard from our speakers this morning. It appears the U.S. Congress is not eager to increase funding, either for HIPC [the Heavily Indebted Poor Countries Initiative] or, indeed, as we will have to find out, for Kosovo or other places of crisis.

Consider the Caucasus, from which I have just returned. It is not in the headlines, but there are still close to a million refugees in those areas. I visited the camps, and the squalor and hardship there are worse than the squalor and hardship suffered by the people of Kosovo, because the people in the Caucasus have now lived in these camps for 10 years. In all there are 22 million refugees around the world whom we have to deal with. And from where does the money come? Where does the money come from for debt relief? Where does the money come from for reconstruction? Where does the money come from for refugees?

So we are forced back to the issue, first of all, of identifying the problems, and then relating them to our focus on the structural and social issues, and on the need for funding, and for the effort required from all of us to make this work. And that is another area where we have changed the focus in the Bank, because we have clearly determined that the Bank cannot do all this alone. It is obvious that we cannot, notwithstanding the fact that we currently lend $30 billion a year, and notwithstanding that we have doubled the work of the advisory services in the Bank. With all that, we still touch only a fraction of the challenges.

And so the Bank is looking much more now at how it works together with, first, the governments of the countries themselves: with the parliaments, the provincial governments, the states, the city parliaments. There is a whole new dynamic, by the way, in terms of democratic development around the world. We are also looking at how we work with the Fund, of course, and with the UN agencies, the bilateral donors, and the other multilateral organizations. We are looking at this in a much more coordinated fashion than we have before, and it is needed.

We are looking at how we work with civil society, which has been burgeoning with the expansion of freedom, with the establishment of market economies, and with the birth of democratic states. And, most significant, we are looking at how we work with the private sector. Private sector flows have changed dramatically in the last 10 years. In 1987 these flows to developing countries were on the order of $25 billion a year, while official development assistance was $40 billion. Ten years later, in 1997, private sector flows had reached $300 billion, yet public flows were still $40 billion. In other words, from being just over half the size of official flows, private sector flows have grown to seven times their size. That changed somewhat in 1998, with a reduction in private sector flows of about $70 billion, but it is still a four- or fivefold difference.

In short, however we focus on the social sector, it is not something that we at the Bank can do alone, or even bilaterally with a government. We have to learn to work effectively with the whole range of other partners. This is quite a big challenge for our institution, and in meeting that challenge we need and appreciate enormously the help of this group. We are very, very grateful to you for the work that you do on Capitol Hill, and for the work that you do generally, in spreading understanding of our needs and of the importance of our institution to the position of the United States internationally. It is very important that the United States continue to have a strong influence in the Bretton Woods institutions. It is very important that we be able to rely on the United States for leadership. It is very important that our legislators be educated, and that they be ready to recognize that giving money for overseas development assistance is not charity. It is an integral part of the development of the countries that receive it, and without that integral and safe development, we are not going to have a prosperous United States, and we are surely not going to have a stable world.

These issues become very clear when you get out into the field. They are very clear to me after four years as the Bank's president. And your committee, which has been working now since the mid-1980s, has played a very, very important role in getting this message across. I hope you will recognize the role that the Bank has played and that our affiliate, the expanded IFC [International Finance Corporation], is playing, about which you will hear at lunch from my colleague Peter Woicke. He has taken on not just the responsibility for the IFC, in terms of the corporate sector, but the whole responsibility for private sector activities within the Bank Group. This is a response not only to increased international investment, but also to the establishment of capital markets and domestic investing in developing countries themselves, which has doubled or trebled the size of international financial flows.

So we are trying to gear up. We think the challenges are enormous. We feel the pressures for money. We feel the pressures of a limited budget. And we feel the pressures of an ever-expanding series of challenges. It is not an easy moment for the Bank or for the Fund, but I do believe that this focus on structure and on the social activities is the correct one for us. It is a focus that parallels that of the Fund, and it needs to be kept in mind at the same time as one looks at the financial and macroeconomic considerations. It certainly gives us enough to do, and I hope it gives you enough reason to continue to support us in the Congress and in other places.

With George Carey, published in *The Globe and Mail* (Toronto)

JUNE 17, 1999

> *This piece appeared just before the Cologne Summit of the Group of Eight industrial countries, where debt relief was at the top of the agenda. Together with George Carey, Archbishop of Canterbury, Wolfensohn calls for unity and common cause for all those seeking to help the world's poor.*

More than 1.3 billion people today live in extreme poverty. Nearly 1.4 billion lack access to clean water. Three billion live without basic sanitation. In 1999, 11 million children under 5 will die of preventable disease. For those children who live past 5, more than 250 million will work instead of going to school.

Several hundred million of these poor live in countries where crushing debt stands in the way of lasting poverty reduction. How did we get here, and what can we do to reduce burdensome debt in the poorest countries?

For decades, developing countries in every part of the world borrowed money from governments and international development organizations to invest in their future. In many countries this lending contributed to important gains in human and economic development. Life expectancy, infant and maternal mortality, and literacy improved significantly in even the poorest countries.

But such improvements did not take place everywhere, and for a number of reasons dozens of poor countries find themselves severely in debt. That the vast majority of this debt is owed to governments and government-owned organizations is important, for it means that we—all of us—are not only providers of development lending, but also creditors. It is up to all of us to come up with answers.

There is reason for optimism. We are, perhaps for the first time, working together as a world community on important issues of development. We are discovering that we are truly neighbours, that we share the same future. And we are finding that economics and spirituality—each fundamental to human dignity—are inseparable, and have much to learn from each other.

The concrete benefits of the global campaign to end the debt crisis have been extraordinary. The vigorous advocacy of churches and non-governmental organizations (NGOs) has helped place the issue of debt on the agenda of the international community, and expanded the range of practical ideas required for finding a practical solution. These ideas, along with initiatives of international development organizations such as the World Bank and proposals by various G8 countries whose leaders will gather tomorrow in Cologne, will form the basis of what we expect will be a strengthened plan—and new money—to deliver more debt relief to more countries more quickly.

Unfortunately, sometimes the passion all of us bring to this issue has created the perception that creditors, in the form of governments and international organizations such as the World Bank, stand on one side of a great divide, with dedicated churches and NGOs squarely on the other. In reality, we share the same dream: to eliminate poverty. We will differ over details, but we must not overlook the fundamental principles on which we agree.

It is perhaps important to establish at the outset that we both firmly believe that debt, when it contributes to poverty, is a moral issue. We both care about the child who will be born in Mozambique today, and the effect severely high debt could have on her future. No poor country should ever lack the resources to educate its children or treat its sick because of debt. But our morality—indeed, our humanity—is tested not only by our solutions to daunting problems, but by the commitment and good will we bring to solving them.

Debt relief must complement, not replace, development assistance. Poverty is related to many factors: crumbling schools, overstretched health care, impassable roads, polluted air and water, poor governance, lack of investment and, sometimes, severe indebtedness. We must address all these causes within a comprehensive development strategy that combines debt reduction and aid. Financing debt relief by cutting development assistance would be a cruel hoax on the poor.

Resources freed from debt service must be better directed at fighting poverty. Donor governments and multilateral institutions must continue to work with civil society to design a tighter link between debt reduction and poverty, and to build this link firmly into any future debt-relief plan.

Relief must be provided only when there is common agreement that freed resources will, and can, be used wisely and productively. There is, simply, too often a lack of capacity to allocate these resources productively. In a world in which development assistance has dwindled to its lowest levels in 50 years, we cannot afford to waste a single dollar. Strict accountability at every level will increase confidence that the poor really will benefit from debt relief.

Sound economic policies matter. The right economic decisions enhance the effectiveness of aid and build the foundation for long-term, equitable growth. But these policies must be designed transparently and with the participation of the people who will be affected by them. NGOs and religious organizations can and must play a critical role in developing and implementing these policies.

Finally, it is a tragic fact that unless we act decisively on all the factors that perpetuate poverty, including unsustainable debt, next year there will be a larger proportion of people living in poverty than today—and larger still in 15 years. The challenge for all of us is to ensure that the extraordinary momentum generated for debt reduction goes beyond the debt question and beyond the Jubilee commemoration of 2000 to a long-term campaign to end poverty. We know what we can do if we work together.

Wolfensohn on Debt Relief

"... *Make no mistake, debt relief is very important to least developed countries. . . . the heavy debt burden many LDCs faced before HIPC [the Heavily Indebted Poor Countries Initiative] certainly hampered their development. But debt relief by itself cannot be effective without sustained aid flows. Breaking out of the debt trap and moving toward sustainable growth is not a one-off result. . . ."*

From "A New Compact to Meet the Challenge of Global Poverty,"
address at the Third United Nations Conference on
the Least Developed Countries, Brussels, May 14, 2001

Address to the Board of Governors at the Annual Meetings of the World Bank
and the International Monetary Fund

WASHINGTON, D.C. | SEPTEMBER 28, 1999

In this strong and heartfelt call for partnership, Wolfensohn lays out the case
for creating coalitions of all parties in the development arena and proposes the
Comprehensive Development Framework as the basis for that improved
cooperation. The speech also mentions for the first time the World Bank's
watershed report, Voices of the Poor, *which reported on interviews of*
60,000 poor people in 60 countries. The report would feature frequently in
Wolfensohn's speeches in coming years.

Mr. Chairman, Governors, Ladies and Gentlemen:

I am very pleased to welcome you to these Annual Meetings of the World
Bank Group and the International Monetary Fund. I would like to express
my appreciation to our chairman, Mahesh Acharya,* whose work in Nepal
shows a deep understanding of many of the issues I wish to address today,
and to my colleague and friend [IMF Managing Director] Michel Camdessus.
We work ever more closely together, and I salute the remarkable team he
leads.

Mr. Chairman, I have had the privilege of addressing you on four previous occasions. In 1995 I spoke of the challenge of development, of the
need to educate girls and address the burden of debt. I saw the need for
the Bank to reorganize within and to embrace partnerships outside with a
wholly new vigor—partnerships with other official aid and development
institutions, with civil society, and with the private sector—to listen to and
work more closely with the governments and people of the countries we
serve.

In 1996 I emphasized our role as a Knowledge Bank. I spoke, too, of the
"cancer of corruption." The Bank committed itself to join with concerned
governments to fight corruption wherever we found it, and since that time
we have been pushing ahead vigorously with that agenda. Later in the year,
with our partners in the IMF, we articulated our approach to debt forgiveness for the poorest countries. The Heavily Indebted Poor Countries Initiative has made a real difference, and at these Meetings, following the changes
suggested at this year's Group of Eight Summit in Cologne, further progress
has been made.

---

* Governor of the World Bank and the IMF for Nepal.

In 1997 I spoke of the "challenge of inclusion," of the need to think of development in human terms and to bring the weakest and the most vulnerable from the margins of society to the center stage.

A year ago, with the Asian financial crisis dominating our concerns, I spoke of "the other crisis," the human crisis of those condemned to poverty as well as those who had found hope and seen it roughly snatched away. I spoke of the special role of our institution in dealing with the impact of the crisis on people, and of the urgent need to look beyond financial solutions, to consider the social and the structural together with the macroeconomic.

Taking Stock at the Millennium

Mr. Chairman, as we meet today, one year later, it is tempting to take comfort in thoughts of a financial crisis passed, while for millions that other crisis still lives. It is tempting to put off the needed reforms, while for millions those reforms still matter. It is tempting to talk of safe passage, while for millions of poor and unemployed there is still no sight of harbor.

We meet today on the threshold of a new millennium. We must take stock and ask ourselves some fundamental questions. Will we seize the moment to raise our sights for a better world? Will we begin to judge our efforts not by the prosperity of the few but by the needs of the many? Will we be prepared to hold ourselves accountable, to make the effort necessary to bring about change?

For what is the millennial world we see? It is a world where, over the last 40 years, life expectancy has risen more than in the previous 4,000; a world where a revolution in communications holds out the promise of universal access to knowledge; a world where democratic culture has opened up opportunities for many; a world where 5.7 billion people live in market economies, compared with 2.9 billion only 20 years ago.

But look more closely and we see something else. Incomes per capita will stagnate or decline this year in all regions except East and South Asia. In the developing world, with the exception of China, 100 million more people live in poverty today than a decade ago. In at least 10 countries in Africa, the scourge of AIDS has reduced life expectancy by 17 years. There are more than 33 million cases of AIDS in the world, 22 million of them in Africa. One and a half billion people still lack access to safe water, and 2.4 million children still die each year of waterborne diseases. One hundred twenty-five million children still are not in primary school, and 1.8 million people die annually of indoor air pollution. The information gap is widening. And the world's forests are being destroyed at the rate of an acre a second.

Mr. Chairman, the picture is mixed and the challenges are great. But this is a moment in history when we can set a new course to a world of greater peace, equity, and security. It is a time not just for review, but for action.

Hearing the Voices of the Poor

My colleagues and I decided that, in order to map our own course for the future, we needed to know more about our clients as individuals. We therefore launched a study titled *Voices of the Poor* and spoke with poor people about their hopes, their aspirations, their realities. Teams from the Bank and from nongovernmental organizations have gathered the voices of 60,000 men and women in 60 countries. Let me share with you our findings.

Poverty is much more than a matter of income alone. The poor seek a sense of well-being, which is peace of mind; it is good health, community, and safety; it is choice and freedom, as well as a steady source of income. Well-being is having the chance to grasp new economic opportunities, something the poor feel much less able to do today than a decade ago. Well-being is personal security. More women are working outside the household now, trying to make ends meet, but gender inequity at home persists, and domestic violence is on the rise. And corruption is a daily fact of life as the poor try to access public services and make a living.

What do the poor reply when we ask what might make the greatest difference to their lives? They say, organizations of their own so that they may negotiate with government, with traders, and with NGOs; direct assistance through community-driven programs, so that they may shape their own destinies; local ownership of funds, so that they may put a stop to corruption. They want NGOs and governments to be accountable to *them*.

Let me share with you their world in their own words:

- An old woman in Africa: "A better life for me is to be healthy, peaceful, and to live without hunger."
- A middle-aged man in Eastern Europe: "To be well is to know what will happen to me tomorrow."
- A young man in the Middle East: "Nobody is able to communicate our problems. Who represents us? Nobody."
- A woman in Latin America: "I do not know whom to trust, the police or the criminals. Our public safety is ourselves. We work and hide indoors."
- A mother in South Asia: "When my child asks for something to eat, I say the rice is cooking until he falls asleep from hunger, for there is no rice."

These are strong voices, voices of dignity. Many represent a new generation seeking control of their lives. These people are assets, not objects of charity. They can build their future, given opportunity and hope. They are talking about security, a better life for their children, peace, family, and freedom from anxiety and fear. As we sit comfortably here in Washington, we must hear their aspirations, for they are no different from our own.

No, the crisis is not over, Mr. Chairman. The challenge has barely begun. Next month our global population will reach 6 billion. On current trends we will not meet the International Development Goal of halving poverty by 2015, nor will we meet the goal of universal primary education by 2015. On current trends we will not meet the goal of reversing the current loss of environmental resources, both nationally and globally, by that date. In 25 years' time, those 6 billion people on our planet will grow to 8 billion. Of the 6 billion today, 3 billion live on less than two dollars a day, and 1.3 billion on less than one dollar a day. These extraordinary statistics may rise to 4 billion and 1.8 billion, respectively. This is not a legacy to leave our children.

The number of conflicts seems likely to be higher, the quality of our environment poorer, the disparities between rich and poor wider. The voices of the poor will be louder. But will they be heard?

Becoming Doers of Development

Mr. Chairman, what have we learned about development? We have learned that development is possible but not inevitable, that growth is essential but not sufficient to ensure the reduction of poverty. We have learned that we must put poverty front and center. We have learned that we must take the social and the structural hand in hand with the macroeconomic and the financial. We have learned that, for development to be real and effective, we need local ownership and local participation. Gone are the days when development can be done behind closed doors in Washington or in other Western capitals, or in any capital for that matter.

At a recent meeting in Stockholm to assess progress on the Comprehensive Development Framework, President [Benjamin] Mkapa of Tanzania said, "Ownership of development policies and programs is not only an understandably nationalist yearning, an inherent and sovereign right, but it also creates the most fervent disposition and conditions for hard work and for self development, both at the national and the local level." "Our people must be encouraged and facilitated," he said, "to be owners of their development: not just beneficiaries, but *doers* of development."

We must heed this call as we plan our development agendas in the years ahead. But we must go further. We must recognize our own role in helping, not hindering, those *doers* of development by better coordinating our own activities. It is shameful that Tanzania must produce 2,400 quarterly reports a year for its donors. It is shameful that Tanzania must suffer 1,000 missions from donors a year. And Tanzania is by no means alone.

So how do we proceed? Mr. Chairman, it was in recognition of the need to better coordinate our efforts, to recognize the holistic nature of development, and to put the country firmly in the driver's seat that we launched the

CDF this year. Our aim was simple: to merge the social and the structural aspects of development with the macroeconomic and the financial, so as to establish a much more balanced and effective approach; to bring the players together so as to leverage all our activities; and to work with the broad development community—the United Nations, the European Union, bilateral donors and lenders, regional development banks, civil society, and the private sector—to build a new generation of genuine partnerships.

What are the results so far? Together with our partners, we are piloting the CDF in 13 countries. We are learning to cooperate and to coordinate our work better at the local level. After discussions with many ministers, I believe that the approach of the CDF is now widely supported—not as a blueprint, but as a process through which we pursue long-term, results-driven development, with the country in the driver's seat and in partnership with the broad development community.

Very shortly, the Development Assistance Committee of the Organisation for Economic Co operation and Development will report on its review of bilateral and multilateral initiatives along lines similar to the CDF. It will conclude that the need for partnership and more coordinated efforts is widely recognized and accepted.

I am delighted, too, that we have reached a historic agreement with the IMF to develop common poverty reduction strategies with our client governments. We will take a balanced approach, linking macroeconomic and financial parameters with the human, structural, and social aspects, in one document that will guide the programs of each institution.

Strengthening Governance

But, Mr. Chairman, in the course of the last 12 months, I believe we have also learned something else. We have learned that the causes of financial crises and of poverty are one and the same. Countries may come up with sound fiscal and monetary policies, but if they do not have good governance; if they do not confront the issue of corruption; if they do not have a complete legal system that protects human rights, property rights, and contracts, that provides a framework for bankruptcy laws and a predictable tax system; if they do not have an open, well-regulated, and transparent financial system, their development is fundamentally flawed and will not last.

What use is the lawbook if the judges are corrupt, if the poorest and most vulnerable expect only brutality from the police? What use is constitutional protection, if women face discrimination in the marketplace and violence at home? What use is the foreign investor, if there are no accounting standards and requirements for transparency, no laws governing contract, and no predictable and fair tax system? What use is privatization, if there are no social safety nets to deal with unemployment, and no rules to protect the public from private monopoly? These holes in institutional development and governance and the lack of adequate and fairly paid staff allow policymaking, service delivery, and accountability to corrode.

Mr. Chairman, we have learned, both from our general experience and from our pilot CDF programs, that strengthening the organization, human capacity, and structure of the state, at both the central and the local levels, is the first priority in our challenge to reduce poverty. We have learned that when we sequence the steps of the CDF, we must give the greatest emphasis first to strengthening governance and to building capacity in government and civil society.

That decision is confirmed by a recent UNDP [United Nations Development Programme] survey of 150 resident coordinators of development assistance. Over half gave top priority to the need to strengthen governance and build capacity. It is supported by a recent survey of over 3,600 private firms in 69 countries, which identified the need for strong institutions and rulemaking. It is supported by our own consultations with the poor, who repeated the same cries over and over: too much corruption, too much violence, too much powerlessness and weakness. They long for a system that gives them equity and voice. And if they cannot have this through the ballot box or through government, they want it through informal organization outside government.

What will it really take to move from powerlessness to a democratic culture? from weakness to capacity for action? from violence to peace and equity? First and foremost, it will take real commitment from the leadership of each country, both the elected leaders and those with financial power and influence. It will take a willingness to reform systems of government, regulations, and institutions. It will take strong support for building capacity. It will take police forces that are no longer seen as agents of oppression rather than of protection and security. It will take strong local institutions to bring government closer to the poor. It will take empowering local people to design and implement their own programs, because far less is lost in corruption when a community manages its own resources.

Whether you look at it at the government or the community level; whether you look through the prism of financial crisis or of human need; whether you speak to investors and bankers or to the dispossessed, governance and capacity are key. With poverty reduction front and center of our agenda, our work at the rock face must be governance, institutions, and capacity building.

Studies are already showing what we surely knew intuitively, that good governance is associated with higher GNP per capita, higher adult literacy, and lower infant mortality, and that bad governance—lack of accountability and transparency, corruption, and crime—is the number-one impediment to development and poverty reduction. Weak governance threatens to undermine the HIPC Initiative, which will work only if the resources that are freed are purposefully used to reduce poverty. With weak governance there will be no progress in education, health, water, energy, or rural and urban development. Weak governance threatens to marginalize countries and whole peoples from the economic mainstream and to keep them there on the margins. For if lending is effective only in countries with sound policies and sound institutions, who will lend to the poor performers?

At the Bank we propose to give great emphasis in the years ahead to the question of working with governments to strengthen structure and governance. Do we have all the answers? No. Do we have all the expertise? Certainly not. We can achieve success only through partnership with others in the development community, including civil society and the private sector. Within the next few months we will join with the UNDP, which has special skills and experience in this area, and with others to look at what each of us is doing to improve governance and capacity building. We will assess the strengths and experience that each of us brings and determine how we might all go forward together.

Mr. Chairman, such an agenda requires that we focus on the interrelatedness of the systems that make societies function effectively. It requires that we focus on sound public governance systems with checks and balances, and that governments take up the fight against corruption. It requires building legal and judicial systems that protect the rights of citizens and their endeavors, going beyond big-ticket government and business deals. Corruption is a core poverty issue, because it robs from the poor the little they have. We must focus on financial and banking systems that inspire equal confidence in global investors and in peasant farmers with small savings, especially women. We must have modern corporate procedures, including accounting, audit, and disclosure policies at the highest level. We must focus on microcredit schemes, on finance for small and medium-size enterprises, and on microinsurance schemes that work both in times of crisis and in ordinary times.

We must train well-organized and well-motivated civil servants and civic leaders who see the purpose of their jobs in delivering to the communities they serve. And we must remember that this training rests in turn on effective teaching and effective learning. We must concentrate on building strong local official *and* civil society institutions that inspire trust. For there can be no doubt that strong institutions at the local level are the real key to effective poverty reduction.

It takes more than changing formal rules to build these institutions. It means changing the informal rules and norms. It means building people, building values, and building skills and incentives that can support peoples committed to change.

A new model is emerging in Africa, called the Partnership for Capacity Building. It has taken just two years to move from concept to action. It is African-led and will be implemented by Africans. It involves the direct support and collaboration of the Bank, the IMF, the UNDP, and the African Development Bank, and it is rooted in partnership with the private sector and civil society. We have pledged $150 million to supporting this endeavor. We will all join with our African colleagues to support them in a coordinated and urgent effort to achieve their objectives.

But we must remember President Mkapa's enjoinder. We must create *doers* of development. Too many capacity-building efforts have foundered in the past because they have not been rooted in local ownership.

Building a New Development Architecture

Mr. Chairman, I have spoken at length about the complexity of reaching our goals at the country level. But we know that nations are dependent on one another; they are no longer the sole masters of their destinies. We also need *global* rules and changes in *global* behavior. We need a new international *development* architecture to parallel the new global financial architecture.

What might such an international development architecture look like? First, it would be a coalition built on the cooperation of all the players: the United Nations, governments, multilateral institutions, the private sector, and civil society. It would be a coalition between recipients and donors and the citizens of donor countries, a coalition based on results. There must be effective performance in utilizing development assistance, corruption-free and reaching the poor. Voters want to see that their assistance makes a difference. The goodwill exists; performance is what is needed.

Second, it would be a coalition in which we recognize that, yes, we must break the chains of debt, but we must also have the resources to go much further and break the chains of poverty. The HIPC debt forgiveness we have already announced is the beginning of our challenge, not the end.

Third, it would be a coalition that recognizes that we must have a trade system that works, with rules and norms that are fair, comprehensive, and inclusive. We need a Development Round of trade negotiations for the 21st century.

Fourth, it would be a coalition that recognizes that the environment knows no borders. We need to implement international agreements on climate change, desertification, and biological diversity, just as we did with ozone depletion. We must move to action on these global conventions. We must ensure that the Global Environment Facility is fully funded to do its work.

Fifth, it would be a coalition that recognizes the power of modern research to democratize health, to harness new vaccines to eradicate AIDS, malaria, tuberculosis, and polio.

Sixth, it would be a coalition to make the information revolution truly universal, to bridge the growing knowledge gap, to connect all developing and transition economies to the world and to each other, to be a real vehicle for sharing and learning via satellite, e-mail, and the Internet. For there is no doubt that the technological revolution will have an enormous impact on the substance of development.

Mr. Chairman, globalization can be more than the unleashed forces of the global market. It can also be the unleashing of our combined effort and expertise to reach global solutions.

We need to build *coalitions for change:* coalitions with the private sector, which will bring investment, create jobs, promote the transfer of technology and skills, and foster social responsibility; coalitions with civil society and communities, to mobilize the kind of grassroots support we have seen behind the debt-relief campaign and extend it to health, to education for all, to participation, and to poverty reduction; coalitions with governments, to assist them in taking charge of their own development agendas with the participation of their citizens; coalitions with each other, to put an end to the turf battles, the waste, and the duplication; coalitions with religious communities, with trade unions, and with foundations, to benefit our common work; coalitions of commitment to the seven United Nations pledges on sustainable development, gender, education, infant and child mortality, maternal mortality, reproductive health, and the environment. I pledge to you our intention to work with all our partners to help build those coalitions for change, so that, when we meet next year in Prague, we will have begun to put in place that new development architecture.

Meeting the Challenge

Mr. Chairman, I have outlined a complex agenda. Is the Bank gearing up to meet this challenge? I believe, unequivocally, yes. On governance we are already spending over $5 billion a year, working on civil service reform, budget management, tax administration, decentralization, legal reform, judicial reform, and institution building. We are working with over two dozen countries on anticorruption programs. We are helping train judges; we run public national workshops that bring corruption into the bright glare of sunlight; we even train investigative journalists, conscious that a free and professional press is a society's voice.

On the sharing of knowledge, we have made dramatic progress over the last four years. Our Knowledge Bank brings us closer together through distance learning using satellite connectivity. And it takes knowledge to faraway places by closing the information infrastructure gap, by reaching students through the African Virtual University, and, through our WorldLinks program, by connecting schoolchildren in the industrialized world with their brothers and sisters in the developing world.

We have undertaken a major project to clear slums, through programs built on the efforts of the local people, by introducing land titles and self-sustaining projects for infrastructure. With the World Wildlife Fund we have built a powerful alliance to save our forests; with the private sector, the United Nations, and foundations we are building a Global Alliance for Vaccines and Immunization, an AIDS Vaccine Task Force, and a malaria initiative. With over 140 different partners we have already wrestled river blindness into submission—a marvelous example of what we can do together. And we are working with local communities to build partnerships from the bottom up, through local democratic institutions as in India. We have learned that the best and most effective projects are those that are locally based and close to our real clients, people in poverty in rural and urban communities. We have learned that local ownership and involvement must be central to our new development architecture.

Is the Bank up to the challenge? I believe we have 10,000 extraordinarily gifted and committed staff in the Bank, the International Finance Corporation, and the Multilateral Investment Guarantee Agency. It has been a tough year, and I want to thank them and their families for the contributions they have made.

Mr. Chairman, we stand on the threshold of a new millennium. So much that could be possible is within our grasp. Will we have the courage and the leadership to reach out and grasp it? Will we finally recognize that we live in one world? Look around. We are linked by financial systems, by communications, by a shared environment, by trade. Migration knows no borders, nor does crime, nor drugs, nor do war and peace. Only national budgets, Mr. Chairman, stop short at frontiers. Only national elections pay little heed to that larger world.

We need leadership to explain to our peoples that our national interests are international. We must reaffirm our commitment to development and make a real commitment to each other to act on the generous statements made by so many of the leaders of industrialized countries toward the developing countries. We must find the commitment to meet the recommended level of 0.7 percent of industrial-country GNP for official development assistance. And leaders of developing and transition economies must reaffirm their commitments to carry out their promises for good governance, equality, and growth.

These commitments, Mr. Chairman, have a human and moral aspect as well. There needs to be a passionate rededication of each of us to each other as we enter the next century. All of us have to assume a responsibility for global equity, which is the only assurance of peace.

How can one not be moved by the comments of the poor, like those I shared with you earlier? By the father from Eastern Europe when he says, "Poverty is humiliation, the sense of being dependent on them, and of being forced to accept rudeness, insults, and indifference when we seek help." And by the voice of Bashiranbibi, an agricultural laborer from South Asia, when she says, "At first I was afraid of everyone and everything: my husband, the village, the police. *Today I fear no one.* I have my own bank account. I am the leader of my village's savings group. I tell my sisters about our movement."

Mr. Chairman, we must look forward, we must commit ourselves to bring about the day when the poor of the world, the hopeful youth, the aged, the street children, the disabled, the rural workers, the slum dwellers, will all be able to cry out, *"Today I fear no one. Today I fear no one."*

1999: FACING THE NEW MILLENNIUM
WITH CLARITY OF MISSION

Message from the president and chairman from the 1999 World Bank *Annual Report*

OCTOBER 1999

This Chairman's Message covers the year from July 1998 to June 1999 and talks about the Bank's growing partnerships as embodied in the Comprehensive Development Framework.

Our *Annual Report* is always an opportunity to pause and take a good, hard look at where we have been, what we have learned, and where we should be going. This year all the more so. As the special moment of passage that is the new millennium approaches, we are more than usually challenged to confront our future with a better understanding of our past. We must invigorate this special moment with an exceptional clarity of mission.

It is two years since the financial crisis of the late 1990s began in East Asia. Since I last reported to you, we have confronted further dangers in Russia and in Brazil. Now there are signs of recovery in a number of countries, some of them remarkable. Elsewhere, the pain lingers on. If we can harness the energies of lessons learned in this tough classroom of crisis, I am optimistic that we will deal more effectively with such challenges in the future.

Most important, what we call the "financial crisis" is now understood to go far beyond that. At the core of the various crises have been the very structural and social building blocks of society, and, of course, bearing the brunt of these crises have been the millions of citizens who found no refuge. Institutional and governance reform and the provision of some harbor for the most vulnerable have been central to the Bank's work of the past 12 months. Crisis has changed and challenged the very way in which we work and the instruments and necessary flexibility we have to do that work. And we have been flexible: the Bank has developed new lending approaches, and our levels of efficiency and quality are up, as you will read in the pages of this report.

Crisis has also alerted us to focus intently on the interrelatedness of policy and structure, and people. I am quite convinced that we will not get one right without the other. And this is clearly true at all levels of society. The Comprehensive Development Framework that we are piloting is the Bank's vision of how we might take this understanding forward. It is a formulation that stresses partnership, shared goals, and an integrated approach to what needs to be done. In the driving seat of both developing and implementing this agenda is—and must be—the country itself. The Bank's role will be defined by what we can best bring to the mix, as I hope will be the role of our many other development partners. We have found broad support for this comprehensive approach, and I thank those who have enthusiasm for the partnership that this requires of all of us.

But just as crisis has worked to rally us around a wider and deeper agenda, it has also called our attention to the sobering fact that the number of people in poverty is rising. Yes, the fight against poverty has made gains: life expectancy has risen, infant mortality has dropped, and there are more girls in school than before. But achieving our agreed goal to halve the incidence of poverty by 2015 now requires a strengthening of effort. In many of the poorest developing countries, progress on poverty reduction and sustainable development is lagging. These silent crises require as much energy of us as those crises that grab the headlines.

To do all this will take partnerships the likes of which we have not seen before. I am convinced that our work with the private sector will leap ahead as the millennium turns and companies understand the scale of corporate social responsibility that will make a real difference. Partnerships with civil society will and must underpin everything we do, as new areas of work in governance, postconflict, environment, cultural heritage, and the development of social capital become very much a part of the Bank's workaday agenda. This report is as much about the Bank and its multiple partners as it is a Bank report, and that is as it should be.

The fight against poverty is not a fight for glory. It is about equity and social justice, about the environment and the resources we all share, and about peace and security. It is a fight for a better life for all of us and for our children who will live in this very interconnected world.

CULTURE IS THE BASE OF DEVELOPMENT

Remarks at Culture Counts: A Conference on Financing, Resources, and the
Economics of Culture in Sustainable Development

FLORENCE, ITALY | OCTOBER 4, 1999

> *In a very accessible and eloquent speech, Wolfensohn demonstrates his
> appreciation of the cultural wealth of poor countries. He makes the case that
> preservation of indigenous cultures is "not an optional extra—it is an essential
> element in the development process."*

Deputy Mayor Brasca,* Signora Marcucci,† Distinguished Colleagues, Ladies and Gentlemen:

May I first of all thank you, Minister Dini,‡ for your remarkable address, and
for your friendship and for the support your government has given not only
to this conference, but to the whole issue of culture and development over
many years. We would not be here today were it not for you, and were it not
for the help of Director-General Bonetti,§ for which we are very grateful, Minister [Vincenzo] Petrone of the Directorate-General for Development Cooperation, and Minister Melandri,** and all of those associated with the Italian
government in this effort.

I would especially like to thank Franco Passacantando, the Executive Director of our Bank for Italy, who has ensured that I am here. I am grateful to
him for that.

This is a remarkable gathering in a remarkable place. And we are all, I think,
enormously indebted to the municipality of Florence and to the regional government of Tuscany for all they have done to make this possible. I should also
acknowledge our other partners, represented here by Hernan Crespo-Toral of
UNESCO [United Nations Educational, Scientific, and Cultural Organiza-
tion], who is clearly our leader in all of our activities in the area of culture, and
without whom the world would be a much poorer place.

I should tell you how personally moved I am to be here. You may or may
not know that I was born in Australia. And Australia, when I was growing up,
was not exactly the cultural center of the world. In fact, everybody there referred to England as home, and the great hope of many young Australians was
to go to England, because that was the source of all knowledge.

---

* Alberto Brasca, deputy mayor of Florence.
† Marialina Marcucci, former vice president of the Tuscan region.
‡ Minister of Foreign Affairs and former Prime Minister of Italy Lamberto Dini.
§ Director-General for Cultural Promotion and Relations of the Italian Ministry of Foreign Affairs Gianfranco
Facco Bonetti.
** Italian Minister of Cultural Heritage and Activities Giovanna Melandri.

I see Lord Rothschild here, who for many years ran the cultural activities in England. No disrespect to you, Lord Rothschild, but to me it was strange. We in Australia lived on the edge of Asia, but Asian culture had no impact on us. I was taught nothing of the aborigines, nothing of our local culture. I had to learn a rather distant British history, study the kings and queens, and as a consequence I failed history and failed a lot of my studies. It was of total disinterest to me.

So I took refuge in music, and later music became my passport. Through music, I was able to meet friends, develop an international association, subsequently run Carnegie Hall in New York, and come to the understanding that culture was the thing that united us all.

And I felt very timid the first time I came to Florence, because I felt that this is part of my history, but I am ignorant of it. So I set about learning. And I found, for myself, that life was enriched by this cultural voyage. It was, if you like, elitist in one sense, but it was also very basic. It was history; it was part of my formation.

And then I became president of the World Bank, and I started traveling. And on my first trip to Africa, I visited Mali. And in Mali I discovered a place called Timbuktu. I had always thought Timbuktu was a creature of my father's imagination. I don't know whether you have the same idiom in Italy, but in Australia, if your father wants to get rid of you, he says, "Go to Timbuktu." I thought it was some amazing place unrelated to reality. And I discovered that, once, Timbuktu was a great center and that Mali once had had an empire that stretched to Egypt.

And I met with some young Malians, and I saw them dance, and I talked with them. And for them this ancient past was becoming part of their reality. It was their birthright, it was their strength, it was something on which they could build, notwithstanding the fact that theirs is one of the poorest countries in Africa. And I started to think that maybe culture is important to others, not just me. It may not be Etruscan, and maybe it is not the culture of the Renaissance, but it is a national culture.

And then I went to the hills of Guatemala, and I met there with Mayan elders who told me of their long history. They told me of how, before the West was doing astronomy and mathematics and working out the principles of engineering, they were already engaged in these practices and building vast monuments and studying the stars, and they were developing their own concepts of philosophy and humanism. This was a totally different culture, now dramatically weakened, but nevertheless fighting to exist.

To my shame, I then saw a school that the World Bank was building next door to the room in which the elders were meeting with me. It was a red brick schoolhouse with a tiled roof, with no allusion whatsoever to Mayan culture. It could have been in any suburb of the United States or European capital. And I thought how crazy it was that, with no additional cost, but with a little bit of sensitivity and a little bit of understanding, we could have linked that educational institution to the history of the Mayan culture.

And so it is that, over the five years of my odyssey at the Bank, I have come to learn that culture indigenous to the countries in which we operate is a fundamental base on which development can occur. It is not all related to this palazzo; it is related to the country's own indigenous history. These are histories that themselves are rich, that are important, that form the basis for the people of these many different countries and, for us, of a global future. And so I have become deeply committed to this issue of culture—not as a matter of elitism, not as a passport to dinner tables where one can meet brilliant and accomplished people, but as a basic element in development.

We at the Bank have an interesting challenge. There are 6 billion people in the world today. Of those 6 billion, 3 billion live on less than two dollars a day. A billion, three hundred million live in absolute poverty, on less than one dollar a day. In the next 25 years that 6 billion will grow to 8 billion. And, if we do not change what we are doing, 4 billion of that 8 billion will live on less than two dollars a day, and 1.8 billion will live in absolute poverty.

The demographics and the count of 8 billion are correct and given. The issue for us is how we can help improve the lives of the 1.8 billion and of the 4 billion. This is not a theoretical challenge. This is the challenge of the first 25 years of the next millennium.

And so my colleagues and I at the Bank have tried to think how we can deal with this challenge. The first aspect is, of course, money. Financial assistance is the issue that we read about in the context of the Asian crisis, and the Russian crisis, and the Brazilian crisis, as we put together macroeconomic packages and fiscal packages, as we talk of restoring financial strength. And financial assistance is, of course, crucial to growth.

But there is a whole other side that one needs to deal with. It is the social side: the human, the political, the structural; legal systems, justice systems, financial systems; education, health, power, water, communications; rural strategy and urban strategy, as more and more of the poor move into towns and cities.

And there are still other essential elements, and among them are the environment and culture. You *cannot* come up with a plan for development that ignores the environment and ignores culture. That is the world we live in. That is the world that we need to preserve and to create.

Let me just share with you a recent experience that we have had in the Bank. We decided that we would go out and talk to poor people. We went out to 60 countries, and we interviewed 60,000 poor people. We conducted one-on-one interviews to find out what it means to be poor, what it is that people want. And what they want is not just money. It is what they call a sense of well-being. It is good health, it is care of the spirit, it is family and community, and happiness. It is a choice of freedom, as well as a source of steady income.

And when you listen closely to what they say to us, you find they are concerned about threats to their security, about physical survival, about crime, violence, and corruption. They are concerned about their vulnerability, their weakness in terms of their ability to negotiate and to bargain, and they are concerned about their social connectedness, their need to have a social context, their need to have their culture.

A woman in Ukraine said to us, "Without these simple human signs of solidarity, our lives would be unbearable." It is the richness of the spirit, it is the richness of their history that these people want, not just money. They want security, they want a chance for their children, they want identity. They want the same things we do, these 1.8 billion people who 25 years from now may live in absolute poverty.

We at the Bank are deeply moved by this study. It has confirmed to us what we have been thinking in recent years. It has confirmed to us the importance of our relationship with UNESCO, of our activities with the government of Italy and with other partners in this room, and it has become a central element in our own development programming.

And what is this culture? Let me quote to you from the World Commission on Culture and Development, in a 1995 report titled *Our Creative Diversity*. It says that "culture is a whole complex of distinctive spiritual, material, intellectual, and emotional features that characterize the society or societal group. It includes creative expression, oral history, language, literature, performing arts, fine arts and crafts, community practice, traditional healing methods, traditional natural resource management, celebrations and patterns of social interaction that contribute to group and individual welfare, and, of course, material or built forms such as sites, buildings, historic city centers, landscape, arts and objects."

That, of course, is a very broad definition. But it is clear that culture is not something that is an optional extra, it is not a luxury, it is not something that is added on after you give someone money so that person can eat. The poor tell us that *all* of that is part of poverty and wealth. Why should poor people be any different from those of us privileged to be in this room? These are not animals; these are people. And the preservation of their culture is not an extra. It is an essential element in the development process. And that, of course, is why we are so anxious at this meeting to participate in discussions with you, to see how we can do a better job and how we can move forward together.

Of course, not all culture and not all history are remarkable. In a quite spectacular address at our Bank-Fund Annual Meetings last week, Professor Wole Soyinka, who is a Nobel laureate and a Nigerian, talked about Christiane Amanpour, who, as a CNN reporter, is part of the global culture. In preparing a report on Ghana, its history and its present, Amanpour discovered that young girls were still being taken in as "brides of the gods" by religious ministers. As they reached the age of about 10, these young girls became essentially slaves, on the basis that this was part of the culture and part of the area's history. And, in an astonishing interview, she spoke to the ministers, who quite openly talked about their slaves and about these girls, who were treated in the most despicable ways. This was part of their culture, they said. This is something that they needed to have to deal with their sense of cultural history.

Professor Soyinka went on to point out that "culture is a matrix of infinite possibilities and choices." He says, "from within the same cultural matrix, we can extract arguments and strategies for degradation or ennoblement, for enslavement or liberation, for the suppression of productive potential or the enhancement." And, indeed, we have to be realistic in knowing that there is choice in culture. But that choice must be understood, it must be opened, it must be made transparent, and it is for the current generation to choose.

We have had quite some experience in our institution in promoting cultural endeavors. We seek, first of all, to engage this cultural heritage in all of the things we do in our normal development activities. And, second, we try to create activities that are especially designed to promote culture, such as restoration of cities or cultural programs. But it is in our normal programs that culture can play such an important role. Let me give you some not very remarkable examples of our efforts.

In Guatemala we set up health clinics, which were very badly needed. But the local people refused to go to them because they were used to going to their own traditional healers. So we had this wonderful set of health clinics and no clients. We therefore invited the healers to come and work in the clinics alongside the medical practitioners, and the moment we did that, we had full houses. The endorsement was there and people came.

In Pakistan we decided that we should build houses for people. So we put out a tender, we picked the lowest bid, and we built thousands of concrete, one-story houses. No one went into them. We had forgotten that everyone there built two-story houses. Why? Because in the winter people can live on the top story, where they have the benefit of the sun, and in the summer, when it is very hot, they have it cool in the lower story. So we went around and added a story, and then everybody used our houses.

In Africa one of the first issues that I faced was that of literacy. In that same trip to Mali I described earlier—I will never forget it—my wife and I went to a school, and there we saw a group of young Malians learning French. And on the walls there were these wonderful posters in French showing an ambulance coming to an accident, where a car had hit a fire hydrant, and one of the kids in the poster was calling out, "*Au secours!*" The only problem was that these kids in rural Mali had never seen an ambulance, had never seen a fire hydrant. Few of them had seen a car. So for them learning French was like learning a language from another planet. There was no relationship between what they were doing and their immediate environment. And so now we, together with the Library of Congress, the International Federation of Library Associations, the New York Public Library, the Carnegie Foundation, and many others, including some international nongovernmental organizations, are dealing with indigenous languages and putting libraries into villages and towns that relate to the local culture.

We are also linking, in many countries through our World Net program, schools in developing countries with schools in developed countries. I will give you a personal example. I was in Uganda visiting and then traveled directly to Wyoming, a state in the West of the United States, in the Rocky Mountains. I was asked to speak by the local chamber of commerce. They said, "What can we do?" I said, "Well, why don't we link your school here in Wyoming with a school in Uganda?" A totally preposterous notion: the Wyoming people had never heard of Uganda, and the people in Uganda had never heard of Wyoming. But, in fact, three months later, with assistance from a Ugandan insurance company and help from the telecommunications people, we started a program of linking schools in the developed world with schools in the developing world. We now have 400 schools linked together, crisscrossing the world.

The advantage of this is not just that the Ugandans learn something from American culture; it is also that American culture learns something from Uganda. We have linked schools in France and Spain to schools in Latin America and Africa. And these kids are now growing up conscious of their culture, and they are sharing their culture on equal terms with boys and girls in other countries. This story shows that cultures do not need to be static or limited just to villages or a single location. With modern technology the possibilities now exist for interconnectedness, for kids in Wyoming and in Canada and other places to obtain enrichment from activities going on in the developing world.

These are issues that we need to face as we enter the new millennium. It will be a millennium of linkage. There will be pressures to have singular values, pressures of globalization, pressures of McDonald's, pressures of Coca-Cola. What is crucial for us, as we think about culture and development, is to recognize that the maintenance of heritage, of culture, of individual history is a mandatory building block on which development within countries and around our globe needs to occur.

From my odyssey of the last five years, I have become convinced that there is a world outside Australia, a world outside Florence. It is a world of 4.8 billion people, a developing world that in 25 years will be 6.8 billion people. This is a world that we have to preserve, a world of richness, a world in which people need to build on their heritage. We are working in places from India to China and in Fez, Bangkok, Timbuktu, and all over the world to try and give people the sense of identity, the sense of belonging, the sense of family. It requires all of our help from civil society, from the private sector, from governments. But, most important, it requires help from all of you.

We are here not just to take advantage of the chance to come to another conference. We have a responsibility, as a result of this conference, to take from here the message, and try and make people understand, that culture is not an adornment, not a luxury, not elitism. Culture is humanity.

Thank you very much.

Wolfensohn on Culture

". . . The issue of culture and development is not one that we regard as controversial. We start from the proposition that you cannot have development without a recognition of culture and of history. In a world that is becoming increasingly globalized, in a world where there are pressures for cultural homogeneity across all our countries, what is abundantly clear is that it is essential for us to nurture, to prize, to revere, and to support the culture and the history of the countries in which we operate. Very simply, we do not believe that you can move forward unless you recognize the base and the past from which we have come.

"This is not some wild, exotic idea. This is not a view of an elitist. This is a view that you find in villages and in slums and in parts of countries where people, however bereft of physical resources, are turning back to their culture and their history . . ."

From an address at a conference on Culture and Sustainable Development: Investing in the Promise of Societies, Washington, D.C., September 28, 1998

Remarks at the Ninth International Anti-Corruption Conference

DURBAN, SOUTH AFRICA | OCTOBER 11, 1999

Building on his 1996 "cancer of corruption" speech, Wolfensohn urges developing countries in this speech in South Africa to take action on corruption. Inaction, he warns, threatens foreign aid by donors who are increasingly demanding that their money be used wisely.

Mr. Chairman, Your Majesty, Mr. President, Distinguished Colleagues, Ladies and Gentlemen:

First let me say how delighted I am to be at this meeting. I want to congratulate the organizers and my friends in the other institutions, particularly Transparency International, on the work they have done.

Let me say, too, that, as far as our institution is concerned, there is nothing more important than the issue of corruption. I say this not because it is in the headlines today or because it is a subject that the press deals with, whether it be in Asia or in Russia or on the continent of Africa. I say it because we at the World Bank start with the issue of poverty as central to our objective. And on that issue we are very worried. We are worried because the incidence of poverty is not diminishing; it is increasing. And at the core of the incidence of poverty is the issue of equity. And at the core of the issue of equity is the issue of corruption.

We have today, as I think you all know, 6 billion people on our planet, 3 billion of them living on less than two dollars a day, and 1.3 billion of them living in absolute poverty, on less than a dollar a day. In 25 years we will have another 2 billion people sharing our planet, and we might well have as many as 1.8 billion people living in [absolute] poverty. And the 3 billion people living on less than two dollars a day now could grow to be as many as 4 billion.

What this means is that the issue of corruption is not just the focus of some interest group. It is not some issue on the periphery. It means that we have got to change things if we are going to have a better and more peaceful world. And it means that we are going to have to confront an issue that President [Thabo] Mbeki* [of South Africa] talked about last night, namely, that our work in development is not just about the monetary values we apply to things. It is about trying to return to something that has essential value; it is about social justice and equity. It is about a return to values. It is about a return to a system that is likely to lead to a better life for more people.

We have just done a study at the Bank to find out what poor people think. We have had individual discussions in 60 countries, with 60,000 people, and what is interesting is the consistency with which these people respond. What is also interesting is the centrality of corruption in their comments:

- In Malawi a poor fisherman said that every cabinet minister has a big vessel for catching fish.
- In Ecuador the poor said the government should make sure that congressmen do not steal.
- In Uzbekistan someone said, "Unless I pay 25,000, I can't get a position, and therefore I am still pulling a cart in Tashkent."
- In Bangladesh someone said, "No one can count on the judgment of the commissioner, since he does not work for the poor. He is biased toward the landlord."

Our report goes on to say the following:

Again and again, in country after country and site after site, poor women and men spoke of corruption. It took many forms: corruption in the distribution of seeds, medicines and social assistance for the destitute and vulnerable; corruption in getting loans; corruption in getting teachers to teach; corruption in customs and border crossings; corruption in the construction of roads; corruption in getting permission to move in and out of cities or stay in certain areas; corruption in street and market trading; and corruption in identity cards. In many places the poor reported having to pay managers, hooligans, and the police "protection" money to save themselves from the worst forms of harassment, theft, and abuse.

This study takes corruption down from the level of megacrime to the level of a disease that permeates society. And it is felt by the poorest levels of society. During the Asian crisis the stories in the headlines were about putting together multi-billion-dollar packages, and the press played up whether the package was $17 billion or $42 billion or some other amount. In the policy discussion the issues were whether capital market reforms should be introduced and what kind of macroeconomic adjustment was needed, and everybody had their own theory. Meanwhile what was going on behind the scenes was devastation for the poor.

For the first time in Thailand, children were being forced to stay out of school to protect their homes from people coming back to their villages expecting support, and theft arose. There were huge increases in the number of children being sold into prostitution. People who had worked for years in small and medium-size enterprises in Korea found themselves without jobs, without credit. There were massive increases in the numbers of the unemployed.

And so, as was later demonstrated, the real impact of the crisis was not felt by the rich or even the middle class. It was the poor that suffered. And so the issue of corruption, at all levels, becomes the issue not only for us at the World Bank, but for every government, for all members of civil society, for every corporate official, for every individual.

The question then becomes, What do we do about it? What can we do to bring about the societal change that President Mbeki spoke of last night? And what is clear is that the task is not just for a single person to take on. It is not even for a single conference to achieve. What is great about this conference is that we have, in this room, representatives of all sectors of society, and the first thing that we have to do is come together and recognize it.

As president of the Bank and leading a very committed team, I, too, have had to think, What is it that we at the Bank can do? Surely, we get blamed for most things, and we frequently get blamed for the existence of corruption. In fact, if there is something corrupt in a project in which we are operating, more often than not I get a letter blaming *us* for having allowed it to happen. More often than not, if a government official steals something, it is blamed on a lack of control and supervision in *our* practices. Let me say to these critics that we at the Bank have moral standards no less than anybody else. In fact, we feel deeply that corruption is the thing that can make the difference in whether our projects are effective or ineffective.

But imagine yourself running the Bank and trying to decide what it is that you can do to make a difference. What can we, as an institution, do to bring about a change in societal values, in a whole series of countries, globally, in developed and developing countries alike, but in our case particularly in the developing and transition economies in which 4.8 billion people live? Two of those countries alone, China and India, account for 2.2 billion. In the remaining 2.6 billion we have more than 140 different governments and systemic arrangements with which to deal—more than 140 presidents and parliaments, tens of thousands of government officials. And all these countries have different regulatory frameworks, different traditions, different weightings between who has power and who does not.

So, as a practical matter, we have decided a few things, which I would like to put in front of you today. The first is that we have to recognize the issue of corruption as central. It was only three years ago that a president of the World Bank and a head of the International Monetary Fund first mentioned the word "corruption" in public. Why? Because, when I arrived at the Bank, I was told, "You don't talk about the C-word, because it is a political issue. The Bank is owned by governments, and your charter does not allow you to enter into the political field. And corruption is something that affects politics, so stay away. Deal with your projects, but don't talk about the C-word."

Well, three years ago, we redefined corruption and said that corruption was not just political, but the single most significant factor in bringing about development, equity, and social justice. And six months later every minister at the Development Committee‡ meetings was making a speech on corruption, even those from countries where one might have expected them to be somewhat embarrassed about it. But today everybody talks about corruption, and we have put it at the center of every finance ministry's agenda. That was an enormous step forward.

The second thing that emerged in those discussions, as we told the ministers, was that no statement from the World Bank or the Fund or any international body, not even from my dear friend [UN Secretary-General] Kofi Annan, will ensure that every country gets rid of corruption. Corruption can only be dealt with, in my judgment, by a combination of commentary and assistance, in part from the outside but, most importantly, from the inside, within countries themselves. It can be *assisted* from the outside—the Bank and other organizations can help. But the real motivation, the real engine, has to come from the inside. And, typically, that means from the top. There must be changes at the top, because people will not believe it *unless* there are changes at the top. But the reason that one can have changes at the top is that there are forces driving them from below.

There must also be partnerships; there must be coalitions for change. And so we, as an institution, felt that the best thing we could do was to assist in the building of coalitions and in the forging of that interest in corruption and inequity. Get it out there. Get it open. Make it transparent.

We have recently completed the first stage of a really fabulous initiative, led by Daniel Kaufmann in our organization, in which, three months ago, we brought to the Bank seven country teams from Benin, Ethiopia, Ghana, Kenya, Malawi, Tanzania, and Uganda. And we said to them, You tell us what are the problems in your countries. You come up with what you think is the course of action. You tell us what you want to do, and we will try to help. And I might at this moment pay tribute to my predecessor, Bob McNamara, who has been carrying this fight for years and who voluntarily attended every day of the sessions, which was an enormous encouragement to us all. So we started with a blank worksheet, which we called a country-action matrix, on which the teams were to list the problems, the actions to be taken, by whom they would be taken, the resources needed, the expected results, and by when those results were to occur.

And we gave each of the teams that piece of paper, and for a week we sat and worked with them. What was extraordinary was both the interaction and the convergence of ideas, both in terms of how one goes about addressing the

---

‡ The Development Committee is a grouping of finance ministers representative of the Bank's member countries that meets twice a year to discuss and advise on development issues.

issue of corruption and in terms of what to do about it. These were not ideas imposed by the Bank, nor were they ideas coming from the countries' leaders. These were ideas that emerged from five people representing different sectors of society in each of seven countries. After that we continued the discussions, not in Washington but by satellite, every week, so that we had a weekly video-conference with the seven countries, run from Washington but with each of them interacting from their own countries, taking up a different aspect of the issues each week. And now we have an action plan in each country, and we will be meeting later today on those action plans. Then, in nine months' time, we are going to come back and see where they are.

This for me was a most extraordinary initiative, because it was driven from within. It strikes a balance among government, civil society, and the private sector, and it is owned and recognized and transparent. And, using a set of diagnostic survey tools, which are really rather remarkable, we are going out to different people in the society, from individuals to governments, and saying, Tell us about corruption. How does it impact you? In your judgment, how much does it cost to become a customs officer? How much does it cost to become a judge? How much does it cost to become a minister? What, in your judgment, is the cost of doing business? What is the cost of getting a contract?

And you would be amazed—amazed—at the results and the convergence of the replies. People know what these things cost, whether it be 17 or 12 or 5 percent of the position's salary. They tell you that, "So-and-so got a ministry cheap," or "So-and-so became a judge cheap." And with the transparency that comes from this exercise, and the prominence that is being given to the results, we have an opportunity to try to deal with issues that are not fictitious, but rather are practical, clear, and targetable.

The reason I am commenting on these rather practical ways of getting at this issue is that the speeches have to end. What we have to do is dive in. And

---

Wolfensohn on Corruption

". . . [W]e cannot do the most effective work in countries on corruption by indicating how it should be dealt with or by setting forth reform mechanisms. Of course, we do this, but corruption can only be addressed from the inside, in our experience. It is only when the citizens themselves decide they want to rid the country of corruption that it really happens. . . ."

From "Parliamentary Actions and Cooperation for Action," address at the Parliamentary Network of the World Bank conference, Athens, March 9, 2003

we are diving in at the level of the awareness of society itself, on the issue of transparency and on the issue of societal reform. Corruption does not exist outside a framework. You have to look at it within the framework of governance. You have to look at how a government is organized, how strong the government is, what the capacity of the people is, what the regulatory framework is, how many ministries there are. You have to ask, Is there a legal system that works? Are there honest judges? Is the financial system properly supervised? Are there capital markets? Is there transparency? Is the country's police force an agent of oppression, or an agent of support for the people?

One also has to deal with the structural issues. It is impossible to deal with corruption outside of structural reform. And that, too, needs to be dealt with transparently. So, at the Bank, we have a couple of really important initiatives, in which we are trying to provide assistance within the countries. We try first to analyze the situation, and then we agree on the course of action that the countries themselves wish to bring about. We in the Bank are only a supporting player, but we can help and we are doing those things.

Let me clarify one other point about the role of the Bank. And that is that corruption is now affecting the sources of funding and the international balance on development assistance. At this very moment, in parliaments in developed countries, the voters of those countries are saying, "We do not want to give money to any form of development assistance if it ends up in an offshore bank account." They are reading the headlines. They are reading about Russia. They are reading about Africa. They are reading about Asia. They are reading about virtually every part of the world, and not just about the people in the countries in development or transition, but also about the companies in the developed countries that are subject to the OECD agreements.[§] And what they are saying is, "Unless we can see that there is fairness and a realistic attack on corruption, we are not going to provide the money." There is the issue for us: it is not just a problem inside this or that country; rather it is a structural issue inside the whole system.

And so what I would like to say to you in closing is that we at the Bank are deeply involved at the country level. I believe we have some practical things that we are trying to do, and, equally significant, what we are trying to do is keep the balance of development assistance flowing. And at that level, too, corruption becomes a central and vital issue.

We are very happy to be part of this conference, and I thank you for the invitation to come here.

---

§ The Convention on Combating Bribery of Foreign Public Officials in International Business Transactions of the Organisation for Economic Co-operation and Development entered into force in February 1999.

POSTCONFLICT COUNTRIES AND DEFINING NEW COOPERATION IN THE HUMANITARIAN AGENDA

Remarks at the Center for Strategic and International Studies

WASHINGTON, D.C. | NOVEMBER 2, 1999

In these remarks Wolfensohn addresses the critical issue of closing the gap in the delivery of humanitarian aid at the cessation of conflict and the beginning of reconstruction. He draws on the World Bank's recent experience in assisting recovery in several postconflict situations including Bosnia and Herzegovina, Timor-Leste, Kosovo, and the West Bank and Gaza.

First of all, I am very happy that [UN High Commissioner for Refugees] Sadako Ogata is here. She is my heroine in the whole UN system. She is a remarkable woman, and if she has spoken to you, as I know she has, there is probably very little for me to say, because what there is to know about conflict and postconflict, Sadako Ogata knows and acts on. I think we are all very fortunate to have her in the UN system.

Let me say that nothing is more important to us at the World Bank—or more complicated—than the issue of dealing with postconflict situations. I just got the *New York Times* for this morning, and, to give you an idea of the sort of challenge, let me read to you what is happening in Timor-Leste at this very moment in a 40-man committee led by Klaus Rohland,* one of our colleagues.

The article says:

> Even before the recent violence that destroyed most of East Timor's buildings, the creation of a newly independent society and economy here presented a harsh case for development.
>
> Apart from roads, ports, airfields and power plants, East Timor has almost none of the basic elements of a functioning nation: no budget or banking system, no judiciary or law enforcement, no civil service, no government institutions.
>
> Its educational, health care, trade and agriculture systems are in a shambles. Most of its people are subsistence farmers; most are illiterate.

That's not a bad starting point for a problem, but it is not unique. And Klaus Rohland is now out there with a team of 40 people from 30 institutions for the purpose of trying to see how you can deal with a postconflict situation where there is practically nothing to build on.

---

* World Bank country director for Papua New Guinea, the Pacific Islands, and Timor-Leste. Timor-Leste (formerly East Timor) had recently won its independence from Indonesia.

We had already started on this issue three months ago, when we brought to Washington a number of Timorese to instruct them in the most simple and basic elements of administration. And we said, of course, that when the conflict was over, it could not just be left at that. We did not know how it would emerge, but what was particularly important to us was to make sure that the first element in postconflict reconstruction was established. And that was to develop an infrastructure of people in the local community who could take hold and who could seek to develop a framework in which a society could function. In the case of the Timorese, everything had been done in the past by the Indonesians; the interdependence was totally with Indonesia.

Then take Kosovo, where we are also working. There, too, we confronted a situation where everything had been done from the center, in this case Belgrade. Kosovo had been starved of money. It had been starved of investment. And as one visits the country—or, rather, as one visits the region—one becomes peculiarly aware that the antecedents to this conflict and to the tragedies that occurred there were, in fact, the result of interdependence with an unwelcome partner. Yet there was total dependence on that partner: total dependence for trade, total dependence for administrative functions. There are few systems of government in Kosovo, few people in an administrative capacity. So, as much as we would all like to think of an autonomous Kosovo, in fact the reconstruction is already constrained by history, because of the relationship with the former Yugoslavia and with the Serbs. In such cases the first thing one has to do is to get a grip on the total picture: a total picture of the political framework, of the structural framework, and of the economic framework.

And I say "a total picture" because all these elements touch on the very critical issues of bringing in aid and subsistence food to people, and meeting the essential needs of protection and habitation. These are the sorts of things that Mrs. Ogata addresses with such vigor. But they are certainly also not sufficient for dealing with the question of postconflict reconstruction. And as one addresses these humanitarian needs, simultaneously one has to try and build for the society a framework where there is some continuity going forward, where there is some systemic reform that allows you to start right at the beginning with the issues of comprehensive development.

I should tell you that although the Bank started 54 years ago as a reconstruction agency after World War II, some time after that we lost our way. We came into being as the IBRD, the International Bank for Reconstruction and Development, formed because of the problems created by that war. But as countries emerged and as the Western world as we know it developed, the need for the Bank to think in terms of postconflict reconstruction became more distant. And so the institution became one that dealt instead with issues of development. It dealt with the 4.8 billion out of the 6 billion people on our planet, to use current numbers, who live in developing countries. And we focused on the issue of poverty, on the 3 billion of those people who live on less than two dollars a day, and the 1.3 billion who live on less than one dollar a day. And we took our focus off of reconstruction to focus on the issues of poverty.

But we soon learned that poverty and inequity are, in fact, the cause of conflict, or at least one of the causes of conflict. Let me be clear, since this is an academic environment. If this were the Rotary Club, I might get away with it, but I guess it isn't, so I'll take my Rotary Club speech and tear it up. But let me say that *one* of the principal causes of conflict is poverty and inequity. I think I can say that with some certainty. And for us at the Bank, dealing now in 39 cases of countries affected by conflict, we are finding that our issues are coalescing once again, and in more and more countries, into the issue not just of poverty but of postconflict.

The fact that a country is in a postconflict situation is not something that changes the nature of the challenge on poverty and development. It surely exacerbates the problems, as we have seen in Timor-Leste. The approach we take in postconflict situations is similar to the approach we take to general situations of development and even the transition from central planning. So, to keep our minds clear, we have developed a methodology that is fundamentally geared to looking at a comprehensive framework. Of course, it has different manifestations in the case of postconflict, as illustrated by the description I just gave on Timor-Leste. But it is coherent and consistent with the way in which we go about development in general.

Let me give you some examples. When you look at development in general, it is very difficult to conceive of just pouring money into projects and thinking that you will have effective development. We have learned this the hard way in very different places, from Russia to the countries in Africa.

The first thing that you have to think about is how to establish a continuing structure. How can you, first, have an element of government? Can you train people who can carry forward the essence of government? Because without a trained and growing force of people who understand the essential elements of government, in any postconflict situation you cannot have continuous movement forward.

The second thing is the establishment of a system that protects rights, that creates a framework in which one can operate. And there you think in terms of a legal and justice system. In much of the work that we have been doing, the assurance of rights to property, the protection of the rights of individuals, the establishment of a sense of order in which a society can function—these are prerequisites to any form of development in a postconflict situation.

And so it was when I was in Bosnia that one of the first things that I saw to—and Sadako will remember—was the reconstruction of the Supreme Court. You might think that would be a luxury in a country like that. It is not a luxury. It is a necessity to establish the framework within which you are operating.

It makes it sound simple to jump very quickly through this as I am doing, but you need a legal system and a justice system, and that in itself is a highly complex issue, because to have a justice system work, you have to have laws. The judges have to know what the laws are. You have to have lawyers who know what the laws are. You have to have law books. You have to have a framework in which it is all operating. You have to build on what you had in the past, even though very often people do not want the system they had in the past, but instead want to move to a new system. That is tough enough in the absence of conflict. It is extraordinarily difficult at a time when you still have ethnic confrontations and human confrontations. But, the fact is, you need a basic system, and you need a basic form of keeping order.

One of the issues facing us now in Kosovo is that of police. How do you administer justice? Do the police become an instrument of oppression, or do they become protectors of the rights of people? And what we have learned, in a 60,000-person study that we have just done of poor people in 60 countries, is that they regard the police, almost to a person, as an instrument of oppression rather than as a protector of rights. So managing that in an environment where rights have been violated, as typically they have been in postconflict situations, is very difficult.

Jump now to Gaza and the West Bank, and remember the problems we had over the establishment of the local police. What is the local police force in Gaza and the West Bank? It used to be the Israeli soldiers. It is now an arm of the Palestinian Authority or the future Palestinian government. This is highly controversial in the local community. It is obviously necessary in terms of keeping order, but is it an instrument of political oppression, as it is seen by some of the Palestinians? It very much depends on whom you talk to as to which side you come down on.

It is the same with the establishment of the court. It has taken us several years to convince President [Yasser] Arafat about the appointment of a new chief justice, which he has now done. We have been talking for probably three years about the creation of a legal system in that country. And we have had the Australians go over there and draw up a strategic development plan for the rule of law. But getting it adopted affects the people who are already in power and the influence arrangements that exist in any postconflict situation. I mention this only as an aside, to demonstrate that when I say, "establish a legal and a justice system," it is easier said than done. But it is surely an essential element.

Then you have to have a financial system. You must have something that at least gives some transparency and order to the establishment of the society in terms of its finances. Take, again, the case of Bosnia, and Sadako will remember the problems we had in trying to get a functioning system for payments. Although it was agreed that it had to be done, the putting together of a central banking arrangement became a *cause célèbre* in the Bosnian situation. It raised again all the issues of who is going to be in control. On the other hand, how do you run a society without a functioning payments system and a methodology by which you can have some form of banking system?

So we are focusing on that. And if you start with banking, you also need to be thinking about such issues as the control of corporations, the registration of companies, and the transparency with which corporations operate. This is necessarily a framework that applies in ordinary countries, but it surely applies in spades in a postconflict situation as you try and get the framework established.

And then there is the issue of corruption. Corruption is never far away in any country. But in a postconflict situation, power is typically vested in the hands of a few people. Some of them are impeccable. Many of them are remarkable. But around these central units, our experience has been that you have to be very, very careful, not only in dispensing funds for aid and assistance, but also in terms of the flow of funds generally.

Here we get to the question of fiscal policy. We have a problem in raising money in these situations, which I will get to in a minute, which is exacerbated because many of the finance ministers say it is not our job at the World Bank to put money in for ongoing costs. This is a complaint that Mrs. Ogata and I have run into constantly. In Kosovo, for example, the UN management is running perhaps $40 million or $50 million shy of what they need to pay the people who are working there between now and the end of the year. But when you go to the potential donor governments to try and raise the money, they tell you it is not their job to pay for working capital. Let them get it themselves from tax collection, because that's the way it works in France or Germany or the United States or any other respectable country. But to go into a postconflict situation and talk about tax collection—the very idea is nonsensical. You can do something in terms of sales taxes. You can do something in terms of visible taxes on transfers. But just think about going to collect taxes in a postconflict situation. They will shoot you as soon as look at you.

My friend [IMF Managing Director] Michel Camdessus and I have actually been to tax authorities where they train people with machine guns—I am not joking—because tax collection has to be done by force. Well, in a postconflict situation, that is a little difficult because everybody has got a gun.

I am surely not making light of the situation, nor am I trying to dramatize it. What is crucial for us is to convince the donors and those who put up the money that it is different in a postconflict situation, that you cannot apply the same rules that you can in the case of normal, orderly development where things are going all right.

Let me stop there without getting into the issues of education and health and roads and communications and all the other things that go to make up societal development. But at the front end, this issue of structure and of getting adequate people, the issue of getting training, the issue of getting funding—all these pose us our most serious problems.

The World Bank, again, was founded as a bank for reconstruction and development. The founders decided that we could only lend to a country when it was in shape, when its payments were up to date, and when you could have appropriate lending programs that would pass the screens that we have on the way to presenting a proposal to the Board. The country had to be not only up to date on its payments with us but up to date with everybody else, according to the cross-default provisions.

And so, when Sadako Ogata comes to me and says, "You're doing $30 billion of business a year, why can't you spare us $20 million for this country? Why not just write a check?" the answer is that if the country's finances are in order, we can lend you a billion. But if they are not in order, for us to find even $10 million or $20 million is damn difficult. Because our shareholders, who are full of excitement and enthusiasm while the conflict is going on—as they were in Kosovo, as they were in Bosnia, as they are in Timor-Leste, as they have been, but much less, in the Great Lakes district [of Africa] and in Burundi and in Sierra Leone—when the story is in the newspapers like this, people come out and say they will give support. While the conflict is on the front page, you have a chance of getting promises. But the problem then is to collect. And then you find there is often a gap between the statements made by the ministers—and I think it is all in good faith—and the way the system actually functions. And so we have this gap between the humanitarian assistance during the conflict and the humanitarian assistance during the reconstruction.

If everything is in place, the Bank can come in with terrific programs for reconstruction. Hopefully, during the period of crisis there are funds available for humanitarian needs. But that period between the humanitarian crisis and the commencement of the reconstruction, this gap period that we discussed at a recent meeting at the Brookings Institution, poses for us an extraordinarily difficult problem.

And so it is that during that gap period what we are looking for is ways in which we can get trust funds to come in to try and bridge the gap, and sometimes we are successful and sometimes we are not. It is easier to raise trust funding for European-based problems than it is for African-based problems. But even in the case of Europe it is not fully successful. Even in something as dramatic as the Kosovo conflict, which was on the front page of all the papers and where tens of millions of dollars were squandered every day in bombing, if you try and get half a day's costs to carry you through the end of the year, [UN Secretary-General] Kofi Annan will tell you that he has not got it. Forty to fifty million dollars is still needed to allow the administrator to pay for the ongoing costs of government as we make the transition in Kosovo.

This is a huge problem for us, and it is a problem that we are facing really around the world in these postconflict areas. It is not, however, an insuperable problem. The numbers are not that great. But, at the margin, if you do not get it, and if there is a gap in the system, which is where the problem is, the numbers become enormous.

The World Bank earns $1.2 billion, roughly, a year. But our shareholders tell us to put $300 million of that into IDA [the International Development Association], put $200 million to $500 million into debt relief, and try and put another $500 million to $700 million into general reserves to allow for growth. And, by the way, they say, help us with Gaza and the West Bank, and this, and this, and this. As a result, I am at this moment looking at a margin of $37 million in funds that I can dispose of next year.

So, here we are, an organization with a balance sheet of $155 billion, or $280 billion including the IFC and MIGA.[†] And we are looking at a total of $37 million in discretionary funds to carry us through between now and next June. It is preposterous.

On the other hand, the wheels of government are such that getting money out of governments takes a major effort. Often the cycle for getting money for these transitional funds is the same as that for getting money for IDA or for other longer-term activities. This is a massive problem for us in obtaining funding for the period between conflict and reconstruction, quite apart from the organizational issues.

And, frankly, that is where we need your help. Now, I know that there are people here from the business sector, so let me say that I am not telling you all this as a deterrent in terms of investment. I am giving you the facts. The fact is that there is a lot of business to be done in these countries. I am from the busi-

---

† The International Finance Corporation and the Multilateral Investment Guarantee Agency are both part of the World Bank Group.

ness sector, and I see the opportunities in these countries not as a matter of charity but as a matter of good business. In these countries you can come in very early to establish a framework of business. And you can get some guarantees from us and from governments in terms of some of the basic rights that you need.

We are looking at trying to assist companies in moving in. We are prepared to go in with you through the IFC, which is our investment arm at the Bank, so that you have some ability to go in with some cover. And in terms of general business, in terms of trading, those companies that have valor and have a sense of looking beyond the immediate conflict have, I think, a real opportunity to build a base for future development.

I do not come to the business community as a matter of charity. I happen to think it is good business to have a stable world, but that is a much longer argument to make to you. I think it is a matter of us joining with the business community in looking at these situations, and I have run into some wonderful young people working for companies in these countries, who are going in excited because they have a chance to do something that links business with humanitarian and social objectives.

It is a wonderful thing to send a young executive to try and set something set up in these countries. It does not all have to be handed on a plate. And when you go there and you see the human despair but also the hope, and you come upon people who have fought to get themselves independent and to get the opportunity for a better life, you know you are working with an extraordinary group of people who will be anxious to work with you to try and develop the fabric of that society.

It is not like investing in Alabama or California. It is surely very different. But it is still something that is worth doing. And the establishment of business enterprises in these countries, starting in our case with small- and medium-size enterprise, whether it be for the widows in Bosnia or for returning servicemen in Burundi or in Uganda or in Sierra Leone, there is the possibility to take the next step and bring in the international knowledge and skills that many of you have in many areas, and surely in the area of natural resources. The ability to deal with issues of natural resources and mining in many of these countries is extraordinarily important.

In the case of Gaza at the moment, there is the prospect of oil. In Kosovo there is the reconstruction and the involvement of the mining concern, where massive investments that were previously made under the former Yugoslavia are lying there now ready to be rebuilt. It is an area in which there can be a re-creation of employment and activity. It is not a hopeless case. It is, in fact, for many people the most exciting case that you can have. You can make money, and you can do good at the same time.

And we at the Bank are ready to be your partners. We want to be your partners in every sense: in terms of the structure, in terms of information, in terms of dealing with government, in terms of getting your help to find out what it is that you need to do business effectively, because everything is flexible in these environments. We want to get the structure straight, but we have had numerous examples now of companies coming in and getting the best shot right at the beginning, and we can help.

And so I would urge you, in some of these situations, to find some of your younger people and provide them this fantastic opportunity for them to develop. Give them a chance. Give them a few dollars. Give them the backing. Those people will become presidents of your companies someday because, if you can do it in those conditions, you can do it anywhere. It is not something to turn your back on. It is a business opportunity, but it is also a moral and a social responsibility. And you have a great partner in the Bank. You have a greater partner in Sadako Ogata. You have a great partner in the UN system. And you typically have great partners in those people in the countries who have fought for their freedom, because they do, more than anything else, want to develop their country.

So it is different from normal investing, but it is not something that you should turn your back on, because there is an excitement in this reconstruction. You can really feel that, apart from making money, you can help in nation building, and in doing that help secure the future not only of the people in those countries but of your own children as well.

GLOBAL TRADE AND THE DEVELOPMENT ROUND:
SEIZING THE DAY

Remarks at the Third Ministerial Meeting of the World Trade Organization

SEATTLE | NOVEMBER 30, 1999

The Seattle WTO meeting is remembered as the site of antiglobalization
protests, elements of which would soon come to the 2000 Bank-Fund
Spring Meetings. In this speech Wolfensohn urges action on trade and
spells out why fulfilling the WTO's next round of international trade
talks will benefit poor countries.

Mr. Chairman, Your Excellencies, Distinguished Colleagues:

I would like to thank [WTO Director-General] Mike Moore for asking me to
join you today. I share his conviction that this must be "one family, where
everyone has a seat at the table." Today I want to speak for those family members who are not always the first to be heard at this table: the poor countries
and peoples of the world.

Four Underlying Principles

Let me begin with the principles that I believe must underlie our discussions.

First, to speak for the poor today is to speak for the peace and stability of
our global future. Half the world's 6 billion people today live on less than two
dollars a day. Half of a far larger world population may well be living in
poverty 25 years from now. We must act now to help the world's poor become full partners in the potential gains from world trade. This is not just a
moral imperative. It is intensely practical.

Second, the trade agenda cannot be debated in isolation. We must look at
the options for trade expansion in the wider context of a holistic approach, such
as the Comprehensive Development Framework that I have outlined elsewhere. We must recognize the interconnections of national and international
policy initiatives, including trade initiatives. We must recognize trade liberalization as an integral part of a broader strategic effort, as part of a broader set of
partnerships—partnerships for building a better future for our world's children.

Third, the new Development Round of trade talks must move beyond the
narrow negotiation of mutual concessions. We must seize the day and work
flexibly and creatively toward a world trading system that really makes a difference for developing countries. It makes no sense to urge poor countries to
reform their economies, to urge them to compete and "pay their way" in the
world, while denying them the *means* to compete. But, in practice, this is what
we do, by restricting their market access in areas like agriculture, construction,

and textiles. It is precisely these areas where many developing countries have comparative advantage. Granting access may be temporarily tough for protected industries in developed countries, but in the long run it will benefit us all. It will contribute to the peace and security we surely all seek. It is time we took those tough steps.

Fourth, we need to make special efforts to ensure that we build a genuinely inclusive system. A number of developing countries have been very successful in competing in world markets. But they remain a small minority. We cannot afford to compound the old division of rich countries versus poor countries with a new division between the successful few and the marginalized many of the developing world. We live in an increasingly interconnected global economic and geopolitical environment. In such an environment, the welfare—or lack of it—of the poorest can destabilize the prospects of the wealthier. Inclusion matters for us all.

Five Areas for Action

On the basis of these principles, let me now suggest five areas for priority action if the Development Round is to fulfill its promise.

First, we must expand market access for all exports from developing countries. Manufactures from these countries to the industrialized world face barriers four times higher than those from other industrialized countries. And barriers are even higher for manufactures flowing *between* developing countries. These barriers hurt both North-South and South-South trade. They stunt the growth of competitive manufacturing exporters in the developing world. They deny millions of people the benefits of freer trade. They cannot stand. A first step would be to endorse Mike Moore's call for completely liberalized access for the exports of the 48 least-developed countries. And we should add to that group all the countries eligible for debt relief under the Heavily Indebted Poor Countries Initiative. Voices may be raised against this idea. But it would surely send a signal of our commitment to greater fairness toward the most vulnerable.

Second, we must quickly reduce agricultural protection in high-income countries. Trade expansion in agriculture has lagged far behind that in manufactured goods: agricultural trade grew at a rate of under 2 percent a year between the mid-1980s and the mid-1990s, compared with nearly 6 percent a year for manufactured goods. Agricultural protection in the OECD countries—even after the reforms of the Uruguay Round*—causes annual income losses

---

* The Uruguay Round of international trade negotiations, concluded in 1994, led to the creation of the World Trade Organization. The member countries of the Organisation for Economic Co-operation and Development (OECD) include most of the world's high-income countries.

for developing countries of nearly $20 billion a year. This not only penalizes the two-thirds of the poor in developing countries who work in agriculture: it also penalizes consumers in developed countries.

Third, we must work collaboratively to support the capacity of the poorest countries to participate in international trade negotiations—not just to be present at the table, but to have a voice and to be heard. Some developing countries are well equipped to take part, but many are not. Too many lack even representation at Geneva.[†] Many more lack the full range of domestic expertise needed to be effective partners in the debate. The Bank is working in this area through the WTO 2000 project, and I want to thank a number of developed countries, notably the Netherlands and the United Kingdom, for their support. The Integrated Framework for the Least Developed Countries—a cooperative effort involving the WTO, the International Monetary Fund, UNCTAD, the ITC, the UNDP,[‡] and the Bank—is also playing a valuable role. But let us imagine an even greater collaboration. Let us find ways for the high-income countries and the better-equipped developing countries to provide more technical support to the negotiating efforts of the poorest.

Fourth, we must anchor trade liberalization firmly within the wider context of the global development effort. This means taking coordinated action on the part of the development community as a whole—the members of the "coalitions for change" I have referred to elsewhere: action to structure comprehensive assistance programs that get maximum results for developing countries wishing to take advantage of the world trading system. These programs should go far beyond support for trade expansion, to support institutional reform, regulatory reform, and the development of physical and social infrastructure. They should be programs that work *with* trade expansion to deliver better lives to people.

Fifth, we must make trade liberalization work most effectively for the poor. The state of our knowledge about the practical impact of different patterns of trade liberalization on poverty is still far too limited. To make the Development Round work, we need to know more, and we need to sharpen our focus on the links between poverty and trade. This is an area where the Bank would be happy to work with the WTO, the IMF, and other partners to increase our knowledge. Knowing more would allow us to do more—and to do it better.

---

† The WTO's headquarters in Geneva is the main forum for international trade negotiations.
‡ The United Nations Conference on Trade and Development, the International Trade Centre, and the United Nations Development Programme, respectively.

Deepening Partnerships, Broadening Opportunities

Mr. Chairman, if we seize the day in this Development Round, we have the power to open up world trade in new and dramatically beneficial ways. We have a great opportunity now. Making the most of it will demand collaboration, creativity, and flexibility. I pledge to you today that we in the World Bank will do everything we can to help ensure a successful outcome. And I look forward to further deepening our partnerships with the IMF, the WTO, the United Nations, and other multilateral and bilateral agencies. I look forward also to deepening our partnerships with the private sector and civil society. We must come together to help all countries share more fully in the international trading system.

All this we must do. But we must never lose sight of the fact that whatever we do here is a means toward a wider set of ends: toward broadening the opportunities for *all* peoples to share in the potential for global prosperity; toward helping to eradicate the human, social, and economic degradation of poverty; and toward building a world that holds out the promise of peace and security for future generations. These must be our underlying goals. These must be our unifying sources of inspiration when the negotiations get tough. And these must form the frame of reference that guides our work, and by which we judge our efforts, today, tomorrow, and as we go forward into a new millennium.

Excerpts from an address to the United Nations Security Council

NEW YORK | JANUARY 10, 2000*

> *The UN Security Council's first meeting on HIV/AIDS in Africa was historic, both as a major recognition on the United Nations' part of AIDS as a development and a security issue, and because it marked the first time a World Bank president addressed the Council. In his remarks, Wolfensohn urges world leaders to break the "vicious circle of AIDS, poverty, conflict."*

One does not have to be a social scientist or a diplomat to know that people who live in orderly, well-governed, representative societies where there is economic opportunity, social justice, human rights, and declining poverty are less likely to be fighting, less likely to be angry, less likely to be frustrated than those who live in chaotic or poorly managed societies, where opportunity is denied, where poverty is pervasive, and where there is little hope of good or effective government.

We believe that combating poverty, giving opportunity to citizens, and providing effective development programs are the true key to security and peace. If this belief is justified, we should be in closer touch with this august body.

As we meet here today, much is at stake. We will be judged by our actions on three broad counts:

First, we will be judged on whether we are serious about Africa's development and inclusion; whether we are serious about working with Africans to give their continent a chance in the 21st century; whether Africa, which suffered so badly so long under oppression and racism, can at last free itself of poverty and integrate with the modern, open global economy. Africans must lead, but we must partner with the strong new generations in Africa to build the institutions, the structures, the rule of law, the human rights, the governance that are needed for people to take hold of their future. Only if we beat back AIDS can Africa take that step.

Second, we will be judged on whether we globally understand the nature of human security and sustainable development. Security develops from within societies. If we want to prevent violent conflict, we need a comprehensive, equitable, and inclusive approach to development. A culture of prevention needs to permeate our work. Security, empowerment, and opportunity must be recognized as key to freedom from poverty—just as freedom from poverty is key to security. Communities that are driven apart by disease are weak communities.

---

* As published in *Presidents & Prime Ministers*, January-February 2000.

Weak communities are subject to strife. Beating back AIDS in Africa will support a culture of peace.

Third, we will be judged on whether the international community can face up to global challenges. AIDS is a global issue. It forces us to bring all our understanding together—of security, health, economics, and social and cultural change. It forces us to bring all actors together—from developed and developing countries, communities and governments, business and NGOs [nongovernmental organizations], science, faith, and civil society.

Across the world, there is a wave of concern about whether we can come together and deal with the pace of globalization. How we beat back AIDS will show whether we are truly able to lead jointly to face global challenges.

AIDS in Africa is not only claiming lives; it is changing the very nature of development. As one farmer in southern Africa put it, "Today, we are spending more time turning the bodies of the sick than we are turning the soil."

More than 13 million Africans have already died of AIDS, 23 million are now living with HIV/AIDS, and 10 million African children have been orphaned by AIDS. The 21 countries with the highest rates of HIV are all in Africa. The arithmetic of risk is chilling. A child born in Zambia or Zimbabwe today is more likely than not to die of AIDS.

Many of us used to think of AIDS as a health issue. We were wrong. AIDS can no longer be confined to the health or the social sector portfolio. Across Africa, AIDS is turning back the clock on development. Over the last four decades in Africa we have seen life expectancy increase by 24 years, and education and health programs extended to improve literacy and give greater opportunity. We have seen the growth of a new generation of African leaders, greater voice for the people, and more democratic regimes. But today Africa is in crisis of a type never seen before. Nothing will put Africa back more quickly, reverse the gains, and throw countries into turmoil than the current AIDS epidemic.

In too many countries the gains of life expectancy won are being wiped out. In too many countries more teachers are dying each week than can be trained. Judges, government officials, military personnel, women and girls, and the young are being ravaged with an enormous economic reversal of development gains.

Nothing we have seen is a greater challenge to the peace and stability of African societies than the epidemic of AIDS. African leadership must recognize it, they must fight it, and they must overcome social mores and admit that their countries are at war. We must support them. The Security Council must take note. Together we must act.

In AIDS we face a war more debilitating than war itself, because in so many countries it is seldom spoken of, because it does not catch the headlines, because the voices of its victims do not reach the corridors of power.

We face a major development crisis and, more than that, a security crisis. For without economic and social hope we will not have peace, and AIDS surely undermines both.

We need to break that vicious circle of AIDS, poverty, conflict, AIDS. For the truth is that not only does AIDS threaten stability, but when peace breaks down it fuels AIDS. Of the countries in Africa with the highest prevalence of AIDS, half are engaged in conflict of one kind or another.

AIDS spreads through the military. It spreads even when conflict ends and when populations move. It spreads rapidly among refugees, 75 percent of whom are women and children, making them especially vulnerable. There are too many refugees in Africa.

It is a grim picture. But that is the reality of AIDS. To beat it, we must be convinced of two things:

One, that we can win. We can stop its spread. We can prevent new infections. We can treat those who suffer. In time we can hope to find a cure. I propose to confidently hold up the prospect of a world free of AIDS. For that, we know, we need a world free of poverty.

Two, we must build on the dignity of the human individual and the capacity of her community. For far too long, all over the world, and in too many places still, AIDS is faced with silence, shame, and denial. If we fail, that will be the reason.

Care, not fear. Dignity, not denial. This is where winning starts, in families, communities, governments, nations. And we in the international community must work together with only one purpose in mind: winning. Each institution must bring its best strengths, aligning with others and adding value.

We have come a long way. UNAIDS [the Joint United Nations Programme on HIV/AIDS], in which the World Bank was a partner from the outset, was a major innovative step. The Partnership Against HIV/AIDS in Africa, launched here at the UN last month, brings us even further. And we are partnering with many African governments in new ways.

We pledge to walk together with Africa on this journey, knowing it will be long. Each step of that journey demands that we do things differently. When we think about security, we must think beyond battalions or borders. We must think about human security, about winning a different fight, the fight against poverty. The World Bank is ready and anxious to work with the Security Council now and in the future on a broad range of issues affecting human security.

We must shine a spotlight on the AIDS issue, put it front and center. Break the silence; destigmatize it. And build coalitions with governments, the private sector, and civil society to fight it.

We must find innovative ways to make care and treatment available, including affordable drugs. The science is difficult and the market incentives are weak, but we must create new win–win strategies with the private sector in order to address this critical market failure.

We must speak openly about sex and gender inequalities, and about rape.

We must raise more resources, recognizing that it makes no sense to give aid with one hand if we do nothing to stem AIDS with the other.

We must put prevention at the center. We estimate that the cost of prevention is between $1.50 and $3.50 per capita per year, compared with over $7 per capita per year needed for basic treatment—and, of course, the cost of treatment per patient is astronomically higher.

Africans must lead. I say it again because it is so crucial. We know it can be done and done successfully. We have the examples of Uganda and Senegal, important strides in Malawi and elsewhere, and further afield we know of the groundbreaking work in Thailand. And we must acknowledge that, without peace and stability, in Africa the chances of staunching this epidemic will be much slimmer.

Three months ago in Lusaka, the World Bank launched a new strategy for HIV/AIDS in Africa. I bring it to this table. This strategy declares AIDS a top priority for the Bank in Africa and commits us to an unprecedented effort, in partnership with UNAIDS, to support countries and communities in this struggle.

We will mainstream AIDS in all our work in Africa, recognizing that AIDS and development are inextricably tied together; we will back this commitment with increased funding and with a long-term partnership.

We must recognize that, if we provide the resources and the enabling environment, solutions will come from communities. No community wants to dash the dreams of its children. AIDS will do nothing to change that bedrock bond between generations. But communities need financial support, and their programs need to be scaled up. We estimate that the total sum needed for prevention in Africa is on the order of $1 billion to $2.3 billion, and yet at present Africa is receiving only $160 million in official assistance for HIV/AIDS. Every war needs a war chest, but that provided by the international community is woefully empty.

I have told all my offices in Africa that we will provide governments with the maximum available funding to create and implement programs. We can make a very big difference, but we cannot do the job alone. We will discuss AIDS at the meeting of the Development Committee[†] in April, and I hope that there, too, we can see action on the issue of resources.

We must build a coalition for change. As surely as if we mobilized for peace, we must now mobilize for war: a war against AIDS, a war for Africa's future and for our own.

Let me leave you with the voice of a young African woman whose village has been all but destroyed by AIDS. "We do not think," she said, "that life will become any better for our children and even for generations to come." I believe that with a concerted international effort we can prove her wrong. Let us align our strengths to one day see a world free of AIDS.

Together, we can extend local information programs, educate for safer behavior, distribute condoms. Together with the private sector we can expand low-cost treatments.

We know it can be done. But we do not have much time. The cost of inaction will be great. The cost of action is relatively small, but the rewards are priceless: a better chance of peace and stability and hope for millions who now live with none. That is surely the true meaning of security.

---

† The Development Committee is a grouping of finance ministers representative of the Bank's member countries that meets twice a year to discuss and advise on development issues.

EMPOWERMENT AND VOICES OF THE POOR: CAN ANYONE HEAR US?

With Clare Short, foreword to Volume I of *Voices of the Poor,* published for the World Bank by Oxford University Press

MARCH 2000

> *Wolfensohn teams up with then-U.K. Secretary of State for International Development Clare Short to introduce this new three-part series of books, which are based on thousands of interviews with poor people around the world.*

[. . .] *Can Anyone Hear Us?* brings together the voices of over 40,000 poor people from 50 countries. The two books that follow, *Crying Out for Change* and *From Many Lands,* pull together new fieldwork conducted in 1999 in 23 countries. The Voices of the Poor project is different from all other large-scale poverty studies. Using participatory and qualitative research methods, the study presents very directly, through poor people's own voices, the realities of their lives. How do poor people view poverty and well-being? What are their problems and priorities? What is their experience with the institutions of the state, markets, and civil society? How are gender relations faring within households and communities? We want to thank the project team led by Deepa Narayan of the Poverty Group in the World Bank, and particularly the country research teams, for undertaking this work.

What poor people share with us is sobering. A majority of them feel they are worse off and more insecure than in the past. Poor people care about many of the same things all of us care about: happiness, family, children, livelihood, peace, security, safety, dignity, and respect. Poor people's descriptions of encounters with a range of institutions call out for all of us to rethink our strategies. From the perspective of poor people, corruption, irrelevance, and abusive behavior often mar the formal institutions of the state. NGOs [nongovernmental organizations], too, receive mixed ratings from the poor. Poor people would like NGOs to be accountable to them. Poor people's interactions with traders and markets are stamped with their powerlessness to negotiate fair prices. How then do poor people survive? They turn to their informal networks of family, kin, friends, and neighbors. But these are already stretched thin.

We commend to you the authenticity and significance of this work. What can be more important than listening to the poor and working with our partners all over the world to respond to their concerns? Our core mission is to help poor people succeed in their own efforts, and the book raises major challenges to both of our institutions and to all of us concerned about poverty. We are prepared to hold ourselves accountable, to make the effort to try to respond to these voices. Obviously we cannot do this alone.

We urge you to read this book, to reflect and respond. Our hope is that the voices in this book will call you to action as they have us.

Wolfensohn on Empowerment

". . . If we do not protect their rights and give them opportunity, the poor will continue to be a liability. If we can give them the opportunity and the access to use their skills and their assets, if we can empower the poor—not to give them charity but to give them equity, justice, and the possibility to fulfill their human capacities—then we will have peace. . . ."

From an address at a conference on Empowerment, Security, and Opportunity
Through Law and Justice, St. Petersburg, Russia, July 9, 2001

ENSURING SAFE WATER FOR ALL THROUGH PARTICIPATION, INNOVATION, AND INCLUSION

Remarks at the Second World Water Forum: From Vision to Action

THE HAGUE | MARCH 22, 2000

In this address in the Netherlands, Wolfensohn outlines the importance of water to development, and how access to water often distinguishes the wealthy from the poor. He talks about how water can be a source of conflict, but also a catalyst for cooperation and peace, as shown in the Nile Basin Initiative.

Your Royal Highness, Distinguished Guests, Ladies and Gentlemen:

I am delighted to be here for the concluding session of what I understand from the Crown Prince* and my Bank colleagues to have been an exciting and fruitful forum. We must now put into practice the lessons that have been shared this week and focus on the way ahead.

There is no subject more important than water—for people, for growing food, for the environment. Every time I visit one of our client countries, I am struck by the magnitude of the challenge portrayed so well in the World Commission on Water's report to this forum. There is no way we can continue with business as usual. By 2025 we will need 40 percent more water for cities and 20 percent more for food than we use today. Yet already the environment is overstressed.

In [the Republic of] Yemen, once regarded as the garden of the Arabian peninsula, the introduction of diesel pumps over the last 30 years risks literally pumping the country dry. In the basin around Sana'a, for example, four times more water is pumped out every year than is recharged by streams and runoff. Water tables are sinking several meters every year, and, as in many other cities of the developing world, poor people pay five times more for a bucket of water than it costs people in The Hague or in Washington, D.C.

This kind of scenario is not restricted to Yemen. It is estimated that 10 percent of the world's food is grown with water from aquifers that are being depleted faster than the rate of recharge. What does this mean for ordinary people in the developing world? Let me share with you what some of them have to say about it:[†]

- A farmer in Kenya: "Water is life, and because we have no water, life is miserable."

---

* Willem-Alexander, Crown Prince of the Netherlands and chairman of the World Water Forum.
† The quotations that follow are from Volumes I and II of the World Bank study *Voices of the Poor*.

- A young man in Russia: "How can we sow anything without water? What will my cow drink? Water is our life."
- An old woman in Ethiopia: "We live hour to hour, wondering whether it will rain."

These voices of the poor offer poignant witness to their concerns and needs. In many parts of the world, access to water distinguishes the poor from the nonpoor. When I was in Vietnam recently, some children told me that poor people were those without access to safe drinking water. Indeed, lack of access to water is synonymous with poverty throughout the developing world.

Some countries have made progress. In Côte d'Ivoire and Benin more than 70 percent of people now have access to safe water. But elsewhere the situation is dismal. In Eritrea only 7 percent of people have such access, in Cambodia the figure is 13 percent, in Mozambique 24 percent, and in Paraguay 39 percent. If we do not meet this challenge, we will not succeed in our broader mission of alleviating poverty for the 3 billion people who live on less than two dollars a day. Good intentions are not enough. We must do development differently, by grounding it in equity, in justice, and in new partnerships, as well as in solid economics. In the case of water, this means full-cost pricing matched by carefully targeted subsidies for the poor.

Institutions and Participation

We must look at our institutions to see how we can give stakeholders a real stake, how we can use water more efficiently, and how we can make service providers more accountable. Take, for example, the Hermosillo aquifer in the state of Sonora, in Mexico, where the situation is quite similar to Yemen's. The introduction of pumps has boosted agricultural output. But the water table has fallen below sea level, and the aquifer is being destroyed by saltwater seeping in from the sea.

In recent years, however, there has been encouraging progress, thanks to a new federal water law, which stresses integrated water resources management at the basin and aquifer level, participatory management, and the use of tradable water rights. What has happened in Sonora is remarkable. First, there is a new partnership. It is the water users who make the decisions, while the government provides information and helps with enforcement. Second, users now have clear property rights and an incentive to manage the water sustainably rather than engage in a race to the bottom. The result? Farmers have voluntarily decided to reduce extraction by 50 percent, so that usage and recharge are in balance. Water is used much more efficiently, and low-value uses have stopped. Amazingly, regional income and employment have actually increased even as pumping has been reduced.

What does the World Bank do with this information? We share it, distilling the lessons learned in places like Sonora and using them to inform groundwater management reforms in other parts of the world. For example, we took two Turkish officials to Mexico to see how farmers' associations were managing their local irrigation networks. They were impressed by what they saw, and they went back to Turkey determined to make similar changes. Today Turkey runs its irrigation systems the same way. More recently, the huge state of Andhra Pradesh in India has, with support from the World Bank, done the same.

Technological and Financial Innovation

Institutional reforms of this kind are not enough on their own, however. Technology also has an important part to play in finding more efficient, more environmentally friendly ways of ensuring that there is enough water for people, for food, for energy—and for nature.

We also need financial innovation if we are to meet the enormous demand for water. The World Commission estimates that annual investment will have to double over the next 25 years, from some $70 billion today. This cannot be done unless the private sector plays a much larger role in the provision and financing of water services.

Yet most water utilities in developing countries are still financed and run by governments. A few of them are well managed. But most lose half of their water through leakage and generally provide terrible service. A few hours' supply each day is the norm. And who suffers most from such systems? Go into the *pueblos jovenes* of Peru, the *favelas* of Brazil, or the *bairros populares* of Mozambique. Everywhere you see the same thing. It is the poor who don't have service. It is the poor who are at the end of the empty pipe. It is the poor who must buy water from vendors at many times the price paid by better-off people who have service.

In recent years a number of countries have made a decisive change. In many cities, from Abidjan to Buenos Aires, the authorities have transferred the water utilities to private companies. The most obvious advantage is that the private sector brings in money: about $30 billion during the 1990s. It also brings in know-how. But, more important, the private sector brings in transparency and accountability, because for the first time there is a contract between supplier and consumer.

The Challenge of Inclusion

Less tangible is the impact of these changes on poor people's sense of dignity and self-worth. This was vividly brought home to me a few years ago when I visited a large water and sanitation project that the Bank is supporting in the *favelas* of Brazil. The project, which is now self-sustaining, brings together the local community, the private sector, and nongovernmental organizations.

With my host, the vice governor of the state of Rio de Janeiro, I went from one makeshift home to the next, talking with the women who live there and who used to carry water on their shoulders from the bottom of the hillside to their dwellings at the top. One after the other, they proudly showed me their running water and flushed their toilets and told me how the project had transformed their lives. And as I walked around, more and more of the women came up to me displaying pieces of paper showing charges and receipts for a few *reais* a month. I watched and listened for a while until the vice governor said, "What they're showing you, Jim, is that this is the first time in their lives that their name and address have appeared on an official notice. This is the first time their existence has been officially recognized. This is the first time that they have been included in society. With that receipt they can get credit to purchase goods. With that receipt they have recognition and hope."

As I walked back down the hill from that *favela,* I realized that this is what the challenge of development is all about: inclusion, bringing people into society who have never been part of it before. This is why the World Bank Group exists. This is why we are all here today: to help make it happen for people.

What conclusions can we draw from Yemen, Mexico, Turkey, Côte d'Ivoire, Argentina, and the *favelas* of Brazil? To my mind, they provide powerful evidence that the principles set out in Dublin‡ in 1992 were the right ones. The challenges remain holistic management, inclusive governance arrangements, and a recognition that water is an economic resource. We must now move from analysis and vision to action, if we are to meet the twin objectives of poverty reduction and environmental sustainability. Dublin was a broad, participatory process, and the hundreds of consultations that prepared the ground for this forum—and the forum itself—are testimony to the soundness of the approach.

I am struck by the similarities between this process and the way the Bank has been rethinking its broad approach to development through what is known as the Comprehensive Development Framework. Working with many partners, including Eveline Herfkens [UN executive coordinator of the Millennium Development Goals campaign] and the government of the Netherlands, we seek to allow developing countries to decide on their own priorities in an informed, transparent, and participatory way.

We need to apply the same kind of participatory approach to resolving tensions over the use of water in many of the world's 300 or so international rivers. As you know, it is these tensions that have given rise to the suggestion that the wars of the 21st century may be fought over water rather than oil.

When we hear the words "water" and "conflict" in the same sentence, it is often in the context of the River Nile. Instead, in this forum, we have heard of a visionary and courageous initiative of the Nile riparian states, exploring

---

‡ The International Conference on Water and the Environment was held in Dublin in January 1992.

win-win opportunities and joint development in the Nile Basin. With such cooperation, the aspirations of the peoples of the basin—rich in their cultures but too many of them desperately poor—are more likely to be achieved.

Although future conflict over water is possible, water can also be the focus for cooperation and peace. To this end we are working with many partners in moving away from the zero-sum game implicit in the notion of "sharing water" to the win-win possibilities of "sharing benefits." In southern Africa, for example, the Lesotho Highlands Project, which provides water and power to South Africa, is resulting in a net, permanent 5 percent increase in Lesotho's GDP.

Dams are another example of how participation and partnership can help address the thorniest of problems: in this instance, when and how to plan, build, and operate dams. The World Bank has been an active partner, with the IUCN, in establishing the World Commission on Dams, so ably chaired by Minister Kader Asmal** from South Africa. There are many remarkable things about this commission. One is the highly participatory process that led to its formation and the key role being played by people of great stature from developing countries in forging consensus. A second is the breadth of views among its members: it includes the chief executive of one of the world's leading engineering companies, leaders of movements opposing dams, environmental activists, water resource managers, and government officials. For the Bank it is a new departure—and a recognition that we have to develop new approaches to this and other critical and controversial development issues.

We are following the same participatory approach in designing a new Water Resources Strategy for the Bank, which we plan to present to our Board later this year. All of the material from the six broad-based regional consultations that are part of this exercise is on our Web site, and I invite you to read it and send us your views.

One of the messages we heard time and again during our consultations in Brasilia, Sana'a, and Manila is that we at the Bank talk holistic management but don't yet walk it. This may have been the case in the past, but it will not be so in the future. I am pleased to tell you that we have appointed lead water resources specialists in four of our six regional divisions, to bring consistency and integration to our work on water resources. And we recently constituted a Water Resources Sector Board—the equivalent of a water resources ministry inside the Bank—to provide leadership to staff across the institution and to manage our portfolio.

** South African minister of education and former minister of water affairs and forestry.

I should like to pay particular tribute to the Global Water Partnership, of which the Crown Prince is patron. It is becoming a powerful network of regional partnerships, with the regions in command, defining what to share with others and how to improve their own performance. The donors who have underwritten the partnership deserve our special thanks.

Finally, as the Vision Commission has ably laid out, we face an enormous challenge over the coming decades in ensuring that every person has the water services he or she needs for health, for food, and for energy. As the commissioners and many others have said this week, we need a new "water movement." And what better place to launch it than here in the Netherlands, where the struggle with water has been a constant of history, and where, the Crown Prince tells me, the oldest democratic institutions, dating back to the 14th century, were created to manage water?

As we launch this important new initiative, we must recognize that it addresses just one part of a much broader agenda. Our overarching goal remains to bring together all the elements that will enable us to eradicate the human, social, and economic degradation of poverty; all the elements that will help us build a peaceful and secure world for future generations; all the elements that promise people healthier and more prosperous lives. These aspirations underpin this forum and provide us with our common source of inspiration. They also provide a framework to guide our work as we move from vision to action.

"IT IS DIFFICULT TO TALK REASON WHEN PEOPLE ARE ON THE BARRICADES"

Remarks at the Multilateral Development Banks' Meeting on the HIPC Initiative

WASHINGTON, D.C. | APRIL 4, 2000

> *This speech contains some of the most detailed remarks Wolfensohn made on debt relief and the Heavily Indebted Poor Countries (HIPC) initiative. Ahead of expected street protests at the annual Bank-Fund Spring Meetings, he calls for a sensible approach to relieving the debts of the poorest countries.*

Let me say first, thank you, Masood,* and good morning to everybody. You come at a time when we are under a fair amount of pressure in this building, as a result of quite a confluence of forces. As you know, within a week we will have demonstrators here in what they call "Seattle, Part Two," the aim of which is to demonstrate that certainly the Bank and the [International Monetary] Fund, and multilateral institutions in general, have no place in the equitable development of the world.

It is not a particularly authentic group of demonstrators. It is led by Ruckus, which is a group whose purpose is to disrupt meetings, and they go to training camps for a couple of weeks and learn how to climb buildings and how to create demonstrations. Then they distribute on the Internet the location of the next party, which is now in Washington. But, sadly, there are some other events occurring, including a demonstration by the labor unions about the WTO [World Trade Organization] and China; a second demonstration about debt, which will be on Capitol Hill; and then, next weekend, at the [Bank-Fund Spring] Meetings here in Washington.

Now, why do I tell you that? I tell you that because in it all is a constant reference to debt. It is a mix-up of Jubilee 2000. It is the feeling that the rich have it over the poor, and that the way to put everything right is by demonstration and by immediate debt forgiveness. In the middle of all that, what we have to do, of course, is to try and keep our heads, and try and talk reason. But it is difficult to talk reason when people are on the barricades and when our political masters are anxious to be responsive. So quite a number of our ministers want to go out and talk to them, and we are already getting letters from ministers that are less supportive rather than more supportive of the speed and effort of all the multilateral institutions in debt forgiveness.

What I am trying to do with my colleagues is to prepare for the Spring Meetings, during which we hope to get across to the finance ministers that, if HIPC I [the first version of the HIPC Initiative] was a burden, HIPC II is an

---

* Masood Ahmed, deputy director of the Policy Development and Review Department of the International Monetary Fund.

enormous challenge. It will cost a total of $28 billion in present value, of which $14.1 billion is to come from multilateral creditors. For the World Bank Group the cost is $6.3 billion, leaving $2.3 billion to the IMF and the remaining $5.5 billion to other MDBs [multilateral development banks]. That is a huge burden for us, which is possible to bear only if we can write off the debt to the Bank[†] of more than $1 billion by taking it out of our earnings over a period of five years, although our capital is limited. Also, we have the right, if we want to, to forgive debt to IDA [the International Development Association] up to the level of $80 billion, which is the debt outstanding owed to IDA, because we do not have to repay that.

The only problem is that, if we do that, we will not have any more money coming in to lend out through IDA. And so the easy short-term answer for us is to say, "All right, we will write off $5.6 billion in IDA," at net present value. And there is no doubt we can do that. But then IDA does not get the repayments it expected, on the basis of which the IDA deputies were planning their future expenditures on loans. So for us it is a problem—one that is manageable, but at the cost of deeply wounding IDA in the future. It delays the problem for us, in that future loans made by IDA will then need to be funded by the IDA donors. It is not an immediate crisis, but it is a future crisis.

Because ours is a problem we can handle, all our attention has been given to raising trust fund monies for organizations other than ourselves, because we do not face the crisis that they do. And we have raised, give or take, $2 billion, which is available to all of you as we seek to distribute it. The critical sum at stake is the U.S. contribution of $600 million plus, the first $200 million of which would be for the next year, and which broadly affects the Americas, whereas the European monies broadly affect the African countries. Crucial in all of this is the demonstration taking place on Capitol Hill this week, which might be of some use to us in getting additional funding for the contribution of the $600 million, so that we could have $200 million this year for funding the Americas' portion of the debt forgiveness package.

All of this, however, concerns the next two or three years. And the point that I will be making to the ministers is that the ownership of many of your institutions does not lie with them; it lies, in fact, with the developing countries themselves. Therefore it is not just a question of the wealthy countries putting up capital for existing institutions.

There is the separate question that, for many of your institutions, your participating shareholders do not have the ready money to be able to build the

---

† The International Bank for Reconstruction and Development (IBRD), the oldest and largest affiliate of the World Bank Group.

capital and maintain the financial integrity of the institutions. And therefore the only way to solve that problem is through contributions to the trust fund from the wealthier countries, to allow for the sustenance of your institutions and the writing off of the debt with some support from the trust fund.

Now, the sad reality is that the ministers as a group seem to be more concerned with the politics than with the financing, and so the rhetoric is all very good, but the writing of checks is not up to the level of the rhetoric. And I am going to make myself a nuisance yet again to the ministers this time, pressing the case of your institutions once more of the urgent need for trust fund support, so that financial integrity can be maintained. I will start with the Inter-American Development Bank and then make the case for the other institutions. I will base my case on the unfairness of calling for global debt reduction while doing nothing about the capital of these institutions.

There are the additional issues of packaging, the focus on poverty, and the comprehensive nature of the programs, on which I think reasonable progress is being made. But it seems to me, at the moment, that the focal point—which must be of concern to you, and is of concern to us—is less on the holistic nature of how we do it, that is, tying it into poverty and Poverty Reduction Strategy Papers and anything else that they want to put on us. Rather it seems to me that the focal issue at the moment is finance, and that is, for the moment, a reality.

What the ministers, I think, are insisting is that we all take a look inside our institutions to see how far we can go, and that varies according to institution. As I say, the amount that the IBRD has to forgive can probably be taken out of earnings over a period of years, while we are at the level of the last summit. The problem that we face, and that all of us face, is the prospect of the next round, which Jubilee 2000 and others are calling for, which would entail 100 percent debt relief. This is very attractive politically and is being pushed by Jeffrey Sachs[‡] and a bunch of others who do not look at the implications for our institutions.

There the drama, of course, is that 100 percent debt relief would raise total debt forgiveness by the multilateral creditors from the current $14.1 billion—the level we have established under HIPC II, which is half of the total of $28.2 billion—to $43 billion. Now, $43 billion, spread around this group, is completely impossible in terms of leaving our institutions with adequate capital. If the present round is already causing problems, then more than doubling the amount will be terminal for many institutions, unless support is given. And

---

‡ A leading proponent of debt forgiveness and, at the time of this speech, professor of economics at Harvard University.

so my task at these next meetings is to convince the ministers that 100 percent debt relief, even for the 32 existing HIPCs, without assistance, is not doable.

An additional problem is this: If we forgive debt for the 32 countries, what about all the others? If we are changing the basis on which one judges whether a country is HIPC-eligible, what about the next 10 countries, or the next 15 countries, who just missed the cutoff? They will now say, "Well, look, it's terribly unfair for you to forgive the debt completely of these countries who didn't do very well. We have tried very hard to be good citizens, and now you are going against us by not including us in this wonderful holiday that you are going to give for the millennium."

Total outstanding claims of all multilateral institutions on the 40 HIPCs are about $70 billion in nominal terms. If one includes the nearly eligible countries, that figure doubles again, at least. And by the time it is all finished, everybody will want debt relief, and there will be no longer any recognition that, if you ever borrow something, you have to pay it back. That would be very convenient for the borrowers, but not very good for the international financial system.

So we are in the middle of a very curious debate at the moment, in which, quite honestly, I am trying very hard to get our political masters to understand that the slope is very steep, and that these easy political jumps from HIPC I to HIPC II to total debt relief are in fact not easy jumps at all. They have huge implications, particularly on intermediary organizations such as ours.

I will be fighting the good fight in the next two weeks. You will hear a lot of rhetoric in Washington about debt, about the international institutions, about 100 percent debt relief. And I think I understand the case. I am very anxious to hear from you as to whether you think I do or not, or what the implications are that you would like me to represent. But I will be doing my best in the next two weeks to try and get the ministers to understand.

One of the things I have been thinking about is whether to try and get this group to take a stand after the meeting, by putting together a signed and agreed case to put forward and distribute to the ministers, so that your voice is heard. I think that would be a very useful action to take, both politically and practically. And, in fact, each of you may wish to make a special case for your institution. In that way we will have on record the absolute limits of this debt forgiveness program for institutions that have based their future on the assumption that they will be repaid, which is not a whimsical idea in the banking business. No bank can withstand somebody coming in and saying, "Forgive the debtors."

So I believe that, first, after this meeting, my colleagues will report to you. Second, I think it is important that we get a more present voice from this group, and you can decide whether you will do it jointly or individually. But surely, I think, there needs to be more political pressure and representation, both through your ministers and directly, to your shareholders and, in particular, to the donor countries, the wealthy countries. That is something that we should probably be planning for the period between the Spring Meetings and the Annual Meetings this fall in Prague. So I would come back to you on that, and I would strongly recommend that, in addition to everything else we are doing, we consider a more forceful campaign, so that our voice is heard and so that the line is drawn.

I would be very happy and anxious to hear your comments and questions and observations as to whether I have the story right, or whether I have it incorrect, and whether there is any guidance you can give me on what I might do at the Spring Meetings.

Excerpts from an address at the World Bank Early Childhood Development
Conference 2000

WASHINGTON, D.C. | APRIL 10, 2000

In this welcoming address, Wolfensohn focuses on an issue that has always been close to his heart and to that of his wife Elaine: early childhood education and what he calls the "pivotal importance of those early years."

Thank you very much, and good afternoon, ladies and gentlemen. You can see the success I have been having in reaching to the outside by the police that are outside the building at the moment.

It's quite hard in these circumstances to get one's voice heard, but I want to reemphasize what Ruth* has said to you, which is that never in the history of our institution have we sought to reach out more than we have in these recent years, and never have we recognized more the need to have an interchange of views with an audience such as this. We believe that we're moving on the right track in what we're doing.

This week will give us a chance to look at three different issues: today and tomorrow, the issue of early child development; for Wednesday and Thursday, the issue of child labor; and on Friday, the issue of street children.

There are many subjects that we could discuss this week, but these are three core issues that are of relevance to us—relevant not just in the sense of their intellectual importance, but relevant to us in terms of the types of plans and activities that the Bank should be engaged in. And so it is particularly valuable to us to start with the early years, the early childhood development years. In the last five years, with a lot of assistance under the leadership of Mary Young,[†] we have come to recognize what all of you already know, and that is the pivotal importance of those early years. We started with the scientific findings, which tell us, first and foremost, that the development process in those first five years puts a mark on children for the rest of their lives. This is something that is well known to this audience.

But when we looked at our own activities, and particularly at the issue of poverty, we discovered in the demographics that the people who are hit most are the women and children. And when you project forward to the challenge that faces us in the next 25 years, during which we will see 2 billion more people added to our planet of 6 billion, the challenge is even greater. The 4.8 bil-

---

* Ruth Kagia, former education director at the World Bank.
† Mary Eming Young is the lead child development specialist in the Human Development Network at the World Bank.

lion living in developing countries will grow to close to 6.8 billion, because
the 2 billion new arrivals will be added almost entirely to the developing
world. The fact of 2 billion more children coming in that next 25 years poses
to us the question of what strategy, what plans we should adopt given that our
objective is poverty alleviation?

And here one has to recognize that what impacts children most in terms of
their health and education is what happens in those first five years. If you lose
the fight in those first five years, there's not much one can do to make up for
it in the subsequent years. So that first five years of early childhood development is something to which we have now given additional focus, and where
we have participated in the action plans of a number of countries. It's more
than 10 percent of our ongoing portfolio, and it's something that we wish to
press further on.

We are, of course, extremely conscious of the difficulties. None of this can be
done by our edict. None of it can be done just by us making a decision that early
childhood development is an important thing. It gets into cultural practices. It's
very much a familial activity. Unless one can enter the house and participate in
the actions of that household, not physically, of course, but intellectually speaking, not much is likely to change. Unless we can help project these ideas so that
they are embraced within the household, we are setting ourselves a tremendously
difficult task for the future. In many societies, existing cultural practice leads to inadequate attention being given to the children, and too many of them, as you
know, die today for lack of food and from exposure to disease.

I first saw this when I was in Bangladesh. A government official there told me a statistic—I know not whether it's right or wrong—that 25 percent of the children who are lucky enough to reach primary school are already physically and mentally handicapped when they get there. And we know that 125 million kids around the world don't even reach primary school. That is a stunning statistic when you are thinking about pouring more resources into primary education. It means that a quarter of the children will be literally unable to take advantage of the opportunities that are offered in primary education, even assuming they get there.

These are the sorts of issues you will be facing in your discussions in these next two days, and they are discussions that impact us very much. They impact us in the sense that, first of all, we know that we at the Bank can't do it alone. Second, we need an interface with our peers, such as we're having in these next two days, and with people that know more about these issues than we do. And, finally, we know that, to be effective, we have to work in partnership— partnership with governments, partnership with families, partnership with civil society, partnership with other organizations engaged in this activity, with the UNICEFs, with the activities of donor governments around the world. We at the Bank have to be part of that partnership.

But we as an institution do have some leverage in terms of being at the cutting edge of government policy and being able to influence some of the ways in which our client countries think about these issues. We don't claim to be the leader. We don't claim to have all the answers. But we are a factor, and what we ask of you in these coming days is the opportunity to exchange views with you, so that together we can come up with a program to which each one of us can contribute.

NEW CHALLENGES FOR DEVELOPMENT IN THE MIDDLE EAST

Remarks at the 30th-Anniversary International Board of Governors Meeting, Ben-Gurion University of the Negev

ISRAEL | MAY 23, 2000

This address reflects Wolfensohn's long-standing interest in the Middle East and the economic situation in the Palestinian territories. He reminds the audience that, "when you talk about peace, you have to talk economics and hope."

This to me is a remarkable opportunity and one that my father, if he were still alive, would have been very proud of. He actually recruited Ben-Gurion into the Gedud in 1917.* My father was the recruiting officer in the Gedud, and I grew up with the names of the past: not only Ben-Gurion but Shertok, later to become Sharett,[†] and many others who were part of that unit. And to now come to a university named after so distinguished a leader, and to be asked to address you on its 30th anniversary, is something that I find very moving.

I also find it quite moving to be here with my friend Ambassador Indyk.[‡] He and I went to the same *shul* in Australia. It is sort of remarkable that two Australians who could not get work in Sydney wind up somewhere halfway around the world in the Negev. It just shows that this is a country of opportunity, and very soon I hope that we will get a job with Omar Salah[§] that will allow us to live the rest of our lives in great comfort.

The World Bank is an institution that I am very proud to lead and that you probably do not know a lot about. It is an institution that was founded some 55 years ago, essentially to look after the reconstruction following World War II. It gradually mutated into other forms of activity, the most prominent of which has been working in the developing world, trying to bring about equitable development throughout our planet.

The task today is not so easy. We have a planet of 6 billion people, of whom 4.8 billion live in the countries with which the Bank is concerned. Of the 6 billion people on the planet, as I understand my friend Sadako** said this morning, 3 billion live on less than two dollars a day and 1.2 billion live in absolute poverty, on less than one dollar a day.

This is a difficult problem, but one that we seek to address. Our institution is owned by 183 countries, and it has done about $450 billion in lending since

---

* David Ben-Gurion was chief architect of the state of Israel and its first prime minister. The Gedud Ha'Avodah (Labor Battalion) was founded after World War I to help Jewish immigrants into Palestine find work.
† Moshe Shertok (later Sharett) was Israel's first foreign minister.
‡ Martin Indyk, U.S. ambassador to Israel.
§ Founder and chairman of the Century Investment Group, Amman, Jordan.
** Sadako Ogata, United Nations high commissioner for refugees.

its creation. We lend about $20 billion or $30 billion a year, and we have affiliated institutions that deal with the private sector and with investment insurance, and we have another affiliated institution called the International Development Association, which makes concessional loans to the very poorest countries. Altogether the Bank is an institution of nearly 11,000 people, with offices in a hundred countries, now all linked by satellite so that we have voice data and video communications with our offices, and we are running some 400 videoconferences a month now. So if you go to Côte d'Ivoire and you want to see someone in New York or in Nepal or in Brazil, we can set it up on our system. It is truly a World Bank.

All of that sounds rather glamorous and interesting and well financed, were it not for the fact that, in the next 25 years, we will have another 2 billion people coming onto the planet. So in 2025 the world will have 8 billion people, and 97 percent of those additional 2 billion people will be living in developing countries. So instead of 4.8 billion we will have 6.8 billion people living in the parts of the world we deal with. And the question is, What will happen to poverty?

Meanwhile we will have another shift in that 2 billion more people will move into cities and towns. That in itself will be a major demographic change, and we will be faced with all sorts of new problems in how to run countries, how to run states, and how to run cities. And there the essential issue will be, How can we bring about growth first? Because, without growth, one cannot do a lot to bring about positive change. And when we do have growth, how can we use it to reduce poverty?

And why should *we* reduce poverty? What is it that is relevant about an institution like the World Bank or about the United Nations' agencies or about the bilateral agencies that are concerned with the issues of poverty? Why should we be interested? Does it come from the Judeo-Christian belief in giving charity, or is it out of self-interest? Is it for a broader purpose? My judgment, having now worked in the institution for five years and having joined it for this reason, is that the issue of development and the issue of improvement of economic life are inextricably tied to the issue of peace. And nowhere can I say that with greater feeling than in the Middle East, because political agreement and the signing of peace treaties mean something only if economic development and opportunity go along with it.

We are linked in a very complete way. Let me start not in Israel, but from the point of view of the United States or any of the developed countries. The world is no longer two worlds of developed countries and developing countries. To start with, the numbers belie that. But, in the world of economics and trade, 18 percent of the world's products come from developing countries. In another 25 years it will be 30 percent. So the growth is there.

Aside from the growth and the trade linkages, the globe is linked by the air that we breathe, by health, by crime, by drugs, and by finance. We need only think back to the Asian financial crisis and recall that, the next day, it was felt in Israel and Egypt as it was felt all around the world. The world is linked by migration, by all sorts of political trends and influences that simply do not recognize borders. This is not just an issue for the Middle East; this is a global issue. We at the Bank are dealing with it in Bosnia and Herzegovina and in the Central African Republic and the Congo; in Ethiopia and Eritrea; and on the India–Pakistan border and in Central Asia. And we are dealing with issues of politics *and* issues of economics, which are fused in a very real way.

We have just completed a study called *Voices of the Poor,* in which, over seven years, we went out and talked to poor people, 60,000 of them in 60 countries. And what was remarkable was that we found that people are the same everywhere. They are the same as all of you. You have kids; you have a family; you want a certain sense of well-being; you want security; you want a right to represent yourself; you want a voice. And it is the same with poor people. What they do not have is the right to represent themselves. They do not have a voice. Many of them said they do not know whom to trust, the police or the criminals.

Corruption affects poor people much more than rich people. Suppose you are living on two dollars a day and you or your spouse needs health care. If it is going to cost you a dollar under the table, it means the difference between feeding your family and not feeding your family. If you are making $10,000 a year, you can afford it. But poor people cannot. If their health goes, it means the difference between livelihood and no livelihood. And what they want is education and opportunity for themselves and their kids. None of them want charity. They want a chance.

I have now been with my wife to 105 countries. I have been in more slums and villages than I knew existed, and I found that the best people you meet are in those slums and villages. They know what they want. It is the basic needs. They have a very clear view of what is needed. And if you get into the issues of community development and you trust the people in the towns and villages, you never lose a penny because they watch each other, they represent each other, they own the projects, they get them done, and they are more effective.

So I come to this world with that perspective, and I then look at the countries and the areas in which we are operating. But there is one additional overlay, because this world is not static: we have moved from an agricultural revolution to an industrial revolution and now to a digital revolution.

This is clearly a new age, a Third Age, an age that allows me to be linked with my offices by satellite, talking to 10 to 12 people at a time. We are establishing 50 different learning centers now, each complete with 30 seats in a classroom like this one, with an adjacent classroom with 30 or so computers, all linked by our satellite networks so that, wherever you are in the world, you can have a class. This is the way the world is going.

But, more important than that, it is supporting new industries and presenting new challenges, because unless the countries now in development can catch up, they will soon be a generation behind. So, for these countries, the challenge of the digital age is a challenge also of either jumping a generation or falling back a generation. And we are seeking to respond to that new challenge of the digital age in wonderful ways. In fact, one of my colleagues was recently in Addis Ababa, in Ethiopia, talking to a group like this one about connectivity, e-systems, and e-business. And he said to this group of Ethiopians, "Do you know anything about the Internet or Internet sites? Have you heard of it?" And one man put up his hand and said, "I have a site."

And my colleague said, "How do you have a site here in Ethiopia? What business can you do from here?"

"I sell goats."

"How do you sell goats on your site?"

"It is really very simple. There are a lot of Ethiopian taxi drivers in New York, Chicago, and Washington, and they like to buy goats to give to their families. So I have a site on Yahoo, and every day I go to the cybercafé, and I check in and I am doing a wonderful business."

We have another example, in India, where one of our clients put up a computer monitor and a touchpad on the wall of his factory, which was next to a slum. No training, no instructions. First the bigger kids came along and started playing with the computer. And, by the way, we have this all on film. Next we saw that boxes had been put there for the younger kids to stand on so that they could reach the touchpad. After a week they were in touch with the Disney Channel and many others. After a month they had their own Web site, and every day, from 7:00 in the morning to 7:00 at night, you would see people using that computer.

This age is an age where we are increasingly finding computers in villages, not because we are putting them there, but because they are being demanded. We recently had an African woman come over to one of the exhibitions we had at the Bank, in South Africa, one hour north of Cape Town. They went in a helicopter—my wife opened the center—they had no water and no power, but they had a shed, a solar dish, and a computer. And they were using it for all sorts of purposes.

I give you those examples to say to you that this is a real revolution that is occurring, and one that is opening up not just opportunities but the possibility of freedom. And the place where we are looking at this most intently now is China, because the role of Internet and the role of greater productivity will have the single most important impact on political developments in that part of the world, as it may well in the Middle East.

I give you all that by way of background, because these are the sort of things about which we are thinking, and to remind you that the world is a complicated and large place. I have not even mentioned Africa, which has its problems at the moment: 25 percent of the continent is engaged in conflict; there are 23 million cases of AIDS; there are 10 million orphans, and the number is growing exponentially.

And now we come to the Middle East and North Africa, an area of 280 million or so people in a world of 6 billion, with a combined GDP of, give or take, $600 billion out of a global GDP of $30 trillion. Israel, with about $100 billion in GDP, represents one-third of 1 percent of the world's GDP. The whole region may account for 2 percent. I mention this not to downplay what happens here, because the Middle East and North Africa are very important, particularly to the people who live here. But from a global perspective it is a relatively small part of the world. However, in terms of its complexity and in terms of its politics, you have managed to take it to an extreme unmatched anywhere. And daily events set new standards for what one can do if one has the history of our peoples in this area.

It is, of course, more than a joke. It is a very real challenge to Israel and its Arab neighbors at this time, because the issues of equity and social justice are also issues of peace. And when we talk here in the region about treaties, they have to be backed by discussion of growth, of social justice, and of equity, if you are to have peace.

My friend [former Palestinian finance minister Mohammed Zuhdi] Al-Nashashibi knows this very well. We have talked about it many times. And my Jordanian friends know it as well. This is not a question about being Jew or Muslim or Arab. It is a question of us all being human beings with the same aspirations and hopes as the 60,000 people in poverty whom we interviewed.

It is necessary to stand back. It is not a question of *will* there be peace in the region; it is only an issue of *when* there will be peace. Because if there is no peace, there is no future, and if there is no future, your kids will not live in tranquility. There will not be the sense of well-being that I talked about, there will not be the opportunity, and there will not be the future. That is the issue we are facing. It has demonstrated itself as a series of challenges in many ways, in the last days and in the last months and in the last years. But what it needs is a conviction that one must move forward.

And for Israel, with an income per capita of $17,000—and, I might add, with inequity growing in this country, in terms of the spread of wealth—outreach to its Arab neighbors is not just a question of charity. Outreach is a question both of charity and of social justice; it is also a question of self-interest. There is no choice. With a market of close to 300 million people—and the Arab world has not taken advantage of intraregional trade to any significant degree—the prospect of peace opens up an opportunity for intraregional trade within the Arab world but also with Israel.

Would you prefer to have a border, with Lebanon or with the Palestinian territories, where there are no people, or one where business is thriving? Would you prefer to have a border where there are deserts, or one where towns are functioning? Would you prefer to have a town where people are busy, happy, and constructive, or one where there is 40 percent unemployment?

Think not just about social justice. Think about self-interest. I like to feel that justice and equity are part of the Jewish tradition. They are part of the Christian and the Muslim traditions as well. They are part of the human tradition. And never were they more needed than they are today.

When you talk peace, you have to talk economics and hope. And that is the issue that we are privileged to work with in the Bank. And it is an issue that needs contemporaneous treatment along with military and peace agreements. We have discovered in the Bank that it is also part of a broader development challenge. Development is not an instant fix, as Mr. Nashashibi knows very well. And, to my Jordanian friends, the issue of equitable development is not just an issue of putting money in. You have to have structure; you have to have a legal system; you have to have a justice system; you have to protect property rights; you have to have a financial system that works; you have to have a social system that helps the people who cannot help themselves; and you have to fight corruption.

You have to do all those things simultaneously. We are thinking about education, about health, about water, about power, about transportation, about environment, about cultural policy, about rural strategy, about urban strategy, and you cannot just pick one and say, "I will deal with that and not worry about the others." You have to have what we call a comprehensive development program, and it is not an instant fix. It is a medium-term program in which you have to move on these things progressively. And that is not just true for the Middle East; it is true globally.

So the challenge of development, once you recognize it, is not just a matter of bringing in investment. The receiving governments and the people that are in fact running the areas that are developing have an equal, if not greater challenge. They have to put it together in a way that can protect rights, create harmony, create equity, and bring about equitable growth and development. This is not a one-way street. This is not an issue of writing a check; this is an issue of real partnership and real development.

And each region of the world has its own individual characteristics. In this part of the world, as change occurs, many issues are being faced, including issues of the particular forms of governance in the region. Some countries have been democracies; some have not. Some have been monarchies, some dictatorships, or at least under centralized control. And with the development of public interest groups, of civil society, of information, these countries themselves are finding that there is a need to move from centralized control to new forms of governance. That takes time. It has taken time in developed countries to develop government that works. It will take time in developing countries as well.

But what is great about this moment is that there really is an opportunity for a speedier interchange of ideas, speedier support in terms of capacity building and speedier transfer of resources, both financial and intellectual, to try and bring about change. What is needed on the part of everybody in the world today is a sense of focusing not just on the immediate or on what is happening in our own countries, but recognizing that, more than ever in history, we are part of a global community, part of a global pattern, and part of regional patterns. It is a very exciting time.

The point that I would leave you with is this: for you in the audience, this is, I hope, an interesting framework within which to view the present issues. For your children, it is the difference between having peace and not having peace. This is not a theoretical issue—not in the Middle East, and not globally.

If I can try out my Hebrew, let me say this: *Lo alecha hamelecha ligmor, ve lo atah ben chorin lehipater mimenah,* which, for the benefit of my friends from Jordan, means, "It is not incumbent upon you to complete the work, but neither must you avoid doing all you can." That is the task that faces us.

Thank you very much.

PEACE AND POVERTY

JUNE 2000–AUGUST 2002

DEVELOPING COUNTRIES IN AN EVOLVING WORLD FINANCIAL SYSTEM

Remarks to the Harvard Business School Global Alumni Conference on "Business Without Walls"

BERLIN | JUNE 14, 2000

> *At this meeting of fellow alumni of the Harvard Business School, Wolfensohn recalls his training there and urges the audience to recognize the economic potential of the developing world and the interconnectedness of the world economy today. He proposes that the ongoing discussion of a new international financial architecture go further, to consider the need for a new "international development architecture."*

Let me first of all say that, I think, given the distinction of the speakers who will be joining you later in the session, it is not necessary for me to get down into the detail of European integration, the United States' relationship with Europe, or the other issues that were so clearly postulated before you. But I will allow myself the privilege of trying to tell you how, as president of the World Bank, I have a sense of the backdrop against which you are looking at these issues.

I think this may be the first and only time at this conference where we will have a chance to take a look at the world, not just as Europe, which was so well presented to us earlier, but as a world, to try and give you a little sense of the scale, a little sense of the issues, at least as I see them. I hope to get you thinking not just about the United States and Europe, but about our globe.

Five hundred million people coming together in Europe with 250 million in the United States is important, but our planet has 6 billion people on it. That is important because, in the developed world and in the developing world together, we have a total global output of $30 trillion. And it is important to get a sense of the scale.

The 1.2 billion people who live in the so-called developed world—which comprises Europe, the United States, and the other OECD countries[*]— represent approximately 80 percent of that $30 trillion, or about $24 trillion. The other $6 trillion comes from the 4.8 billion people in the developing and transition economies.

It is important that you get these dimensions in your head, because we have got to change our thinking from what it was when many of us graduated. In fact, when I graduated in 1959, there were 3 billion people in the world, and there are now 6 billion. And as we look forward in the next 25 years, we are going to add another 2 billion people to the planet, so we will have 8 billion people. How many of them will come to Europe and the United States and the

---

[*] Member countries of the Organisation for Economic Co-operation and Development.

other OECD countries? About 50 or 60 million. Europe, in terms of population, will remain the same size it is now. Virtually all—96 percent—of the additional 2 billion people will go into the developing world, including the countries in transition from central planning. So from a developing world of 4.8 billion, we move to a developing world of, give or take, 6.8 million. And meanwhile our developed economies stay the same size, plus 50 million or 60 million.

It is important when you think about new markets, when you think about our planet, when you think about financial systems, and when you think about stability that you think about the future and about the world our children are going to live in. That is going to be a world of 26 megacities, cities of 10 million people or more, and over 500 cities of a million people or more, and, as I say, most of the growth will be concentrated in the developing world.

The developing world, which today represents 22 percent of the world's GDP, will by then account for 30 percent. But, regrettably, it is a world that, as you know, is unstable. It is a world that is prone to difficulties, a world, as was mentioned earlier, in which there is a lot of communication and information, which makes clear to people that the world is rather inequitable.

In fact, 3 billion of the 6 billion people now living on the planet live on less than two dollars a day. A billion, two hundred million live on less than one dollar a day. And I will not go into the statistics of the half the world who have never made a phone call, or the 2 billion people who do not have sanitation, or the billion and a half who do not have water, or the millions of kids who are not at school. But it is clearly an inequitable world.

And you might ask, why am I starting off by talking about the developing world, when we have just had a map of Europe shown to us, and when most of us at Harvard Business School were trained to look at business opportunities, entrepreneurship, development, size of markets, capital markets—all the things that I grew up in and worked in? Well, it is for one simple reason. It is that the world does not have any walls. And you cannot think of the developing world as being outside our world, somehow behind the walls.

We have to change our thinking. Look at what happened in the Asian financial crisis. Disturbances in Thailand, Korea, and Indonesia had an immediate impact not just in Cairo and Delhi, but in New York and London, on the capital markets in which we operate. In the last 20 years the extent of external borrowing by those countries has moved from $600 billion to $2.5 trillion, in terms of outstanding obligations. Trade has doubled in the last 10 years. The interrelationships between markets, if you needed a demonstration or proof, came most recently, as I say, in the Asian financial crisis.

But we are not just linked by finance. We are linked today by communication, by technology—where, by the way, the developed world has practically

90 percent of all hosts and of Internet connectivity, where New York City has more than the rest of the developing world put together, but where there is enormous growth and where there is enormous potential in the developing world. And we are linked by environment. Every one of us is subject to global warming. Every one of us is affected by the destruction of forests in places you do not know about, but where forests are being destroyed at the rate of an acre a second. We are affected by biodiversity. We are affected by crime. We are affected by terror. We are affected by migration. Someone earlier gave a greeting in Turkish. I came last week from Turkey and was told that there are 2.5 million people of Turkish extraction now living in Germany alone. And if you look at the United States, and you see the movement from Latin America to the United States, and as you look forward in terms of the integration of Europe, you think in terms of migration. You think in terms of the flows of people.

This is a world dynamic that is different, certainly from the world of 1932, and even different from the world that I graduated in. But it is the world of the new millennium. And in this city, where I was on the night that the Wall came down, you have a remarkable example also of the changes in the world in which we live.

Had I been talking here 15 years ago, I would have been talking of East-West confrontation. For those of you who were in Berlin and went by Checkpoint Charlie, as I did last night, there was not a color picture of a G.I. there back then. There was Checkpoint Charlie. And it was a cold experience. And we divided our world into two worlds.

Today, what happens in Russia and in the rest of the former Soviet Union is crucially important because, first of all, there are the remains of an enormous political machine. There is a real attempt now under President [Vladimir] Putin, I believe, to enter the market economy in a very focused way. And it is in all our interest that Russia succeed.

As I said, I have just been to Turkey. It is in all our interest that Turkey succeeds, not because of the chance of a recurrence of communism there otherwise, but because there is a movement of fundamentalism that can be addressed most effectively in Turkey. So Turkey is important to Europe. Russia is important to Europe. China is important to Europe.

The first thing you have to understand is that there is a connectivity today, a linkage—as, indeed, the title of this conference suggests—that has never been more meaningful than it is now. And most of us are not ready for it.

We look at Europe and we are experts on European integration. We look at NAFTA [the North American Free Trade Area], and, with limitations, we have some sense of American integration. We see regionalism developing in different parts of the world. But are we ready for the real question, that of the 4.8 billion in the developing and transition economies who are now part of our world? They are indeed part of our world in that they are growing faster and will soon represent 30 percent of world GDP; they are part of our world because, whether it be crime or terror or drugs or trade or finance or health or environment, that *is* our world.

And so I put it to you, as you enter this conference: Do not be too narrow in your thinking, because what happens in that world will determine whether we live in peace or whether we do not. That is the world your children will have to be concerned about. And it is a world in which we have to set some rules, in which we have to try and deal with some issues so as to make it more predictable, more certain, more effective, more balanced, and more equitable.

And here we come to one of the elements of that task, which is the international financial system. Efforts are being made today to make the international financial system a better functioning system, a system of greater transparency, a system of greater integrity, a system in which there is greater predictability, because it was thought that if they had known more about what was happening in Korea, Thailand, and Indonesia, the foreign banks—some of them led, perhaps, by some of you here—would not have loaned perhaps as extensively as they did. Would they have loaned $80 billion to the Indonesian private sector? That would be surprising if they had known all the facts.

But the issue is not just information. The issue, in the countries in which we are operating, is also that just designating a new financial system, just setting rules, without training people in governance, without training supervisors, without a change in culture, is a step in the right direction, but it is only one step.

And what about the countries in which there is not a functioning legal system, where there are no bankruptcy codes, where the judges can be bought, where the legal systems do not work, where corruption is rife? How can you have an effective financial system unless you deal with the fundamentals of governance, the legal system and the judicial system, issues of corruption, issues of strengthening integrity, and building managerial competence? You cannot.

So do not be misled into thinking, as we talk about the new international financial structure, that it begins and ends with that. It does not. There is a need for a much greater sense of development, which I call the international *development* architecture, which includes not just finance but structure as well, and moves to education, health, infrastructure, environmental policy, cultural policy—all the factors that go into making a society work.

And there is a need for trained people, and I should perhaps tell you that the World Bank has drawn heavily on the Harvard Business School. Indeed, as [Harvard Business School Dean] Kim Clark knows, for the last three years we have had our own six-week program that we have put 600 of our top people through, and where we bring in outsiders to join us so that, for our own sake, we can take a better look at ourselves and be more open-minded and more effective in the way we do things. And then we make those same people go and live for a while in a developing country, not in a hotel but in a slum or a village out in the field, so they can sense what poverty is, and sense what development is, so that they can bring a different orientation to their work.

But I should tell you of one Harvard graduate we hired, whom we sent to Uzbekistan, and he claimed to be an agricultural expert. And he came to a field where there was a farmer with a whole bunch of sheep, and, very confidently, as befits a Harvard graduate, he said, "If I can tell you how many sheep there are in your field, will you give me one?" And the farmer, in perfect Russian, said, "Yes, I will." And the Harvard grad took one quick look, and he said, "There are 875." The farmer said, "That is the most amazing thing I have ever seen. Take one." So the Harvard man bent down, picked up an animal, started to walk away, and the farmer then called to him and said, "Excuse me, sir. If I can tell you where you did your training, will you give it back?" And the Harvard man said, "Yes, I will."

"You went to the Harvard Business School."

"How did you know?"

"You just picked up my dog."

I just wanted to make the point that there are some practical elements that we all need to have, even with the extraordinary education that we are all lucky enough to have from our alma mater.

But, seriously, it is important that we build the level of competence and capacity, and here we are entering a new age in terms of technology and distance learning, because the other big difference I am finding as I travel around the world is that there is absolutely no doubt that we have moved from an agricultural to an industrial revolution, but we are now in a digital age.

And as we look at the world without walls, I look at my own institution, where we have succeeded now in linking all our 100 offices overseas by satellite, voice, data, and video. We are running 400 videoconferences a month now, and shortly we will reach 500. We are establishing distance learning facilities in countries throughout the world. We are setting up global gateways for information and knowledge.

One of my colleagues—and this is a true story, the other was not—had a recent experience where he went to address a group in Addis Ababa, Ethiopia, and he said to the group, "I am here to talk to you about e-commerce." And, of course, there is not much penetration of Internet sites in Ethiopia. So he said, "Do any of you know what an Internet site is?" And a man put up his hand and said, "Well, I have a business on the Internet." And my colleague said, "How do you possibly have an Internet business?"

"I sell goats."

"How do you sell goats on the Internet?"

"Well, there are a lot of Ethiopian taxi drivers in New York, Chicago, and Philadelphia, and it is our tradition in Ethiopia to send goats to our families on holidays. So I have opened a website, and every day I go to the cybercafé in Addis, I check my Web site, and I am doing a hell of a business selling goats to taxi drivers in the United States for delivery in Ethiopia."

I could give you literally dozens of examples of the impact that the Internet is already having in the developing world. But it is also a huge challenge, because if we do not bring those 4.8 billion people, soon to be 6.8 billion, into that world, they will fall further behind. But if we do, it holds within it the seeds of a major jump forward.

And so for us in my organization, and many in the development field, when we talk about worlds without walls, we are talking about worlds without walls in an Internet age. And that is a big difference from when I went to Harvard Business School.

We have got to change our thinking. My only plea to you at this conference is to think not just in terms of the United States and Europe, but in terms of the orientation of that marketplace to a world that is five times the size of the United States and Europe combined, and in which most of you now have a bigger stake than ever before.

My last statistic: 10 years ago, in 1990, around $40 billion was invested each year by the private sector in that developing world, and about another $60 billion came from agencies such as mine. In 1997 that figure for private sector investing peaked at over $300 billion, and ours had decreased from $60 billion to approximately $50 billion. So, as recently as 10 years ago, total private sector investing—that means direct investment, bank lending, and portfolio investment—was only two-thirds the size of official transfers. Today the marketplace has shown that it is now at least five times the size. And even in the wake of the Asian crisis, foreign direct investment in the developing world has continued to grow, to reach $170 billion in this last year.

If you need proof that this is a world without walls, think only of these numbers. And as you think of the challenges of the next millennium, do not just think of them as being in the United States and Europe, but think of them in terms of a world in which the developing countries will have six out of every seven people on the planet, and where the six are not behind walls, but are part of our universe.

Thank you very much.

THE ROLE OF INFORMATION TECHNOLOGY IN A KNOWLEDGE-BASED GLOBAL ECONOMY

Address to the United Nations Economic and Social Council

NEW YORK | JULY 5, 2000

In this address Wolfensohn is speaking to an ECOSOC (UN Economic and Social Council) chamber at a high-level policy dialogue with representatives of finance and trade institutions. He describes how information and communications technology can be used to support development on a daily basis. Wolfensohn says the choice is not between "bread and computers," adding that countries need both to survive and succeed.

Mr. President, Your Excellencies, Ladies and Gentlemen:

It is a great pleasure to be back with you today to discuss this very important issue and to share the podium with my friends Louise Frechette and Secretary Summers,* as well as Eduardo Aninat, Rubens Ricupero, and Mike Moore.† The subject that we are discussing today has been very well framed by the introductory remarks of the deputy secretary-general and the secretary of the Treasury, and theirs is similar to the framework that I would also like to set out. When we look at information technology in the context of the global information-based economy, we must not lose sight of the fundamental issue of poverty and development, and we must, as was pointed out earlier, recognize that information and communications technology is not some magic bullet that will solve that problem.

We have to look at poverty within the context of its reality. There are 3 billion people in the world living on less than two dollars a day, and a billion-plus people living in absolute poverty, on less than one dollar a day. The challenge facing us in the next 25 years, as 2 billion more people join us on our planet, raising the global population from 6 billion to 8 billion, practically all of them in the developing countries, is how to address the challenge of poverty and equity. So the question for us today is this: To what extent does Internet technology and modern, knowledge-based communications technology affect this basic challenge—the challenge of poverty?

On that point, in our own organization we have gone back and looked at the results of our recent study, titled *Voices of the Poor,* to see what it is that makes a difference to poor people. As many of you know, the issue is not just money; it is also knowledge and it is also opportunity. What we need to do if we are to affect the future of our planet, if we are to affect global poverty, is

---

* Deputy secretary-general of the United Nations, and U.S. secretary of the Treasury, respectively.
† Deputy managing director of the International Monetary Fund; secretary-general of the United Nations Conference on Trade and Development; and director-general of the World Trade Organization, respectively.

to give people living in poverty the opportunity to help themselves, and to make the assistance that we give available in a more organized and efficient manner. To implement those hopes, we need to address the question of information and communications technology.

At the World Bank we are seeking to understand how we as an institution can adapt from our original purpose, that of a financial institution with growing experience in development, to being an institution that is both a money institution and a knowledge institution. It is very important that we conceive the development challenge as involving both those essential factors.

In April of this year there was a high-level meeting of experts here at the United Nations to address the question and scale of this problem. For those of you who have not read their report, I suggest that you do so, because it provides some background to the issue of the so-called digital divide: how, of a world population of 6 billion, 276 million, or fewer than 5 percent, are Internet users, and of those 276 million, 90 percent live in the developed world. As the report points out, there are more Internet hosts in New York than in all of continental Africa, and more in Finland than in Latin America and the Caribbean. As we look at the issue of investment in information infrastructure, we find that the OECD countries[‡] are investing an average of $130 per capita in their own countries, and Sub-Saharan Africa is investing $9 per capita. I give you these stark figures not to recite to you a lot of statistics, but simply to tell you that the gap exists and that it is wide, and it presents a major challenge.

The second thing I would put to you is the issue that these experts raised: whether or not we should address this challenge, why we should address it, and whether we should address it now. The debate can be framed in the question, "Do you want bread or do you want computers?" and the answer is that you want both. One has to look at Internet technology within the context that Larry Summers and Louise Frechette have framed it, within the context of the development framework: we cannot forget growth, we cannot forget legal and justice systems and structural and financial systems, we cannot forget education and health, we cannot forget rural strategy, we cannot forget anything in our development paradigm. But we can look at information technology and see how it can assist us in terms of advancing our methodology to meet the challenges of poverty. That is the central issue for this Council meeting.

In our own institution, we have concluded that there is no way that we can come up with some broad, Olympian plan for what is going to happen with

---

‡ Member countries of the Organisation for Economic Co-operation and Development.

technology. We all have to, first of all, recognize that this is a challenge and an opportunity and then work together in a flexible way in the coming years, to try to meet the objectives set forth by this expert panel calling for connectivity to all communities in the world by 2004. But we must try and find innovative ways in which we can learn together and cooperate in a wholly new endeavor. There is no past paradigm for how we might work together using Internet technology. In fact, if we were to look at our paradigms in the past, they are probably contrary to what is needed. The bilateral institutions, the multilateral institutions, civil society, and the private sector have barely cooperated at all on the development agenda.

In today's world we find civil society constantly attacking Mike Moore and myself and the IMF for all the things that we do, whatever we do. This is hardly a basis for cooperation. Bilateral agencies frequently don't talk to the multilaterals, and even within the UN system there is not always the cooperation that we need. For Internet technology to work, we have to start afresh, because we need each other, and because information and knowledge need to be shared. That is absolutely crystal clear. And in a fast-evolving world, we need to learn from each other about those innovative practices that have already borne fruit.

Let me give you some very specific initiatives in which we at the Bank are engaged and in which we invite ownership, participation, and help. Why am I addressing these immediate practical initiatives? Because we don't have an overall plan. We have only our series of initiatives from which we want to learn and which we want to develop. And we invite the participation and help of all of you. Let me just start with *info*Dev [the World Bank's Information for Development program]. This is an association of private sector and public institutions to try and finance innovative practices in developing countries in the use of technology. They relate to marketing; they relate to sharing information.

We have even had a recent experience in the slums of India, where we put on a wall in a slum area a computer monitor, under glass, and a touchpad built into the wall; it was made available to the kids and to the adults in the slum to see what they would do with it. No information was given on how to use it. All we had was a camera to see what would happen, to see whether the existence of the computer itself—programmed in English, not even in the local language—would have an impact. In the first few days we discovered that boys from 6 to 12 years old were approaching the computer, and then the 16-year-olds. Next we saw boxes. Why boxes? So that the little kids could stand on them and reach the touchpad. The parents, the women at least, never came near. After one week, the kids had invented their own language for the cursor and learned how to use it, how to click. And within a month they were onto the Disney Channel and were preparing files in a language that was unknown to most of them, but there were some kids who knew some English and they came together. We are now doing 150 of these examples around India to try and test how the existence of this capacity will make a difference.

We have also done things in Africa. Larry talked about his experience in Côte d'Ivoire. I had an experience in Côte d'Ivoire where I went to visit some coffee and cocoa plantations, and then to a village where I was duly made a chief with my beautiful robes, sitting with my brother chiefs in the hut. They said, "Would you like to see our computers?" I said I would be delighted, and

I went, and there I saw two Ivorians, one testing the quality of the cocoa and coffee being brought in, and the other with a computer, getting information from Reuters on prices, which was then sent out on telephones and pagers so that people in the communities, the same poor people whom I had visited in the morning, had price information when they came to sell their goods.

I could go on and on with these examples, but I will give you one last one. The same *info*Dev representative went to Ethiopia to talk about e-business. He said, "I suppose none of you know what an Internet site is." Someone put up his hand and said, "I do. I sell goats on the Internet." The *info*Dev representative said, "How do you sell goats over the Internet?" He said, "There are Ethiopian taxi drivers in Chicago, New York, and Washington, and it is our tradition for them to buy goats for their families in Ethiopia, so I sell them goats on the Internet from my cybercafé, and I have a great business going."

Why am I telling you these stories? Because they show that there is no way that we can plan the evolution of the use of the Internet in developing countries. We have dozens and dozens of examples, from getting information on how to deal with an invasion of ants in Ecuador to learning how to sink wells. Let us just make sure that we get the technology out there, so that the knowledge is available and that people can use it.

As a second point, let us make sure, in our work with governments, that the regulatory framework is such that people can have access at low cost. Let us not have a tool that is so costly that poor people cannot use it. Let us ensure, as part of the policy of all your governments, that Internet accessibility is central and basic for poor people, because there is no sense having the technology if it costs too much to access. That can be done by establishing appropriate arrangements for customs and taxes in advance, as has been done in Estonia and in Costa Rica and in Brazil. There are many examples that we can follow.

What else have we done? We have established a framework now for linking high schools around the world, called the Global Distance Learning Network. Already 35,000 kids in 15 countries are linked, and we are aiming at 3.5 million by 2004. High schools and teachers are linked from the North to the South and from the South to the South, enriching the education process. And teaching the teachers to use computers is important. In Africa we have a virtual university now in 14 countries teaching degree courses in computer science and in business from the west coast of Canada, from the east coast of the United States, and from Dublin. This week I opened an expansion of the Global Distance Learning Network to 13 countries. We hope to have 50 by the middle of next year. What are they? They're classrooms that are linked by satellite to each other and to the world. We had a conference with all 13 of these locations simultaneously last week as we opened it. We cut the ribbons simultaneously in 13 different locations, from Asia to Africa, and, adjacent to that, a room with 30 computers to link to the rest of the world.

These are the types of things that one can do. But what is most important is that all of us come together to pool our knowledge and our experience. This, in my judgment, is the biggest challenge of all. It is the need to use technology to bring about the cooperation that should exist among all of us. I don't think any of us today could take a subject—say, judicial reform—and claim that in any country we would know all the organizations cooperating in that reform. We surely could not do it on a global basis. All of us work in little silos. By chance we may have the information, because of good people in the field. But the first thing that we could do is establish a common information base on what is going on with whom and in what countries, so that with a press of a button you could get information on what everybody is doing in any particular subject area in any part of the world.

We already have a framework for this in our own organization, so that we can get that kind of information now within the Bank. But I must tell you that until two years ago we did not have it in the Bank. We did not know what one department was doing in relation to others. So we are now pushing forward an initiative called the Global Development Gateway. In the next six months we will be approaching all of you, not as a World Bank initiative, but as an initiative that all of us must own, so that nongovernmental organizations can participate, so that each of you can participate, so that each country will have a gateway for its country knowledge. We are working in 13 countries already, to prepare the gateway and to provide knowledge and places where information can be exchanged—communities for the exchange of information. You will be able to go in and point to a country on the screen and get the latest information on what is going on, the latest news from a hundred different news locations. We already have this in place. We will have pages for mayors: for the last year, we have already been linking 300 mayors in Latin America every Saturday morning through the Monterrey Institute of Technology, giving courses to mayors on how to run their towns and cities. These are both synchronous in that they provide teaching in real time, and asynchronous in that the discussions go on all week. They focus on everything from running a fire department to drawing up a budget.

The potential is enormous, but we ourselves must start getting together an orderly framework of information, and we must start to trust each other in terms of sharing knowledge and experience: good knowledge, bad knowledge; good experience, bad experience. We must try and save ourselves from making the same mistakes others have made, and we must develop best practice and provide the opportunity for the creation of communities.

We are working with major international organizations to come up with the prototype for development of the gateway. It is already essentially developed. We will be coming to all of you to offer this as a framework for both developed and developing countries to participate in the exchange of knowledge. Let me point out that this is not just information going from developed to developing countries. Accessibility and information on the Internet are equal. There is just as much to be learned from the experience of developing countries, maybe more, than from the experience of developed countries trying to act as professors. This is a crucial change in terms of the development experience, and it is something that all of us must grasp.

Don't let people talk to you about the Internet being a luxury. It may not be an alternative to bread, but it does give us the opportunity of bringing knowledge and opportunity to people at all levels throughout the world. It is time to grasp that fact. It is time for us to pledge to each other, whether we be in international institutions, bilateral institutions, the private sector, civil society, or among the leadership in the countries we serve, to come together and make sure that this new age—not the agricultural revolution, not the industrial revolution, but the digital revolution—improves equity for poor people throughout the world. I hope that today adds fervor to that endeavor.

Thank you very much, Mr. President.

Foreword to *World Development Report 2000/2001,* published for the World Bank by
Oxford University Press

AUGUST 2000

> *This foreword to the 2000/2001* World Development Report *recommends action in three areas: promoting opportunity, facilitating empowerment, and enhancing security.*

Poverty amid plenty is the world's greatest challenge. We at the Bank have made it our mission to fight poverty with passion and professionalism, putting it at the center of all the work we do. And we have recognized that successful development requires a comprehensive, multifaceted, and properly integrated mandate. This Report seeks to expand the understanding of poverty and its causes and sets out actions to create a world free of poverty in all its dimensions. It both builds on our past thinking and strategy and substantially broadens and deepens what we judge to be necessary to meet the challenge of reducing poverty. It argues that major reductions in human deprivation are indeed possible, and that the forces of global integration and technological advance can and must be harnessed to serve the interests of poor people. Whether this occurs will depend on how markets, institutions, and societies function—and on the choices for public action, globally, nationally, and locally.

The Report accepts the now-established view of poverty as encompassing not only low income and consumption but also low achievement in education, health, nutrition, and other areas of human development. And, based on what people say poverty means to them, it expands this definition to include powerlessness and voicelessness, and vulnerability and fear. These dimensions of human deprivation emerged forcefully from our *Voices of the Poor* study, conducted as background for the Report, which systematically sought the views of more than 60,000 men and women living in poverty in 60 countries.

These different dimensions of poverty interact in important ways. So do interventions to improve the well-being of poor people. Increasing education leads to better health outcomes. Improving health increases income-earning potential. Providing safety nets allows poor people to engage in higher-risk, higher-return activities. And eliminating discrimination against women, ethnic minorities, and other disadvantaged groups both directly improves their well-being and enhances their ability to increase their incomes.

The 20th century saw great progress in reducing poverty and improving well-being. In the past four decades life expectancy in the developing world increased 20 years on average, the infant mortality rate fell more than half, and fertility rates declined by almost half. In the past two decades net primary school enrollment in developing countries increased by 13 percent. Between 1965 and 1998 average incomes more than doubled in developing countries, and in 1990–98 alone the number of people in extreme poverty fell by 78 million.

But, at the start of a new century, poverty remains a global problem of huge proportions. Of the world's 6 billion people, 2.8 billion live on less than $2 a day, and 1.2 billion on less than $1 a day. Six infants of every 100 do not see their first birthday, and 8 do not survive to their fifth. Of those who do reach school age, 9 boys in 100, and 14 girls, do not go to primary school.

These broad trends conceal extraordinary diversity in experience in different parts of the world and large variations among regions, with some seeing advances and others setbacks in crucial nonincome measures of poverty. Widening global disparities have increased the sense of deprivation and injustice for many. And social mobility and equal opportunity remain alien concepts for far too many people.

Future demographic changes will add to the challenge we face in further reducing poverty. In the next 25 years roughly 2 billion people will be added to the world's population—almost all of them (an estimated 97 percent) in developing countries, putting tremendous pressure on these societies. Clearly, much must be done to reduce poverty in its multiple dimensions and to promote human freedom, today and in the years ahead.

While current and future challenges remain daunting, we enter the new millennium with a better understanding of development. We have learned that traditional elements of strategies to foster growth—macroeconomic stability and market-friendly reforms—are essential for reducing poverty. But we now also recognize the need for much more emphasis on laying the institutional and social foundations for the development process and on managing vulnerability and encouraging participation to ensure inclusive growth. And while domestic action is critical, we have also learned that global developments exert a potent influence on processes of change at national and local levels—and that global action is central to poverty reduction. We have taken a fresh look at our work through the Comprehensive Development Framework, which converges with the views and findings of this Report.

Based on its analysis of ideas and experience, this Report recommends actions in three areas:

- *Promoting opportunity:* expanding economic opportunity for poor people by stimulating overall growth and by building up their assets (such as land and education) and increasing the returns on these assets, through a combination of market and nonmarket actions

- *Facilitating empowerment:* making state institutions more accountable and responsive to poor people, strengthening the participation of poor people in political processes and local decision making, and removing the social barriers that result from distinctions of gender, ethnicity, race, religion, and social status
- *Enhancing security:* Reducing poor people's vulnerability to ill health, economic shocks, crop failure, policy-induced dislocations, natural disasters, and violence, as well as helping them cope with adverse shocks when they occur. A big part of this is ensuring that effective safety nets are in place to mitigate the impact of personal and national calamities.

Advances in the three areas are fundamentally complementary—each is important in its own right, and each enhances the others. Drawing on this framework, countries need to develop their own poverty reduction strategies, in a manner consistent with preservation of culture. Decisions on priorities must be made at the national level, reflecting national priorities. But action must also take place with local leadership and ownership, reflecting local realities. There is no simple, universal blueprint.

Action at the local and national levels is not enough, however. The evidence of the past decade vividly reveals the importance of global action, both to ensure that the opportunities from global integration and technological advance benefit poor people, and to manage the risks of insecurity and exclusion that may result from global change. Five actions are key:

- promoting global financial stability and opening the markets of rich countries to the agricultural goods, manufactures, and services of poor countries
- bridging the digital and knowledge divides, thus bringing technology and information to people throughout the world
- providing financial and nonfinancial resources for international public goods, especially medical and agricultural research
- increasing aid and debt relief to help countries take actions to end poverty, within a comprehensive framework that puts countries themselves—not external aid agencies—at the center of the design of development strategy and ensures that external resources are used effectively to support the reduction of poverty
- giving a voice to poor countries and poor people in global forums, including through international links with organizations of poor people.

Public action must be driven by a commitment to poverty reduction. The public and private sectors must work together—along with civil society—both within and between countries. While we have much to learn, and while the world continues to change rapidly, the experiences reviewed in this Report show that there is now sufficient understanding to make actions to reduce poverty truly effective.

We are living in a time in which the efforts and issues surrounding poverty reduction are subject to great scrutiny. In the aftermath of protests and in the midst of controversy, this Report offers real substance to the public debate and brings the dialogue to the foreground, where indeed the goal of a world without poverty belongs.

With Peter Seligmann and Mohamed T. El-Ashry,* published in
BusinessWorld (Manila)

AUGUST 29, 2000

In this essay, Wolfensohn and his coauthors announce the launch of the
Critical Ecosystem Partnership Fund, which aims to provide poor people
with job alternatives while conserving biodiversity.

Over the last 10 years, the international community has spent some $4 billion
to conserve biological diversity. This has paid for a lot of good work and we
have scored some important wins. But overall, we are failing to stem the lethal
dynamic of chronic poverty, growing population, and unbridled consumption
which is destroying species a thousand times faster than ever before. We need
to do conservation differently if we are to cope with the potentially catastrophic
impact of these pressures on the natural systems that support life on earth.

Let us start with one of the success stories. Along the coast of Brazil, the
pressures on the Atlantic rainforest are gradually receding as local communities,
private groups and state governments work together to put in place an action
plan to safeguard the unique habitat they share with 20,000 different kinds of
plants, of which more than 8,000 are found nowhere else in the world. They
have come to understand and explain to others that there are viable alternatives
to deforestation. Increasingly, they see more opportunities in protecting the
forest—for tourism and other productive uses—than in cutting it down.

Africa and Asia also offer compelling examples of how we can turn the destructive tide by working together and setting priorities. Projects with strong
community support show that it is possible to fight poverty by protecting the
ecosystems that underpin water resources, agriculture and rural livelihoods.
Unfortunately, there is far more evidence to the contrary: of outright destruction proceeding apace in the face of what are too often uncoordinated attempts to do the right thing.

The result is that some 12% of mammal species and 11% of bird and plant
species are threatened with extinction. This is bad news for us all but particularly for poor people in the developing world. For them, conserving biodiversity is not just about long-term welfare. It is about survival because so many
of them depend on the habitats that support biodiversity for their daily needs.

Deforestation in the Sierra Madre watershed in the northern Philippines
poses a threat to the region's biodiversity and people, but also to those in
Metro Manila hundreds of miles to the south who depend on the Sierra Madre

---

* Chairman and chief executive officer of Conservation International, and chairman and chief executive officer of the Global Environment Fund, respectively.

Mountains for their water supply. Meanwhile, the fury of Hurricane Mitch [in 1998] vented on the bare hillsides of Central America set back development in many parts of the region by 40 years.

It is easy to throw up our arms in despair. We have swapped national debt for nature, negotiated international conventions, signed solemn agreements, and implemented hundreds of projects. What more can we do? Our three agencies have taken a look at what works and what does not, and tried to come up with a practical approach to better safeguard biodiversity by complementing the many efforts already under way.

If we are to make a real difference we must involve poor people and communities more centrally in the management of their lives and the stewardship of our shared natural resources. In other words, we need an approach that places ordinary citizens front and center in the fight to conserve biodiversity.

Where to begin? All species and their habitats are important. But some areas are more richly endowed than others. Some 60% of all terrestrial species are found in 25 so-called "hot spots" which make up just 1.4% of Earth's total surface area. The list includes places like Madagascar, West Africa, and the tropical Andes in South America. All are in critical condition and offer enormous returns in terms of species conserved. Arguments about economic efficiency bolster biological ones in suggesting we need to focus more attention on the natural wealth of these places.

Action at the grassroots and geographic focus are only part of the solution. We also need to learn to work together in new, turfless ways. For too long, conservation groups and funding agencies have divided the natural world up into pizza-like slices, with each doing its own thing and failing to coordinate with others working just across the river or mountain range. In the Mayan forests of Central America, park service teams on either side of national borders have no contact with each other, yet they are working on the same ecosystem and confront the same problems. This makes no sense.

We must find ways to share our visions, to set priorities together and to forge a consensus about how to go forward.

To this end, our three organizations have joined together to create the Critical Ecosystem Partnership Fund with a target of $150 million. This is a new source of money exclusively for civil society groups working to protect biodiversity in the hot spots. The aim is to help agencies and communities pull together more effectively and have a greater impact by providing information about what others are doing and underwriting crucial activities that otherwise would not be funded.

The Fund will be flexible enough to ensure that conservation investments achieve maximum impact.

Streamlined decision-making procedures will allow quick responses to new threats and for urgent smaller-scale projects.

Grant guidelines will be available on the Internet and applications can be submitted online.

We have to move fast if we are to create realistic alternatives for poor people and thereby relieve the growing pressures on the natural environment. This new Fund—the Critical Ecosystem Partnership Fund—will help us find solutions that allow poor people to have a better way of life while at the same time conserving the biodiversity on which the long-term survival of us all depends.

Address to the Board of Governors at the Annual Meetings of the World Bank and the International Monetary Fund

PRAGUE | SEPTEMBER 26, 2000

In the first Annual Meetings speech of his second five-year term, Wolfensohn appeals for action to address what he calls a "world scarred by inequality." He praises the Czech Republic's transition process and uses human anecdotes to illustrate development challenges. Acknowledging the protests outside the meeting hall, Wolfensohn says he shares the demonstrators' passion but cautions that dialogue must be built on constructive and mutual respect.

Mr. Chairman, Governors, Ladies and Gentlemen:

I am delighted to welcome you to these Annual Meetings of the International Monetary Fund and the World Bank Group. I extend a very special welcome to the delegation from San Marino, which becomes the Bank's newest member country this year.

I would like to thank our chairman, Trevor Manuel,* for his support and for his powerful speech. He has shown that rare combination of leadership in the fight for freedom and sound economic management after freedom has been achieved. I would also like to thank the governors and the Board of Executive Directors for their partnership in the work of the Bank.

May I also express my admiration for all that [IMF Managing Director] Michel Camdessus has achieved over his years of leadership at the IMF, and thank him for his friendship and his close collaboration. I look forward to working in the same close relationship with Horst Köhler, and I believe we have made a great start. I am looking forward to our joint visit to Africa, as Horst has mentioned.

Let me emphasize how strongly I share what Horst has just said about our joint understanding of the complementary roles of the Bank and the Fund. Our shared objective is to improve the quality of life and reduce poverty through sustainable and equitable growth. In pursuit of this common goal, the Bank's core mandate is to reduce poverty, particularly by focusing on the institutional, structural, and social dimensions of development. It thus complements the Fund's focus on macroeconomic issues in pursuit of its main objective, which is to promote and maintain international financial stability. Let me underscore how closely these are intertwined. If we fail to confront the flawed structures and social tensions that undermine macroeconomic stability,

---

* Chairman of the Development Committee and minister of finance of South Africa.

the poor will be the first casualties. At the same time, as we pursue fiscal responsibility, our first priority must be protecting the poor.

I would also like to thank the Czech Republic and the people and authorities of Prague for hosting these meetings. They have done a magnificent job under difficult circumstances. I thank President Václav Havel, who so uniquely encapsulates in one person, one voice, the hopes and dreams of a generation. His words today were indeed inspirational, and we shall always remember his call for a renewal of values.

The Czech Republic has felt the pain and the difficulties of the transition process. But it has been a pioneer and is firmly committed to building the institutions, the market structures, and the governance that are essential for equitable growth. And our Meetings here in Prague, at the heart of Europe, symbolize the great significance of the movement for European integration.

This is the sixth time I stand before you as president of the World Bank Group—and my first address in my second term as president. I have learned much in the last five years, during which Elaine and I have traveled to more than 100 countries. I learned from a woman in the *favelas* of Rio de Janeiro, who participated in a self-sustaining community water and sewerage program, that development is not about charity; it is about inclusion and empowerment. I learned from a shrimp farmer in the Mekong Delta, robbed of his livelihood by environmental degradation in the mangrove swamps, that hard work can be for nothing if we do not address environmental challenges. I learned from a Muslim religious leader in Côte d'Ivoire, on one of my very first trips for the Bank, that if you give the poor money with one hand and take it back in debt service with the other, you do little to alleviate poverty. This simple lesson was the basis for the creation of the Heavily Indebted Poor Countries Initiative.

Above all, I have learned about a common humanity. People in poverty want for their children what we in this hall want for ours: education, good health, security, and opportunity. They want voice. They do not want charity. They want a chance to make a better life for themselves. They want respect for their human rights. We are all here to work for that common humanity and, above all, to fight against poverty with passion.

But, to overcome poverty, passion is not enough. We must act, and act effectively. And we must commit ourselves for the long haul. I believe the fundamental changes of the last decade, challenging and difficult as they have been, provide us with a real opportunity for a dramatic advance in the fight against poverty. That opportunity is now, and we must seize it.

We have deepened our understanding of what poverty is and of how to generate equitable development. We are changing our institution and the way we do business to deliver our services more effectively, transparently, and with greater accountability. But we will make progress in fighting poverty only if we all work together—developing and developed countries, international institutions, civil society in all its forms, and the private sector. Ours must be a partnership to leverage the fight against poverty. Ours must be a partnership to build a new internationalism to match a globalized economy.

Outside these walls, young people are demonstrating against globalization. I believe deeply that many of them are asking legitimate questions, and I embrace the commitment of a new generation to fight poverty. I share their passion and their questioning. Yes, we all have a lot to learn. But I believe we can move forward only if we deal with each other constructively and with mutual respect. In this context, I am very grateful to President Havel for having organized a colloquium for dialogue recently here in Prague.

The World at the Millennium

We stand at the beginning of a new millennium and at the end of a decade during which globalization has accelerated dramatically. This is a time to assess where we have been and where we are now, as well as to provide a vision for the future. This is a time of great opportunity, but also of tremendous challenges. We must treat globalization as an opportunity and poverty as our challenge.

But what do we mean by globalization? Globalization is about an increasingly interconnected and interdependent world. It is about international trade, investment, and finance growing far faster than national incomes, making our economies more and more closely integrated. It is also about international financial crises: as we saw in the East Asian experience, instability in one country can affect us all. It is about technologies that have already transformed our ability to communicate in a way that would have been unimaginable a few years ago. It is about illness, and I think particularly of HIV/AIDS, malaria, and tuberculosis. It is about crime, about violence, about threats and terrorism, which do not respect national boundaries. It is about new opportunities for workers in all countries to develop their potential and to support their families through the jobs created by greater economic integration.

But globalization is also about workers in developed countries who fear losing their jobs to countries with lower wages and limited labor rights. It is about workers in developing countries who worry about decisions that affect their lives being made in faraway head offices of international corporations. In short, globalization is about risks as well as about opportunities. We must deal with these risks at the national level by managing adjustment processes and by strengthening social, structural, and financial systems. And, at the global level, we must establish a stronger international financial architecture and work to fight disease, to turn back environmental degradation, and to use the advances in communications to give voice to the voiceless.

We cannot turn back globalization. Our challenge is to make globalization an instrument of opportunity and inclusion—not of fear and insecurity.

The last decade has not only seen an acceleration in globalization; it has also seen real progress in the quality of policies in developing countries. Around the world more children are attending primary and secondary school. In many countries people are living longer, fewer infants are dying, and more mothers are living to know their children. In many countries inflation has fallen, markets have been liberalized, and investment has risen strongly.

The economic outlook is promising, with incomes per capita in developing countries likely to grow at well over 3 percent a year. This would be the highest rate of sustained growth in decades, and faster than in the developed countries. Indeed, a large number of people in developing countries are seeing the fruits of the combination of these improved policies and globalization.

But, for too many, that optimistic picture is still a mirage. In too many countries, population growth has wiped out gains in income per capita. In too many countries, HIV/AIDS has wiped out improvements in life expectancy and caused incalculable grief and hardship. In too many countries, weapons, war, and conflict have wiped out development. And, at the global level, we cannot be complacent about the outlook, particularly in the face of volatility in oil and commodity prices and wild swings in exchange rates.

We live in a world scarred by inequality. Something is wrong when the richest 20 percent of the global population receive more than 80 percent of global income. Something is wrong when 10 percent of a country's population receives half of its national income, as happens in far too many countries today. Something is wrong when the average income for the richest 20 countries is 37 times the average for the poorest 20—a gap that has more than doubled in the past 40 years. Something is wrong when 1.2 billion people still live on less than a dollar a day and 2.8 billion on less than two dollars a day.

With all the forces making the world smaller, it is time to change our way of thinking. It is time to realize that we live together in one world, not two. Poverty anywhere is poverty in our community, wherever we live. It is our responsibility. It is time for political leaders to recognize that obligation.

And the stakes could not be higher. The conflicts that have so plagued development are not simply accidents of history. Conflicts are much more likely in countries with severe poverty and extreme dependence on primary commodity exports. Violent crime is more likely in countries with wide income inequality. And what is true within a single society today will be increasingly true in all, as international conflict and terror spread in a globalized world. The fight against poverty *is* the fight for global peace and security.

What Have We Learned About How to Fight Poverty?

In facing these challenges we must act together, and we must draw on the lessons of experience. What lessons have we learned?

We have learned that poverty is about more than inadequate income or even low human development; it is also about lack of voice and lack of representation. It is about vulnerability to abuse and to corruption. It is about violence against women and fear of crime. It is about lack of self-esteem. Poverty, as discussions with 60,000 poor people in 60 countries have taught us, is about lack of fundamental freedom of action, choice, and opportunity.

We have learned that market-oriented reforms, if combined with social and institutional development, can deliver economic growth to the poor. We have learned that economic growth is the most powerful force for sustained poverty reduction. Growth is central, but it is not enough.

If we are serious about fighting inequity, we must also help poor people build their assets, including education, health, and land. We must get infrastructure and knowledge to poor areas, rural and urban alike. We must confront deep-seated inequalities and bridge gender, ethnic, social, and racial divides. We must protect poor people from crop failures and natural disasters, from crime and conflict, from sickness and unemployment.

Development must be comprehensive. It must embrace education and health, but also good governance, the fight against corruption, legal and judicial reform, and financial sector reform. It must embrace infrastructure provision and environmental protection as it must also embrace sound economic policies. All these elements depend on and reinforce each other.

We have learned and this is fundamental—that development cannot be imposed from above. There is no universal blueprint for development. It must be home-grown and home-owned. Without a comprehensive approach, developed by and adopted in each country, we will not achieve the development that is vital for a peaceful, equitable world.

We are applying what we have learned. Over a year ago, recognizing the importance of a comprehensive approach, we launched the Comprehensive Development Framework. Holistic, long-term, and country-owned, the CDF is already being implemented in a dozen countries.

Last year, with the IMF, we began supporting our partner countries in their work on poverty reduction strategies—strategies that are country-driven and poverty-focused. Our comprehensive framework and the poverty reduction strategies embody an approach to development that is gaining strong recognition in the development community.

There is one key element that runs right through this approach: participation. Participation delivers powerful results at the project and the program level. And it can create the social consensus that is the foundation for social change and reform. It is a part of freedom. Where better than here in Prague, home of the Velvet Revolution, to underscore the central importance of participation? Where better to reaffirm what poor people across the world say they want: freedom, participation, and voice in creating a better life for themselves?

Participation can take many forms—and it works:

- In Bangladesh we are supporting nongovernmental organizations that are taking the lead in microcredit programs serving more than 5 million poor people, 90 percent of them women.
- In Uganda we have provided matching grants to community groups, with the result that school attendance and use of health facilities have improved dramatically.
- In India the deepening of democracy has advanced participation in the smallest towns. Reforms have greatly strengthened representation by women in local councils.

With the support and leadership of our client governments, we are working with communities, local governments, the private sector, and civil society to support community-driven development:

- In Indonesia more than 2,000 villages and community groups are developing their own proposals to receive local funding.
- In Benin women are working together to protect the forests and make them sources of income rather than sources of fuel.

And, at the national level, we are helping to build strong institutions to ensure that poor people can participate in, and benefit from, their economy and society. We must make state institutions more responsive to the poor. We must recognize that, in too many countries, fighting poverty is also about fighting the vested interests of an economic elite that has undue influence on policies, regulations, and laws. If we embrace a comprehensive approach, working in partnership with governments, and if we achieve this participation, this equity, and this inclusion, then we will have democratized development.

The Information and Communications Revolution

Today we have a unique tool at our disposal to enable the involvement of all, on a scale undreamed of even several years ago. The information and communications revolution will transform development as we know it. This revolution promises a historic opportunity to redraw the global economy through broad and equal access to knowledge and information; through enhanced empowerment and inclusion of local communities; and through economic growth, jobs, and improved access to basic services. And so, over the last five years, we have been focusing on how to harness the power of information and communications technology and of knowledge to accelerate development:

- We are working with governments to foster policy, regulatory, and network readiness, through our analytical and advisory work and through our grant facility, *info*Dev [the Information for Development program].
- We are linking development leaders globally through our Global Development Learning Network, which provides training and creates broad learning communities.
- We are connecting students and teachers in secondary schools in developing countries with their counterparts in industrialized countries, through our World Links for Development program.
- We are using information and communications technology to create a "university without walls" and to link Sub-Saharan African countries directly with global academic faculty and learning resources through the African Virtual University.
- Through the Global Development Gateway and the Global Development Network, we are promoting the generation and sharing of knowledge. We are supporting knowledge networking, global research, and communities of practice from the grassroots up.
- Finally, we are developing many practical applications for use by poor communities worldwide, to bring them knowledge in their local languages, to build communities, to create businesses, to assist in medical treatment, and to link them with each other and with the world.

The information and communications revolution offers an unprecedented opportunity to make empowerment and participation a reality. And poor people across the world are demanding action. In response to our *Voices of the Poor* study, many groups have asked us, as a key priority, for increased access to information and communications technology. We must work toward the day when, through the Internet, through distance learning, through cellular phones and wind-up radios, the village elder or the aspiring student will have access to the same information as the finance minister.

Communications technology gives us the tools for true participation. This is leveling the playing field. This is real equity.

A Bank That Is Delivering

Throughout its history, the Bank has adjusted to the changing external environment, from post–World War II reconstruction to the challenges of global development. That change continues today. Let me tell you a little about what we have done over the last five years to build on the enormous contributions of my predecessors, and on the solid base of the past.

In the last five years we have continued to focus our lending on the social sectors such as health, education, and social protection; those loans now make up about a quarter of our portfolio. Five years ago our lending in the global fight against HIV/AIDS was small; as of today we have committed about $1 billion, including $500 million recently made available for programs in Africa. Five years ago we were not engaged in postconflict activities; today we are involved in over 35 countries. Five years ago we had not thought of the HIPC Initiative; today we have agreed to debt relief for 10 countries, and we are doing our utmost to reach 20 countries in all by the end of the year. Five years ago we did not work on anticorruption programs; over the last five years we have engaged in over 600 anticorruption activities. Five years ago we focused only on "doing no harm" to the environment; today we have an environmental portfolio of $15 billion, including climate change and biodiversity programs.

We are working with governments to improve governance and the climate for investment. We are working to build sound regulatory environments so that the private sector can contribute more effectively to building infrastructure. The International Finance Corporation is working, through its innovative projects and growing portfolio, to expand the frontier of investment opportunities. So, too, is the Multilateral Investment Guarantee Agency, whose guarantee coverage has risen from $600 million five years ago to over $1.5 billion today.

There are those who say we promise more than we deliver. But we have focused on results and we have delivered. In 1995 I said we would become a Knowledge Bank, and we have made great strides. In 1996 I said we would fight the "cancer of corruption," and we are now one of the leaders in that fight. In 1997 I spoke of the "challenge of inclusion," and we are working more than ever to bring the weak and most vulnerable from the margins of society to the center stage. In 1998 I spoke about the need to balance essential economic growth with social and structural development and called for a new, Comprehensive Development Framework; since then we have piloted this approach, and we are introducing the poverty reduction strategies on a more global basis. And in 1999 I spoke of the importance of governance and capacity building and of partnering with others. We are working on these issues every day, day in and day out, and achieving great results.

We work constantly to improve the quality of our programs. Over the last five years the share of lending operations with outcomes rated satisfactory or better by the Bank's independent evaluation unit has increased significantly. Five years ago 34 percent of our projects were at risk. Today that figure is down to 15 percent. We are closer to our clients: we now have half of our country directors and 2,300 staff in the field. And we are more transparent, disclosing over 85 percent of our country assistance strategies, up from none five years ago.

We are a different Bank, doing development differently. Are we there yet? No. But are we more than halfway through a major reform program? Yes. And in the next five years we will focus still more sharply on implementation.

We are ready and able to take responsibility for the social and structural agenda, working with the IMF in supporting countries' programs. We are working with our colleagues in the UN system and the other multilateral development banks on selectivity and the division of labor among us. We are working with governments, helping them to take their own policies and institutions forward rather than simply implementing our projects.

All this calls for a further change in our business strategy: less micromanagement, more working with governments to help them set the broad parameters. We will continue conditionality, but we will streamline it and focus on fundamental principles. We will support fully owned country strategies, with program loans that align donor support with the government's budget and policy cycles. For this purpose we are introducing the Poverty Reduction Support Credit.

Both in our projects and in our programs, we will be flexible in responding to the specific needs of particular countries. We will be looking for innovative ways to support regional programs with advice, financing, and grants. We will work with our development partners to harmonize and coordinate our procurement, environmental, and reporting standards and procedures to reduce the administrative burden on clients. We believe that this is the route to scaling up and to more speedy, flexible, and effective implementation.

Let me also make very clear that we will both continue and deepen our work in overcoming poverty in middle-income countries. We cannot ignore the 1 billion people living on less than two dollars a day in these countries. We will continue to bring both money and knowledge to work in education, health, and social protection in poor communities.

We will continue to build on the synergy between our lending and our nonlending services, which is critical to promoting reform. We will continue to work with national and regional authorities to improve the climate for the investment and jobs that are crucial for poverty alleviation. Over time their access to markets will grow. We cannot simply ask these countries to rely on volatile capital markets to fund their fight against poverty. Our partnership must be long-term, committed, and poverty-focused—in bad times and in good.

This is a demanding program, and our budget is highly constrained. Let me take this opportunity to express my deep gratitude for the dedication and professionalism of our management and staff who, during this period of transition, have worked so hard. I believe they are the most dedicated, talented development team in the world, and I applaud them and their families. I am immensely proud to work with them.

Moving Forward: Responsibility and Opportunity

I have spoken of opportunity, of security, of empowerment. I have spoken of participation, transparency, and accountability. But what of responsibility? Two years ago we published a study on the effectiveness of of aid. The results were clear. Countries with good policies that receive aid use it well. In countries with bad policies, aid is wasted. More countries have been putting in place policies that promote sound growth. And more countries have been doing well. More and more developing countries are keeping their side of the bargain.

But what about the developed world? Some countries are shouldering their responsibilities magnificently, and we are extraordinarily grateful to them. But many are not. I believe we need to focus on several priority areas as we move forward:

- Many developed countries have fallen far below the internationally recognized targets for aid. They must increase their aid.
- Developed countries must provide the resources for deeper, faster, and broader debt relief. If we want to move rapidly on the HIPC Initiative, we must look to the rich countries for resources. This initiative should not be funded by reduced or more costly support for other low- or middle-income countries.
- Developed countries must dismantle their trade barriers to poor countries. Our estimates indicate that the annual costs of all trade barriers by industrial countries are more than double total annual development assistance.
- We must explore innovative instruments, including grants, for such pressing issues as HIV/AIDS, the environment, basic education, and health. We at the Bank must build up our Development Grant Facility.

- Multilateral and bilateral donors must work together to simplify their procedures and reduce the cost of doing business.
- Finally, we must recognize that there are more and more issues whose resolution requires action at the global level. We must act together.

Now is the time. The budgets of rich countries have never been stronger. Technology has never been more dynamic. Growth prospects have rarely been brighter. Public action in all countries must be driven by a new commitment to poverty reduction.

The demographic challenge is before us. Over the next 25 years nearly 2 billion people will be added to today's world population of 6 billion, and almost all of that increase will occur in developing countries. In 25 years Europe's population will be roughly the same as today, but that of the developing world will grow from 5 billion to almost 7 billion.

Without that commitment to development, we will not hold back the tide of deprivation, want, and despair. We will not create that equitable world, nor will we ensure peace and stability for our children. All of us here today know that we can and must do more.

We Have a Historic Opportunity

This new world, our greater understanding of it, a wiser development community, and a changing international institutional environment mean that, through working together, doing development differently, and giving voice to the voiceless, we now have a chance to make the next decade one of real delivery in the fight against poverty. The opportunities and promise of a global economy, the information age, and life-saving and productivity-enhancing technologies are all ours to seize. We must work together to harness the benefits of globalization to deliver prosperity to the many, not just the few.

This is not just a new economic program. It is an obligation, an obligation based on shared moral and social values. It is an obligation that is also based on enlightened self-interest. It is an obligation to the next generation to leave them a better world: a world of equity, a world of peace, a world of security.

Message from the president and chairman from the 2000 World Bank *Annual Report*

OCTOBER 2000

This Chairman's Message covers the year from July 1999 to June 2000. Wolfensohn explains to shareholders how the Bank's antipoverty strategy has evolved on the local, national, regional, and global levels.

A new millennium is beginning. For the World Bank, it is a time to ask ourselves, how can we improve our effectiveness in the fight against poverty? It is also a time to act: with urgency and with responsibility. Urgency, because roughly two billion more people will be joining us on this planet in the next 25 years, and we must be ready for them. Responsibility, because the 2.8 billion poor who currently live on less than two dollars a day are our fellow human beings, and not just a statistic.

Achieving a world free of poverty is an enormous and complex undertaking. And solutions are far from simple. The challenges are multidimensional; they call for people, groups, and institutions to come together to play a wide range of roles in a collegial, collective effort. It is only with strong coalitions—local, national, regional, and global—that we will succeed in fighting poverty; that much is clear.

What does it take to reduce poverty?

Our strategy, at the *country level,* is rooted in a wealth of lessons from development experience. Some of the key lessons are that development assistance leads to progress in sound policy and institutional environments; that economic growth is crucial but must be accompanied by government action targeted to meet poor people's needs and to address the social costs of reform; that reforms cannot be imposed from the outside but must be "home-grown"; that communities must have a voice and play a role in their own development; and that open economies grow faster than closed economies. Our recent work on poverty—economic analysis as well as consultations with poor people—reveals that people in poverty are an asset, not a liability. It is imperative that we give them opportunities, that we empower them, and that we ensure their security.

Drawing on these lessons, our work is guided by the following principles:

- *Country ownership:* A country's progress depends fundamentally on the country itself directing the policy agenda. Actions taken without broad buy-in have too often turned out to be unsustainable. Success requires that consensus building by all stakeholders be part of the action agenda.
- *Long-term integrated approach:* To achieve sustainable growth, crucial for poverty reduction, poverty reduction strategies must be multidimensional. These strategies must address macroeconomic as well as social, environmental, and

institutional needs. Progress must occur on all fronts, ranging from governance, anticorruption, and judicial and financial systems to health, education,
and transport policies.

- *Partnership:* Collaborative relationships, shared objectives, and a mutually
  agreed-upon division of labor are crucial. We need to go beyond aid coordination: we need to align strategies, be selective, draw on mutual expertise, and reduce wasteful competition and duplication among donors.
- *Results focus:* It is crucial to have development outcomes as our guides, and
  these must flow directly from the long-term vision. Countries must set
  poverty reduction targets, lay out public policy actions to achieve them,
  and work with civil society to monitor progress.

We put forward this vision last year to the global community under a pilot
approach we call the Comprehensive Development Framework (CDF). I am
heartened that it is increasingly a shared vision. More countries and more partners are testing the CDF approach and participating in this work-in-progress.
Our work with these countries in fiscal 2000 has advanced: their interest
creates the learning ground; their experience will define the way forward. Continuing this theme is our joint endeavor with the International Monetary Fund
to help those countries eligible for debt relief, under the Heavily Indebted Poor
Countries Initiative, to produce Poverty Reduction Strategy Papers.

Our strategy to fight poverty also requires action at the global level. There
is much that can be done to promote disease reduction globally through
greater use of cost-effective vaccines; to raise awareness of the impact of HIV/
AIDS on development; to address transnational challenges such as the prevention of financial crises; to provide concerted debt relief to poor countries; and
to preserve the world's natural resources. Each of these efforts could have a
profound impact on poverty. In addition, empowering people with knowledge and technology could have far-reaching benefits. The Bank has taken
important steps to advance the concept of the "Knowledge Bank," including
efforts to develop the framework for a Global Development Gateway, being
conceived as an Internet-based vehicle facilitating the provision and exchange
of information.

At both country and global levels, our emphasis is on demand-driven services and aid effectiveness. The past year's decline in lending relative to the
previous year's record volume attests to this evolution. Emerging market
countries have needed substantially less financial support thanks to the strong
recovery of global financial markets and a resumption of access to private capital. Other countries are indeed in need but lack the circumstances (national
peace as well as sound policies and institutions) that would permit an effective
use of financial aid. Lower lending also reflects smaller-sized operations,

through which the "New Bank" has responded to country needs to adopt pilot approaches and build institutional capacity as prerequisites to successful development efforts. The Bank has, moreover, increased its reliance on non-lending services in the policy dialogue, recognizing their key role in building support for development efforts.

I cannot stress enough the importance of partnerships. The task ahead is too formidable for any single institution or set of institutions to tackle. Every one of us has a role to play: private sector, public sector, civil society, nongovernmental organizations, academia, religious groups, multilateral and bilateral donors, and development organizations. If we are to achieve the United Nations–based international development targets, we all need to work together. Halving poverty levels by 2015 is possible, but only if we concert our efforts in a new way.

It is my firm conviction that the Bank has a crucial role to play in this challenge. As a cooperative, we enjoy the backing of nearly every nation of the world in pursuing our mission. As a development institution with a half-century of experience across countries and sectors, we have a vast array of lessons that we continue to build on every day. As a global institution with offices throughout the world, we have an unparalleled reach, growing in leaps and bounds in this age of communication, which is helping us get closer to the people we serve, and to share knowledge that is key to empowerment and progress. As a strong financial institution and leader in capital markets, we mobilize funding on good terms and tailor it to meet long-term development needs typically unmet by private creditors. And, as a multinational employer, we are blessed with a rich pool of skills and talent, a group of people with an unequaled professionalism and devotion to fighting against poverty. I am enormously indebted to them.

The World Bank's track record shows clearly that we are making a difference, and that we are learning and adapting to client needs. Our task is to build on all that we have achieved. We, as a global community, can go down the business-as-usual path and see the numbers of poor grow steadily, decade after decade; or we can innovate and follow the path with more unknowns but infinitely more promise. For the Bank the choice is clear: we have embarked on a path of change, and we are committed to listening, learning, and acting in partnership until more and more people partake in the many opportunities that the new era of growth, technology, and global development has to offer.

WHY PUBLIC-PRIVATE PARTNERSHIPS MATTER FOR DEVELOPMENT—AND ARE GOOD FOR BUSINESS

Keynote speech at the Fifth German World Bank Forum

BERLIN | NOVEMBER 27, 2000

In these remarks, Wolfensohn praises the Bank's relationship with Germany and spells out why he thinks public-private partnerships are so important to development. He also talks about the innovative Business Partners for Development Program, a partnership among business, government, and civil society.

Let me start by paying tribute to Minister Wieczorek-Zeul* for the relationship that we at the World Bank have with Germany, which has enriched our activities in the Bank and brought about a much closer relationship between Germany and the Bank, and, I think, a more interdependent relationship—one in which she feels very comfortable in criticizing me and I feel occasionally very comfortable in modestly making suggestions to her. So it is an equal partnership, as you can see, and one I certainly enjoy. There is a new force in the field of development, with four new women ministers, and I can only tell you that four women ministers are more powerful than all the other ministers. And, of course, she is at the center of that activity.

Let me set the framework for a minute, not by speaking about the actual activities of the Bank, which I will have an opportunity to talk about at dinner, but rather to give you my perspective on why I think public-private partnership is so important. I start with the belief that, for businesspeople to be involved in the issue of development, they must recognize not just an appeal to their moral position or their social position or their ethical position, but that it is also helpful to have a sense of the economics and the self-interest of business in promoting development. This is not to diminish the moral or social reasons, but it stands to reason that, to engage business actively in development, one has to make a case for why development is important. That case to me is very, very clear and has become clearer now that I have spent five and a half years in the Bank, and many of you coming from the private sector already know this.

The case is rather simple. There are 6 billion people in the world, and 4.8 billion of them live in developing countries. Those 4.8 billion, who make up 80 percent of world population, have about 20 percent of total global income of $30 trillion. The other 20 percent have 80 percent of the income.

So, first and foremost, business looks at the developed markets because they are the most profitable and the most concentrated and very often the most competitive. In the developing world, however, it is clear that, in terms of trade,

---

* Heidemarie Wieczorek-Zeul, German minister for economic cooperation and development.

in terms of exports, and in terms of business opportunity, there is today a real potential. The numbers show that the private sector internationally has taken an interest in that potential, not just in ever-increasing trade, but also in investment. And, as Heidemarie observed, 10 years ago private sector foreign investment in developing countries was about $30 billion a year, including portfolio investment and lending. It was then half the size of official development assistance, which was $60 billion. Last year official development assistance was at $53 billion, and private foreign direct investment alone in developing countries reached close to $200 billion. If you add in bank lending and portfolio investment, it was something on the order of $250 billion. So, from being half the size of official development assistance 10 years ago, depending on the statistics you use, private sector foreign investment is now four or five times its size, and at its peak it was seven times its size. So the private sector is showing its interest in developing countries by this enormously expanding investment. That is not salesmanship; that is fact.

The second thing is that, as we look forward 25 years, world population will have grown by 2 billion people. We will have a world not of 6 billion but of 8 billion, and of those 2 billion people who will be added to the world, all but 50 million will be living in the developing countries. Meanwhile Europe will be the same size that it is today. It will be different: it will be older; it may have different demographics because of immigration, different characteristics; but in terms of population it will be about the same size. You can vary these numbers by 10 million or 20 million, but broadly speaking that is the situation.

There are two reasons why the private sector needs to look at this challenge. First, because if the developing world does not develop but instead stays poor, there is no way the world will have peace. That is just a simple assertion on my part, but I believe it to be true. One cannot conceive of a global economy, with communications, with finance, with crime, with drugs, health, environment, and immigration and with the Internet, that remains so unequal. In such a world you don't need an army to create problems anymore. All you need is a bit of terror, a bit of crime, and immigration. There is really no way, in my judgment, that business cannot be interested in stability, and so it has to think about the developing countries simply as a defensive measure.

As an offensive measure, which is much more interesting, the creation of a marketplace of 6.8 billion people, which is increasing in size and in scope and in depth, is the place, many would say, where the future growth and development of markets will come from. Many macroeconomists would argue that, both in percentage terms and in absolute numbers, we should be looking for disproportionate growth in the developing world. I believe that to be the case also.

Now, if this growth is to be accompanied by greater equity, by a greater sense of social peace and social justice, many of us have to play a part. It cannot be done by the German development ministry alone. It cannot be done by the World Bank alone. What we need to do is to try and find ways to work together on this problem. The World Bank and the official institutions can do a lot to create the climate. As I mentioned earlier, it is essential to have a framework that attracts business. You need good governance, you need a legal system, a financial system, and a judicial system; you need to combat corruption, not just in the developing countries themselves but also in some of the developed countries, as the OECD[†] has demonstrated, so that bribes are not deductible for tax purposes.

There is a need to address this corruption and to build the framework, and we can help with that. On issues of governance it is essential that business speak its mind and that Western practices—transparency in accounting and better governance—are also conveyed to developing countries. Clearly we have to deal with the issues of job creation and investment and help countries build their capacities. Here what we are discovering is that, in our attempts to bring business along, in our attempts to bear social responsibilities, there is a tremendous interest, on the part of both large multinational companies and medium-size companies, in reaching out to help build the societies in which they operate. This is not just throwaway charity. This is creating a climate in which business can be done more effectively as well as creating a more stable environment in which to move forward. And whether it be providing schoolchildren with Internet access and knowledge-based centers, or training apprentices, or dealing with issues about equity (which companies can contribute), we are finding a growing understanding on the part of business about that responsibility.

We have at the Bank something we call the Business Partners for Development Program, and it consists of just four subjects that we thought we would bring businesses together on. One is natural resources: how oil and mining companies can enhance prosperity in communities, and water and sanitation, which the minister mentioned earlier. Bringing the private sector into that work is central to the future.

Again, these are not throwaway activities. These are real activities that can contribute to stability and growth in these countries. And I would invite any of you who are interested to get in touch with us, because we can provide you with a huge amount of information about the countries in which we are operating. We can also provide you with information on investment opportunities and partnership opportunities with the Bank and with our related organizations.

---

† The OECD (Organisation for Economic Co-operation and Development) Convention Against Bribery of Foreign Public Officials in International Business Transactions went into effect in February 1999.

Peter Woicke, who is here tonight, is in charge of the IFC [International Finance Corporation] and the Bank's private sector activities generally, and either tonight or later, either directly or through the minister, we are ready to discuss your interests, either in terms of direct investment or in terms of partnership, to try and broaden your interest into issues of social responsibility and working with communities.

I want to leave time for questions, but let me just touch on two other things. One is the role of civil society today. I remember going to the WTO [World Trade Organization] meetings in Seattle and saying to Mike Moore, the head of the WTO, that if only he did things as intelligently as we did at the Bank, he would have no problems. Three months later, in Washington, he came up to me and said, as we tried to get through the lines of the demonstrators, "What was that you said to me in Seattle?"

I would say to you that we were the first target, but business is second, and you should not underestimate the need to interface with civil society in this world in which we are all going to operate. This issue has already manifested itself against McDonald's, against Kentucky Fried Chicken, and against certain oil companies, but the need to interface and engage in discussion with civil society, I predict to you, will become a very key issue as you move forward in business.

We at least have some interface with civil society, as many of you do, too, but on issues of the environment, social justice, and the way that companies are run, international industrial societies and banks are the next target. I urge you to consider that this issue, too, can bring us together, either as a force for positive development or as a source of big trouble for all of us. And I raise this issue because it is my judgment that this is another area in which we could all work together and exchange experience. This is not just a question of dealing with business opportunity; this is also a question on which, I think, you may well find a convenient partner in the World Bank Group with whom you can deal.

So, for all of these reasons, I am a big supporter of public-private partnership. I congratulate the German government for its efforts, and I merely want to say, in addition to what has been said earlier, that we stand very ready to work with you. We look forward to our contact with you, not just next year but in the intervening period, and I hope that I may have sketched for you some good reasons why you might find it useful to think about the 6.8 billion people who will be here in 25 years. I'm happy to know that many of your companies are already leaders in the developing world. A number of companies represented here are already among the most multinational in the world. For those that are among that number, we need you, and, for those that are not, we welcome you and hope that we can work together.

Thank you very much.

Remarks at a reception to celebrate International Women's Day

WASHINGTON, D.C. | MARCH 8, 2001

In these remarks at an internal event at the World Bank, Wolfensohn
returns to the issue of gender. He speaks about the importance of education
for girls and women and talks about the Bank's efforts to hire more women
in management and at senior levels.

I want to, first, thank all of you here for the invitation to be with you. And I want to recognize the appearance of a few brave men in the audience and thank them for being here. I also want to recognize the fact that this group gets larger each year, which is a wonderful tribute to the organizers and to all of you.

I will speak from my heart because I haven't prepared a speech. I've had a speech prepared for me, but I want to just share some observations about my time here at the Bank and some general observations on things that I've learned.

The first thing is that, when it comes to gender issues and discrimination in the institution, I feel that we have come a long, long way in the years that I have been here. And that is not just as a result of my contribution, which [World Bank Managing Director] Mamphela [Ramphele] was kind enough to recognize, but as a result of all your efforts and of the efforts of many people who are not here.

The discussion has changed. When I first came, I certainly felt the image of the Bank on my brow. When I went to the Beijing conference, Bella Abzug* attacked me, in a way that only Bella could, about the role of the Bank and about the responsibilities that I'd assumed. That was not an easy meeting for me, because it made me look at what our institution had really achieved.

Many people said to me, "Here you are going out and trying to deal with issues of poverty—issues where women are central, both in terms of who is affected by poverty, and in terms of who can help you and help communities get out of poverty. Yet you lead an institution that does not have anything like the representation it should of women in its management. Here you are claiming to address the questions of poverty. Yet when you look at your institution's history and the way it does things, gender is something that is put in sometimes to tick off in a box. It is not really at the heart of your thinking or of your beliefs."

Bella put that to me, and so did others. When I came back to Washington and started looking into what they had said, it was very clear to me that this

---

* The Fourth World Conference on Women was held in Beijing in September 1995; Bella Abzug was a former U.S. congresswoman from New York and an outspoken advocate of women's rights.

conference had in itself been a microcosm of many of the things we were try-ing to deal with. We were an institution that *did* have discrimination, that *did* have a practice of male domination; where sexual harassment, regrettably, was not unknown; and where, at the core of the beliefs of the institution, there was not that gut feel that women are both the object of our exercise and the solu-tion to the exercise.

I think we have come a long way in five years. We are not yet where I want us to be, but we have clearly made some progress. And just as this group is increasing in number, so, too, I think the people who are clear on the issues are increasing in number.

And the issues themselves *are* clear. The people most affected by poverty are women and children, especially women who are vulnerable. When we talk of people who don't have water, it is not just that they don't have water. For many women, it is two and three hours a day going to find water, and having to carry it to their abodes, if that's what they can be called. When we talk about poor sanitation and disease, it is the women who bear the brunt. When we talk about food, in so many societies it is the women who find it and pre-pare it, and are the last to eat it, after their husbands have eaten.

When we look at questions of poverty, as was pointed out in the Bank's *Voices of the Poor* study in 60 countries, violence against women is a central issue, and this is something that was not previously so clear to me. The other issues were the vulnerability of women to a husband's death or divorce; their lack of access to property in terms of equal participation or even shared par-ticipation; their lack of opportunity to get financial resources; and their lack of educational opportunity, reflected in the fact that so many more girls grow up without education than boys.

On the issue of AIDS, so many women around the world are defenseless against a disease that is not just another disease but a killer. They are affected by the inability to talk about issues of sex—the unwillingness of leaders to talk about it, the unwillingness of men to talk about it—and by their vulnerability to the results of their men's philandering.

We at the Bank can be very proud that we are addressing every one of these issues. We are addressing the issue of poverty, of course, every day. But we now have in perspective issues of water, of health, of attacking AIDS and get-ting those issues out into the open—issues of food security, the question of fuel and alternative fuel supplies, so that women don't have to spend their time gathering fuel and then live in dwellings where they must inhale fumes that come from poor sources of power.

We in the Bank, I think, are now recognizing that gender is not just some-thing that you add to a project, nor is it a separate set of projects. Gender is part

of every project. This comes out in our *Engendering Development* study[†] and is starting to take hold in our organization.

This is not just a moral issue, or an issue of ethics or of values. It is an issue of both practical economics and growth. There is no doubt that it is more important to educate a woman than to educate a man. Everyone from Gandhi to [IMF Managing Director] Horst Köhler would tell you that whereas educating a man is educating a man, educating a woman is educating a family.

It's also true that, if you can get equal access to resources for a country's women, even if you do nothing else in that country, you strengthen the economy. In Africa it has been estimated that equal access for women, by itself, can raise GDP by 20 percent.

So whether the issue is population, or AIDS, or community development, it is the women who are at the center. And it *is* a moral and an ethical issue, but it's also an issue of straight economics and a straight question of how best to address the questions of poverty and growth.

I am very proud that we have also been able to increase the number of women in the Bank's management. We have a target of 30 percent of women in management and 45 percent of women at levels of GF and GG [internal

† *Engendering Development: Through Gender Equality in Rights, Resources, and Voices* was published for the World Bank by Oxford University Press in January 2001.

Bank staff grades] by fiscal 2003. I can give you statistics that document that we're on the road to gender equality at the Bank. And here I want to pay special tribute not only to Karen but also to her colleague Anette Pedersen,[‡] who has really given me the works whenever I would start to forget the importance of this issue.

So today I want to salute International Women's Day. I want to salute all of you. I want to recognize that the battle's not won, but I think we're surely doing better than we've ever done. We can now talk about these issues without feeling insecure, without feeling that it's a show. Together we can really make International Women's Day a chance to reflect each year on our true progress, not just for women but for humanity.

Thank you very much.

---

‡ Karen Mason, director of the PREM (Poverty Reduction and Economic Management) Gender and Development Group at the World Bank; Anette Pedersen, former senior adviser on gender equality and diversity at the World Bank.

With Horst Köhler, published in the *International Herald Tribune*

MARCH 14, 2001

Based on a visit to Africa in February 2001 with the managing director of the International Monetary Fund, this essay speaks optimistically about Africa's future. Together the two leaders urge the international community to mobilize in support of Africa's development.

Africa's leaders are committed to far-reaching changes that will help the continent escape from the vicious circle of poverty and share in the prosperity enjoyed by so many elsewhere in the past two decades.

Africa knows that exceptional efforts will be needed to restore peace to countries engulfed by conflict, tackle the AIDS crisis and stem the spread of malaria and tuberculosis. Governments will have to push ahead with effective economic and social policies and invest in human and physical capital.

The need for decisive action could hardly be more urgent. Almost half of all Africans live on less than $1 per day. AIDS has reduced life expectancies sharply in some countries.

At the same time, development aid to Africa has fallen from $32 per head in 1990 to $19 in 1998, despite evidence of the effectiveness of such assistance in countries with sound economic and social policies.

We have just returned from a joint visit to Africa, where we met with 22 heads of state and with civil society leaders, and spoke candidly about the problems they face. We were deeply impressed by a new spirit of leadership and determination, a recognition that Africa's future lies in its own hands.

The international community must rise to the challenge of helping Africa. It is simply unacceptable that while the developed world enjoys unprecedented prosperity, one in seven African children will die before his or her fifth birthday. It is time that politicians and voters in rich countries realized that without a bright future for the poor, the future cannot be bright for the rest of the world.

On our visit we heard from national leaders how they intended to achieve their vision. They recognize that there can be no more "business as usual." They are convinced that peace must come from within Africa. They know that good governance and a level playing field are essential to set Africa on the path to prosperity.

Central to their efforts to reduce poverty are higher economic growth, improved access to education and health services, and containing the devastating effects of AIDS. We heard a new emphasis on bolstering private investment and exports through homegrown policies, good governance, better use of technology and an efficient infrastructure.

But the challenges are daunting. Without real help for their reform efforts, further debt relief and external financing, they will not progress fast enough to make a real difference.

International support is vital. Take trade. Sub-Saharan Africa accounts for only 2 percent of world trade. Yet research by the World Bank and others shows that granting free access to industrial countries' markets for these African countries—particularly for agricultural products and textiles—would result in growth for Africa worth billions of dollars per year.

We strongly endorse free market access for poor countries to industrial countries' markets, where tariffs on meat, fruits and vegetables can exceed 100 percent. The European Union's decision to phase out trade barriers is an important step in the right direction.

Developed countries could help by reducing their agricultural subsidies. The industrial nations of the OECD [Organisation for Economic Co-operation and Development] spend more than $300 billion a year on these subsidies, roughly equivalent to the entire GDP of sub-Saharan Africa.

Rich countries' governments must honor their aid commitments. Aid is not charity but a vital investment in global peace and security. We would gladly join a campaign to convince industrial nations to move to the long-standing United Nations target for official development assistance of 0.7 percent of GNP within 10 years.

Current levels of foreign aid, at some 0.24 percent of yearly GDP, fall far short of this promise. The difference between these figures is worth a hundred billion dollars a year.

And we must work with the countries involved to make sure that Africa does not again fall into a debt trap.

We at the World Bank and the International Monetary Fund regard debt relief, especially for the poorest countries, as crucial to our mission of alleviating poverty. Last year we led the debt reduction initiative that brought $34 billion in debt relief to 22 poor countries, of which 18 are in Africa. We have been working with national governments to develop comprehensive poverty reduction strategies, drawing on the experience of civil society groups, as well as donors, in their preparation, to ensure that money goes where it is most needed.

We recognize that we have more to do. In the coming months we will be supporting countries in their efforts to use debt relief for poverty reduction. In particular we hope to see debt relief extended to countries emerging from civil conflict and trying to put themselves back together again.

The World Bank has committed half a billion dollars to fight AIDS, and will commit more once that is spent. At the same time, in line with African

proposals to reduce conflict in the region, we will be moving swiftly to cut assistance to aggressor countries.

We will step up our work with African governments to build an enabling environment for private investment, both domestic and foreign, which is so important for economic growth and poverty reduction. We will respond to leaders' requests to help build their capacity through technical assistance and training on a larger scale.

The fight against poverty requires courage, commitment and sustained effort. It requires new partnerships and a spirit of cooperation. It will succeed only if it is based on a strategy designed by the affected country itself. Governments, together with their people, must be in the driver's seat.

We have great expectations. With Africans themselves insisting on leaders who govern for the good of people rather than for themselves, the sharply disappointing experience of the last 40 years can become a thing of the past.

This will be all the more possible if the international community mobilizes behind African countries willing to work for the benefit of their people.

LOCAL ACTION IN A GLOBALIZING ECONOMY: IMPORTANT ROLES FOR MAYORS AND CITY ADMINISTRATIONS

Remarks delivered by videoconference from Washington, D.C.

MARCH 21, 2001

This address, delivered by videoconference to a mayors' conference in the Netherlands, focuses on urban development. Wolfensohn describes the Bank's work in The Cities Alliance initiative and urges the sharing of knowledge to solve common urban problems.

Mr. Chairman, Mr. Minister of State, Mr. Mayor, Ladies and Gentlemen:

Let me say, first of all, how very happy I am to be with you today and how sorry I am that it is by the medium of a videoconference rather than by being with you personally. For, indeed, the subject that you're addressing today is one that is very dear to my heart and very dear to the hearts of many of my colleagues here in the World Bank Group.

As we look at the demographics of our world and the concentration of people within it, it becomes very clear that we have to give increased emphasis to management and the provision of services at the local level. We are facing a worldwide population increase of 2 billion people over the next 25 years, from 6 billion to 8 billion. We also know that, in that same period of time, 2 billion people will move to cities and towns.

This demographic fact changes very significantly the way in which we as an international development agency work, and it changes, of course, very significantly the way in which democratic groups come together to manage themselves. No longer is administration something done only from some central government. Instead it is distributed through states and through cities and through towns. And we ourselves are trying to adapt to the new conditions and to set up programs through which we can be helpful to those city administrators who have this very heavy responsibility.

I pay very great tribute to you in the VNG* who, for so many years, since 1912, have brought together the cities and towns in your own country to share experiences and to explore together how to deliver services in a more effective way. We are very grateful to you and to your government for the attention that you are giving to municipal international cooperation, so that we can work with you in the years ahead to try and strengthen the local units that deliver services to citizens.

* Dutch initials of the Association of Netherlands Municipalities.

We at the Bank have, as you know, a primary responsibility to deal with central governments. Indeed, under our charter, we work directly with central governments. But, more and more, we're finding that those central governments are ready and indeed anxious to see us work with their states and with their cities in implementing programs.

We ourselves have set up a remarkable program, The Cities Alliance, in which the Netherlands is a very active participant, to address such questions and to plan such projects as Cities Without Slums, a program where over the next 20 years we want to take 100 million slum dwellers and improve their lives. We're also working on city development strategies in more than 50 cities at this time, and we're seeking to achieve our objectives not just by sharing our experience, but also by setting up horizontal connections of the type that you have pioneered in your own country.

Quite recently, I was in Monterrey, Mexico, where every Saturday morning we are running distance learning courses for 1,500 mayors of cities and towns throughout Latin America. We cover everything from preparing budgets to running the fire department to dealing with water and sewage issues. And the format is really very simple. A class is held, given by a professor in Spanish, with materials prepared by the Bank and the Monterrey Institute of Technology, and it is interactive, using video, downloading of software, television, radio, and the Internet.

But the most important thing about this program—and this came through to me when I met with a number of the mayors—is not so much the teaching itself; rather it is the coming together of a network of people who can communicate with each other, sharing their ideas and their questions on an ongoing basis. So, for instance, between sessions, in the middle of the week, someone may be saying, "I'm having problems with my police cars," or with my ambulances, or with collecting sewage, and the next morning they will have 50, 60, or 100 answers from others throughout the network telling them what they would do in that situation and offering help.

This rather simple idea is now expanding dramatically, and we have come to learn that, certainly from the World Bank's point of view, although we have some experience to offer, it is the experience on the ground, among practitioners, among people who face these problems every day, that is the base element in building knowledge and in allowing people to develop their own skills and apply that knowledge. It's for that reason that we are enormously excited about this particular initiative, the coming together of the group that is within this church, to discuss how an international expansion of this initiative can take place. I want you to know that, so far as the Bank is concerned, we are ready to stand behind you in every way that we can, to work with you to develop appropriate programs and an appropriate interchange of ideas and experience that can benefit those in the developing world.

We, of course, are especially interested in the developing world, because that is our function. And we have 4.8 billion people, out of a global population of 6 billion, who are, if you like, our clients. What is fascinating is that, in the next 25 years, as I said earlier, another 2 billion people will join us on this planet, and this additional 2 billion will go nearly entirely to the developing world. All but 50 million will, in fact, be added to the number that we have to serve. And, clearly, within that group there will be major agglomerations resulting from more and more people moving to urban areas.

This challenge is a very serious one, but, if we face it correctly, we can make those cities a source of intellectual activity and vitality and opportunity that can meet the needs of their citizens. We have to keep the cities open and well provided with services. We have to provide opportunity. We have to allow freedom of mobility and of trade. And we need to create the supporting services that will allow people to flourish and their children to grow, with proper education and health care.

These things are all much more easily talked about than done. As we look toward the future, we see 500 cities in the world each with a million people or more, and maybe as many as 10,000 cities with 100,000 or more. The problems of these cities cannot be met just by the Bank, nor, indeed, by the managements of the cities and towns on their own. There is a need for all of us to come together and to learn together. There is a need for horizontal associations that can bring together those who have the experience and those who are learning and seeking to develop.

We ourselves are testing a couple of new projects: one involves a relationship between Hai Phong and Seattle, and the other between Montreal and several West African cities. These initiatives are not something new. You have heard of sister cities very often in the past. But for us they have a new focus, one that is geared to the issues of poverty and development, to transferring information and assistance to those governments still in development from those who have already been through their development phase and have emerged into fully functioning and effective local governments.

This challenge that you're addressing today is not just another mechanical challenge. It's not just another organization. I truly believe that what you are doing can make a huge difference in terms of the outlook for poverty in our world. And the outlook for poverty is really the outlook for peace. If we don't address the issues of equity and justice, we will have no peace in any of our cities, not in the Netherlands and not in the developing world.

So I take pleasure in joining you in something that I regard as an exceedingly important endeavor, one that can take your knowledge and experience and make it available to those who need it for their development. I thank you for allowing me to participate with you today, and I can assure you that I and my colleagues at the World Bank will always be ready to be of assistance and to work at your side.

THE CHALLENGES OF GLOBALIZATION: THE ROLE OF THE WORLD BANK

Address to the Bundestag

BERLIN | APRIL 2, 2001

Wolfensohn delivered this speech to Germany's parliament less than two years after it returned to its historic seat in Berlin. The address resembles an Annual Meetings speech because it covers such a wide range of Bank activities and offers a snapshot of the World Bank in the spring of 2001. Wolfensohn speaks of the importance of community-driven development and explains the Bank's role across the board in low-income countries, in middle-income countries, and on the global level.

It is a pleasure to address you again in this beautiful city. I would like to thank Ms. [Christine] Scheel, chairwoman of the Finance Committee; Mr. Rudolf Kraus, chairman of the Development Committee; and Mr. Hans-Ulrich Klose, chairman of the Foreign Committee, for your kind invitation.

Minister Wieczorek-Zeul* plays a very important role in the relationship that the World Bank enjoys with Germany. I am delighted to have had the opportunity to meet with her again. We have had, and continue to have, a deep and long-standing association, in which we both share common perspectives, and in which her department and my colleagues in the Bank work effectively together in our common fight against poverty. I am also glad to see Professor Ernst-Ulrich von Weizsäcker, chairman of the Enquête Commission, here today.

You have just heard my friend [IMF Managing Director] Horst Köhler outline the role of the International Monetary Fund. As he mentioned, we recently returned from a joint mission to Africa. I want to join with him in saying not only that these were extremely productive discussions with 22 African heads of state, but also that Horst and I both came away from that trip with a very strong sense of how African leaders are now taking charge of their continent and their countries.

African development can only result from a partnership in which the leadership and basic responsibility are borne by Africans. And the role of the international institutions and bilateral donors must be to give wholehearted support, with knowledge and experience, and to give liberally in terms of material resources and access to markets.

It is a supreme irony that, just at the time when African leaders are putting the right policies in place and are showing results, overseas aid to Africa has fallen from $32 per person in 1990 to $18 per person in 1998. We must reverse

---

* Heidemarie Wieczorek-Zeul, German minister for economic cooperation and development.

that trend. I join Horst in saying that it is time for a concerted appeal to the heads of governments and major aid donors, to make it clear, once and for all, that development assistance is not charity, but a vital investment in global peace and security.

Current levels of foreign aid, at some 0.24 percent of annual GDP in the donor countries, fall far short of the 0.7 percent target that developed countries have promised to meet. The difference between these figures is $100 billion a year. For millions of poor people, this is the difference between life and death. And it is surely an amount that, if correctly used, could make the achievement of global objectives possible.

Never was this more necessary. With each passing decade the challenge intensifies. Today half the world's population lives on less than two dollars a day, 80 percent of the global population owns only 20 percent of global GDP, and within countries there is a massive imbalance between rich and poor. And the challenge does not end there. Over the next 25 years, 2 billion people will be added to the planet, almost all of them in the developing world. We will go from a world of 6 billion people to a world of 8 billion people, with maybe over 6.5 billion living in the developing world. How many people will be condemned to live on less than two dollars a day then? How the international community answers that question will be the key determinant of whether our children will live in a peaceful world or a world of rising conflict.

The Road We Have Traveled

Let me make some brief remarks about how the World Bank has changed, how we fit into the international development architecture, and where we are headed. When I look back over the last six years since I came to the World Bank, I see an institution that has been undergoing a process of continuous renewal, with significant results.

In 1995 there was no comprehensive mechanism in place for debt relief for the poorest countries, by either the multilateral institutions or other creditors. Today 22 countries have begun receiving debt relief under the Heavily Indebted Poor Countries Initiative, 18 of them in Africa, for a total of $34 billion. The total external debt of these countries will be reduced by two-thirds, lowering their indebtedness to levels below the average for all developing countries.

After receiving HIPC debt relief, these countries will spend about 2 percent of their GDP on debt service—well below the level in other developing countries—compared with about 7 percent on social expenditures. More countries will join the first 22 by the end of 2001. We hope that the remaining countries eligible for relief under the HIPC Initiative will emerge from war or conflict so that they, too, can complete the program.

Let me take this opportunity to pay tribute to the far-reaching proposals that Germany has made, beginning with the 1999 HIPC review and culminating with the pledges made at the [1999] Cologne Summit [of the Group of Eight]. Chancellor [Gerhard] Schröder's leadership in the events leading up to Cologne deserves our deepest admiration. I am also extremely grateful for Germany's pledge of $226 million to the HIPC Trust Fund.

But agreements on debt relief alone are not enough. They need to be linked with explicitly articulated development strategies targeting poverty reduction. We are helping countries prepare such strategies in the form of Poverty Reduction Strategy Papers. Today we have interim PRSPs with 32 countries and have completed PRSPs with 4 countries.

Development is not about a quick fix or a silver bullet. Nor will it endure if it does not have broad-based support. What is significant about this new approach, embodied in the PRSPs, is that it is comprehensive and long term and involves the participation of all the players, including the private sector and civil society. As such it stands a much better chance not only of surviving major political shifts, but also of reaching deep into communities and societies where real change takes place. We now need to broaden this approach further by including in it measurements of results and accountability for performance by governments, the international and bilateral institutions, civil society, and the private sector, so that we can track progress as we go forward.

There have been other important changes in the Bank's work and its focus. HIV/AIDS has infected more than 50 million people worldwide and killed close to 21.8 million, over 17 million of them Africans. Six years ago the Bank was committing $35 million to fight HIV/AIDS; we have now moved to a commitment of $1 billion, an almost 30-fold increase. And we will make more money available as effective programs are developed.

We are working on HIV/AIDS prevention and working through public education programs, local clinics, and village groups, but we have also been active on the issue of treatment and the cost of retroviral drugs. And we are all too conscious of the fact that HIV/AIDS and other communicable and deadly diseases can only be addressed after dealing with health service delivery systems in general, and in this aspect we have been, and will continue to be, engaged.

We are also stepping up our work on postconflict situations. Six years ago we had 15 postconflict operations in place; today we have 35, and we are looking at how the Bank can get involved in postconflict countries at an earlier stage. Our best contribution will be to work with countries and regions to create the growth and social equity that will help prevent conflict.

Six years ago, we in the Bank did not speak about corruption—it was seen as too political and, for many, an impossible challenge. Today we are working on anticorruption and good-governance programs in 95 countries, and we are a leader in many aspects of this work.

Six years ago, there was little or no focus on community-driven development. Today we have over $1.5 billion in commitments: projects such as the nutrition project in Mozambique, which has radically reduced the incidence of malnutrition there, and the social funds in Malawi. Our objective is to see these kinds of community programs replicated all across Africa and throughout the developing world.

We believe that people who live in poverty should not be treated as a liability, but rather as a creative asset, one that will contribute more than anything else to eradicate poverty. They do not want charity, they want a chance, and community-based development programs provide such an opportunity.

Our experience in reaching out to communities in India, China, and countries in transition from central planning has been very promising. Today over 70 percent of our projects involve civil society and communities in some way, up from less than 50 percent in 1995. In all these endeavors, the key is to move from projects to programs that can be replicated and expanded on a national scale.

These are just some of the changes we have made to better sharpen our poverty focus. And the results have been impressive.

Over the last few years our development impact—our most important bottom line—has improved dramatically. The quality of our portfolio is at its highest level in two decades, which by itself translates into billions of dollars in more effective development spending for the people we serve. As measured by our independent Operations Evaluation Department, project effectiveness rose from 66 percent to 77 percent between 1996 and 2000: an impressive figure for an institution whose core business—development—always involves considerable risk. We expect this figure to improve further as we judge the effectiveness of projects commenced in the last five years. The quality of design of our projects has also improved, and improvements extend to project implementation, too.

No other international institution has embarked on such an ambitious reform plan over so short a period with such dramatic results. Have we succeeded in all areas? No. Much more remains to be done. But we have achieved an enormous amount with the dedication of our staff, and we have put in place the foundation for further change. We now have a tremendous opportunity to build on that progress.

But budget constraints are now causing enormous stress and anxiety among our staff. Doing development differently—with a more participatory approach and with more emphasis on the complex issues related to *human* development—takes much more time and more resources. And yet, uniquely among the international financial institutions, our budget is the same today in real terms as it was four years ago, despite the expansion in what we deliver and its higher quality.

Other demands are made on us. As a sustainable environment becomes an increasingly important public good, including it in the country programs puts increased requirements on Bank staff. The Bank's focus on gender issues has similar effects, calling on staff to do more.

Costs are also rising. The Bank has the most comprehensive environmental and social safeguard policies of any of the multilateral development banks. We have a leadership role to play in this area, and we intend to play it. Make no mistake, we will not water down our safeguards as some have alleged. But enhanced compliance with the safeguard and fiduciary standards, which are essential for sustainable development, has also increased our costs. We must recognize the higher quality and the benefits for our clients, but we must also recognize the costs. These need to be fully funded, and our clients must be helped to build the capacity to put these policies in place.

The New, Renewed Bank

How can we further sharpen our focus on poverty and maximize the catalytic role we can play in the development community?

In January of this year we discussed with our shareholders—of which Germany is a prominent and important member—a strategic framework for how we will carry reform forward over the next few years. Underscoring that agenda are five fundamental ideas that we are operationalizing in all our work:

First, the Bank must retain a global competence and a global diagnostic capacity. But this does not mean we must do everything ourselves. Under the Comprehensive Development Framework and the related PRSPs, we want to see more *selectivity* and a much better division of labor among all the players: international institutions, the United Nations, bilateral donors, nongovernmental organizations, and the private sector. Selectivity is at the heart of our work going forward. It should be based on comparative advantage and on accountability.

Second, we must focus in our work on how, in partnership with the development community, we can help achieve the Millennium Development Goals. Let me remind you of what these are:

- reducing by half the proportion of people living in extreme poverty by 2015

- a two-thirds decline in infant and under-five mortality, and a three-fourths decline in maternal mortality
- universal primary education for all by 2015
- gender equality in education by 2005
- national strategies for sustainable development by 2005, and
- ensuring that the current loss of environmental resources is reversed globally and nationally by 2015.

Third, within that overall framework we must focus on two areas in particular: *building the climate* for investment, jobs, and sustainable growth, and *empowering poor people* to participate in development by investing in them and through them. These must be the main drivers as we move toward greater selectivity.

Fourth, we must continue to gear all our work to the fact that development must be country owned and country driven. We must listen to the voices of the poor. As our interviews with 60,000 poor people in 60 countries confirmed, they do not want charity, they want a chance. Development must be done *by* them and *with* them, not *to* them.

And fifth, we must recognize that it is no longer enough to talk to governments alone. We must embrace *all* the players: civil society—including NGOs, whether foundations, universities and research institutions, or faith-based community groups—the private sector, bilateral donors, the other multilateral institutions, and developing-country governments themselves and their parliaments.

The Challenges of Globalization

I believe we must treat globalization as an opportunity, and poverty as our challenge. What do we mean by globalization? Globalization is about an increasingly interconnected and interdependent world; it is about international trade, investment, and finance that have been growing far faster than national incomes. It is about technologies that have already transformed our abilities to communicate in ways that would have been unimaginable a few years ago. It is about our global environment, communicable diseases, crime, violence, and terrorism. It is about new opportunities for workers in all countries to develop their potential and to support their families through jobs created by greater economic integration.

But it is also about international financial crises, about workers in developed countries who fear losing their jobs to countries with lower labor costs but limited labor rights. And it is about workers in developing countries who worry about decisions affecting their lives being made in the faraway head offices of international corporations.

Globalization is about risks as well as about opportunities. We must deal with these risks at the national level by managing adjustment processes and by strengthening social, structural, and financial systems. And, at the global level, we must establish a stronger international financial architecture and work to fight deadly diseases, to turn back environmental degradation, and to use communications to give voice to the voiceless.

We cannot turn back globalization. Our challenge is to make globalization an instrument of opportunity and inclusion—not of fear and insecurity. Globalization must work for all.

The World Bank's Role in Low-Income Countries

Let me first address our role in the low-income countries. I have already spoken of debt relief, and we must push ahead with that process as vigorously as possible. But we must also recognize that debt relief by itself is not a panacea.

The Bank has a crucial role to play in working with governments to put in place good and strong governance, effective legal and judicial systems, and a robust financial system, and to assist in the fight against corruption. Without these initiatives it will be impossible for countries to attract foreign and domestic private investment, which are so crucial as engines of growth and poverty reduction.

We need to continue our work in the rural sector, home to 70 percent of the poorest, and our work with the Consultative Group for International Agricultural Research. Our partnership with CGIAR is perhaps one of the oldest and most significant and effective we have.

We must recognize that gender equity and security are the bedrock of development. Equity for women and education for girls are perhaps the two most important development tools of all.

We need to help put in place safety nets for the vulnerable, as we are doing around the world, and work with governments to focus on education, health, and nutrition. We need to step up the fight against HIV/AIDS, malaria, and tuberculosis, and to work with governments to meet their basic infrastructure needs: potable water, sanitation, electric power, roads, and telecommunications systems.

Our recent work also confirms that participation in development matters. The CDF and the PRSPs have put national ownership and national consultation at the very heart of their approaches. We need to build on these.

We will push ahead with streamlining conditionality, focusing more on outcomes and less on itemizing what steps a government must take to reach them. We know that no list of conditions can replace domestic commitment to reform. In this regard our new instrument, the Poverty Reduction Support Credit, by focusing on programmatic lending, will reduce conditionality.

Above all we must recognize that debt relief is not a substitute for much-needed development assistance. It is tragic that, just when many governments have begun to put in place policies to foster growth and reduce poverty, the flows of aid have begun to shrink. Aid works when governments act in a responsible and accountable manner, and we can do more to make it work for more people.

Industrial countries must also get serious about trade. Barriers to developing-country exports in industrialized-country markets continue to put poor countries at a severe disadvantage. Industrialized countries spend more than $300 billion a year on agricultural subsidies. That is roughly equal to the total gross product of all of Sub-Saharan Africa. Yet even today developed-country tariffs on meat, fruits, and vegetables—all primary exports from the developing world—can exceed 100 percent. Debt relief without increased market access is a sham.

We must push ahead with donor coordination and harmonization. I said two years ago that it is shameful that a country like Tanzania must produce 2,400 quarterly reports a year for its donors, and suffer over 1,000 missions from different donors each year. Since that time the development community has made some progress on donor coordination with the bilateral donors and the regional development banks—but not enough.

The World Bank's Role in Middle-Income Countries

We need to remain engaged in middle-income countries. After all, 80 percent of the world's poor live in these countries. Let there be no mistake, we are not about to turn our back on them. Not only are these countries important for global financial stability, but many of them have yet to put in place crucial structural and social reforms that will move them to the next stage of development.

Helping these countries meet their development challenges is central to the Bank's overarching mission of tackling global poverty; it is also central to the realization of the Millennium Development Goals. Developments in these countries are also important for poverty reduction elsewhere.

At the request of our Board, we are reviewing our plans dealing with the scope and nature of our support and the principles of costing of services. We do not intend to replace sources of funding available from private markets.

The economic well-being of the middle-income countries can translate into trade opportunities for low-income countries. On the other hand, financial instability, environmental degradation, and the proliferation of communicable diseases can have deleterious effects far outside their own borders.

The Bank's engagement will be focused on the provision of secure long-term funding and advisory services, creating the right policy and institutional framework, and addressing weaknesses in social, structural, and sectoral policies and institutions. With its global reach, broad sectoral knowledge, and specific engagement with the private sector through the IFC [the International Finance Corporation] and MIGA [the Multilateral Investment Guarantee Agency], the Bank Group has comparative advantage in advising on overall priorities and actions to improve the investment climate.

Will we be crowding out the private sector? I do not believe so. Many of these countries may have a credit rating, but they do not have continuous access to international capital in the amount they need or on terms that are manageable for them. Moreover, as our own research and experience shows, World Bank lending has a catalytic effect: it crowds *in* private capital. It doesn't crowd it out. But here again let me stress that we will be selective, focusing on areas where we have comparative advantage and working closely with partners.

The Global Agenda

I have outlined the Bank's agendas in the low-income and middle-income countries. But much more remains to be done globally. Globalization is an opportunity to reach global solutions to national problems. Concern for the environment is a given starting point, which is already embedded in our work. Within our Strategic Framework, there are three areas in which we are sharpening our focus and capabilities. The first is communicable diseases. Disease respects no national boundaries, and it impoverishes and poses tremendous obstacles to development.

Bank-supported programs can provide the essential country-level framework on which effective global action can be based. I have already spoken about the Bank's work on HIV/AIDS. But we are working in many other areas, from malaria to tuberculosis. Every year 3 million children die from measles and hepatitis because they lack access to immunizations. We are involved in major alliances such as the Global Alliance for Vaccines and Immunization. We also provide seed capital, both intellectual and financial, for new initiatives of a public goods nature.

Second, trade expansion has been a leading factor in global integration. Over the last 30 years, several developing countries have participated in trade liberalization, but the gains from trade have been uneven. Low-income coun-

tries, particularly in Africa, have been less able to capitalize on liberalization
and growth in world trade. We see a catalytic role for the Bank in increasing
trading opportunities for Africa and other developing countries, to boost their
capacities to negotiate with the World Trade Organization and with industrial
countries.

Third, the Bank's analytical and advisory role is essential, supporting national policies to strengthen market institutions and infrastructure. This has
considerable potential for creating large gains from trade. I believe that the
Bank has a major role to play in working toward a level trading field for
developing countries. We must work to ensure that the next round of
international trade negotiations will be a development round.

Fourth, the financial crises of 1997–98 have brought about broad agreement that international standards, especially in financial systems, are a necessary foundation for robust economies. The Bank continues to participate in
various forums: with the Fund, with the Bank for International Settlements,
and other partners, for capacity building at the institutional level. We are in-
tensively engaged in these areas. We will also participate fully in efforts to end
abuses of the system by criminal acts and money laundering.

Finally, I believe that our work in bringing knowledge and information to
developing countries is as important as—if not more important than—capital
as an engine of development. This means not only our work in bridging the
digital divide or establishing a Global Gateway to radically transform the development business, but also making available our development expertise. Our
technical assistance and capacity-building work will be key in our support to
developing countries. We will press ahead vigorously with this work.

Nor should we neglect the importance of culture in a globalized world. We
hear or read almost daily about the fear of cultural homogenization. These
fears are real. We must not lose sight of the importance of culture and cultural
heritage in a rapidly shrinking world.

Looking Ahead

There are more challenges ahead, and bigger ones. As I observed earlier, in
the next 25 years world population will rise by 2 billion, to a total of 8 billion
people, with 98 percent of that increase in the developing world. The population of Europe will shrink, while that of the United States will go up a little,
but largely from migration.

Last year more than 47 percent of the global population—about 2.8 billion
people—lived in urban areas. By 2020, 4.1 billion, or 55 percent of global
population, will live in urban areas. Already today there are 20 megacities with

populations of over 10 million. By 2015 there will be 26, with enormous environmental and human consequences.

If we all act together now, we may succeed in achieving one of the most important of the Millennium Development Goals: that of halving the population living in poverty by 2015. The education and gender equality goals are also likely to be achieved by a considerable number of developing countries in several regions, and a few countries are on track to achieve significant reductions in infant and under-five mortality.

But the fact remains that, if present trends are an indication, none of the goals on health and education—the two-thirds decline in infant and under-five mortality, the three-fourths decline in maternal mortality, and universal primary education for all by 2015—are likely to be achieved at the global level without a more concerted, powerful campaign.

Never was there a better time for such a campaign. Knowledge about what sustainable development entails has never been better. The budgets of industrial countries have never been stronger. Technology has never been more dynamic. Our goals have never been clearer. We must seize this moment.

Public action in all countries must be driven by a new commitment to reducing global poverty. We must work together to harness the benefits of globalization to deliver prosperity to the many, not just the few. We must recognize that "business as usual" will no longer do. We must build the development dialogue on engagement and listening. As we go forward, the voices of the poor must be our guide.

Time is short. We must be the first generation to think both as nationals of our countries and as global citizens in an ever-shrinking and ever-more-connected planet. Unless we hit hard at poverty, we will not have a stable and peaceful world. Our children will inherit the world we create. The issues are urgent. The future for our children will be shaped by the decisions we make, and by the courage and leadership we show today.

Address at the Fourth Global Partnership Meeting to Roll Back Malaria

WASHINGTON, D.C. | APRIL 18, 2001

These comments were presented at the launch of the action phase of the Roll Back Malaria campaign, a new partnership of the Bank with the World Health Organization, the United Nations Children's Fund, and the United Nations Development Programme. Wolfensohn speaks of the human toll of malaria and the need for partnerships to tackle the disease.

Mr. Doryan,* Mr. Minister, Dr. Brundtland,[†] Other Distinguished Colleagues on the Panel, Your Excellencies, Ladies and Gentlemen:

We are very happy to have the opportunity of hosting this fourth meeting of the Roll Back Malaria campaign. I am particularly proud to have all of you here with us, including the representatives of our partner organizations the UNDP and UNICEF, and, indeed, so many of you who have made a tremendous contribution to this campaign.

As Mr. Alnwick[‡] said, today is an opportunity for us not just to reflect on the progress that we've made in the last several years, but most particularly to talk about the action phase, to move from discussion to implementation. It is also an opportunity to learn from each other what we are doing and what we have been doing, and, more significant, what we *can* do in terms of this dramatic development problem, which is also a human problem.

Over 3,000 people are dying from malaria every day, most of them children, and the economic costs in Africa alone are estimated at $12 billion a year. This makes malaria not only an immense problem on the human scale, but immense as a development challenge as well. Malaria is said to reduce GDP growth in the affected African countries by more than 1 percent a year, and this in a continent that is struggling to build GDP growth so that we can attack the questions of poverty. So this is a large and important issue.

Indeed, at the recent meeting of African leaders at which you, President Rawlings,[§] made a very stirring speech, this recognition of the crucial importance of this campaign was made evident. And, in fact, the representation at that meeting was such as to give us confidence that African leadership is very much behind the approach that we're taking.

---

* Eduardo Doryan, vice president for the Human Development Network at the World Bank.
† Gro Harlem Brundtland, director-general of the World Health Organization.
‡ David Alnwick, project manager of Roll Back Malaria.
§ Jerry Rawlings, former president of Ghana.

Now, what is so significant about this work? It's clear that it's not just the money being invested, though money is important. We in the World Bank now have about $450 million invested in various forms of antimalaria programs, in 56 projects in 46 countries. But we're ready to roll out additional funding, mainly through our affiliate the International Development Association, for this work. That funding is really at the call of you, your health ministers, and your finance ministers, whom no doubt you can influence in this effort.

Funding for this program will be coming, we hope, not just from the World Bank but, with Jeff Sachs'** help, through grants from around the world from all the people he knows who are ready to give. But we also recognize that, even if we get the monetary resources—if we can link the grants, the lending, and the other funding in whatever form it comes—that alone will not be sufficient. The fight against malaria is not just a matter of killing mosquitoes or providing bed nets or bringing in the drugs that are required. All that is, of course, important. The medical aspects, the focus on the disease itself, are crucial, as is prevention. But it has to go beyond that in two very important respects.

First of all, the effort has to be national in scope. It has to be rolled out on more than a project basis. The numbers are too great to think in terms of a project here and a project there. We simply have to deal with this, as we do so many other development issues, by creating programs that are replicable, that are communal, that are owned by the people they serve, and that can be rolled out on a broad scale.

Any of us could take a small area and attack malaria by delivering bed nets, by solving the problems of getting drugs, and so forth, and, by focusing on the problem, we could make that area safe. And projects like that do work, and that makes you feel terrific. We tend to do a lot of that in the Bank and in all our work. But with the population in Africa alone anticipated to rise from about 600 million to 1.1 billion in the next 25 years alone, and with 2 billion more people worldwide in the next 25 years being born in the developing countries, many of which are affected by malaria, projects alone are not sufficient. We have to come up with programs that are communal, that provide education, and that can engage all sectors of society, not just medical officers. And it starts with the planning of public works, with water supply. In every single project that we're engaged in, we need to think in terms of the impact on malaria.

We have to scale our projects in terms of whole communities, so that communities recognize the problem and are educated about malaria, so that they

---

**Jeffrey Sachs, then-professor of economics at Harvard University.

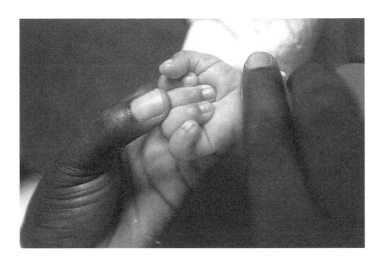

know how to deal with it. They must no longer simply accept as a fact of life that 3,000 people will die of the disease every day, mainly kids under five years old. That is not a necessity. It is a fact, but it's something that we must join together to fight against.

Here the partnership that we have to build is not an uncommon partnership. It's a partnership first and foremost with governments. Governments must give this work the priority that it needs and deserves. It needs to be more than a health priority. It needs to be a priority that is embedded in government policy at all levels and is perceived as such. In Africa such an awareness is already growing in the case of AIDS, which indeed may be more visible than malaria in some ways today. It needs to be communicated through the public media that malaria is a killer of a million people a year, and that its costs are huge when measured by the loss of jobs, the loss of efficiency, the loss of GDP, and the loss of human contentment and human happiness.

That is where we have to place this issue, so that governments can play their essential role. But governments alone can't do it. It has to be done together with nongovernmental organizations, with civil society in its broadest forms, and with church groups, which have played such an important role in building health delivery systems and which need to be embraced in a more coordinated manner, through voluntary cooperation, than perhaps has been true up to now.

We at the Bank have been dealing with the faith-based organizations and with civil society in many of the countries in Africa, and most notably, I'm happy to say, in Tanzania, where we recently had a meeting with faith-based groups on this subject. So we are ready to reach out to all aspects of civil society and to the private sector. For the private sector, cooperating in the fight against malaria is not just a matter of charity. It's a matter of self-interest. It's in their interest to keep families healthy, to create an environment in which fewer jobs are lost, and to build a healthy society in which to operate. It's good business as well as good societal behavior.

What we need to do, and what we're going to learn from each other in the course of these next few days, is to learn of the initiatives that have been taken, to learn from each other, in the presentations that will be made, what are the types of programs that work, that can be replicated, that can be owned, and that can be developed in scale.

Keep in mind the importance of replicability and scale and ownership. We're not interested in programs that can solve the problems of 1,000 well-placed, well-financed families. Or rather, we are interested, but that's not the issue we're facing today. Dealing with 1,000 families who have enough money and have walls around them and bed nets to stop the mosquitoes is one thing. The more significant thing is how to deal with the sort of people we saw in the short feature that was shown to us today.

We need to engage academia, and we need to engage the drug companies and the vaccine companies, and we need to give a focus to this war in which we're engaged. This fight is similar to, if I may say so, so many of the problematic wars and conflicts in Africa. They do not get the attention in the press that they deserve. They do not get the sense of priority. They do not get the impetus that they deserve, as if life were cheaper and human suffering less significant when it's happening in Africa and in other poor countries. Suffering is the same in whatever family and in whatever economic stratum it occurs. And we have today the responsibility and the opportunity to lift the level of awareness and to create the momentum and build on that momentum, because this is truly a fight. It is truly a war.

We have to work with governments on taxes and tariffs. We have to work in terms of setting priorities. We have to look at the debt relief issues, which Mr. Alnwick has already mentioned, and on which I believe we've already made significant progress. And we need, in fact, to use today as another starting point, no longer for analysis but for implementation.

I want to say to you that, so far as the Bank is concerned, we're ready for that challenge. We're anxious to be part of it. We respect greatly the leadership of Dr. Brundtland and WHO [the World Health Organization] and those who are setting the course for us. We're anxious to be a good partner, and we welcome you to this meeting.

Thank you very much.

Remarks at the World Bank Group Infrastructure Forum 2001

WASHINGTON, D.C. | MAY 2, 2001

In this address, Wolfensohn describes how building infrastructure—roads, water and sanitation systems, and the like—is integral to development and to meeting basic human needs. He warns that if developing countries fail to attract enough investment to build the infrastructure that their growing populations will need, a crisis could occur within the next 25 years.

Let me first welcome all of you and say what a pleasure it is to see this auditorium filled with people who are like-minded and concerned about the subject of infrastructure, or, from our point of view, the subject of infrastructure and poverty. Let me also thank our distinguished panel. It is a privilege to have them with us and a reflection of the great interest that this seminar has evoked. Let me start by giving you a brief overview of the way that we at the World Bank are looking at the question of infrastructure and of our role in the world. Our role, put simply, is to address the question of poverty and development.

For many of you from the private sector, the great opportunities of the past have been in the developed world. But as we look at the demographics— 6 billion people on our planet, 4.8 billion of them living in developing countries—one has to think in terms of numbers and needs and contrast that at the same time with economic advantage.

Roughly 80 percent of the world's population today receive 20 percent of world GDP, and 20 percent of the population receive 80 percent, out of a $30 trillion economy globally. In other words, roughly $6 trillion for 4.8 billion people. And among that same 6 billion people there are 1.2 billion living on less than a dollar a day, and 3 billion living on less than two dollars a day. At the broadest level, that is the challenge that we are facing—but that is not the whole story.

Among those countries that the World Bank deals with, two—India and China—account for 2.2 billion of those 4.8 billion people. And within that whole range of countries there are of course very significant within-country inequities between rich and poor.

If that were not already a tough enough situation to face, it is also a dynamic situation. Within the next 25 years we will add another 2 billion people to the planet, moving from 6 billion to 8 billion. All but 50 or 60 million of them will be born in developing countries. So in another 25 years we will have a planet of 8 billion people, with 6.8 billion, more or less, in developing countries and just over 1.2 billion in the developed world.

In my days in the private sector, we would have seen this as a real market opportunity. It is certainly the area of the world that is going to grow the fastest. But it is also an area of the world that is plagued with difficulties in terms of reputation, in terms of the ease or otherwise of making investments, and indeed, on current trends, in terms of financing. What we have seen in the last two years is a continuation of direct investment, which has grown to around $170 billion to $180 billion a year. We have seen portfolio investment also return to the positive column; we have seen a very modest amount of bond financing, and commercial bank financing has virtually disappeared.

At one point, at its peak in 1997, foreign investment to developing countries reached something on the order of $300 billion, with close to $100 billion coming from the banks. That, in net terms, has been reduced to virtually zero now. And as we face this great challenge going forward, we find that the financing element is going against us even as social and development needs are in fact increasing. In that environment, the role of the World Bank becomes more important, not only in terms of scale, but also, and far more important, in terms of the alternatives. We, along with the bilateral institutions and the regional development banks, are forced to look at where it is that we should put our money, how we should place that money, and how we can face this challenge.

It is not as simple a matter as identifying a project and putting some money up and doing it. We have concluded that, if there is to be satisfactory and long-term development, you cannot just do a project here and a project there. It needs to be something that we can approach more fundamentally.

So we are looking at such issues as strengthening governments and strengthening governance. We are looking at legal and judicial systems to try and make sure that they operate in an effective and honest way. We are looking at establishing financial markets and ensuring that they function in an equitable and honest way. We are looking at corruption, which is a huge issue that we all face every day, not just in developing countries but also in developed countries. We are trying to get the developed countries to change their laws so that bribes are no longer tax deductible—because that sends the wrong message to the people with whom we are trying to work.

All this is at the level of structure—and I haven't yet talked about projects—and then you have to get to the people. You have to get to the people because our purpose is to deal with poverty as it is reflected in the lives of people.

We at the Bank did a study that we found pretty interesting, called *Voices of the Poor*. We discovered that people around the world are probably no different from the people in this room, and not surprisingly. They want peace, they want security, and they want opportunity. The women don't want to get beaten up; violence against women is something that is unfortunately all too

prevalent in the developing world. Women want equal opportunity, which is wholly appropriate. They want services. They want to know whether they should trust the police more than they can trust the criminals. They want to be protected against corruption. They want a chance—they don't want charity.

That is the base from which we are working. When we come to our own analysis of what is to be done, the question becomes, "How do we do this? What do we look at? Do we look at education? Do we look at social programs? Do we look at health? What is it that we need to do to put the package together? What priorities do we deal with?"

Well, there are certain priorities that impose themselves. AIDS in Africa is an issue that has to be attacked directly. There are 25 million cases, 10 million orphans—and it is growing exponentially. The very issue of AIDS is a showstopper in Africa and, unfortunately, in some other areas, including some parts of the Caribbean, some parts of South Asia, maybe even some parts of eastern Europe.

There is also the issue of tuberculosis, the issue of malaria, the issue of water-borne diseases. All these things we have to look at as single issues because they are all showstoppers. There is also the issue of armed conflict: when there are 30 countries affected by war, it makes it pretty hard to get things done in those environments.

So there are a number of global issues that we need to address—and that we are addressing—in this rather complex matrix that we are looking at. And then there are the demographics. In the next 25 years, 2 billion people will be moving into cities and towns, according to the best estimates that we have. That movement will bring with it new forms of management: distributed management from the center of the country to the provinces, to the localities, to the towns. And how do you deal with that? We are looking then at the importance of Internet technologies, and at technology as a basis on which it might be possible to put this all together. We have a lot of things on our minds in terms of structure: in the legal, judicial, and financial areas, the education and health strategy; the rural strategy; and the urban strategy.

Of course, there is the question of infrastructure. At what point does one bring in infrastructure? If we are so concerned about the social issues—and we are—what has happened to projects? What has happened to roads? What has happened to power and to water? You come to the conclusion, without having to give it a lot of thought, that unless you have the infrastructure base down, it is very difficult to do any of the other things.

You will all have dozens of examples of how health is affected by sewerage, by water, by wastewater management in all its forms, by water-borne diseases. These are issues that probably everyone in this room has images of. I carry around with me images of the slums I visited in Latin America. In the *favelas* in Brazil, when women have water delivered to them for the first time on commercial terms—because poor people, as you know, pay more for water than rich people—they find, first, that their health improves; second, that they live a much better life; and third, that they have far more time, since they no longer have to spend four hours a day walking down the hill and back up the hill, fetching water.

The same is true of power. If you can have power delivered to your home, you obviate the need to collect wood that you burn indoors and asphyxiate yourself. If you can get clean power to communities, that has advantages both in terms of the women's time and in terms of the health of the family.

In primary education, particularly girls' education, you can have funding that provides for the possibility that the family can let the girls go to school, but we have discovered that the factors that ensure the greatest attendance of girls at school are rural roads and toilets. If you provide toilet facilities, and if you provide rural roads, that, curiously, is key to improving girls' education. That is not the only key, but without that you cannot get girls to school. If you want to expand education, and if you want to have Internet access, you need communications, and you need power.

There is not a single area that I was talking of before that doesn't require basic infrastructure to make things work. So this conference for us is not just a conference about things and about projects. It is a conference about people who have these social and human needs. Unless we deal with the infrastructure issues, there is no way that we get to the human requirements and no way that we can satisfy the issues of poverty.

That is why for us the issue is of such crucial importance. This audience is composed of people from our institution, other institutions, and the private sector. It is very, very clear that this is not just an institutional activity. This is a public-private partnership, in which we will participate in a number of different ways: with the World Bank as a financier, MIGA as an insurer, and IFC* as a co-venturer. In each of these areas we are dependent on you, but I hope you can find some benefit in working with us.

Indeed, the schedule that has been set out for the next few days gives us a chance to explore together the ways in which we can work to meet these infrastructure needs. I want you to understand that the rhetoric of people, the rhetoric of social demands, the rhetoric of poverty is also the rhetoric of infrastructure. We have to have the infrastructure base and attend to those needs in a growing environment—and that is particularly so in the developing world. In an environment that is changing both in terms of demographics and in terms of concentrations of population, if we do not act now, then in 25 years a crisis will occur.

I want to say to you that a crisis 25 years from now is actually a crisis today. It is a crisis today because, unless we deal with the infrastructure needs now, unless we take part now in an enormous investment undertaking estimated at $800 billion a year—which is up from a previous estimate of $600 billion per year, which in turn was up from the one I saw before that—it will be upon us before we realize it. Whatever that number is or may become, it is enormous in terms of size, in terms of management capacity, and in terms of the ability to plan and implement.

So this is not a subject that can be left to deal with in a leisurely way for 25 years. This is today's problem that needs today's solutions and that has a great urgency about it. I will close simply by saying that, to us, the infrastructure sectors are central. Without them the social, the educational, and the health requirements cannot be met.

The urgency is immediate. It demands better analysis and then better practical associations between the public and private sectors and civil society to try and deal with a problem that will in fact determine whether 25 years from now we will live in peace or in conflict. I thank you for being here, and I thank again our speakers, and I hope that you have a great few days.

---

* The Multilateral Investment Guarantee Agency and the International Finance Corporation are both part of the World Bank Group.

Published in *The Washington Times*

JUNE 24, 2001

Just days ahead of the UN Special Session on HIV/AIDS, Wolfensohn sounds the alarm on AIDS's march through Africa and other parts of the globe. He urges countries to contribute generously to the proposed new global trust fund for combating AIDS, and he highlights the World Bank's new Multi-Country HIV/AIDS Program for Africa, which aims to help African countries scale up prevention, care, and treatment.

Last year alone, AIDS killed almost 3 million people around the world. More than 5 million became newly infected with HIV, nearly 4 million of them in Africa. The HIV/AIDS epidemic is spreading at alarming rates in other regions as well. In Eastern Europe, and South and Southeast Asia, there is evidence the disease is taking deadly hold of people and their communities. In the Caribbean, AIDS has become the major cause of death among men under the age of 45.

As heads of state, policy-makers, U.N. agencies, health experts, civil-society groups and others converge on New York for the U.N. Special Session on HIV/AIDS, these facts should command the world's attention. Under the leadership of U.N. Secretary General Kofi Annan, this high-level global meeting will underscore that HIV/AIDS is no longer just a health problem, but a global development problem, threatening to reverse many of the gains made over the last half-century. More than that, it is an international security problem, and, as such, it needs a war chest and a rigorous strategy.

A growing consensus has emerged among U.N. agencies, donors and stakeholders that a global trust fund offering grants for the prevention and treatment of HIV/AIDS and other communicable diseases is the only way to surmount the very large financing gap threatening to defeat the fight against AIDS. But as such, we want to ensure that the proposed fund provides financing over and above existing foreign aid. To reallocate those funds would simply be a shell game.

I hope and trust that governments, charitable foundations, the private sector, civil-society and other groups attending this special session will respond generously to the challenge of checking the spread of HIV/AIDS and contribute significantly to the war chest that will be needed.

While money alone will not solve the problem, it is a vital part of the solution, and funds earmarked for confronting the epidemic are currently much too low. Total global support for HIV/AIDS in developing countries last year

was probably under $1 billion, less than a third of the estimated need in Africa alone.

Dramatic reductions in prices of anti-retroviral drugs are key to treatment. But even they do not provide the magic bullet. At $400 to $500 a year, down from $10,000, they are more affordable, but still well out of reach for the vast majority of infected people in developing countries where per capita income is less than $500 per year, and where governments spend less than $5 per person on health care.

Prevention is key. But prevention is costly as well. What is needed is at least $9 billion per year.

The World Bank, in partnership with African governments, has launched the Multi-Country HIV/AIDS Program (MAP) for Africa, which over the past year has provided $500 million in new money to help 10 African countries scale up effective prevention, care and treatment. The MAP makes significant resources available to civil-society organizations and communities, which have developed some of the world's most innovative HIV/AIDS interventions. Next year, we plan to finance another $500 million to reach 15 more African countries.

Moreover, the bank has unveiled a new $150 million fund to fight HIV/AIDS in the Caribbean, and $40 million in recent lending has also gone to support HIV/AIDS prevention and care in Bangladesh.

These reflect a solemn pledge I made last year that there will be no limit to the amount of funding we are willing to provide, and that no national HIV/AIDS program will be stopped because of lack of funding. I reaffirm that commitment. But no one on its own—not the bank, donor agencies, national governments, non-governmental organizations or the private sector—will be able to provide the scale of money and support needed to engage HIV/AIDS at the global and country level and ultimately prevail. For this reason, the bank strongly supports the establishment of the global fund within the context of meeting the International Development Goals. These call for a halving of the proportion of people living in extreme poverty by 2015 and also urge greater strides in reducing infant, child and maternal mortality.

Treatment, prevention, implementation—all these are needed. But there is one more essential element in our strategy. Leadership. In too many countries, AIDS, sex, rape and condoms are subjects rarely mentioned. In too many communities, men believe that sex with a virgin will cure them. The human tragedy surrounding that belief is staggering—in South Africa today, 95,000 children under the age of 15 are HIV-positive, most of them girls. More and more leaders are beginning to break the silence. We need others to follow suit. Rich countries must set an example by putting up funds and offering help to those who speak out.

Collectively we have the resources, and we surely have the need. All we lack is the political will. Let us join with the G-7 [Group of Seven] and the U.N. system to commit to a global fund. Let us also invite civil society into this global campaign against HIV/AIDS. Its contribution could be enormous. Civil society has played a pivotal role in all countries that have had success against HIV/AIDS. At the global level, representatives of civil society should be involved at all stages in the design, decision-making and implementation of HIV/AIDS-related activities. At the country level, civil society should have a direct role in AIDS governing bodies, and those bodies should channel a significant share of HIV/AIDS resources directly to the local level and to community organizations.

So, let us all join arms and show we are not powerless against this epidemic. Let us mobilize the money, the political will and the battle plans to turn the tide of this global threat. Let us then make this U.N. Special Session on HIV/AIDS a pivotal moment in the fight.

Keynote address at the launching of the International Consortium
for Cooperation on the Nile

GENEVA | JUNE 26, 2001

*This address, about the 11 countries of the Nile Basin cooperating in using
the river's waters, captures the imagination. Wolfensohn speaks to the history of the Nile with its pharaohs, kings, and plundering and destruction.
The aim of the initiative, he says, should be not just to change history in
the Nile region but also to "help to change Africa."*

Mr. Chairman, Ministers, Distinguished Guests, Colleagues, and Friends:

I am extremely pleased to be invited by the Nile Council of Ministers to open
this extraordinary event, the first meeting of the International Consortium for
Cooperation on the Nile. Let me say to you, Mr. Chairman, that the task of
setting the tone for this event is a very difficult one indeed, after listening to
those 11 young people representing the countries of the Nile, because I think
they have said it all. Anything that one might say, after their presentation of
hope, of expectation, of partnership, of joy, and of community, would be anti-
climactic. So let us not leave this gathering with recollections of anything I
might say, but with recollections of what the children have said. As one child
said of the Nile, "I love him, he loves me, I care for him, and he cares for
me." What more do you need to indicate the bond between the Nile and its
people today, and the future generations who will live along that great river
tomorrow?

I am so moved by what has been happening here today that I would like to
give you my personal impressions and feelings about the Nile Basin Initiative.
This is more than just another international consultative group, more than just
another meeting where the World Bank, the UN system, and others come to
work together with your countries, Mr. Chairman. This is a historic opportunity to ensure that cooperation, prosperity, peace, and inclusion triumph over
poverty, conflict, and exclusion in a region of great need. This is an occasion
on which all of us are coming together with a sense of purpose, and, in my
case, with a sense of feeling like a mere speck in history.

I have been reading many books on the history of the Nile. As we look
back in history at this river system and its peoples, as we think of the 300 million people drawing life from the Nile today, as we think of the prospect of
600 million people drawing life from the Nile in another 25 years, as we think
of 10 countries bound together by one of the world's great rivers coming together for the very first time in a consultative group meeting, we can see that

your Council of Ministers has taken a very bold step. It indicates that the past is behind you and that your future is together.

We in the international community have a chance to join you now, at this historic moment, to lay the foundations for a future of prosperity and peace. We join you in a way that is different from previous consultative groups that I have participated in, because this is not a group of experts coming together to try and sell a program to a group of recipients. This is a case where the 10 Nile Basin states themselves have come together. And you have done a truly magnificent job in preparing for us this briefing document that sets out your program for cooperation. It is masterful in its clarity and clear in its direction. It is something that all of us would wish to have on coming to a consultative group meeting.

As we read this remarkable document, we are struck by the fact that the ministers said in 1999 that the initiative is guided by a shared vision "to achieve sustainable socioeconomic development through the equitable utilization of and benefit from the common Nile Basin water resources." It is marvelous in its simplicity, but remarkable in the fact that your countries have come together in support of this shared vision. As we further reflect on this document, we find that not only have you agreed on a shared vision for the Nile Basin, but you have established policy guidelines and prepared a basin-wide Shared Vision Program of seven projects. You then break down your activities into subsidiary action programs, for investments in the Eastern Nile Subsidiary Action Program and the Nile Equatorial Lakes Subsidiary Action Program. You have clear policies and plans and an organization that is committed to pursue those policies and plans in a transparent manner and a manner based on trust.

If ever there was a consultative group that deserves support, it has to be this one, because it really does have all the elements necessary for success. What is fascinating about this initiative is that it does not just deal with the issue of water. As the two ministers start by saying, "This is an issue of people, this is an issue of poverty, this is an issue of peace."

I believe that the benefits of this initiative can go well beyond the river itself. There are clearly direct gains from managing the river together: you can responsibly produce more food and power, you can reduce the devastation of drought and flood, and you can protect watersheds, wetlands, and habitats. By working together, you can reduce the real costs you are incurring from the historic effects the river has had on relations between countries—costs from isolationism, costs from seeking self-sufficiency in food and power, and even military costs—diverting attention away from the overarching challenge of poverty.

Finally, as you work together to manage and develop the river and to conserve the environment, and as you build trust and relationships, other doors will open. Beyond the river, there will be growing incentives to reduce conflict, and opportunities to work together more broadly: to link your roads, railways, and power grids and to boost trade and investment flows.

If any of us is concerned—indeed, as we all are concerned—with the future of Africa, this initiative can be seen as a microcosm of the challenge of Africa. These 10 Nile Basin countries include 4 of the 10 poorest countries of the world. In this region we see great poverty and exclusion. We see inadequate education. We see HIV/AIDS. We see widespread conflict. We see a lack of utilities provision. We see markets that are too small to be developed on their own. We see the need for coming together and for integration to bring about appropriate economic development. As the children have said, and as the ministers have said, this initiative must move forward while preserving the special culture of the region. This is not an American initiative or a European initiative or a Canadian initiative. This is an African initiative. It is an initiative that starts with the river, but which encompasses the social, cultural, and human aspects of development.

And what could be more exciting than to bring about cooperative development in a region so steeped in history? As I am finding in the history books, some of that history is positive and some less positive. It is a history that goes back to kings and pharaohs, to remarkable traditions, to the very origins of our own species and of civilization in East Africa, and to long-gone plunderers who have fought over this river, fought over its resources, and brought destruction to the area.

Together, we are all now a mere speck in this history. We just happen to be here, at this time, at this meeting, when we can make a difference in history. Together, we have an opportunity to be a part of the future history of the Nile. This opportunity is given to very few people. It is perhaps the first time in history that we have the scientific and the technical resources, the capacity, the knowledge, and the experience to come together. And we have more. We have the will. We have growing trust. As the ministers have emphasized, trust cannot be forced; it must be nurtured and developed, particularly because of that history.

This is a remarkable—and fragile—first step. But it is less fragile than history might dictate, because your nations have come together bound not by mistrust, but by trust and hope. Your countries have already given much thought to defining the way forward, and you are telling us what you need to do. You need to recognize and understand each other's interests and to explore the many ways in which those interests converge. You need to bring civil society together, within and across borders, creating a Nile community, fostering the exchange of knowledge and ideas, and pooling skills and capital. You need to pool other resources, perhaps even co-financing and co-owning infrastructure for river regulation and for power generation and transmission, thereby building trust and interdependency. You need to promote private sector investments and joint ventures across borders. You need to rationalize food, energy, and other production within a regional and not a national context, to exploit comparative advantage across the basin. You need to design and adopt innovative ways of sharing the *benefits* from the river—merely sharing its waters will not be enough. You need to promote the movement of labor to wherever jobs can be created. You need to work together to find solutions to conflict throughout the basin, for you know that you must not pass on to your children the legacy of conflict that too many generations have inherited. And you need to move to action without delay.

These are not things that are being said by some outside group trying to impose its ideas. These are the deliberations of the ministers themselves. And if we look at the project descriptions in detail, every line is characterized by this desire to work together for a common future. It is a very, very impressive program indeed. But the Nile states need support. For all of us in the development business, this is an opportunity not only to back a project or a program—but to change history.

We in the development community also need to come together at this meeting and in the consultative group tomorrow, to pledge the other side of this partnership. We must be prepared to work with the Nile states, to plan development that considers the river as one system, that optimizes the production of food and power, that shares costs and benefits, and that seeks to resolve and avoid disputes. We must be prepared to help identify innovative public and private financing mechanisms, which might include co-financing and joint ownership of assets across borders. We must be prepared to work with the Nile states as you make difficult choices. If you need to build dams, for example, we must help to ensure that the best options are chosen, that voice is given to the people affected, and that the environmental impacts are minimized and mitigated. We must be prepared to build capacity and to build and strengthen institutions, both national and international.

We all must recognize that conflict prevention and poverty alleviation are inextricably linked, and we must be prepared to look for new instruments, if needed, to support development. In the Nile Basin the alternative to cooperation is unthinkable; it would impose enormous costs on the people of the basin—and for the rest of the world. We all must recognize that investment in poverty alleviation and cooperation in the Nile Basin is not charity; it is an investment in development, peace, and global security.

This is not going to be an easy course of action, because the problems of Africa remain: the problems of governance, the problems of legal and judicial systems, the problems of financing, the problems of education, the problems of health. None of these broader issues will go away because we talk about cooperation on the Nile. They are there, and together we must confront them at the same time. But there is a real chance to carve out an island of integrity and of hope in the Nile Basin Initiative. By facing these challenges together, we have a real opportunity to promote development that is characterized by trust, by transparency, by equity, by well-implemented projects, and by common purpose. This is a chance not only to change history in the Nile Basin, but to help to change Africa.

I must acknowledge the remarkable work of the UNDP and CIDA* and the work that is being done by the European Union, by the Global Environment Facility, and by the individual bilateral donors. The World Bank is here not as a leader, but as a supporter of the Nile Basin Initiative, working in partnership with all of the countries of the basin and all of the donors.

This meeting, ministers, launches your journey, and I know that there will be sufficient support committed for you to take the first steps along this road, with financing for your Shared Vision Program of cooperation among all 10 states. As you advance, it is clear that the investments necessary to meet your development needs, both in developing the resources of the river and in linking your countries together with physical and social infrastructure, are very large. With the plans you are developing, you may need to see investments of several billion dollars secured in the first five years. Over the next 20 years, as cooperation grows and opportunities expand, you may need to see many times this sum. Although today these numbers may seem large, 20 years from now there will be perhaps half a billion people living in the Nile Basin states, and together we must face the challenge of meeting their needs.

I commit to you today, ministers, the continued support of the World Bank. As your cooperation grows, the World Bank will be prepared to underwrite a substantial share of your cooperative investment needs, and, along with the international community, we will seek to provide whatever level of financing can be effectively absorbed. We will be there for you throughout this program. I want you to know that I say that with complete sincerity. I look forward to working with all of you.

I regard it as an enormous privilege, on behalf of my colleagues at the World Bank and on my own behalf, to declare this meeting open.

Thank you very much.

---

* The United Nations Development Programme and the Canadian International Development Agency, respectively.

Closing remarks at Public Sector Day, World Bank headquarters

WASHINGTON, D.C. | SEPTEMBER 12, 2001

These remarks are of historical import for their weight and gravity, coming
one day after the September 11 terrorist attacks on the World Trade Center
in New York and on the Pentagon, only a few miles from World Bank
headquarters in Washington. In the wake of the attacks, Wolfensohn
reminds World Bank staff at a meeting of public sector experts that they
have a unique opportunity to make the world a better place.

Thank you all very much. It has been quite a time these last 24 to 48 hours. I
had intended to talk to you today about many things, before the tragedy that
occurred yesterday morning. They are of very different levels of seriousness
and immediacy, but, given that I get this group together so very rarely, let
me try and deal with a number of them and then find time for questions, if
you have any.

This has not been the easiest summer for me, given the vitriolic criticism
both in journals and in the press, but what is remarkable is that, in the last
10 days, there has been a very considerable outpouring of support. I take this
as an indication that there is some support for what I am trying to get done
here, which I can only do with all of you. So these attacks in the press, which,
while personalized, are really attacks on all of us, are incidental in terms of
what we are trying to do.

Let me for a moment deal with the tragedy of yesterday, and deal with it
on a number of levels. We have tried to review a number of lessons that have
emerged.

The first is, of course, that we are in a whole new world. It is not a world
that is unexpected. I was making a speech in New York on Monday in which
I talked of the new forms of terror and violence. I said that armies were no
longer necessary; that one part of globalization was that terror could be conveyed by small groups with good planning and could wreak the same havoc
that was wrought earlier by amassed armies. Little did I realize that, within
24 hours, an example that exceeded anything I had even dreamed of would be
forthcoming here in the United States.

I was dealing then in my remarks with the issue of globalization, saying
that globalization is not just something that has to do with economics or with
jobs or trade. It has to do with violence. It has to do with stability. It has to
do with finance. It has to do with health. I had seen just in the days preced-
ing that my compatriots in Australia had just been confronted with 400
Afghan refugees on Christmas Island; some Afghans had also been caught

running through the Channel Tunnel. So the notion of distance, the notion of country, and the notion of being behind walls, with which many of us grew up, is just gone, just absolutely gone. And it is very clear that it went yesterday in a way that will bring home the reality of it to everyone in this country and around the world.

In fact, I have been in the last few days very active, again, on the Middle East process, and it is having a big impact there at this very moment. Everything is being reappraised in light of this tragedy, and we have to come to terms with it in the Bank. I think there are several levels that we have to come to terms with.

First of all is the security for all of you, and so our security arrangements are being revamped and reexamined at this moment. We have some emergency measures in place, but clearly we have to go to a different level of security for all of us, and we will do that because it is part of the new reality. After yesterday, there is no way that we can avoid it, and we will need your help, your guidance, and your advice on that.

We already had pretty good systems for fire, and we had pretty good systems for ground-level bombs in the building, including plans to get people in or out if there was an explosion. But we didn't have any great understanding of what to do if an aircraft is coming at the building, or whether there are other forms of destruction that could be wreaked upon us. So security concerns come first, and we will certainly be dealing with that.

The second thing that I think we need to deal with is how we come together as part of a global institution, and at this time, I think, unilateralism has become evidently much less attractive than working for global solutions through global institutions. If there was ever a moment when there needs to be a reaffirmation of the role of global institutions, it is now. And it needs to be reaffirmed at all levels, because globalization means that there is a need for new measures of governance, new measures of organization.

I think that, for all of us in the Bank, there is both an opportunity and a responsibility to do better and to work with greater conviction on our mandate, which is to try and make the world a bit better and to deal with issues of poverty. As I have said a number of times before, the conquest of poverty is really the quest for peace, and this linkage is something all of us have to understand and reconfirm for ourselves. The Bank has a unique role to play in this, and we have to lift our level of seriousness and stop looking at our navels and start looking out the window at the things we need to be doing. We need to stop pampering each other and recognize that we have a role in world peace, which needs to reach a new level of discussion than what has so often occurred inside the institution. I nearly said something that I would have been

criticized for, but I think you probably know that I am concerned about the level of dialogue in our institution and our concern for ourselves, which is justifiable, but which surely needs to be balanced by our concern for the job that we are doing.

The third thing is that, if we are going to do this job, we have to come together in a way that is different from the way we have before. We have to be a global institution that takes account of the fact that we are different, that this room is full of very different people. men and women, management and staff, but, equally, people of different races and different religions. We have to recognize that we are one staff, that we should not allow ourselves to be engaged in any form of racial or religious bias or prejudice, and that we should come together as a single team supporting each other. We have not been very good at that kind of mutual support. Ever since I arrived at this institution, I have been deeply concerned about the cynicism and the lack of generosity that we have toward each other. It has struck me very vigorously since I have been here, and I think that, in light of recent events, we have a chance to start again and build the sort of spirit that we need.

Why am I saying these things? Because I actually feel somewhat freed by the criticism. I don't know what else people could say about me, so I might as well tell you what I think. But what I think is extremely well meaning, and in light of the events of the last 24 hours, I think extremely serious. We could be at the beginning of a really terrible period. President Bush talked of war. Who knows what is going on at the moment? We hope and pray for peace, but, whatever happens, something changed yesterday, and we must all take that seriously if we are going to contribute in the way that we would like to.

As to this particular group and what you are doing, I think you know that, after I was here 12 months or so, I reached a very simple conclusion: unless you have governance in its broadest sense—which means strengthening the instruments of government, strengthening capacity, having legal and judicial systems that work, having financial systems with the capacity to serve rich and poor and bridge the issue of equity—and unless you attack the problem of corruption, no amount of money and no program is going to work. It seemed to me just blindingly clear that, without the structure, without the framework, you couldn't deal with the question of poverty and equity. It is not such a brilliant idea, but it seemed to me a very obvious idea and one that I thought the Bank Group had given much less attention to than it should have.

So it is not surprising that, in the Comprehensive Development Framework and the Poverty Reduction Strategies, countries are saying that the top three items on our agenda are all within the framework of your work. In fact, I learned what I have learned from visits to countries. So, for me, it is absolutely, transparently clear that your work—running parallel with the other work that is done in the Bank—is a precondition for effective poverty alleviation.

If you read the *Voices of the Poor* study, as I have done now several times, and you hear those voices, what people want is protection of their rights. They want voice. They want a fair chance. They don't want corruption. They want to know the difference between the police and the criminals. Women want to be protected against violence. They want a chance for their kids. They want balanced economic development, and these are all the things that you are concerned with, whether it be on taxes or customs or legal or judicial reform or strengthening government. They are all part of that issue. And so I am very proud of the fact that this group has gotten larger, and I am particularly proud of the effectiveness of what you are doing. I think you will find that the demand continues to grow, and, as I get around the world, there is no question that this contribution is appreciated more and more.

It is not a high-volume dollar business, but that should not be the basis of our judgment anyway. The judgment of the effectiveness of what we do should be quite separate from the number of projects or the number of dollars that we put before the Board. So I just want you to know that I will most assuredly continue my support, not just because you are good-looking and attractive, but because I have said repeatedly it is what I believe.

This also becomes part of the debate on the so-called New Bank versus the Old Bank. Peripherally, it becomes a part of whether I am judged a complete bastard or something less than that, but what I am is what you get. What I am is someone who is absolutely convinced that a comprehensive, long-term approach to development that is integrated, that takes advantage of the contributions of the other international institutions and the bilateral institutions, of the private sector and civil society, and that does it with the ownership and leadership of the local government—that is the way to go. Individual projects without the sort of framework that you provide just will not work. The money will be stolen, the projects will be ineffective, and it is just not going to get done.

You are at the very core, it seems to me, of an approach to development that a number of people would like to turn back. They are saying that it is mission creep, that it is lack of focus, that it is lack of understanding, that it is adding complexity to the development paradigm. My answer to that is that what they are saying is nonsense. I do not believe it. Having a comprehensive view does not mean we have to do everything ourselves. We can select the things that we have the best competence in and let others do the rest. Having the capacity to understand a complex issue doesn't mean that you have to be active on every aspect of that complexity. We do not have to do everything, but some institution has to have an overall view of the development paradigm.

It is a bit like having a general practitioner come and conduct the first examination, and then you can have your specialists deal with the specialists' issues. There is a need for a general practitioner in the international development business, and there isn't anyone but us. The regional banks cannot do it. The UN system cannot do it. Bilateral agencies cannot do it. And to waste the singular advantage of our institution by saying that we are too broadly spread or lack focus, or to respond to the cheap criticisms that we get, would, I think, be a terrible mistake for the global move against poverty.

So I just want to conclude by saying to you that, from my point of view, I am going to stick with this thing and work with you to try and bring about the sort of advance that we want, that I am really counting on you to try and push the work that you are doing, and that I have no doubt that the demand will continue. And I would like to urge you, in your interaction with your colleagues and with your family, to think about the terrible occurrences of the last

24 hours and become adjusted to the new reality of the post–World Trade Center and the post-Pentagon and the post-Pennsylvania disasters.

It is a different world today. It is a world in which we have to become adults pretty quickly, and I know I can count on you. I hope we can work together, because we are a very important organization, and we are very privileged to have the responsibility that is given to us.

Well, this has been probably longer and more philosophical than you want, but I haven't slept much. In any event, it is what I think, and I will be glad to answer some questions.

Thank you.

2001: THE URGENCY FOR ACTION ON POVERTY IS PRESSING

Message from the president and chairman from the 2001 World Bank *Annual Report*

OCTOBER 2001

This Chairman's Message covers the year from June 2000 to July 2001 and reminds shareholders of the challenge of halving global poverty by 2015.

The poverty reduction agenda has advanced significantly over the past year, with development partners coming together as never before. We must now build on that momentum. Progress in reducing poverty remains slow: too many girls still do not go to school; too many children die before the age of five; and too many poor people lack opportunity.

The urgency for action is pressing. Nearly half of the world's people live on less than $2 a day, and their numbers will grow in the next 25 years, as nearly two billion more people are added to developing countries' populations. The stakes are high, as poverty touches all and drives prospects for no less than global peace. How can we scale up successes enough to meet the international development goals for 2015? Only with concerted action can we make a difference.

Progress Is Evident at the Country and Regional Levels . . .

Over the past year, I was privileged to visit India and Africa, which, between them, hold 55 percent of the world's poor. They offer striking examples of the ways in which societies are transforming.

In India's Andhra Pradesh state, rural women are engaging in open discussions—unthinkable a few years ago—on how to confront the problem of HIV/AIDS. In the same state, e-government has cut the time taken for land registration from 6 months to 20 minutes. Elsewhere, empowered grassroots communities are successfully implementing the country's education projects, now covering 50 million children.

Africa is on the move. On a first-ever joint trip by the heads of the World Bank and the International Monetary Fund, [IMF Managing Director] Horst Köhler and I met with 22 African presidents. We were deeply impressed by their conviction that Africa's future lies in its own hands, and by their commitment to far-reaching change. Leaders stressed the need to deal with conflict and governance, combat HIV/AIDS, and pursue stronger regional cooperation.

Middle-income countries, too, are addressing poverty-related concerns ranging from inequality and governance to urban pollution and rural infrastructure, and are increasingly adopting sound macroeconomic policies.

Developing countries, on average, have begun to enjoy higher per capita growth rates than industrial countries.

. . . and at the Global Level . . .

A remarkable development of the past year is the unprecedented alignment of partners around a common global development agenda, embodied in the Millennium Declaration adopted by leaders of the world's nations. Common guiding principles for development partnership, too, as outlined in the Comprehensive Development Framework, have gained growing acceptance by the United Nations and, most recently, by the Development Committee for application also in middle-income countries. These principles emphasize a comprehensive approach, country ownership, partnership, and a focus on results. Other major steps forward are the European Union's decision to adopt the Poverty Reduction Strategy Papers approach, as well as growing efforts among all donors to harmonize aid procedures and untie procurement.

. . . but 2015 Is Approaching, and All Must Act

Halving the percentage of those in poverty by 2015 is an immense challenge. Global action is a moral imperative; all have a responsibility.

Developing countries need to ensure sound policy and institutional environments and an attractive investment climate. Equally crucial are inclusive policies, to allow the benefits of growth to reach poor people.

Donor countries need to remove trade barriers and open their markets. They need to provide debt relief and new concessional finance, multilaterally—foremost through an adequate 13th Replenishment of the International Development Association and funding of the Heavily Indebted Poor Countries (HIPC) Initiative—as well as bilaterally. An increase in aid is crucial, from the present 0.22 percent of gross national income of the world's rich countries to the 0.7 percent share to which they have committed. And concerted international efforts must help fight major global problems and strengthen the structures needed to help countries avoid crises and integrate into the global economy.

Action and progress, moreover, will need to be built on a solid base of global growth and sound macroeconomic policies.

The World Bank Is Committed to Concerted Action

Guided by the 2015 poverty goal, we have strengthened the poverty focus of our efforts. This has meant intensified support to the HIPC Initiative, helping

23 of the world's poorest countries shift about $1 billion from annual debt service to spending on basic social services. It has also meant helping the governments of poor countries take the lead in preparing poverty reduction strategies developed with national consensus, and especially involving civil society and the private sector. The role of business in job creation is crucial; we have expanded our work in microcredit and our support for small and medium-size enterprises.

We have radically transformed the way we do business. A persistent focus on quality has vastly improved the effectiveness of billions of dollars of Bank lending. We are also responding more quickly and flexibly to client needs and have substantially strengthened our knowledge sharing with clients.

We have made partnership—with countries and with other development agencies—intrinsic to all that we do. A key priority is the ongoing initiative for the harmonization of donor policies and procedures to reduce costs for developing countries.

And we have stepped up collaborative efforts to address such enormous development challenges as HIV/AIDS, conflict, environmental decline, and the digital divide. These efforts have included innovative support to help Africa fight HIV/AIDS and become more competitive.

In fiscal 2001 the Bank articulated a Strategic Framework for action over the next three years. The Framework sets two priorities: strengthening countries' investment climates, and helping them empower and invest in poor people. It emphasizes selectivity—within and across countries as well as at the global level—and partnership.

What counts, ultimately, is impact. Outcomes of individual Bank-financed operations have improved markedly. But achieving the broader impact of an overall Country Assistance Strategy is a long-term endeavor, involving players and factors beyond the control of any one institution. The coming together of the development community on a common set of development goals provides a solid basis for progress. The Bank is committed to action to help realize this vision. I am deeply indebted to my colleagues, whose commitment has earned us our position of strength today. I rely on them to take the Bank forward, in concert with our partners.

In closing, on behalf of the Board of Directors and Bank staff, I would like to pay tribute to the late Ibrahim Shihata, who died on May 28, 2001. As Senior Vice President and General Counsel from 1983 to 1998, Ibrahim was a brilliant lawyer and dedicated officer of this institution. History will recognize his landmark contributions to the Bank Group and to the cause of poverty reduction in our client countries.

Published in *BusinessWorld* (Manila)

OCTOBER 15, 2001

> *While commending the increased international cooperation seen in the imme-*
> *diate wake of September 11, Wolfensohn argues that the "greatest long-term*
> *challenge for the world community . . . is that of fighting poverty and pro-*
> *moting inclusion worldwide." Poverty, he says, may not lead directly to con-*
> *flict or terrorism, but "we know that exclusion can breed violent conflict."*
> *He outlines an agenda for meeting that long-term challenge and calls for*
> *a "global coalition" to carry it out.*

The horrifying events of September 11th have made this, for many, a time of reflection on how to make the world a better and safer place. The international community has already moved strongly to do so, by confronting terrorism directly and increasing security. We have also seen real collaboration aimed at averting global recession. These are signs of a rising cooperative spirit seeking international responses to international problems.

One step further. But we must go one step further. The greatest long-term challenge for the world community in building a better world is that of fighting poverty and promoting inclusion worldwide. This is even more imperative now, when we know that because of the terrorist attacks, growth in developing countries will falter, pushing millions more into poverty and causing tens of thousands of children to die from malnutrition, disease and deprivation.

Poverty in itself does not immediately and directly lead to conflict, let alone to terrorism. Rather than responding to deprivation by lashing out at others, the vast majority of poor people worldwide devote their energy to the day-in, day-out struggle to secure income, food and opportunities for their children.

And yet we know that exclusion can breed violent conflict. Careful research tells us that civil wars have often resulted not so much from ethnic diversity— the usual scapegoat—as from a mix of factors, of which, it must be recognized, poverty is a central ingredient. And conflict-ridden countries in turn become safe havens for terrorists.

Our common goal must be to eradicate poverty, to promote inclusion and social justice, to bring the marginalized into the mainstream of the global economy and society.

We can do this through steps that help prevent conflicts. Take the example of the Nile Basin Initiative. It is no secret that water shortages pose a challenge to development and peace in North Africa and the Middle East. The initiative is a coming-together of the ten countries of the Nile River Basin, providing a vehicle for cooperation on a program of sustainable water use and development. This is a good example of multilateral action to prevent conflict and to work directly for poverty reduction.

Equally important, we can help peace set down roots in societies just emerging from conflict. For example in Bosnia, where international support is helping communities come together at the local level on small-scale projects, creating jobs, and bridging ethnic differences.

Or in post-conflict societies like Cambodia, East Timor and Rwanda—where the international community is helping to rebuild infrastructure, re-integrate soldiers into the society and workforce, and restore the capacity of governments to manage their economies. Success may take years of hard work, but the alternative is a never-ending cycle of violence.

Central to conflict prevention and peace-building must be strategies for promoting social cohesion and inclusion. Inclusion means ensuring that all have opportunities for gainful employment, and that societies avoid wide income inequalities that can threaten social stability. But inclusion goes well beyond incomes. It also means seeing that poor people have access to education, health care, and basic services such as clean water, sanitation and power. It means enabling people to participate in key decisions that affect their lives. That is what we mean by empowerment.

But can we really make progress against poverty? Recent history tells us that we can. After increasing steadily for 200 years, the total number of people living in poverty worldwide started to fall 15 or 20 years ago. Over twenty years, the number of poor people has fallen by perhaps 200 million, even as the global population grew by 1.6 billion. This has been a direct result of the better policies that developing countries have been putting in place.

And progress extends well beyond income measures. Education and health have also improved. Since 1970, the proportion of those in the developing world who are illiterate has fallen sharply, from 47% to 25%, and since 1960, life expectancy has risen from 45 to 64 years.

Yet we must not underestimate the challenges that remain. Half the developing world—some 2 billion people—live in countries that have seen little growth in the last two decades. And even in those developing countries that have been doing relatively well, hundreds of millions of people are marginal to the progress of growth. As a result, well over 1 billion people, around 20% of the population of this planet, live on less than $1 a day.

And the scale of the challenge is not only immense, but rising. In the next thirty years the population of the world will increase from 6 to 8 billion. Virtually all those 2 billion will be in the poor countries of the world.

In the wake of the tragedy of September 11th, facing these challenges, and taking multilateral action to meet them, are more important than ever. What should be our agenda?

Agenda. First, scale up foreign aid. This may be much harder in an international economy that is slowing, but the needs and the stakes were never greater. Aid to Africa fell from $36 per person in 1990 to $20 today. And yet it is Africa, a continent that today is making great efforts to improve, that may feel most sharply the poverty fallout of the terrorist attacks. We cannot let Africa fall off the map as we turn our attention elsewhere.

Second, reduce trade barriers. The WTO summit must go ahead,* and it must be a development round, one that is motivated primarily by a desire to use trade as a tool for poverty reduction and development.

Substantial trade liberalization would be worth tens of billions of dollars to poor countries, and yet we know that at times of economic downturn there are increased pressures for protectionism. We must fight these pressures.

Third, focus development assistance to ensure good results. This means improving the climate for investment, productivity, growth, and jobs; and empowering and investing in poor people so that they can fully participate in growth.

And fourth, act internationally on global issues. This includes confronting terrorism and internationalized crime and money laundering, but also combating communicable diseases like AIDS and malaria, building an equitable global trading system, safeguarding financial stability to prevent deep and sudden crises, and safeguarding the natural resources and environment on which so many poor people depend for their livelihoods.

And all this we must do with developing countries in the driving seat— designing their own programs and making their own choices.

But we must also bring in the private sector, civil society, faith-based groups, and international and national donors. Ours must be a global coalition— to fight terrorism, yes, but also to fight poverty.

Whether we take up that challenge is up to us. Some generations have had the courage. Others have turned away. Which course we choose will determine not just our future, but whether our children and grandchildren can live in peace.

---

* The Fourth World Trade Organization Ministerial Conference was held in Doha, Qatar, the following month and would launch a new round of multilateral trade negotiations.

Statement at the International Monetary and Financial Committee meeting

OTTAWA | NOVEMBER 17, 2001

*In the wake of the September 11, 2001, attacks in the United States, the
Bank-Fund Annual Meetings planned for later that month in Washington
were not held. In early November a shortened version of the meetings took
place in Ottawa, where Wolfensohn delivered this statement to the International Monetary and Financial Committee.*

The tragic events of September 11 give renewed emphasis to our efforts to
make the world a better and a safer place. The challenges are obvious: continuing and strengthening the fight against poverty, strengthening the global
economy, and combating money laundering and the financing of terrorism.
These challenges are reflected in the agenda of the IMFC today and the Development Committee* tomorrow. In each case an effective response requires
close collaboration, driven by the spirit of mutual trust and confidence. We
can draw on a growing, but still fragile, new asset: an international recognition
of global interdependence. The recent events have underscored again the fact
that we live in one world. In this environment, global governance and global
institutions play a crucial role. The World Bank and the IMF with their universal membership provide a unique institutional setting in which to tackle the
problems ahead. I would like to reiterate Horst's [IMF Managing Director
Horst Köhler] point that both Bank and Fund are ready, with your support
and guidance, to take up their responsibilities.

The Outlook, Risks, and Vulnerabilities

Before September 11, the prospects for the world economy had already weakened, driven by a slowdown of activity in industrial countries. In the aftermath
of September 11, the economic outlook has become still weaker and subject to
significant risks, and investors and consumers have become much more cautious.

Against this background there is some evidence that the economic downturn will be deeper and longer lasting than expected. There will be a dramatic
fall in trade, which is expected to grow by less than 2 percent this year, compared with 13 percent in 2000.

The events of September 11 have placed specific burdens and immediate
pressures on several countries. First, the number of refugees and displaced

---

* The Development Committee is a grouping of finance ministers representative of the Bank's member countries that meets twice a year to discuss and advise on development issues.

persons will increase considerably. This will affect in particular Afghanistan and its immediate neighbors. Second, receipts from tourism are hit exceptionally hard because increased security concerns have limited travel. Tourism centers in the Caribbean, in eastern and southern Africa, and in South Asia, but also in the Middle East, will feel the impact particularly sharply. Third, increased risk aversion has led to a substantial reduction of financial flows to emerging market economies. At the same time, spreads have increased significantly, with the greatest impact on those countries that have already been subject to financial pressures.

The steep drop in global demand will have a broad-based impact on developing countries. Their immediate economic outlook has weakened significantly. The dramatic fall in trade will be reflected in lower export receipts and in a further drop in commodity prices, which have deteriorated for the fourth year in a row. This will be felt in particular in those countries in Africa that rely heavily on agriculture and other commodities.

The Policy Response of the International Community

Although these developments are darkening the short-term prospects and there remain many uncertainties, we all expect that—after some delay—the world economy will recover. Most industrial countries have responded to the weakening outlook by strengthening demand through monetary or fiscal easing. It may take some time until these measures have their impact, but the measures being taken are helping to move the world economy in the right direction. The industrial economies must be vigilant and ready to act, because the risks of a severe downturn are real, and there is room to strengthen this policy response if the weakening should turn out to be deeper than expected. In addition, many developing countries have improved their macroeconomic framework and launched crucial structural reforms by opening their economies and strengthening their institutions. A pickup in global demand should immediately improve their economic outlook.

The situation calls for a broad policy response from the international community to help to bring the world economy back to a satisfactory growth path and to support those countries that are immediately affected by the recent events. Industrial countries, in particular Europe, Japan, and the United States, have a responsibility to help get the world economy back on a sustainable growth path. Developing countries must continue in their efforts to strengthen their policy frameworks and institutions. But the global institutions must also help in four ways in dealing with the immediate impacts of September 11:

- We must put in place support mechanisms for countries that suddenly find themselves hosting large numbers of new refugees.
- We must support countries that are highly dependent on tourism and that have to bear the impact of September 11.
- We must continue and intensify our efforts to provide financial and other support for reform in the countries most affected by the shock to international capital markets.
- Finally, we must contribute to the international efforts to curb financial abuse and the financing of terrorism.

The Bank is cooperating closely with the IMF and other international institutions. In response to the changes in the world economic situation, Horst and I have emphasized in a joint statement our support for low-income countries. Together with our partners, the Bank Group has been working with clients to assess the consequences for country programs and the ways it might best respond to help foster continued development and poverty reduction. Countries may need to rethink some aspects of their development programs and priorities. The Bank stands ready to support them both with analysis in assessing the impacts of the events on poverty and in identifying new vulnerabilities, and with financial assistance, where needed.

This assistance can and will take a variety of forms. We will be discussing the specific implications for the Bank and IDA [the International Development Association] at the meeting of the Development Committee tomorrow.

Sustaining Poverty Reduction in Low-Income Countries

Poverty may not immediately and directly lead to conflict, let alone terrorism. Yet we do know, from experience and research, that great desperation and a lack of opportunity can breed civil wars that spill over borders. Now, more than ever, our common goal must be to eradicate poverty and promote inclusion and social justice, to bring the marginalized into the mainstream of the global economy and society.

Weakening global growth, falling commodity prices, increased refugee flows, and loss of tourism earnings will adversely affect most of the world's poorest countries and keep millions of people from climbing out of poverty. In economies that stall or fall into recession, the number of people living on less than one dollar per day will actually increase.

We have an agenda, and we should have an action plan. The actions of developing countries themselves are, of course, paramount in determining progress in the fight against poverty. International support for development will have only limited effects if governments in developing countries do not share the commitment to poverty reduction. Countries must help themselves through well-designed development strategies, as well as reform to policies, institutions, and governance. But that is not enough; even with the right policies in place, many countries will fall short if they do not receive greater international support. I suggest the following four priories for international action:

- First, promote better policies and governance in developing countries. As uncertainty and the economic downturn reduce private sources of funds, it is more important than ever that developing countries accelerate reforms to improve their investment climates and to enable poor people to participate in the process of growth. If it supports such reforms, additional financing from the international community will be a real help in implementing pro-poor programs and encouraging private investment.
- Second, reduce trade barriers. Now, more than ever, we must support the new WTO [World Trade Organization] negotiations and ensure that the next round is indeed a development round, motivated primarily by a determination to make trade an effective engine for poverty reduction and development. The new trade round must become a success. Horst and I have emphasized this in a joint statement. Trade liberalization could provide an additional cumulative income in developing countries of some $1.5 trillion over a decade and increase annual GDP growth in the developing countries by an additional 0.5 percent over the long run. Rich countries must open their markets to the exports of developing countries.
- Third, scale up foreign aid. This may be harder in an international economy that is slowing, but the needs and the stakes were never greater. Aid to Africa has fallen from $36 per person in 1990 to $20 today. It is Africa, a continent that today is making great efforts to improve, that may feel most sharply—particularly through reduced commodity prices—the poverty fallout of the terrorist attacks. We cannot let Africa fall off the map as we turn our attention elsewhere. If countries in Africa make their own efforts, through sound policies in the framework of a coherent development strategy, a doubling of ODA [official development assistance] and high concessionality will be needed to support low-income countries if they are to reach the 2015 poverty goals.
- Fourth, act internationally on global issues. This includes confronting terrorism and internationalized crime and money laundering, building an equitable global trading system, safeguarding financial stability, and protecting the natural resources and the environment, while also combating communicable diseases like AIDS and malaria.

The Bank is ready to take a global lead in helping countries reduce the impact of September 11 on the poorest countries, in line with our mission to fight poverty, in close partnership with other institutions. We will be discussing this more fully at tomorrow's meeting of the Development Committee.

For the heavily indebted poor countries, an important window of support is debt relief under the enhanced HIPC Initiative. This initiative is providing relief to 24 countries. We are committed to press ahead with the further implementation of the initiative, including bringing additional countries to their decision points as soon as country circumstances permit. We have also been concerned about the effects of exogenous shocks on the debt sustainability of HIPCs. In those cases where, at the completion point, we find that their debt sustainability may be jeopardized because of such shocks, we, together with the Fund, have now put in place the operational procedures to top up their debt relief, if necessary. Debt relief will continue to be a key instrument, but it should not replace new development assistance and aid flows.

The support is based on country-owned poverty reduction strategies. So far the Boards of the Bank and the Fund have endorsed 38 interim poverty reduction strategies and 8 full poverty reduction strategies. Bank and Fund staffs are cooperating closely in supporting these country strategies, which are increasingly used as a basis for wider donor coordination.

Combating Money Laundering and the Financing of Terrorism

Money laundering and the financing of terrorism are a problem of global concern and have an adverse impact on development. The September 11 events have demonstrated the urgent need for a more systematic approach to these problems.

The main focus of the Bank will be on helping countries strengthen their defenses against financial abuse and money laundering through enhanced support for capacity building. The Bank has been providing technical assistance to a dozen member countries on anti-money-laundering [AML] issues. This number is expected to increase significantly as the Bank steps up its involvement with a specific focus on diagnostics, capacity building, and training, building on work launched earlier this year with the IMF, which leads the AML efforts of the international financial institutions. Bank and Fund staffs are examining how the issue of the financing of terrorism could be reflected in the recently developed AML methodology, which is being tested in several countries and will become a standard feature in the Financial Sector Assessment Program. Follow-up to FSAPs will include technical assistance, capacity building, and training programs, particularly in the context of action plans for those countries that most need to upgrade their legal, judicial, and financial supervisory standards. The Bank is also developing a program to disseminate AML training materials to governments, central banks, other financial institutions, and nongovernmental organizations. It is expanding its staff working in this area.

The analytic and diagnostic work carried out by the Bank, other IFIs [international financial institutions], and donors provides the underpinnings for the AML efforts. Several elements of Bank economic and sector work are likely to be especially important in this respect. Country economic analysis, strengthened by FSAP diagnostics, will provide focus to follow-up work. Furthermore, under the Bank-Fund Reports on the Observance of Standards and Codes initiative, staff are collaborating with the Financial Action Task Force on Money Laundering of the Organisation for Economic Co-operation and Development to develop an AML module that will complement other governance-related ROSC modules in the areas of accounting and auditing and corporate governance. In addition, the Bank is working internally and with borrowers to strengthen due diligence on country procurement and financial management systems, to help ensure that development funds do not inadvertently find their way to terrorist organizations. With this objective in mind, Bank staff is trying to advance the scheduling of country financial accountability assessments and country procurement assessments to the extent possible.

Coordination of Conditionality

Finally, I want to underscore the proposal that Horst mentions in his progress report on streamlining conditionality. Last year Horst and I set out a vision for the roles of the Bank and the Fund and their enhanced partnership. To implement this vision, the Bank and the Fund recently carried out a joint review of our collaboration, with the objective of better focusing our lending conditionality in close partnership with the country concerned. We have identified a number of proposals, building on the principles that have guided our collaboration in the past.

These proposals we are pursuing together are designed above all to simplify and streamline the conditions we attach to our lending. They will therefore bring major benefits to our borrowers. To achieve this streamlining in a cost-effective way, we are pursuing a clear allocation of lead responsibility between our two institutions for different issues, allowing each to focus on its core areas of expertise and mandate. Over time, the proposals may involve substantial changes in the way staffs of both institutions approach their tasks.

Remarks at a townhall meeting at World Bank Group headquarters

WASHINGTON, D.C. | JANUARY 14, 2002

> *Poverty Reduction Strategy Papers (PRSPs) are written by developing-country governments to describe the macroeconomic, structural, and social reforms they intend to undertake to promote growth and reduce poverty, as well as associated external financing needs. Two years after the introduction of the PRSP approach, Wolfensohn outlines the progress so far and the challenges ahead. He urges the audience to find ways of strengthening the PRSPs, but only in a way that keeps them based on the aspirations of the countries themselves.*

Ladies and Gentlemen, Friends and Colleagues:

I am delighted to join Horst Köhler* in welcoming you all to this important conference. Our shared purpose is to reflect on the Poverty Reduction Strategy Paper approach we initiated a little over two years ago, and collectively to develop concrete ways to improve its impact.

When I say impact, I mean something very simple: better lives for poor people. Let me be very clear that the PRSP approach itself and, I believe, our discussions in the coming days must have one overarching goal: to do everything possible to support poor people in their efforts to live fuller, more secure, more productive, happier lives. All of us here today form part of a wider global community of commitment, dedicated to fighting poverty in all its multiple dimensions. And because I see the PRSP approach as a critical weapon in this fight, I cannot overstress the importance of this conference.

Our community of commitment has become even more important in the light of tragic recent events. In our post–September 11 world, the need to address poverty—and its consequences in terms of despair, alienation, and violence—has become not only a moral imperative, which it surely is, and not only a social and economic necessity, which it also surely is, but also a central concern for everyone who strives for national and global security and peace. We can no longer afford—we could never afford—to turn our backs on or offer quick palliatives to the world's poorest. We are therefore presented today with both a tremendous opportunity and a stark challenge: to rededicate ourselves and our efforts to attacking the scourge of poverty and all its horrifying consequences—most especially for the poor themselves, but also for all of us in our still-too-divided planet. To those who still believe that we can ignore or merely pay lip service to the plight of the 20 percent of the world's population living in direst poverty, I say, "Go to Ground Zero."

---

* IMF managing director.

I therefore find it heartening today to see so many representatives of our developing member countries, of civil society, and of donors gathered together to deliberate about what has worked—and what has perhaps not worked, or not yet worked—in the first two years of experience with the PRSP approach. We may have differences about some of the specifics of the approach. But I believe that we all share a common purpose: to do the best we can to support poor countries and poor people in their efforts to claim for themselves a better life, a better world.

I mentioned a wider global community. It is right to pay tribute to all those who are not with us today but who have participated in the PRSP approach: dedicated leaders, public officials, and parliamentarians in poor countries; representatives of donors and international and local NGOs [nongovernmental organizations] working at the grassroots; and, most important, poor people themselves, who have helped to inform country poverty reduction strategies. They have all enriched our early experience with the approach. They deserve our thanks.

Let me also thank all those individuals and organizations that have contributed specifically to this conference by providing written comments on the PRSP approach, or by participating in the regional workshops that have led up to today's event. Many of you are here today, but many more are not. You all deserve our gratitude.

As Horst Köhler has rightly said, a better life for poor people and their children depends on action on many fronts beyond the purview of this conference. I totally agree with him. But we also totally agree that the PRSP framework is a critical element in the wider effort to enhance the opportunity for which poor people cry out, and the social and economic justice that they deserve. Like Horst, I have traveled widely as part of my responsibilities, and I have seen how much poor people want to do—and can do—to build better lives for themselves and their families. I see the PRSP approach as a framework for helping to liberate their energies, to enhance their access to the tools they need—be it credit or rural roads, be it decent heath care or education—to do that job.

With these thoughts in mind, let me spend a few moments, as one who was "present at the creation" of the PRSP approach, discussing what I see as some of the major achievements of the past two years, and some of the challenges that lie ahead.

Early Achievements of the PRSP Approach

Looking back, it is astonishing how much has been achieved, given the scale of the task. As you know, the approach is rooted in the concept that countries themselves and their citizens need to own their poverty reduction strategies. It is also based on the concept of partnership: partnerships *within* countries—among government, NGOs, the private sector, and the local communities in which poor people live—together with partnerships *between* countries and their external supporters, but always with the country in the lead. And the approach is posited on the concept that strategies need to be comprehensive, long term, and focused on tangible results for their intended beneficiaries. These ideas are at the heart of the Comprehensive Development Framework, which I had begun to advocate a year or so before the PRSP approach was developed. And they are embodied in the strategies that countries themselves have prepared or are preparing.

But we all knew from the beginning that achieving broad-based ownership and vibrant partnerships and developing comprehensive, results-oriented strategies would not be easy. It is therefore remarkable that 8 countries have already completed their first PRSPs, and that nearly 40 more have prepared interim PRSPs.

I am not here today, however, to base an assessment of achievements simply on numbers of strategy documents produced. The numbers are signifiers of a wider achievement: the way in which countries have seized ownership of the PRSP process. They have repeatedly told us how much they welcome having the space to take the lead in framing their own strategies and policy agendas. And they have proved that these are not idle words by the dedication and intense effort they have shown in undertaking a task that would tax the resources of any country, rich or poor.

The extent to which the PRSP approach has taken hold in just two years is perhaps its most remarkable achievement so far. But there have been other early achievements, both on the part of countries themselves and on the part of their external supporters.

First, the concept of country ownership founded on broad-based participation has led to a more open and widely diffused policy debate about priorities and how to realize them in practice. This is an ongoing process, and I would be the last to suggest that early experience with it has been uniformly ideal or anything like it. But we have seen greater involvement of groups hitherto underrepresented—including line ministries, civil society organizations, women, and poor people—in policy discussion. We have seen their contributions having an effect, putting new priorities on the policy agenda. And I believe that the ongoing nature of the PRSP process itself will help institutionalize this expanded policy dialogue, helping to enhance both strategies and their grassroots outcomes for the poor and neglected.

Second, the PRSP approach has elevated the importance of poverty reduction as a political and policy priority. While many countries were already dedicated to reducing poverty—and emerging country strategies draw on their prior, home-grown experience—the PRSP approach has put poverty reduction front and center in the panoply of national goals and objectives. In this respect, the Enhanced HIPC [Heavily Indebted Poor Countries] Initiative[†] has also been an important catalyst, as countries have sought to ensure that the proceeds of debt relief are well spent on programs to enhance the prospects and liberate the energies of poor people. If substantial, sustainable poverty reduction is to be achieved, and if poor countries and their external supporters work together to reach the Millennium Development Goals, bringing about a better understanding of poverty and providing a new impetus to attacking it are surely worthy early achievements.

Third, the international donor community has responded remarkably to the PRSP approach. The UN system, multilateral institutions, bilateral donors, and NGOs are working to help make the approach work—and to work better as it evolves. Several donors—including, but not confined to, the European Commission, the United Kingdom, the Netherlands, and the Nordic countries—are already actively working to align their assistance with national poverty reduction strategies. This is not an easy task. As I know from my own experience, existing country assistance programs have a certain momentum—sometimes a certain inertia—of their own. But both the will and the action to support the approach are, I believe, real and growing. The presence of so many donor organizations here today—multilateral, national, nongovernmental—testifies to the breadth of donor commitment. Given the centrality to the PRSP approach of partnerships, this is crucial support indeed.

Speaking only for my own institution, we are putting our money where our mouth is. Let me mention only three quick examples. We have taken the decision to draw on country-owned PRSPs to frame our own support programs as set out in our Country Assistance Strategies. We have introduced a specific lending instrument, the Poverty Reduction Support Credit, to provide focused assistance dedicated to helping countries to realize their poverty reduction priorities. We have set up, with the initial generous support of Japan and the Netherlands, a Poverty Reduction Strategies Trust Fund to help build the capacity of PRSP country governments and NGOs to prepare and implement poverty reduction strategies. I know that other donors will also wish to support the Trust Fund.

---

† In 1999 the international community endorsed enhancements to the HIPC Initiative, allowing more countries to qualify for HIPC assistance, accelerating and deepening the delivery of relief, and strengthening the link between debt relief and poverty reduction.

But let me stress that I have no illusions about where we stand today. We are barely into the woods, let alone out of them. The issues paper before you is frank about the problems encountered with the PRSP approach and challenges for the future, many of which have been raised by many of you here today. It is one of the great strengths of this effort that it is an evolving one, based on a process of learning by doing. It would not be surprising if the discussions over the next few days did not add to the list of issues presented in the issues paper. But I would hope that your identification of issues would be matched by your thoughtful creativity in proposing ways to handle them.

Because I hope and believe that your discussions will focus frankly and constructively on areas for improvement, I shall not prejudge them by offering you detailed thoughts on this topic today. But let me single out just three general challenges that I see emerging as we move forward together.

Challenges Ahead

First, there is a group of challenges associated with the nature of the PRSP approach. I have already said that the task of developing a comprehensive long-term poverty reduction strategy based on broad participation would tax the resources of any country, rich or poor. Achieving domestic consensus and building external partnerships in support of a set of well-specified, well-costed-out priorities that eschew quick fixes is a formidable endeavor. And implementing these priorities consistently over time, possibly in the teeth of entrenched interest groups, will pose new challenges of its own. Countries will need all the support we can give them in meeting these challenges inherent in the approach.

Second, a better life for poor people requires stimulating economic growth that is pro-poor. This is both an analytical and an intensely practical issue. Countries preparing PRSPs have told us that it is the policy question with which they struggle most. Because country circumstances vary widely, there can be no one-size-fits-all prescription for pro-poor growth. The idea that every country is unique in its experience and potential is one of the great strengths of the PRSP approach, but uniqueness also presents enormous challenges in terms of policy development: there are no off-the-shelf blueprints that can guarantee successful pro-poor growth. But we can—and must—share ideas and experience. All of us, poor countries and the international community, need to work together on supporting national efforts to achieve pro-poor growth, and learn from both successes and mistakes—while always remembering the uniqueness of individual country conditions.

Third, effective implementation of national poverty reduction strategies will depend critically on good governance. Capacity building—and external support for it where necessary—will be crucial for success, as will actions in areas ranging from developing effective public expenditure management to the attack on corruption. The PRSP approach has already proved to be a spur to greater transparency in government. Transparency, and its sister accountability, need to be strengthened. Here I believe NGOs can play an important role. But countries' efforts, in these and other areas critical for success, will need to be matched by donor efforts, in the form of enhanced financial and technical support. We as donors need to walk the walk, not just talk the talk, with respect to stepping up our assistance to countries' poverty reduction efforts. In this last connection, I look forward to the upcoming Financing for Development discussions as an opportunity to make progress.

A More Fulfilling Future

Let me end by restating my conviction that country-owned poverty reduction strategies—based on broad citizen participation and assent, comprehensive in scope, long term in perspective, results-oriented in approach, and supported by external partners—are a critical weapon in attacking the scourge of world poverty and enhancing national and global security and peace. The task of this conference is to find ways to further strengthen the PRSP approach, but never to forget that these and subsequent efforts must always be based on the aspirations of poor countries and poor people for a more fulfilling future. It is their efforts that the rest of us must support, their dignity that we must help sustain and strengthen, and their destiny that we must honor—and see as inextricably bound up with our own.

I wish you every success in your discussions. I look forward to their outcomes. And I shall do everything in my power to maintain and strengthen the frank and constructive dialogue about how best to make the PRSP approach serve the needs of poor countries and peoples that this conference is designed to foster.

Thank you very much.

Keynote address delivered at the Woodrow Wilson International Center for Scholars

WASHINGTON, D.C. | MARCH 6, 2002

In one of his best speeches in the aftermath of the September 11 attacks, Wolfensohn speaks passionately about how the "imaginary wall that divided the rich world from the poor world came crashing down." The Washington Post *ran an editorial the next day about the speech, titled simply, "There Is No Wall."*

Ladies and Gentlemen:

I am delighted to be here at the Woodrow Wilson International Center, addressing this event co-hosted by the Bretton Woods Committee.

Eighty-four years ago in this city, Woodrow Wilson spoke of war and peace to a joint session of Congress: "What we demand," he said, "is that the world . . . be made safe for every peace-loving nation which, like our own, wishes to live its own life, determine its own institutions, be assured of justice and fair dealing by the other peoples of the world. . . . All the peoples of the world are . . . partners in this interest, and for our own part we see very clearly that unless justice be done to others it will not be done to us."* Two weeks from now, in Monterrey, Mexico, leaders from across the world will meet to discuss financing for development, where we must all hope that the words of President Wilson will resonate. For rarely has there been an issue so vital to long-term peace and security, and yet so marginalized in domestic politics in most of the rich world.

Our challenge, as we go forward to the Monterrey conference and beyond, is to persuade political leaders why that marginalization must end, why justice must be done to others if it is to be done to us, and why "all peoples are partners in this interest." Never perhaps has the chance for concerted action been greater, or the prize more worth the winning. The horrifying events of September 11 have made this a time of reflection on how to make the world a better and safer place. The international community has already acted strongly, by confronting terrorism directly and increasing security. But those actions by themselves are not enough. We will not create that better and safer world with bombs or brigades alone. We will not win the peace until we have the foresight, the courage, and the political will to redefine the war.

---

* Wilson's speech, in which he announced his Fourteen Points for the basis for a just and lasting world peace, was delivered on January 8, 1918.

We must recognize that, while there is social injustice on a global scale both between states and within them, while the fight against poverty is barely begun in too many parts of the world, while the link between progress in development and progress toward peace is not recognized, we may win a battle against terror, but we will not conclude a war that will yield enduring peace.

Poverty is our greatest long-term challenge: grueling, mind-numbing poverty that snatches hope and opportunity away from young hearts and dreams just when they should take flight and soar; poverty that takes the promise of a whole life ahead and stunts it into a struggle for day-to-day survival; poverty that, together with its handmaiden, hopelessness, can lead to exclusion, anger, and even conflict; poverty that does not itself necessarily lead to violence, but which can provide a breeding ground for the ideas and actions of those who promote conflict and terror.

On September 11 the crisis of Afghanistan came to Wall Street, to the Pentagon, and to a field in Pennsylvania. And the imaginary wall that divided the rich world from the poor world came crashing down.

Belief in that wall, and in those separate and separated worlds, has for too long allowed us to view as normal a world where fewer than 20 percent of the population—the rich countries in which we here live today—dominate the world's wealth and resources and take 80 percent of its dollar income. Belief in that wall has too long allowed us to view as normal a world where every minute a woman dies in childbirth. Belief in that wall has allowed us for too long to view the violence, disenfranchisement, and inequality in the world as the problem of poor, weak countries and not our own.

There is no wall. There are not two worlds. There is only one.

The process of globalization and growing interdependence has been at work for millennia. As my friend [Nobel economics laureate] Amartya Sen has pointed out, a millennium ago it was ideas—not from the West but from China, from India, and from the Muslim world—that gave the intellectual basis for much of science, for printing, and for the arts. It was the great Mughal Emperor Akbar, a Muslim, who in the 16th century called for religious tolerance and openness.

There is no wall. We are linked by trade, investment, and finance; by travel and communications; by disease, by crime, by migration, by environmental degradation, by drugs, by financial crises, and by terror. Only our mindsets continue to shore up that wall, too set in our ways, too complacent, or too frightened to face reality without it. It is time to tear down that imagined wall, to recognize that in this unified world poverty is our collective enemy. Poverty is the enemy we must fight. We must fight it because it is morally and ethically repugnant. We must fight it because it is in the self-interest of the rich to join the struggle. We must fight it because its existence is like a cancer, weakening the whole of the body, not just the parts directly affected.

And we need not fight blindly. For we already have a vision of what the road to victory could look like. Last year, at the Millennium Summit of the United Nations, more than 140 world leaders agreed to launch a campaign to attack poverty on a number of fronts. Together we agreed to support the Millennium Development Goals. By 2015, we said, we will

- halve the proportion of people living on less than one dollar a day
- ensure that boys and girls alike complete primary schooling
- eliminate gender disparity at all levels of education
- reduce child mortality by two-thirds
- reduce maternal mortality by three-quarters
- roll back HIV/AIDS, malaria, and other diseases
- halve the proportion of people without access to safe water, and
- develop a global partnership for development.

How could anyone take issue with these goals? How could anyone refuse to stand up and say that, for my children and my children's children, I want that better world? And yet there are those who legitimately ask, "Can we win a war against poverty? And if we can't be sure, should we wager our resources?"

To these people I would ask, "Can we afford to lose? How much are we prepared to commit to preserve our children's future? What is the price we are willing to pay to make progress in our lifetime toward a better world?"

And to the doubters I would say, "Look at the facts. For the facts show that, despite difficulties and setbacks, we have made important progress in the past, and we will make progress in the future."

Over the past 40 years, life expectancy at birth in developing countries has increased by 20 years, about as much as was achieved in all of human history before the middle of the 20th century. Over the past 30 years, adult illiteracy in the developing world has been cut nearly in half, from 47 percent to 25 percent. Over the past 20 years, the absolute number of people living on less than one dollar a day, after rising steadily for the previous 200 years, has for the first time begun to fall, even as the world's population has grown by 1.6 billion. Driving much of this progress has been an acceleration of economic growth in the developing world: the average income of those living in developing countries has doubled over the past 35 years.

These are not just meaningless statistics. They indicate real progress in real people's lives:

- in Vietnam, where the number of people in poverty has halved over the last 15 years;

- in China, where the number of rural poor fell from 250 million to 34 million over two decades of reform;
- in India, where the literacy rate for women has risen from 39 percent to 54 percent in just the last decade;
- in Uganda, where the number of children in primary school has doubled;
- in Bangladesh, where dramatic strides have been made to achieve universal primary education, and enrollment of girls in high school has risen to about par with boys, in an environment where girls have long faced huge barriers;
- in Brazil, where the number of AIDS-related deaths has been cut by more than a third;
- in Ethiopia, where 6 million people are now benefiting from better education and health services.

These advances have not come about by chance. They have come through action: first and foremost, action by the developing countries themselves, but also from action in partnership with the richer world and with the international institutions, with civil society, and the private sector.

"But," some would say, "should we wager our resources on success, knowing that there has also been failure?" True, much of the growth and poverty reduction worldwide over the past 20 years have come in the two giants of the developing world, China and India, with progress, too, in other parts of East Asia and Latin America. And too many countries are being left behind, especially in Sub-Saharan Africa. There is too much inequity between countries and within countries, too much exclusion, too much war, too much internal strife, and now AIDS threatens to reverse many of the gains made over the last 40 years. And these challenges will only grow over the next 30 years, as the global population increases by 2 billion, to a total of 8 billion people, with almost the entire increase going to developing countries.

Therefore, as we in the international development community—international institutions and bilateral agencies, governments and nongovernmental organizations—look to the challenge before us, we must also look objectively back at the past, and do so with humility. For too many poor people, the Cold War years were years when development stalled or even reversed, when leaders became enriched at the expense of their people, when monies were lent for the sake of politics, not development.

We have seen failure, yes, and we have seen the politicization of aid, and we must never forget its corrosive impact. We have learned that policies imposed from London or Washington will not work. Countries must be in charge of their own development. Policies must be locally owned and locally grown.

We have learned that any effort to fight poverty must be comprehensive. There is no magic bullet that alone will slay poverty, but we know, too, that that there are conditions that foster successful development: education and health programs to build the human capacity of the country, good and clean government, an effective legal and justice system, and a well-organized and well-supervised financial system.

We have learned that corruption, bad policies, and weak governance will make aid ineffective, and that country-led programs to fight corruption can succeed.

We have learned that debt reduction for the most heavily indebted poor countries is a crucial element in putting countries back on their feet, and that the funds released can be used effectively for poverty programs.

We have learned that we must focus on establishing the right conditions for investment and entrepreneurship, particularly for smaller enterprises and farms. But that is not enough for pro-poor growth: we must also promote investment in people, empowering them to make their own choices.

We have learned that development is about the long haul, reaching beyond political cycles or quick fixes, for the surest foundation for long-term change is social consensus for long-term action.

These lessons and principles should give us heart, for more than ever today, bilateral and multilateral donors, governments, and civil society are coming together in support of a set of shared principles. More than ever today, a new wind is blowing though the world of development, transforming our potential to make development happen.

In this new world, development is not about aid dependence. It is about a chance for developing countries to put in place policies that will enable their economies to grow, that will attract private investment, and that will allow governments to invest in their people, promoting aid independence. It is about treating the poor not as objects of charity, but as assets on which we can build a better and safer world. It is about scaling up, about moving from individual projects to larger programs, building on successes and then replicating them, as in the successes of community-driven development and microcredit, where the poor are at the center of the solution, not at the end of a handout. It is about forging a new partnership between rich and poor based on mutual interest and mutual support.

And it is developing countries that are leading the way. Listen to what African leaders are saying in the New Partnership for Africa's Development: "Across the continent Africans declare that we will no longer allow ourselves to be conditioned by circumstance. We will determine our own destiny and call on the rest of the world to complement our efforts."[†]

These leaders, and leaders and peoples like them through much of the developing world, are recognizing what must be done to allow their countries to develop. They are committing themselves to good governance, to improving the investment climate, to investing in their people. And the marked improvement in policies in much of the developing world since the 1980s shows that they are serious and are having an effect.

In some countries these improvements in policies and governance have generated growth led by the private sector, which involves poor people. By building a more favorable environment for productivity and development, they are creating jobs, encouraging growth in domestic saving and investment, while also spurring increases in foreign direct investment flows. They are not sitting back, waiting for development to be done to them. They are helping to finance their own development, and they recognize the crucial importance of building human capacity within their countries.

But they cannot do it alone.

I have spoken of one side of the new partnership, the leadership in the developing world. But there is also a need for leadership in the developed world, which must grasp the opportunity presented in Monterrey to take the next important step to create that more stable and peaceful world.

What is it that leaders in rich countries should do?

First, they must assist developing countries in building their own capacity in government, in business, and in their communities at large. And, in doing so, they must listen to the expressed needs of developing countries, so that they help to build individual programs that are relevant and can make a real difference. This is not pro forma work. This is work that requires real commitment and passion.

Second, they must move forward on the issue of trade openness, recognizing that, without market access, poor countries cannot fulfill their potential no matter how sound their policies. The European Union's lead on the Everything but Arms agreement and the United States' lead on the African Growth and Opportunity Act[‡] should be followed by action by other rich countries now, and the benefits extended to all low-income countries, to end the trade

---

† The New Partnership for Africa's Development (NEPAD) is a vision and strategic framework for Africa's renewal that arose from a mandate given to the five initiating heads of state by the Organisation of African Unity to develop an integrated socioeconomic development framework for Africa.
‡ The Everything but Arms initiative would grant duty-free access for all goods except arms to the world's 48 least-developed countries. The African Growth and Opportunity Act was enacted by the United States in May 2000.

barriers that harm the poorest nations and poorest workers. And this action does not need to wait on agreement by the World Trade Organization.

Powerful political lobbies will be ranged against any such action. But it is the task of political leaders to remind their electorates that lowering trade barriers does not cost the rich countries anything in the aggregate; what they gain from freer trade in these areas far exceeds any short-term costs of adjustment. There is little sacrifice required and no excuse for failing to take action that would leave all countries better off.

Third, rich nations must also take action to cut their agricultural subsidies, which rob poor countries of markets for their products. Farm support in the rich countries goes mainly to a relatively small number of agribusinesses, many of them large corporations, and it amounts to $350 billion a year—six times what the rich countries provide in foreign aid to a developing world of close to 5 billion people.

Yes, there are powerful political lobbies ranged against this action, too. But the fundamental truth is that agricultural subsidies constitute a heavy burden on the citizens of the *developed* countries, as well as a barrier to primary commodity producers in the developing world. With skillful political leadership, they can be cut back. But we need that leadership. Reducing these subsidies would have the additional benefit of yielding significant budgetary savings for the governments of rich countries—savings far greater than would be necessary to make room for very substantial increases in aid, together with any internal compensation that may be necessary.

Fourth, rich countries must recognize that, even with action on trade and on agricultural subsidies, there is still a fundamental need to boost the resources flowing to developing countries. We at the Bank estimate that it will take on the order of an additional $40 billion to $60 billion a year to reach the Millennium Development Goals. That is roughly a doubling of current aid flows, to about 0.5 percent of the combined GNPs of the rich countries, which would still be well below the 0.7 percent target agreed by global leaders years ago.

Budgetary realities may make it impossible to double aid overnight. But if the new partnership is to work, we must commit ourselves to matching the efforts of developing countries step by step, with a phased-in increase in aid—say, an additional $10 billion a year for the next five years, building to an extra $50 billion a year in the fifth year.

As part of this support, donors must also conclude an agreement for the funding of the International Development Association for the next three years. This program, which provides long-term support for countries with incomes per capita below two dollars a day, is critical for those living in desperate poverty. I believe that an agreement is close on this vital program; the time has come to put it in place. The poor should not be asked to wait.

Does anybody really believe that the goal of halving absolute poverty by 2015 is not worth this investment? An extra $50 billion in aid would cost only an extra one-fifth of 1 percent of the income of the rich countries. It would reverse the decline of aid as a percentage of their GDP that has taken place over the last 15 years. Contrast that with the fact that, today, the world's leading industrial nations provide nearly 90 percent of the multibillion-dollar arms trade. And the arms they produce are contributing to the very conflicts that all of us profess to deplore, and which we must spend additional monies to suppress.

Let me repeat:

- We should do this because it is ethically right.
- We should do it because it will create a better, more understanding, more dynamic, and indeed more prosperous world for our children and our children's children.
- We should do it because it will increase the security of all of us, rich and poor.

We know that disease, environment, financial crisis, and even terror do not recognize national boundaries. We know that imaginary walls will not protect us. If we want to build long-term peace, if we want stability for our economies, if we want opportunities for growth in the years ahead, if we want to build that better and safer world, fighting poverty must be part of our quest for national and international security. I do not underestimate the challenge of securing an extra $50 billion for development. But I know, as do many others, that this is the right place to put our money. The conquest of poverty is indeed the quest for peace.

We must not let our mission be clouded by debates over issues where no debate is needed. Let's have effectiveness. Let's have productivity. Let's ensure that the money is well spent. Let's ensure that programs and projects are not corrupt. Let's ensure that women are given an important place in the development process. Let's ensure that projects are locally owned. Let's use all the instruments at our disposal—grants, loans, and guarantees. These are not issues for debate. They are issues on which the principles are all agreed. These are not issues to hold up action. These are issues on which we can all close ranks and move forward.

Time is not on our side. But perhaps, for once, public opinion is.

There are those who say, "You will never get support for extra aid in a climate of economic recession and budget cuts. You will never persuade people to look beyond their pocketbooks." I for one do not believe it. I have seen people at their best and at their least selfish in difficult times.

And I believe there is a sea change since September 11. People everywhere are beginning to recognize that military solutions to terror are not enough, that people must be given hope, that we must build an inclusive global community, and that we must make globalization work for common humanity, not for commercial brands or competitive advantage. This understanding is growing. Three months ago a poll of 23,000 people in 25 countries showed overwhelming support for the view that fighting poverty and addressing the gap between rich and poor should top the international agenda.

My friends, for centuries, we have focused on issues of war and peace. We have built armies and honed strategies. Today we fight a different kind of war in a different kind of world, a world where violence does not stop at borders, a world where communications sheds welcome light on global inequities, a world where what happens in one country or region affects all the others.

Inclusion, a sense of equity, empowerment, anticorruption—these must be our weapons of the future.

I believe we have a greater chance today than perhaps at any other time in the last 50 years to win that war and forge that new partnership for peace. Together we must promote the understanding that policy can no longer exist in tidy boxes labeled "foreign" and "domestic," and it can no longer budget a miserly tenth or a quarter of a percent of GDP on aid. Together we must persuade finance ministers that, when they discuss their budgets, they must, alongside their defense and domestic spending, give equal weight to international spending.

But we must go further. We must change the mindsets that build the walls. Across the world we must educate our children to be global citizens with global responsibilities. We must celebrate diversity, not fear it. We must build curricula around understanding, not suspicion, and around inclusion, not hate. We must tell our children to dare to be different, to be international, intercultural, interactive, global. We must do better with the next generation than we have done with our own.

Let me end, as I began, with the words of Woodrow Wilson, words that reach out across cultural and national divides: "You are not here merely to make a living. You are here in order to enable the world to live more amply, with greater vision, with a finer spirit of hope and achievement. You are here to enrich the world, and you impoverish yourself if you forget the errand."

Thank you.

FINANCING DEVELOPMENT FOR PEACE THROUGH ENDURING PARTNERSHIPS

Address at the International Conference on Financing for Development

MONTERREY, MEXICO | MARCH 21, 2002

The Monterrey Conference on Financing for Development followed the news of pledges by the United States and the European Union to increase their aid to developing countries. Wolfensohn welcomes the boosts to aid and calls on both rich and poor countries to do their part in development. He calls for reforms to agricultural subsidies and for trade reform to benefit poor countries. For more information on the Financing for Development conference, see www.un.org/esa/ffd/.

Distinguished Excellencies, Delegates, Ladies and Gentlemen:

Please allow me to thank both our host, President Vicente Fox of Mexico, and [UN] Secretary-General Kofi Annan for organizing this Conference on Financing for Development.

As most of you know, the World Bank has been very closely involved in the financing for development process. We believe this is a great opportunity to reinforce our collective commitment to expand the opportunities and resources necessary to halve world poverty by 2015 and meet the other Millennium Development Goals.

It is apt that we meet here in Monterrey. For Mexico today exemplifies much of what can be achieved from open markets, capacity building, the creation of a favorable investment climate, good fiscal and monetary policies, an attack on corruption, and a commitment to democracy. Mexicans should be proud of their progress. But Mexico also shows how resilient inequality and exclusion can be. Development is a long road. We must not underestimate the challenge ahead.

This conference brings together heads of state and of government; foreign, finance, development, and trade ministers; civil society, business leaders, and international institutions for perhaps the first time at an international meeting. And for perhaps the first time at an international meeting there is greater consensus than ever before about what needs to be done.

We must not squander that opportunity. Nor must we forget why we are here. All people have a right to human dignity. That is why we are here.

All people have a right to control their own lives. Yet for billions poverty snatches that right away. That is why we are here.

People have a right to opportunity: in education, in trade, in building a better future for their children. That is why we are here.

We must not fail them.

I have spoken before of an imaginary wall that separates the rich world from the poor. For too long, belief in that wall, and in those separate and separated worlds, has allowed us to view as normal a world where fewer than 20 percent of the population—the rich countries—dominate the world's wealth and resources and take 80 percent of its income.

There is no wall. There are not two worlds. There is only one. Here at Monterrey we must rid ourselves of that wall once and for all. Here at Monterrey we must recognize the link between progress in development and progress in peace, so that generations to come will point to Monterrey and say, "Something new began there. A new global partnership was born at Monterrey." And we will remember, and we will tell our children, "We were there and we did not fail." For the opportunity is ours to seize.

What is this new partnership? It is an understanding that leaders of the developing and the developed countries are united by a global responsibility based on ethics, experience, and self-interest. It is a recognition that opportunity and empowerment—not charity—can benefit us all. It is a recognition that we will not create long-term peace and stability until we acknowledge that we are a common humanity with a common destiny. Our futures are indivisible.

We have the makings of just such a new partnership before us. A new generation of leaders is taking responsibility in developing countries. Many of these leaders are tackling corruption, putting in place good governance, giving priority to investing in their people, and establishing an investment climate that will attract private capital. They are doing it in the private sector, in civil society, in government, and in local communities. They are doing it not because they have been told to, but because they know it is right. We must support more and more countries in taking that path. And in the rich countries growing numbers of people are beginning to understand that poverty anywhere is poverty everywhere, that imaginary walls will not protect us. And their leaders are listening.

I very much welcome, as should we all, the recent decisions by President Bush and the leaders of the European Union to boost aid spending. There is no debate that our efforts need to be focused and effective. On this we are all agreed. Too much money has been squandered in the past by decisions borne of politics, not development. I look forward to the forthcoming discussions on increasing the effectiveness of the development community as a whole.

Your excellencies, we have come a long way in just a week. But we must not stop there. This is not just about resources. It is about scaling up, about moving from individual projects to programs, about building on and then replicating, for example, microcredit for women or community-driven development. It is about development in which the poor are at the center of the so-lution, not at the end of a handout.

It is about recognizing that any effort to fight poverty must be comprehensive. We know there is no simple formula that alone will defeat poverty, but we know, too, that there are conditions that foster successful development: education and health programs that build the human capacity of the country, good and clean government, well-functioning infrastructure, an effective legal and justice system, and a well-organized and well-supervised financial system.

It is about recognizing that debt reduction for the most highly indebted poor countries is a crucial element in putting them back on their feet, and that the funds freed up by debt relief can and must be used effectively for poverty programs. And we must push ahead with the HIPC [Heavily Indebted Poor Countries debt relief] program.

We know that, in countries with good governance and strong policies, aid can make an enormous difference. Yet we know, too, that corruption, bad policies, and weak governance will make financial aid ineffective, even counterproductive.

We must support nations in building their capacity so that *they* can create an investment climate and invest in their people, so that *they* can create jobs, so that *they* can increase productivity and boost investment in health and education. This is not about rich countries telling developing countries what to do. This is about creating a chance for developing countries to put in place policies that will enable their economies to grow, policies that are home-grown and home-owned. For the surest foundation for long-term change is not development by fiat, but social consensus.

But we at the World Bank estimate that, even if developing countries do all these things, it will take somewhere between $40 billion and $60 billion in additional resources a year to meet the Millennium Development Goals. We have made a fine start. But we must not stop here. Let us work together for results, and let us build the pressure for additional funds as we succeed in using effectively the funds now promised.

Nor can we shrink from taking action on trade. We must keep urging rich countries to tear down their trade barriers that harm the world's poorest workers, depriving them of markets for their products. Yes, there will be powerful lobbies ranged against any such action. But it is the task of leaders to remind their electorates that lowering of trade barriers will not cost the rich countries anything in the aggregate. Rather they will gain from freer trade in these areas, and the gains will far exceed any short-term costs of adjustment. There is little sacrifice required, and no excuse for failing to take action that would leave all countries better off.

Rich nations must also take action to cut their agricultural subsidies. These subsidies rob poor countries of markets for their products, and their cost is six times what the rich countries provide in foreign aid to the developing world. Trade and agriculture must be a crucial part of the new global deal.

Your excellencies, in one week alone we have seen new commitments on resources, and we have heard new words on interdependence. In recent months we have seen the launch of a promising new trade round. We have had a taste of what is possible.

But we do not have much time. In 25 years 2 billion more people will join us on our planet. The challenge will be greater, the pressure on resources will be more acute, and the chances of success may be slimmer.

Let us not have come this far to stop now. Let us build on this momentum as we move forward to Johannesburg.* Let us tell our children, "We seized the moment. We did not fail."

---

* The World Summit on Sustainable Development took place in Johannesburg about six months after the Monterrey conference, in August and September 2002.

PARLIAMENTARY ACTIONS AND COOPERATION
FOR POVERTY REDUCTION

Address at the Third Annual Conference of the Parliamentary Network
on the World Bank

BERN, SWITZERLAND | MAY 10, 2002

*Striking up new partnerships with key constituencies in development was a
hallmark of Wolfensohn's presidency. Here Wolfensohn addresses a meeting
of the Parliamentary Network on the World Bank, an independent international network of 450 members in 90 countries, which aims to encourage
policy dialogue and the exchange of views between legislators and the Bank.
It is also a platform for parliamentary coordination and advocacy on international development and poverty eradication.*

Thank you very much, Mr. Koenders and Mr. Frey.* It is very nice to see
you and my other friends again. When I was first in Switzerland in 1959–60,
doing some teaching in Lausanne, I dreamed of becoming a Swiss citizen. I
was told that this could be possible if I knew some people in Bern. Never did
I imagine that I would one day be standing in the Swiss Parliament itself, in
this important place, giving an address.

This is a pleasure for me because I feel that Switzerland has contributed
enormously during the 10 years of its participation in the World Bank. It has
been a very constructive partner with us. We have done many things together,
and I see [former member of the Swiss parliament] Walter Frey at the back,
who has just returned from Vietnam. After my seven years in office, he told me
that things are actually working in the field. I said, "I told you so," to which he
replied that, "In Switzerland, seeing is believing, but touching is even better."
He has seen that, with our work in Vietnam, there is in fact a far greater contact with the people with whom we are working. I believe that all of you, as
parliamentarians, can most assuredly continue your observations and your criticisms of the institution. But I think that I can report to you that there has been
real progress, progress toward what Mr. Frey was talking about: toward participation and a true sense of trying to make our institution democratic.

That is the reason that we are particularly happy to have the opportunity to
be with you here today, and also to have our colleagues in Burundi, India, and
Uganda with us by satellite. Let me tell you quickly where I think we are in
relation to the development process that is ongoing. We had our meetings
in Monterrey,† as President [Abdoulaye] Wade [of Senegal] told you. These

---

* Bert Koenders, member of Parliament, the Netherlands, and chairman of the Parliamentary Network on the
World Bank, and Claude Frey, chairman of the Foreign Affairs Committee, Switzerland.
† The International Conference on Financing for Development was held in Monterrey, Mexico, in March 2002.

meetings not only discussed NEPAD [the New Partnership for Africa's Development], the African initiative, but spoke also about a new partnership that is very similar in form to that of NEPAD. The partnership is very simple to describe but very difficult to achieve. It says basically that developing countries should undertake to manage their countries on a basis of building the capacity of their administration, and of dealing with the question of legal and judicial reform so that human and property rights can be protected. These countries should also have a financial sector that is transparent and makes funds available from the highest level of business down to microcredit. This would be a transparent and deep financial system. Finally, this partnership also involves the combat against corruption, a cancer that affects so many parts of the world, including the developed world.

This was the set of undertakings given by the leaders of the developing world—not conditional, not imposed, not insisted upon, but offered. These undertakings were offered because it makes sense for the citizens of developing countries to live in environments where they can enjoy equal access, equal opportunity, and voice. That was on the one side.

The other side included the undertakings that were given by the developed countries. They simply said, "If you do those things, we will assist you on capacity building, we will open our markets to trade, and we will increase development assistance." This is a very simply stated partnership, but one where there is a mutual requirement to ensure that the conditions are fulfilled. This is, of course, an issue that relates not only to the signatories of this agreement, the administrators. It is a set of conditions that apply on both sides, and this brings us directly back to the parliamentary bodies.

In this partnership, it is impossible for either side to perform without the support of the parliamentary bodies. Therefore parliamentarians are facing a situation where the leadership on both sides has made undertakings to have a form of partnership that requires support from the parliamentary bodies. It is clearly stated; it is out there and now it needs to be done. It is for the parliaments to decide whether they are willing and able to meet the conditions on each side. I can tell you that it is already being done in some countries and not being done in other countries. It is typically, in my experience, a tough thing to try to introduce legislation on legal and judicial reform, to replace judges and change legislation, and to try and change a culture that may not have been at the highest level of judicial procedure, equity, or justice. These things are easy to state but difficult to implement.

The same is true of corruption, particularly in countries where corruption exists on both sides of the partnership, from the head of state down. I have had dozens of discussions in 120 countries on the subject of corruption.

These discussions are very often the same, and the language used is always the same:

  "Corrupt? Not us."

  "Me? No."

  "The head of state? Impossible."

  "Parliament? Never!"

  "The legal system? Incomprehensible."

Nothing, it seems, ever happens in any country. In fact, we know the opposite is true. People may look at you as if to say that only a handful of minor civil servants are involved in corruption, but both sides know that corruption often goes to the very top. This is not an issue that the World Bank can fix by edict or that any individual can fix by declaration. It requires momentum building, to deal with something that is very often deeply ingrained in the functioning of the society. We are often told that a customs official cannot refuse bribes if he is not paid enough to live on. How can a government official fulfill the needs of his family if he is paid half of a living wage?

These are issues that are very well known to you. To me, they represent very serious challenges to this partnership. I am concerned that because the partnership is now very clearly stated, it can be very easy for neither side to perform. Or, in the event that performance is not up to the standard that the donor countries are looking for, they can say, "Look, you have not done what we said. Where is the honest legal system? Where is the corruption being eradicated? Where is the organization? What have you done on capacity building?"

This agreement that was reached in Monterrey, which on the surface is wonderful, requires an enormous and consistent pattern of behavior, and it will not change the current situation overnight. I therefore simply say to you that what is now most critical is that, since these undertakings have been given, we work together over a period of years in order to ensure that they are met. In other words, I would add the dimension of time to the agreement that was signed. This will not happen overnight. It requires consistent and effective work by the parliamentary bodies to make sure that it gets done, because the pressure for countries to act comes from the parliamentary bodies, which sometimes need to clean up their act themselves. It is therefore quite important that this group, which understands these issues and is committed to this sort of program, can take a program that is clearly stated but also recognize that it is a challenge that will take 5 to 10 years to implement. The changing of a culture is not completed overnight. We need to be honest with each other that these cultures do not change overnight, any more than the culture of the World Bank has changed overnight. It has taken time to change our culture into a listening, nonaggressive, consultative culture that also listens to cultural differences. It has taken me seven years with my colleagues to try and turn the ship around, and I believe that we have succeeded. It is no easier in a country, and it takes time, commitment, and honesty to say what the real problems are.

This leads me to the second point. What we have decided at the Bank is the philosophy that we have discussed tonight. We decided at the spring meetings that we have had all the discussion and debate we need, and it is now time to implement what we know needs to be done. There is no debate on the fundamentals.

For our next meeting, we have decided to take two or three specific objectives and see whether each side has performed. These objectives are based on the consultative process of the Comprehensive Development Framework and the Poverty Reduction Strategy Papers, which have led to discussions with governments, with our colleagues in the international institutions, with civil society, with the private sector, and with parliamentarians. I do not go to a country now without seeking permission to see the parliamentarians.

The problem of consultation between partnerships and the administrations of the country is not a problem that the World Bank has created. It is something that was there before us. You can blame us for not consulting with you. You can say that it would be so much better if we were to deal with parliamentary committees than with the administration. After all, you have the power. But I would ask you to consider for a moment that it is not we who create our relationship with the administration. We are obligated to deal with the administrations of the countries with which we deal. They are our shareholders and our governors. The Bank governor from each of the countries is not a representative of the parliament. It is the finance minister or the development minister. They are the people who are my bosses, according to statute. When I come to visit parliaments, and it varies by country, I have to obtain the approval of the ministers. Can you imagine me coming to a country and setting up independent meetings with parliamentary supervisory bodies without the approval of my host? It is simply not possible.

If you open the doors, I am willing to speak to parliament. We want to consult. Who, after all, is more representative of civil society than elected parliamentary bodies? But you have to help us by dealing with the government officials if you want a broader and deeper contact. We will welcome you at the Bank. We will do anything that is reasonable. As you know, we have done it very often for gatherings like this and for other groups.

The effectiveness of either the Bank or the Fund in dealing with parliamentary bodies is a function of your existing domestic relationship between the parliament and your administration. That is something that I cannot solve.

It is something that I can be supportive of or be ready to follow enthusiasti-cally. I would, however, urge you not simply to shoot the messenger. We are there to try and work with you, because we know that if we want to do some-thing, it needs parliamentary support. I must tell you that, in many cases, when something does not happen, the administration says that it is the parliament that will not approve it. We are ready to fulfill any undertakings, but I would urge you to think in terms of that linkage, which is essentially a domestic problem and your problem. We will be supportive, but we ask your help.

Let me now move on to what we are doing in terms of our development strategy and this partnership. We are going to focus on three specific things. First, we are going to set up a fast track on education in 10 countries. This is because our own research and the general principles arising out of the Millen-nium Development Goals have shown that education is clearly central. We are therefore going to take 10 countries at varying levels and try and see how we can work within the framework of this partnership. We will look at the in-hibitions, the need for funding, and how we can frame programs that are not one-year programs but 10-year programs.

Remember that you cannot change an education system in one or two years. We have to start at the beginning and retrofit some of what we are doing over a protracted period. But the key change that we will have in the world is with the education system. So we are seeking to do this, and we will then confront the donors and say, "In these 10 countries, this is the additional support that we need." It will be practical, not theoretical. We can then see what it feels like to commit to 10-year programs in countries to ensure that they get uni-versal primary education for boys and girls.

The second area that we are prioritizing is health care, and in particular HIV/AIDS. We are giving priority to HIV/AIDS because we have an inter-national trust fund and assistance from the Bank. There is actually a lot of money available for fighting HIV/AIDS, but what are the inhibitions? Are they social, cultural, administrative, or due to a lack of will? I nearly always wear an AIDS button when I go to certain countries, because although they are full of AIDS problems, people do not recognize that it is the main chal-lenge they face. We are therefore going to focus on it and see what the op-portunities and the difficulties are.

The third thing that we will look at is rural development, and in particular the enfranchisement of local communities. We have discovered that making poor people not the object of charity but instead part of the solution, by giv-ing responsibility to the people in poverty and in the field, is the most effec-tive way of leveraging up our activities that we have. Very often this can be done through existing levels of governance. In India the *panchayat* level of government is very effective in running things, but this is not true in all countries. Sometimes it has to be done directly.

So, from our point of view, you can expect no more philosophy. At the partnership level we will take these three specific areas and bring them to the Annual Meetings and to Johannesburg,[‡] where of course, we will add the other issues of sustainability and environmental considerations that will be part of the Johannesburg conference.

I believe that we are now at the stage in the development paradigm where we have established that it should be consultative, that it should include parliamentary bodies as well as civil society and private sector. The donors need to get their act together in order to work better together. The partnership between the developed countries and the developing countries is now set up within a framework, and we are now going to test it in practice. I believe that this represents real progress. It means that we will be coming back to you in order to see, in many cases, whether the parliamentary bodies are also prepared to act. This will be a test of the relationship between the administration and the parliamentary bodies, because all of us have to work together. This is the message that I want to give you. We have moved from philosophy to action, and we look forward to working with you. I will be delighted to take questions if there are any.

Thank you very much.

---

‡ The World Summit on Sustainable Development was held in Johannesburg in August and September 2002.

TIMOR-LESTE: THE STRUGGLE AGAINST POVERTY AHEAD

Letter from Dili, Timor-Leste

POSTED MAY 21, 2002

Wolfensohn was on hand for the ceremonies, as were UN Secretary-General Kofi Annan, Indonesian President Megawati Sukarnoputri, and former U.S. President Bill Clinton, as the tiny Southeast Asian state of Timor-Leste (formerly East Timor) officially won its independence. These excerpts from his letter to World Bank staff, written the same day, feelingly convey the emotions—excitement, joy, and pride, including pride in the Bank's contributions—of that historic occasion.

East Timor gained its independence at midnight last night, and today, the first day in the life of the world's newest country, was one that none of us who witnessed it will ever forget. We saw people hug and cry as they watched their flag raised for the first time on their independent soil. We heard them shout "Viva Timor-Leste!" as they celebrated. We watched, this morning, in a moment rich in symbolism, as the new Parliament was sworn in, in the building used two years ago as a temporary "tent city" by the first joint assessment mission—a mission made up of Timorese, Bank and other experts, who began work even as Dili was still smoldering.

It has been an intensely emotional couple of days. The last time Elaine and I were here in Dili, we arrived in a city without roofs, where most buildings were burnt shells, where life had come to a standstill. There were few cars, no animals, no shops, one restaurant, and almost no supplies. Our staff flying in often had to fill a shopping list before they left Darwin [Australia]. There were only mobile telephones.

The office was a single room in the former central bank, and several of our staff lived in another room there for several months, sleeping on stretcher beds and sometimes living off military rations. Visiting staff stayed with families, in an effort get some cash to local people, so they could rebuild their homes. Working hours were long and intense—usually late into the night—reflecting the huge needs of the Timorese and our equally huge desire not to let them down.

In two years, the change is nothing short of miraculous. In Dili now, there are not only cows and goats and chickens by the road in from the airport, but roofs on the houses, well-stocked shops, and even traffic jams. But the greatest change is in the people.

Today, Elaine and I ate lunch with all our staff in the office. The national staff told some of their stories, their hopes and fears for their country. They told what independence meant, in terms of new opportunity, of former suffering, of their dreams. Almost everyone in the room cried. Some of the words of Diana, Divaia, Roberto, Felicidade, and Fernando are reprinted here* just as they were said, because I would not paraphrase such feelings.

Let me just say that it was a day that moved me deeply, a day that reminded me again of why I do this job and, I hope, why we all work at the World Bank. It's a special place, with the opportunity to do huge amounts of good, and to benefit the lives of millions of people who need a hand. I heard this again today, as our Timorese colleagues laid out their wish-list for their country: peace, better health care, better education, jobs, no corruption, opportunity, a chance to rise above poverty.

These are the great goals of development, shared by people around the world. They are central to our work, the reason for our focus on poverty, and why we must continue to insist that people of a country be allowed to determine their own future and not have things dictated from outside. It will take time, of course, to achieve all these goals, in Timor or anywhere else. They have their political independence, but it took many years to win. The struggle for economic independence, the struggle against poverty, may be long and hard too.

I hope we can all remember these voices, which I am sure you have heard as well, in different languages and in different places. They should be with us when we think of the impact of our work, of really scaling up to change things for the better by reaching more people more quickly.

I wish you could all have been here. You would have choked with pride, as I did, to be associated with such a fine group of staff, and with such remarkable outcomes. This little office in many ways shows what's best about the World Bank: our ability to work as a team, to deliver quickly, to care deeply, and to be energetic and creative—and above all, to believe in people and empower people.

I want to thank the East Timor team—in Dili, Sydney and Washington for what they have done for the people of this country. And I would like to thank the people of newly independent East Timor, including our national staff, for all they have done for us. They have inspired us and challenged us, and by their words today, they have rewarded us more than I can say.

---

* A transcript of some of the staff's comments accompanied the original letter.

TOWARD EDUCATION FOR ALL:
WHAT CAN THE G-8 DO?

Remarks at a press conference at the Council on Foreign Relations

WASHINGTON, D.C. | JUNE 12, 2002

*At this press conference Wolfensohn announces the Fast Track Initiative to
help developing countries accelerate their progress under the Education for All
program, which was launched in 1990. He urges rich countries, and in particular the Group of Eight (G-8), which would shortly be meeting in
Kananaskis, Canada, to support developing countries in their quest to put
all primary school-age children in school.*

Let me say at the outset that I'm very happy to share the platform with colleagues who are on the front line of this initiative and to thank them for their
support. The World Bank is announcing this initiative today, but I would like
you to know that, in announcing this, I am speaking on behalf of a lot of people who have been consulted and who have participated and will participate
in this initiative.

Of course, Oxfam [International] has been extraordinarily supportive, both
in making the case and in implementation. But we've also had extensive discussions with UNESCO and UNICEF,* with a number of national governments, and with the European Union, and I want to say that this is an initiative
that has gained a lot of coherence and support from others, and it is not just
something that we're dumping on the international community today or, indeed, on which we are seeking to assert primacy.

On the other hand, I think it's important that, prior to the upcoming
meetings of the G-7/G-8, we take the steps that were already indicated at
the time of the Monterrey meetings [the 2002 Financing for Development
conference] and, in particular, at the time of the [Bank-Fund] Spring Meetings, where we had an Education for All paper distributed to all the ministers, in which we spoke of the importance of moving from concept to
reality, of getting beyond the talk, of which we've had a lot, and into actually doing the job.

And so what we're announcing today is not rocket science. It is simply saying, Let's now identify those countries that have an overall strategy for national
development in their countries, that have an education strategy that is doable,
and let's get behind them. Let's say to them that, if you have those conditions
in place, if you are anxious to move forward, to be participants in this program, and to demonstrate that you can manage and achieve the program, then
we will seek to provide you with the necessary financing.

---

* The United Nations Educational, Social, and Cultural Organization and the United Nations Children's Fund.

And so we have done a review of all 88 countries, but in particular 47 of the poorest, and we have concluded that there are 18 countries that should immediately get on the fast track for this partnership between the governments and the administrators of the education programs and the international community. These 18 countries—and we've given you a list—have within them 17 million children who have not seen the inside of a school and whom we want to get into school. In addition, in 5 of the larger countries whose education programs and national strategies are at different stages of development, we want to provide immediate technical assistance and help, so that they can come up with an overall national framework that we can get behind and support. And these countries have another 50 million kids out of school.

These countries that we have identified have either existing programs or programs that will need to be brought up to speed, and we are asserting that these countries should receive long-term commitments to ensure that they get universal primary education. This program amounts to breaking the back of the problem of primary school education in these countries and ensuring a partnership between those who wish to offer the education and those who will finance it.

This is not a free-money activity, however. This is not just saying that money will solve it all, because money doesn't solve it all. It is money associated with intelligent programs, properly administered and correctly assessed.

That is the partnership that we're looking for. But what we have not been able to do until this moment is to give the assurance of the financial resources, and this is an attempt to ensure those financial resources that will parallel the professional activities of people like those sitting at the table here.

So we're very excited that this should go forward. We estimate that, for all 47 countries, something on the order of $3 billion will be required on an annual basis. This is a sum that is well within the context even of the additional funding that was pledged in Monterrey. It clearly addresses an issue that is at the base of the development process, and so we're very hopeful that we can get both an endorsement and specific support.

We are not suggesting a new fund. That in itself would probably take several years to negotiate. So we've decided to avoid the notion of a new fund, and it's really not necessary. What is necessary is to have an annual consultative process in which we review the progress and ensure that continuing financing is available, and we in the Bank are deeply committed to try and make this work. And I'm very happy to have the chance to announce the initiative to you today.

Remarks at a reception for new staff, World Bank headquarters

WASHINGTON, D.C. | JUNE 27, 2002

> *Throughout his presidency, Wolfensohn took time out to address groups of new staff arriving to work at the World Bank. He used the occasions to introduce himself and to get to know the newcomers, but most important, to inspire them in their work as a team that would be "united in the dream of contributing to a better world."*

I want to welcome all of you because, as you will find out, the Bank is the institution it is only because of the people that participate in the institution. Other than that, it's some buildings and some bureaucratic regulations, which we gradually change and which I hope you can help us change even more radically, to make ourselves into the sort of business that I hope has attracted you here. Because, as I've said many times, this is more than a job that you've come to do. This is a real chance to serve mankind and to participate, particularly in the period that I think most of you are going to be working here, in something that is going to be incredibly interesting and incredibly testing.

If I were going to be here in 25 years' time, to give you your 25-year pin, I would say that, when you joined the World Bank, there were 6 billion people in the world, 5 billion of whom were in our constituency, which is the developing world. And now—that is, in 25 years' time—the number is 8 billion, of whom 7 billion are in the developing and transition economies.

You're here today to deal with the problem of 3 billion people already living on less than two dollars a day, and a billion, two hundred million living on less than one dollar a day. You have to deal with them and their problems, and you will also have to deal with 2 billion more people coming down the pike. And you will have to do that in an environment in which Europe will become smaller and older and very different in terms of its makeup, in terms of the nationalities that are part of it. You will be looking also at a United States that is different—larger, yes, but demographically different and different in terms of nationalities, and probably also older.

So it is the youth, the future of the developing world who in many ways are the clientele that we serve, but it's a clientele that is generally less than well endowed, because those 5 billion people in the developing countries have only 20 percent of the world's GDP. And the real test is whether you can help bring about greater equity for those people and for those countries that house the largest share of the poor of the world. How we deal with social justice and equity, how we deal with the education of those young people, how we deal with the enfranchisement of women, how we deal—and I'm very happy to see here our new executive in charge of disabilities—with persons with disabilities, how we deal in so many ways with the issues that confront us. These things will determine the future of our planet. And we need to address them not just as a matter of conscience, although that in itself would be enough, and not just as a question of morality and social justice, although those would be adequate reasons to do it, but because fundamentally, and this is the question that you're all going to have to address, the question of poverty is a matter of self-interest, because it is, for all of us, the question of peace.

If we do not address the questions of social justice and of poverty, there is no way that we'll have peace on the planet. We've seen elements of that on September 11, but we didn't need September 11 to show us that where there is poverty, there is always a place in which problems can be fomented. You'll be working in a world where there are people who want to foment problems, a world that no longer has walls, a world in which living in the United States or Australia or Europe is no longer different from living in Africa or Asia or Latin America, because what happens in those countries affects every other country. We're linked by education, by trade, by finance, by crime, by health, by environment, by drugs, by terror. There is no way to hide on this planet that you're going to be working on.

In a very real sense, you're in an institution that may be the best placed of all the global institutions to have a key role in determining how we approach these economic and social issues on a global basis. There is no organization that can match us in terms of breadth and understanding of those global issues. Now you're part of that team, and you have to carry your weight in whatever part of that process you participate. You're not just working for a paycheck, and you're not just working for yourself. There's some element of what you're doing that is really working for humanity. I don't say that just to stimulate you or to have a nice rounded phrase, but because it happens to be true.

The role of our institution is a really serious one, and it's one that is backed by self-interest, by morality, by ethics, by social justice, and by what's right. And what's right is to confront the issue of poverty on a global basis and the question of social justice on a global basis.

I hope that you'll stay for many years. I'm sure that as members of the Staff Association or as individuals you'll have your gripes, that you will think management is lousy, that there will be many things that you think are ridiculous, that there are many rules that you don't understand, and, if that is true, change them. You're not a prisoner. We need your advice. If you've got good ideas on how things can be changed, speak up. Retribution is not nearly as bad as you hear it is. Some people think that if you say anything unattractive, you're fired within minutes. Well, actually you have at least a few days, and in those few days, I'd urge you to fight like hell. And if you get fired for voicing crit-icisms, come see me and I'll promote you.

What we really need is a group of people—and we have some very young people in their first jobs, others who have worked with us for various periods of time—who have the interest of the Bank at heart. What we really need is people who want to bring about change and who are united in the dream of contributing to a better world.

So I wish you luck. I hope you enjoyed the orientation program. But more than that, I hope you enjoy the work that you're going to do, and I hope that you'll get great satisfaction for yourself and for your families, and that when I'm long gone, I can look back and say I knew that group that came in in 2002, and they're now running the institution and they're doing a better job than I did. I will take great joy in knowing that I met you tonight and that you'll carry all this on.

So I salute you and thank you for coming and wish you a great stay at the World Bank.

Thank you.

Address to the Rwandan National Assembly

KIGALI, RWANDA | JULY 15, 2002

In these remarks in the Rwandan capital, Wolfensohn addresses the trauma of the Rwandan genocide of 1994 and speaks of the economic side of the country's rehabilitation. He offers the World Bank's help in rebuilding what he calls a "society of hope."

Mr. Speaker, President Kagame,* Mr. Chief Justice, Members of this Assembly, Members of the Diplomatic Corps, of Civil Society, and of the Private Sector, and Friends:

Let me first of all thank you for your welcome and say what an honor and privilege it is for me to have the chance to address this cross section of the community in this august assembly, which is itself a reflection of the democratic spirit in this country.

Let me say also that this is for me a long anticipated visit to your country, and that even after being here for only 24 hours, I have learned a great deal that you cannot learn in books or in reading history or reading political papers.

The first thing that you become aware of in this country is the dominance of the sense of history, a history that is very difficult for all citizens of Rwanda, a history that did not start in 1994 but that was already building up in 1959, 1963, 1967, 1973, 1991, when Rwandan citizens witnessed and the world looked on at activities that cannot and should not be sustained, and which themselves gave the possibility of the 1994 occurrence. And this tragedy, which I was reminded of during my visits to Armenia and Timor-Leste—and to the Holocaust Museum in Washington, reflecting the wartime experience of the Jews and the Roma and others—all of these made me feel just how deep and how strong these emotions must be in your country.

Today I have had the chance to get some glimpse of that history. I have been in the Demobilization Center in Muhazi, where I met with ex-combatants who were coming back to be reintegrated into society. And I went to the [genocide] memorial in Gisozi, where I looked at some of the exhibits and read the explanatory material, which starts by indicating that the objective of that memorial is not only to remind people of what happened, but also to build a future of education for your people and for reconciliation.

So the thing one becomes aware of as a stranger to this country, but as someone who, through his organization, has been involved in it, is the crucial

---

* Paul Kagame, president of Rwanda.

importance of reconciliation and the remarkable work in which your country is engaged, under the leadership of your president, to reunify the country and give it internal strength. And for that I congratulate you and express the hope that it will long continue and strengthen.

But what I have learned about human behavior is that if you try to change it and make it more rational and give it more hope, there has to be an economic component that goes along with that. And that is true whether the people are Palestinians or Timorese, whether it is someone who is downtrodden in Latin America or some other part of the world. To stop the feeling of anger and conflict, you have to have hope. You have to have some economic activity that gives you a better chance for life, for yourselves and most particularly for your children. It is in that context of hope, that context of building an economic future, that I hope the World Bank Group has been able and will continue to give some support to your nation.

We are not a political organization. We are not geared to enter into the political fray, either the reconciliations you need to make outside this country or, perhaps more important, the reconciliations inside. We can help technically, we can help with funding, but we are not on the front line of peacemaking. What we can do is work with your government, with this Assembly, and with society generally in trying to give you the assistance that you need to build that society of hope.

You have already demonstrated that, economically, you can take steps to build a future for your people by enabling your economy to grow. I must commend you on the 5 percent increase in economic growth in 2000, and last year's increase of 7 percent. But given population growth of 3 percent a year, and given a desire to catch up and build from your present base, you need greater growth, and for that you need a whole variety of things. Those are the sorts of priorities and interests that are reflected in the work that you have done with us in the preparation of your strategy—we call it the Poverty Reduction Strategy—which is a strategy designed to build that economic hope and that social hope for your people.

And what is that strategy? Is it different here than it is anywhere else? My answer to you is that it is not different here than in other places, and to explain that I want to position your country just for a moment in the context of the world as a whole. When I look at Sub-Saharan Africa, I see a continent of 46 countries with more than 600 million people, 10 percent of the world's population. And I see that that 10 percent receives less than 1 percent of the world's income and less than 1 percent of the world's trade.

Since I have been at the Bank, together with my colleagues I have tried to say to the richer countries and to the other countries that are also in development—

the other 5 billion people in our world of 6 billion people—I have tried to say to them that, notwithstanding that Africa is small in terms of its share of economic power, it is rich in terms of natural resources and in particular of human resources. And you must take an interest in Africa, because you cannot have peace globally, you cannot have prosperity globally, unless you have peace and prosperity in Africa.

Now, unfortunately, making that case is not easy. The world tends to think that issues of conflict, issues of development, are more important in the North than in the South. There has been greater interest in the conflicts in the Balkans and in Kosovo and in the Middle East and in other places than there has been in Africa. And so it is really necessary that African leadership come out and say for itself, "We don't want favors. We want a partnership. And we don't want to be treated as third-class citizens, because we are not. We want to lead our countries into the 21st century, and we want to do it standing upright and not with charity, but with leadership that is African leadership and choice that is African choice."

And that assertion has now been made in the NEPAD initiative, the New Initiative for Africa's Development, in which your president is playing a leading role. And it is an important statement because it is one that applies to your country as well as to other countries on the continent. And it says very simply, "We want a partnership, but we want a partnership that is based on us having strengthened capacity; on having a legal and judicial system, Mr. Chief Justice, that is honest, that is straightforward, and that gives justice to all; a financial system that is clean and transparent and solid; and a system that fights corruption, that does not stand for corruption, in a continent that has been racked by corruption for too long."

These are not conditions that have been imposed by Western donors. This is not an outside prescription. This is the prescription given by African leadership itself about its desire for its future. And it says, "If we can do that, as we plan to do, we expect a partnership. We want support on capacity building and increased development assistance." And it says further, "And we want to do that on an ongoing basis, judging the effectiveness of what we do, because we Africans don't want to waste money, either. We want to control our destiny, and we want to do it effectively for the benefit of our people."

For me, this statement was enormously important, and it was ratified in a way in the meetings that we had in Monterrey [the 2002 Financing for Development Conference] where all the developing countries came up with a similar agenda, a new partnership between the developed and the developing countries. And I believe that, within that context, very much the same is being asserted by your own government, reflecting your position as a landlocked country in this great continent of Africa, with 8.7 million people anxious to ensure hope and destiny for themselves.

And I say this to you, to bring it from the general down to the specific, because it is sometimes easy to think that the world you live in is the world. Your country is the world to you, but it is small in terms of the continent and in terms of global activity. I know this because I grew up in Australia, and I thought everything important in the world was Australian, and I am used to feeling that sense of pride about my country. But when you enter the world, you have to relate what you are doing to global forces and to regional forces, and therefore what I believe your government is doing is to prepare yourselves for regional integration, for regional leadership, and for participation in the development of economic and social programs in the region and in the continent.

Now, I know from our experience here—with more than $800 million worth of projects, in infrastructure, in rural development, in health, in education, and more recently in assisting the reintegration of combatants and in the building of a consensus in the country—I know that there is enormous quality in the Rwandan people, and I know that the efforts you are making to reunify the country are being well met. And what I was anxious to say to you today was that, within the global context of this new partnership, we will continue to give you support in every way we can in your efforts to lead your people to the future that the 21st century offers.

This is a future that is only to a limited degree for the people in this room. It is for all of our children—my children and your children. It is a future that is built on good education, on education that is not education to hate but education to love; an education that is broad, not narrow. It is built on health services that can give proper strength to your youth. It is built on technological developments that can allow them access to the world on the Internet and through other forms of communication. It is a possibility for them to trade with the world. It is a possibility for them to build a region, not just a country. And it is a possibility for them to lead in the region, and to remember the past, but build for the future.

Mr. Speaker, let me speak from the point of view of the Bank. We have our office here in Kigali, and we have some remarkable young Rwandans who are working with us, and we intend to build that office with strength. And I want to say to you and commit to you that we stand ready to be of assistance to you. We are not here as professors, we are not here as policemen, we are not here to lecture. We are here to share with you your challenges and, I hope, Mr. Speaker, to contribute to the Rwanda of hope and prosperity that all of you are seeking.

Thank you, Mr. Speaker, for giving me this chance to address you.

RICH, POOR SHOULD JOIN HANDS FOR
SUSTAINABLE DEVELOPMENT

Published in *China Daily*

AUGUST 26, 2002

This essay appeared in the press worldwide just days before the World Summit on Sustainable Development in Johannesburg, South Africa. Wolfensohn calls for fighting poverty and for building a better world, but for doing so in a sustainable way that will not come at the expense of the environment.

JOHANNESBURG: Last spring, the UN [Financing for Development] summit in Monterrey spurred poor countries to commit to improve their policies and governance in exchange for promises by rich countries to deliver more aid, and open their markets to trade. The World Summit on Sustainable Development in Johannesburg this week gives us the chance to put those words into action.

What should the world expect from Johannesburg? Perhaps the best way to answer that is to look ahead and imagine what kind of world we want, not just now, but for our children, and our children's children. Are we going to leave as our legacy a poorer globe that has more hungry people, an erratic climate, fewer forests, less biodiversity, and is even more socially volatile than today?

According to the World Bank's new *World Development Report 2003,* the next 50 years could see the global population swell by 50 percent to 9 billion people, and the world's gross domestic product increase fourfold to US$140 trillion. Given current trends in production and consumption, social and environmental strains threaten to derail development efforts and erode living standards unless we design better policies and institutions. Development policies will need to be even more closely focused on protecting our forests, fisheries and farms and making them more productive. Misguided policies and weak governance have contributed to environmental disasters, growing income inequality, and social upheaval in some countries, often resulting in deep deprivation, riots, or refugees fleeing famine or civil wars.

If we stay on the road we are on, the signs do not appear very encouraging. By 2050, the world's annual output of carbon dioxide will have more than tripled while 9 billion people—3 billion more than we have today and mostly living in developing countries—will be tapping into the earth's water, adding more stress on the world's already-strained water supply. Meanwhile, food needs will more than double, a grim prospect for Africa where food production is currently falling behind the pace of population growth. All this in a world where extinction already threatens 12 percent of all bird species, and a quarter of its species of mammals. Globally, 1.3 billion people already live on fragile lands—arid zones, wetlands, and forests—that cannot sustain them. By

2050, and for the first time in history, more people will be living in cities than in rural areas. Without better planning, the stresses from immigration and population shifts across the globe could create new social upheaval and desperate competition for already scarce resources.

Yet these trends also offer opportunity, if world leaders and policy makers meeting in Johannesburg muster the courage to pledge—and follow through on—bold actions over the next 10 to 15 years. Most of the capital stock and infrastructure—housing, shops, factories, roads, power and water services that will be needed by the growing population in coming decades—do not yet exist. Better standards, increased efficiency, and more inclusive means of decision-making could mean that these assets are built in ways that put fewer strains on society and the environment. Similarly, as population growth slows, economic growth will translate more readily into lower poverty and higher incomes per capita—provided that development over the next few decades has been handled in a way that does not destroy the natural resources that underpin growth, or erode critical social values, such as trust. We must strive for the Millennium Development Goals, which map out a world where poverty is cut in half by 2015, and in so doing we will lay the basis for a virtuous cycle of growth and human development in the poor nations of the world.

If individual incomes in the developing world grow by an average of 3.3 percent annually, they would reach US$6,300 a year by 2050, nearly one-third more than that in current upper/middle income countries. And such growth is already viewed as a modest goal by some leaders in the developing world. Over the past two decades, we have seen growth in many East Asian countries at an annual average of nearly twice that rate. What would this mean for ordinary people? Their basic human needs for shelter, food and clothing could be affordably met. Life expectancy would rise to 72 years in poor countries, compared with 58 today in those nations with the lowest incomes. The number of children who die before the age of five would drop dramatically, and the number of people who can read and write would rise to nearly 95 percent.

Of course, this dramatic economic growth would pose potentially enormous risks to the natural environment, and these risks are greatest in developing countries. Given that rich nations are the greatest consumers of our common resources, they have a special responsibility to help the developing world address these risks. We all must protect our forests and fisheries from overexploitation. We must halt soil degradation, and ensure our water supplies are used efficiently. We must protect biologically diverse ecosystems, as they underpin the flow of goods and services essential to our economies and societies. We must limit emissions from factories, cars and households. That is why the challenge of delivering sustainable development must be met locally, nationally, and globally.

Developing countries need to promote democracy, inclusiveness and transparency as they build the institutions needed to manage their resources. Rich countries should increase aid, support debt reduction, open their markets to developing country exporters, and help transfer technologies needed to prevent diseases, and especially to increase energy efficiency and bolster agricultural productivity. Civil society, meanwhile, can act as a voice for dispersed interests, and provide independent oversight of public, private and nongovernmental performances. A socially responsible private sector, supported by good government, should create incentives for companies to pursue their interests while advancing environmental and social objectives. And the international community must work together on global issues, such as climate change and biodiversity.

If we wisely safeguard our vital resources, key among them the environment, and social stability, then we will attain the growth rates essential to reducing poverty in ways that will last. It would be reckless of us to successfully reach the Millennium Development Goals in 2015 only to be confronted by chaotic cities, dwindling water supplies, increased emissions, and even less crop land to sustain us than we have now.

PART THREE

SECURING THE 21st CENTURY
SEPTEMBER 2002–MAY 2005

Address to the Board of Governors at the Annual Meetings of the World Bank
and the International Monetary Fund

WASHINGTON, D.C. | SEPTEMBER 29, 2002

*Building on the summits of recent months in Monterrey and in Johannesburg,
Wolfensohn calls for unity in achieving the Millennium Development Goals.
On the trade front, he calls on rich countries to dismantle their domestic
agriculture subsidies that rob poor countries of opportunities to export
their way out of poverty. He reiterates that the development community
must pay special attention to the issues of inclusion, participation, and
empowerment.*

Mr. Chairman, Governors, Honored Guests:

It is my pleasure to welcome you to these Annual Meetings. I would like to
extend my appreciation to the United States authorities for making our meeting in Washington possible and the D.C. Police Department for all their help.
I also thank my friend, [IMF Managing Director] Horst Köhler, for a collegial
and cooperative working relationship in the last two years and for his thoughtful speech this morning. To our newest member country, Timor-Leste, I join
Chairman Macki* in welcoming you to the Bank. Please accept our best
wishes for every success in your efforts to build your nation.

Mr. Chairman, two years ago, when we gathered, I spoke of the opportunities and challenges of development. These have been a tough two years.
In the rich world, collapsing stock markets and corporate scandals have
shaken confidence and mutual trust. In the developing world, people have
been badly hit by continuing wars and conflict, by falling commodity prices,
and by a slackening of demand for and continuing restrictions on their trade
with rich countries. There has been a heavy human toll in Africa and Latin
America.

Yet, in the face of these difficulties, much of the developing world has
shown strong resilience. This is a tribute to the progress that has been made in
shaping and implementing policies. Many countries have taken on the problems of dislocation inevitably involved in reform. They have worked to improve institutions and governance. And through these difficulties and our
collective action, we have in many ways seen the best of people. We have seen
a coming together, a recognition that international problems require international responses.

---

* Ahmed Macki, governor of the IMF and the World Bank from Oman.

A New Global Partnership for an Interdependent World

On September 11th last year, the world finally came to recognize that there are not two worlds, rich and poor. There is only one. We are linked by finance, trade, migration, communications, environment, communicable diseases, crime, drugs, and certainly by terror. Today more and more people are saying that poverty anywhere is poverty everywhere, and their voices are getting louder. Their demand is for a global system based on equity, human rights, and social justice. It must be our demand, too. For the quest for a more equal world is the quest for long-term peace—something that military power alone can never achieve. And the world is beginning to listen.

We have seen a year in which the commitments reached at Doha, Monterrey, and Johannesburg have laid a new basis for a global deal.[†] The development community has confirmed the Millennium Development Goals as our framework for action. In pursuit of these goals, we have witnessed the emergence of a global partnership built on a consensus that the world is interdependent. Our thinking and our action must be local, regional, and global, and we must work and act together. And we have reached a remarkable consensus on what is needed for successful poverty reduction.

First and foremost, developing-country leaders have asserted that the responsibility for their future is in *their* hands. It is they who must drive their countries' development and create a constructive environment, to encourage growth that is equitable and just for poor people, indeed for all people. This growth must be based on sound social and economic policies—investment in health and education, especially early childhood education; effective legal and judicial systems; clear tax and regulatory frameworks implemented so as to fight corruption at all levels; strong and well-regulated financial systems—thereby creating the conditions for entrepreneurship, productivity, and jobs. And it must involve empowering the poor so that they can shape their own lives. Poor people are assets, not liabilities.

In Monterrey and Johannesburg, developed countries agreed to work in partnership with the developing countries, to help them build capacity, increase overseas development assistance where it is effective and well managed, open markets to trade, and reduce agricultural subsidies. They reaffirmed their commitment to the Millennium Development Goals for poverty and hunger, education and health, gender equality and the environment.

---

† The Fourth World Trade Organization Ministerial Conference, which launched the Doha Development Round of international trade negotiations, was held in Doha, Qatar, in November 2001; the United Nations Conference on Financing for Development was held in Monterrey, Mexico, in March 2002; the United Nations World Summit on Sustainable Development was held in Johannesburg, South Africa, in August and September 2002.

Mr. Chairman, together we have set 2015 as the deadline for our results. We must now, together, move beyond words and set deadlines for our actions. We have said we are mutually accountable. It is time to implement. It is time to deliver. If the goals of 2015 are to be achieved, each of us must act now. In doing so, we must recognize that development is not about quick fixes. Bringing lasting change requires vision. It requires time and patience. It requires a long-term commitment. It requires focus and discipline. And it requires us to measure effectiveness.

Some may say we need to learn more before we act. To them I would say, Of course, we will learn more as we go along, but there is already strong evidence on what works and what does not. We know enough to begin implementation *now*.

A New Multilateralism for Better Development Results

What must each of us do? Let me start with the rich countries. Deliver on the Doha agenda. We know that rich-country barriers to trade are too high. Bring down the tariffs, and cut back the nontariff barriers that all too often are covert protectionism. Keep to the Doha timetable. But there is so much that rich countries can do without waiting for Doha. We know that agricultural subsidies in rich countries, at $1 billion a day, squander resources and profoundly damage opportunities for poor countries to invest in their own development. There should be a fixed timetable for their elimination. Seize the opportunity, at the World Trade Organization's Cancún meeting in 2003, to make firm commitments on subsidies. But I urge you to act sooner. Deliver on the welcome commitments of increased aid made at Monterrey, and the excellent response to the financing shortfall for the HIPC [Heavily Indebted Poor Countries] Initiative made at Kananaskis.[‡] We see an emerging willingness to increase aid that is productively used. Untie aid, and move to better coordinate and harmonize development programs and policies. The fragmentation of donors' efforts has long plagued the effectiveness of aid. Many of the failures blamed on borrowing countries actually represent the failure of donors to coordinate their efforts. Better development multilateralism will deliver better development results.

What must developing countries do? They must continue to build capacity, good governance, and good institutions; to push ahead with legal, judicial, and financial reforms; and to invest in their people. They, too, must focus more on results, monitoring outcomes and managing programs so that the goals for growth and poverty reduction can be achieved. For many countries the New Partnership for African Development shows the way.

What must the Bank do? We must focus on making good on our promises to work toward the Millennium Development Goals. Although as an institution we have changed greatly over the last decade, we must do more. We must become more transparent. We must support developing countries in building their capacity. Although we have been a leader in measuring the results of our projects and programs, we must measure our results more rigorously, and, with others, we must be held accountable against broader country goals and the Millennium Development Goals. We are anxious to move ahead with efforts to harmonize and coordinate our work with the International Monetary Fund, the United Nations, the multilateral development banks, and other donors.

All partners in development must pay special attention to inclusion, participation, and empowerment:

- *inclusion,* because we cannot expect reforms to be sustained, if the poor are excluded when choices and trade-offs are made
- *participation,* because poor people know best what makes a difference in their lives
- *empowerment,* because we will not have lasting change unless the poor acquire the assets and means to shape their future.

---

‡ The annual summit of the Group of Eight took place in Kananaskis, Alberta, Canada, in June 2002.

Societies the world over are changing. People demand to know, to be consulted, to have a say, to have a voice. Unless we build on their strengths, we will forgo the most powerful force for implementation. But actions by governments of developing and developed countries and by international institutions are only part of the solution. We must all do more to enhance the role of civil society and the private sector. The old multilateralism was government to government. The new multilateralism must include the voices of the private sector and civil society. We must all be more accountable—better partners, better listeners, better deliverers. And we must keep track of our actions.

A Comprehensive Strategy for Poverty Reduction and Sustainable Development

We have made real progress in reaching broad agreement that development must be addressed comprehensively, with developing-country ownership. For most poor countries this approach is embodied in their poverty reduction strategy, following an approach that is transforming development strategy and partnerships in many countries. Similarly for middle-income countries, the Comprehensive Development Framework is proving effective.

For the first time we have a tool, the Development Gateway, that can enable us to collate information and learn more about projects going on in development around the world. As the Development Gateway shows, over 63,000 development projects are currently under way worldwide, not including those programs undertaken by civil society or church groups. All too often, projects in the same sector in the same country are run by many varied agencies, who are not talking to each other. We must use the Development Gateway to track our actions so that we can better coordinate our efforts.

Mr. Chairman, we have come a long way. We do not have to start from scratch. We already have implementable programs. The Education for All Initiative, for example, will enable us to work together to enroll some 17 million children in school for the first time. We have programs on HIV/AIDS: as of today, 20 developing and transition economies have developed and are implementing AIDS strategies that build on prevention, care, and treatment. We have programs for clean water and sanitation. But we need to scale up these initiatives, so that we can have national, regional, and global impact. And we need donor support to implement them. Let our progress on education, AIDS, and clean water be a first test of our commitment to partnering for results.

To move implementation forward, we must agree to set deadlines now if we are to meet the 2015 goals. But we must go further: 2015 is only a staging post on a much longer journey. Over the next 50 years we will likely see world population grow from 6 billion to 9 billion, with almost 95 percent of that increase going to the developing world. Food needs will double, annual output of carbon dioxide will triple, and for the first time more people will live in cities than in rural areas, placing an enormous strain on infrastructure and on the environment.

If we are to meet the 2015 goals and to go on reducing poverty effectively, we estimate that the world economy will have to grow at an average annual rate of around 3.5 percent. That implies a $140 trillion world economy by 2050.

Mr. Chairman, if we cannot protect our environment and make such growth ecologically responsible, we will not have sustainable development. If we retain the current distribution of income, in which 15 percent of the world's population controls 80 percent of the world's income, we will not have sustainable development. If we continue to exclude the disenfranchised—women, indigenous people, the disabled, street children—from playing their rightful role in society, and if we ignore their human rights, we will not have sustainable development. And if we do not have sustainable development, we may not have long-term peace. That is the challenge that together we must meet.

We Must Act Now

Mr. Chairman, I cannot conclude without saying that I am extremely proud of the staff in the World Bank Group. They are united by a desire to fight poverty with passion. I thank them, from the bottom of my heart, for their hard work and commitment.

My friends, together we have the chance, the responsibility, and the privilege of shaping the planet of the future. We are not hapless bystanders. We can influence whether we have a planet of peace, of social justice, of equity, of growth—or a planet of unbridgeable differences between people, a planet of wasted physical resources, of strife, of terror, and of war.

Ours can be a time of a new renaissance of values, of justice, of freedom from want and from fear. We must set our horizons high. We must not be distracted. We must act *now* on our promises. We must deliver with a sense of urgency. This is our responsibility and our destiny.

Thank you.

Message from the president and chairman from the 2002 World Bank *Annual Report*

OCTOBER 2002

*This Chairman's Message covers the year from July 2001 to June 2002.
Wolfensohn refers to the watershed Monterrey conference the previous March
and the new Monterrey Consensus, which calls on both wealthy and poor
countries to do their part in supporting development.*

A New Global Partnership for Development

As a result of the events of the past year, more people than ever before have
come to realize that no wall divides rich and poor nations. There are not
two worlds—there is only one. And in this world, poverty is our collective
enemy. This has been a year of tremendous challenges. But it has also been
a period of reaching out, of standing together—a time of commitment to
shared goals.

The Millennium Development Goals (MDGs) represent an expanded vision of development with essential objectives, including halving world poverty
by 2015. At the International Conference on Financing for Development in
Monterrey, Mexico, in March 2002, the international community committed
itself anew to achieving those goals. It formed a new global partnership—the
Monterrey Consensus—that marks an important watershed in its aspirations
to achieve the MDGs. Both developing and developed countries will play important roles.

Developing countries recognize that they must commit to good governance and sound policies, building the conditions for investment and empowering their people in the development process. They have pledged to
use aid funds to build human capacity, focusing on education and health
programs. They have pledged to fight the corruption that drains resources
away from productive activities. They have taken the initiative to identify
priorities and generate their own development policies while representing
all constituencies, including women and the disadvantaged, in the process.
The development community is committed to increasing the quantity and
effectiveness of its support to developing countries as they move forward in
these areas.

Developed countries acknowledge that they must provide more and better
aid, improve policy coherence, and, critically, move forward on trade policies
in support of development. In particular, it is essential to address policies that
limit markets for developing countries' products. Without greater access to
global markets and the growth in trade that follows, many developing countries

will be severely constrained, not realizing their potential for investment, private sector growth, job creation, and sustainably higher incomes.

We in the development community are all agreed that the essential conditions to foster successful development include education and health programs that build human capacity; an effective system for infrastructure provision; good and clean government; effective legal and judicial systems; and well-organized and well-supervised financial systems.

The Monterrey Consensus was a historic step forward. At last developing countries saw the promise of a turnaround in access to trade and in the volume of aid, as an additional $12 billion was pledged by donor countries over the next three years. The challenge before us now is to translate the new global development partnership into action, redoubling our efforts on the part of developing countries and the broader international community.

What matters most is results. Over the past decades, impressive gains have been made in many countries in life expectancy, literacy, and poverty reduction. Because of better policies in developing countries, together with improved performance-based allocation in recent years, aid is more effective today at reducing poverty than ever before. But there is more to be done. With good results, we can open the door to increased resources for fighting poverty. Both developing and developed countries are now in a position to take the next steps toward achieving the Millennium Development Goals.

Essential to those steps is the need for developing countries to use the new resources committed at Monterrey effectively. Donors should harmonize their lending policies and procedures and untie aid, so that borrowing countries are not mired in unnecessary requirements and reports and can obtain resources more efficiently. Donors should also commit to helping developing countries build capacity in government, business, and communities, listening to their expressed priorities.

The Monterrey Consensus is in line with the development strategy that the World Bank Group has been progressively pursuing in recent years. The Bank's knowledge resources, based on more than fifty years of development experience, have played a vital role. There is now a broad acceptance of the Comprehensive Development Framework and Poverty Reduction Strategy Papers by low-income countries and our development partners. I believe that country ownership of this approach will increasingly broaden to embrace national parliaments, civil society, and the private sector. Country-led comprehensive processes enable clients to do an increasingly good job of setting clear priorities for policies and actions needed to deliver faster growth and poverty reduction. In each case, these priorities will need to reflect the country's unique circumstances and needs and will often go beyond political cycles.

Focus on Poverty Reduction and Improvements in Education

This year the Bank has played a leading role in relieving poor countries of debt in order to increase their resources for poverty reduction. Twenty-six countries are now benefiting from the Heavily Indebted Poor Countries (HIPC) Initiative, having received about $41 billion from all creditors in nominal debt-service relief over time. Five more countries will soon be receiving relief under this program. Together with other forms of relief, HIPC cuts the total external debt in these countries by two-thirds. These countries can now spend between three and four times more per year on key social investments, such as education and health, than on debt-service requirements.

Education is at the heart of poverty reduction. At its Spring Meetings this year, the Development Committee* of the World Bank Group specifically endorsed an Action Plan for accelerating progress toward Education for All, which aims to provide every girl and boy with quality primary school education by 2015. The case for faster progress toward this goal is clear: 113 million children of elementary school age in developing countries have either never set foot in a classroom or dropped out of school shortly after enrolling. The Bank has subsequently invited 18 countries to join an Education for All Fast Track [Initiative] and is working with 5 other countries to qualify them for the program. This is an initiative designed to help developing countries meet the 2015 education goal. Many more countries are expected to benefit from this initiative in the months and years to come.

We must continue to increase resources for poverty reduction in the poorest countries, for which the International Development Association (IDA) remains the largest source of concessional financing. Its catalytic role can now be even greater with the 13th Replenishment of IDA (IDA13), which stresses working with other development partners and a strong focus on results. IDA13 represents an 18 percent increase over IDA12, and reconfirms the commitment of IDA donors to addressing the goals highlighted at Monterrey. The increased grant funding within IDA is especially welcome, and we are grateful to the donors for this new development.

In the past year, the World Bank Group has developed and communicated its strategy, approach, and priorities and established many of the procedures

---

* The Development Committee is a grouping of finance ministers representative of the Bank's member countries that meets twice a year to discuss and advise on development issues.

and tools needed to translate those broad directions into concrete actions that can be monitored. With our strategy established, our focus will continue to be on implementation. We will work to scale up our impact because of the scale and urgency of the global poverty challenge. Where the Bank has been successful in the past, we know that country leadership and our strong partners in development have played important parts. We will continue to work with our partners to find more effective ways to help clients formulate their policies and build institutions. By sharing and applying the Bank's considerable knowledge resources, we can assist our development partners and client countries in identifying successful poverty reduction efforts and in carrying them out on a wider scale. I am especially grateful to the management and staff of our World Bank Group for their selfless efforts.

In a changed world, the new partnership of nations can make the difference in the lives of poor people. The time for action is now. The opportunity is here. We must stand firm in our fight against poverty and aim to achieve a drastic reduction of it in our lifetime, for the sake of our children. We must commit ourselves to a poverty-free and inclusive world with renewed vigor.

Keynote address at the Lifelong Learning Conference

STUTTGART, GERMANY | OCTOBER 9, 2002

In this address Wolfensohn speaks to the importance of literacy and its role in enabling adults to function in a modern economy. The pace of techno- logical change, he stresses, requires people, whether in wealthy countries or poor countries, to keep learning throughout their working lives.

President Adamkus, Minister President Teufel, Mr. Mayor,* Members of the Government, and Friends:

Let me say first of all how grateful we are to the authorities of Baden-Würt- temberg and to the city of Stuttgart for their welcome and for their generosity in hosting this conference, which we in the Bank have been looking forward to for a very long time. For us this is an extremely important meeting, and not just another World Bank meeting, because it comes at a time when the world is faced with many challenges and when, after the meetings in Monterrey and Johannesburg,[†] there has been a significant focus on several things.

The first is that the world is an unequal world. Of the 6 billion people cur- rently living on our planet, over 80 percent share between 15 and 18 percent of the economic benefits, and some 15 to 20 percent enjoy 80 percent of the benefits.

But it goes beyond that, because the difference is not just monetary. The difference is also reflected in technology and in knowledge—not indigenous knowledge, the knowledge needed to live in one's community, but the knowl- edge that can make one competitive in a global economy and that can improve living standards in the developing countries in which so many poor people live. It's a world of inequality, as has been addressed by many commentators as well as politicians and economists. And, after the tragic events of September 11 in the United States, many in the developed world have come to recognize that these two worlds, developing and developed, are not separated by a wall, but in fact are one global community. What happens in the developing world has a significant impact on the world in which the wealthy live.

It's become fairly common wisdom, though not totally agreed, that if we do not deal with the question of poverty and the question of social equity and jus- tice, it's unlikely that we will have peace in the years ahead. Certainly that is my

---

* Valdas Adamkus, president of Lithuania; Erwin Teufel, prime minister of the German state of Baden- Württemberg; and Wolfgang Schuster, mayor of Stuttgart.
† The Conference on Financing for Development was held in Monterrey, Mexico, in March 2002, and the World Summit on Sustainable Development in Johannesburg in August and September 2002.

belief. And the issue becomes even more stark when one considers that, in the next 25 years, our planet's population will grow from 6 billion to 8 billion, and all but 50 million of those additional 2 billion people will live in developing countries. In 2025, therefore, we will have a world of 8 billion people, 7 billion of them living in developing countries. And Europe and Germany will be smaller and older, and the two great giants, India and China, with a total of 2.3 billion people today, will continue to grow. But many, many countries will be left behind, and the global framework will be one that may provide a foundation for crime, for terror, for disruption, but also a clear and positive linkage in terms of the possibilities for trade and finance and for investment.

In short, we have a great disparity in this world, and the genesis of this conference was that one of the principal ways to try and deal with the question of poverty, of development, of markets, and of peace is to deal with the question of education. And both in Monterrey and in Johannesburg there was very wide agreement that education is at the center of the development agenda. So a lot of the talking on that subject is behind us, and the question has become, How can we deal with the many subjects of development and, at this conference, the particular subject of education?

We at the Bank started some years ago, as did the United Nations, to think about how we can address this question. And the United Nations at its Millennial Assembly decided that, at least at the first level, we should move to get education for all, so that every child, boy or girl, would have the opportunity to go to primary school. There are today some 120 million or 130 million children out of school, more girls than boys, and it was decided that we would set ourselves the goal of getting all kids into school by 2015, because it was judged that education was going to be a very important driver of development.

We also addressed the question not just of kids in school but of adult education as well. And we found that, with the exception of India and China, in the developing countries something over 20 percent of the men were illiterate and something over 45 percent of the women were illiterate. But then we came to look again at what it means to be illiterate. Literacy is defined as the ability to read, but the ability to function in a modern economy, the literacy of skills, is a very different thing. And we discovered, not surprisingly, that that gap was very great in the developing countries.

We also discovered that 15 percent of the world had 80 percent of the computers and did 91 percent of the world's investment in research and technology, and 40 percent of the world did 1 percent of that investment. And so all the things that we were discovering made us believe even more that getting all children into primary school was not the only challenge; we also had the challenge of adult education and the challenge of a growing technology gap, which was giving the developed countries greater opportunities for advancement and exposing the poorer countries to the risk of falling further and further behind.

And that led us, of course, to ask how we could use technology not just for the rich but for the poor, to catch up on some of the areas in which the poor did not have the opportunities. So we looked at secondary education, and we looked at tertiary education, on the understanding that you need good primary, secondary, and tertiary education if you are going to have a comprehensive system. We also noted that, in order to have good primary education, one has to have good preschool education.

But then we further concluded that, in the modern world, even getting a substantial portion of the population educated is not enough. And this was where we came upon the notion of lifelong learning. We came to see lifelong learning as a series of stages. For those who are illiterate, lifelong learning can take them to the next stage, that of reading. For those who have a secondary school education, it can take them to the next stage. But we also discovered to our surprise, or at least to my surprise, that, even in a place like Baden-Württemberg, at a certain level the question of lifelong learning still applies. It applies equally to developed and to developing countries. The pace of technological change, the pace at which our world is changing, presents even the citizens of this land with the challenge of how to keep up with science and technology. And so we decided to have this conference here for all the reasons that Minister President Teufel described: the region's deep commitment to education, its 80 tertiary-level institutions including three of the oldest universities in the world, and its great commitment to technology.

My first trip after I came to the Bank was to Mali, one of the poorest countries in the world. I discovered there that Mali once had a very rich culture. And so now we are seeking to help the Malians build their education system with a sense of that history.

It is the same in Central America, where history surrounds you anywhere you look. As the world becomes more globalized, the differences between cultures become more important, not less important, for building identity and for building a planet where one can live with some sense of hope and optimism.

So there are many, many aspects to this question of increasing lifelong learning—not just technology, not just making a living, but adjusting to an ever-changing world. These are the things that I hope we will discuss at this conference, where we can experiment, where we can speculate with each other about the sort of things that we might do.

But, before closing, let me just touch on some of the things that we at the Bank are now experimenting with and, indeed, applying as ways of bridging this gap between the developed and the developing countries. We now have 100 of our offices linked by satellite. We're running 1,200 videoconferences a month. We're hitting 86 countries a day, on average, covering everything from agricultural advice to economic advice. We're linking people in Nepal with people in South Africa. Every Saturday morning, in a program that we've started with Mexico's Monterrey Institute of Technology, we're reaching 1,500 mayors of towns throughout Latin America, offering programs in Spanish about how to run their towns. Lifelong learning is essential for the newly elected officials among them, because many of them have never been officials before at all. They have come to office totally untrained, and often in a new democratic environment, where responsibility is diffused. So they need to be linked not just to the professor who teaches on Saturday morning, but to a website where they can ask questions of each other and of the authorities and build together a knowledge base that is effective.

We're working with an initiative that we started in Africa called the African Virtual University. We're running courses throughout Africa, including this year degree courses, which will be offered in computer technology and business administration.

When we came to the postconflict reconstruction of Timor-Leste and Afghanistan, the very first thing that we did, at the request of the governments, was to put in distance learning centers, linked by satellite. My first task in Kabul was to open a distance learning center, so that we could have learning for the new people in the government, and the same in Timor-Leste. We did this because it is not just the leaders who require additional learning, but also the trade union leaders, the administrators, the teachers, the doctors—and all of this is now becoming possible because of new technology.

We are also linking schoolchildren around the world. I recently came back, Mr. President, from a visit to Uganda to a house I have in Wyoming, in the western part of the United States, and I was asked to speak at the local chamber of commerce. So I made my usual pitch about development. And they said, "What can we do?" I said, "Well, why don't you link the Jackson Hole High School with a high school I just saw in Uganda, so that kids here in the mountains, in the Rockies, can learn something about Uganda, and the kids there can learn something about the Rockies, and you can all work together?" We now have 135,000 children linked in 20 countries, and we're training 20,000 teachers. Why do you have to train teachers? Because the kids know more about computers and learning than the teachers do. And if you don't train the teachers, you can't get the programs going, and so on.

All I'm trying to suggest, without giving you a catalogue of all the things we're doing—and there are many other initiatives that we have taken—is that technology now gives us a chance to deal with the issues of knowledge and advancement in a way that has never before been possible. Take one state in India, Andhra Pradesh. By the end of this year, 18 million people there will be linked by fiber-optic cable. Every village and town will have computers. There will be 25 different sorts of e-government, and a huge potential for schools and education. I mention this because I think the added dimension in lifelong learning that comes from technology gives us a tremendous potential in terms of bridging those gaps I spoke of, the income gap and certainly the knowledge gap, and the two are linked.

Finally, we can learn a lot from the people in poverty themselves: indigenous knowledge, knowledge of how to deal with problems, knowledge of how people in poverty cope, how they deal with issues, because my experience has been that they know a lot more about poverty and development than we do. So this is not just a one-way street. This is an opportunity for us to learn as well, if we are open-minded enough to be lifelong learners ourselves.

So, Mr. President, I believe that this will be a very interesting conference, one in which, while we have a lot of initiatives, we do not claim to have the answers. And we look forward to working with you and to learning something about what we believe will be a key not just to education but to world peace.

Thank you very much.

Remarks at a seminar of the Operations Evaluation Department

WASHINGTON, D.C. | NOVEMBER 6, 2002

The Operations Evaluation Department is an independent unit within the World Bank that assesses what has worked at the Bank and what has not, how borrowers plan to run and maintain projects, and the lasting contribution of Bank projects to a country's overall development. At this OED seminar Wolfensohn praises outgoing OED head Robert Picciotto and welcomes his successor Gregory Ingram. He also stresses the recently expanded role of evaluation to take account of progress toward the Millennium Development Goals.

OED has come a long way from being something that was just historical in terms of its observations to something that is active in the way it influences current activities, and we've gone a long way in terms of bridging the gaps toward assessment, even without, as Bob Picciotto has often pointed out, an adequate database on some of the things that we were seeking to measure.

But we are now moving to a new area, an area of evaluation that is not just of our own projects and against our own expectations of those projects, but against a new dynamic of how what we're doing relates to the Millennium Development Goals. And that has not just an impact on the evaluative function, but a significant impact on the way we conceive the work that we're doing.

Is our work limited to projects within the purview of the Bank, or does our work relate to the totality of work that is being done in the development field? How do we look at having a more coordinated effort among the Bank, the other multilateral and bilateral institutions, the regional banks, and civil society and the private sector for that matter, all working within a framework set by the country's government to meet the goals that are now agreed internationally? If we are involved in a development project in, say, education, how do we now evaluate that project not just against our own immediate goals, but against the goals of meeting a larger set of expectations that have been agreed by the international community?

This is important because the Bank will get a significant share of the blame or credit if the Millennium Development Goals are or are not achieved. People will come back and say, "Well, the World Bank obviously didn't do its job," even though we're only a small part of the development paradigm.

So, as we move forward, Greg Ingram and his team have to expand what it is they are looking at in terms of the evaluation of our own activities, to include not just the immediate focus, but also how we are playing our role as part of an integrating function in the development community, and how what we're doing fits into and assists and helps scale up the efforts toward achieving the Millennium goals.

This is shifting ground, but it is also a new challenge for OED in the coming years, because the questions that are going to be asked are not just, "Did your project do satisfactorily" but, since we're the Bank, "How did you impact the achievement of the Millennium goals?" So we may be comfortable about where we've been, but we have a new set of challenges for where we're going, and I'm sure Greg and all of you involved will be able to assist us.

Again, I want to thank you for the effort in the past and say that I think we've obviously made tremendous progress. There's been a great integration of OED and QAG [the Bank's Quality Assurance Group], of course, with the operations, and I wish you good fortune as we go forward in taking on this new challenge that's been handed to us by the Development Committee* and indeed by the global community at large.

So I look forward to hearing these presentations, and I pass it back to you, Greg, and I'm going to sit in the audience.

Thank you very much.

---

* The Development Committee is a grouping of finance ministers representative of the Bank's member countries that meets twice a year to discuss and advise on development issues.

COOPERATION AND PARTNERSHIP: HARMONIZING
THE ACTIVITIES OF DEVELOPMENT AGENCIES FOR
POVERTY REDUCTION

Remarks at the High-Level Forum on Harmonization

ROME | FEBRUARY 24, 2003

> *This address was delivered at the first of a series of annual meetings aimed at*
> *seeing how development agencies and other institutions could cooperate better*
> *and eliminate overlap and duplication of effort. Wolfensohn tells the audi-*
> *ence of heads of multilateral and bilateral institutions that the collective*
> *achievement of the group is greater than any single organization's efforts,*
> *and he urges a "coming together" on common objectives.*

After such erudite introductions, there is not a lot to add to open this conference, but let me give you some perceptions from the point of view of the
Bank and draw on the admirable comments that were made earlier.

Our starting point at the World Bank has been at the global level, where
we, like you, have become very much aware that the task of achieving the
Millennium Development Goals is a very daunting one. It's daunting because,
as President [Benjamin] Mkapa [of Tanzania] said, we need to integrate not
just the provision of funding, but also trade and global policies in a way that is
likely to give us a chance to be effective.

And as President Mkapa also said, there is a gap between the resources that
are needed to achieve these goals and the funding that is already in sight.
We're operating at a level of $50 billion or so a year [in total official develop-
ment assistance], and the need is probably somewhere between $100 billion
and $150 billion.

We've been told, very correctly, by our shareholders in the Bank and by
many of you and by many of your parliaments, that there is no way that more
funding is going to be provided unless we can demonstrate that the monies
that are already being used are being used effectively. That is at the core of this
meeting—a demonstration of how we are either using or not using effectively
the monies that are being given to us. And that involves, of course, many
things; many things are related, as some of the earlier speakers have said, to
strengthening capacity in the governments of the countries themselves, because all of us are dependent on these countries being in the driver's seat and
being able to administer and carry forward the programs in those countries.

I don't think any of us is thinking any more about running development
programs from Washington or other developed-country capitals. It's clear
that local ownership and participation are central. And we must, as President
Mkapa said, give all of the help that we can in building capacity and giving the
assistance that the recipient governments demand. But when we came to take
a look at our own behavior and, rather timorously, at the behavior of many of

our partners, we discovered that we, as an institution, were perhaps not as co-operative, not so minded to partnership, and not as good a listener as perhaps we might be. So we decided that we would have a personality change, a culture change. And this was not easy, and it's still not easy, because what we are now seeking to do is to listen, to simplify, to harmonize, to follow, to lead, to do whatever is necessary in the situation involving development, and we're doing it for very simple and obvious reasons.

As you know, we have started to collect information on what all of us in the development community are doing. We started an entity called the Development Gateway, which, because it was in the World Bank, was looked upon skeptically by many, both in this room and in civil society. So we spun it off so that it could be independent. But that Gateway has been very interesting. In the last 10 years, we discovered, more than 400,000 projects have been undertaken by the collective international community, and we think that something on the order of 80,000 projects are still going on out there.

If you go into the Gateway and you look at any country at random, and let's say you're interested in that country's activities in education, you'll probably find that there are 20 or 30 competing or parallel projects going on. Certainly, in the case of our institution, when we present to our Board the programs that we want to get through the Board, we very rarely mention the other 20 projects that are going on.

This is ridiculous on the face of it. We're not cooperating, we're not coordinating, and we're not learning from the experiences of others, and in some cases we're not even learning from our own experience.

So we confronted a very fundamental reality, which was that if we go on the way that we're going, we're really not going to make a hell of a lot of progress. And so we decided that, as a matter of course, understanding what others were doing, in the multilateral sector, in the bilateral sector, and in civil society and the private sector, was an essential prerequisite to effective development

As we thought of the challenge and the problems of the Millennium Development Goals, we also recognized that looking at issues on the basis of projects was not adequate, because there was a huge need for consistency and time in order to be able to reach the goals that we're seeking. In fact, with the Millennium goals we're talking about a 15-year time frame in which we have to keep going. So the issue of management, the issue of bringing all of this together, the issue of controlling it, and the issue of harmonization became, for us, central, because we were aware that we certainly couldn't do it alone, and we became very much aware that nobody can do this alone.

That led to the very obvious conclusion that we had to change, and in the last few years we have really tried to do that. But there are these perceptions on the part of all of us about each other that are, unfortunately, quite fixed. The nongovernmental organizations think that we're terrible. We think some of the NGOs are terrible. Some of you think we're terrible. Some of us think you're terrible. So we're getting stuck in these old, outdated perceptions about each other, which are difficult to get through.

And so the first thing to do is say, "Listen, there's no way any of us can do it alone. Let's come together." And that means a big culture change for many of us, and central to that is harmonizing our efforts.

At my first meeting of the United Nations Development Programme, I remember the leader at the time saying that he thought, after I'd been at the Bank and had been saying this for a few months, that this was a very constructive thing, and they looked forward to coordinating the activities of the World Bank.

I said, "Wait a minute! I didn't say you could coordinate us. I said we'd cooperate."

And I guess all of us feel the same way: none of us wants to be coordinated. We all want to have our own independent views, but we must come together in a way that shows some consistency, some harmony, and some sense of each other. And so the first people who have to change is us, and that, I guess, is the purpose of this meeting, to try and see how we can change in order to make the work of people like President Mkapa and his colleagues on the ground more effective. And so I think this meeting is incredibly important. My colleagues will explain to you later some of the changes that we've made, and we will discuss some specific examples of activities where we've worked together. And I pay tribute to the DAC* and the OECD Working Group for the enormous advances that they've made. And I think that we and the regional development banks have also made advances.

But what I hope might emerge from these two days of meetings is an understanding of each other, so that we are prepared to look at each other with different eyes, and prepared to come together to set some objectives to emerge in the final statement that can be practical, that can be focused, and that we can review a year from now to evaluate our achievements and hold ourselves mutually accountable. Because the last point I'd make is that achieving the Millennium goals, dependent as that is on each of the countries, is from our point of view a matter of mutual accountability. We have tried, under pressure from our shareholders, to evaluate the Bank's contribution to the Millennium goals, and I must tell you it's tough to get a framework of

---

* The Development Assistance Committee of the Organisation for Economic Co-operation and Development.

measurement of an individual organization's contributions to these goals. I think we'll be able to make some progress toward that, but the end result is only going to be a collective achievement, and that means harmonization, and that means coming together.

My colleagues and I are really thrilled to be part of this meeting. We look forward to contributing, we look forward to learning, and we look forward to coming out of this meeting with a final statement that is a statement for action and for cooperation and partnership.

Thank you, Mr. Chairman.

SCALE UP THE GLOBAL FIGHT AGAINST TUBERCULOSIS:
A KILLER RETURNS

With Gro Harlem Brundtland, published in the *International Herald Tribune*

MARCH 25, 2003

In this essay, Wolfensohn teams up with World Health Organization
Director-General Gro Harlem Brundtland to call for action in ending
tuberculosis. The two leaders urge the Group of Eight, whose annual summit
would be held three months later, to expand the fight against tuberculosis.

Ten years ago the World Health Organization declared a global emergency to
battle the resurgent epidemic of tuberculosis. The international community is
making steady headway in coping with the crisis, but "steady" is too slow.
Two million people die from tuberculosis every year, worn down slowly and
painfully by an infectious disease that destroys their lungs and wastes their bodies. The epidemic is still growing in Africa and countries of the former Soviet
Union.

Tuberculosis thrives on poverty and social disruption. It is a close compan-
ion of AIDS as it takes advantage of the weakened immune systems of those
who are infected with the AIDS virus. The emergence of drug-resistant strains
has revived the centuries-old reputation of tuberculosis as the "Captain of
Death." Yet there is an effective weapon against this killer.

The directly observed treatment short-course, known as DOTS, ensures
that people suffering from tuberculosis are fully treated with a powerful combination of drugs under the regular supervision of health workers or community volunteers. The treatment costs $10 or less for six months of drugs and
uses primary care services. Over the past few years, DOTS has turned the tuberculosis tide in several countries and more will follow suit. Since 1993,
10 million tuberculosis patients have been treated successfully worldwide,
more than 90 percent of them in developing countries. A total of 155 countries have now adopted the DOTS strategy, which is vital to ensuring high
cure rates and preventing the spread of infection. China and India have shown
remarkable progress in expanding population coverage while maintaining high
cure rates. Some 50,000 new tuberculosis patients are put on effective therapy
each month in India alone. In China, active tuberculosis cases fell by 35 percent
in areas applying DOTS over the last decade. Other countries, such as Peru
and Vietnam, have already surpassed 2005 targets for tuberculosis detection
and treatment.

But only a third of all people with tuberculosis are being treated under
DOTS programs. We must move much faster in scaling up and reaching out
to communities at greatest risk. The life and hope of those living with the
AIDS virus are being extended by treating them with anti-retroviral medi-

cines. DOTS must become part of the treatment package for the millions of people infected with both the AIDS virus and tuberculosis. We must also improve health systems so that they can respond faster to public health threats. Community and political leaders can be mobilized far more.

The countries with the highest tuberculosis burdens, together with the Group of Eight governments, the World Health Organization, the World Bank, nongovernmental organizations, foundations, universities and committed individuals such as George Soros and Bill Gates,* are supporting the Global Plan to Stop Tuberculosis and are committed to the Stop Tuberculosis Partnership. The new Global Fund to Fight AIDS, Tuberculosis and Malaria is a major new contributor to this work and is bringing still more energy to the fight. Through these partners, hundreds of millions more dollars are now available for DOTS expansion, innovative responses to AIDS-associated tuberculosis and drug-resistant tuberculosis, and research and development for new diagnostics, drugs and vaccines. Even so, this is still well under the $1 billion more that is needed annually to change the trajectory of tuberculosis control. As Group of Eight leaders prepare to meet in France in June, they should unite in scaling up the fight against tuberculosis and other major diseases. Millions of lives hang in the balance.

---

* Founder and chairman of the Open Society Institute and the Soros foundations network, and co-founder of the Bill & Melinda Gates Foundation, respectively.

Statement at the World Trade Organization General Council Meeting on Coherence

GENEVA | MAY 13, 2003

Wolfensohn uses his first address before the WTO General Council as an opportunity to spell out why, as he sees it, trade and development issues go hand in hand. He notes in particular what he calls the "eye-catching statistics" that the wealthy countries spend $300 billion to subsidize their agriculture while giving only about $50 billion in development assistance.

Mr. Chairman, Mr. Director-General,* My Colleague Horst Köhler,[†] Your Excellencies:

You must understand that, after eight years at the World Bank, it is the peak of my expectations to come and speak to this group, which, I know, beavers away at the issues of trade and speaks a language that I scarcely understand but know to be important.

To arrive here and, after a significant briefing by my colleagues, to try and get the language right is a hazardous task for someone who's just come from Bhutan.

I tell you that because, in Bhutan, issues such as trade and finance are all measured in terms of human happiness, and I nearly stayed there because it seems so much simpler than the work that you're doing here, or indeed the work that we do at the Bank. But nonetheless I came back because Dr. Supachai gave a remarkable presentation at the IMFC meetings,[‡] and indeed my colleagues and I have, in recent years, sought to build the relationships that we have with this distinguished body.

Putting it in my own terms, the reason we are here is that our daily work, in terms of poverty alleviation and the advocacy we are engaged in, both in Monterrey and in Johannesburg,[§] in relation to the questions of poverty and the improvement of social equity and the achievement of the Millennium goals, about which my colleague Horst Köhler has spoken, has at the center a range of important contributions that we speak of regularly. When we speak of Monterrey and Johannesburg, we talk of a partnership between the developed and the developing countries, we talk about the undertakings on the part of developing countries to improve governance, to have legal and judi-

---

* Supachai Panitchpakdi, director-general of the World Trade Organization.
† Managing director of the International Monetary Fund.
‡ The International Monetary and Financial Committee meetings were held in Ottawa in November 2001 in lieu of the regular Bank-Fund Annual Meetings, which were not held following the September 11 attacks.
§ The International Conference on Financing for Development was held in Monterrey, Mexico, in March 2002; the World Summit on Sustainable Development was held in Johannesburg in August and September 2002.

cial reform, to have financial sector reform, to build capacity, and to fight corruption.

With NEPAD [the New Partnership for Africa's Development], the African countries have taken actions not because they are forced on them, but because the countries themselves have decided that these are essential preconditions to development. The developed countries, for their part, have said, "If you do those things, we will give you support and capacity building, and we will increase the development assistance that is made available, provided that it is spent effectively." They also said, "And we will open our markets for trade."

Today it is this issue of trade that we are addressing. And when we talk about coherence, it is integral to the work that we are doing in the Bank that trade be considered alongside each of these other considerations. Yet all too often trade is treated as a subject for specialists, without being integrated into a coherent discussion. We at the Bank don't even attend the meetings as observers in relation to trade. I'm not seeking to do that because, frankly, I go to enough meetings. But it would be sensible to have people around the trade negotiating table who are addressing the fundamental question of development, and we would like to be present to make whatever contribution we could in terms of trade, just as Dr. Supachai and the WTO should be present in the meetings of our bodies.

But it is impossible to consider the question of economic development and the question of equity, about which Horst Köhler has spoken, without an integral consideration of the question of trade. It makes absolutely no sense to help countries boost their agricultural production if they have no markets for that production. It makes absolutely no sense to boost industrial production if tariffs and other inhibitions to trade do not permit the sale of those manufactures.

The opening of markets in developing countries to manufacturers from more efficient and more productive developed countries is also something that, as a matter of policy, should be adopted, but one also has to understand the fragility of these countries and the need for proper sequencing and the importance of giving them support, so that they can adapt to the new conditions of free trade as they are set up under the WTO agreements.

So, at whatever level, the issue of a coherent approach to development includes necessarily the issues of reformation of the economic structure, reformation of the social structure, and reformation of the trading structure. And that is indeed what you're engaged in, in the Doha Round [of multilateral trade negotiations], and why it's necessary to integrate the considerations that the IMF addresses with the work that Horst and his colleagues are doing, and the work that we at the Bank are doing into the work that you are doing. And may I say that my own judgment is that we have come a long way at the staff level, but

I am absolutely delighted that we now have a chance to engage at this level, where I think the exchanging of ideas is all too infrequent.

So I'm delighted to be here, and there are three particular areas that I'd like to address. The first, in terms of what we think is important, is the issue of coherence between trade and development in the field of agriculture. My colleague Horst Köhler has already addressed a number of these issues, and you are very familiar with the rhetoric.

We speak quite often of the $50 billion or so that is available in overseas development assistance, and of the $300-plus billion that is provided in the developed countries in agricultural subsidies. We frequently cite the rather amusing statistic that the average European cow lives on a subsidy of $2.50 a day, at a time when 3 billion people in the world are living on less than $2 a day. And, for the benefit of my Japanese friends here, the average Japanese cow lives on a subsidy of $7.50 a day. These are, of course, eye-catching statistics, but they do, in fact, reflect the imbalance between current subsidies and our professed belief in free and open access to markets in agriculture. And given, as Horst reminded us, that poverty is so often a rural phenomenon, it is for us at the center of our considerations in terms of the alleviation of poverty. What we are looking for, as a matter of advocacy for poor people, is what many of you are seeking, namely, a better deal in terms of agriculture, and one that would allow for effective development and effective addressing of the question of poverty. We also recognize that this is not just a North-South issue, that the South-South issue is equally important, that 25 percent of world trade is between South and South, and that development is already taken into consideration in your deliberations and recognized as important. We also recognize that freeing up markets will affect some people favorably and some people badly, relative to existing preferences, and that there will be a need for a period of adjustment.

We have looked at a series of issues within the agricultural area:

- One, of course, is the cutting of subsidies in OECD countries, especially those subsidies that have the greatest impact on production, and instead using transparent, decoupled payments to support farmers' incomes and meet rural development objectives.
- Another is a formula for tariff cutting that results in genuine cuts in tariff levels and tariff escalation in all countries, and that gives credit for liberalization that is undertaken between negotiations.
- Another is the conversion of tariff rate quotas in agriculture and specific duties to ad valorem tariffs, which provide more transparent protection.
- We also suggest development of a safeguard mechanism that protects poor producers against import surges, while encouraging tariff liberalization.

- Finally, we advocate the adoption of liberal unilateral rules of origin under preference schemes such as the Everything but Arms agreement and the African Growth and Opportunity Act,** especially for clothing and textiles, with these rules harmonized across countries.

Let me add here that, of course, while agriculture is at the center of what we have in mind here, it's not the only thing that matters to developing countries, and that the service sector, your work on TRIPs [trade-related aspects of intellectual property rights], on public health, and the antidumping discussions are all central to the work that we are engaged in. And these are all areas where it is obviously essential that we have cohesion in the discussions that are being undertaken here.

Let me now speak to the issue of a rational framework for special and differential treatment [for developing countries], which is an area on which, although I have spent now some hours on it, I will not set myself up as an expert. I'm sure all of you know a great deal more about it than I do. I did, however, ask my colleagues to do a research paper for me to see if there was a way in which we could make some contribution, and, like the Fund, we, too have explored this issue. And we have come up with some approaches that might be relevant and useful, and which we're submitting to the director-general, but which essentially approach this issue not on the basis of individual treatment, but instead suggest some more generalized approaches for consideration. We are also exploring the possibility of all exports from low-income countries entering the OECD countries tariff and quota free, and we note that doing so would simplify rules of origin.

We recognize the problems faced in the poorest countries in implementing the WTO rules, the issue of capacity and resources, and let me say here that we've been working for some time with the Secretariat to support training and capacity building, using distance learning. We have devised some answers to this problem together, which I believe have shown some merit and have been quite useful in the work that you're doing.

We've also recognized that, if you get rid of special and differential treatment, in the poorer countries that have been asked to accept WTO principles there is a significant concern about fragility. Therefore the issues of timing and support and contributing to the safety net are ones on which we at the World Bank can help. As you make your decisions in relation to trade, we are a natural

---

** The Everything but Arms initiative of the European Union, approved in February 2001, grants duty-free access to the world's 48 least-developed countries for all goods except arms; the African Growth and Opportunity Act was enacted by the United States in May 2000.

partner to assist the countries affected in terms of that safety net and that necessary support.

Also, as my friend Horst mentioned, in our work with countries on their Poverty Reduction Strategy Papers and in the strategies that we're setting forth, the whole question of trade has been integral. Indeed, it is taking an increasingly important place in the work that we are doing.

Finally, of course, there is the question of better integration and cooperation between us at the institutional level. The fact that this is the first time in eight years that I have come here suggests that each of us is going in our own different ways. We know, however, that we cannot go our separate ways on this issue of trade, and it's important to bring not just us, but also UNCTAD, the UNDP, the ITC, and the OECD†† all together, under the leadership of the WTO. Progress on the trade front is crucial for all of us in terms of achieving our individual objectives, and so the need to enhance the relationships among us is apparent. I looked at the work that we're doing on the Integrated Framework in conjunction with the WTO. Specifically, I looked at the action plan for Senegal, which is not just an action plan on trade, but an action plan that relates to how the economy functions, to capacity building, to the physical resources needed to take advantage of trade opportunities, to the whole question of development, the whole issue of education, of training, even of health, and it gets into the questions that we're dealing with here. So it is sort of nonsensical that we haven't had a better approach to improving the coherence of our endeavors until today, and we are indeed extraordinarily happy that this new approach has been suggested by your director-general to build on the work of our staffs. It is something that we are more than happy and indeed anxious to be supportive of.

So let me say in conclusion, Mr. Chairman, our mandate from our Board is the alleviation of poverty, and within the question of alleviating poverty we have a number of issues to address, but central among them is the question of trade. We cannot deal with poverty without dealing with the question of trade, and so we welcome very much the opportunity to exchange views with you here, we look forward to continuing discussions, and I want to say how much I appreciate the chance of coming and being with you to open this new dialogue.

Thank you very much, Mr. Chairman.

---

†† The United Nations Conference on Trade and Development, the United Nations Development Programme, the International Trade Centre, and the Organisation for Economic Co-operation and Development.

Keynote address at the German World Bank Forum

BONN, GERMANY | MAY 20, 2003

> *This speech in Bonn at the annual German World Bank Forum focuses on knowledge, research, and the use of science and information in development. The Forum, which has been held regularly since 1995, brings together about 350 German leaders to discuss development issues.*

Well, thank you very much, Mr. Chairman and Madam Mayor.*

She's actually my mayor, because I'm an honorary citizen of Bonn, I think, and I advise you all to come to the Beethoven Festival. I advise you all to come and look at this dynamic city. I'm really learning my script very well about Bonn and can only be supportive and grateful for the opportunity to be here once again where, in fact, the World Bank Forum started six years ago. So we're very grateful to you, Madam Mayor. We're very grateful to our friends in Nord Rhein-Westphalia, to Minister President [Peer] Steinbruck, and to you, Dr. Berkel, and to Deutsche Telekom, particularly to Mr. Schutz,[†] and indeed especially grateful to all of you, many of whom have come multiple times to our meetings.

The discussion today on the knowledge economy is extremely important and, I must say, is something of a welcome relief to me from the last couple of weeks. For, in the course of discussing the World Bank and the issues of development lately, most of the discussion has been about Iraq, about the slowdown in the international economy, about geopolitics, and about the strains in the North Atlantic alliance. The focus has been on immediate pressures of a geopolitical nature, which have tended to push aside the questions of development and the issues that we typically address at these meetings.

It would be easy for me now to give you a very long talk on what I have learned in the last couple of weeks from meetings with the Group of Eight and with heads of government. And I'm tempted to talk about that subject. But then I was told that that's not the subject of today's meeting. Today's meeting is about the knowledge economy. And so my frustration will be relieved tonight at dinner, if anybody comes, when I'm told that I can have a fireside chat and give you all indigestion about my views on the global scene, and, I hope, generate some discussion on broader subjects. Because you cannot look at the knowledge economy, you cannot look at any sector, in terms

---

* Bärbel Dieckmann, Mayor of Bonn.
† Officials at Deutsche Telekom.

of how it's going to be effective or ineffective if you don't position it within the context of the world in which we're currently living. And it is fair to say that the world in which we're currently living poses some problems that are somewhat different from the ones we've faced in the last six years. So tonight I'll have a chance, for those of you interested, to talk a little bit about those broader questions, and I very much look forward to an exchange of views.

But today is not for that purpose. It's to tell you instead a little bit about the Bank and the knowledge economy, because in past meetings we have not in any intensity addressed this question of the importance of knowledge to what we do and to the general principle of the two-part Bank: the Bank that is a money bank and the Bank that is a knowledge bank. And this distinction between the two parts, which, obviously, subsequently fuse as a partnership between knowledge and money, is really the subject that I'd like to spend a few moments discussing with you now, because it's something that I hope you, as friends of the Bank, will understand as you think of our institution, which has evolved significantly in the last eight years toward becoming that knowledge-based institution.

If I cast my mind back on history, of course, we've seen very substantial progress as a result of technological advances in the last couple of hundred years. I normally speak of the 2.8 billion people in the world who live on less than two dollars a day and the 1.2 billion who live on less than one dollar a day, and those numbers are, of course, correct. But what is also correct is that, in the last 100 years, from 1892 to 1992, when the measurement was done, real annual income per person worldwide grew from $650 on average to close to $5,000 on average. And life expectancy grew from a mere 27 years to 61 years. So we should not ignore the fact that technology and knowledge and science have brought us a long way, notwithstanding the fact, which we, of course, bemoan but also view as a challenge, that we now must deal with the question of poverty on a pretty large scale.

So when we sat down some eight years ago, my colleagues and I, to look at the world, we took a look first at ourselves as an institution and then at the world outside. And let me share with you what we found, because it's been quite a voyage of discovery. Eight years ago we were making the assumption that we *were* the Knowledge Bank. We were making the assumption that, with 50 years of history, we really knew everything, or, if not everything, nearly everything. And we made the assumption that we were there to tell the world all about development, and some people would even have said that we were slightly arrogant in the way we did it. Some people here might have said we were more than slightly arrogant, that we were very arrogant in the way we went about it.

And the so-called Washington Consensus,‡ if not born at the Bank, was carried through there as a sort of prototype example, which our institution could fit comfortably on any given country and everything would work. And whether it was privatization or whether it was the issue of opening capital markets or whether it was a framework for political development, we had the knowledge and we were there and we were the World Bank.

Fortunately, a few of us sat down and said, "Well, is this true?" And we discovered a number of things. The first was that our knowledgeable people were leaving our institution with their knowledge. When they left, they were taking their files with them. Why? Because no one was gathering that knowledge. And they were concerned that the thing that they'd spent their life's work on was going to be buried in a vault somewhere, never to be retrieved, and that the history of their experience was going into a mountain. And so, not surprisingly, our best people, when they left the institution took the information, took their knowledge with them, so that they could have something that would remind them of their period at the Bank, and it was lost to our institution.

We also discovered that half the people in our institution were consultants. Now, consultants have absolutely no incentive to give the knowledge they had to us at the Bank, because if they gave us all their knowledge, we wouldn't need them any more. And so we had a group of consultants who would advise us, but who were extraordinarily careful to keep the information to themselves, because otherwise they wouldn't be reengaged. They would do this or that individual project, but, in terms of sharing experience, there was an inbuilt rigidity in the organization.

The third thing we discovered was that our people were not renewing their knowledge. We looked at the career development of people in our institution, and they came in at their peak as young professionals and very well trained, but we were not putting enough effort into reinvigorating their knowledge and giving them a chance to learn, to study, to go work with other companies or with institutions around the world. And so we had this situation where people were coming in and, instead of engaging in lifelong learning, were repeating what they'd already known, as strengthened by the other young people who came in who had the same experience. What I'm describing is, unfortunately, not solely the experience of the Bank but is true in many organizations that don't give enough attention to the question of nurturing knowledge.

---

‡ The term "Washington Consensus" was coined by John Williamson in 1989 and refers to economic reforms in 10 areas that most of official Washington (including the international financial institutions and most major economic think tanks) at that time agreed that developing countries with debt problems should pursue.

We also discovered that our people who were dealing with the question of poverty knew very little about poverty. Very few of them had done more than visit projects. And so we thought we would try and do two things. First, to try and change the orientation of the institution to one that would value knowledge and value change, we started a program, which 600 of our top people have now gone through, about understanding change, understanding knowledge, and understanding the importance of that second bank, the Knowledge Bank. And second, we asked our people to go spend a week in a slum or in a village, living in poverty, so that they would understand what it was that they were talking about. And this had a profound impact on our institution.

Now, none of this has to do with Internet technology or regulation. It has to do, very simply, with an orientation that says that, if you're going to be a Knowledge Bank, you'd better manage the knowledge. You'd better think about how you're going to preserve the information and how you're going to spread it.

And so, after about a year of this, we held a Knowledge Fair at our institution, which I will never forget. We said to people, "Look, if you have knowledge of a particular area, why don't we try and build a knowledge base?" And, as some of my colleagues here will remember, we had a fair in which people set up booths, saying, "We have a justice system," or "We have a transportation system," or "We have a health system," and people would come to these booths and sign up to say, "I will give you some of my information so we can build a database." And this was extraordinarily exciting because we had 60 or so of these booths around our institution where people would come up and say, "I know something about this. I'd like to sign up for an exchange of information."

Well, that was the beginning for us of what was truly an adventure, which has gone incredibly quickly and has enormously enriched our institution. It has led us to the developments in the Global Gateway, about which you'll hear tomorrow, in which we said, basically, "How many projects have there been in our institution? What has been our experience? What is the good experience? What is the bad experience?" And we discovered, if I have the number right, that a total of 400,000 separate development projects had been launched, by both the Bank and others in the development field, in the last 10 years. And we discovered that at the time there were 63,000 projects currently going on in the development business. We discovered, looking at it by country, that if you went to Bangladesh or Burkina Faso and you were interested in, say, primary health care or secondary education, there were, in addition to the projects we had, perhaps 15 or 20 that others had, and which we knew very little about until we started to consolidate and bring together this information.

All this has led not only to a change in our own institution, but, I think, to something that is not measured in terms of growth in lending but which has been for me maybe the most significant development in the last eight years. And that is the bringing together of not just our knowledge but the knowledge of the international development community, of the private sector, and of civil society. Because why make the same mistakes twice? Why not profit from the experience of others?

It led us also to say that it's not just the professionals who know about this. Let's start with the poor. So we started a study five years ago called *Voices of the Poor,* in which we interviewed 60,000 poor people in 60 different countries to find out what they knew about poverty. We did it because that was our business, to try and deal with the question of poverty. So what was more logical than to talk to poor people? Except that we had not done it before in an organized way.

And what we discovered about poor people has been at the core of the way in which our own development paradigm is now working. We discovered that poor people are no different from rich people. They don't want charity; they want an opportunity. Women don't want to be beaten; they want to live a civilized life and to have opportunity. They all want an opportunity for their children. They want a sense of standing. They want voice. They want a chance to work in a protected environment. They want freedom from crime. And they want a chance to develop themselves and their kids.

You may say that that is an obvious set of conclusions, but it was an enormously enriching one for us because it allowed us then to conceive of our own approaches, not as financial approaches, but as approaches based on the people with whom we were working. It allowed us to change our perception of poor people from being the object of the problem or the object of charity to becoming the engine of the solution. Because if you do not have a community base to work with, if you don't build on the knowledge of the people, there is no way of getting an inclusive approach to development.

I wanted to tell you this because it has brought about a huge change in the nature of our organization. It is now much more humanistic. It is now much more based on people. It is now much more based on experience. Of course, there is still an understanding that, without economic growth, without structure, it's very difficult to do anything about development. But the crucial element in the work that we're doing is that of gathering experience and bringing it together in a coordinated way, bringing together poor people, governments, civil society, and the private sector in a shared knowledge experience so that we don't have to keep making the same mistakes over and over again, and so that together we can move forward, using knowledge as the most important resource we have.

That has been really a significant change for us, and we have won quite a number of prizes for what I think is doing the obvious. People say we're terrific at knowledge management. Various American academies keep putting us in the top 10 for doing something that seems to us incredibly logical. But, in fact, for us it was something that we were assuming but not managing as effectively as we could. And, of course, the possibilities that technology has opened have enriched our ability, as some of our speakers have said today, to gather this information, to use it, to make it accessible, and to cross-reference it. As a result, now, in the case of the Global Gateway, in which we've had such support from this region and from the German government and others, that information can be accessed and used.

Technology has also led us to two more strong developments. One was the greater emphasis that we now put on research, to take this information and try and get cutting-edge research, whether it be on conflict or education or water, so that now, as some of you know, we are doing a plethora of research reports, not just alone but with partners and with research institutions throughout the world. We've put together a group of, I think, some 300 research institutions—not all of them developed-country research institutions but also institutions in the countries we work in. And, using technology today, much of the research that we're doing is joint research in various parts of the world, so that, again using technology, we can bridge this geographic gap.

Beyond that is the issue of how we then interface with our clients. And here we came immediately to the understanding that the low- and middle-income countries were very far behind the developed countries. The numbers were quite astonishing to us. I remember looking at research and development expenditure in low-income and lower-middle-income countries, and even in upper-middle-income countries, and finding that the total was only 7 percent of R&D expenditure worldwide, with the high-income countries doing the other 93 percent. And 99 percent of all patents were coming from the wealthy countries, and a mere 1 percent from the poor and middle-income countries.

We also looked at education and, not surprisingly, discovered that average years of schooling in the lower- and middle-income countries was half what it was in the developed countries. We also looked at schooling and income and, not surprisingly, discovered that the best-educated people made the most money, and the ones without much education made less.

And so we started a series of initiatives. We decided that, if today you can do research anywhere in the world, we would start Millennium Science Institutes, to try and keep developing-country scientists and researchers in their own countries, doing not just economic and social research but research in the natural sciences, much of it geared much better to being done in those countries than to doing it in another place. I think, for example, of the work that's being done in the Amazon on the environment. If you go to the Amazon and see the research centers that we're supporting there—which the German government, by the way, is supporting also—you couldn't imagine it being done anywhere else, because it couldn't be done any better.

In our work in science and in agriculture, together with the Rockefeller Foundation and some others, 50 years ago we set up a group called the Consultative Group on International Agriculture Research, or CGIAR, which has within it some 40 different agricultural research centers, whose work brought about the Green Revolution. And this research is done not in the United States and not in Germany, but in the countries themselves. And that perhaps more than any other single research organization has affected the growth and quality of life in the developing world.

And so we are trying to bring together the knowledge that is there and the applications that we've been working in. But we then discovered, as so many of you know, that there's a big gap between knowledge and application. My first trip to a CGIAR institution was more than 35 years ago when I went to Mexico. I was then on the board of the Rockefeller Foundation, and we had new varieties of corn that grew twice as tall as the traditional varieties. And the question then was, How do you convince the farmer to plant a seed that he's never seen before? And I remember going literally barefoot with some of my colleagues across the fields, and we discovered that just telling them was not good enough. You essentially had to bribe a couple of farmers to try it. And then they would teach their colleagues, once they saw that this corn really was twice as high as the other.

Long after that very simple experience that I had all those years ago, we are still seeking to engage with the users of knowledge, so that knowledge is not just something in books but something useful, because of the ways in which it can be applied. And there, too, I think we have made very significant strides, whether it be the example of Botswana, as we heard earlier, or whether it be in terms of encouraging countries in terms of their adoption of research practices, although in some cases we have been very successful and in others not. I think only of the examples that others here have mentioned: how 40 years ago Korea and Ghana were at the same level of income per capita, and since then Korea's has gone up ninefold while Ghana is still where it was. But we're now working with the Ghanaian authorities, belatedly, to try and see if we can encourage what they're doing right.

So this reaching out became something that we needed to do, but we also needed to make ourselves accessible. And here we had, again, another advance, because we decided that, if we've got all this knowledge, we had better make it available and become an international knowledge institution. So we decided that we would link every one of our offices by satellite, and that we would have, as we now have, more than 100 videoconference facilities in our offices. We're running 1,500 videoconferences a month. We're averaging 80 countries a day. Whether you come into our office in Côte d'Ivoire or in Botswana or in Brazil, you can today meet face to face not only with professionals but with other government people or civil society people around the world.

In Mexico, we have extended our teaching by not just relying on our own network, but by using the Monterrey Institute of Technology's network, which was already quite extensive. Now every Saturday morning, Madam Mayor, we link with a thousand mayors of towns and villages in seven countries in Latin America, working on such things as budgeting or sewage collection or water. And this learning continues through the week, because we provide the mayors not only the knowledge that we have through Monterrey, through the professors who work with them on Saturday, but also a Web page and a chat room that goes on during the week. And here the thing that we did not anticipate came into play, which is that mayors ask questions, which are then answered by other mayors. A community of mayors is being built, so that you have not us trying to convince somebody, but South–South cooperation, which is just infinitely better and infinitely more effective.

We also had decided that we wouldn't just leave it to our own offices, but that we would establish a network of distance learning centers. I established a target of 100 distance learning centers. My colleagues at the time thought I was crazy. I said I want centers that have 30 seats, double screen, an adjacent room with 30 computers, and a place where people can meet. We now have 54 of these centers around the world, and we're running a huge variety of classes and interchanges, on everything from how to fight corruption to how to deal with water issues along the Nile. This is a daily occurrence.

And, beyond that, we now have a virtual university in Africa, with 14 universities connected, running degree courses in various languages—in Spanish, French, Portuguese, and English, but also in some cases in Wolof, Hausa, and Swahili.

These are extraordinary developments in terms of using the kinds of technology that Deutsche Telekom is involved in, but which for us is now becoming a tool in relation to our broader issue of how to use knowledge as an asset that is just as important, if not more important, than money. And the curious and remarkable thing for us is that, in these last few years, as we've been recognized for the work that we've done on knowledge, it has all seemed just essentially so logical. What is so remarkable about what we've done? Well, there's nothing really remarkable except that we hadn't done it. And now we've done it. And I must tell you that it is transforming our institution and the attitudes of the people in our institution, encouraging them to care about knowledge and to learn from people, not just within the Bank but from the outside, because the most cherished thing we have in our institution now is better know-how. And this changes the culture of the institution, because it makes us more modest. Once you're exposed to the creativity and the knowledge of the outside world, you can't be as arrogant as you were before.

I don't want to claim victory yet for what we're doing. We're expanding all the time. We have 200,000 schoolchildren linked on computers, with 30,000 teachers in 30 different countries. All the time we're looking for new ways in which we can do more. But I do want you to know that an evolution is taking place in our institution. And while it may not sound dramatic, for us it is a huge change in orientation and is changing the nature of our organization.

For those of you who know our organization and have been loyal and have come to our meetings, we thought today would be a good opportunity to present to you this somewhat unseen development in what we're doing, to bring to your attention that it's not just high-tech, it's not just razzle-dazzle. It is a commitment to the fundamental belief that money is important but that knowledge and know-how and partnership are even more important.

Finally, let me say that this has led us further into a better understanding of culture, and let me recognize Mr. [Michael] Hoffmann [director-general in the German Ministry of Economic Cooperation] and others that are here from the German government, who have shown tremendous support for us in this endeavor to make knowledge a central activity.

It is an extraordinarily powerful tool, and it is one that we're seeking to build on. With its own technological developments and its own commitment to development, Germany is a remarkable partner for us to have. And I want to thank all of you for being good partners with us, and I especially want to thank our hosts of today, our German government colleagues, for the support that we've received in this endeavor.

Thank you very much.

Remarks at the Bretton Woods Committee Annual Meeting

WASHINGTON, D.C. | JUNE 12, 2003

At this meeting held at the U.S. State Department, Wolfensohn's speech followed remarks by U.S. Secretary of State Colin Powell. In the address, Wolfensohn comments on the United States' new Millennium Challenge Account, which would provide increased development assistance to those developing countries that have taken certain concrete reforms.

This is a very important moment in the life of the World Bank, and I am enormously grateful to the secretary of state for such a vivid and encompassing description of the way development is now looked at. And I hope that in these few moments I can tell you where the World Bank fits into that description, and to say thank you, not only to those at the dais here but all of you, for the interest that you are showing in the Bretton Woods institutions [the World Bank and the International Monetary Fund], because never before have we needed you so much as we need you today. And we are extraordinarily grateful that an independent and well-informed group such as this is there for us to count on.

Much of the debate over the development paradigm has now taken place. At the time of the Millennium Assembly of the United Nations, it was recognized that the key objectives for the planet in the coming years could be described in the Millennium Development Goals. And those goals, which every head of state signed, spoke of halving world poverty by 2015. They spoke of dealing with issues of the human condition and the environment, and they established quite meticulous and specific goals that countries should attain.

The Millennium Assembly left open exactly how we would get there, but that assembly was followed by a number of other meetings: the annual meetings of the Group of Eight and, in the interim period, the meetings in Monterrey and Johannesburg.* Those meetings in turn were followed by Africa's own contribution, the NEPAD [the New Partnership for Africa's Development], which set out a form of compact or partnership or understanding of the kind that the secretary of state was talking about.

The concept of the Millennium goals is really quite simple: the leaders of the developing countries—home to 5 billion of the 6 billion people on our planet—agreed to take into their hands, on behalf of their people, the job of

---

* The International Conference on Financing for Development was held in Monterrey, Mexico, in March 2002; the World Summit on Sustainable Development was held in Johannesburg in August and September 2002.

running their countries and being accountable for them. And they have said in various different ways—at Monterrey, at Johannesburg, and in NEPAD—exactly the same thing: "We want to run the countries, as we should. We want to have a form of governance that we decide on, as we should. We want to strengthen the capacity of governance. We want to have legal and judicial systems that protect rights. We want financial systems that are clean and that allow for development, from microcredit through to major corporations. And we want to fight corruption. And, with that backdrop, we then want to have our own plans for development, plans that are comprehensive."

Whether these plans are called comprehensive frameworks or poverty reduction strategies or national plans matters little. But they should encompass education, health, infrastructure, the environment, the protection of culture, and the protection of the values of people in the society. And they should be built on what I call the structural necessities of good governance: legal and judicial reform, financial sector reform, and fighting corruption.

Countries are doing these things, first of all, because they believe it's the right thing to do for their people, and, second, because they understand that, if they do them, they will receive the assistance of the developed world. But these are not conditions being imposed by the Fund or by ourselves or by any other international institution. They are suggestions and indications coming from the countries themselves, because they think they are right. In the case of NEPAD, which includes 47 countries in Sub-Saharan Africa, the countries say not only that these are the right things to do, but also that they want to have peer review among the African countries, so that they can monitor each other on how they are moving toward this set of objectives. This is not the police force of the Bank or the Fund. This is peer review because it's right. That is a hugely significant change in the eight years I've been at the Bank.

On the other side, the rich world has said, "If you do all of that, we will help you with capacity building. We will help you with the kinds of structural reform that you want. We will try and deal with our own people who participate in corruption, because corruption has two sides. And we will increase the level of aid and open our markets for trade, because we understand that trade is a crucial element in the development process."

With these two sets of undertakings on either side, we are now right in the middle of seeing whether it is going to work. We will see whether the developing countries are able to uphold their commitments, and whether the rich world will respond.

In the context of this arrangement, however, came September 11, and in the couple of years since then we have seen, I think, a growing awareness that these two worlds, developing and developed, aren't separated by a wall but, in fact, are totally interdependent. Whatever the demonstrators might wish when they come out with their signs condemning globalization, the fact is that in recent years it has become absolutely evident that, while we define these worlds as two worlds for the purposes of the bargain, in fact they are interdependent. Whether it is on finance, whether it is on health, whether it is on migration or the environment or crime or drugs or trade, it's very clear to this audience, as it has been clear to us at the Bank for a long time, that each depends on the other. It is also clear that, in the pursuit of this new bargain, this partnership, it's not just one side looking to the other for charity or for help; rather it is something that is in the self-interest of everybody to address.

If anyone still doubts that it is one world, they should only recall the image of the World Trade Center collapsing, and words like "Afghanistan" and "Islamic fundamentalism" echoing at the center of Wall Street. That is enough to recognize that, whether it be Wall Street or the Pentagon, the walls do not exist. And if they did exist, they have now fallen down.

We now share a pretty clear understanding of what needs to be done, and at the Evian Summit [of the Group of Eight], which I attended, there was yet another restatement of those propositions, with some additions on certain key areas. AIDS, as the secretary said, is central. Water is another area that was regarded as central for this particular set of meetings. But there was also a recognition that the Millennium goals, in relation to poverty, education, health, and environment, remain nonetheless to be addressed.

And so we find ourselves at the Bank trying to assist the countries that have stated what they want to do. Sometimes that requires money, and, equally, sometimes it requires experience and knowledge. The Bank is doing two things that you need to be aware of. One is the provision of funding through the International Development Association, through the Bank itself, through the International Finance Corporation, and through the Multilateral Investment Guarantee Agency. And the other, which is integrated with the first, is the provision of services to help build capacity and to help countries reach the position that they are striving for.

The Millennium Challenge Account is also important in this context. It says that grant funding will be made available for the top 15 or 20 countries, those that meet the 18 criteria minus one, as the secretary said, with the exception of corruption, which all must meet. Those countries that make it into that privileged group will get assistance at the rate of $5 billion a year from 2006 onward, which will be provided as a grant. It is, in a sense, the prize that countries get for being top of the class. And that is great, commendable, and valuable.

But another 125 countries in the developing world, which we and the Fund and, to a degree, the U.S. Agency for International Development and other agencies have to deal with, are either on the cusp of qualifying for that assistance or a long way from it. We cannot leave them behind, because our job is not just to give prizes to the top 20, although we will do that. It is to consider the totality of the countries and address the very difficult issues of how to deal with countries that are in the process of change.

Two countries come to mind at the moment. One is [former Governor of the Central Bank of Brazil] Arminio Fraga's country, Brazil, where President Lula [da Silva] has come in with a remarkable opening series of positions and directions that he wishes to follow. There may be a lot of things to worry about in Brazil, but there is absolutely no question that we have to help Brazil succeed. The notion of a Latin America with an unsuccessful Brazil is simply not possible. And, with its neighbor Argentina, we also have to be certain that we do everything that we can, notwithstanding some frustrations, which [IMF First Deputy Managing Director] Anne Krueger here is familiar with, to bring Argentina to the point where it joins the countries in that group or at least espouses that as its objective.

The other country is Nigeria, where one in four Africans live, which has been through a period of corruption perhaps since its independence in 1960. Nigeria's president will, in the course of the next week, I hope, announce a clean cabinet, a cabinet designed to stand up to corruption and change the culture in the country, to bring it to the point where it is recognizably approaching that favored group. Nigeria is certainly not going to get money from the Millennium Challenge Account. But with one in four Africans living there, someone has to come in to provide assistance, and, I might tell you, the work that we're doing with the president of Nigeria at the moment has nothing to do with money. It has a lot to do with arguing, cajoling, helping, supporting, trying to bring about the conditions under which Nigeria will succeed, because one cannot imagine a successful Africa without a successful Nigeria. And the same is true for Kenya, in East Africa, which is now emerging from the period under President [Daniel] arap Moi and has a chance of moving forward.

One of the things we are discovering is essential as we try and bring about change in these countries is this: The countries in the developing world want to know for sure that the rich world is there to support them, not just once or twice within the current political framework, but over the long term and in scale. If they don't have that assurance, they are unlikely to respond. How can you get a country to agree to put every child in school, if you cannot say to them, "In addition to what you generate in your budget, we will be there for the next 10 years to give you funds that you can use for budgetary support, to pay teachers, so that you can reach your educational objectives"? If instead you tell them, "Well, we can do two or three years' worth of support," how can any legitimate president agree to change the system? How can he do that when in three years' time he may have to either drop the education program or re-work the whole budget?

What is it, then, that will convince these leaders that we're serious? They look at that partnership I have described, one of the key elements of which was the Doha Round [of multilateral trade negotiations]. What are they currently looking for in terms of bona fides from the rich world? When I was at Evian, I spoke to the leaders of the developing world, and they asked a legitimate question: "If you in the developed world think that trade is so important, why are you providing only about $50 billion in aid, while at the same time you are giving $350 billion in subsidies to your agricultural producers, and spending $900 billion on defense? You're making some very useful steps forward, with $5 billion in new aid from the United States and $8 billion from Europe. But you're still giving less than 0.25 percent of your GDP for development assistance, and you promised us 0.7 percent 20 years ago," which would be $170 billion a year. "And now you're telling us," they say, "on agriculture and on the other things we care about, that maybe there will be some bilateral deals. But you're running away from the very essence of your side of the partnership. And you're creating all sorts of questions in our minds about whether money will or won't be available to us, and we don't see the move toward an extra $50 billion or $75 billion, if we need it and if we qualify."

We have heard [U.K. Chancellor of the Exchequer] Gordon Brown talking about $50 billion in extra assistance, and we find [French economic minister] Francis Mer being very supportive of this move forward of the partnership. But the developing-country leaders are not yet convinced that this partner-ship is real. What they see is a predominant interest on our side in conflict and postconflict reconstruction. They see a spotty record on Afghanistan, and they see a focus on Iraq. They see a focus on real wars—although if those wars hap-pen to be in Africa, they get a lot less attention. What they don't see is a focus on the war against poverty, what I call "the other war." This other war is not front-page news. And this is where I think this committee and this group be-come important.

I remember the contract I signed long ago with Paul Volcker,[†] when he agreed to join my firm. We took a taxi to my apartment, and in the taxi we signed the contract, which consisted of 32 yellow pages that our lawyers had

---

† Upon Volcker's retirement in 1987 as chairman of the U.S. Federal Reserve Board, Wolfensohn persuaded him to become chairman of the board of his new firm, James D. Wolfensohn, Inc.

written—and we never looked at the contract again. What I'm saying is that, if you have an agreement with someone, if you come to a personal understanding, and if both of you have a passion about what it is you want to accomplish, you write a contract, but then you put the contract in the bottom drawer and you grab the idea and you run with it. You don't look at the contract any more. You make it work.

It's what I call the "period beyond contract." We're in that period now, in the contract between the developed and the developing world, where we need the passionate commitment of our government and other governments. We need to make sure that these agreements are carried out, not as a matter of contract, but as a matter of commitment and as a matter of belief—belief that this is the right thing to do and is in all our interests. And for me that is the testing point we find ourselves in at this moment.

I see in the contract a clear delineation of what everybody should do. What I have yet to see is enough passion to do it. What we saw from the secretary of state this morning was passion at the level I'd like to see it. If we had more people like the secretary expressing that passion, we'd have no problems. But even at this time of financial stress, when there is limited growth, when we know that we cannot deal with the question of development in a contractionary economic environment, we can still be making steps toward it. What we need today is the passionate commitment of people to make that contract work.

We need to put Monterrey and Johannesburg in a bottom drawer and be able to get on with it. We need to know that the culture has changed, to recognize that there is no wall, that we are interdependent, and that the right thing to do for our kids and for peace is to make all this work.

What we're trying to do at the World Bank—your World Bank, given that this is the Bretton Woods Committee—is to be advocates for that position and facilitators of the achievement of the contract that has been agreed. We're dealing with both sides. You may hear mostly about our work for developing countries, but we also need desperately the partnership that has been articulated with the developed world.

I believe the statements by [French] President Jacques Chirac at the Evian Summit were exactly along the lines that we need. I believe the statement by Secretary Powell and the statements by President Bush are exactly on the side that we need. But we also need a demonstration that there will be delivery, and Cancún[‡] is an essential building block for that demonstration, and another

---

‡ The World Trade Organization's Fifth Ministerial Conference took place in Cancún, Mexico, in September 2003.

is our upcoming [Bank-Fund] Annual Meetings, when we will look at the scale and the phasing in of funding, and the issue of how one gets to scale, and the issue of long-term commitments. That is still a matter of doubt for many people in the world.

And so we need your help, but we're a lot further along than we were 10 years ago. We have a much greater understanding. There are more and more people talking about the issues. But what we need now is the passion and the commitment to make it work, and this body can make a big difference, and I'm extremely grateful to you for your existence and for the help you give us.

Foreword to the 2003 Multilateral Investment Guarantee Agency *Annual Report*

PUBLISHED JUNE 30, 2003

In this foreword, Wolfensohn ties the role of the Multilateral Investment Guarantee Agency to the Bank's aim of achieving the Millennium Development Goals. MIGA serves as a catalyst, increasingly promoting foreign direct investment—a key driver of growth—into developing countries through its guarantees, technical assistance, and legal services.

The past fiscal year has been an especially challenging one, as a multitude of factors—including the conflict in Iraq and the SARS [severe acute respiratory syndrome] epidemic—have led to considerable global anxiety and uncertainty. This marks the second consecutive year that has been beset by troubles, and it means that the challenges facing the world's developing nations are all the more urgent. The impact of the ongoing economic malaise is undoubtedly being felt most acutely by the poor.

In this context, the institutions of the World Bank Group have an especially important role to play. The Millennium Development Goals, which aim to halve the number of people living in poverty in the world by 2015, remain as critically important targets. As economies around the world retrench, and markets stand still or retreat, it is vital for public institutions to step forward and try to bridge the gap. We remain committed to the mission of alleviating poverty, and to helping people help themselves and their environment by providing resources, sharing knowledge, building capacity, and forging partnerships in the public and private sectors.

MIGA continues to occupy a key position in achieving this mission. There remains an urgent need for private investment flows to developing countries. However, the uncertainties in the geopolitical environment greatly influence the risks that people are prepared to take in terms of investment and in terms of the larger outlook on their activities. This is precisely where an institution like MIGA makes a major difference.

This past year has seen MIGA's guarantee program maintain its level of coverage issued from the previous year's levels. Given the external environment, and the decline in foreign direct investment levels to developing countries, this is a noteworthy achievement. At the same time, the Agency has been able to support more projects in more countries than in fiscal year 2002, and has been able to deliver solid results in the Agency's priority areas of supporting investment into the world's poorest countries, particularly Sub-Saharan Africa; between developing countries; for small and medium-sized enterprises; and for complex infrastructure projects.

MIGA's technical assistance program continues to be extremely relevant, and the Agency has had a strong year in this regard. As foreign direct investment levels have been declining around the world, owing in large part to the hesitation of investors, the importance of host countries having a healthy investment climate cannot be understated. MIGA's capacity building and advisory services provide significant value to governments, and the Agency's suite of online services continues to expand its reach, enabling governments to actively promote opportunities quickly and efficiently to the investment community throughout the world.

Looking to the future, I see the role that MIGA can play only increasing in importance. Foreign investment will remain a crucial ingredient for all countries seeking to achieve economic development and poverty reduction. And MIGA's ability to catalyze investment, by helping investors mitigate risk and supporting host countries' investment promotion efforts, is unique and valuable.

In closing, I am delighted to note that by the end of MIGA's General Capital Increase subscription period, which closed in March 2003, the Agency's shareholders either contributed or pledged 97 percent of the $850 million in new capital that was being sought. This additional capital, along with the $150 million contributed by the International Bank for Reconstruction and Development, will considerably strengthen MIGA for the coming years, and allow the Agency to increase its scope and impact.

Remarks at the conference on Roma in an Expanding Europe:
Challenges for the Future

BUDAPEST | JULY 1, 2003

Together with financier and philanthropist George Soros, Wolfensohn here calls attention to the need to address the development needs of the Roma people, traditionally known as "gypsies." The meeting in Budapest would lead to the launch in February 2005 of the Decade of Roma Inclusion.

Mr. Chairman, George,* Prime Ministers, and Friends:

Let me first thank our hosts in Hungary and you, Prime Minister [Péter] Medgyessy, for all that you have done to make this meeting so successful. Let me thank also our colleagues in the European Union for their joint sponsorship of this meeting with the Soros Foundation and the World Bank.

I have been sitting quietly, wondering what I could add after the remarkable sequence of speeches made by those who have attended the conference and by the political leadership of the region. I suppose the first thing that one should observe is that this is truly a unique occasion: to have nine government leaders, one after the other indicating their commitment to our joint programs; to have nine government leaders recognize, publicly and in the presence of Roma leadership, the need to resolve an issue that has been with us for centuries, and to establish the sense of urgency that has been attested to by all, is something that is clearly remarkable.

Also remarkable were the opening statements—the articulate and eloquent statements by Roma youth and Roma women—and the summary of the proceedings by Dena Ringold from our World Bank team, to whom I owe an enormous debt for the work that she has done in preparing this conference. It was truly a beginning to this endeavor that moved my heart.

As was mentioned by Mr. Rudolf Chmel, Slovakia's minister of culture, the substance of the conference has made me feel that the statistics on the Roma condition are important, but that people are more important, that the heart and soul and the humanity conveyed today are what matter. I was touched by [United Nations Development Programme Administrator] Mark Malloch Brown's comments, when he mentioned how, in our crazy world, we globalize and people turn up in the strangest of places. I suppose the first globalized citizens were in fact the Roma, because they have been spread across several regions perhaps longer than anybody else. In the context of today's unpredictable world, I was struck by Mark's reference to Mr. [Simeon]

---

* George Soros, founder and chairman of the Open Society Institute and of the Soros Foundations Network.

Saxe-Coburg Gotha of Bulgaria, a prime minister who was a king; to George Soros, a Hungarian who emigrated to the United States and is now a tycoon; and to myself, a poor Australian Jewish boy now running the World Bank.

We are all here to deal with the question of the Roma. We are united not because of our backgrounds, but because this is an issue that speaks to us all at a human level. And it is at the level of humanity—not coercion, or conscience, or moral persuasion—that we come together. Finally, we have come together because we have come to recognize, as we look around the world, that it is just impossible to let this issue persist in the way that it has.

We in our institution deal with poverty around the world. Today 5 billion people out of a total world population of 6 billion live in developing countries. An estimated 3 billion are living on less than two dollars a day. These 3 billion people account for half of humanity. And, in grappling with persistent poverty, we talk of Sub-Saharan Africa, as Mark said; we talk of the issues in South Asia; and we talk in very similar terms about the problems of indigenous people, about the problems of gender rights, about the problems of education, of opportunity, of prejudice and the frustrations that flow from it, and of the terror and of the wars that come about when poverty is allowed to exist and when people have no hope.

We describe the world of the Middle East and the world of Africa, of Kashmir, and other places in these terms. And then we come to Europe—rich Europe, with an economy of about $9 trillion—and there in the midst of Europe we find the same problem, described in the same terms: problems of inequity, problems of social injustice, problems of prejudice, problems of ignorance, problems of not caring.

In this context, it simply is not right that the Roma issue should not be dealt with. Fortunately, as we contemplate the accession of central and eastern European countries into the European Union, and as European citizenship is offered to all, and will thus be offered to 5 million more people of Roma origin, we now have to confront this issue head on. Of course, in the face of economic challenges, it is difficult to bring about change when there is limited growth, and we all share that conundrum. But what is clear is that much can be done, and much will be done, about the injustices facing our Roma colleagues, which all of us are determined to confront.

What I found deeply moving in Prime Minister Medgyessy's introduction, as well as in the speeches of the other leaders, was that they all went beyond national work and national initiatives and spoke to the need for regional attention. Everyone spoke in terms of humanity. This conference is not a political gathering. This is a gathering that reflects a very real change, a very real recognition.

If we can carry that recognition from this chamber—with pride and with a sense of commitment—out into the world that sometimes buffets us and makes us forget these things, then this Budapest meeting will surely be one of historic proportions. This is an event in which, under the leadership of the Hungarian prime minister, we have agreed on a course of action: one that is visible, that can be measured, and for which we all will be judged accountable.

Today we agreed to pursue the following two initiatives: One is to pursue a decade of Roma inclusion, to run from 2005 to 2015. This will in no way reinvent initiatives already taken, nor will it replace successful efforts already under way. Instead this initiative will help us understand those ongoing efforts, learn from them, and build on them so that we can bring to the attention of the European and global public this decade of progress that we will all plan for.

And why will it take a year for us to define and outline this? Because we do not want to present today an empty program. We want to come back to you in a year with a program that has been analyzed, negotiated, and enriched, and that is practical and pragmatic, and for which we can be held accountable. This is not a year's pause; this is a year's work.

This will be done under the leadership of Prime Minister Medgyessy together with his colleagues from the other countries, all of whom agree that this is a useful initiative. Each leader will appoint representatives to work on this, but they will remain personally involved and committed. Also, the initiative will engage the full cooperation of the European Union, the Soros Foundation, the World Bank, and other interested groups that wish to join us.

But, most important, this initiative will constitute a true partnership with the Roma people. Roma leaders and representatives will shape, contribute to, and guide our decisions. I think today we saw evidence of the intellect and the passion of these leaders. I am well aware that some who have not spoken today, but to whom reference has been made, such as Nicolae Gheorghe [coordinator of the Roma Center for Social Intervention and Studies], who has made his own huge contribution, should be recognized and included in what will be an inherently open process. And we will be back with that plan in 12 months or so.

The second initiative will be an education fund, which we will design in consultation with the same group. I think we agree with what has been said: that housing and unemployment are equally important, as is health, as is gender, as are so many of the issues that arouse advocates for social justice. But, as a particular and singular initiative, we are committed to this education fund.

So, as we launch these initiatives and get the organizing group started, I think it is fair to say that all of us, including the Roma leaders whom I have spoken to, believe that this has not just been another meeting. This is an epochal event that will make a lasting difference in the lives of the Roma people.

Of course, it is easy to be cynical; it is easy to say, "Well, what is different?" What is different is all of you in this audience. The future of this depends on each of your contributions. The future of this depends on us going out of here changed, optimistic, and prepared to work. Certainly, I can speak with conviction for my own organization, where our mission is to fight poverty with passion, and where we measure our success in terms of human results. For us this is a cause that we embrace warmly, a cause that is central to the human spirit, and a cause that we will succeed in addressing in this coming year and in the years ahead.

Again thank you, Mr. Prime Minister, for your leadership.

Foreword to *Accountability at the World Bank: The Inspection Panel 10 Years On*,
published by the World Bank

JULY 2003

In this foreword, Wolfensohn marks the 10-year anniversary of the Inspection Panel, which was set up in 1993. More on the panel can be found at www.inspectionpanel.org.

Almost a decade ago, the World Bank Board of Executive Directors took a bold step to increase the transparency and accountability in Bank operations, by establishing an independent inspection mechanism—known as the Inspection Panel. The Panel is a three-member body created in 1993 to provide an independent forum to private citizens who believe that they or their interests have been or could be directly harmed by a project financed by the World Bank. The Panel is the first body of its kind to give voice to private citizens in an international development context.

The creation of the Inspection Panel provided, for the first time, a vehicle for private citizens, and especially poor people, to access directly the World Bank's highest governing body—the Board of Executive Directors—and to seek redress for what they may perceive to be harmful operational consequences of the World Bank. The process for addressing claims—which has been developed and is still being fine-tuned by the Panel—has empowered and given voice to the people who may have been adversely affected by World Bank–financed projects. The Panel has evolved as an independent, thorough, and thoughtful mechanism for addressing compliance, and it has enabled the World Bank to listen to complaints brought forward by people, consider the Panel's assessments of those claims, and adopt better policies and operational procedures to implement successfully the Bank's poverty reduction mission.

Since the Panel began operations in September 1994, 27 formal Requests for Inspection have been received. The texts of these Requests made to the Panel are publicly available at the Panel's Web site: www.inspectionpanel.org.

As we move into the 21st century, accountability and transparency in Bank operations are even more important than they were 10 years ago, and the Bank continues to be at the forefront of efforts to ensure that in this context development policies and procedures truly benefit poor people. More specifically, through the Inspection Panel, the Bank seeks to ensure that its operational policies and procedures, which are intended to protect the interests of those affected by its projects, are adhered to in project design, preparation, and implementation. It is a testament to the Panel's success that 10 years after its inception, even more of the Bank's projects meet its own high standards and objectives. Today the Panel's success has provided other international financial institutions (IFIs) the example and value of an independent accountability mechanism upon which to model their own accountability mechanisms. Indeed, most IFIs regard the World Bank's mechanism as the standard of excellence to follow in their own efforts to improve transparency and accountability.

This publication traces the Panel's evolution and reviews its experience over the years, focusing primarily on the Panel's practice. Case studies highlight the Panel's impact on the ground, and range from the Bangladesh Jamuna Multipurpose Bridge Project to the Uganda Bujagali Hydropower Project to the Yacyreta Hydroelectric Project [on the Argentina-Paraguay border]. Also discussed are eligibility issues and the Panel's effect on World Bank practice and policies. The publication underscores the Panel's value not only to the Bank but more importantly to the people the Panel serves—the world's poorest people. It also illuminates the Panel's fundamental contribution to the World Bank's efforts to enhance its effectiveness, accountability, and transparency. These achievements are due in no small measure to the Board of Executive Directors, to Bank staff, and especially to Panel members and members of the Panel Secretariat, who formulated and implemented the specific mechanisms of the Panel's operations and who reviewed and investigated cases over the years.

In all the cases discussed in this publication, the Bank seeks to ensure that our operations remain beneficial to the poor people of the world and that we do indeed have a favorable impact on their lives. We aim to reduce poverty with passion, and to address the concerns citizens express regarding our operations forms a major part of the contribution the Inspection Panel is making to development. That is what development is about, and it is why this publication by the Panel is an invaluable document that everybody must make an effort to read.

Five years ago, I wrote for the Panel's first publication, *The World Bank Inspection Panel: The First Four Years,* that "by giving private citizens—and especially the poor—a new means of access to the Bank, the Panel has given voice to those we most need to hear. At the same time it has served the Bank itself through ensuring that we really are fulfilling our mandate of improving conditions of the world's poorest people. The Panel's value both to the Bank and the Bank's beneficiaries and stakeholders has proven itself repeatedly and cannot be overestimated." This statement remains as true today as it was then.

Foreword to *World Development Report 2004,* published for the World Bank by Oxford University Press

AUGUST 2003

> *This foreword to the 2004* World Development Report *describes how involving recipients can improve delivery of basic services to poor people and communities.*

We enter the new millennium with great hopes. For the first time in human history, we have the possibility of eradicating global poverty in our lifetime. One hundred and eighty heads of state signed the Millennium Declaration in October 2000, pledging the world to meeting the Millennium Development Goals by 2015. In Monterrey, Mexico, in the spring of 2002, the world's nations established a partnership for increasing external assistance, expanding world trade, and deepening policy and institutional reforms to reach these goals. Foreign aid, which declined during the 1990s, has begun to increase again.

But the first few years of the 21st century bring heightened challenges. HIV/AIDS and other diseases, illiteracy, and unclean water threaten to dash the hopes of millions, possibly billions, of people that they might escape poverty. Tragically, conflict has undermined development in many countries. Peace and development go hand in hand. And even as we learn how to make development assistance more effective, aid continues to be criticized for not being effective enough.

This year's *World Development Report,* the 26th in the World Bank's flagship series, helps to reignite and reinforce our hopes by confronting these challenges. Development is not just about money or even about numerical targets to be achieved by 2015, as important as those are. It is about people. The Report focuses on basic services, particularly health, education, water, and sanitation, seeking ways of making them work for poor people. Too often, services fail poor people. These failures may be less spectacular than financial crises, but their effects are continuing and deep nonetheless. The Report shows that there are powerful examples of services working for poor people. Services work when they include *all* the people, when girls are encouraged to go to school, when pupils and parents participate in the schooling process, when communities take charge of their own sanitation. They work when societies can curtail corruption—which hurts poor people more than it hurts the better off—particularly when it hits basic health services, which poor people need desperately. They work when we take a comprehensive view of development—recognizing that a mother's education will help her baby's health, that building a road or a bridge will enable children to go to school.

Services work especially well when we recognize that resources and their effective use are inseparable. More effective use makes additional resources more productive—and the argument for aid more persuasive. External resources can provide strong support for changes in policy and practice that can bring about more effective use. This is how we can scale up to achieve the Millennium Development Goals.

To improve service delivery, the Report recommends institutional changes that will strengthen relationships of accountability—between policymakers, providers, and citizens. These changes will not come overnight. Solutions must be tailored not to some imaginary "best practice" but to the realities of the country or the town or the village. One size will not fit all. But I am convinced that this new way of thinking about service delivery, and indeed about development effectiveness, will bear fruit, particularly when matched with adequate resources and a desire to assess what works and what does not, and to decide what must be scaled up and, indeed, what must be scaled down.

In short, this year's *World Development Report* is central to the World Bank's two-pronged strategy for development: investing in and empowering people, and improving the climate for investment. Next year's Report will focus on the second of these. Together, these reports form part of the World Bank's contribution to meeting the challenge the global community has set for itself—to eradicate poverty in our lifetime.

Foreword to *2003 Annual Review: Small Business Activities*, published by the International Finance Corporation

SEPTEMBER 2003

In this foreword to an annual International Finance Corporation publication, Wolfensohn describes why small and medium-size enterprises are critical for creating jobs and opportunities in developing countries.

It is very clear from my travels: effective overall development requires strengthening the local private sector, especially in the poorest countries where almost *all* business is small business.

Sparking growth of these smaller local firms is one of the keys to the sustained employment growth that is so crucial to both poverty reduction and the building of stable, democratic societies. Today there are many proven ways to develop local businesses, and there is an urgent need to scale up these models, spread them around, and share their lessons widely. Few things are as important as the vast numbers of new jobs that would result.

To get there, we must take a comprehensive approach, one that closely weaves together the key needs of small businesses—by increasing their access to capital, by providing greater access to business services, and by improving the business enabling environment in which they operate.

We cannot underestimate how daunting a challenge this is. But with increased effort in recent years, the World Bank Group and our partners have together been making some good progress in this area. In the last year we have launched several new initiatives, bolstered other existing ones, and taken some good partners and models to new places where they are much needed. For its part, IFC has sharply increased efforts to create and strengthen sustainable SME [small and medium-size enterprises] and microfinance institutions. In Cairo, for example, I was pleased to help launch its North Africa Enterprise Development facility this year. Like IFC's other technical assistance ventures of this kind, it is a true multidonor partnership, bringing a wide range of tools and expertise together to help small businessmen and women succeed despite the odds.

This year we also embarked for the first time on a promising new collaboration in Africa between IFC and the World Bank's concessional lending arm, the International Development Association (IDA). Partly modeled on the World Bank's recent approach to fighting HIV/AIDS on the African continent, it is a coordinated, multicountry initiative that will start off in 10 countries. Building on the World Bank Group's experience, it seeks long-lasting, locally driven results, with careful measurement of our impact along the way. There is great potential to replicate this model in other countries in Africa and elsewhere.

In these or any other efforts to fight poverty, the methods used must be far-reaching and systematic, and we must make tangible improvements. There is no simple formula to raising living standards, but SME development has an important part to play, and I am encouraged by the progress that is being made. The true challenge now is the biggest and most important one of all: to increase the scale and reach of this work, and achieve even greater impact.

Remarks at the Youth, Development, and Peace conference

PARIS | SEPTEMBER 16, 2003

At this first meeting of its kind, Wolfensohn addresses a group of young people from all over the world and engages them in dialogue about development issues, jobs, opportunity, and hope as they perceive these in their different countries. An encounter occurred at this conference that Wolfensohn would often speak of later: upon hearing Wolfensohn declare that the young generation was "the future," one youth responded, "Mr. Wolfensohn, we are not the future. We are the now."

Let me, first of all, thank all the speakers and the organizers and their staff for your work. And I want to thank all of you for coming to this meeting, which, in a way, is an experiment for both sides. I guess none of you have ever sat down for two days with my colleagues from the World Bank, and I guess none of my colleagues have ever sat down for two days with such an intelligent and good group.

I think the reason why we all came—and, underneath, there is probably quite a lot of suspicion and concern as to why this thing is happening at all—is a feeling we all share that the world is not in the sort of shape that any of us would like. Whether we're young or old, if we have some sense of social conscience and a desire for peace, for equity, and for the future, then we recognize, I think, on each side of this discussion, that we can't do it alone. We recognize a need to come together, all of us who share a fundamental belief that the world is in lousy shape and that we can do a lot better. Some time soon, and you'll be amazed how quickly it happens, you in this room will be confronted by 20-year-olds who will be looking at you and saying, "What the hell did you do 20 years ago?" In my case it's, "What the hell did I do many more years ago than that?" But I do have children who look at me much as you do, and it brings home to me the fact that this is something that does involve a transition, and that it is important that we get together and work on it.

I should tell you, just for the record, that I was also once a student leader. I, too, once was out complaining about multinational corporations, about people trying to take Australia away from me, about many of the things that I think are on your mind. So let me say simply that I've been there. I hope I haven't forgotten it completely. Age does take its toll, and it is wonderful to be reminded today of the issues that, frankly, are ever present for most of us, but of which I hear a particular point of view coming from this group. It is a group that is significantly multinational, and I'm especially pleased that representatives of the disabled community are joining us. Their needs and interests are something that I have long been concerned with, and I regard them as a part of the general community and not some fringe element.

Let me make a couple of comments first of all and then hope that by the dessert, as you put it, we can end up with something that is edible and that engages us sufficiently to want to come back at some future time. I believe we should come out of this with some specific things to do, with responsibilities for both sides. This is not just an audience looking at an actor in the World Bank and waiting for him to do something. This is something that will only work if the work is carried out between us. Let's also stipulate up front that we're all too busy to make Hollywood projects, and that we want to build into this both measurement and assessment at an early stage, so that we all know whether the things we do are going to be effective. Then, if they're not effective, we can find that out quickly.

I think also, on the basis of the engagement, there's not much that separates us. We all want to come out of this with something. And I don't think there is a single silver bullet that will solve all the problems. But I do think that, from the range of issues that have been discussed, there are quite a number of things that we can do together right off—things that can both have a useful impact in themselves and help build the sort of mutual confidence that will be essential if this dialogue is to be fruitful.

Before I get to the question of youth and youth participation, let me spend a couple of minutes on what has been preoccupying me in my preparations for the [Bank-Fund Annual] Meetings coming up in Dubai. Because youth, or the youth agenda, is not something that exists on its own. Rather it is something that exists within a framework, a framework of global commissions and of attitudes, a framework that includes the breakdown of governance as it exists today. And that is something that we cannot stipulate that we're not interested in. So, as I go to Dubai, I have a few very things clear in my mind about the way the world is.

First of all, it has not been in great economic shape. There's some evidence now of a bit of an uptick, but nothing dramatic. We live in a world in which, as I need hardly tell you, 5 billion people out of a population of 6 billion control only 20 percent of the resources, and the other 1 billion people control 80 percent. Looking ahead, in the next 25 years 2 billion more people will come onto the planet, and all but 50 million of them will live in developing countries. So when you find yourselves, 25 years from now, facing that next group of 20-year-olds, it will be a world of 8 billion people, 7 billion of whom will be in developing countries. The question is, To what extent will that essential inequity, reflected structurally in that simple 80-20 split, be affected by that growth in population?

As someone mentioned earlier, there will also be 2 billion more people living in cities and towns 25 years from now, rather than in rural areas. There will be big demographic shifts as a result, and many more changes in terms of how we govern ourselves. Among the rich countries you'll have a Europe that is older and smaller in population. In the United States you'll have maybe 40 million more people, but 70 percent of that growth will come from immigration and, significantly, Latin American immigration.

Today we have a lot of wars. We have a lot of conflicts. And we have a unity in the world that people of my generation never grew up thinking was there. When I was growing up in Australia, although we young people had some antagonism toward England and the United States and the other capitalist countries, thinking they were probably trying to attack us and ruin us, we basically thought we were part of the rich world and that there was a wall between us and the poor world.

I think today the real meaning of globalization, to me, is that these two worlds are now linked in every possible way, by terror and crime, in health, education, and the environment, so that all of us sitting in this room are not part of two worlds—we're part of one world.

The reason I'm giving you this background is that, in 2000, when the Millennium Development Goals were set, all the leaders of the world signed onto this concept and said, "We *are* all one world. We have to deal with these Millennium goals of poverty and education, of health and the environment." Then, in Monterrey and later in Johannesburg,* a deal was struck between the developed and the developing countries. The developing countries said, "We're going to manage ourselves better. We're going to build capacity. We're going to have more democratic systems in government and put aside corruption. We know we have to do that." The rich countries, in return, said, "We're going to open our markets for trade, and we're going to give you increased development assistance. And we're going to be interdependent."

The fact is that this is not happening, and this is something that all of us have to get over. This meeting in Dubai will be coming on the heels of the disappointment at Cancún,† and meanwhile there's no real evidence of a lot of extra money coming in for development assistance. There is talk of another $16 billion over the next three years, but the numbers are crazy. We've got a $32 *trillion* global economy, and the rich world takes $26 trillion of that. And the rich countries are spending about $300 billion a year for domestic agricultural subsidies and $800 billion a year for defense, and only $55 billion a year for development assistance.

So we're going to be bouncing on the end of a pin in Dubai about development assistance, trying to get money for education, trying to get money for health, trying to get money for youth employment, trying to get money for disabilities, trying to get money for debt relief. It all has to come from the same $55 billion. At the same time the rich countries are not prepared, at this moment at least, to give up the $300 billion in agricultural subsidies to make a more equal partnership.

You cannot *get* to the question of carving out special work for youth and special work for education and special work for AIDS until we get our leaders to understand that those are not different battles. There is no way that I can promise you that we will go forth and solve the youth problems first, when every issue gets back to this question of resources. It all comes from the same limited pot of resources, and so the decision whether to give debt relief is also a decision about whether to give new development assistance. The decision to free markets for trade is a decision to give up tariff income and support for rich farmers.

So there is no sense in us kidding each other that we can have an isolated discussion on the question of youth and its relationship with the World Bank,

---

* The International Conference on Financing for Development was held in Monterrey, Mexico, in March 2002; the World Summit on Sustainable Development was held in Johannesburg in August and September 2002.
† The World Trade Organization's Fifth Ministerial Conference took place in Cancún, Mexico, in September 2003 and failed to reach agreement on developed-country agricultural subsidies.

or about carving out of the existing pot of money more advantages for youth of the types we've been discussing, unless we can move the world to understand that this basic balance doesn't work. That's the first battle I have to fight in Dubai. Some years ago it was agreed that the developed countries would give 0.7 percent of their GDP each year for development assistance, which would be $180 billion a year today. We're now at $55 billion. And of that $55 billion, only half reaches the developing countries in cash. The rest goes to expenses, consultant fees, scholarships, emergencies, and debt relief.

That is the reality, and I'm sorry to give you such an extended introduction. I do it not to avoid the question on the table, of how we're going to work together to address the issues of youth. I do it to be honest with you that we have to deal with the question of getting domestic electorates to understand that the issue of global poverty, the issue of equity, the issue of global youth, which is a most vulnerable part of all that is affected by this, is all part of that same issue. And our leaders are not there.

So the first fight that we have to fight together is the fight for getting a different balance. In my opinion, the first fight for this group, as an international group, is the fight to get people to understand that, if your kids are not going to accuse you of inaction 20 years from now, we have to deal with that fundamental issue. It is not just a question of you saying to me we've got to have formal and informal education—we do. It's not just a question of saying that we also have to have job creation, that we need microcredits, that we need training in entrepreneurship, that we want to keep people employed in their home countries so that they don't have to migrate. . . .

I understand these arguments incredibly well. But I'm just telling you that taking money from one pocket and putting it into another pocket to satisfy the needs of some group is not the solution. It is something that we can play around with, and indeed we should give greater emphasis to the role of youth and the pressures of youth. I am prepared to work toward that and will work toward that. But, trust me, the fundamental issue is not that. The fundamental issue is the importance of bringing about a different balance between the developed and the developing world. This is not an excuse I'm giving you. We *should* address the other issues. But if you want to succeed, it won't be by shuffling a limited deck of cards. What we have to do is expand the number of cards. I hope you'll at least consider that point, and, hopefully, we can engage on it, because one of my requests to you will be that we work together on that issue, and not just on the issues that you all have raised with me.

Now, let's get to those issues. On the issue of youth participation in our work, there is no problem as far as our institution is concerned. It may be a problem with some people in the institution, because we are not used to having

young people around sticking their nose in and criticizing. But we are prepared to go through that, and indeed we've already started. We've started with
a group in Peru, and I hope that some of my Peruvian friends are here. As has
been mentioned already, we want to start bringing groups of young people
inside the Bank and giving them access to our offices, access to the projects,
input in project design, and input on monitoring. That is something that I'm
prepared to commit to here. And one of the monitorable goals that we have
is that, by June of next year, we will have set up two or three of these groups,
parallel to our friends in Peru, in each of the regions. That will give on-the-
spot, direct access in a practical way to people in the institution.

The second thing that I'm prepared to commit to is additional pressure to try
and give voice to youth participation when setting national poverty reduction
strategies. I am prepared to do that and to push it. Let me tell you, not all governments are prepared to listen. I need hardly tell you that, because you have
had a fair amount of experience with it yourselves. But we will, in a practical
sense, work with you and your colleagues on the country assistance strategies
and on the poverty reduction strategies that we're doing. We will work with
you country by country, so long as you set up the mechanism by which to do
it and to check whether a full discussion has taken place. And if it has not, you
will decide who are the appropriate people to deal with and how we can bring
them in. That way we will put in place something that is definable, monitorable, and measurable, and I think we should try it and see how it works.

The third set of issues you've come up with is a series of individual suggestions
about what you think is important in terms of priorities. In health, the issues
you've identified start with nutrition and go through to sexually transmitted diseases, AIDS, and the whole question of access to health care. We're working on
this set of issues continuously, and we will continue to do so. The problems are
well known to you. The average North American spends $15,000 a year on
health. In Africa it's $5 a year. So we have quite a ways to go in terms of reach-
ing equilibrium on the health issue.

The question of education for all is one I'm going to be addressing
frontally at Dubai. When we set the Millennium goals, we were told there
were 115 million kids not attending primary school, and we said by 2015 we
want to have them all in school. We came up with what we call the Fast Track
program, which takes only those countries that have a good education program, a good, integrated holistic strategy, and were ready to go. We came up
with seven countries that met the criteria, and we said to the rich countries
that we needed money to cover these countries for 5 to 10 years, because they
have to hire and train teachers, and in some cases to build schools. We have
managed so far to get funding for only three years, and to a level of only

70 percent of what is required. This is not just a tragedy, it is downright dishonest, and I will be saying so in Dubai.

But the issue, again, is not to get the money taken out of some other valuable activity and put into education. It is to get additional monies, yet what we are hearing now is that, from most of the European countries, there will be a reduction in development assistance, not an increase. The European Union is planning to put up another $6 billion over the next three years, and the United States about the same: $5 billion over three years. However, these amounts are tiny when you set them against the other needs for which they're going to be used: Iraq, Afghanistan, Congo, Gaza and the West Bank. All of these conflict situations, as you will see, will eat up the funds available.

Take the United States alone. We are lobbying to get the incremental $3 billion for the U.S. contribution this year. Yet President Bush came on television a week ago to request from Congress a further $87 billion for the next 12 months in Iraq and Afghanistan, on top of the $70 billion already spent. Whatever you think of the rights or wrongs of the Iraq war, that is $157 billion in spending, which the Congress will pass—with some argument I'm sure—over the next period. Where will it come from? What other programs will be hit? Everyone will come back and say, "We must be fiscally conservative. Let's look at what projects we can cut." And you can be sure it will include development. . . .

The problem is that the issues and the interventions that you've addressed so beautifully here today are not headline issues. The headline issues are conflict, terror, things that you can photograph. What you can't photograph is lack of progress in terms of employment, of youth, of poverty. You can get coffee table books showing you those pictures, but it's not a headline.

What I would like to suggest, finally, since there is a range of these issues, is that, over the next three months or whatever period your organizers are prepared to suggest, we take each of these reports that you have prepared and review them one by one. Because it's impossible today, I think, realistically to say, "Yes, we'll buy this, this, this, and this, and no to that and that." I think what is needed for this process to be credible is for us to take some reasonable period—three months might be a good time frame—to go through and come up with an action plan, to which we can then agree between ourselves, in addition to the points that I've already made. Then, by way of follow-up, we will report back to you, either by Internet or by whatever means you think is appropriate, on where we've come.

I would like in the next 12 months to do all that is necessary both to agree the things that we're going to do and to have a chance of some progress, and then meet again 12 months from now, for those who are prepared to come back after the dessert, and have another meeting. I'm prepared to give my time to do it, but I think that it only makes good sense if we have set ourselves specific targets during this period of time and then see what the results of our efforts are.

Let me say one other thing. We at the Bank do have probably the best system of information exchange, and for at least visually keeping in touch, that exists anywhere. We have more than 100 sites available for videoconferencing, so that it is not necessary for us all to communicate by traveling to each other's countries these next 12 months. We're running 1,500 videoconferences a month, reaching roughly 80 countries a day. If you are interested in this, we could, in three months' time, beyond the working group, have a broader interface with other members of this group in your various cities and capital cities. Most of you, I would guess, would be able to reach one of those sites, though we may have to deal with a few others in other ways. But we could easily within that period of time come together with our first global conference, not as a big affair with cameras and with press, but as a working conference and as an opportunity to touch base with each other. Again, if your leadership and all of you are interested in doing that, I would suggest that, at whatever time we set—three months or whatever—let's get together for a global conference to report on what we've agreed to do, take stock, and set the next measures and objectives that we're going to deal with.

That is the sort of thing I would like to come out of here with. I can promise you that, from our side, we will perform. If all of you think it's worth doing, we would be very happy to be the other side in that pocket. So maybe that's not a headline, but to me it's progress.

The last thing I would say is that, from our point of view, we need this constituency, not because it's a personal achievement for us to do it, but because if you are not involved, we're leaving out the active participants. I just ask you to think: in 20 years' time, when you're standing here with the next crop of young people coming through, will you wonder whether you should or should not have taken advantage of this possibility. The chances are I won't be around, actively anyway, unless I do another four terms, which seems unlikely. But I will be able from somewhere to look back and say that this was the beginning of something really important. And I think that in 20 years, when there are 1.8 billion people around between the ages of 15 and 24, we will look back and say we made a very good step today to ensure that those young people of tomorrow lead better lives than we do.

Thanks very much.

A NEW GLOBAL BALANCE:
THE CHALLENGE OF LEADERSHIP

Address to the Board of Governors at the Annual Meetings of the World Bank
and the International Monetary Fund

DUBAI | SEPTEMBER 23, 2003

*In a poignant speech at the Annual Meetings in Dubai, Wolfensohn
describes a "world out of balance" and delivers a ringing call to restore that
balance. The speech came just one month after the terrorist bombing of the
UN compound in Baghdad, in which the World Bank lost a staff member.
The Dubai meetings also marked the first time the joint Bank-Fund
meetings were held in the Middle East.*

Your Royal Highnesses, Mr. Chairman, Governors, Distinguished Guests:

It gives me great pleasure to welcome you to this remarkable city of Dubai for
the Annual Meetings of the World Bank and the IMF. I would like to express
my profound appreciation to the government and people of the United Arab
Emirates for their warm hospitality, their magnificent preparations—one has
only to look at this extraordinary hall—and their commitment to making our
meetings a success.

Thank you, Chairman Villiger,* for your remarks and for your leadership
of these meetings. I wish also to thank my friend [IMF Managing Director]
Horst Köhler and our colleagues in the IMF for another year of working together in close and effective partnership.

The Region and the World

We meet in the Middle East for the first time—and at a vital moment. The
eyes of the world are on the region. They are also on us. We meet, 184 nations strong, with a responsibility to show leadership and to set a clear course
for development and peace.

We meet in the shadow of conflict and loss. The horror of the attack on the
UN compound in Baghdad is seared in memory, and we were reminded of it
by yesterday's attack.[†] We mourn Sergio de Mello, an exceptional humanitarian who dedicated his life to development and with whom we worked closely
in many postconflict countries. We mourn also Dr. Alya Sousa, our Bank col-

---

* Kaspar Villiger, chairman of the Board of Governors and governor of the IMF and the World Bank for
Switzerland.
† Sergio Vieira de Mello, UN special envoy to Iraq, and Alya Ahmad Sousa, a UN employee seconded to the
World Bank office in Baghdad, were among those killed in the attack on the UN headquarters in Baghdad on
August 19, 2003. A second attack on the headquarters occurred on September 22.

league, whom we lost to terrorism. She was a committed professional who took pains to look after her co-workers, an outstanding person.

I visited with both of them just days before the attack. Like all of you, I feel for the families of those killed and injured in the blast. How sad our world has become when peacemakers become the targets. We honor Sergio, Alya, and all who have died—by continuing their work.

I can assure you of the Bank's commitment to help the people of Iraq, just as we have worked to support the people of Afghanistan, Bosnia and Herzegovina, Kosovo, Timor-Leste, and the West Bank and Gaza. One result of our effort is the needs assessment that we and our IMF and UN colleagues will deliver to donors in Madrid next month. We look forward to assisting with the reconstruction process in the years ahead.

The Bank has been at work in this region for more than half a century. Our first loan here was, in fact, to Iraq in 1950, for flood control on the Tigris and Euphrates Rivers. The projects we support today finance low-income housing in Jordan, microcredit for women in the Republic of Yemen, capacity building for a new nation-state in the West Bank and Gaza, and cooperation among 10 Nile Basin countries to provide water for 300 million people today, and 600 million just a quarter-century from now. We also assist Saudi Arabia with reimbursable technical assistance.

Knowledge and the exchange of ideas are key to our collaboration. That is why we have prepared, together with scholars and experts in the region, four new reports on employment, trade, gender, and governance. That is why our website and its wealth of development experience are available also in Arabic.

This is an ancient region that has given civilization so much, in science, mathematics, culture, and religion. Yet it is also a young region, where an astonishing 60 percent of the people are under the age of 25. I would like to offer my remarks today particularly to the young people of the Middle East—and of the world. Last week, in Paris, I met with youth leaders who represented organizations with more than 120 million members worldwide. The meeting included rural youth and street kids, children orphaned by AIDS and civil conflict, youth from the excluded Roma community, and young people with disabilities. They met in peace and with mutual respect. They asked why our generation could not do the same. They said, "We are ready to be part of the solution, to be partners." "But," they also said, "we do not want a future based only economic considerations—there must be something more." They challenged us about values and beliefs.

My colleagues and I were inspired by their passion and idealism. We invited four of their representatives to join us here today to witness our shared commitment. Soon young people will start working in the Bank's country offices, to help review projects and suggest initiatives—as is already the case in Japan and Peru. We will also ask governments to make it possible for youth to participate in discussions of poverty reduction strategies. And we will come together in 12 months' time to take stock of how far we have come in our partnership.

Mr. Chairman, by 2015 there will be 3 billion people in the world under the age of 25. They are the future. But, as the young people in Paris said most forcibly, they are also the *now*. And their expectations of us are high. To respond to them, we must address the fundamental forces shaping our world. In many respects, they are forces that have caused imbalance:

- In our world of 6 billion people, 1 billion own 80 percent of global GDP, while another billion struggle to survive on less than a dollar a day. This is a world out of balance.
- Over the next 25 years, 50 million people will be added to the population of the rich countries, and about 1.5 billion to that of the poor countries. Many will experience poverty, unemployment, and disillusion with what they will see as an inequitable global system. A growing number will leave their home countries to find work. Migration will become a critical issue.
- Rich countries today spend $56 billion a year on development assistance, but $300 billion on agricultural subsidies and $600 billion for defense. The poor countries themselves spend $200 billion on defense—more than what they spend on education. That is another major imbalance.

Developing economies are projected to grow at twice the rate of the developed economies. But many will need help to bridge the gap between rich and poor. Pressures on the environment and on natural resources, such as water, will become central issues. Interdependence will be more evident. Opportunities will expand, but so will the dangers.

Three years ago, world leaders gathered at the Millennium Summit to assess the future. They made a commitment to cut poverty in half by 2015. They agreed on Millennium Development Goals for health, education, and equal opportunity for women. They set targets for the environment, from the air we breathe to the preservation of our forests and oceans. These are remarkable goals. Many leaders spoke of them as morally right. They are our human responsibility, but they are also in the global interest.

The leaders agreed on a bargain, one that was later spelled out in meetings in Monterrey and Johannesburg.‡ Developing countries promised to strengthen

---

‡ The International Conference on Financing for Development was held in Monterrey, Mexico, in March 2002; the World Summit on Sustainable Development was held in Johannesburg in August and September 2002.

governance, create a positive investment climate, build transparent legal and financial systems, and fight corruption. Developed countries agreed to support these efforts by enhancing capacity building, increasing aid, and opening their markets for trade. There was unprecedented agreement on the bargain and the actions required to achieve it. What have been the results?

The developing countries' policies and governance have never been stronger. As I mentioned, their economies as a group are growing significantly faster than those of the rich countries. But this good news should not blind us to other important realities.

Progress on poverty differs sharply across regions. China, with its 1.3 billion people, will achieve most of the Millennium goals. India, with a billion people, is on track to meet the poverty goal. But, in many other countries, the goals will not be met. Sub-Saharan Africa, with 600 million people, will fare the worst. The number of people living in absolute poverty there will increase, not decrease. Only half of Africa's children will complete primary school; one in six will die before they reach the age of five, many from AIDS. Like the young people I met in Paris, I ask, Why?

Part of the reason is that reform is not happening fast enough in the developing nations. There is still too much cronyism and corruption. In nearly every country, it is a matter of common knowledge where the problems are and who is responsible. Frankly, there is not enough bold and consistent action against corruption, particularly at the higher levels of influence.

What about the developed countries' part of the global bargain? Here, too, there has been progress: Commitments were made in Monterrey toward an increase in aid of around $16 billion a year by 2006. Substantial amounts were pledged to fight HIV/AIDS and malaria, and for conflict prevention and reconstruction. We see better allocation and use of resources, including enhanced donor harmonization—as in the Rome Agreement earlier this year [at the High-Level Forum on Harmonization in February 2003]. But these actions, while laudable, do not match the promises made.

In Dakar [at the April 2000 World Education Forum], donors said no sound primary education project would go unfunded. They committed to an Education for All initiative requiring several billion dollars of incremental grant funding over a 5- to 10-year period. Yet today, under the [Education for All] Fast Track Initiative, only seven countries have received promises of funding, and only for a total of $200 million over three years, reaching fewer than 5 percent of the 115 million children who are not in school. This naturally leads developing countries to wonder where the additional resources will come from to help them open schools, hire teachers, and plan for secondary as well as primary education. They worry that resources needed to meet other goals will not be forthcoming, that debt relief will not be sufficient, and that monies will go to deal with the latest crisis or to fight drugs or terror, rather than to long-term development. They worry that only half of existing aid flows actually reach them in direct cash transfers for their programs. And they worry that their repayments of debt are crippling their capacity to grow. Developing countries feel they have made significant efforts to fulfill their part of the global bargain. But they do not see enough delivery on the other side.

The recent impasse at Cancún is a case in point.§ Two-thirds of the world's poor people depend on agriculture for their livelihood. As the developing countries see it, rich nations put forward proposals that did not respond to their central demands in this crucial area. They also found unacceptable a view of negotiations in which they are expected merely to respond to rich-country proposals. At Cancún, developing countries signaled their determination to push for a new equilibrium. They signaled that there must be greater balance between the rich and powerful, and the poor and numerous. They signaled that, for there to be peace and sustainable development, there must be a different set of priorities. There must be greater cooperation.

The fact is that aid today is at its lowest level ever. It has fallen from 0.5 percent of the combined GDPs of developed countries in the early 1960s to about 0.22 percent today—and this at a time when incomes in developed countries have never been higher. Against this background, the Bank has taken a close look at how progress toward the Millennium goals could be accelerated—through better policies, more effective use of aid, and higher aid levels. Our analysis, based on current plans, leads to two conclusions: First, aid is being used more effectively today than ever before, because of improvements in many developing countries and in the allocation of development assistance. Second, developing nations could easily absorb double the extra $16 billion promised in Monterrey for 2006. And this is a conservative estimate. The $50 billion in additional aid per year proposed by Chancellor [of the U.K. Exchequer Gordon] Brown could be put to effective use very quickly. The prospect of such funding would encourage developing countries to make more rapid reforms. Leaders are more likely to take action if they know that resources are forthcoming on a consistent basis. They will not move if the financing and the benefits of reform cannot be assured.

Action on trade is equally important. It is inconsistent to preach the benefits of free trade and then maintain the highest subsidies and barriers for precisely those goods in which poor countries have comparative advantage.

§ The World Trade Organization's Fifth Ministerial Conference took place in Cancún, Mexico, in September 2003 and failed to reach agreement on developed-country agricultural subsidies.

Developing countries also need to help themselves on this point, since they pay substantial tariffs in trade with each other.

Restoring balance to our world will not happen unless there are serious efforts to build greater public understanding about the importance of poverty and inequity. My generation grew up thinking that there were two worlds—the haves and the have-nots—and that they were, for the most part, quite separate. That was wrong then, and it is even more wrong now.

The wall that many people imagined as separating the rich countries from the poor came down on September 11 two years ago. We are linked today in so many ways: not only by trade and finance, but by migration, environment, disease, drugs, crime, conflict and, yes, terrorism. We are linked, rich and poor alike, by a shared desire to leave a better world to our children, and by the realization that, if we fail in our part of the planet, the rest becomes vulnerable. That is the true meaning of globalization.

We know elections are won and lost on local issues. But it is global issues—and especially poverty—that will shape the world our children live in. Leaders must make the case for development. It is a domestic as well as an international issue.

Learning about other countries and cultures and respecting their values and aspirations are imperative. We need to teach our children about the rest of the world. The young people I met in Paris live as global citizens. They have a grounding in their own cultures, but they respect the cultures of others. So do the young people of Dubai. Last Sunday, the Bank convened a conference at the Women's College here. We brought together by videoconference young women students in Afghanistan, Ethiopia, Jordan, Turkey, Uganda, the United States, and Yemen. We asked them what issues they would like to discuss. They said, education of girls, respect for different cultures and religions, stereotypes, dreams, gender equity, ethics, art, and unity through diversity. This was the view of young women students right here. They are global citizens. And Dubai can be very proud of them—as I am.

We can feel encouraged that a global poll conducted earlier this year indicated that many people around the world now see the connection between poverty and stability. In some cases they see it more clearly than their leaders.

Mr. Chairman, I have suggested how nations can rise to their responsibilities. So, too, must development institutions. Together, working with governments, civil society, and the private sector, we have supported the developing countries in their achievements over the last 40 years: increasing life expectancy by 20 years and reducing illiteracy by half. But now, with just 12 short years left to reach the Millennium goals, multilateral and bilateral organizations must raise their game.

That means moving away from single projects—we at the Bank call them feel-good projects—and instead going for results on a larger scale, not in 5 villages but in 50 or 500—or 5,000. Speaking for the Bank Group, I can say we are taking a hard look at how we can do better, how successful programs can be scaled up. We now have more than 2,500 staff in the field, closer to our clients. We are speeding up project preparation time. Success rates in the projects we support have risen from 71 percent in 1995 to 85 percent last year. Policy performance and good governance are now priorities in our country dialogues. We are driving hard on AIDS, education, and water and expanding our efforts in basic infrastructure. Working with the IMF and our partners in the Heavily Indebted Poor Countries Initiative, we are providing some $52 billion in debt relief to 27 low-income countries. And we continue to respond to the needs of middle-income countries, where many of the world's poor people live.

We are leveraging technology, with over 100 of our offices now connected by satellite. We do 1,500 videoconferences every month and reach more than 60 countries every day. The Development Gateway has about 100 partners helping to build capacity and provide an information base for the development community. We are introducing a new "client card," which gives policymakers and team leaders the same Web-based information we ourselves use to manage projects, provide financial information, and undertake research on a confidential basis. It is a powerful tool for implementation and, above all, transparency.

Our other members of the Bank Group family also are making progress: the International Financial Corporation is encouraging private sector investment in small and medium-size enterprises, including in Africa, and introducing new approaches such as carbon emissions trading. The Multilateral Investment Guarantee Agency has continued to increase its focus on low-income countries. last year over half of its guarantees were in nations eligible for concessional lending from the International Development Association.

In the poll I mentioned earlier, people said they see the Bank as becoming more client-oriented, effective, and relevant. But they warned us to continue our efforts to be less bureaucratic and more flexible—and to deliver more results. We take this feedback seriously. Next spring we will be cosponsoring, together with the Chinese government, a conference in Shanghai on how to enhance efforts at poverty reduction. We will study how to take successful programs and scale them up, how to enable poor people to be the central force for change and not objects of charity, and how to manage programs over time for results that truly make a difference. I hope many of you will join us in Shanghai.

Taking our efforts to the next level is the challenge for the international community. It is the challenge for the Bank, and our world-class team is determined to take it on.

A Time for Action

Mr. Chairman, it is time to take a cold, hard look at the future. Our planet is not balanced. Too few control too much, and too many have too little to hope for. There is too much turmoil, too much war, too much suffering. The demographics of the future speak to a growing imbalance of people, resources, and the environment. If we act together now, we can change the world for the better. If we do not, we will leave greater and more intractable problems for our children.

We must rebalance our world to give everyone the chance for a life that is secure, with a right to expression. That means equal rights for women, rights for the disabled and disadvantaged, the right to a clean environment, the right to learn, the right to develop. These are not exotic objectives. All of us want the same, rich and poor alike. There is no better time than now to join in a common effort to make a better world. You are the global leaders who can make it happen. Delay is reckless. This is a time for courage and action—for a new vision of the future.

Mr. Chairman, I do not speak as a dreamer or a philosopher. Like all of you, I, too, have a family and worry about their future. We have the resources to make a difference. We know how to make a difference. We have the courage to make a difference. We must now act to make a difference.

We all share one planet. It is time to restore balance to the way we use it. Let us move forward to fight poverty, to establish equity, and ensure peace for the next generation. Let us respond to the youth from Paris and the students in Dubai, telling them that they can trust us, and that we will act today, here, in Dubai.

Thank you.

Message from the president and chairman from the 2003 World Bank *Annual Report*

OCTOBER 2003

> *This Chairman's Message covers the year from July 2002 to June 2003 and recaps the past year's progress at the Bank. In particular, Wolfensohn talks of the importance of partnership.*

The past year has been one of extraordinary global anxiety and uncertainty, including the continuing economic slowdown, the conflict in Iraq, and the impact of a new disease, sudden acute respiratory syndrome (SARS). In this context it is more important than ever that we work with our development partners to redouble efforts to reduce world poverty.

The pledges made at the International Conference on Financing for Development at Monterrey in March 2002 underscored the importance of the collective effort needed to attain the Millennium Development Goals (MDGs), including the goal of reducing poverty by half by the year 2015. The Monterrey Consensus provides a framework of actions and accountabilities for all parties, developed and developing countries alike. All are agreed that we must now focus on implementation and augment the impact of our collective efforts.

For the World Bank this has translated into a special focus on implementation in four priority sectors that are key to meeting some of the MDGs: education for all, HIV/AIDS, water and sanitation, and health. Working with our partners in these areas, we have learned a number of lessons that can be applied going forward. First, support must be based on country-driven programs set in a sound policy environment. Second, where the right policy environment exists, the international community needs to be ready to provide the additional support to help countries meet their targets. Third, resources must reach countries in the right form—that is, aligned with their budget cycles, untied from donor-driven imperatives, and with simplified and harmonized donor procedures. Meeting the MDGs not only will require more development assistance but also will require that assistance to be used even more effectively.

The approach embedded in the Comprehensive Development Framework (CDF) and Poverty Reduction Strategy Papers (PRSPs) helps us all respond to the challenge of improving development effectiveness—and that approach is increasingly taking root in many of the poorest countries. We also have begun to better understand how the CDF principles can be applied in middle-income countries to address issues of poverty and equity. In addition, we are making special efforts to assist the group of low-income countries that suffers from weak policies and governance, including those countries with long-standing conflicts. Without progress in those countries, the MDGs will not be met.

In partnership with others, the Bank's support to the poorest countries has included debt relief through the Heavily Indebted Poor Countries (HIPC) Initiative. Over time this will reduce debt stocks and debt-service burdens by an estimated $40 billion from all creditors.

In the past year our own internal review of HIPC has indicated that there are areas where we can improve the initiative even further—and action is under way to implement the changes. The 13th Replenishment of the International Development Association (IDA13) agreement to provide grants to the poorest and most debt-vulnerable countries is also a significant step forward.

Monterrey underscored the central importance of trade in attaining the MDGs. At the Doha meeting on trade last year, the international community made a commitment to collective action that holds the promise of truly integrating trade with development.

As we approach the halfway mark of the Doha Round, the challenge of translating that commitment into concrete results looms large. Agriculture is the most crucial and most difficult issue on the agenda—and market restrictions and subsidies in agriculture are the most important external impediments to tackling poverty in the developing countries. In fact, the amounts of aid needed globally by all the developing countries to reach the MDGs represent a fraction of what is spent on agricultural subsidies by developed countries. Action on the trade agenda is a top priority for the international community.

Private sector investment and productivity are also needed to accelerate growth and achieve the MDGs. For vital investments in sectors of the economy such as infrastructure, for example, much of the investment continues to come from the public sector, which funds 75 percent to 80 percent of the estimated $250 billion to $300 billion of annual infrastructure investment in developing countries. Throughout the developing world, more than 1.2 billion people lack access to safe water, and nearly twice as many do not have improved sanitation. Given the scale of the needs, the World Bank Group, with the support of our Board and in partnership with many other development actors, will increase our investment in infrastructure. And through our focus on policy reform and capacity building, we will aim to leverage additional financial support from both public and private sources.

Our actions must lead to development that is sustainable. The World Summit on Sustainable Development, held last year in Johannesburg, South Africa, emphasized the need to move toward a sustainable future, combining environmental responsibility with social equity. The Bank Group will continue to take fully into consideration the effect of our development programs on future generations.

Strengthening our partnerships has become a core objective of the Bank in recent years. Two principles have been key in our search for better coherence and cooperation. First, in the interests of efficiency and effectiveness, the Bank has sought to work increasingly closely with all relevant partners, deferring to their work and judgments in areas where they have comparative advantage. Second, at the country level we have stressed the principle that all partners must align behind country-owned strategies. Ultimately, increased effectiveness and a better chance for sustainable and successful development can be ensured when the countries truly steer their own development with the full support of the international community.

During the past year we have made important inroads in that regard. But we all must step up our efforts if we are to meet our joint goal of cutting poverty in half by the year 2015. I can assure you that the dedicated and talented staff of the World Bank Group is committed to this endeavor in the period ahead.

This address details the Bank's work on Iraq and the needs assessment the Bank put together for a donor meeting on Iraq held in Madrid earlier in the month. Turning to the global picture, Wolfensohn describes a world out of balance where the 1 billion people in rich countries have 80 percent of the world's wealth and the 5 billion in the poor countries have only 20 percent.

Let me start with some words about Iraq, and I will deal with it expeditiously, so that I can then turn to some other important matters.

The role that the World Bank has been asked to play in the reconstruction of Iraq is one that we are long accustomed to. You will remember that the formal name of the World Bank is the International Bank for Reconstruction and Development, and frequently in recent years we have been called upon to deal with reconstruction in postconflict situations. And that is the basis on which we were called into Iraq.

We were asked to come up with a needs assessment—essentially a plan for reconstruction—and that we have done, jointly with the International Monetary Fund and with our colleagues in the United Nations. Our assessment led to an examination of 14 different subject areas, ranging from governance to health and education to infrastructure. We completed that study some weeks ago, so that at the beginning of October a preliminary meeting was able to take place, followed a week ago by the meetings in Madrid.

What that analysis showed was that a five-year reconstruction plan in these 14 areas would take time, attention, and $36 billion. To that was added the assessment of the [Coalition Provisional] Authority, which looked at some issues that were outside the scope of the Bank's purview, in particular security and energy. A few other minor items were also discussed there, but the conclusion there was that in that same five-year time period some $56 billion would be required.

It was not said how that $56 billion would be funded. Some hoped that additional resources would be made available as a result of Iraq's own budget surpluses, particularly if oil could be exported at high prices. But the decision was made not to count on that money, because a lot had to be done first to get the country running. We therefore decided to look at a stand-alone basis for funding, and the conclusion, as I said, was that $56 billion was needed. In Madrid the United States confirmed its contribution of $20 billion, and although the extent to which it will consist of debt rather than grants is yet to be determined, there was a strong indication on the part of the administration that it

would be largely grants. And there was indication of interest in additional funding in excess of $13 billion.

Was the Madrid conference a success? I would have to say that, given the need of $56 billion over a five-year period, starting out, as we did, with $33 billion, is pretty good. Frankly, even a $20 billion front-end contribution, available immediately in cash, would have been a decent start, but it is much better that we had the additional funding that we did. It offers plenty of chance to get things organized over a two- or three-year period toward the ultimate reconstruction, the details of which will no doubt change during that five-year period both in terms of its extent and in terms of how it is done.

What soon became clear was that certain parameters were fundamental, the first being security. [UN Secretary-General] Kofi Annan, in a very good and very short speech, indicated that the security question was paramount as a condition for UN involvement. And, of course, there is the residual and indeed ever-present question of governance—how the CPA would eventually relinquish its current position and its objectives to an Iraqi government under an Iraqi constitution.

But the conference itself was, I would have to say, generally a success. The parties that one would have expected not to contribute at least turned up, although in fact they did not contribute. And that was not surprising. I was asked when I came back whether I was surprised. I said, "How can you be surprised if they're still debating the politics? Why would you expect them to pull out a checkbook?" So what happened is what happened, and $33 billion is a very sporting amount of money.

Another very important overhanging issue is that of Iraq's outstanding debt. I was very anxious to ensure that the meeting not conclude just on the basis of new money, without considering that existing debt. Iraq's GNP is on the order of $15 billion, and the country's outstanding debts are somewhere upward of $120 billion and possibly as much as $150 billion. And that is even before one adds the claims from the last war, of which there are at least $40 billion currently outstanding, and possibly more.

So if one looks at the economic viability of the country, there's absolutely no doubt that in this current year it will be essential, as was indicated by the G-7 in Dubai,* to deal with the question of overhanging debt. You cannot have a country that has a ratio of outstanding debt to GDP of 800 or 1,000 percent. We get worried about countries where it's 70 percent, and when it tops 100 percent we get very concerned. And when it's 150 percent, as in some of the countries in the Heavily Indebted Poor Countries Initiative, the country becomes eligible for debt relief. So in Iraq's case resolving the debt overhang is clearly an integral part of the solution. And when one talks about success, it has to be success in relation to the immediate need for funds, true, but also in relation to the work that's being done this year on debt relief.

Fundamentally, there are, as I think you know, some serious social problems remaining in Iraq. The damage is not to a significant extent a result of the war. Rather, the damage is a result of 20 years of neglect. Twenty years ago the GDP per capita of this country was something in excess of $3,500 per person. Today it's somewhere between $400 and $600 per person. No one knows exactly, but it is of that order, and one hopes it will be $700 next year.

Meanwhile the human statistics are really horrendous. Infant mortality runs at 100 per 1,000, which means that 1 in 10 infants die. Mortality among children under five, after they survive infancy, is 50 per 1,000. And maternal mortality is 294 per 100,000. To give you an idea, that compares with 41 per 100,000 in Jordan. Therefore the social conditions in the country are of great interest and concern to us.

The question is also asked, "How quickly can you get this money out? When are you going to start?" And, I'd have to say, a large part of that depends on security. We've seen what's happened in these last few days. It's not a question of being cowardly. I've said I'd be perfectly happy to go in and have

---

* The finance ministers and central bank heads of the Group of Seven countries met in Dubai in September 2003.

meetings in the Green Zone personally, and maybe take someone along with me. But if I sent 20 or 50 people out there, they would not have the benefit of bulletproof cars and a phalanx of people to protect them as I would, and they wouldn't be staying inside the palace as I would.

What is difficult for me, particularly, is that I was there two weeks before the bombing in August, and, unfortunately, tragically, in addition to Sergio and his team, we lost one of our Bank colleagues,[†] and three other people were very badly injured. I think we, along with everybody else, are really apprehensive about sending colleagues in while the security situation is difficult. I know President Bush said yesterday that Iraq is a very dangerous place. I think he used the word "dangerous" 15 times. And if that is anywhere close to true—even if he used it 5 times—it's dangerous. And it makes it very difficult to commence the sort of work that we have to do until the security is available.

Nonetheless, there is a lot of preliminary work we can do. We've set up videoconference facilities. We can meet outside Iraq. What is crucial is the transfer of responsibility and the ability to put something together with the Iraqis themselves, so that reconstruction can proceed on a more secure basis and with greater ownership by the Iraqi people.

That is a snapshot of the Iraq situation, so let me now provide a snapshot of what I think are the other important problems. One of those is, of course, the global environment in which all of this is taking place. And there, again in a snapshot, my belief is that, for the stability both of that region and of our planet, the issue of poverty and the issue of equity have become central.

We see several serious imbalances in the world today. There are 6 billion people on the planet, 5 billion of them in developing countries, the other 1 billion in the rich countries. The rich countries have 80 percent of the wealth, and the 5 billion have 20 percent. That's the first imbalance. The second imbalance is that, of the 6 billion, approximately 3 billion people live on less than two dollars a day, and 1.2 billion live on less than one dollar a day.

The world's answer to these imbalances is to deal with them on the basis of the Millennium Development Goals, and, on that basis, what has happened since 2000 has not been totally successful. The Millennium goals, you will remember, are the set of objectives that were set in 2000 at a conference held at the United Nations by the heads of all the member countries.

Considering both the morality of the situation and their own self-interest and that of the planet, the leaders came out with a Millennium statement,

---

† On August 19, 2003, terrorists attacked the UN headquarters in Baghdad, killing 22 people including UN Special Envoy to Iraq Sergio Vieira de Mello and Dr. Alya Sousa, a UN employee seconded to the World Bank.

which identified poverty as the central issue. Certain other things about the environment were added, but fundamentally they set these goals because they said—and I have reread many of the speeches—"Look, it's morally right to do this, but it's also in everyone's self-interest, because globalization means that we are all in this together, and that we have to think differently, and no longer just in domestic terms."

No one, I think, doubts the difficulty of going beyond domestic political issues in any individual country. And I think global poverty will be a small part, if any, of the U.S. presidential debate. Insofar as it affects domestic issues, it will come up, although it is probably not going to be formulated in that way. In any case, the leaders agreed in 2000 that we would halve poverty in the world, and that we would get all the children into school—worldwide there are 150 million kids not in school. They agreed that we would improve infant and maternal mortality, and that they would work toward a better world environmentally.

Later, at the March 2002 Financing for Development Conference in Monterrey, it was agreed that the way to do all this for the developing countries was to strengthen their governments: build judicial systems that protect rights, build financial systems that work, and fight corruption. These were understood as a set of preconditions to growth, and they are not something imposed by anybody. The Monterrey agreement was subsequently reendorsed by the African countries in an agreement called NEPAD [the New Partnership for Africa's Development], because every one of the leaders, or at least the enlightened leaders, of the developing countries said we cannot go forward unless we do that. And some progress has indeed been made in countries on the basis of the Monterrey Consensus.

In return, the rich countries said, "If you do that, we will help you with capacity building, we will open our markets for trade, and we will increase development assistance." Well, the history on that set of objectives has not been terrible, but it has not yet been compelling. The Bush administration has, in fact, indicated that, over the next three years, the United States will increase its development assistance by 50 percent. It will add $5 billion to the assistance that it's now providing. And the European Union has said that it would add, give or take, $7 billion or $8 billion over that same period.

But what happened at Cancún[‡] was, at the very least, a disappointment compared with the undertakings that were hoped for. And, unfortunately, despite the increased expectations, we have already run into some problems. Take, just as one example, the issue of education for all, trying to get kids into

---

[‡] The World Trade Organization's Fifth Ministerial Conference took place in Cancún, Mexico, in September 2003 and failed to reach agreement on developed-country agricultural subsidies.

school. Although the initial target involved 25 countries, we identified 7 countries, accounting for only 4 percent of children out of school worldwide, for financing. And we came up with fairly modest demands: maybe as much as $800 million a year over a 10-year period of incremental funding, because of concern about the money going out of one pocket and into another. Well, we have succeeded, with a lot of trouble so far, in raising $207 million for the first three years, and we're almost to the brick wall.

We are going to have another go in a month's time. But the fact is that today, with less economic growth than we would want and many other distractions, the money is simply not flowing. And I must say that it's unlikely that the developing countries will take the steps that are necessary, be it on social reform or even on corruption, if they don't see the benefits. It's one thing to make a bold move when you know that, if you get the support, you can look confidently to the future. But it's unclear whether the support will be there, and this is an issue of great significance.

Meanwhile the world does not stand still: in the next 25 years world population will grow by another 2 billion, give or take a couple hundred million. And all but 50 million of that increase will go to developing countries. So in 2025 we will have a world of 8 billion people, 7 billion of whom are in developing countries.

It is my strong belief that unless we deal with the question of equity and the question of stability and the issue of hope, there is no way that we can guarantee peace and security to our people, wherever they are in the world. Knocking off the heads of fundamentalist terror organizations is no doubt meritorious, but it will not deal with the question of fundamental stability.

The other thing you should know is that, in 2025, the world will have more than 3 billion people under the age of 25—in fact, under the age of 23. I've been working on a new initiative with youth, and in Paris I met with a group of these young people, who through their organizations represent a couple of hundred million. I started to talk to them about the future, and they said, "Listen, we're not the future—we're the *now*. We are here now, and there are 3 billion of us today. And there are 1.8 billion of us under the age of 15, and another 1.2 billion between 15 and 23. And we're the people who can either make the world or ruin it."

I think you've seen—whether it be child soldiers or people who have never had a job—that the issue of stability is tied very closely to the question of development and the question of hope. And here I think we've got it really wrong. When Mars passed close to Earth recently, I started to write a piece in which I said the following: If a Martian came down and had a look at where we are in relation to the Millennium goals, he would go back and report that we're crazy. We have a $33 trillion global economy. We have an interest in helping the developing countries. The Martian would say, "Well, I see that they are all linked on one planet—by the environment, by health, by trade, by commerce, by drugs, by terror, by crime, by migration. And yet, in response to the threat that they themselves have identified, the rich countries are putting only $56 billion into development assistance, only half of which is in cash. And meanwhile they are spending $350 billion on domestic agricultural assistance, through either tariffs or subsidies, and $800 billion on defense."

So, if you accept my analysis, we have this curious imbalance between the likely future of those kids I saw in Paris and the future of our own kids. We ourselves may not have to worry so much, except for [former World Bank President] Bob McNamara, who seems to have eternal life and youth. But for the people living 20 or 25 years from now, this issue is going to be *the* issue, and it is not a speculative issue. It is a train coming straight down that track. And we are not addressing it as we should. And this issue of imbalance of resources and imbalance of our interests is something that I think this Council could fruitfully explore.

I love coming to the Council to say these things. I still have a few friends here. Most of them think I have gone off the rails, because I used to be a perfectly understandable investment banker with a thing about music. Now they see me coming here and talking about poverty and about these other issues. And they wonder—they certainly hope that I'll stay in Washington, but they wonder—how has this affected me?

All I can say to you, my friends, is that after eight and a half years in this job, I really passionately believe that this issue of poverty and this issue of equity are the issues that need addressing as much as or more than any other that we face. It is my hope that, by having the opportunity to talk to you here tonight, and respond to your questions, we can do even more on this Council to address this issue, which is the issue of our day, and the issue that will determine whether we have security and peace.

Address to the United Nations High-Level Dialogue on Financing for Development

NEW YORK | OCTOBER 30, 2003

As Wolfensohn notes in his opening remarks, this address marked the first time a World Bank president had addressed the UN General Assembly. Wolfensohn reminds the audience of the Monterrey agenda and of the need to work together in the global fight against poverty.

Mr. President, Mr. Secretary-General, Distinguished Colleagues:

This for the World Bank is a historic occasion: the first time the president of the World Bank has addressed the General Assembly. And it is, of course, significant that we should come together on financing for development—a subject that unites us, a subject on which our partnership is being tested and proven each day. I am delighted to be here in the presence of the secretary-general [Kofi Annan], whose leadership on these matters is so important and so crucial to a better world, a peaceful world, and a world in which development can take place.

Let me say by way of early observation that we are enriched by the various meetings that have been held by this body. The work on the environment, the work on gender, the work on social issues have given the international financial institutions an agenda that is enriched by the observations of this body and its partners.

I have come to speak about where we are in our efforts to fulfill the joint undertakings of the developed and the developing countries of the last several years. Developing countries undertook to strengthen capacity, to strengthen their legal and judicial systems and financial systems, and to fight corruption. All of these tasks were undertaken at [the March 2002 Financing for Development Conference in] Monterrey and reaffirmed, in the case of Africa, in the New Partnership for Africa's Development. In return, wealthy countries indicated that they would assist in capacity building, that they would provide additional development assistance, and that they would open their markets for trade.

Some progress has, in fact, been made on both sides. The countries that are developing have taken steps toward strengthening governance, toward building the infrastructure of their legal and financial systems, and to a degree toward fighting corruption.

But I think it is not unfair to say that there is still much to be done. As I commented in my speech at the Bank-Fund Annual Meetings, there are really no secrets in the countries represented here. Everyone knows the steps that need to be taken, and the issue is to take action. Everyone knows where the gaps in structure are and where those who are corrupt are to be found. It is difficult to move forward, but it is essential if the aims of Monterrey are to be met.

But, on the other side, the encouragement to action is that of a better world, a better opportunity, which needs to be supported by the wealthy countries, and progress here has at best been mixed. Yes, we have seen, and are delighted by and grateful for, the $18 billion in additional funding promised over the next three years. And, yes, we have seen discussions taking place on opening to trade. But, again, it is fair to say that, with the problems that emerged at [the September 2003 World Trade Organization ministerial conference in] Cancún and with the reassessment of countries' financial needs, this is something that needs further and significant attention.

We in our institution are concerned about the imbalance that exists in the allocation of resources and the allocation of interest in the development process: an allocation that leads to annual worldwide spending of $800 billion on defense, yet only $56 billion on development assistance. The imbalance can also be seen in relation to the movements of people around the world: remittances from migrant workers overseas now total $80 billion a year, dwarfing the development assistance coming from the governments of the developed countries.

It is not a lack of good will; it is not a lack of intent. We are seeing good progress and leadership on the part of our colleagues in the United States and in the European Union. But, if indeed we are to succeed with the Monterrey agenda, we must each of us—developed countries, developing countries, and international institutions—lift our game. And we in the Bank are looking at ourselves, at how we can increase our effectiveness, and how we can build a more coordinated effort and follow up on the Rome* agenda.

I am delighted to have met, within the last couple of weeks, with the local representatives of the United Nations Development Programme. I thought the meeting was highly constructive. And I want to assure all of you here, in this chamber, that the desire of our institution is to work intimately and closely with the UN system, because we believe that no results can be possible in terms of the Monterrey agenda unless we work as partners, you and us together with our friends in civil society and the private sector.

I think there has been progress, but I must say, Mr. President, I think there is very much to be done in today's environment.

Thank you so much.

---

* The High-Level Forum on Harmonization, held in Rome in February 2003, sought to improve cooperation among development agencies and other institutions and eliminate overlap and duplication of effort.

With Gordon Brown, published in *The Guardian* (Manchester)

FEBRUARY 16, 2004

This essay, co-written with the U.K. chancellor of the exchequer, was published the day the U.K. Treasury hosted a meeting of government officials, religious and civil society leaders, and celebrity activists to prepare to make 2005 a "year of development." Brown and Wolfensohn paint a picture of what will happen without more action on the Millennium Development Goals, and they call for world leaders to take further steps on trade, debt relief, education, and aid.

In London today, governments, faith groups, charities and business will come together and examine how the world can meet its 2015 millennium development goals; 2005 will be a crucial year that will determine whether the world keeps its promises or breaks them.

Five years ago, every world leader, every major international body and almost every single country signed up to eight millennium development goals—at the heart of which is a definitive commitment to ensuring education for every child, the elimination of avoidable infant and maternal deaths and the halving of poverty. But by next year, the first goal, for girls' education, will go unmet—and world leaders face a stark choice.

Either resources are made available now to tackle poverty, or targets set in a fanfare of publicity will once again be missed and the world's poor left further behind. Seventy countries will have failed to achieve universal primary education by our target date. Yet the promise we made on education for sub-Saharan Africa was to be met by 2015, not—as now predicted—2129.

Instead of cutting child mortality by two-thirds by 2015, 30,000 children continue to die unnecessarily each day from avoidable diseases. Yet the promise we made on child health for sub-Saharan Africa was to be achieved in 2015, not—as it now looks—2165.

Without greatly increased growth, sub-Saharan Africa, the Middle East, North Africa, Latin America, the Caribbean and the transition economies of Europe and central Asia will all fail to see their poverty halved. Yet the promise made to sub-Saharan Africa was for 2015, not—as now seems likely—2147.

When we know the scale of the task, and the promises we made, we cannot wait for some other time and some other people. The world must act together now. But there is another reason why 2005 is a vital date: it is the 20th anniversary of Live Aid,* an event that marked for many the moment when the world woke up to the enormous challenge of tackling poverty.

Yet 20 years on, the great divide between rich and poor countries has grown, is growing and will continue to grow—and in Ethiopia, where Live Aid began, there are today only 7,000 doctors for 67 million people, and spending on health is no more than two dollars a year per person.

Twenty years on, with needs even more pressing, we must yet again awaken the conscience of the world. For the sake of Africa and the world's poor, Britain's G8 presidency of 2005† must become, in the UK's view, a development presidency.

To have a chance of meeting the millennium goals, a new deal between developing and developed countries must be forged. It is in the interests of developing countries to tackle corruption and undertake a sequenced opening up to the investment, trade and growth that will provide jobs. And working with the World Bank and the IMF, developed countries must improve the quantity and quality of development aid. Our offer should be that countries willing to reform will have the resources they need to tackle illiteracy, poverty and disease.

So what does the detail of such an agenda for development look like?

First, the world trade talks—which can reduce agricultural protectionism and thus poverty in developing countries—must be pushed forward. Developing countries would gain nearly $350bn by 2015 as a result—enough to lift 140 million people out of poverty.

Second, so that all highly indebted poor countries shed the burden of unsustainable debt, the next stage of debt relief must be properly financed.

Third, there is no single more effective anti-poverty strategy than education, and we must push much harder to deliver the agreed "education for all" goals, including 80 million new school places in Africa.

Fourth, substantial extra resources must now be available to eliminate preventable diseases—TB, malaria and HIV/Aids.

And because these noble challenges need to be financed together, bold initiatives must be explored—including the UK government's proposal for a new international finance facility, through which donors from the richer countries would raise funds on the international capital markets to double aid from around $50bn a year to $100bn.

We must act, not only because it is morally right, but because it is now essential for stability and security. Many of us grew up thinking there were two

* The Live Aid concert took place on July 13, 1985, in London and Philadelphia simultaneously and raised an estimated $100 million to relieve hunger in Africa.
† The United Kingdom will host the 2005 Group of Eight summit at Gleneagles, Scotland, in July.

worlds—the haves and the have-nots—and that they were quite separate. That
was wrong then. It is even more wrong now. We are linked now in so many
ways: by economics and trade, migration, environment, disease, drugs, conflict
and—yes—terrorism.

It is only by addressing these global issues now—and tackling poverty—that
we can shape the better world we want our children to inhabit. Meeting and
mastering these challenges can unite all people of goodwill. Let the days and
the months leading to 2005 become a time of action.

HUMAN RIGHTS AND DEVELOPMENT: TOWARD MUTUAL REINFORCEMENT

Remarks at a dialogue organized by the Ethical Globalization Initiative and New York University Law School

NEW YORK | MARCH 1, 2004

In these remarks Wolfensohn addresses the Bank's role in the promotion of human rights through its development agenda. He points to the common ground between the development and human rights communities and appeals for joint action against what he calls a "lack of focus" on basic human needs.

Thank you very much, Mary,* and thank you, Philip,† for being here, and thank all of you for attending this gathering. I'm very happy that it is being held in a room named after a very good friend of mine, Lester Pollack [chairman of the board of NYU Law School], whose name is on a plaque by the door, and happy that we're here to inaugurate it. I also must acknowledge Mary's team and Phillip's team and my own team for the work that they've done in preparing for this meeting.

Let me start by saying that Alfredo Sfeir-Younis [senior adviser to the managing director at the World Bank] gave me three versions of a speech. It's very lengthy, very complicated, and frankly beyond me. He knows so much about this subject that I think he assumed that I would be able to enter immediately into a discussion with human rights activists at the highest possible level, relate it to the work of development activists, and emerge with some searing insights that I could leave you with that would set the tone for the entire day. Sadly, I'm unable to do that because I'm really not there yet. And one of my hopes is that, in the course of the day, we may, with my colleagues, elucidate just what some of the issues are and what is the way forward in a debate that I've never fully understood.

What I'd really like to do is just to give you my feelings about this issue of human rights and development, and share some of the thoughts that go through my head as I think about the subject and as I try to lead our institution in a way that will profit from the activities of human rights activists. Indeed, the approach is one I have discussed with Mary many times, comparing the rights-based approach to development with what it is that I imagine we at the Bank are doing already. I've said to Mary a number of times that I think there's a tremendous coalescence between what we do every day in our institution and what the human rights community is doing. Perhaps we do not speak as much

---

* Mary Robinson, director of the Ethical Globalization Initiative and former UN high commissioner for human rights.
† Philip Alston, professor of law at NYU specializing in human rights.

about rights as we should, but in fact we are giving effect to the agenda of the human rights community.

I did take the trouble last night to read each of the declarations and the covenants on human rights that have been agreed to by the United Nations. There's quite a volume of them, but I did decide that if I was going to come to this meeting it might be worthwhile to read them. And it was a profitable activity, because I started circling with my pen, first, the elements of the Universal Declaration,[‡] and then of the covenants, with which you are all, of course, very familiar: on civil and political rights; on economic, social, and cultural rights; on the right to development; and the various other human rights instruments that have been added since.

Going through it in that way, starting with the preamble to the Universal Declaration and looking at the various articles, you, of course, start with the right to life, liberty, and security of every person. You then move to issues of the recognition of rights before the law, or what we would incorporate in our work under the heading of legal, social, and judicial reform, and from there to various aspects of what that law should be and the right to nationality.

And, when I read about that right to nationality, I thought about something we at the Bank did six months ago. We held a conference in Europe along with six central European governments on the Roma peoples. We didn't call it a rights conference, but we did gather together the representatives of 12 million people whose countries will be joining the European Union, yet who suffer, in many cases, by not even having passports. We had what I thought was a fantastic conference, and I never mentioned the words "human rights." But it just jumped out at me as I thought of the many activities we do every day that seem to be in keeping with human rights.

I then looked at Article 17, on property rights. I looked at the right of freedom of thought, conscience, and religion. And again I thought of the activities of our own institution in seeking to reach out and to have a dialogue on faith and development. Over the last five years we have pulled together, for three separate meetings, faith leaders from around the world. We have engaged in this dialogue despite the view expressed by some that such a dialogue pollutes our institution, by having religion as an aspect of our activities.

The declaration also goes on to talk about culture, and I had the same experience on culture. We held a conference in Florence on culture and development, and we expected a couple of hundred people to attend, but 700 turned up for a four-day conference. And, that, too, was resisted by many of

---

‡ The Universal Declaration of Human Rights, adopted by the United Nations General Assembly in 1948.

our shareholders as being exotic, elitist, and not the sort of thing that a development institution should do.

I remind you of all that because we at the Bank work for the same people who wrote this document, and their application of the principles to which they have so vigorously attested, I might tell you, in actuality sometimes varies with the notions that they had in mind when they signed it. And I raise that point, too, because we are not an institution just composed of my colleagues and myself, who are able to do whatever we'd like to do. We're an institution that is owned by and, to an extent, dominated by the very same people who wrote the Declaration of Human Rights and the addenda thereto.

I've said to Mary many times, "You know, one of the things we have to do in our institution is to try and get some things done, but to some of our shareholders the very mention of the words 'human rights' is inflammatory language. It gets into areas of politics and other areas, and they become very concerned. So we decide to just go around it, and instead we talk the language of economics and social development."

And then I continued to read the Universal Declaration and came to the point where it refers, as you know, to social security, equal employment, the right to adequate standards of living, motherhood, children, education, and international order. All these are things that, if you had asked me to indicate what is the agenda of our institution, I would have told you before rereading this document were part of the charter of our institution. It's actually what we do every day. We have a motto just inside our door that says that we should fight poverty with passion and that we should do it every day.

And I have 10,000 colleagues, some of whom probably have never read the Universal Declaration of Human Rights, and certainly have not read the covenants in detail as I can now claim I have. They come in and together we deal with this development agenda in a way that is, we think, pretty strong. Our people feel morally pretty strong and indeed feel they are no less strong on these issues than the rights activists. They actually think, correctly or not, that they're on pretty high moral ground and that their job is to deal with the question of poverty. And when you look at what they're dealing with, I will tell you candidly, it is everything that is in this document of the rights agenda and the covenants thereto.

I was really fascinated last night when I read this, because—and I have only mentioned a couple of issues—I could see in this document that if I had read it thoroughly *before* I had articulated the program of our institution, this document could have been the framework that would have led us to the framework of our poverty reduction strategy, or the Comprehensive Development Framework, or the interconnection of rights. The declaration refers to the interconnection of rights, and we have said that our approach to poverty and development is an interconnected process. It is one where you need to have all the parts functional, because if you don't, you're going to fail to give adequate attention to those things, and that will make the achievement of your objective on poverty unattainable.

So there are an enormous number of parallels between what we've, perhaps, lucked into, or groped toward, over our 50 years and the integrated world development approach that those concerned with human rights have articulated, as I found in the human rights literature, which I also read some of last night. And which, I might add, I have been pumped full of in the last few days by my friend Alfredo, whose main job in our institution is not to ensure that all my colleagues are educated but, as I discovered, to educate me. Every week I learn something new from Alfredo, and so you should know that that white-bearded gentleman over there is a great factor in our institution, and he feeds me this stuff intravenously. And it's having an effect, as it is on many in our organization.

But then I thought, why then are we arguing, both here and within our organization? Why is there any heat in *this* debate, when all of us face a much more difficult and significant problem? We can argue with each other and debate, as I know we will today, on the correct approach to each of the five subjects on the agenda. And it will, I think, demonstrate a considerable commonality of interest between the two communities and I hope, at the end, bring about a methodology for moving forward in a better, more complementary, and mutually supportive way.

As Mary has said, when I came to the Bank, I found we were not allowed, as Peter Eigen§ well knows, to mention the word "corruption." It was called the "C-word." I was told within days of coming to the institution, by the general counsel and in great secrecy, "Don't mention the C-word." And I said, "What's the C-word?" He said, "Corruption."

Well, maybe we need to mention the "R-word," which is "rights." And maybe, coming down the line, we will talk much more about rights as we move forward. But, in the case of rights, the reason we have not used the word is not, I think, that there is any difference of view. Rather, I think, there has been, because of the history of our organization and because of the way we have to move things forward with our Board and with our client countries, a tendency to approach the matter from an economic and from a social point of view. We may stake out objectives that are articulated in the Declaration and in the covenants, but we don't refer back specifically to this document, but

§ Founder and chairman of Transparency International.

rather pick up things from the document within the context of seeking to address the question of poverty.

Let me return now to the thought that I just touched on a moment ago. Why is it that we're debating while Rome is burning? There is an issue that I think each of our communities needs to face. Our shareholders who set the Millennium Development Goals also set, as a result of the meetings in Monterrey and Johannesburg,** a basis on which those goals might be achieved. And the issue is that we have, in most cases, very little chance of achieving these Millennium goals for lack of interest and support and priority being given to the question of achieving them at this time.

There's a fair chance that we will achieve the poverty goal, as measured by the statistics. But, if you read the statistics, you will see they are strongly biased by China and India. If you take a look at the 47 countries in Sub-Saharan Africa, you'll find that the statistics are, in fact, going in the other direction. Or look at the goals for primary school education, which, by the way is mentioned many times in the covenants as well as in the initial charter. We started with the fact that there are 130 million kids around the world who are not in primary school, the majority of whom are girls. And so, we thought, let's make the first target for the Millennium goals that every child should be in school, because no one can disagree with that.

I probably should have said back then, and may well have said, "Look, every child has the right to primary school education. They have the right. It's written right here. And we just want to support that right. It's a right that is agreed to by all the nations of the world. So let's get on with it."

Well, I did that, and we came up with 18 countries plus 5 more large countries, which would have allowed us to tackle the question of how to finance those countries that have an integrated approach to education, an interdependent approach to education, as the charter says, that have an effective program, and that have the means of applying that program, and lack only the resources.

And we calculated that for these countries we needed a couple of billion dollars a year for a period of 7 to 10 years, as supplemental support for this right to education and for this education objective, to achieve this Millennium goal. Well, we succeeded in the first round of trying to get money for this in reducing the number to seven countries, with fewer than 7 percent of the kids involved. And we succeeded, if that's the word, in putting together a total of $200 million for three years.

** The International Conference on Financing for Development was held in Monterrey, Mexico, in March 2002; the World Summit on Sustainable Development was held in Johannesburg in August and September 2002.

And then my friend Jean-Louis Sarbib[†] who'll be talking to you later, went back and got what I think he calls a catalytic fund for a few hundred million dollars, to see if we could come at it again—a catalytic fund that will allow us, if we're lucky, to get this small number of kids into school.

Now, there the issue is as we define it. It's not the issue of advocacy. It is the simple fact that today people are really not interested in pursuing these goals if it requires extra finance. One hears various numbers. There's the $5 billion more that is being put up by the United States to increase its commitment from $10 billion to $15 billion, and there's another $8 billion to $12 billion that will be forthcoming from the European Union. And people will tell you that last year saw movement forward, with an increase of $6 billion in available funding for development assistance. And, in fact, if you look at the statistics, it goes from $52 billion to $58 billion. But I asked my colleagues, since I used to be in the business of analyzing numbers, to take those numbers apart.

So we took them apart. What is this $6 billion increase? Three billion of it is debt relief, which is a zero contribution. It is money that would not have been paid back anyway and is now written off. So, in fact, of that $58 billion, $6 billion is debt relief. Another $2 billion is an increase in the money going to consultants and scholarships. So that makes $8 billion. And $2 billion more goes to Pakistan and Afghanistan in special transfers, and we're not yet talking about the special transfers to Iraq, which also will probably embellish and strengthen the numbers. So, far from being an increase, when you really dig into it, it's at best a "wash". And when you do the same analysis for the whole $58 billion, which we had done already some months ago, you'll be lucky to find $26 billion to $28 billion of it in cash.

Against that you have agricultural subsidies by the developed countries, which Mary alluded to, of $300 billion plus. And you have expenditures on the military and defense. In 1999 those added up to $800 billion, and we estimate that today it is probably $1 trillion. Those are the statistics. And then we talk about achieving the objectives because the world is united in support. It's nonsense. We're spending on the military 20 times what we're spending for development. And the developing world itself, by the way, is spending $200 billion a year on military expenditure. That is largely China and some of the other large countries, but it is still much too high in Africa and other places as well.

Forgive me for this diversion, but I thought it was important that, before we beat each other up, we understand that we have a common enemy, which is indifference. It's the lack of focus on what both of our communities, the

---

† Senior vice president, Human Development Network.

development and the rights-based communities, think about. And it is here that, I think, together we could make a big contribution, by joining together to put pressure on our leaders to make this world a better place through a more focused and more effective effort both in terms of development and in terms of rights.

I look forward to the results of these discussions very much. And I can assure you that, from the point of view of the Bank and the International Finance Corporation—and you have Peter Woicke [executive vice president, International Finance Corporation] here who will be addressing the private sector activities—we are deeply committed and interested in trying to clarify the role of rights in development. We want to explore how we can go beyond language to try and make our work more effective, and how we can, from the point of view of advocacy, join together to get some results. I simply have added the dimension that, when our two sides are talking about our respective disciplines, let's not forget that there are people out there who care about neither rights nor development.

Thank you, Mary, for letting me join you.

Foreword to *World Development Indicators 2004*

PUBLISHED BY THE WORLD BANK, MARCH 2004

This foreword to the Bank's premier annual statistical publication makes the case for the importance of solid statistics in setting goals and measuring progress in development efforts.

Development is about people. But to measure development and see its effect on people, we need good statistics. Statistics that tell us that life expectancy in the last 40 years has gone up 20 years in developing countries, more than in all the time before that. That literacy has improved. That infant mortality and maternal mortality have decreased. And that fewer people are living in extreme poverty.

However, the statistics also tell us that malnutrition and disease still claim the lives of millions of young children. That millions more never receive a primary education. And that in countries at the center of the HIV/AIDS epidemic, life expectancy has been falling. Of the 6 billion people on the planet today, 5 billion live in developing countries. But in the next 30 years the world's population will grow by 2 billion—from 6 billion to 8 billion—and all but 50 million of them will live in today's developing countries. What will their lives be like? We hope, much better than today.

The Millennium Development Goals set specific targets for improving people's lives. They were proposed and adopted by the General Assembly of the United Nations—not as vague and lofty statements of our good intentions, but as a practical guide to what can and should be accomplished by the international community in the opening quarter of the 21st century. That is why they were presented so clearly, with precise, quantified targets, based on widely accepted statistical indicators. Setting goals and measuring progress toward them in a transparent process is a proven management technique for holding our focus, avoiding wasteful diversions of effort, and encouraging robust public discussion of both means and ends.

Since the adoption of the Millennium Development Goals, another important step in deepening the international consensus on development was the Monterrey Conference on Financing for Development. At Monterrey developing countries recognized the need to put reducing poverty and achieving the human and environmental goals of the Millennium Declaration at the center of their development programs. Developed countries accepted an obligation to uphold their share of a partnership for development by providing resources, opening trade, and relieving the burden of debt on the poorest countries. That consensus requires monitoring not only the outcomes in developing countries—but also the policies and actions of rich countries and development agencies to meet their commitments.

A comprehensive development strategy calls for a comprehensive set of statistics. Any user of *World Development Indicators* recognizes the many gaps in sound, available information. At the World Bank we are committed to working with our partners to improve the quality and availability of development statistics. This effort starts with strengthening national statistical systems in developing countries. But it must be matched by a commitment of the international community to provide the necessary technical and financial support.

The World Bank's mission statement asks us to "fight poverty with passion and professionalism for lasting results." Ultimately, it is the results that count. If we act now with realism and foresight based on good information, if we think globally and allocate our resources accordingly, we can make a lasting difference in people's lives.

Published in the *Toronto Star*

MAY 3, 2004

This op-ed describes the role that a free press can play in spurring economic development, fighting corruption, and supporting public health outreach efforts. It was timed to run in newspapers worldwide on World Press Freedom Day.

As we mark World Press Freedom Day on May 3, this year's campaign theme, "Press Freedom Pays," provides an excellent opportunity to reflect on the catalytic role that an open and free media can play in economic development, and particularly in the fight against global poverty.

We know from Freedom House* that out of a global population of six billion people, only 1.2 billion people live in countries with access to a free press, 2.4 billion have access to a partially free press, and another 2.4 billion live without a free press. In other words, around 80 percent of the world's population does not have access to a fully free press. It is striking that the majority of those people live in the developing world.

These imbalances in press freedom reflect broader imbalances between the rich and poor countries.

Some of these broader imbalances include: One billion of the total world population own 80 percent of global wealth, while another billion struggle to survive on a dollar a day. Two billion people have no access to clean water; 150 million children never get the chance to go to school; and more than 40 million people in the developing countries are HIV-positive, with little hope of receiving treatment for this dreadful disease.

What is the connection, then, between press freedom and economic poverty? A large part of the answer lies with corruption, and the fight against it. Studies by the World Bank, for instance, show that the higher the level of press freedom in countries, the greater the control over corruption and thus the greater focus of scarce resources on priority development issues.

A free press not only serves as an outlet for expression, but it also provides a source of accountability, a vehicle for civic participation, and a check on official corruption. A free press also helps build more effective and stronger institutions.

By fostering transparency and accountability in both public and private spheres, the media in poor countries are being increasingly recognized as a

---

* Freedom House is a nonprofit, nonpartisan organization that publishes ratings of countries according to various measures of freedom.

"development good" capable of contributing to improved government accountability and more effective use of resources.

But a free press not only pays off in the fight against corruption. It also pays
off in supplementing traditional school education (e.g. radio math lessons), in
improving public health efforts (HIV-AIDS education campaigns), and in supporting institutional change and market development (sharing of timely and
relevant information). Further, there is a strong positive correlation between
greater voice and accountability, and improvements in incomes, infant mortality, and adult literacy.

That is why we must continue the push for press freedom and there is still
much to be done. In many countries, particularly in transition and developing
economies, the independence of the media can be fragile, and even shackled.

Policies on access to and dissemination of information, and other legal regulations that foster a culture of openness, transparency and accountability are key.
Ultimately, they help to promote good governance and more equitable growth.

The World Bank is contributing to this effort. Through the World Bank
Institute, our learning arm, we have delivered training programs reaching over
3,000 journalists. These programs include specialized courses on economic
journalism, health, and environment. Most programs are offered using distance

learning technologies, such as videoconference, interactive television and the Internet to broaden the outreach to participants in more than 50 countries.

By addressing critical health issues like HIV/AIDS we have spurred journalists to find new ways of covering this pandemic in their countries. And investigative journalism courses help them tackle the issues of corruption in a professional way.

There is no longer any doubt that the media's contributions are invaluable to advance economic progress, fight corruption, address the great imbalances between rich and poor, and ultimately reduce poverty worldwide.

Let us then make sure that press freedom continues to pay, especially for the billions of poor people who need it most.

Closing remarks at the Annual Bank Conference on Development Economics

BRUSSELS | MAY 11, 2004

> *In this speech at the World Bank's annual research conference on the economics of development, published in the conference proceedings, Wolfensohn argues that the issue of peace and development is "consuming us." He describes the arrival of 2 billion people in developing countries in the coming three decades as a "train that's coming down the track" and an issue that needs attention.*

Let me, first of all, say thank you to the prime minister [of Belgium Guy Verhofstadt] for hosting this conference. We are very grateful to you, and I am very happy indeed that we have so many people from different spectra of society at the meeting.

My impression is that we have done more than enough analysis to know what it is that would get us to the Millennium Development Goals. We can keep analyzing it, but one keeps coming back to the proposition that developing countries and developed countries each have responsibilities, and they are fairly clearly laid out, although on the points of emphasis some people differ. Developing countries, in terms of governance, need to build capacity and strengthen their legal systems, they need to strengthen their financial systems, and they need to fight corruption. These are conditions precedent to development. As for the developed countries, at Monterrey, Johannesburg, and Doha* they said they would help build capacity, open their markets for trade, increase aid, and try to help on the issue of corruption, given that it's not a one-sided issue.

This commitment has been analyzed in many ways, and subsidiary issues, such as the level of aid and the pace of openness of trade, have consumed us. Most world leaders understand that the issue is not one of two worlds, but one of one interconnected world. And if that needed to be brought home, it was probably brought home best on September 11, and more recently in Madrid.†

The leaders that I've met and many people elsewhere all understand that we are in a different sort of world today, and that spending $900 billion a year on

---

* The International Conference on Financing for Development was held in Monterrey, Mexico, in March 2002; the World Summit on Sustainable Development was held in Johannesburg in August and September 2002; the Fourth World Trade Organization Ministerial Conference, which launched the Doha Development Round of international trade negotiations, was held in Doha, Qatar, in November 2001.
† Terrorists exploded bombs on four commuter trains in Madrid on March 11, 2004.

military expenditures, $300 billion or $350 billion on agricultural subsidies and tariff protection, and just $50 billion or $60 billion on development is crazy. I said jokingly the other day that, if we spent $900 billion on development, we might have to spend only $50 billion on military expenditures. No one has bought that yet. The point is that we are out of balance. But there are many leaders who, I think, would like to do something about it.

What are the inhibitions? What is inhibiting the wealthy side of the house? Well, the first thing is that, I think, at the moment, everyone is concerned about growth. It looks as though it's picked up, but in the last days at least the stock markets are reflecting some indecision. But overriding it all is Iraq, the situation in Palestine, and the issue of terror. It is very hard in the press and in public debate to get beyond these highly visible issues and to get people to focus, in terms of action, on anything but these critical visible issues. If you look at the European or the American press, the headlines are about the latest crisis, the latest problem, the division between the United States and some of its allies and between Europe and some of its allies, the participation, and the fragmentation of view. And so, if peace is a key component in terms of development in Africa, resolution of these issues is needed. And addressing confrontations between extremists of one side or another and the rest of the community, wherever it is, is fundamental to getting back to the issue of what sort of peaceful world we want, and what sort of world we want for the young people who are here today, and what sort of world they want.

This issue of peace and development is an issue that is consuming us. It consumes most political debates in different countries, as do the issues of security, job security, and the future for much of the population of the rich world. It is in this context that I would like to comment on the observations made by Prime Minister Verhofstadt, who has made some extremely important suggestions for a more regional and representative approach to governance. My slight worry is that even if you have a regional and more representative approach to government, while you have individual country interests, as focused as they are on their own issues at this moment, although I think you'd get a better debate, whether you'll get better action as a result is not clear.

I think that reorganizing is a good thing to do, but the fundamental problem in terms of the wealthy countries is their preoccupation with more visible issues rather than the fact that 2 billion more people will populate the planet in the next 25 to 30 years, all but 50 million of them in developing countries. For me, that is the real issue. That's the train that's coming down the track that's going to hit us, even more than some of the other, more visible issues that we face today, with the possible exception of the confrontation, as perceived by some, with radical Islam. So that is the first point I'd like to make.

The second point is that I think that if we are going to seriously address the questions of reaching the [Millennium] goals, we have to think a step beyond institutional reorganization. In May in Shanghai we will be discussing the issue of scaling up. How do we take successful projects and initiatives and take them to scale? How do we get beyond fixing 50 schools in a country to fixing 5,000 schools? How do we go beyond 100 community development programs to 10,000 community development programs?

It's not surprising that we chose Shanghai to have this discussion, given China's success in scaling up. My interim conclusion is that the big change we have to make is to stop thinking about poor people as the object of charity or as the problem, and think about enfranchising them and saying they are part of the solution. China got this right in many of the projects I have seen. Giving responsibility to the people who are most concerned in order to have local ownership, and doing it on a broader scale, is something we have to develop far more significantly, and I hope it will come out of the discussions in Shanghai.

The third thing I want to say, for the benefit of the young people who are here, is that we at the World Bank were late in addressing the issue of youth. But, surprisingly, I think we are now ahead of most other institutions. We have 2.8 billion people in the world under the age of 24. We have 1.5 billion under the age of 15. We have to create a billion new jobs in the coming years. And there is no way that we will have peace unless we can give hope and opportunity to young people.

Nearly a year ago I met in Paris with a group of young people, and I gave a sort of patronizing introduction about the future that we were going to give to them. And the first person who spoke said, "Mr. Wolfensohn, we're not the future. We're the *now*. And please understand that at 17 we're different than you were at 17." And he added, "My younger brother, who's 12, is different than I was at 12. And so you have to take into account what we think, because we can help you with AIDS, we can help you with education, we can help you with understanding, we can help you with peace."

I am relating this story, because I am delighted that we have young people with us here today, and at least in my organization, we weren't doing enough in relation to young people. But, by the end of this year, in 20 of our offices we will have permanent groups of young people between 15 and 23 who will be commenting on all our projects and working with us.

Let me finally say, in relation to the developing countries themselves, we've focused on trade and we've focused on aid; we've focused on what the rich countries are or are not doing. But developing countries also have problems. I look particularly at those countries that are faced with huge problems of governance. As I get around the world and talk a lot about corruption, I hear a lot of discussion about corruption. But, frankly, in almost any country, within 24 hours you can know whether the president is a crook, whether the prime minister is a crook, whether his wife is getting 10 percent, whether the family is getting 10 percent, which minister is a crook, which chief justice is a crook. It doesn't take a genius to find out what the real structure is. You sit down and talk with many leaders in these countries, and you know that the people close to them may be the worst offenders. So we really need to buttress reformers in developing countries who are trying to bring about a change.

Two major initiatives are under way today, one in Nigeria and one in Brazil. In Brazil President Lula [da Silva] is trying to change the culture in terms of equity, social justice, and the balance between rich and poor. I think it is a remarkable effort. In Nigeria a group under the finance minister and a dozen other people are tackling the issue of corruption and governance.

So there are initiatives taking place, and there are success stories in the developing world. We should not forget that in the past 40 years we have made huge progress in terms of poverty, life expectancy, and many other statistics. We are not entirely on track—but we're not entirely off track either. And there are huge supporters, like the prime minister and [European Commission President] Romano Prodi, to whom I must pay public tribute for what he's done for development. There are many good leaders in the world who are moving together. What we need to do is follow the track, take some of those engines that are off track and put them back on, and, above all, act now and get up enough speed to get us to the goal that we're seeking.

THE SEARCH FOR VALUES IN A WORLD OUT OF BALANCE

Commencement address at Brandeis University

WALTHAM, MASSACHUSETTS | MAY 23, 2004

One of the best commencement addresses Wolfensohn gave during his tenure, this speech calls on the Brandeis graduates to stand up for social justice. He reflects on the Anglo-centric education he received as a youth in Australia and spells out the need for the youth of today to learn more about the world around them, including China, India, and the Muslim countries.

Mr. Chairman, Mr. President, and Distinguished Graduates of the Class of 2004:

Let me first of all say, on behalf of all of us who are honored, what a sense of gratitude we all feel for the recognition put upon us by this university. It is a great moment for all of us, and I feel deeply privileged that I am the one who is allowed to speak for such a remarkable group of colleagues here on the platform with me, any one of whom I am sure could do a better job than I will do. But let me say also that, for all of us, this opportunity to be at Brandeis, at a university with such a distinguished history and with such a clear sense of direction, seeking social justice at a time when our world cries out for it, is a very, very special moment.

This class of 2004 is really the first millennial class, having entered as freshmen in 2000, and I congratulate you. And you have seen many things in your four years here, but highlighted among them must be the experience of 9/11, when the world was shocked and when our world changed.

I was remembering my own graduation just about 50 years ago, as I looked at the class of 1954 here and wondered if I looked as youthful as they do. But 50 years ago I was in distant Australia, and, for me, the world was a very simple place. There was the rich world, and there was the poor world. I imagined that there was around Australia, and around the United States and around Europe, a sort of wall.

I was educated to learn about the kings of England. I learned a bit about the Boston Tea Party. I learned all sorts of facts that seem now irrelevant. I learned nothing about Islam; I learned nothing about China. I learned nothing about India, nothing about Africa, nothing about Latin America.

And I came to do my postgraduate work in this country because I couldn't get into university in England. So I came to a little-known university down the road here, where the first thing that happened to me was, as I entered Harvard, the sister of a friend of mine asked me where I came from, and I said Australia. And she said, "But when did you come?"

I said, "A week ago."

And she said, "But you've learned the language so quickly."

So that was my international world. I must also tell you that I had hoped at that time to go and compete in some international games in Russia. I was told by the Consul-General in Sydney that I had a choice. If I went to Russia, I could not go and study at Harvard. This was in the days of Joe McCarthy, the days of the Cold War, and the world was clearly divided between the rich and the poor, and between East and West.

On 9/11, somehow, this world, which has become ever more connected, was visibly seen to be united. Events in Afghanistan and events of terrorism throughout the world came upon us, not only on Wall Street, but in the Pentagon and in the fields of Pennsylvania, and we came truly to recognize that our world is linked: by trade, by finance, by the environment that we share, by health, by education, by migration, by crime, and, yes, by terror. And all of a sudden we were united, visibly, as that wall came down in the image of the World Trade Center collapsing. And so we are today in the throes of coming to terms with being one world.

And you, as the graduating class of 2004, are not staying at the university, as I read in the *International Herald Tribune* coming back from Europe yesterday. I read that the smart people, your professors and faculty, are staying here inside the university, worrying about parking tickets, while all of us go out into the world with the challenges that face us. But let me say how grateful we should be to our faculties for what they do for us, and for their research and for their training, and I'm sure I join with you in thanking them for what they've done.

We, however, are going out into the world, and it is a world that is hard. But it is not a world that has failed. In the last 40 years, the life span of people around the world has doubled, and indeed increased more than it had in the previous 400 years. It is a world where literacy has improved in many countries, where poverty is less widespread in many countries, where infant and maternal mortality has improved in many countries, but where our environment, sadly, has not improved.

And we come to confront the challenges that were pointed out back in 2000, the same year you started your courses here, at the Millennial Assembly of the United Nations. There the heads of 200 countries came together and, one after another, proclaimed that the challenges that you will face— that we will face—the challenges of this increasingly globalized world must be met. They laid out the challenges before us and set goals accordingly: halving the percentage of poverty in the world, reducing infant mortality and maternal mortality by two-thirds, getting all children into school, and dealing with the environment and stopping its ruin. These were the challenges that our global leaders set in 2000, and it is not just for our leaders today, but it is for you to try and see whether these objectives can be reached.

What is the world you are entering? It is a world of 6 billion people, not the elite communities just of our universities in the East or elsewhere in the United States, but 6 billion people, 5 billion of whom live in developing countries, 2.8 billion of whom live on less than two dollars a day, and 1.2 billion of whom live on less than one dollar a day.

It's a world where, within those countries, huge inequities exist—inequities that allow the top 5 percent in so many of these countries to have 60 percent of the wealth. It's a world where the billion people in the rich world have 80 percent of global income and global resources, and where the 5 billion people have less than 20 percent. It's a world that is dynamic. The world that you will live in for the next 25 years will be a world that grows by 2 billion people, so that in 2025 or 2030, it will be a world of 8 billion people, 7 billion of them in developing countries. And all of that growth in population, save for some 50 million people, will go to the developing world.

The world that you will know is not a world of London, Paris, Brussels, New York, and Chicago. It is a world that is already known to so many of your graduating class and your graduate students, a world that in this university is represented by 100 countries, a world to which some of you will return to take on leadership positions in those countries.

It's a world in which you will find some 35 countries with cities of 10 million people or more, and 27 of those megacities will be in developing countries. It's a world in which 2 billion *more* people will move into cities and towns from rural areas. It's a world where we will all have to come to terms with the growth that is taking place in the developing world.

I had the chance last year to attend the summit of the Group of Eight leaders in Evian, with President Chirac, President Bush, and many of the other developed-country leaders, but also with President Hu of China, Prime Minister Vajpayee of India, and President Obasanjo of Nigeria. And into the room came President Lula [da Silva] of Brazil, a distinguished social innovator, who is conducting perhaps the most important social experiment in the world today. And, self-effacingly, after six or seven of these great people had spoken, he said, "You know, I'm a trade union leader. And if my parents could only see me now with all of you, how proud they would be, me next to these great leaders." He said, "As I look at President Hu and Mr. Vajpayee and Mr. Obasanjo and the other leaders of the developing world, I wonder: we're invited to the G-8 summit by you every year, but maybe next year we should be the G-8 and invite you, because we represent the 5 billion. We represent, in the future, the 7 billion and the 8 billion."

And this is the world that all of you who are graduating today are going into. As I said, it is not just a world of the elite. It is a world that in 50 years' time will have 40 percent of its GDP coming from developing countries. It is a world in which *you* will have to take the lead, a world that is changing, and a world that needs equilibrium and balance if there is to be peace.

The other thing that you should know is that this is not some distant responsibility that you have. We at the Bank have recently been working extensively with young people throughout the world. And I recently spoke to a group in Paris that represents about 100 million young people, and I was patronizingly talking about what we were going to do for their future. But then a young man from Liberia got up and said to me, "Mr. President, I want you to know that we're not the future. We are the *now*."

And you *are* the now. Of the 6 billion people on the planet, 2.8 billion are under the age of 24, and a billion and a half are under the age of 15. So this is not a world of adults. This is a world of youth. This is a world where each one of you has a responsibility, where each one of you can make a difference. And this world that we're bequeathing to you is not in the best possible shape.

After the Millennium Summit, we all thought that the rich world and the poor world had come to a deal. Developing-world leaders said, "We have to take control of our countries. We don't want direction from you. We surely don't want direction from the World Bank. We want to decide ourselves on our future, and we know we must build capacity. We must strengthen our legal and judicial systems. We must strengthen our financial systems. And we must fight corruption." Many of them are doing just this. And I am sure that some of the young graduates here today will go back to their countries and help lead them.

In return, the leaders of the rich world said, "If you do that, we will help you build that capacity." And indeed they are offering access to their universities, and help and opportunity for people from developing countries. But they also said, "We will increase the development assistance we give you. And we will open our markets for trade." But what have we in the rich world done? We have a round of trade talks that is going nowhere, and we have development assistance that is flat.

You should understand how the world is spending its money today. We are spending $900 billion a year on military expenditure and $350 billion a year on agricultural subsidies, which affect developing countries adversely, and maybe $50 billion to $60 billion a year on development. We should be spending $900 billion on development, and then we would only need $50 billion for military expenditure.

And so all of you have an opportunity to restore balance to our planet, and not just in monetary terms. What we have learned, and what I have seen in recent weeks and months as I travel around the world, is that instead of focusing on the human dimensions of development, instead of focusing on the concerns of the individual that are the same in just about every country, where we have shown in our *Voices of the Poor* study that just about everybody wants the same thing that you want.

We studied 60,000 people in 60 countries to come to the very obvious conclusion that what people want is a chance, they want an opportunity, they want to live in safety. Women do not want to be beaten or battered. They want a chance for their children. They want voice, and they want to invest in their future. If we could allow this for people around the world, we would not need military expenditure to combat terror. And your chance and your task are to work toward this.

But there is one other level that is somehow missing, focused as we now are only on Iraq, Afghanistan, the Middle East, and terror. It is something that you got from this university. It is something that is on the shield of this university, the Hebrew word *emet,* or truth. It is the search for values that Justice Brandeis protected so well, the search for social justice and the belief in values.

Too little today do we see people standing up and saying that what should be done should be done because it is right, because our ethical, moral, and spiritual values demand it. We need again to restore to the premier place in our world, not just economics and not just individual advantage, but what you have at the soul, at the core of this university: a sense of social justice, a sense of what is right, a sense of what is moral, a sense of true human belief.

I wish you great success as you go into this world, and I urge you to carry with you that message from this great university.

Thank you very much.

Opening remarks at the Shanghai Conference on Scaling Up Poverty Reduction

SHANGHAI | MAY 26, 2004

Wolfensohn has said the Shanghai conference was one of the best meetings he participated in during his years as World Bank president. Cohosted by the Bank and the Chinese government, the conference brought together developing countries to learn from each other's successes and failures. This South-South learning, Wolfensohn stresses, shows that the Washington Consensus is "dead." The theme of the speech is "scaling up"—the idea of building on smaller, project-level successes and ensuring their widespread use on the country level.

Premier Wen, Prime Minister Zia, President Lula, President Mkapa, Mr. Mayor,* Distinguished Guests, Ladies and Gentlemen:

Just two years ago, I discussed with our friends in Shanghai the possibility of a conference here to deal with the question of scaling up our efforts on poverty. I thought it would be a modest conference, for specialists and for other people who might be interested in this subject. And so, today, to find this huge number of people here is an enormous surprise and an enormous credit to our hosts, the city of Shanghai, and the government and the finance ministry of China. On your behalf I would like to thank them enormously for their efforts and for their hospitality.

I think it is not surprising that we should have chosen Shanghai. This city is a remarkable part of the history of this country, and today it represents a center of industry, of science, of entrepreneurship, and of responsible government. And I'm reminded of the lament of Deng Xiaoping in 1992 when he said he wished that Shanghai had been given attention during the opening of the economy, because it would have transformed not only the Yangtze River economy but the entire face of China. I think we have only to step outside of this building to see how this city has transformed not only this area but, indeed, the whole image of China in the world.

Let me come to the subject of our discussions here during the next two days. But let me first acknowledge and thank the premier for his additional contributions, financial and moral, to the development agenda, which he announced today. He said that, without peace and stability, there is no possibility of alleviating poverty. And I think that one of the things we will discuss at

---

* Wen Jiabao, premier of China; Begum Khaleda Zia, prime minister of Bangladesh; Luiz Inácio Lula da Silva, president of Brazil; Benjamin William Mkapa, President of Tanzania; Han Zheng, Mayor of Shanghai.

this meeting is the reverse of that proposition: without alleviating poverty, there is no possibility for peace and stability. And so the purpose of this conference is to ask what is it that, collectively, we can do—representatives of the North and the South, ministers, representatives of civil society and the private sector, all of us here—to try and pass on to the young a world that is safe and secure, and vibrant but also stable. That is at the heart of our discussions.

We start with the recognition that, in our world of 6 billion people, 1 billion receive 80 percent of the income and the other 5 billion less than 20 percent. We start with the proposition that, in the next 25 years, 2 billion more people will join us on our planet, and all but 50 million of them will live in developing countries. As a result, in 2025, 7 billion people out of a total of 8 billion will live in developing countries, and by 2050, it will be 8 billion out of 9 billion.

I remember very well in Evian, where I had the privilege of attending the summit [of the Group of Eight], how President Lula entered the room and, in a typically self-effacing way, said how proud he was to be with the leaders of the G-8, but that maybe next year President Hu, Prime Minister Vajpayee of India or his successor, the president of Nigeria, the prime minister of South Africa, and himself should be the G-8, because they represented the 5 billion out of 6 billion on the planet.

President Lula also pointed to the new balance that is needed in our world. He pointed to the fact that today there is an imbalance, and that we have a challenge of poverty before us, the challenge identified in the Millennium Development Goals. He spoke also, then and more recently, about the challenge of youth. Young people now make up just about half the world: there are 2.8 billion people under the age of 24, a billion and a half under the age of 15, and in the next 20 or 25 years, as I said, there will be 2 billion more young people coming onto the planet.

This challenge of youth, together with the challenge of gender and the rights of women and the issue of poverty—as the premier said, of a billion people or more living in poverty—in short, this issue of imbalance is what we will be discussing at this conference. And the important thing about this conference is that it is not just a two-day meeting. We have already spent nine months studying experiences in development around the world. And you have, in the papers before you, summaries of a hundred case studies, which provide evidence of good ideas and not-so-good ideas that can be adapted, learned from, and applied in our development efforts. And I'm thrilled that we have on the platform here the leaders of countries that have contributed good ideas and experience to the effort of broadening the approach to poverty alleviation.

This is not a conference for teaching the Washington Consensus.[†] The Washington Consensus has been dead for years. It has been replaced by all sorts of other consensuses. But today we approach our discussions with no consensus, but instead with an interchange of ideas, with the opportunity to share experiences, with the opportunity to learn from each other. And that is why we have had this process—not just a two-day meeting but a process that has taken many of you on 11 field visits, has had you participate in 20 video-conferences, has had you participate bilaterally with our teams and with teams from the Chinese government. It is a process of putting together—not doctrines, not lessons that we insist upon—but opportunities to exchange ideas on a South-South and a South-North basis. This is a real chance to learn.

But it is more than just an exchange of ideas. What we are trying to do at this conference is to go beyond what we've done so often in the past, which is to succeed satisfactorily in a project here or a project there. My own institution is full of what I call "feel-good" projects. Those are the projects we point to when people ask, "What have you done for youth?" or "What have

† The term "Washington Consensus" was coined by John Williamson in 1989 and refers to 10 areas of economic reform that most of official Washington (including the international financial institutions and most major think tanks) then agreed that developing countries with debt problems should pursue.

you done for saving water?" or "What have you done for the environment?" They are a long list of small successes, of projects that we've done for 100 schools in the northern part of a country, or 200 kilometers of highway, or 10 bridges, or the impacts that we've had with small groups.

We've learned, ladies and gentlemen, that feeling good about individual projects is not enough. The challenges that we face are just too big. It's not 100 schools that we need. It's 10,000 schools. It's not 10 bridges. It's 5,000 bridges. It's not 100 people. It's millions and billions of people. And what we have to understand at this conference is how we can move on from our successes in these feel-good projects and scale them up, so that we can have a real impact and that we can achieve the Millennium goals.

And so it was that, when I came here two years ago, it seemed to me that China was the obvious place to start our explorations, because this is a country that in the last 20 years has lifted 300 million or 400 million people out of poverty. And it's a country that does not look at things in short-term dimensions. It looks at the challenges in long-term dimensions. China has had 10 five-year plans. The government is now looking at the 11th five-year plan, and it is consulting widely. And, as the premier noted, the poverty reduction strategy of several years ago, the seven-year strategy, is now being succeeded by another five-year strategy.

This attention to continuity, this attention to a consistent strategy, this line of thinking that does not allow for forgetting earlier strategies, that makes allowance for political change but that has a consistency, is something from which we need to learn. Because bringing these projects up to scale can't be done in four years or five years. Scale requires time. Scale requires management. Scale requires consistency. And scale requires constantly adapting our experience so as to move forward with our programs and our policies.

And you will find in the hundred case studies that we've looked at that many common themes emerge. The first is that you have to set "stretch" targets. You don't set targets just according to the available money. We in our own institution have often fallen into the trap of saying, "We have X million dollars for such-and-such a country, and therefore we will do a project that spends X million dollars." We should not look at it on the basis of whether we have X million dollars. We should look at it on the basis of what the challenge is, what the stretch target is, what is it that we're trying to achieve, and then look at ways in which, over time, we can reach that target. Because success is not spending $50 million or $100 million. Success is achieving, or at least approaching, the overall strategic target that we are seeking to achieve.

We are putting forward in the papers that you have before you many aspects of this challenge—the challenge of management, the challenge of leverage, the challenge of resources. And for me perhaps the single most important element—which this country knows, which Brazil knows, which Bangladesh knows, which Tanzania knows—is that we should look at development not as something that we professionals dream up and then bring to countries that are developing, to poor people, and give to them. What is essential, and what comes out in all these programs, is that, to succeed, we need to turn the people whom we want to lift out of poverty, not into objects of our charity or our development practices, but into assets, into active participants, moving toward getting out of poverty themselves.

What we need to do in scaling up is to engage the community of people who are poor, and who are searching for a better life, in the solution to their problems. They know more about poverty than we do. They know more about what they need than we do. We can help them in terms of the structure and the approach. We can provide them with infrastructure. We can provide them with resources. But the asset that we have to come to terms with is the people themselves: the young people, the people in poverty, the women, the underutilized people whose lives we are trying to help. You will find in these case studies many examples of how we need to engage the poor as people who are rich in capacity and rich in desire to improve their lives.

We did a study of 60,000 poor people in 60 countries, and you will not be surprised to find that their objectives and their feelings are exactly the same as those of the people in this room. Regardless of country and regardless of condition, they all say the same thing: We want a life that is secure. We want voice. We want a chance to be heard. We want our kids to be educated. We want safety. We do not want charity—we want an opportunity; we want a chance. And we want to contribute to our better life.

Our task at this conference is not complicated. It is to try and find ways in which, over a long period of time and with management skills that some of us lack, we can present—by working with these people—programs that are replicable, that people in poverty can own, and where together we can achieve a better future for all.

I just want to give you one example from this country. The example is from the Loess Plateau, which I first visited, I think, nine years ago now. And I saw in front of me valleys that were stark, that had no trees, and that were filling the Yellow River with sediment from the water coming down the hills. And it looked arid, it looked terrible, and the people were living in the worst of conditions on the tops of these hills. But there was a plan, and the plan was to take, in each of these valleys, in an area the size of Switzerland, a hundred thousand people who—and you, Mr. Premier, may have seen this—would go in, in teams of 100,000, and terrace these hills. They'd pick up the rocks by hand. There would be one machine, one bulldozer for the entire area. And on the top of each hill they had a little monument, which said, "World Bank Project Number 1," or "World Bank Project Number 20," and the signatures of the team leader and the finance person and the other people in charge.

And when I went back recently, these arid areas looked like Switzerland. They've got grass. They've got trees. They've got animals. They have houses. And 3 million people have now come from the tops of the mountains into the valleys, in areas where any of us would enjoy having a holiday. Not only that, but the Yellow River is cleaner.

This is not magic. This is a simple idea carried forward by the diligence of people, an idea that works year after year. And we see the results in terms of poverty alleviation and in terms of hope. Our task is to make this world a Loess Plateau, an area that is green, that is full of hope, that allows people in poverty to use their spade, or their pen, or whatever it is they have, to find their way from the conditions of poverty to conditions of hope and opportunity.

Our conference is not just another conference. Our conference is about peace. It is about the future of our planet. It is about moving to scale. It is about social justice. It's about what is morally right. It's about hope. And I am very happy that I can be with you for these next two days and beyond.

Thank you very much.

Address at the First International Conference on Corporate Governance
and Economic Growth in Russia

MOSCOW | JUNE 3, 2004

> *Wolfensohn comments on Russia's development potential and says Russia*
> *has the opportunity to set "stretch targets" that go beyond a doubling of its*
> *GDP. He draws on his just-completed trip to China to talk about the*
> *parallels between the Russian and Chinese development strategies.*

Mr. Prime Minister, Mr. Chairman,* Ladies and Gentlemen:

It's a daunting task to open this conference in the presence of what I think
must be the greatest accumulation of experts on the subject of corporate governance that I have ever seen. It must be the persuasive powers of Chairman
Potanin or the joys of Moscow that has brought us all here. But for those of
you who are not familiar with the folklore of corporate governance, you have
before you at this conference just about everybody that matters—or at least
that think they matter—at these conferences.

So we have, I think, an opportunity to express to you the current range of
views on corporate governance, and I am very happy to share this platform at
the opening session with my friend Don Johnston,† with whom five years ago
we started a joint program of conferences around the world, including Russia, to deal with this question, and also Jean Lemierre,‡ who, as you all know,
has played such an important role in the developments in this country.

This is not a group of people coming here to lecture on corporate governance. It is an exchange of ideas. It is an opportunity for a group of people
who have had the opportunity to explore and experiment with mature systems
of corporate governance to give you, the Russian entrepreneurs and businessmen, a chance to appraise and to look at overseas experience. It is not a tem-
plate from Washington or Europe that should be imposed. It's something that
we wish to present to you for your consideration as to whether or not you
think it should be adopted within the framework of Russian society.

I started to look at this issue by reading President [Vladimir] Putin's address
to the government on May 26 of this year, and I think it's important for us to
set the framework of how we see the position in this country, which is, of
course, taken from no better source than your president. He says at his opening,
"Our goals are absolutely clear: high living standards in the country, with lives

---

* Mikhail Fradkov, prime minister of Russia; Vladimir Potanin, chairman of the Interros Holding Company.
† Donald J, Johnston, secretary-general of the Organisation for Economic Co-operation and Development.
‡ President of the European Bank for Reconstruction and Development.

safe, comfortable, and free; a mature democracy and a developed civil society; the strengthening of Russia's position in the world; and substantial growth in living standards for our citizens." He then went on to say that, since Russia came into being in its modern form, it has gone through three different phases. The first was dismantling an old system. The second phase was cleaning up the mess from that dismantlement. And the third phase, which he said you have reached only recently, is the development of the modern Russian state.

These were his observations, not mine. He also commented on the progress that has been made in the last four years. So we as your friends from overseas understand that we come at a time when growth is important, when poverty eradication is important, when social justice and equity are important, and when Russia is seeking to establish its position in the international community that befits its wealth of natural resources and of human resources.

I've just come from five days in China, and I'd like, for a moment, to digress and tell you about that experience—not to challenge you to imitate the neighbor with whom you have the longest border, but merely to indicate some of the things that struck me in that few days that I spent there. I had the privilege of meeting with President Hu Jintao, with Premier Wen Jiabao, with the economic ministers, and with the governor of the central bank, and the issues they are facing are very much the same as those you face. They talked of the need for economic growth, of having taken some 300 million to 400 million people out of poverty, and of the residual challenge they face in the country's far western areas, and in the northeastern industrial zones, which lack adequate recovery. They talked of the need to move from highly centralized economic activity to more diverse activity in small- and medium-size enterprises, and, in particular, they focused on the question of alleviating poverty in those areas where they find it.

We were talking about, of course, poverty interventions. But our discussion with the economics people was about how to create an investment climate in China in which foreigners and domestic investors would all have the opportunity of building enterprises, drawing on equity contributions domestically and internationally, and allowing China to attract international investment and international debt financing. I think you know that more than 30 percent of international flows of funds are now going to China. China in the last four years has transformed itself from a country where most investors had little confidence to a country that has attracted the attention of the international investor community both to the internal possibilities of the country and to the external possibilities.

China's share of global trade has already moved from 2 percent to 4 percent, and the projections are that in 2017—only a little more than 12 years away—the shares of China and the United States will be the same, at 12 percent each. And the objectives that they're looking to are stretch objectives, as befits a country of 1.3 billion people, but as also befits a country that is trying to reduce poverty.

So it's interesting to come from China to here, because the resonance in President Putin's remarks is exactly the same: let's deal with the question of growth; let's deal with the question of investment; let's deal with the question of poverty; let's deal with those areas of the country that are falling behind; let's take a look at housing and education and health care. But then comes the big question mark: how to create a climate for investment. That is what this conference is about. The president suggested a stretch target of doubling GDP over the coming years, but for a country like Russia to have a GDP of $400 million to $500 million, against a China that is already at $1.5 trillion, against a Europe that is at $10 trillion, and against a United States with $12 trillion, will require Russian businessmen and others to set stretch goals that are far beyond what we are now thinking of. It requires rational leaders to recognize that, in these next four years and beyond, Russia's natural resources and, most particularly, its human resources give it an opportunity to set stretch targets even beyond the doubling of GDP.

Russia has a huge landmass. It has huge resources. And what it needs now, frankly, is an unlocking of the human capital and the corporate capital and the entrepreneurial capital, so that Russia is not just a country that is fighting to advance itself, but becomes a country that is in the lead in terms of its investment environment, and a country that has set itself optimistic targets that are beyond the perception of most people today. Outside this country there is, of course, recognition of the huge oil and gas reserves that exist here, and much of the country's growth is distorted by the growth in the oil and gas industry. But the hidden gem, the hidden treasure of this country is, in fact, the human treasure. That is what gives Russia the ability to invite investment into this country in a way that will make it competitive with other parts of the world and unlocks both the human capacity and the physical capacities that this country enjoys.

That requires a real act of faith. That requires maturity in terms of economic development. And it's not surprising, I suppose, that it comes in fits and starts, and you should bear in mind the remarkable achievements of the last 12 years. But in my judgment you need to be thinking more urgently about the achievements of the next 12 years. Now is the moment to really open up the economy and the corporate sector to development at a level that befits a country as large and as talented as this. You've got to throw off a lot of inhibitions. This debate that you're going to be considering—and it is for you to decide—is not a debate about what are the best laws, what are the best regulations. You've got laws and regulations. It's about whether Russian corporate society wishes to broaden its outlook, wishes to throw itself open to internal competition, wishes to attract investment, and wishes to grasp the opportunities that are available to you.

Russian investors and foreign investors are all the same. You don't invest in a company where there is someone running it who has an advantage over you, who can sell out your assets at any time, who can take off-balance-sheet transactions and profit for himself. Why invest in such a company? You can go to lots of other places where your investment is protected. So why come to Russia if you have doubts about the quality standards of investors? If you look at the level of debt accumulation in 2001, although it's grown since, private sector borrowing by Russian companies was only 11 percent of GDP. The figure for Chinese companies meanwhile was 150 percent, that for Chilean companies was 140 percent, and that for Singaporean companies was 140 percent. You don't have to be a genius to recognize that people lend to companies where they know what's going on, where there is transparency, and where they have a chance of being repaid.

What is also important is the framework of the judicial system. People will lend to you if their rights are protected. People will not lend to you if they do not have their rights protected. We've had this problem recently in Indonesia. Rights have not been protected. Bankruptcy laws were not in existence, much less applied. So investment has gone down. If you have protection, investment goes up. None of the things that we will be discussing in the course of the next two days is the work of an intellectual genius. It's something absolutely straightforward. If the concentration of power in a country is so great that small- and medium-size enterprises don't get a fair shake, you will not have small- and medium-size enterprises. We need to promote small- and medium-size enterprises because that's where the jobs are. It's a challenge for Russia, but it's not like sending something to the moon. It's something that can be done if the will is there.

And, in the course of the discussions we'll be having these next two days, you will have the opportunity to learn from the experience of others, but not with any insistence that you do exactly as they have done. The thing that President Putin said in his speech that struck me was the following. He said very clearly, "I realize that this growth pattern is a very complex task, but we can resolve it, and we can only resolve it ourselves. It depends only on ourselves whether we can really become a society of free people—free in economic and political terms. It depends only on ourselves whether we can resolve priority national tasks—that we know quite well."

Let me say that that is my view of this conference. The results depend on you, and we look forward very much to participating with you in open discussion.

Thank you very much.

ENSURING ACCOUNTABILITY IN ACHIEVING THE MILLENNIUM DEVELOPMENT GOALS

With Rodrigo de Rato, foreword to *Global Monitoring Report 2004*,
published by the World Bank and the International Monetary Fund

JUNE 2004

> *Together with the new IMF managing director, Wolfensohn introduces the*
> Global Monitoring Report, *a new joint Bank-Fund annual study that*
> *measures the international community's progress on achieving the Millen-*
> *nium Development Goals.*

This Global Monitoring Report is the first in a planned series of annual reports assessing the implementation of policies and actions for achieving the Millennium Development Goals (MDGs) and related outcomes. These reports will underpin regular monitoring by the Development Committee, the joint Ministerial body of our two institutions, of progress on the policy agenda; and they will aid the Development Committee in setting priorities for action and defining the accountabilities of the key actors—developing and developed countries and multilateral institutions. The *Global Monitoring Report* is being published in order to disseminate its findings and messages more widely. We expect to publish these reports each year and to maintain the momentum toward achieving the MDGs by 2015.

This report has been prepared jointly by the staff of the World Bank and the International Monetary Fund, in close collaboration with partner agencies—other multilateral development banks, the United Nations, the World Trade Organization, the Organisation for Economic Co-operation and Development and its Development Assistance Committee, and the European Commission. It is particularly encouraging that we now have such a broad partnership supporting this effort. We hope that this first report will spur further interaction on policies and actions to meet the agreed development goals.

The findings of the report provide a sobering assessment of progress toward the MDGs, and of progress in meeting the commitments made at [the March 2002 Financing for Development Conference in] Monterrey. As the report makes clear, on current trends, most MDGs will not be met by most countries. This is not to downplay the impressive progress made in some countries, particularly large ones such as China and India. But there are many that are falling behind, especially in Sub-Saharan Africa. And we can do better even in countries where progress has been good. There is an urgent need to scale up actions, building on the foundations laid by past successes and lessons learned from past mistakes. The report identifies where the need for action is most critical.

The report provides a range of evidence on the improvement of policies and institutions in developing countries. We have seen evidence of this improvement directly, through our own visits and interactions with people in countries in all parts of the developing world. In Africa, for instance, the New Partnership for Africa's Development has asserted a new accountability, and there are now many countries that have taken credible steps to strengthen their policies and governance with a clear sense that there is now an unprecedented opportunity for accelerating progress on development results. More needs to be done to deepen and sustain reforms, but we believe that we have the basis for scaling up in many countries.

As the report shows, in contrast to the improving performance in many developing countries, the developed countries are falling behind on two critical fronts that are vital to accelerating progress and scaling up results—trade and aid. We cannot overemphasize the importance and urgency of reinvigorating the Doha Round [of multilateral trade negotiations], including agreement on improved market access for agriculture and labor-intensive manufactures that are so critical to the prospects of the poorest countries. The other area for priority attention is the quantity and quality of aid. There is a clear need to increase the volume of development assistance in support of countries implementing sound macroeconomic, structural, and institutional policies to accelerate progress toward the MDGs. In parallel, we need political commitment on the agenda to improve the quality of aid—to align aid better with country-owned priorities, to make it more predictable and flexible, to focus it on results, and to harmonize aid practices and procedures.

The report also highlights the need for continued attention to how international agencies, including our own, can strengthen their support at the country, regional, and global levels. There is clear recognition of the importance of strong results orientation in what we do individually and collectively. Refining and strengthening institutional roles in low-income countries, including deepening the process of preparation and implementation of Poverty Reduction Strategy Papers,* is a priority area for attention. At the same time, we need to continue to adapt approaches and instruments to the evolving needs of middle-income countries.

In sum, this first *Global Monitoring Report* is, in our view, an important and credible step in putting in place a framework for results and accountability that will enhance the international development community's review of progress on and priorities for achieving global development goals.

Foreword to *Mind, Heart and Soul in the Fight Against Poverty,*
published by the World Bank

JUNE 2004

In this short piece, Wolfensohn describes how the faith community and
development institutions like the World Bank can work together to reduce
global poverty.

No challenge to today's global community has higher importance or greater
urgency than the fight against poverty. And nothing is more central to success
in that fight than to engage the many sectors of the global community, working together, in new and dynamic partnerships. This is a challenge beyond the
capacity of any single organization or indeed any segment of society. The faith
communities around the world represent vital elements in this partnership.

That almost half of the people alive in the world today live daily with
poverty, disease, and hunger and have few opportunities, little access to the
most basic services, and muffled hope for a better future is a scandal and a
shame to all of us. Millions of people who have seen their lives improve in the
past decades are testimony to the key fact that poverty can be overcome, but
the numbers of those who have yet to see progress are greater still.

The global community has committed itself to changing this picture, most
dramatically in the formal commitment of the leaders of all nations to the Millennium Declaration in 2000. This commitment is inspirational and, still more,
is the commitment to measure and judge progress continuously by continuing
to shine a spotlight on the specific and tangible Millennium Development
Goals. There are no grounds for complacency, however, as we are still far from
achieving the Goals, though the year set for their achievement—2015—is fast
approaching. We have far to go.

The central mission and purpose of the World Bank are to work towards a
world "free of poverty," and our programs and staff efforts are uniformly directed to this end. However, we are keenly aware that many others, above all
the people who struggle each day to improve their lives, are equally engaged
and committed to the same endeavor, to a common end. There is today a
much keener appreciation than even a decade ago that, across organizations,
across countries, across religious and ethnic groups, we hold many values and
goals in common.

Different institutions and sectors have their role to play in working on the
global challenges of the Millennium Development Goals, and diversity, local
initiative, and creativity are essential to success. Nonetheless, there is much evidence that the overall sum of efforts often achieve less than they ideally should.
A central reason is that many are poorly informed about what others do, mis-

apprehend their efforts, or even work consciously in different directions. We therefore are looking more and more to thoughtful and creative ways to bring greater coherence, knowledge, and creative partnerships to the overall development agenda and action, to listen and learn from one another, so that indeed the sum of efforts adds up to the sum of real progress that we seek.

The vast and complex array of institutions founded on a central belief in God, and with spiritual goals at their center, share with the development institutions a commitment to addressing the problems of poverty. Historically, they have played a critical role in the development and provision of both education and health services across many poor countries and communities. Moreover, their contributions to reconstruction in countries and regions wracked by conflict, their capacity to influence land use, and, although less well known, their significant role in directing investment of financial assets are without exception remarkable. The most troubling issue facing humanity today may well be the HIV/AIDS pandemic, and here, too, faith communities have been essential partners, both in raising awareness about the complex practical and ethical issues around the pandemic, and in working, from the global to the community level, to combat it.

Where faith and development institutions have combined their efforts and worked toward common ends, remarkable results can be achieved. The experience suggests two conclusions: first, that the engagement of faith communities in the fight against poverty is vital to success in achieving the Millennium Development Goals; and second, that there is great scope for new and different forms of collaboration that take advantage of the respective strengths of the different communities in a mutually reinforcing manner. Yet these efforts are too little known, and the lessons, good and bad, have engendered too little reflection.

This book recounts a series of experiences that involve common efforts of institutions from different sectors and realms, especially faith institutions, working to fight poverty and improve the lives of poor communities. The cases cover different regions of the world, and they range widely in terms of sectors and type of interventions. What all have in common is that shared objectives brought uncommon partners to work together and to achieve results that had eluded the institutions working individually. The book offers practical lessons and inspiration, and hopefully will lead the way both to more analysis of such uncommon partnerships and to new and creative ways to combat problems and work toward common objectives with new means and in new combinations.

Wolfensohn on Faith

". . . *The thing that our study* [Voices of the Poor] *showed us was that the groups that are most trusted in poor communities are the faiths. But they can't deliver everything. We have been working very hard to try and build a relationship with the faiths, not to have the faiths say that the World Bank does everything perfectly, because we don't, but to try and recognize that the unity that we need is a unity that is based on the individual poor person, and not on our debate as to who has the turf and who does what.*

"As I was coming over here, I recalled a couple of incidents that were very important to me and my relationship with the church. One of those was in Jamaica, when I was going to the slums. The police said to me that it was not safe to go in. I said, 'Well, I can't come and look at poverty and deal with the questions of Jamaica unless I go into the slums.' A man called Father Albert turned up with a vehicle . . . and the two of us went in, and we left the police outside. With him, I met the young people, and I met, I might add, the mafiosi from each side of the camp, and I finished up having drinks with them and planting a tree, all because of not the physical strength but the spiritual strength of one man.

". . . *The one thing that I think really unites us is a common sense of humanity and a common sense of the issues of poverty.*

"Why do I say that? I say that because the central role of our institution is the issue of poverty. It is the conquest of poverty. That issue of poverty is, I think, the central role of your organization as well. Indeed, it's the question that [Bernard] *Cardinal Law* [archbishop of Boston] *put to me: 'What do we do to deal with the question of poverty and equity in this newly globalized world?'"*

From "Globalization, Equity, and Faith,"address at the Conference on Humanizing the Global Economy, sponsored by the Bishops' Conferences of Canada, Latin America, and the United States, Washington, January 28, 2002

ENERGY NEEDS FOR THE NEXT 25 YEARS
AND CLIMATE CHANGE

Excerpts from remarks at a conference sponsored by the Brookings Institution
and the Pew Center on Global Climate Change

WASHINGTON, D.C. | JUNE 25, 2004

> *Wolfensohn discusses the energy needs of developing countries and the
> challenge in meeting them in the next few decades. His remarks also address
> the recently published* Extractive Industries Review *report, which urged
> the World Bank to stop support for oil and coal projects and instead focus
> on renewables.*

I'm finding that I'm getting so old, in relation both to Brookings and to the
environment. I was with Maurice Strong* in Stockholm at the beginning of
the international environmental activities, when we first started to talk about
climate change, and so I come here in front of you as an almost antediluvian
representative, but one who has the privilege of representing an institution
where we take this issue very, very seriously, and where I'm delighted to have
the chance to remind you that the issue is related to development.

All of you, I think, know that the Bank is concerned with the 5 billion people in our world of 6 billion who live in developing countries and who have
roughly 20 percent of the world's wealth. You're aware that in the next
25 years, as world population grows from 6 billion to 8 billion, 7 billion out
of those 8 billion will be in developing countries, with only roughly 50 million added to the rich world. And 50 years hence it will be 8 billion out of
9 billion. So at least we have a growing market in the work of the Bank, and
some growing problems but also, of course, growing opportunities.

During that time, just to give you a sense of the economic base, if today developing countries account for $6 trillion to $7 trillion out of a total global income stream of $34 or $35 trillion, or roughly 20 percent of global GDP, by
2050 we project that developing countries will be receiving 40 percent. And
if world GDP growth averages about 3 percent a year from now to 2050, we
will by then have a $150 trillion global economy. Therefore $60 trillion will
be going to the developing world, or more than eight times what their GDP
is today.

The reason I'm giving you these statistics is that, as economic activity increases with the proliferation of people—and meanwhile, in the next 25 years,
there will be 2 billion more people moving into cities and towns—there will
be tremendous additional pressure both on the environment and on energy
needs. That is the framework within which we are looking at the question of
climate change and sustainable development. It is not static, and, again, that

---

* Senior adviser to the UN secretary-general and to the president of the World Bank.

growth in population is all in the developing world. And you need to have that in the back of your minds as you listen to what we are trying to assert now, which is that the issue of climate change has a disproportionate effect on those who are vulnerable and who live in the developing countries that we represent.

I think it's not necessary for me to tell you how much of total greenhouse gas emissions come from the rich world. It is most of them. I don't need to give you the background of [the December 1997] Kyoto [Protocol], because I understand that that was more than adequately covered yesterday, and you already know about it anyway. But consider the issue from the point of view of the developing countries. These are often countries where people live on marginal land, where a substantial portion of the poor are in rural areas, and where deforestation and changing weather patterns lead to less than optimal usage of land, and indeed the degradation of land. These are also countries where air pollution has a significant impact, and where biodiversity is significantly affected, to the detriment not just of the developing countries themselves but of the world. And we at the Bank are necessarily quite concerned about the impact of climate change on these vulnerable people.

I think you also know that in some parts of the world the actual physical landscape of whole countries is being challenged by a rising sea level. Those of you who have been in the Maldives or in Bangladesh know that the issue of climate change in those countries is not just a question of whether their standard of living will increase or decrease; it is a question of whether they will have somewhere to live at all.

[. . .]

These changes are not as dramatic in many countries, but those of you who have traveled and have seen the degradation of land and the acute difficulty that people face in terms of land use will understand that, for us at the Bank, the question of climate change is not a theoretical question. It's one that is having an immediate and huge impact on the developing world.

I participated in a Security Council meeting on some aspects of this, and, as you know, some people have said that this is as important an issue for the developing world as are some of the more physical threats, be it terror or war. And I believe this. It's very hard to put a number on what a two- or three-degree [temperature] variation would lead to in terms of loss of GDP. But [World Bank Chief Scientist] Bob Watson tells me that it should be between 2 and 9 percent of GDP. Well, that's a pretty good range. But even a 2 percent variation in GDP in most developing countries is huge. And in some countries there is no doubt that the impact of climate change is quite, quite dramatic.

What can we do about it? It's clear that the developed countries can do quite a lot in terms of conservation and in terms of better policy and in terms of research. After four or five abortive attempts to meet with U.S. Energy Secretary Spencer Abraham, I had a one-on-one with him by coincidence this morning. I heard from him about what we should do, that we should undertake massive research and quantum change, in addition to work on renewables and work on better policies. And so why don't we stipulate that I understand what he said and that I've just made the case again.

How we can do that and how quickly we can do that is, of course, a big issue. We would love to have a hydrogen solution. We would love to have a fusion solution. We would love to have atomic energy that is safe. But I think at the moment, in the developing countries, many of which are endowed significantly with coal and, to some degree, with oil and gas, for the foreseeable future the issue that's going to be facing us is how to make best use of hydrocarbons.

We'd love to have enough natural gas. We all know that that would be better. And in Emil Salim's[†] recent report on these industries, he recommends that the Bank get out of coal and oil and that we put our efforts into renewables. And over the last months I have paid a lot of attention to renewables. We've had reports on everything from solar to wind to geothermal to tidal, and I've been out to see these things.

But the bottom line is that renewables currently provide only 2 percent of global energy supply. And if we could raise that to 3 or 4 or 5 percent—and 5 percent is already beyond the range that anybody has projected over the next 15 to 20 years—that would be a great thing to do, and we propose to get busy doing that. But it does not seem that renewables are the immediate answer at any rate. And to that extent, I think, what Spencer Abraham said is right. There is a need for better technology.

I think what we are looking for in the countries in which we're operating, and what we are proposing in the rich world, is that all the science and technology should proceed at as vigorous a pace as is possible to bring about a breakthrough, because clearly a breakthrough would be wonderful. But in the meantime what we need to do is to try and modify policies, try and reduce energy usage as much as we possibly can, and try and clean up the world's act in terms of carbon use.

We have one other problem, which is that somewhere around a couple of billion people, give or take 300 million, don't have any access to energy today

---

† Former environment minister of Indonesia, who led the Bank's Extractive Industries Review, which was published in December 2003.

at all. And this in itself is an issue because it leads to deforestation, because if you have no other energy, you go out and cut down the nearest tree, and that is bad for the environment. It's also bad economically because it wastes those people's time. And then the women are also burning biomass in their homes, and we estimate that a couple of million of them are killing themselves and each other every year because of the diseases that come from inhalation of the noxious fumes that go along with the burning of biomass in a small space.

Poverty, unfortunately, impacts forestry and impacts the environment in which we live. And so, for us, getting electricity or some other form of power to poor communities is in itself an advantage, even if it is from coal-fired plants.

Now, this leads, of course, to the question of cleaning up and the advances that we can make on the use of coal and oil in the generation of electricity. And there the need to clean up the plants, as I think many are doing, including the Department of Energy in this country, to try and get clean coal is a parallel activity that we must hope will continue as we move forward in our efforts in developing countries.

But the notion that any report or any admonition by rich countries to poor countries will persuade them not to use the coal reserves that they have is sheer fantasy. It's not going to happen. It might be wonderful, and it might be a great thing for the environment, but our clients say to us, "Look, you rich countries created this problem. You are profligate in the use of your energy. You, too, burn these fuels, and now you're telling us—as we move, as I remind you, from $7 trillion to $60 trillion in economic activity—that we can't do that. We are the ones, you say, that have to address the problem, while you have no policy and remain profligate, and while you're not spending your money adequately on trying to clean up your act on electricity. We would love to have hydrogen, we would love to have fusion, and we would love to have all these other great things that we're talking about, but don't put the burden on us. And we'd love to have renewables, and we will use renewables, but there is a cost to consider. We're more than happy to do that, but please, please, please, if we're going to use renewables, bring down the cost to a point where it can be attractive to us. Because, remember, we're poor, we're not rich. And that is what we face every day when we go out and try and do the work we're doing."

So I was anxious to come here when I was asked, because I think the issue of the developing countries' confrontation with the question of climate change is, first of all, very real. And it is they who are the most vulnerable, particularly to changes in temperature and water supply. Climate change leads to the unfortunate result that the arid and semiarid areas typically get even drier, and this affects agricultural production. It leads to distortions in developing countries, which are already vulnerable and where the poorest people find that it is their economic activity that is most influenced. It is there that we face the huge challenge of bringing clean water to the 1½ billion to 2 billion people who don't have clean water, and sanitation to the 2 billion or so who don't have sanitation. We also have to try and deal with waterborne diseases, which are also affected by climate change. And here the developing countries are saying to us, "For God's sake, help us, but we're not the cause of this problem. We are contributing to it, but we need a better partnership and a better policy with the rich countries."

This is where we are in the debate, and, if I may speak on behalf of the 5 billion, it's not such an arrogant or distorted request. They're looking for research, they're looking for better policies, and they're looking for partnership. And they're doing it from a point of view that reflects their vulnerability. But what they're not looking for are lectures on "Don't use coal and don't use oil and don't use your natural resources." And they react rather badly to these sorts of suggestions.

So, in the middle of all this, we're trying to weave a path that allows for the best use of renewables, but that also allows for appropriate partnerships on the extraction of minerals and oil and coal. We are looking for the best ways to use renewables at some moderate cost. But the bottom line for us is that this is a huge question for development. I think it is less keenly felt than it should be in most sectors of the community, though I'm sure you in this room understand it. It is a real crisis for developing countries. The issue of climate change affects them more than it does us. It is more than an inconvenience on holidays. It is a question of existence. And I'm very grateful that this group and the Pew [Center on Global Climate Change] are anxious to keep our attention focused on this subject, because there is no way that we can reach the Millennium goals for poverty or for development without addressing it.

Foreword to *World Development Report 2005,* published for the World Bank
by Oxford University Press

SEPTEMBER 2004

*In this foreword, Wolfensohn points to the critical importance of governments
creating better investment climates. Improving the investment climate is one
of two pillars of the World Bank's overall development strategy. The
other—investing in people—was the subject of the previous year's report.*

This *World Development Report* is about creating opportunities for people to escape from poverty and improve their living standards. It is about creating a climate in which firms and entrepreneurs of all types—from farmers and
microenterprises to local manufacturing concerns and multinationals—have
opportunities and incentives to invest productively, create jobs, and expand,
and thereby contribute to growth and poverty reduction. The Report thus
deals with one of the central challenges of development.

Expanding opportunities for people in developing countries is a pressing
concern for governments and for the global community. Nearly half the
world's population lives on less than $2 a day, and 1.1 billion barely survive on
less than $1 a day. Young people have more than double the average unem-
ployment rate in all regions, and population growth will add nearly 2 billion
more people to developing countries over the next 30 years. Improving the
climate for investment in developing countries is essential to provide jobs and
opportunities for young people and to build a more inclusive, balanced, and
peaceful world.

There is good news. More governments are recognizing that their policies
and behaviors play a critical role in shaping the investment climates of their
societies, and they are making changes. China and India provide compelling
examples: investment climate improvements in these countries have driven
growth and the most dramatic reductions in poverty in history. Many other
governments are also taking on the agenda, but progress remains slow and
uneven. Governments still saddle firms and entrepreneurs with unnecessary
costs, create substantial uncertainty and risk, and erect unjustified barriers to
competition.

This year's *World Development Report,* the 27th in the World Bank's flagship
series, looks at what governments can do to create better investment climates
for their societies. Drawing on new research, including surveys of nearly
30,000 firms in 53 developing countries, other new data, and country case
studies, it makes four main points.

First, the Report emphasizes that the goal should be to create an investment climate that is better for everyone—in two dimensions. The investment

climate should benefit society as a whole, not only firms. Well-designed regulation and taxation are thus an important part of a good investment climate. And the investment climate should embrace firms of all types, not just large or influential firms. Small and large firms, local and foreign firms, and low-tech and high-tech firms each have important and complementary contributions to make to growth and poverty reduction.

Second, the Report argues that efforts to improve the investment climate need to go beyond just reducing business costs. Those costs can indeed be extraordinary in many countries, amounting to several times what firms pay in taxes. But policy-related risks dominate firms' concerns in developing countries and can cripple incentives to invest. And barriers to competition remain pervasive, dulling incentives for firms to innovate and increase productivity. Governments need to address all three aspects of a good investment climate.

Third, the Report underscores that progress requires more than changes in formal policies. The gaps between policies and their implementation can be huge, with the vast informal economies in many developing countries providing the most palpable evidence. Governments need to bridge these gaps and address deeper sources of policy failure that can undermine a sound investment climate. Governments need to tackle corruption and other forms of rent seeking, to build credibility with firms, to foster public trust and legitimacy, and to ensure that their policy interventions are crafted to fit local conditions.

Finally, the Report reviews strategies for tackling such a broad agenda. It emphasizes that perfection is not required and that everything does not have to be done at once. But progress requires governments to address important constraints in ways that give firms the confidence to invest—and to sustain a process of ongoing improvements. Persistence pays off.

These findings are supported by detailed analysis and the many examples discussed throughout the Report, which should provide practical insights for policymakers and for others concerned with growth and poverty reduction in developing countries.

Improving the investment climate is the first pillar of the World Bank's overall development strategy. *World Development Report 2005* complements last year's Report, which addressed key aspects of the second pillar of that strategy: investing in people and empowering them to take advantage of opportunities. Together, these two Reports offer sound advice and research that will help the World Bank and our partners realize our common dream—a world free of poverty.

SECURING THE 21ST CENTURY, PROTECTING THE PLANET

Address to the Board of Governors at the Annual Meetings of the World Bank and the International Monetary Fund

WASHINGTON, D.C. | OCTOBER 3, 2004

Wolfensohn's last Annual Meetings address makes the case for why fighting poverty is critical to achieving security in both wealthier and poorer countries. He describes the challenges of the environment, poverty, and giving hope to youth through anecdotes of people he has met in the past year, and he issues an urgent call for world leaders to be more engaged in tackling global issues.

Mr. Chairman, Governors, Distinguished Guests:

Let me warmly welcome you to these Annual Meetings in the 60th year after the founding of the Bretton Woods institutions. I salute my new colleague Rodrigo de Rato as managing director of the IMF. We have already begun to work closely together, and I have come quickly to appreciate his experience and judgment. My colleagues and I would like also to congratulate my friend Horst Köhler on his election as president of Germany, and we thank him for his significant contribution to the work of our two institutions.

The World Bank Group has a long and proud history. We contributed to global reconstruction after World War II before taking on our new role, that of seeking to reduce poverty throughout the world. We have been an agent for growth with equity.

With only $11 billion contributed from shareholders, the International Bank for Reconstruction and Development has made almost $400 billion in loans. The International Finance Corporation, founded in 1956, has brought $67 billion into the emerging markets. The Multilateral Investment Guarantee Agency has issued $13.5 billion in guarantees. The International Centre for Settlement of Investment Disputes, meanwhile, has helped settle disputes in 159 cases worldwide.

On the strength of donor contributions and reflows from borrowers, the International Development Association has committed $151 billion. The countries eligible for IDA's concessional lending are home to 80 percent of the world's poorest people, those who live on one dollar a day or less. IDA is a truly remarkable instrument, designed to be effective and accountable. I hope our shareholders will increase their contributions to the next replenishment. We must keep IDA strong.

I am proud of our achievements over the last 10 years. We may be 60 years old, but we are young. We are a united institution, determined in our goal of "fighting poverty with passion." We seek to support our clients as partners, respecting their diverse cultures and aspirations. We ourselves are diverse, with staff from more than 140 countries. More than two-thirds of our country directors are now in the field, with our offices linked by satellite, making video-conferencing and distance learning a part of all our lives. We are one of the most modern global businesses.

During these years we have sought to put our client countries clearly in the driver's seat. We listen more and lecture less. And we are not afraid to be self-critical.

We provide financing for projects, but also knowledge, offering our global experience to clients. Our greatly expanded World Bank Institute plays a key role in this respect. So does our affiliate the Development Gateway, which makes available on the Internet information on development projects as well as a synthesis of experience.

We have broadened our approach to development to make it truly comprehensive. We have confronted the issue of debt with the creation of the Heavily Indebted Poor Countries Initiative, and we have attacked corruption, working with governments in more than 100 countries.

Our strategy is based on two pillars: investing in people, and creating a stable business climate so that investment is facilitated and jobs are created. Working with the private sector is a central part of our Group's activities. We continue to benefit from both the support and the criticism of a vibrant civil society throughout the world.

Development is about people. We focus on the important role of women and youth in development and on the special needs of indigenous communities, the Roma, and other excluded minorities. We support the special needs of people with disabilities.

The environment is also central to our work, for we know that true and lasting development without preserving our planet is simply not possible.

We know that we can be effective only in partnership with others. We have reached out to the United Nations and to all other multilateral and bilateral agencies. To further improve our effectiveness, we are strengthening harmonization with others.

We have much to do. It seems that the challenges and problems are never ending. But great progress is being made, and I would like to thank all my colleagues for their extraordinary work and commitment. There is no more dedicated or more able group of people working to improve the world than our team at the World Bank Group.

Let me also express my profound appreciation to the executive directors of the Board, and to their predecessors, for their many constructive contributions. They play a vital but sometimes difficult role as officers of the institution and as representatives of their countries.

An Insecure World

At Annual Meetings in the past, I have spoken to you on many subjects, including the challenge of inclusion, the cancer of corruption, the importance of comprehensive development, and the need for a new global balance between rich and poor. Today I would like to discuss what is perhaps the most difficult challenge for the coming years. How do we better manage the big global issues: poverty, inequity, the environment, trade, illegal drugs, migration, diseases, and, yes, terrorism?

This year we are reporting record economic growth in developing countries. And yet, somehow, we feel less secure about the future. Deep down, there is a nagging concern about the way the world is evolving. One need only look at the cement barriers surrounding these buildings to understand the big difference from past years. They are not there for protestors. They are there for terrorists. A computer found in Pakistan showed that the Bank and the Fund have been targeted by al Qaeda. Terror has reached our door.

In recent times we have seen things that cause us to question our basic humanity: bloody wars in Afghanistan, Iraq, and large parts of Africa; unspeakable loss of life in Darfur, Sudan; despicable acts of terror in Bali and Madrid; growing violence between Israel and the Palestinians of Gaza and the West Bank. In Beslan, Russia, we have seen children taken hostage and shot in the back. In Baghdad innocent men are brutally beheaded on television.

In reaction, we have become preoccupied with security. It is absolutely right that, together, we fight terror. We must. The danger, however, is that in our preoccupation with the immediate threats we lose sight of the longer-term and equally urgent causes of our insecure world: poverty, frustration, and lack of hope.

Over the past decade, Elaine and I have visited more than 100 countries. We have met with poor people in all of them: in villages and shantytowns, in remote rural areas, and in slums. Just like all of us in this room, they want to live safely and peacefully. Women want to build their lives, free of violence against them both inside and outside their homes. They want education for their children. They want voice and respect. They want to retain their cultural integrity. They want hope.

They want security, but they define it differently than we do. For them it is not about concrete barriers and military force. For them it is the chance to escape poverty.

If we want stability on our planet, we must fight to end poverty. Since the time of the Bretton Woods Conference, through the Pearson Commission, the Brandt Commission, and the Brundtland Commission, through to the statements of our leaders at the 2000 Millennium Assembly, and continuing today, all confirm that the eradication of poverty is central to stability and peace. It is still the challenge of our time.

We Can Meet the Challenge

We know that development works. In the last four decades, life expectancy in developing countries has increased by 20 years, and adult illiteracy has been halved, to 22 percent. The Bank's chief economist, François Bourguignon, and I have published a paper for these Meetings that looks back on the lessons of development over the last decade, and looks ahead to the challenges of the future.

We can build on these lessons. At a conference in Shanghai that we organized with the Chinese government earlier this year, developing countries shared their experience of what works and what does not. Over 100 case studies showed that we can accelerate development rapidly if poor people are treated as agents of change, not as objects of charity.

Many of you participated in the meetings in Doha, Monterrey, and Johannesburg.* There the developed countries made promises on aid, trade, and debt relief. And let me add that we are very supportive of the proposals on aid and debt reduction that have been put forward by the United States, the United Kingdom, France, Brazil, and others. The developing countries, for their part, promised to do much more to build capacity and institutions, strengthen legal and judicial frameworks, improve financial systems and transparency, and fight corruption.

Next year we will meet at the United Nations to review progress in achieving the Millennium Development Goals—with 10 short years to go until 2015. Thanks to China and India, we know that the overall objective of cutting poverty in half will likely be met. But we also already know that most of the other goals, for most countries, will not. Africa, in particular, will be left far behind. What are we going to do about it? What are our children going to do about a world that, in 2015, threatens to be even more out of balance, even more insecure, than it is today?

---

* The Fourth World Trade Organization Ministerial Conference, which launched the Doha Round of international trade negotiations, was held in Doha, Qatar, in November 2001; the United Nations Conference on Financing for Development was held in Monterrey, Mexico, in March 2002; the United Nations World Summit on Sustainable Development was held in Johannesburg in August and September 2002.

I believe, Mr. Chairman, that we must raise our game as an international community. We must do a better job of managing the key global issues that will determine our future. As I see it, there are three urgent priorities:

- protecting the planet through better stewardship of our environment
- scaling up effective poverty reduction, and
- educating our youth differently for the 21st century—and giving them hope.

Let me touch on each of these briefly.

Protecting the Planet: Environmental Sustainability

We must promote growth with a full awareness of the natural systems on which all life depends. Economic growth does not have to come at the expense of the natural environment. They work together.

We all must do a better job of protecting our planet's fragile environment and addressing global warming. It has been three decades since I attended the Stockholm environment conference, and despite progress made in some areas, the way we have abused the earth since that time is alarming.

People in the rich world have overused and wasted tremendous amounts of energy. The average U.S. or Canadian citizen uses nearly 9 times more energy than the average person in China, and 12 times more than the average African. And, as the climate changes, it is the poor in small island states, in Latin America, South Asia, and Sub-Saharan Africa, who will be the most vulnerable to ravages of drought and floods.

Forests are being cut down relentlessly. Of the world's species, a quarter of the mammals and a third of the fish are either vulnerable or in danger of immediate extinction. Ninety percent of the big fish in the oceans have already been killed off.

Mr. Chairman, we have proved ourselves better at menacing the planet than at preserving it. This was brought home to me two weeks ago, when we had a visit from a poor but proud farmer who lives near Machu Picchu in the Peruvian highlands. He was in Washington for the opening of the National Museum of the American Indian, along with thousands of other representatives of indigenous peoples. As part of the opening celebrations of the museum, we at the Bank had a forum on culture and development.

Our visitor was wearing a traditional woolen knit hat and dress, and his face was weathered by years of living at windy, high altitudes. Speaking in his native Quechua, he told me that his mountains were "sad." The glaciers formed on them for thousands of years had been the smile on the face of the mountains, and those glaciers are now getting smaller every year. As they recede, there is no water to refill the lakes and rivers. The animals suffer—the alpaca yield is half the normal size. The income of his valley has dropped 50 percent. Farmers are abandoning their homelands. So this man from Machu Picchu had a simple question: "Can you help me get my glaciers back?"

For those who doubt the impact of global warming, this was an urgent cry for help. For him this was not some abstract, long-term issue. It was an issue of immediate concern. For him, it was a matter of security.

Perhaps his cry for help is being heard. I welcome the recent decision of the Russian government to ratify the Kyoto Protocol. Let us build on this effort and other signals of support to get political commitment from our leaders to fulfill our common responsibilities to which we agreed at the Johannesburg Summit.

Environmental challenges affect all of us, but poor people are particularly vulnerable. We must give higher priority to renewable energy. New and clean technologies can allow the poor to achieve the benefits of development without having to face the same environmental costs that the developed world has imposed. We must keep the promise to preserve our planet.

Scaling Up the Fight Against Poverty

The second urgent area where we must keep our promise is in scaling up poverty reduction. We all know the basic facts. Half the people in the world live on less than two dollars a day; a fifth live on less than a one dollar a day. Over the next three decades, 2 billion more people will be added to the global population, 97 percent of them in developing countries, most of them born into poverty.

Over the past decade a quiet revolution has taken place in the effectiveness of development assistance, with countries taking ownership of their own programs, with aid being focused on good policies, and with increasing coordination among donors. Taken together, these changes can help us double or triple the impact of aid in the coming decade.

We can also multiply the effects of these projects to reach more people. As you know, this has been a real issue for the Bank and our partners. We complete a project for 5 schools, or 100 miles of road, or 10 community programs—we call them feel-good projects—when the need is for 5,000 schools, or 10,000 miles of road, or 5,000 community programs. At the Shanghai conference, we learned how we can build on small, successful projects and scale them up. Common to all of them was consistent management over a period of years, simple replicable models, and full participation of poor people.

I have seen it happen. In 1996, while visiting China, I met a woman from the Loess Plateau, an arid, mountainous region where we were supporting an agricultural project. Living in a cave, she had no power or running water and little prospect of improving her life. This spring I had an emotional reunion with her, and she told me about how her life had improved, how she now has two caves, with doors, windows, water, and power. She told me about how she had bought her son a motorcycle, how her son had found a wife, and how she herself was now looking to educate her daughter.

She was one of 3 million people who found hope through a series of 32 similar projects in the plateau completed over 10 years, projects carried out by thousands of individuals with spades, literally turning rocky land into arable soil. The area is no longer dry and threatening; it is lush and full of crops and animals. We and our Chinese partners provided management for 10 years, repeating the process while benefiting from lessons learned. These lessons are now being implemented elsewhere in China for the benefit of millions of people living on marginal lands.

The message is clear. We can scale up poverty reduction and thus build a more secure world.

Youth and Education

Poverty, of course, is of major concern to young people—and youth is the third global issue that I believe we must deal with urgently. Almost half the world's population is under the age of 24. Half of the 14,000 new HIV infections that occur each day are in young people aged 15 to 24. More than 50 percent of young people of working age cannot find a job. With alarming frequency, youth are becoming involved in conflict, either as victims or, just as tragically, as soldiers.

What, then, can we do for them and for ourselves to lead to peace? One thing I have learned is that we must engage young people themselves in finding the solution. Last month, when I met with youth leaders from 83 countries in Sarajevo, I was struck by their genuine desire to build a better future of harmony, respect, and peace. The young Bosnians, Serbs, and Croats I met were eager to put the country's past behind them. But they felt it was the adults who were holding them back. Just as they did in Paris the year before, they told me they are not the future—they are the *now*.

We must support our youth through education to create their better world. And it begins with early childhood development, because we know that a child's future is largely determined in the first six years of life. I am very proud that the Bank is a leader in this field. We have invested over $1 billion in childhood education, and we make our global experience available to all through our Web site. We are also actively pursuing the Millennium goal of getting all children into primary school by 2015. But we have to recognize that education is not just about getting kids into school. Content and quality are key—and children need to *stay* in school.

Children in developed and developing countries also need to learn more about each other. I fear that today there is too much education for hate, which will not be reversed in later years.

Providing children with a quality education is not only the right thing to do; it also has a huge development impact. If the 115 million children now out of school in developing countries were to enroll, some 7 million new HIV infections could be avoided over the next decade. That is why, two years ago, we launched the Fast Track Initiative—to accelerate access to primary education for children not in school today.

What has been our experience? We estimated that $3.6 billion in additional aid flows is needed each year, for the next seven to eight years, to ensure that all children complete primary school. That comes to $1,200 per class of 40 children to pay for the teacher, books, and classroom, or just $30 a year for each child who is not now in school. Compare this with the $150 we spend for every man, woman, and child on military and defense expenditures. Sadly, the international community has not yet been able to mobilize the money. We are letting the children down on the promises made in Jomtien in 1990, in Dakar in 2000,[†] and again in Monterrey in 2002.

We are simply not keeping our promise.

Global Leadership for the 21st Century

Mr. Chairman, these issues—protecting our planet, scaling up the war on poverty, and educating our youth—are among the most critical for a more secure world. We know what needs to be done. Why is it not happening? I think it is not happening because, as an international community, we are not managing global issues well enough. And yet, more than ever in the past, the most important issues facing us are global, not domestic, and long-term, not short-term.

This is how our system works today: First, at a sequence of global meetings, we agree on objectives, on everything from environmental targets to the importance of gender equity to education. In recent years, under the remarkable

---

† The World Conference on Education for All was held in Jomtien, Thailand, in March 1990; the World Education Forum was held in Dakar, Senegal, in April 2000.

leadership of Secretary-General Kofi Annan, the United Nations has convened a number of international conferences. In 2000, as we all know, the UN Millennium Assembly set goals for 2015, and they were adopted unanimously.

Then, national governments, supported by international agencies and other responsible institutions, try to achieve those objectives. Every five years or so, another global meeting is held to review progress. Usually that meeting concludes that we have not achieved the objectives. New targets are set, blame and praise are attributed, and we set out on the next five years.

During those five years, various groupings of heads of state and ministers spend a day or two per year discussing one or another of the global targets and commitments. The most visible annual gathering is the G-8. But there are many others: the G-10, the G-20, the G-24, and the G-77. And there are regional groupings of leaders in Asia, Africa, Latin America, Europe, and elsewhere. Although these meetings have contributed to the enormous gains in development over the past decades, we are falling behind on the goals we have set. We need stronger leadership, and we need more continuous engagement on the key global issues.

Actually, this was the original idea behind the G-7 when it first met a quarter century ago. It reflected a recognition by the leaders of the major industrial economies that they needed to set aside two days a year and consider long-term global issues. Their meetings are hugely visible and highly important. They bring the attention of the entire world to the key issues of the day. But global challenges have only grown more demanding in the last 25 years. And the balance between the developed and the developing world has changed greatly for the worse and is set to change further.

Perhaps the G-8 leaders, who have achieved so much, would consider coming together on a more frequent basis, with a broad representation of leaders from other parts of the world, to seek new ways of supporting ur gent global issues. In this way they could report on global progress, publicize efforts in pursuit of the goals, and help ensure that promises are fulfilled. In today's world, every one of us is not only a citizen of his or her nation, but a global citizen. Without greater visible engagement by our global leaders, we will not make the breakthroughs we need to ensure real security and peace.

Promises to Keep

Mr. Chairman, we are one world. Damage to the environment somewhere is damage everywhere. Poverty somewhere is poverty everywhere. Terror somewhere is terror everywhere. If there is a bombing in Bali, or Madrid, or Moscow, we all get scared. We all feel insecure.

Making our planet equitable and safe is an issue that we all need to come together on, and we need global leadership and political will to do it. That is the only way we can keep our promises to the farmer of Machu Picchu, the woman on the Loess Plateau, and the young people in Sarajevo. It is our duty to ourselves. It is our duty to our children. It is the choice we must make for security and peace.

Thank you.

Message from the president and chairman from the 2004 World Bank *Annual Report*

OCTOBER 2004

The past year has brought with it signs of hope and progress, but it has also brought signs of concern in the fight against global poverty.

On a positive note, new data this year show that the number of poor people continues to fall. The proportion of people living on less than $1 a day decreased from 40 percent to 21 percent of the global population between 1981 and 2001. Development indicators are clearly improving in countries that have laid good foundations for growth. In Europe, for example, we saw Slovenia graduate from Bank borrower status and join the European Union along with nine other Bank member countries.

The progress, though, is uneven across the globe. Growth in East Asia has meant that there were 500 million fewer people living below $1 a day in 2001 than in 1981. The number of poor people has also fallen in South Asia and in the Middle East and North Africa, though less dramatically than in East Asia. However, the absolute number of poor people has risen in Africa, Latin America and the Caribbean, and Europe and Central Asia.

This year the Annual Meetings of the World Bank and the International Monetary Fund (IMF) were held in the Middle East for the first time. In Dubai, where we met in the shadow of conflict and loss, I stressed that the world I see today is a world out of balance. Of the 6 billion people in the world today, 1 billion people in the wealthy countries account for 80 percent of the world's gross domestic product while the other 5 billion have 20 percent. While rich countries spend $700 billion a year for defense and transfer $325 billion to their agriculture, they devote just $68 billion to development assistance.

These global imbalances are reflected in the daily lives of poor people around the world. Two billion people have no access to clean water, 115 million children never get the chance to go to school, and some 38 million people, more than 95 percent of them in developing countries, are HIV-positive, with little hope of receiving treatment.

It was only four years ago, in 2000, that world leaders gathered at the Millennium Summit in New York and committed themselves to cut poverty in half by 2015. They agreed on Millennium Development Goals for health, education, women, and the environment.

At our Spring Meetings this year, the Bank launched the first *Global Monitoring Report,* which highlights the policies and actions we all need to reach those goals. The report, a joint effort with the IMF, sounded an alarm bell: most of the goals will not be met in most countries by the 2015 deadline.

So the world is at a tipping point: either we in the international community recommit to delivering on the goals, or the targets we set in a fanfare of publicity will be missed, the world's poor will be left even further behind, and our children will be left to face the consequences.

During the next 25 years, about 2 billion more people will be added to the global population, but only 50 million of them will be in the richer countries. The vast majority will be born with the prospect of growing up in poverty and becoming disillusioned with a world they will inevitably view as inequitable and unjust. Terrorism is often bred in places where a fast-growing youth population has no hope.

We cannot ignore the rise of this more youthful world. In the past year, I met with youth from all over the world at places as varied as Tsinghua University in Beijing and Brandeis University in Massachusetts.

These young people are not only the future—they are the *now*. Almost half the people in the world today are under 24 years old. Nine out of 10 of these young people live in developing countries. A billion of them will need jobs in the next decade. An ever-increasing number will leave their home countries to find work.

We need to face these realities, and we need to act on three issues in particular. First, the world trade talks—which can reduce agricultural protectionism and thus poverty in developing nations—must be pushed forward. Developing countries would gain nearly $325 billion by 2015 as a result, enough to lift 140 million people out of poverty.

Second, aid flows need to rise well above current commitments, and they need to be used more effectively. Although some increases have been made in recent years, almost a doubling of current development assistance levels will be required to meet the Millennium Development Goals. It is essential that donor countries fully replenish the International Development Association (IDA)—the fund that delivers proven results for the world's poorest nations.

Third, we must push forward in relieving the debt burdens of the poorest countries by providing a larger proportion of additional aid in the form of grants rather than loans.

For these actions to be successful, the bargain between rich and poor nations struck at the Monterrey [Financing for Development] conference in 2002 must be more effectively implemented. The developing countries must do more to reform their economies and cut out corruption, and the developed countries must back those reforms with increased support.

In the global fight against poverty, the World Bank is—and should be—playing a central role. The Bank's strategy continues to focus on the two pillars for poverty reduction: empowering people and improving the investment climate. These pillars support the Bank's Country Assistance Strategies and are reflected in the Poverty Reduction Strategy Papers of poorer countries and the development strategies of wealthier ones. The Bank continued its client-oriented approach this year, supporting development of Poverty Reduction Strategy Papers in low-income countries that receive IDA credits, and doing more to tailor its lending instruments for middle-income countries that borrow from the International Bank for Reconstruction and Development (IBRD). We are also continuing to work with countries experiencing weak policies, weak institutions, and often internal conflict through a special initiative known as Low-Income Countries under Stress. Donor partnerships are critical to success.

The Heavily Indebted Poor Countries Initiative gained momentum this year, with progress toward its goal of cutting poor countries' debt to manageable levels. Twenty-seven countries—two-thirds of those eligible—are now participating and are receiving debt relief that will total more than $52 billion from all creditors over time. With our partners, we are working to move beyond debt relief to debt sustainability.

On the AIDS front, the Bank joined with the United Nations Children's Fund; the Global Fund to Fight AIDS, Tuberculosis, and Malaria; and the Clinton Foundation to provide generic drugs at a fraction of the current cost. We are also working with partners to develop HIV/AIDS prevention programs in countries with high risk.

One highlight of the year was the development conference we cohosted with the Chinese government in Shanghai, the culmination of nine months of studying development experiences. Leaders from developing countries shared their successes and failures with other leaders. We learned that feeling good about individual projects is not enough. We learned that we must scale up our development efforts. It is not 10 schools we are trying to help build. It is 10,000 schools. It is not 5 bridges we are trying to help construct. It is 5,000 bridges. It is not thousands of people we are trying to support. It is billions of people.

We at the World Bank believe that the disadvantaged of the world should be seen not as objects of charity but as assets in the fight against poverty. We believe overcoming poverty is a moral, social, economic, and security imperative. We will continue to state this view loud and clear as we work tirelessly to support all who seek to achieve the Millennium Development Goals.

"WE HAVE TO COME TOGETHER
TO DEAL WITH POVERTY"

Address at the High-Level Encounter of the World Council of Churches,
the World Bank, and the International Monetary Fund

GENEVA | OCTOBER 22, 2004

*Wolfensohn's most passionate addresses often centered on finding common
ground with partners. Here he addresses a Geneva gathering called to find
ways in which the World Council of Churches and the World Bank could
work together more closely on development issues.*

Thank you very much, Mr. Moderator, and Sam, and Agnes Abuom, and
Agustin Carstens,* and ladies and gentlemen:

I was really of two minds about coming to this meeting. I have spent eight
years trying to build bridges with the faith-based communities. Together with
the Archbishop of Canterbury, we at the Bank started a process called the
World Faiths Development Dialogue. I approached George Carey, and we
have brought together now, on three separate occasions, some 30 different
leaders representing all of the world's major religions, with the view of having
a dialogue. And the dialogue was based on a perception and a hope that I had,
and that I think Archbishop Carey also had, that the objective of each of our
institutions was to deal with the issue of poverty, with the issue of equity, with
the issue of injustice, and that there had been a breakdown in understanding
between one group and the other.

I say a breakdown, but in fact there was precious little relationship at all
to begin with. There wasn't much to break down. There was a series of perceptions that were held, certainly, about the Bretton Woods institutions,
about the 11,000 people who work for us from 140 different countries—
including, by the way, 1,000 Africans, among them an African woman managing director and several African vice presidents. And I think you would
have to say, if you spoke to the Africans in our institution, that there has
been a significant advance in the last 10 years in the position of Africans in
the World Bank. Our institution was also one of the first to address the question of environment, and much in the same terms, Agnes, that you spoke about.
Our institution was at the forefront of gender considerations, maybe belatedly
but nonetheless significantly in the last 20 years, and certainly since [the 1995
World Conference on Women in] Beijing. I attended Beijing not only as
a matter of conviction, but also as a matter of fear—fear on my part of
what would happen if I didn't do something about the status of women in
the world.

---

* Samuel Kobia, general-secretary of the World Council of Churches; Agnes Abuom, president of the World
Council of Churches and Agustin Carstens, deputy managing director of the International Monetary Fund.

Let me say something on the issue of youth. We know that there are in the world today 2.8 billion people under the age of 24, and 1.8 billion under the age of 14. We have now youth groups in our offices, because I remember what a group of young people told me when I first spoke to them five or six years ago. I was talking to them about their future, and one of them said, "Mr. President, we're not the future. We're the *now*." And, indeed, they've shown us since then that that is what they are.

We've opened our doors and are actively involved in the issue of people with disabilities. We are deeply committed to fighting poverty with passion. Many of the people in our organization have extraordinarily strong faith backgrounds. We feel ourselves, not as outsiders, not as insensitive economic modelers, but, in fact, as a group of people who have chosen to work in these institutions, rather than in the private sector, because we see ourselves as caring about the issue of poverty.

If you were to ask most of the people in our building, "Why did you come here?" they would say to you that they came because they want to make a difference in the world. They would say to you that they go out in the field—and the best jobs at the Bank and the Fund are in the field—because they are there to make that difference. And in my travels now, in more than 100 countries, not just to the palaces and to the offices but to the slums, to the villages, out to the people, I see that our perception of success is measured in terms of people, not in terms of money. That is our self-perception.

And so, when I read a book, which is your introduction to us, that says, "Lead us not into temptation,"[†] and describes us as something other than that, or when I hear us described as being only concerned with economic models, I'm troubled enough to wonder whether I should come here. And yet I came because I think the issues facing us are common issues, and I actually believe, as I indicated to Archbishop Carey and to those 30 other leaders from all faiths, that the issue is not about solving arguments with each other as to our approaches. The issue that we face is the human issue of injustice, inequity, and the human condition, and that we measure our objectives in terms, we would like to say, of poverty eradication.

That is my dream. But, at the moment, the task is poverty *alleviation,* because 200 heads of state decided in [at the UN Millennium Assembly in] New York that we would set a goal of halving the incidence of poverty by 2015, and that was the task that was given to us. And we're not doing a great job even on alleviation, let alone eradication.

---

† "Lead Us Not into Temptation: Churches' Response to the Policies of International Financial Institutions," published by the World Council of Churches.

I can assure you that, when I go to my office every day and when I meet with my colleagues in the Bank, the thing that is uppermost in our minds is the thing that is uppermost in your minds. It is dealing with the question of disadvantaged people in the world. And we do it for several reasons. We do it in some cases for faith-based reasons. We do it in some cases for moral or ethical reasons. We do it because we think it's right. And I suppose some of us do it because we know that, unless one deals with the question of poverty, there can be no peace in the world.

This is not an original notion, this linkage between poverty and peace. For some years I thought it was, and for many years I spoke about it as if it were, until I reread the Pearson Commission report, the Brundtland Commission report, the Brandt Commission report, and the speeches at the Millennium Assembly. And I discovered that what I had thought were extremely incisive, articulate, and brilliant observations had been made for 40 years. So this notion of linking poverty and peace, of linking poverty and stability, is something that has been driving us almost for as long as there has been a World Council of Churches, and as long as there have been Bretton Woods institutions.

But, sadly, the world is not facing these issues other than by making promises. And the reason, frankly, that I wanted to come today was that I think we're in a crisis. I think we're in a crisis because I think that we're pretty high on what we say and pretty low on performance. I think that the statements from the Pearson Commission report right through until the statements that have just been made are consistent, but the follow-up action is slow.

We promised two things in New York: The developing countries promised that they would address the issues of governance in their countries. Agnes, we must look at that as well. This is not just a First World issue. And this is not just my opinion; it is the opinion of the leadership in Africa as embodied in NEPAD [the New Partnership for Africa's Development], and it's the opinion of the leadership of the developing world, as expressed at Monterrey and at Johannesburg.[‡] At both those meetings the talk was of sustainable development and of the need in developing countries to have better capacity, to have better governance in judicial and financial systems, and to fight corruption.

---

‡ The International Conference on Financing for Development was held in Monterrey, Mexico, in March 2002; the World Summit on Sustainable Development was held in Johannesburg in August and September 2002.

I'm not for a moment suggesting that corruption is a Third World issue alone. For every corrupter you need a corruptee, and sometimes they're in different parts of the world. But the simple fact of the matter is that, as you know and I know, in almost any country you go to, you can figure out within 48 hours who the crooks are. That is particularly true in your home country [of Kenya], where I dealt with President [Daniel arap] Moi for six years, trying desperately to make a breakthrough. In almost any country you go to, you can find out whether it's the president who is crooked, or his wife who is crooked, or this or that official who is crooked. You can even find out how much it costs to get something done. But we talk about corruption and we talk about governance, yet in all too few countries is the possibility of reform even there. And, let me say, I'm a minor expert on Kenya. I was run around a lot there and was seen to be a naïve idealist for some time. So the reality is that in the developing world there is still work to be done. Thank God we've got a few good leaders who are now leading us into a new arena.

We also know that levels of aid are not increasing. They appear to have increased in the last two years, from $52 billion to $68 billion. But when you look at the actual flows of cash, as distinct from preattributed funding, the increase is very, very small. We also know that if the wealthy countries devoted 0.7 percent of their GNP to aid, which is what they have promised, it would amount to more than $200 billion a year. In fact we're now somewhere around 0.24 percent, or between $60 billion and $70 billion, about only half of which is in cash.

The other drama is that today, notwithstanding the fact that last year, economically, the world had its best year in 30 years, there are still shadows. We are looking not at the long term but at the short term. The world at the moment is dominated not by faith but by fear. It's dominated by war, by terror, and by short-term challenges. We are spending $900 billion a year on defense and $60 billion on development. If we spent $900 billion on development, we probably wouldn't have to spend more than $60 billion on defense, because that $900 billion would establish a somewhat better world. We're also spending $350 billion on subsidies and protection of agriculture in the developed countries, to protect their rural areas from competition. But rural areas in developing countries are where 70 percent of poor people live.

I came today because I think that whatever we think—whatever you think of us, and, indeed, the much more moderate feelings we have about you, whatever the feelings are—we need to come together on these issues. It's a luxury to beat each other up. The issues are pragmatic. They're pragmatic because we have to come together to deal with poverty.

I have just come from Madagascar and Ethiopia. The image I have of that visit is of the five kids who came up to see me in a rural development program in Madagascar, four of them without shoes, one with a sort of sandal. Two of them were emaciated, and one of them had terrible lesions all over the skin. They looked at me not with smiles, as you hope for with kids, but with blank faces of despair, looking at us as though we could do something to help. I cannot get that image out of my head. We are going to send a health worker, we are going to send an educator to that village, and we will solve, I hope, the problem of those five kids.

But it's not a problem of five kids. It's a problem of more than 40 million people with AIDS. It's a problem of 12 million orphans in Africa alone. It's a problem of 2 billion people being added to the planet in the next 25 years, bringing the total from 6 billion to 8 billion, and nearly all of them, 97 percent, in developing countries. So it is not just the problem of today that is so critical. And it's a question of jobs, and it's a question of trying to find them something to do.

Here, may I say, Agnes, is where I think you may have your biggest misunderstanding about our institution. The issue of culture, the issue of individual voice, the issue of respect for the individual, the issue of faith, the issue of what people want to become complete individuals is something that more than 90 percent, I'm sure, of the people in our organization care about. One of the first things I did on becoming president of the Bank was to start a meeting on culture and development, because I offered the proposition that you could not have development without culture, without history, without faith, without belief. This is not something that is strange to our institution. It is not something that is only owned by the World Council of Churches. There is not a group in our institution that is so economically driven that they're not allowed to have moral values or faith. But if you read this book you have written about the Bank, that's what you think we are. And it's not fair. And it's not correct.

And so I'm pretty passionate about the people in my organization, because they're people like you. They share very often your same faiths. They get involved in the same church politics. They get involved in the same issues of faith. Some of them may even be members of the World Council of Churches, although, if you found them, you'd probably throw them out! These are living people who care about the same issues you care about. And the descriptions of them and of our institution in this book I just think are dead wrong. That's my belief.

The other thing I would say is on this question of human rights to which so much attention is given. What are these human rights? Let me tell you that, for the last five years, I have been dealing with the question of human rights, with Mrs. [Mary] Robinson [former UN High Commissioner for Human Rights] and with many others, on the question of how the Bank could have a rights-based approach to development. If I could agree on a rights-based approach to development with my Board, I would have had it through by now. But we have on our Board quite a number of countries that are not committed to a rights-based approach to development. In most cases, however, it is only a question of language and not of belief.

So what am I doing and what are we doing? We are trying to support and finance the efforts to preserve rights for individuals—rights for women, rights for children, rights not to live in poverty, rights to voice. We're taking the rights issues that you so earnestly want us to take, and, if you look at what we're doing, I believe that there is no institution that is seeking to do more on the protection of rights than we are.

The last thing I'd say is that, on the voting in our institution, this is not an issue for management to decide. If you could persuade the Bank's major shareholders and donors to give up their shareholdings in the Bank in favor of developing countries, I would be the first to applaud. We have come up with alternative methodologies, but it is not my issue. I do not own a vote in the World Bank. But I can tell you that some of the wealthy countries hold strong views as to whether they should give up their voting rights. They're prepared to let us strengthen the offices of developing countries. They're prepared to let us do lots of things. But they also say, "We put the money in. We don't want the borrowers to determine how that money is lent." There is no shortage of good will. It is a question of governance of an institution that already has a long history of seeking consensus on the Board, and that includes the voices of developing countries.

Now, I know that Rodrigo [de Rato] and I and, before Rodrigo, Horst Köhler have been doing our best to push this. The chairman of the committee that's working on it is Mr. Trevor Manuel, the finance minister of South Africa, who is dealing with this issue in a strong way and who is in a position to make things happen. I suggest that, if you have ideas, you should talk to him. This is a shareholder issue. This is not a management issue. And I think certain things can be done, and we have, in fact, suggested certain things. But to the extent that we in management have anything to say, we have taken action. We've appointed Africans, we've appointed other minorities, and we've appointed lots of women.

I'm not suggesting that we're perfect. I guess no one's perfect. Maybe even the World Council of Churches is not perfect in terms of representation. But in terms of direction, I don't think there's much that we will disagree on.

Having said that, I just want to make one last point. It is that we are now at a point of crisis. Perhaps we could declare an amnesty with each other for two years and look at what we could do together. Keep in your heads all the horrible things you think of us, but let's try and think also of the five kids I saw in Madagascar and the millions of kids that are out there that need help. We're a lot stronger working for those kids together than we are by beating each other up. And that is the reason that I came, because it's my earnest hope that we can build on the start we've made and together make life better for many people.

Thank you very much.

TRYST WITH DESTINY: GLOBALISATION CAN BE INDIA'S HOUR OF GLORY

Published in *The Times of India*

NOVEMBER 18, 2004

> *Just ahead of his last visit to India as World Bank president, Wolfensohn penned this op-ed on India's challenges of fighting poverty and narrowing the divide between the fast-growing and slower-growing states. But he also recognizes India's growing importance on the world stage and its "civilisational force."*

When I think about India from the vantage point of someone who has now traversed the globe in the name of development for the past 10 years, I think about not just a nation of a billion people which has made good progress in recent years. I think about the embodiment of an idea whose time must inevitably come.

One-sixth of humanity, no less, hugely diverse and much of it poor, emerges from a history of colonisation and exploitation; a history of mesmerising design and complexity, riches and war and want. Recovering from the trauma of Partition and fuelled by a strong collective sense of destiny, it sets itself a clear agenda for development, aiming to improve the lot of every citizen and to become an influential voice in the world. Then, most remarkably, it opts to achieve this not through any oligarchy-dictated short cut, but through an elaborate and highly inclusive process of democracy in which every individual, rich or poor, educated or illiterate, has a say.

Participation and inclusion are hugely important. We at the World Bank did a study of 60,000 poor people in 60 countries and what they thought about poverty. The $1 a day or $2 a day that they live on was almost the last thing mentioned. What mattered was voice, an ability to contribute to their future, women not wanting to be beaten up, an opportunity for their kids. So, there is a yearning for participation in these countries. A yearning to be heard; a profound value in knowing what's happening around one, in transparency.

I recently read an interview in the *Financial Times* by my friend, prime minister Manmohan Singh, a man I hold in great personal esteem. Speaking in the context of reform, he said: "Few countries in the developing world have been able to implement such far-reaching reforms within the framework of a parliamentary democracy. Public debate and dissent is a source of strength for us, not of weakness. . . . In the long run, a reform programme that has the widest possible social and political support is more enduring." He is so right.

When I think of India, I see a civilisational force that can and must be a voice of weight and reason on the global stage. The international community is already recognising India's potential to play this role. In earlier decades, it es-

tablished its credentials through its leadership of the non-aligned movement. Today, its importance is underscored by such developments as its maturing relationship with the United States, the joint leadership that India, Brazil and South Africa are providing the developing nations in multilateral negotiations, and just this month, the European Union's recognition of India as a strategic partner on par with Canada, China, Russia and the US.

But when I think of India, I also see a very critical role for this country in a very much more immediate fight—the global fight against poverty. The simple fact is that the world cannot win this fight if India does not win it. Despite the impressive gains made by India in the assault on poverty in the last two decades, more than a quarter of India's one billion people are still below the official poverty line; that amounts to more than 250 million people, about a quarter of all the world's poor, living here in India. Perhaps a few hundred million more remain vulnerable to slipping back into poverty by a single shock such as an illness or natural disaster.

That is not all. India's huge numbers of illiterate people, children out of school, people suffering from communicable diseases, and infant, child and maternal deaths all amount to massive proportions of the respective world totals. In the year 2000, the international community set itself what have come to be known as the Millennium Development Goals or MDGs, a set of ambitious targets to improve human development indicators of the type I have just listed by the year 2015. It is obvious how very important India's role is in achieving these global targets. India's recent rapid growth has created a vibrant, confident middle class, and lifted millions out of poverty. But the flow of benefits has been uneven. There are growing disparities between states, and between regions within states. There is a visible urban-rural divide. To resolve these, India must tackle some immediate problems: its antiquated infrastructure, the lack of livelihood opportunities in rural areas, improving health and education outcomes, and ensuring that public services like electricity, water, sanitation and others are efficiently delivered, especially to poor people. And it must recognise that in some states, HIV infections are above 1 per cent—the threshold of a general epidemic.

The key determinant to moving forward on these multiple fronts will be India's ability to mobilise, in a concerted and consistent manner, the right matrix of policies and programmes that will encourage investment, improve livelihoods and incomes, and promote better human development outcomes. The World Bank is ready to partner India in this effort with lending and analytical support.

I see a nation that has the capacity and confidence to address and resolve these challenges. The world believes that India, to quote the great Jawaharlal Nehru [India's first prime minister], has a tryst with destiny. The time has come to redeem that pledge.

With Amartya Sen, published in *The Jakarta Post*

DECEMBER 3, 2004

This op-ed, co-written with Nobel laureate Amartya Sen, shines the spotlight on improving the lives of the 10 percent or more of the developing world's population who are disabled. It ran in several newspapers around the world to mark the International Day of Disabled Persons.

Disabled people are not only the most deprived human beings in the developing world, they are also the most neglected. As the world marks the International Day of Disabled Persons this week, it is important to acknowledge that more than 600 million people in the world live with some form of disability. More than 400 million of them live in developing countries, often amidst poverty, isolation and despair. Not only are they, typically, the poorest of the poor, but they also need more money and help than able-bodied people to overcome their handicaps, and attempt to live normal lives.

As if the many hardships were not painful enough, disabled people can face exclusion and discrimination at the hands of their fellow citizens, even their own families who fear they will be tarnished by association. For example, many disabled children, whether deaf or in wheelchairs, are denied an education. Disabled people are at increased risk of contracting HIV/AIDS due to physical and sexual abuse, and a lack of preventive outreach tailored specifically for disabled people. And yet, experience shows that in countries where people with disabilities have greater access to their broader communities, they can flourish.

It is estimated that at least ten percent of the developing world's population is disabled in one way or another. In fact, some estimates put the figure closer to twenty percent. Not only do these people deserve the right to global attention because of the extreme nature of their deprivation, but it is also important to recognize the impossibility of achieving large reductions in poverty and illiteracy in the world (as demanded by the Millennium Development Goals, endorsed by more than 180 world leaders in September, 2000), unless special efforts are made to bring disabled people into the mainstream.

Take the case of education. An estimated 40 million of the more than 100 million children out of school have disabilities. And yet most of our schools are built without access for children who have physical disabilities, and most teachers are not trained to deal with children who have handicaps of one kind or another, including learning disability.

However, with some basic social help, the terrible consequences of disability can be substantially overcome. It is also important to see that most disabil-

ities are preventable. Only a small proportion of the 600 million people living with disabilities were born that way. For example, malnutrition and lack of access to clean water can lead to blindness.

Other disabilities can result from HIV/AIDS, measles, polio, road crashes, injuries at work or from discarded mines and unexploded ordinance. While a rapidly aging population creates a growing source of disabling conditions, the incidence of disability can be significantly reduced through well-designed social and medical attention.

As we consider how best to respond to the needs of disabled people in poor countries, it is important to understand that simple and inexpensive solutions do exist in many cases. For example, during renovation or restoration efforts in the wake of natural disasters or conflicts, it is possible to make sure that the newly built or repaired buildings are made accessible to people with disabilities, and this can add very little to the costs involved. To take another example, the movements of disabled and old people can often be restricted by high curbs that flank their streets, but, as a good many countries have already shown, these curb designs can be changed at little cost.

Also, many people are in a gray area with mild to moderate mental health disorders or intellectual disabilities or physical handicaps. Policies that can help them join the mainstream of society can certainly be devised. A number of developing country governments are working with national disability groups to overcome restrictive barriers.

In Brazil, which is one of the first developing countries to improve its collection of disability data, surveys showed that large numbers of children with significant visual disabilities simply needed spectacles. The World Bank has been closely involved in these efforts, both in terms of providing glasses, hearing aids, and other interventions, but also in gathering better statistics on people's disabilities and their consequences.

In this latter respect, social scientists also have a responsibility to investigate the incidence of different handicaps and their remedies. But change can happen on a larger scale too. A World Bank funded project in Vietnam is supporting a National Task Force to develop a set of guidelines for inclusive education, and will help teachers improve their classroom practice so that children with disabilities can learn beside other children.

As we approach this year's International Day of Disabled Persons, we have to be determined to bring disabled people out of the shadowy world in which they are typically confined. This task demands more global cooperation, involving national and international institutions as well as organizations of disabled people themselves. The United Nations is working on a Convention on the Rights of Disabled People to help move disabled people from exclusion to inclusion.

Disabled people want what we all want: the chance to get educated, find rewarding work, lead worthwhile lives, and be valued members of their community and in the world at large. These desires need not be just idle dreams, since much can be achieved if we are ready to give this extensive problem the attention and commitment it demands. We need to mobilize the determination to do just exactly that.

Wolfensohn on Disabilities

". . . *My belief about persons with disabilities is that they should not be conceived as a burden, but as an asset, and what we should be trying to do is to educate them so that they can assist with problem-solving. I regard people with disabilities as people who have some limitations, but who very often have great strengths and great drive to fully participate. Our task is to try to ensure that they have the opportunity to contribute . . .*"

From an interview in *Ability* magazine, June 5, 2003

AFTER THE TSUNAMI:
REBUILDING LIVES, ASSETS, CONFIDENCE

Address to the ASEAN Leaders' Meeting on the Aftermath of the
Earthquake and Tsunami

JAKARTA | JANUARY 6, 2005

*In this address only days after the December 26 tsunami claimed the lives of
hundreds of thousands in Asia, Wolfensohn calls on all parties to work together to rebuild the lives of those affected by the tragedy.*

Mr. President:

On behalf of myself, my colleagues, and my institution, and on behalf of the
International Monetary Fund, let me first offer our deepest condolences and
sense of loss to you, your people, and the people of all of the countries affected
by the tsunami disaster. At a time when effective delivery of emergency relief
is clearly the highest priority, we warmly support the leadership role of the
United Nations and will support the secretary-general and his team in any way
that we can.

The enormous force of this international tragedy is one of many reminders
that we are all linked together, by forces that are both visible and invisible:
forces of nature, forces of poverty, of disease, terrorism, crime, and drugs. These
forces remind us all of how tiny we are in comparison with the force of nature
and how, at the same time, we are all indelibly connected.

This means that we must also respond to this crisis in the context of the many
things that link us together, and particularly our efforts to achieve the Millennium Development Goals and a better world for all. We should remember that
the majority of the people killed were poor and unable to defend themselves.

The international response so far has been terrific. It's more urgent than
ever that we work together so that we can deal with this emergency relief stage
effectively.

The reconstruction stage can then also begin quickly. This stage is not just
a matter of financial resources and physical infrastructure, but also very much
a matter of human beliefs and emotional pressures. It's about rebuilding the individual lives of real people and families and children—these are the issues that
we must emphasize. In this context the roles of the communities, civil society,
and the private sector are very important as we work to respond together.

Here in Indonesia, the large-scale Kecamatan Development Program, which
is operational in all regions, including Aceh, is a very useful model. This program calls on local communities to run their own lives, establish priorities for
development, and help in implementing those priorities themselves. Engaging
the people of poor communities in this way makes the development process
real. And we in the World Bank certainly want to work this way, trying to

help people rebuild not only their physical assets, but also their own confidence and hope for the future. We also hope to work closely with other international financial institutions, particularly the Asian Development Bank and the International Monetary Fund.

Let me also stress that this is not a postconflict situation; it is not a situation where there is no government in place, where we would have to seek to build governments and administrative structures. Here, as we have heard so eloquently and articulately this morning, we have existing governments with their own ideas, flaws, and needs. It is a specific aim of our institution to work closely in support of the governments of the affected countries, on their priorities and programs. It is not our objective to try to create unnecessary new organizational structures.

We also believe very strongly that the use of our public resources should be transparent and effective and that it should show clear results. This not only will help in the case of this emergency response, but will also support the governments concerned with the transparent and effective use of public resources in general.

A further important principle, which I believe should be observed not only by my institution but by others as well, is that the support being offered to meet these special needs be continuous, consistent, and additional to whatever we were or are doing already. So many of us come to important meetings and make pledges, yet sometimes the overall level of assistance doesn't increase but instead is just shifted around. It may make us feel good, but we simply cannot take resources away from other critical development issues and put the resources into one emergency after another. The resources must be additional. They must be consistent. This is an absolutely clear-cut message.

Finally, let me add my support to the proposals to establish an early warning system for natural disasters of this kind. The Bank would be very happy to help with this. We are also supportive of the ideas for making debt relief part of the response, and I understand that these ideas will be discussed at a forthcoming meeting of the Paris Club.*

Mr. President, this emergency is an opportunity, an opportunity to demonstrate in a largely visible way to all the world that we are not just bureaucrats, financiers, or administrators. It is a chance to build on the global outpouring of emotion at the human level, so as to create a world with less conflict, more peace, and less poverty. That is certainly the way our institution is approaching this.

Thank you.

---

* The Paris Club is an informal group of official creditors whose role is to find coordinated and sustainable solutions to the payment difficulties experienced by debtor nations.

MERGING GLOBAL KNOWLEDGE
WITH LOCAL KNOWLEDGE

Remarks transmitted by videoconference to the Knowledge Economy Forum

ABUJA, NIGERIA | JANUARY 30, 2005

> *In these remarks on science and technology, Wolfensohn relates the address*
> *to his experience with science as chairman of the board of the Institute for*
> *Advanced Study at Princeton University.*

I am very happy to have this opportunity to be in Abuja with you today by this miraculous medium and to extend to you my warm wishes for what I am sure will be an extraordinarily interesting conference.

There is no subject in which I am more interested than that of knowledge at all levels in the field of development. And of particular interest to me are the initiatives that have been taking place recently in Africa with the establishment of the Nelson Mandela Institution,* as well as the work that so many of you are doing in addressing issues relating to science and technology in Sub-Saharan Africa.

I come to this subject not as a scientist, but as someone who is deeply involved in the field of development and who for the last 18 years has been a chairman of the Institute for Advanced Study in Princeton. This work has given me a wonderful insight into the world of science and technology and made me feel, I must say, somewhat humble in the face of the intellects I have been exposed to. I was not there when [Albert] Einstein and [John] von Neumann were there, but I have been able to see scientists and technicians from many parts of the world meeting and talking about their research and development work and about issues of scientific theory, and through that I've had the opportunity to see just what an impact leadership in science and technology can have on a society.

When one comes to Africa, one is immediately struck by the fact that Africa for years has been behind the rest of the world in its scientific development. In the developed world, there are broadly speaking between 1,000 and 1,500 scientists and engineers engaged in R&D for every 1 million people. In Sub-Saharan Africa, instead of 1,000 or 1,500 per million, there are only 83 per million. Indeed, even in North Africa there are some 400 scientists and engineers per million population engaged in R&D, and Asia has close to 800 per million. This makes for an enormous gap between the developed and the developing countries.

---

* The Nelson Mandela Institution for Knowledge Building and the Advancement of Science and Technology in Sub-Saharan Africa.

One is astonished by these statistics, but then one has to assess what they mean and whether it matters. All of us here at the Bank believe that it matters very much, particularly as we enter the new millennium, and as we look with you toward building a vibrant and exciting Sub-Saharan Africa for the sake of the people of the continent and for, indeed, the world.

Let me jump back for a moment and share with you some of my own experience and why I feel so strongly about this matter. At the Institute in Princeton we looked at the impact of science in the world today, and a number of things came through not only in my work there but in my work with colleagues here at the World Bank. The first is that technology is changing dramatically and is changing the lives of all of us. We at the Bank are now linked with all our offices overseas, running some 1,500 to 1,800 videoconferences a month, and reaching 80 countries a day. This connectivity through videoconference and even greater connectivity using the Internet give us an opportunity to link parts of the world in ways that were unthought of years ago. Sub-Saharan Africa is no longer a long way away. Sub-Saharan Africa is a phone call or an Internet message or a videoconference away.

And this linkage that technology has brought about has, in turn, implications for how science and technology are done. It makes it possible to conceive of joint research programs, of joint consultations, of linking the special knowledge of Sub-Saharan Africa with that in other parts of the world and doing it relatively inexpensively and in real time.

This facility made available by technology is something that we thought we needed to take advantage of. And so, as we considered how the Bank might work in this field, we looked at developing countries and thought of the idea of setting up institutes in these countries, where they can retain their scientists and engineers, where they can work with the understandings that they have developed over the years, not just of the principles of science, which are global, but also with the specific knowledge they have of the challenges that are local. These challenges are in everything from agriculture to medicine to materials and require a local understanding, but they also draw on more fundamental principles of science and technology.

And so we have set up what we call the Millennium Science Initiative, which will encourage scientists and engineers to stay in the countries of their origin. Today, as you probably know, when a young scientist or engineer from Africa is educated outside the continent, there is only a 20 percent chance of him or her going back there to live and work. But if that same engineer, man or woman, is educated on the continent, the likelihood of staying there goes up three times.

So what we need to do is create a framework in which knowledge can be developed locally, with people developed locally, and with institutions that can retain the opportunities for those scientists and engineers to stay where they are needed. Of course, they can still be linked through technology and visits to other parts of the world, so that the science they do can be at the global level, but the application can be local.

This is what the Mandela Institution has in mind, and this is what you have in mind as you come together at these meetings. And the Bank is anxious to be as supportive of this effort as you will wish us to be.

This is not just an activity for the elite, for those who have had the privilege of doing postgraduate work. The impact goes all the way down the chain to primary school, to the earliest levels of education. Again, if I can draw on my experience in the United States, through the Institute for Advanced Study we have established the [Park City] Mathematics Institute in one of the western states, where each year high school teachers are brought together with leading mathematicians. And the purpose is to allow the young teachers to understand the new research in the field of mathematics, to be excited by it, and to bring a new level of confidence and quality to their teaching. So the establishment of the Mathematics Institute has made a whole range of capacities and a whole range of influences possible for the whole educational system of the country.

In the development field one of the often-made comparisons is that of Korea with Ghana. Both countries started at around the same level of income after World War II, but over the intervening years Korea has moved significantly ahead of Ghana. One of the major reasons for that is, in fact, Korea's use of education in science and technology.

I don't need, I think, to convince this audience of the importance of this initiative. But I can say that I cannot see the development of Sub-Saharan Africa without Africans taking on the responsibility and the opportunity of developing their science and technology. Knowledge is at the core of development today at all levels—whether it be in preschool, in education for young children, or in establishing standards. And with this knowledge of science and technology and with the sorts of research institutes I have described, there will be the possibility of creating jobs, of working with industry, of developing a sense of standards that are both international and local at the same time. That can help Sub-Saharan Africa emerge from a period of too little growth to a period of exciting growth, based on modern scientific principles, based on indigenous research, and based on the use of the great resource that Africa has, the very people themselves.

Let me say in conclusion how strongly we feel in the World Bank about the issue of knowledge, of science and technology, in Sub-Saharan Africa. We look forward to working with you to bring about institutes throughout the region, to bring about linkages between local institutions and international institutions, and to bring about fulfilling opportunities for young African scientists to develop their skills within the framework of their local environment but also with the standards of international science.

We know that, if we can work with you to do this, you will yourselves bring about the reduction in poverty, you will create opportunities for work, and you will establish standards that will lead Sub-Saharan Africa to take full advantage of the immense potential of its people and bring about growth and hope for your peoples in the future.

Cover design

Libby Settlemyer, Gensler Studio 585, Washington, D.C.

Photographs

Pages 3, 9, 15, 19, 29, 42, 152, 156, 267, 271, 307, 522 © World Bank; Page 25 © World Bank Photo Collection / Photographer: Shehzad Noorani; Page 71 © World Bank Photo Collection / Photographer: Steven Harris; Page 91 © World Bank Photo Collection / Photographer: Scott Wallace; Page 129 © World Bank / Photographer: Simone D. McCourtie; Page 196 © World Bank Photo Collection / Photographer: Trevor Samson; Page 200 © World Bank Photo Collection / Photographer: Curt Carnemark; Page 202 © World Bank Photo Collection / Photographer: Curt Carnemark; Page 214 © World Bank / Photographer: Simone McCourtie; Page 218 © World Bank Photo Collection / Photographer: Bill Lyons; Page 235 © World Bank/Courtesy: Photodisc; Page 289 © World Bank Photo Collection / Photographer: Ami Vitale; Page 293 © World Bank Photo Collection / Photographer: Scott Wallace; Page 297 © World Bank Photo Collection / Photographer: Curt Carnemark; Page 351 © World Bank Photo Collection / Photographer: Alfred Srur; Page 367 © World Bank / Photographer: Simone McCourtie; Page 413 © World Bank Photo Collection / Photographer: Stan Constantio; Page 423 © World Bank / Photographer: Deborah Campos; Page 441 © World Bank / Photographer: Nazanine Atabaki; Page 451 © World Bank Photo Collection / Photographer: Anatoliy Rakhimbayev; Page 462 © World Bank Photo Collection / Photographer: Eric Miller; Page 475 © World Bank / Photographer: Nazanine Atabaki; Page 516 © World Bank Photo Collection / Photographer: John Isaac; Page 519 © World Bank Photo Collection / Photographer: Masaru Goto

Editorials

Page 41: *International Herald Tribune*, May 11, 1996 © World Bank; Page 70: *The Asian Wall Street Journal*, September 19, 1997 © *The Asian Wall Street Journal*; Page 87: *The Australian,* September 30, 1997 © World Bank; Page 151: *The Globe and Mail*, June 17, 1999 © World Bank; Page 244: *BusinessWorld* (Manila, Philippines), August 29, 2000 © *BusinessWorld;* Page 269: *International Herald Tribune,* March 14, 2001 © World Bank; Page 296: *The Washington*